Ordered West
The Civil War Exploits of Charles A. Curtis

Ordered West

The Civil War Exploits of Charles A. Curtis

Edited and with an Introduction by
Alan D. Gaff and Donald H. Gaff

Number 13 in the War and the Southwest Series

University of North Texas Press
Denton, Texas

Printed in the United States of America.

10 9 8 7 6 5 4 3 2 1

Permissions:
University of North Texas Press
1155 Union Circle #311336
Denton, TX 76203-5017

The paper used in this book meets the minimum requirements of the American National Standard for Permanence of Paper for Printed Library Materials, z39.48.1984. Binding materials have been chosen for durability.

Library of Congress Cataloging-in-Publication Data
Curtis, Charles A. (Charles Albert), 1835–1907.
Ordered West : the Civil War exploits of Charles A. Curtis / edited and with an Introduction by Alan D. Gaff and Donald H. Gaff.
pages cm.
Includes bibliographical references and index.
ISBN-13 978-1-57441-669-5 (cloth : alk. paper)
ISBN-13 978-1-57441-682-4 (ebook)
1. United States. Army—Military life—History—19th century. 2. Arizona—History—Civil War, 1861–1865—Personal narratives. 3. New Mexico—History—Civil War, 1861–1865—Personal narratives. 4. Curtis, Charles A. (Charles Albert), 1835–1907. 5. Quartermasters—United States—Biography. 6. United States. Army—Officers—Biography. 7. Indians of North America—Wars—1862–1865—West (U.S.) 8. Frontier and pioneer life—West (U.S.) 9. West (U.S.)—History—19th century. I. Title.

E607.C87 2017
973.7/8092 B–dc23
2017004008

Ordered West: The Civil War Exploits of Charles A. Curtis is Number 13 in the War and the Southwest Series.

The electronic edition of this book was made possible by the support of the Vick Family Foundation. Typeset by vPrompt eServices.

To Henry and Claudia
With Extra Boba

Contents

Preface

Charles Curtis served in the 5th United States Infantry during the American Civil War, his service including assignments in Arizona and New Mexico between 1862 and 1865. During those years he spent most of his time on garrison duty and had the opportunity to interact with American Indians, both hostile and friendly, as well as notable military figures. Years after his service and while president of Norwich University, Curtis wrote an extensive memoir of his time in the Southwest. This memoir was published in a New England newspaper and remained unknown to scholars of the American Southwest owing to the geographical obscurity and his service outside the main theaters of the war. One of the editors discovered Curtis's story and immediately recognized its potential to contribute to the history of the Southwest, the anthropological study of American Indians in the region, and the military history in a underrepresented part of Civil War literature. A review of the existing scholarship located only two books in print relating to low-level Union quartermasters, confirming the uniqueness of the Curtis narrative, since he often served in that capacity, and reinforcing the importance of assembling his story into a book-length manuscript.

Charles Curtis serialized his experiences as "Army Life in the West" in the pages of the Montpelier, Vermont, *Argus and Patriot*. They appeared in three separate installments each of which contained multiple chapters. The first installment was published between 1877 and 1878, the second followed in 1879, and the third in 1880. Most of this narrative was transcribed directly from archived copies of the *Argus and Patriot*. However, as is usually the case, archives are incomplete and missing elements (e.g., bad or blurred scans) were filled in with the use of interlibrary loan to acquire alternate issues of the newspaper. Since Curtis wrote for a newspaper audience in different installments, his reminiscences did not appear in a seamless timeline. The current editors have taken great pains to honor Curtis's own wish to return his narrative to a chronological form.

While assembling the manuscript into sequential order a few incongruencies became apparent. Unlike the first two installments, where he wrote from copious notes, for the third, Curtis relied on his memories—fifteen years after the events he described. Charles Curtis, himself, would later admit that it would "be impossible for me to follow chronologically the events" described within the third series. During the first two series he had depended upon a notebook, in which he had jotted details of important incidents and adventures, and used it to refresh his memory during the writing of the first installments. Following his arrival at Fort Whipple in 1864, Curtis said that "my journal thereafter took the shape of weekly letters to the East, letters which I then expected would again fall into my hands and furnish the material for a book on Arizona." He confessed sadly, "In this I was disappointed." Although he does not go into details, we can assume that the letters were sent to a young lady who apparently did not reciprocate Curtis's attention and they were subsequently lost. Forced to rely upon his memory, the captain expressed a hope that he could keep his adventures in order.

But as he feared, this lack of notes or a diary led to what he called "several anachronisms and hiatuses." While working on chapter thirteen of the third series, Curtis happened to remember a box of his official papers that had been stored in a closet. He retrieved the box, then "sat down on the floor and for two hours opened and folded papers," searching for dates of events in Arizona. To his chagrin, the astute quartermaster, whose accounts had always tallied perfectly, soon learned "that I had got several incidents reversed in the order of their occurrence and that some very interesting ones had been left out entirely." The passage of fifteen years had resulted in what the author termed "some confusion of the memory," although he claimed the errors were only minor. The project was too close to completion and he could not hope to revise his narrative at this point, but Curtis did advise readers that "should I ever rewrite it for the purpose of publication in book form, I shall change many things."

The few irregularities discovered by the editors while putting the manuscript in order consist of a small handful of "patches" where Curtis used the work of others to fill in portions of his narrative where his notes and memories had failed him. A careful textual analysis of these instances clearly suggests that Curtis was making strategic use of others' work because they had provided details he did not recall or offered descriptions that were better than he could have written. The editors hesitate to call this creative appropriation plagiarism because this was a quite common practice for nineteenth century writers (cf., Robert Macfarlane's 2007 *Original Copy: Plagiarism and Originality in Nineteenth-Century Literature*). Similarly, it might be seen as in keeping with the tradition of telling tall tales in the Old West since these involve Curtis inserting himself into someone else's story or borrowing a few choice sentences from other authors without attribution. Lastly, and perhaps most importantly, given his social status as a university president, Curtis would not have jeopardized his position by stooping to outright plagiarism, but did feel comfortable using an infrequent supplement to his own unique story. The editors have made every effort to identify the sources used by Curtis in this way and have left them in for completeness sake. Curtis relied on two books to add colorful descriptions to his personal narrative: George F. Ruxton, *Adventures in Mexico and the Rocky Mountains* (1848) and *El Gringo; or, New Mexico and Her People* (1857). From the former he used segments on bull tailing, a Mexican waiter, and Padre Abeytia's story, while the latter provided tales of a trailside picnic, Padre Donato's tale, the account of Maria Gertrudis Barceló's burial, and observations on Santa Fe and the New Mexican landscape. Smaller snippets of material came from Major W. H. Emory, *Notes of a Military Reconnaissance, From Fort Leavenworth, in Missouri, to San Diego, in California* (1848) and wartime issues of *The Rocky Mountain News*.

Curtis, like many authors, also took for granted information about events that he did not witness personally or had occurred long before he reached the Southwest. A few of these bits of misinformation include the founding of Santa Fe and Albuquerque, the Battle of Glorieta, and Cabeza de Vaca's supposed journey across New Mexico. These snippets have been retained since they were common knowledge, although inaccurate, at the time Curtis served in the region.

Outside of arranging the narrative into chronological order, eliminating duplicate material, and removing a few anachronisms, a light editorial hand was used on Curtis's writing. Editors improved readability by standardizing spellings and making them consistent throughout in addition to modernizing or supplying missing punctuation. One modernization not undertaken was that Curtis's accented spelling of Santa Fé was retained for flavor and authenticity. They have also provided the correct identifications for individuals whom Curtis only referred to by pseudonyms. He explained that "in all cases where I mention parties still in the army, I do not use their own names, nor have I done so where I have spoken of civilians in any way to make them sensitive." The editors have replaced Captain Curtis's discretion with accuracy (thus Lieutenant Riflebore becomes Lieutenant Samuel L. Barr) whenever clues in the story allow for identification of a particular person. Maureen Gaff provided translations of Spanish words and phrases.

The editors have researched and written an Introduction that includes a biography of Charles Curtis and helps to put his story, and how he came to write and publish it, in historic perspective. They also did extensive research in order to supplement the text with ample notes to assist the reader with points of anthropological, historical, and scientific significance.

Assembling a work of this magnitude necessitates the help of many individuals. Ron Chrisman, at the University of North Texas Press, demonstrated the diligence and professionalism one hopes to have in an editor and his insights and advice contributed greatly to this volume. In a similar fashion, two knowledgable readers, Jerry Thompson and John P. Wilson, both took the time to carefully review the manuscript and offered many thoughtful suggestions for which the editors are grateful. Nora Murphy, archivist at Massachusetts Institute of Technology helped to uncover the mystery of why Curtis's son was exhumed and taken to MIT. Mary Margaret Groberg of the Norwich University Archives helped in the acquisition of photographs of Curtis. At the University of Northern Iowa, the editors would like to thank the Department of Sociology, Anthropology, and Crimology, especially Department Head Dr. Marybeth Stalp, for supporting the acquisition of illustrations for this book. Thanks are also extended to the staff at the university's Rod Library, partiularly Rosemary Meany who was instrumental in locating a portion of the *Argus and Patriot* that was missing from most scans of the newspaper in addition to securing many items via interlibrary loan. University biologist Steve O'Kane, who happens to have experience in the botany of the American West, helped with plant identification.

Megan Schneider, also from the University of Northern Iowa, produced all the maps which have greatly enhanced the book. Research and writing of the introduction and notes was supported by the University of Northern Iowa in the form of a Pre-Tenure Summer Fellowship from the university's Office of the Provost and Executive Vice President for Academic Affairs. Special thanks are due to Curt Witcher, Allen County Public Library's Senior Manager of Special Collections. Carol Nahrwold and her staff at the Allen County Public Library also provided valuable assistance. Maureen Gaff, wife, mother, and silent partner, deserves more of our gratitude than anyone else. Along with reading multiple drafts, proofreading, offering suggestions, and translating Spanish, she helped successfully track down the occasional historical fact with a dogged determination that is the envy of scholars everywhere.

Introduction

People who live east of the Mississippi River have always been fascinated by the Great American West. They have thought it to be a land of mystery and adventure, full of rugged mountain men, bloodthirsty Indians, and innumerable herds of shaggy buffalo. Two main thoroughfares snaked across the seemingly unending plains, rugged mountains, and arid deserts: the Oregon Trail to the northwest and the Santa Fe Trail to the southwest. Miners, ranchers, farmers, entrepreneurs, gamblers, and others followed these trails to their dreams or their deaths. Newspapers in the Eastern states kept their readers spellbound with accounts of frontier tragedies and triumphs, such as the Sioux and Northern Cheyenne victory at Little Bighorn in June of 1876 and the surrender of Chief Joseph and the Nez Perce in October of 1877.

Hiram Atkins, publisher and editor of the Montpelier, Vermont, *Argus and Patriot*, was among those who sought to boost readership and capitalize on this intense interest in Western affairs. As a trustee of Norwich University in Northfield, Vermont, Atkins had become acquainted with Charles A. Curtis, then president of that institution, and knew that he had served as an officer in the New Mexico and Arizona Territories during the Civil War. Atkins quickly persuaded his friend to write a number of pieces for the *Argus and Patriot* in which he would detail his adventures. A low-key announcement of Curtis's upcoming recollections appeared on December 5, 1877: "Next week we shall commence the publication of a series of articles on 'Army Life in the West,' written from the pen of Capt. C. A. Curtis, President of the Norwich University, at Northfield, which will be found to be highly interesting."[1]

Publisher Atkins explained how Curtis entered upon his new task: "The Captain has never made any attempt at fine writing, but simply wrote 'straight on,' as he says, often only the evening before publication, without attempting but the simplest revision." The first installment of "Army Life in the West" appeared on December 12, 1877, and ran for eighteen chapters, concluding on April 17, 1878. Not expecting his recollections to extend beyond his original commitment, Curtis later admitted that he "plunged into what I supposed would be of the most interest to the reader." But when he found that "I had a large circle of interested readers" and, even more importantly, "that the *Argus* was ready to pay for the story," Curtis agreed to write another series the following year.

The next portion of Curtis's narrative appeared on January 15, 1879, and ran through May 14, 1879, encompassing seventeen chapters. Referring with humility to "these rambling and unrevised sketches, put together in moments snatched from the administrative duties of the Military College," Captain Curtis was nevertheless proud of how the public had received his story. He admitted: "It was very gratifying in a recent vacation, when I visited many distant parts of the state, to find how many appreciative readers I everywhere met and to learn that so many had been entertained by them." Curtis even confessed to enjoying his task, being pleased "with the fascination peculiar to living over the old scenes, until I find it difficult to drop the pen." Although his recollections were generally well received by the public, some of the old veterans wondered why he had devoted so much space to "the common details of everyday life." Curtis responded to these critics by stating, "I believe from observation that the interest in these articles lies just in the minor circumstances of an officer's life. People know very little of how the army lives and what it does. If I can enlighten even a few readers, I shall think I have done a good work."

The third and final series of "Army Life in the West" began on January 21, 1880, and ran through an additional seventeen chapters, ending on May 19, 1880. Offering a tantalizing snippet prior to its publication, Curtis teased that, in events covered by this last series, "I was in some Indian warfare and the details of my life there will probably be more interesting than anything I have already told." As his tale unfolded in print, Reverend F. W. Skelton wrote a short note to congratulate Curtis on "Army Life in the West," exaggerating somewhat in his praise:

> It is not saying too much of the accomplished author of these sketches, that they have the charm and freshness of Xenophon's Anabasis. They are full of life and adventure, with not a dull page in them, keeping the attention constantly on the sketch, and no one who begins to read will lay aside the pleasing task until it is completed.

Hiram Atkins promptly published Reverend Skelton's letter, a compliment to both the author and the editor.[2]

Charles Curtis was a rather unique addition to society in the Southwest—a college graduate who had not been educated in medicine, the law, or at West Point—and was an astute observer of both his world and the men who inhabited it. He could convey the perils of crossing a river, then pivot and point out the idiosyncrasies of his fellow officers. Floods, storms, and desert crossings are described in detail, as are bears, fish, and prairie dogs. Nothing escapes his notice. As a young man living among other young men, it is no surprise that the captain's narrative is interspersed with humorous incidents and jokes, with each man trying to outdo his comrades in the mirth department. On the other hand, the portrayal of Apache attacks can be gruesome in the extreme. Yet Curtis is not one of those "only good Indian is a dead one" officers. He is respectful and curious about the culture and history of the Pueblo and Mojave nations, treating their people with dignity and respect. While Curtis has no use for the Mexican people as a whole, he enjoys the company of Lieutenant Colonel J. Francisco Chaves. He was a man of contradictions, yet a man of honor and character.

While Curtis's narrative encompasses three and one-half years during the Civil War, after receiving his commission in April of 1862 he never saw a Confederate soldier. Although he sometimes bemoaned being stuck in New Mexico and Arizona while other officers were winning fame and promotion in bloody battles, we are better off for his singular observations. Although a contemporary of Major John C. Cremony, author of *Life Among the Apaches*, their paths do not seem to have crossed during their service in the Southwest, leaving Curtis's recollections as a wonderful complement to that writer. "Army Life in the West" is a combination of travelogue and military history that is interspersed with anthropological and scientific observations. Above all else it is a well-written human interest story replete with memorable men and women on the American frontier.

Charles Albert Curtis, the son of Charles Stubbs and Amanda Fitz Allen (Ham) Curtis, was born at Hollowell, Kennebec County, Maine, on October 4, 1835. His ancestors William Curtis and wife Sarah arrived in Boston aboard the ship *Lion* in 1632 and settled in Roxbury, Massachusetts. Many of William's descendants lived in Hanover, Massachusetts, so many that it was said that when the town was incorporated in 1727 "no family was so largely represented or owned so much of the territory as did the Curtis family."[3]

The Curtis men had a long tradition of military service in America. Phillip, one of William's sons, served in a company during King Philip's War and was killed on November 5, 1675, near Mendon while attempting to rescue some neighbors who had been taken by the Indians.[4] More members of the Curtis family served in the French and Indian War and the original blockhouse at Hanover was commonly referred to as the Curtis garrison. When the town created a Committee of Correspondence and Safety in 1775, three Curtis brothers served as members. A paternal great-grandfather, William Curtis, and a maternal great-grandfather, Abner Curtis, served in companies raised in Hanover during the Revolution. His mother was a descendant of Captain John Ham who had raised a company in the District of Maine.[5] In addition to military service, other family members owned the Curtis Forge in Hanover, which for decades during the early nineteenth century produced anchors for the United States Navy.[6]

Charles Albert Curtis began his college preparatory work at the North Yarmouth Academy, Maine State Seminary (later to become Bates College), and Lewiston Falls Academy. Popular among his classmates, Curtis "figured as class poet and as the wit of the undergraduate class."[7] He remembered that, at the latter school, "my fellow students fancied me a quasi-military genius and regularly selected me for marshal of their academic processions." In the presidential campaign of 1856, Curtis led a political club that supported the new Republican Party and "perpetrated more mischief than it accomplished good." Most notably, Curtis and a few mates mischievously altered a Republican flag to a Democratic banner, an action that resulted in much blame-calling and finger-pointing in the partisan press. Curtis confessed that the uproar "frightened the reckless perpetrators of the prank into a silence which lasted for years."[8]

Charles A. Curtis as a student at Norwich University. Courtesy of Norwich University Archives.

He had planned to enter Bowdoin College along with a sizeable contingent from the Lewiston Falls Academy, but for some unaccountable reason entered Norwich University, also known as the Military College of Vermont, in February of 1858 and found himself in an environment much to his liking. Classes met from 7:30 A.M. to noon and from 1:30 to 4:00 in the afternoon. The classical course of instruction was so intense that students often transferred to other institutions, such as Dartmouth, Brown, Bowdoin, and Harvard, without losing ground in their studies. Although academic learning was an important component of the Norwich experience, the most appealing to young Curtis was the elite battalion of cadets, which from 1850 to 1861 never numbered more than one hundred. The military organization was unique. There were no permanent officers or non-commissioned officers, only an adjutant who was actually little more than a first sergeant and drilled with a musket like the privates. Temporary officers and non-commissioned officers were appointed daily from the senior and junior class, respectively. This arrangement allowed each cadet, over the four-year course, to serve in every capacity from private to battalion commander. Two adjutants were appointed annually, one serving during the first half of the school year and the other during the latter half. The adjutant's duties included calling the roll, marching the cadet battalion to meals and church, inspecting the barracks and grounds, and reading reports at morning parade. An officer of the day, appointed from the upperclassmen, received reports, kept order in quarters, and acted as mail clerk.

Military instruction, primarily based upon Winfield Scott's *Infantry Tactics*, consisted of artillery and infantry drills, the latter including bayonet, skirmish, and the popular Zouave maneuvers. Fencing was also taught, with an emphasis on sword, sabre, and bayonet. Curtis would later recall, "On the walls of nearly every cadet room were grouped foils, wooden cutlasses, and fencing poles." Lectures concentrated on "the tactical use of the three arms, special operations of war, tactical operations in sieges, [and] field service in war." Professor Alonzo Jackman, who taught mathematics and military science among other courses, took the lead in providing practical experience following years of service in the Vermont militia. Individual cadets had different motives for joining the military program and Curtis noted that "some confessed to the love of a handsome uniform, a pleasure in handling fire arms, sword, and sabre; others to a desire for regular hours for study, meals, sleep, and exercise; and others that they sought the ease of manner, grace of carriage, and erect figure which military drill was here to give."

Whatever their motivation, cadets found their world confined mainly to their barracks and recitation rooms. Young men lived in the South Barracks, a four-story brick structure with passages running the length of the building. Roll call was held on the second floor, the third floor contained a large recitation room, and the fourth floor included the armory. Cadets lived in rooms on the upper floors that opened onto the main passageways. Walls were whitewashed in a sort of brindle color and back-to-back rooms shared a chimney. There were no beds, mattresses or carpets. Cadets slept on wooden bunks, three feet wide, with blankets and sheets. Gun racks were fastened over the bunks where wooden pegs held old flintlock muskets and accouterments. Clothing was hung in closets beside the chimneys. Each morning the bunks were turned against the wall prior to inspection and prayers.

Cadets wore three different uniforms. For dress occasions they donned blue coats, with a "profusion" of silver buttons, blue pants (white in summer), and flat, round caps with silver lace. For drill they changed into "claw hammer" style sturdy cotton coats with three rows of buttons, dark blue pants with a two-inch black stripe on the seams, and high, blue cloth caps with a gold band. The undress uniform consisted of a single-breasted frock coat, blue pants (white in summer), and a soft, blue cap with velvet lace and the letters "N. U." in a gold wreath in front. Feeling that a military academy deserved a military magazine, Charles Curtis (Class of 1861) and George A. Converse (Class of 1863) decided to produce a periodical called *The Reveille*. Converse owned a small printing press, but Curtis had served a brief apprenticeship in the printer's trade so he set the type and operated the press. The first volume of *The Reveille* appeared in two numbers, April and December, in 1860, Converse assuming the role of publisher and Curtis serving as chief editor. Curtis also became editor of a short-lived publication called *University Quarterly* and rewrote the ritual for Alpha Sigma Pi when he joined that fraternity in 1858. He joined the Parthenon Society and acted as poet for that group from 1859 to 1861.

Curtis also became a public speaker, giving an 1859 commencement oration on "Improvement in the Art and Weapons of War" and an 1860 oration on "Military Education."

Physical exercise was also an important component of Norwich cadet life. In addition to regular drills, the cadet battalion would generally conduct a "promenade" during the summer. In 1858 the men marched to Woodstock, a distance of sixteen miles, to celebrate the Fourth of July. The following year the cadets made a similar march to Fairlee for the Fourth. Curtis remembered that on the latter occasion the cadets were led by Robert E. Hitchcock, carrying the sword worn by Colonel Trueman Ransom when he was killed while storming Chapultepec in the Mexican War. There were also sporting teams and, although there is no indication that Curtis played on the baseball team, he was elected president of the "Parade Foot Ball Club."

As the political situation deteriorated in the country in 1860, cadets found their military skills were in demand across the region, even at Dartmouth College, a rival of Norwich just across the Connecticut River. Class recitations began and ended with political discussions as cadets argued in favor of Lincoln, Douglas, Breckenridge, or Bell. Various political clubs organized torchlight processions, sometimes combining with Dartmouth men to swell their ranks. The tenor of the times was captured by the graduation of Samuel W. Shattuck in the Class of 1860; he had served in the Sixth Massachusetts Militia and was immediately hired to tap his expertise as an instructor in military science. Charles Curtis emerged from this tumultuous time with a bachelor's degree in the Class of 1861, but that year's commencement had to be postponed because most of the graduates and upperclassmen had left to instruct and drill the thousands of eager, untrained volunteers who had joined the army.[9]

Curtis returned to Maine on vacation in the spring of 1861 and, like many other former Norwich students, began drilling volunteers. While engaged in this task, he was invited to visit Bowdoin College where students had expressed a desire to form their own cadet battalion. Curtis recalled that "the proposition proved so attractive that I wrote President [Leonard] Woods and asked if I might be allowed to attend Senior recitations and lectures if I accepted the students' offer." President Woods quickly accepted this proposal and Curtis soon found himself in charge of some 150 young men, "intelligent and enthusiastic" but wholly ignorant of military affairs. At first, there were some detractors; boys who remembered young Curtis's unorthodox tactics at Lewiston Academy voted unanimously against his appointment for this important post.

Although they had no uniforms, members of the newly formed student battalion "proved themselves promptly responsive to every command given them, as well as attentive to all lectures and explanations." A few weeks after the formation of the battalion, complete with officers and companies, the drills and evolutions were supplemented by the arrival of boxes of muskets. Battalion commander Curtis saw that the weapons were covered with dirt and oil, so

> I accordingly distributed one rifle with a screwdriver to each student, and then in their presence took one apart and assembled it, requiring them to do the same. When this was done, I gave some further instruction concerning material to be used in cleaning, how to apply it, and how to keep arms and accoutrements in serviceable condition, and then ordered everyone to take his rifle to his room and next day appear in line with it in proper shape.

While at dinner that evening, Curtis was approached by a member of the battalion who seemed eager to learn how to make cartridges. He sent the young man after wrapping paper and the two sat and rolled blank cartridges, using sugar instead of gunpowder, until the student was as proficient as the master. Satisfied at the result and pleased with the youngster's enthusiasm, Curtis accepted another student's invitation for a carriage ride in the country, unaware that he was intentionally being decoyed away from campus.

When the pair returned to campus and began walking toward their rooms that night, Curtis was startled when, "suddenly, from every window and every doorway of every dormitory blazed volleys of musketry filling the air with the rattle of irregular discharge." In the five hours since his dinner, all 150 students had furiously been making and filling cartridges for their new muskets. It quickly became obvious that "every man of the Bowdoin Battalion had purchased powder and percussion caps and worked industriously in the preparation of ammunition." Curtis later admitted, "The constant flash and unceasing rattle of the rifles showed that the boys had wasted no time in their preparation."

As Curtis sat on the steps of the armory, pondering where he had gone wrong, President Woods, Professor Joshua L. Chamberlain, and three tutors came running up and demanded that the fusillade stop. Curtis said that would be impossible, so Woods declared he would put a stop to it and the six men headed for the dormitories. Chamberlain, who had been an avid supporter of the battalion since its recent inception, whispered to Curtis, "The young scamps will have to carry their fun to the end, as the president will presently learn." Curtis captured the moment:

> As we approached Appleton we found the north end in a blaze of light. Flashes of exploding gunpowder streamed from its windows and doorway, wreaths of smoke rose above its roof and floated into the pines in its rear, and the noise was continuous and ear-splitting. We walked toward the door, but instantly the firing party concentrated there and filled the aperture from top to bottom with sheets of flame and the President and his companions flattened their backs against the brick wall and waited.

A voice from overhead cried out, "Oh, Professor! First time under fire! How do you like it?" Bemused, Chamberlain said to President Woods, "Doctor, I think Mr. Curtis is right, the boys will have to fire their last cartridge before they stop." The firing kept up until nearly midnight, briefly flaring up again at two in the morning, when the students finally gave up and went to bed.

Of course, Curtis was summoned to the president's office next morning and the gist of the dressing down centered on Woods's assertion that "firearms should never be intrusted to the hands of ordinary college boys." Following an intense discussion of military discipline and its questionable effect on young men, Woods finally allowed the battalion to keep its weapons with the proviso that arms and ammunition be kept under lock and key in the armory every night. Curtis assembled his battalion, explained the gravity of the situation, and received assurances that no student would ever again fire his weapon without permission. The "Battle of Bowdoin" was over.[10]

In May of 1861 Charles Curtis had offered his services as "drill master" to the State of Maine, but had been turned down.[11]

Undeterred, he began rudimentary instruction for over a dozen volunteer companies raised in the area, including four which would eventually join the 6th Maine Infantry. Feeling that his military qualifications should result in a commission, Curtis did not enlist but joined the 6th Maine as a sort of unofficial drill instructor and secretary to the colonel.[12] On July 17 he accompanied the regiment to Washington, but it arrived too late to participate in the Battle of Bull Run.

Curtis served in Virginia near the Chain Bridge until August and then participated in the Federal advance on Lewinsville the following month when he apparently took command of one of the 6th Maine's companies. His conduct was observed by Colonel Isaac Stevens of the 79th New York Infantry who immediately detailed him on his staff. After Stevens was promoted to brigadier general, he learned that Curtis had no official status. Stevens did offer to obtain a commission for Curtis, but only on the promise that the "lieutenant" accompany him to his new assignment at Beaufort, North Carolina. Although tempted by the offer, Curtis decided to remain with the troops guarding Washington.

About this time Winfield S. Hancock was promoted and assumed command of a brigade at Fort Ethan Allen. His regular staff officers had not yet arrived, so Curtis volunteered to act as temporary aide. On September 28, during a march after dark, some of the Federal regiments fired into one another, not once but three separate times.[13] Curtis gave an account of his actions that night:

> I acted in the capacity of Aide-de-Camp to Brig. Gen. Hancock on that night, several weeks ago, when thirty men were accidentally shot by a part of our own force, and had the equivocal honor of getting a bullet through my military cape and being thrown to the ground by the dead horse of a Cavalryman riding by my side—carrying my own horse to the ground and rolling me in the dust. As soon as I was again mounted I was ordered to advance and let those who fired know we were friends. It was while riding to execute this order that I got a shot through the collar of my cape. I really believe, if there had been no one to see me, I should have "turned tail" and run—for I never imagined that I possessed much courage; but pride restrained me and I succeeded in letting the Massachusetts men know their mistake.

The next day when General George McClellan, commander of the Army of the Potomac, rode up to consult with Hancock, the latter brought out Curtis and introduced him to McClellan. The army commander told the young man, "Your conduct shall not be forgotten."[14]

Curtis was hiding a secret from the generals. He, too, had been shot, struck by a ball that passed through the edge of the left tibia about three inches below the knee and came out just below the knee on the outer side of the leg. Although he had been acting as a lieutenant since his arrival with the 6th Maine, Curtis had still not been officially commissioned and found himself in a delicate situation. He later explained that "being ignorant of my rights to Hospital attendance I did not receive the medical assistance I ought; also fearing that if I left the office I should lose my hopes of a commission, I studiously concealed my situation from the General until Inflammation set in." This decision not to seek treatment resulted in anchylosis, a condition wherein inflammation damaged the bone and cartilage with the resulting fusion or stiffening of the joint.

Unaware of Curtis's injury, Hancock offered him an appointment as assistant adjutant general with but one condition. That office had already been offered to someone else, but that man had said he would probably accept another offer. If the first appointee declined, the job would belong to Curtis. After over a week of waiting, Hancock gave Curtis the necessary paperwork for his appointment and sent him to Washington. The other man arrived literally as Curtis was mounting his horse and accepted the position. Curtis explained his embarrassment, saying, "This of course was a bitter disappointment to me, especially as my friends, and indeed myself, had been so sure of the appointment as to write home that it was a fixed fact." Hancock and his division commander, William F. Smith, were also embarrassed by the situation and both men gave Curtis recommendations to the War Department. A month after receiving his injury Curtis still had not obtained a commission and told his friends why: "The fact is I have no home influence, really I do not personally know a single Congressman or public man in our State and offices are given here to those only who possess political influence or have influential friends."[15] Curtis continued to act as a volunteer aide on General Hancock's staff and with the 6th Maine for the remainder of the year, but forces were at work to secure him a commission. Hancock and Colonel Hiram Burnham of the 6th Maine both endorsed his candidacy in letters to the War Department. Maine's new senator, Lot M. Morrill, had also expressed an interest in the case. On February 8, 1862, Assistant Secretary of War John Tucker wrote to Senator Morrill: "The Secretary of War directs me to inform you that he has read the papers accompanying the application of Mr. Charles A. Curtis, and considering it one of extraordinary merit, has given instructions to the Adjutant General to make the appointment."

Early in 1862 Curtis left his unpaid position in the army and took up residence in Yarmouth, Maine, probably to convalesce from his still-inflamed wound. He expressed impatience at receiving his merited appointment in several letters dispatched to the War Department, the last of which he sent directly to Secretary of War Edwin Stanton, complaining, "This life of idleness to one who has been in service since the war began has few charms for me, I am anxious to again be in service, as I said before, and trust that I shall at once receive the commission which must have been long since made out."[16] The Adjutant General finally issued Curtis a commission as second lieutenant in the 7th United States Infantry on April 14, 1862, but two weeks later inexplicably transferred the new officer to Company F of the 5th United States Infantry. He received his commission on April 30 and swore out his oath of allegiance on May 2 before a justice of the peace in Yarmouth.[17] After over a year of unpaid service in positions of trust and responsibility, in addition to receiving a severe wound that would leave him a cripple, Charles Albert Curtis had finally become an officer in the United States Army.

Lieutenant Curtis left Kansas City on June 16, 1862, and, after a long, adventurous stage ride along the Santa Fe Trail, reached Fort Craig, New Mexico, where he reported for duty on July 4. Later that month, he accompanied the Federal force that drove the remaining Texas troops out of New Mexico following their aborted invasion of that territory. He spent the next few months on assignments at Los Pinos and Peralta, before being assigned to Fort Marcy in November. After a brief stint at San José in June of 1863, Curtis returned to Fort Marcy where he served as acting assistant quartermaster and acting commissary of subsistence. On October 24 he marched his company to the tiny outpost at Los Valles Grandes[18] where, as the only line officer present, he acted as commander, quartermaster, and commissary until June of 1864. The highlight of what Curtis called his "not very eventful" service occurred on November 4 when he "with thirty five men repelled an attack of three hundred Navajos on the post." The only significant change in his status was a promotion to first lieutenant, an appointment he accepted on March 30, 1864.

After being relieved at Los Valles Grandes, Curtis and his company were ordered to march to Fort Whipple in Arizona Territory. They left Los Pinos on June 23 and reached Fort Whipple on July 29. Four days later he was appointed acting assistant quartermaster and acting commissary of subsistence at that post, holding those offices until returned to company duty on April 26, 1865. In the meantime he had been appointed acting commissary of musters on February 23, 1865, and would pair this office with the role of recruiting officer for the 1st Arizona Volunteers, effective June 12, 1865. Lieutenant Curtis remained at Fort Whipple until he departed on leave of absence on October 23, 1865.

On October 25, 1864, Curtis had applied to the adjutant general for an appointment in the Quartermaster Department, pointing out that he had actually been an acting assistant quartermaster since July of 1862. He also confessed, "A severe wound received on the Potomac has somewhat incapacitated me for Infantry service but in no wise impaired my health—never having been unwell since my recovery in the fall of 1861." Captain Allen Anderson approved the application and forwarded it to Washington with the comment, "He is sober industrious and capable. His lameness (the result of a wound received while in the service of his country) although it interferes with the performance of some of his duties as an Infantry subaltern, would not in the least incapacitate him in the performance of staff duties." The three highest ranking politicians in Arizona Territory signed a letter of recommendation for Curtis on January 2, 1865. Governor John Goodwin, Territorial Secretary Richard McCormick, and Territorial Congressional Delegate Charles Poston all assured Secretary of War Stanton that offering Curtis a quartermaster position would be appreciated by his "wide circle of friends." On May 17, 1865, Quartermaster General Montgomery Meigs also endorsed the application, noting, "His accounts were promptly forwarded and are well prepared." Although his application never received approval, Curtis did receive a brevet to captain on September 27, 1865, for "meritorious service during the war." He would later say, "I am not aware to whom I am indebted for my brevet. I applied for a Quarter mastership and received a Brevet instead."

When his leave expired, Lieutenant Curtis reported to Fort Leavenworth, where he was placed in charge of a body of recruits for the 5th Infantry and marched them overland to New Mexico. He was assigned to Fort Sumner, New Mexico, from September 1, 1866, to October 13, 1867, where he helped police the Navajos at Bosque Redondo. Curtis then marched to Fort Reynolds, Colorado, where he commanded the post almost continually until the spring of 1869 when he was listed on army rolls as officially unassigned. On August 19, 1870, Lieutenant Curtis appeared in New York City before an Army Retiring Board that inquired into his ability to continue as an infantry officer. In response to a question from a board member whether he was incapacitated to serve on active duty, Curtis honestly replied, "For movements of celerity, double quick, or long marches, Yes, otherwise not incapacitated." A thorough investigation of Curtis's physical condition and his military service led the Retiring Board to conclude that he should be placed on the retirement list effective December 15, 1870.

Even prior to his retirement, Lieutenant Curtis had rekindled his association with Norwich University. While still on duty at Fort Reynolds, he had been detailed as a professor of military science and tactics at that school, reporting for duty on April 8, 1869, and continuing until August of 1875. At that time he resigned to accept a similar post at St. Augustine College in Benicia, California, although he remained only a year before returning to Norwich. Curtis resumed his professorship but was elected president of Norwich University on October 19, 1876, and remained in that capacity until his resignation on July 1, 1880, shortly after the publication of his military narrative.[19] During his tenure as president, Curtis received an honorary bachelor's degree from Bowdoin College in 1877. In recognition of his contribution to Bowdoin during the spring of 1861, the administration voted that the name of Charles Albert Curtis should be inserted into the catalog as if he had graduated in the Class of 1861.[20]

Prior to his elevation to the presidency of Norwich, Curtis had considered a teaching position at the University of Tennessee.

Charles A. Curtis as Commandant of Cadets at Norwich University. Courtesy of Norwich University Archives.

Then-president Malcolm Douglass recommended Curtis as "singularly well qualified" to teach military science classes. Douglass continued, "He has an acquaintance with Academic detail and the exigencies of Academic life, strengthened and matured by long experience, far beyond what is usually found in Officers of the Army. As a military instructor, a Professor of Military Science, a vigilant Commandant, a thoughtful disciplinarian, it would in my judgement be difficult to find his equal." When President Douglass resigned, he strongly recommended that Charles Curtis be chosen as his successor, advice that was taken by the Board of Trustees. After his own resignation in 1880, the Norwich University Board of Trustees publicly thanked Curtis "for his attention to the interests of the University, and his self-sacrificing efforts in its behalf since he has held the office of President."

After leaving Norwich, Captain Curtis taught military science and tactics at a series of schools, colleges, and universities: Bishop Seabury Mission (Shattuck School), at Faribault, Minnesota (1880–1885); East Florida Seminary, Gainesville, Florida (1886–1888); Kenyon Military Academy, Gambier, Ohio (1888–1889); Marmaduke Military Academy, Sweet Springs, Missouri (1891–1892); Howe Military School, Lima (now Howe), Indiana (1895–1896); and the University of Wisconsin (1899–1907). Prior to taking the Marmaduke position, Curtis seriously considered a proposition to teach school on St. Lawrence Island in the Bering Sea and oversee the introduction of a herd of Siberian reindeer. While employed in a teaching capacity, Captain Curtis also held National Guard ranks of colonel in Minnesota, lieutenant colonel in Florida, and colonel in Wisconsin. As an acknowledgement for his long and faithful service, Curtis was promoted to full captain in 1904.

Charles Curtis had married Harriet Louise Hughes of Ashland, New Hampshire, on May 17, 1866 and she, like a typical army wife, followed her husband on his various assignments. They had five children: Wardon, Lawrence, George, Dorothy, and Barbara. In 1885 Harriet must have tired of the turmoil of an officer's wife and she settled in Madison, Wisconsin, to raise the children in a more stable environment. Charles's professorship at the University of Wisconsin allowed the family to reunite permanently. In addition to his teaching and National Guard duties, Curtis supported the Republican Party and attended a Protestant Episcopal church.

He also joined many service and patriotic organizations, including the Masons, Wisconsin Historical Society, Military Order of the Loyal Legion, Grand Army of the Republic, Society of the Army of the Potomac, Sons of the American Revolution, Alpha Pi Sigma Fraternity, and Scabbard and Blade Society.[21]

In his free time Captain Curtis wrote stories for popular magazines, including *St. Nicholas*, *Wide Awake*, *Youth's Companion*, and *Harper's Young People*, in addition to serialized stories for several newspapers. He wrote one book of fiction, *Captured by the Navajos*, published by Harper & Bros. in 1904, and contributed chapters to *Boy's Book of the Army* and *Adventures of Uncle Sam's Soldiers.* Most of his writing was based upon fictionalized versions of his military adventures.[22]

Headstone of Mr. and Mrs. Charles A. Curtis in Arlington National Cemetery. Courtesy of Michael Patterson and arlingtoncemetery.net.

On April 4, 1907, Curtis suffered a severe attack of pneumonia, but after five weeks of hospitalization he was thought recovered enough to return home. A longstanding intestinal infection became worse and at 2:55 A. M. on May 26 Charles Curtis died from an ulcer of the duodenum at his home in Madison, Wisconsin. A military funeral was held the following day by the University Regiment. An obituary said of Curtis, "He did not mingle largely in social affairs, but when not busied with the duties of his department to which he devoted himself without stint, he was occupied with literary work, military history and fiction." A fellow professor confessed to "a pang of regret of the passing of that unruffled, kindly, upright character, and those who came in closest touch with him feel that they have lost a friend."[23]

Captain Curtis's casket was sent by train to Washington, D. C. where it was transferred to Fort Myer, Virginia, for interment in Arlington National Cemetery. At ten o'clock on Memorial Day, amid thousands of graves decorated with flowers and flags, Captain Charles Albert Curtis, United States Army Retired, was laid to rest. A chaplain said a few words of comfort, the firing party shot off three volleys, and a trumpeter sounded "Taps." He would lie there alone until 1924 when Harriet would join her husband for eternity.

Alan D. Gaff
Donald H. Gaff

Notes

1. *Argus and Patriot*, December 5, 1877.
2. *Argus and Patriot*, February 18, 1880.
3. Dwelley and Simons, *Town of Hanover*, pt. 2, 107–108.
4. Olney, *Passengers on the* Lion, 176.
5. *History of Dane County* 2: 212.
6. Barry, *Historical Sketch*, 139.
7. *Daily Kennebec Journal*, May 29, 1907.
8. Minot and Snow, *Tales of Bowdoin*, 261–62.
9. Minot and Snow, *Tales of Bowdoin*, 261; Ellis, *Norwich University (1898)*, 11, 14–18, 54; Ellis, *Norwich University (1911)*, 1: 123–24, 130–31, 484, 493, 531; 2: 651.
10. Minot and Snow, *Tales of Bowdoin*, 263–71.
11. Unless otherwise noted, subsequent material in this introduction is taken from "Memorandum of papers in case of 1 Lieut. Charles A. Curtis Retired," Letters Received by the Commission Branch of the Adjutant General's Office (1870).
12. *Portland Daily Advertiser*, October 11, 1861.

13. One soldier wrote that, during the second encounter, inexperienced troops fired upon one another when they mistook fireflies for enemy musketry in the darkness. *Philadelphia Inquirer*, November 2, 1861.

14. Powell, *Records of Living Officers*, 158.

15. *Maine Cultivator and Hallowell Gazette*, November 2, 1861.

16. Charles A. Curtis to E. M. Stanton, April 18, 1862, Letters Received by the Office of the Adjutant General, Main Series, 1862.

17. Charles A. Curtis to Major Gausche, April 30, 1862 and Oath of Allegiance, May 2, 1862, Letters Received by the Office of the Adjutant General, Main Series, 1862.

18. Although the exact location of the post at Los Valles Grandes is no longer known, the general site is in today's Valles Caldera National Preserve approximately five miles west of Los Alamos, New Mexico.

19. *Ellis, Norwich University (1911)*, 2: 652.

20. Stanwood, *Class of 1861*, 10; *Bowdoin Orient* 7, no. 6 (July 18, 1877): 62.

21. Ellis, *Norwich University (1911)*, 2: 652; *History of Dane County*, 213.

22. Ellis, *Norwich University (1911)*, 2: 652.

23. Freeman, "Colonel Charles A. Curtis," 225–26.

Chapter 1

The Adventure Begins

A four years' course at the Military College of Vermont had enabled me to offer my services at the outbreak of the late war as military instructor to the volunteers of my native State of Maine and, after a few months' drilling and but a few days before the First Battle of Bull Run, I arrived in Washington with the 6th Maine Infantry. I never held a commission in the Volunteers or bore a musket in the ranks, but had frequent opportunities, nevertheless, to act as volunteer aide and twice as company commander in several affairs on the Potomac. It is not my intention to dwell upon this experience, but simply to mention that it was my good fortune to attract the attention of a general officer and, through his influence, secure, as a reward, a commission in the 5th Regular Infantry. This regiment was located at Fort Craig, New Mexico and, as soon as I had accepted my appointment and, in spite of an application to be allowed to remain on the scene of big movements and grand battles, I was ordered to join my regiment forthwith.[1] Accordingly,

1. Second only to Fort Union in its importance to the New Mexico frontier, Fort Craig protected the northern end of the Jornada del Muerto when it was established in 1854. Named for Captain Louis S. Craig who had been murdered two years earlier, Fort Craig would eventually consist of twenty-two buildings surrounded by a thick wall, all construction being made of adobe bricks. Located on the west bank of the Rio Grande about eight miles from the Jornada del Muerto, the post was designed to hold two companies that would

one day in June, 1862, I found myself in Kansas City, Missouri, looking for a seat in the Overland Stage which left that place once a week.

This route was beset by the marauding bands of the Confederate partisan chief William Quantrill, a man as ubiquitous as Robin Hood and as sanguinary and cruel as a Cheyenne.[2] The principal topic of the conversations of the bar-rooms and saloons in Kansas City was the daring exploits of this somewhat overrated leader; a leader whose existence, like that of Robin Hood, there have been plenty of persons ready to doubt. And there has been much to encourage this doubt, for few men can be found who claim to have seen Quantrill and his death, like his life, was hidden in mystery. He would be reported one day as swimming the Missouri River under the fire of a dozen pursuers and the next day several hundred miles farther west, burning a Kansas village and pillaging the inhabitants of their stock. Almost my first Western adventure was connected indirectly with this notorious chief.

I had found, on my arrival at Kansas City, that every seat in the coach which was to leave the next day had been taken and that there was but one vacant seat left for the following week. I booked myself for that and passed away the time in strolling about the place, making acquaintances and participating in various amusements. One morning I walked down to the levee to see a steamboat from St. Louis arrive. As she drew up to her mooring place, I noticed upon her deck an officer of the army and, as soon as the opportunity offered, I went on board and made his acquaintance. I found him to be Captain Charles E. Farrand, of the Regular cavalry, on his way to Independence

---

attempt to check depredations by Apache and Navajo raiders. During the Civil War soldiers and civilians constructed earthworks intended to provide protection against threats of a Confederate attack that never came. Fort Craig was abandoned in 1885. Thompson, *Texas and New Mexico*, 56–57; Thompson, *New Mexico Territory*, 97–99; Frazer, *Forts*, 98.

2. Described as a "mean and vicious" child, William C. Quantrill became a notorious bushwhacker during the Bleeding Kansas period. He put his experience to work for the rebel army and his guerrilla band captured Independence, Missouri, only a few months after Curtis began his westward journey. Over the years Quantrill's loosely organized band of raiders included such men as George Todd, Bill Anderson, Cole Younger, and Frank and Jesse James. Allegedly commissioned captain and colonel, Quantrill is best known for plundering and burning Lawrence, Kansas, on August 21, 1863, killing upwards of 200 civilians during the attack. Mortally wounded near Smiley, Kentucky, by Union soldiers after the war had effectually ended, Quantrill died in a military prison in Louisville on June 6, 1865. Breihan, *Quantrill*, 17, 50, 54–56, 134, 141; Boatner, *Dictionary*, 675; *Baltimore Sun*, June 10, 1865.

to instruct some Missouri troops.[3] We walked up to the hotel together to procure a conveyance to take the captain and his wife to their destination and, after completing the arrangements, returned to the steamer.

As we went up the plank from the levee to the deck, our attention was attracted by the clatter of hoofs and the clanking of sabres and, looking back, we saw a squad of twenty men halt on the shore, dismount and come on board the boat. While I was wondering what could be the cause of this demonstration, the sergeant in charge advanced to Farrand and told him he had an order for his arrest, at the same time placing in his hands a paper. After reading the order, the captain passed it to me and I found it was an order from the commander of a camp in the vicinity of Kansas City for the arrest of Quantrill, who was said to be a passenger on board the steamer *Excelsior*, from St. Louis to Kansas City, disguised as a captain of the United States Army. Then followed an accurate description of the officer who stood before me, even down to a mole at the corner of his left eye. "Well," said the captain, as I finished the order, "what do you think of that?"

"It appears to be an exact description of you," I replied.

"But I am not Quantrill," he said, with emphasis. "I am a graduate of West Point and have been an officer in the army since 1857."

"My orders were to arrest you and any other persons in your company," said the sergeant, glancing at me as he closed the sentence.

I made no attempt at explanation when I found I was included in the arrest. To me the whole thing was an amusing adventure, whatever it might be to my new acquaintance. I knew I should not have much difficulty in proving my loyalty to the flag, but how it would be with the tall, handsome fellow before me and whether he was the noted guerrilla mentioned in the order, I was by no means sure.

3. Charles E. Farrand graduated from West Point in 1857 and received a commission as second lieutenant in the 7th Infantry on January 2, 1858. He was transferred to the 1st Infantry on June 24, 1858, and promoted to first lieutenant in the 11th Infantry on May 14, 1861. Advanced to captain on October 24, 1861, Farrand served in the Western Theater during the war. Transferred to the 20th Infantry on September 21, 1866, he mustered out of service on January 1, 1871. His father, Eben Farrand, had been an officer in the U. S. Navy, but resigned his commission to serve as a captain in the Confederate Navy. Charles married May Spencer in Chicago on September 19, 1888, but the couple had no children. Charles Farrand died on September 29, 1900, at Arvada, Colorado. Cullum, *Biographical Register* 2: 466; *Denver Post*, September 18, 1900; October 1, 1900; Cook County, Illinois, Marriages Index, 1871–1920.

I could not take sides with him, as he seemed to expect, for I had no knowledge of him whatever. His appearance was in his favor and while he was naturally indignant, as an innocent man might be, there was no bluster or swagger about him.

He at last requested the sergeant to accompany him to his stateroom where he could show his United States commission and the orders under which he was traveling. This was assented to and the sergeant directed two men to remain with me and half of the others to go along the outside of the boat, while he with the rest went into the saloon with the captain. All Western boats have a saloon on the second deck, running the entire length, and staterooms open out of it, each having a second door out on the guards. It was to prevent the supposed Quantrill from making a bolt through his stateroom, from the saloon, that the men were stationed outside.

I waited patiently on my seat for about fifteen minutes, until the party returned, the sergeant having become convinced that Farrand was the person he represented himself to be. With apologies for the inconvenience the execution of his orders had caused, he left us and his party soon clattered and jingled out of sight.

When once more alone, Farrand showed more indignation than he had during the whole interview with the sergeant and for the rest of the day he never ceased to wonder who was at the bottom of "this contemptible trick." About six o'clock in the afternoon he left for Independence and I never met him again, but I afterward learned that a party of his friends in St. Louis telegraphed the military commander at Kansas City that Quantrill was on the steamboat, giving a minute description of Farrand as a practical joke. Whether they were punished for so grave a military offence I never knew, as in a few days I was on the plains and events of the next month reached me only in fragments.

On the 16th of June, 1862, a Concord coach, drawn by six horses and capable of holding nine passengers, drew up at my hotel. I found the passengers were to be six in number, being two in a seat, and consisted of Captain William J. L. Nicodemus, of the 12th Infantry; Lieutenant Hugh Johnson, recently appointed, like myself, and to the same regiment; an army surgeon, Doctor William W. Nassau; and Mahlon Cottrill, whom Vermonters will remember as the owner of some of the principal stage lines in the old coaching days.[4] The sixth passenger was to be taken up farther along the line.

Mr. Cottrill had recently secured the contract to run the mail to Santa Fé and was going out to look after the stock and property of the old contractor, with a view to the valuation and purchase.[5] Our sixth passenger was the old contractor, a former member of Congress, by the name of Andrew Stuart.[6] His precise whereabouts

4. William J. L. Nicodemus was a graduate of West Point in 1858 and was commissioned second lieutenant in the 5th Infantry on January 19, 1859. He served in Utah and New Mexico Territories and was promoted to first lieutenant in the 11th Infantry on May 14, 1861. Commissioned captain in the 12th Infantry on October 24, 1861, Nicodemus was sent east in the fall of 1862 and served briefly as colonel of the 4th Maryland. Assigned to the Signal Corps on February 20, 1863, he served there until August 23, 1865, when he reverted from his Volunteer rank as lieutenant colonel to captain in the 12th Infantry. While overseeing the Signal Camp at Georgetown, D. C., he married Fannie Pettit on December 27, 1864. Nicodemus served in various garrisons until assigned to Western University at Pittsburgh as military instructor. Discharged on December 29, 1870, he became a professor of civil engineering at the University of Wisconsin and died in Madison, Wisconsin, on January 6, 1879. When the 21st New York was formed, Hugh M. Johnson was commissioned as ensign on May 20, 1861, and elevated to first lieutenant on January 2, 1862. He received a commission as second lieutenant in the 5th Infantry on February 19, 1862 and was promoted to first lieutenant on October 21, 1863. Johnson resigned on November 15, 1869. When questioned for the 1890 Veterans Census, he claimed to have been a captain in the 21st New York although no record of him serving at that rank can be located. At that time Johnson was a successful stock breeder in Great Barrington, Massachusetts. He died in Philadelphia on May 13, 1928. William W. Nassau graduated from Lafayette College in 1850 and received his medical degree from the University of Pennsylvania in 1855. He practiced medicine in Davenport, Iowa, until the war, when he was commissioned assistant surgeon of the 2nd Iowa on May 31, 1861. Commissioned surgeon of volunteers on April 4, 1862, Nassau rose to become surgeon-in-chief of the First Division, Seventeenth Army Corps prior to his resignation on January 23, 1863. Doctor Nassau is credited with the establishment of steamboat hospitals on the Mississippi River and its tributaries. He settled in Burlington, Iowa, and died there on May 23, 1891. A native of Bridport, Vermont, at the age of twenty-nine Mahlon Cottrill moved to Montpelier and began work on a stage line. Cottrill secured a partner and bought out his employer, the new business becoming the primary means of transportation between Montreal and Boston until the expansion of the railroads in the state. In conjunction with the stage line, he also had extensive mail contracts and ran the celebrated Pavilion Hotel in Montpelier. Following the death of his wife, the former Catherine Couch, on April 28, 1861, Mahlon set his sights on the West. He established a number of stage and postal delivery lines under various business names, the original line running from Kansas City to Santa Fe. Cottrill died in Kansas City, Missouri, on October 20, 1864. Cullum, *Biographical Register* 2: 477–78; Brown, *Signal Corps*, 36–37; Heitman, *Historical Register* 1: 515, 741; *Herd Register and Breeder's Journal* (January 1903) 13: not paginated; 1890 Veteran Census, Great Barrington, Massachusetts; Hugh M. Johnson Pension Records; Coffin, *Men of Lafayette*, 35; *Pennsylvania Men*, 146; *Town of Montpelier*, 493–94, 520.

5. The firm of Cottrill, Vickroy and Company operated under the name of the Kansas City, Santa Fe and Colorado Stage Company. One editor summarized the operation: "The distance between Santa Fé and Kansas is about eight hundred miles, and there are stations all along the route at convenient distances, for changing horses, accommodation of passengers, &c. From the following number of horses, mules, coaches and men employed, something may be imagined of the magnitude of the business: Number of horses used, fifty; mules, two hundred; coaches, twenty-five; men employed, fifty." Several branches from this main line gave access to southern New Mexico and Colorado. *St. Albans Messenger*, September 18, 1862.

6. Andrew Stuart had received but limited schooling when he began working in a Pittsburgh newspaper office. In 1850 he moved to Steubenville, Ohio, and became editor of

were not known, but, as I remarked above, he was to join us farther along.

Upon assembling at the coach, Captain Nicodemus told us we had better not wear uniforms, but put on civilian apparel, that bands of Quantrill's men would probably overhaul us and if they had no suspicion that we were soldiers would let us pass by, simply relieving us of superfluous valuables. To Lieutenant Johnson's objection that it seemed to look like cowardice to sink our rank, the captain replied that "he hoped none of us would prove cowards if it came to a fight, but he thought it foolhardy to invite attack, when a simple change of clothing would probably take us safely through." We agreed to this and changed our dress, at the same time looking well to our pistols and ammunition.[7]

Captain Nicodemus was a Baltimorean and a graduate of West Point. His traits of character will show themselves as we go on. Lieutenant Johnson had been a dry goods clerk in Buffalo, whom patriotism had taken into the field and whose "Congressional uncle" had secured for him a commission in the Regular Army. A good fellow enough and a brave one, as I had opportunity afterwards to learn, but whose bundle of Ned Buntline, Harry Hazel and Lieutenant Murray's novelettes, stored under his seat for his perusal on the plains, did not convey to the rest of us a high impression of his erudition and literary acquirements.[8] Doctor Nassau was known in the Army of the Cumberland as the "fighting doctor," having at Fort Donelson abandoned the scalpel to take the sword, rally a band of retreating soldiers and lead them into the fight, a thing he was well qualified to do from some previous experience as militia captain and no end of pluck.

Johnson had been sick for some time with dysentery and at first declared his intention of remaining behind for another week,

---

the *American Union*. Stuart served one term in Congress, continued to publish his newspaper for a couple of years and then went into the shipping business. His freight company carried supplies and mail along the Santa Fe Trail during the Civil War. Stuart resided in Washington, D. C. where he died intestate on April 30, 1872, leaving his widow Henrietta to sort out his many business holdings. *Congressional Dictionary*, 827; *Baltimore Sun*, May 2 1872; *Reports of Kansas Supreme Court* 22: 585–94.

7. The caution displayed by Captain Nicodemus was undoubtedly warranted. On the night of September 16, 1862, a party of fifteen guerrillas waylaid the Kansas Stage Company coach, robbed the passengers, and stole everything of value from the mail bags. *New York Evening Post*, October 6, 1862.

8. Edward Z. C. Judson ("Ned Buntline"), Justin Jones ("Harry Hazel") and Maturin M. Ballou ("Lieutenant Murray") were popular and prolific dime novelists of the period. They wrote historical adventures, war stories, maritime tales, and frontier fiction. Cox, *Dime Novel*, 17, 147–49.

but at the last moment placed himself in the coach, on the back seat, with Nicodemus. The latter held the lieutenant in his arms for a great part of the time, over the first 300 miles of our journey—and he was no small burden—and showed him every kindly attention in his power.

The allowance of baggage was sixty pounds per man and, in addition to this, each one of us had a roll of bedding, for sleeping on the prairie. Under the seats and in every available place were bestowed parcels, lunch packages, canteens and two demijohns of Bourbon whiskey, given some members of our party by Mr. Charles Kearney, a Kansas City merchant.[9] Revolvers, two breech-loading carbines and ammunition for the same were placed in convenient loops overhead, for we were quite sure we should be obliged to use them. Only the trip before, at one of the relay stations, the Confederates had taken all the horses from the coach and stables and a month before, when Captain Nicodemus had come in from Santa Fé, bearing special dispatches from General Edward R. S. Canby to Washington, all the passengers had been robbed.[10]

The Eastern reader, accustomed to the green fields and forests, hills, mountains and valleys, springs, rivulets and rivers which surround him on every hand, gets but a faint idea of the plains, mountains, valleys and streams of the Far West. In my own case I know that close reading of Western travel, with careful study of all the physical features of the country between the Missouri River

9. Charles Kearney was a native of Ireland and left for America just before Queen Victoria assumed the British throne, claiming afterwards that he had no desire to live "under petticoat rule." He served as a Texas Ranger in the Mexican War, seeing the opportunities offered in the Southwest. He began freighting to New Mexico Territory and opened stores in Albuquerque and Santa Fe, as well as Westport, Missouri. Kearney's firm became an economic powerhouse and one morning he made $30,000 before finishing breakfast. The Civil War brought his business to a halt, so Kearney unsuccessfully tried his hand at investing on Wall Street. After the war he gave up the mercantile trade and concentrated on real estate and grain trading. Kearney died on January 3, 1898, in Kansas City, Missouri, leaving a widow, the former Josephine Harris, and four children. *Kansas City Star*, January 4, 1898.

10. Edward Richard Sprigg Canby began his advanced education at Wabash College, but was admitted to West Point and graduated in 1839, next to last in his class. Brevetted twice during the Mexican War, Canby was in New Mexico when the Civil War broke out. Commissioned colonel of the 19th Infantry, he commanded the District of New Mexico until 1862 when he was sent east to act as an administrative officer with the rank of brigadier general of volunteers. For part of this period Canby was an unofficial secretary of war under Edwin Stanton. Promoted to major general in 1864, he was seriously wounded aboard a gunboat on the White River in Arkansas. General Canby led the forces that compelled the surrender of Mobile, Alabama, in 1865, remained in the army as a brigadier general, and was murdered April 11, 1873, while at a peace negotiation with Modoc Indians. Heyman, *Prudent Soldier*, 24, 27, 37, 64, 138, 189–90, 219, 231, 375–76; Cullum, *Biographical Register* 2: 590–91.

and the Pacific Ocean, did not fully prepare me for what I met with when I came to march over and actually see the country for myself. I have since crossed the plains on foot from the Missouri to Fort Sumner, New Mexico; I have crossed in a stagecoach from the same point to Santa Fé; I have marched from the Rio Grande to the Pacific; and I have crossed the continent on the railroad; and I feel obliged to say that even when I saw the very things of which I had so often read, I was surprised; so hard is it to break up the impressions made by our home surroundings.[11]

When one leaves Fort Leavenworth, Kansas for the overland trip, on foot or in the stagecoach, for several days' journey the country does not strike him as very different from most of the Eastern States.[12] There may be, if he chooses to examine closely, some trees and shrubs different from those he saw at home, but there is still the verdure; there are still the brawling streams that skirt the roadside or over which the road passes on a bridge; there are the wayside springs and there are the waving forests. But soon the trees dwarf and finally disappear, except the cottonwoods along the river bottom; soon no more springs are seen and, shortly after, an entire day's march may be made without seeing a brook or spring. Now the soldier, who has served in the East and replenished his canteen every time he desired cool water, first learns why the army canteen is covered

11. When General James Carleton needed a place to confine Apache captives in 1862, Captain Joseph Updegraff, 5th Infantry, recommended a site called Bosque Redondo in eastern New Mexico along the Pecos River. The post that would guard these captives would be called Fort Sumner, after General Edwin Vose Sumner who had recently been killed while leading an army corps at the battle of Antietam. While soldiers eventually had adobe buildings, Apaches lived in tents or brush shelters. An influx of thousands of Navajos in 1864 stretched Bosque Redondo past capacity. Although it occupied over one million acres, with access to wood, water, and arable land, the captives did not adapt well to farming. In fact, hostile Navajos raided the Bosque for provisions and livestock, the undermanned garrison incapable of protecting their charges. After the Navajos signed a treaty with the government in 1868, they returned to their homes and the post was auctioned off. Lucien Maxwell bought the site for a ranch and in 1881 Pat Garrett shot "Billy the Kid" in one of the buildings that had been remodeled into a home. Thompson, *New Mexico Territory*, 123–26; Frazer, *Forts*, 104.

12. In 1827 Colonel Henry Leavenworth selected the site for a new western post that would be named Fort Leavenworth in his honor. Located on bluffs on the west bank of the Missouri River, Fort Leavenworth had several missions: protect the fur trade on the upper Missouri, protect traders on the Santa Fe Trail, protect American settlers from Indian raids, and protect the peaceful Indians from ruthless exploitation by whites. To these were later added the protection of settlers on the Oregon Trail and its use as a base for scouts and surveys as far west as the Rocky Mountains. Fort Leavenworth became the base of operations for troops advancing to New Mexico and California in the Mexican War, as well as those sent on the Utah Expedition in 1857. During the Civil War the fort acted as a defense for Missouri and Kansas and was responsible for keeping western mail routes operational. After the war Fort Leavenworth transitioned into an administrative center and remains an important military base to this day. Hughes, *Fort Leavenworth*, 3, 5, 15–22, 35–40, 58, 64, 67–69.

with cloth. It is that by saturating the woolen cover and leaving the cork out, the rapid evaporation of the water on the outside may cool that inside. In nearly all parts of the Far West water is brought into the houses in the evening, of a temperature too warm to be palatable and is cooled in water pots covered with woolen cloth or in those which are slightly porous, so as to emit a constant moisture, or in canvas buckets which do the same. The water thus cooled in the night is drunk during the following day.

As the march continues, the grasses change. Timothy, bluegrass, clover, etc. have all disappeared and are succeeded by the rich and burling buffalo grass and soon this yields in New Mexico to the grama grass. The country gradually grows drier and the cactus begins to be seen on every hand. Insect life grows more venomous and rattlesnakes abound. One officer who marched with me from Fort Leavenworth killed sixty-four rattlesnakes before we reached Bent's Old Fort and that without hunting for them.[13] Often we were compelled to march thirty and sometimes forty miles in order to reach water. As we approach the Rocky Mountains and its spurs, we see for the first time the *piñon* (a small pine bearing edible seeds) and juniper trees. These are about the size of the apple tree and seen at a long distance away, on the dry and otherwise barren mountainside, look like orchards irregularly set out.

In New Mexico the whole country is dry and utterly incapable of cultivation except by irrigation. There are grasses which grow luxuriantly during the fall rains and cure on the stalk retaining all their nourishment through the year. This makes the country excellent for raising sheep and cattle. Nearly all vegetation, even the grasses, is armed with thorns, and tarantulas, scorpions, centipedes and other poisonous insects abound. Harmless lizards rustle

13. In 1833 William Bent, one of the Southwest's most famous traders, constructed an adobe fort on the north bank of the Arkansas River a dozen miles west of the Purgatoire River. Originally named Fort William, it soon became known as Bent's Fort. One author explained its significance this way: "In the heart of Indian country and buffalo hunting grounds and at the crossroads of key overland routes, it was a fur trading center and rendezvous for traders and Indians; a way station and supply center for emigrants and caravans; and the chief point of contact and cultural transmission between whites and Indians of the southern Plains." The fort became headquarters of Bent, St. Vrain and Company, but this trading empire lost its importance during the Mexican War when it became a government supply depot and scared away the Indian trade. Following a cholera epidemic in 1849, William Bent partially destroyed his fort and moved farther down the Arkansas where he built Bent's New Fort to distinguish it from his original site, now called Bent's Old Fort. By the Civil War, the Old Fort had been rebuilt and was in use as a stage station. *Soldier and Brave*, 103–106.

Captain Charles A. Curtis in 1866. Courtesy of Norwich University Archives.

and gleam through the grass on every side and the horrid rattlesnake sounds his warning or hisses his defiance as we pass him on the road.

Unaware of what lay ahead, we drove out of Kansas City to begin our journey on the morning of June 16, 1862. The road for many miles was crowded by the incoming empty and outgoing loaded ox wagons which do the commerce of the plains and which leave and arrive at the towns on the Missouri River (or did until the railroads put an end to their traffic) like ships at a seaport. Trains generally numbered twenty-five wagons and were drawn by five yokes of oxen each. The drivers were usually Mexicans, for the most of these trains went to New Mexico and, as the stage rolled past them, each dusky driver was seized with a desire to attract attention by his vociferations and the repeated pistol-like cracking of his buckskin "popper." The whip lashes were several yards long and the constant "popping" of all the drivers in a train was something like the firing of a bundle of Chinese crackers.

The road across the plains is a natural one, on which no work is done. When it becomes gullied by the rains, it is only necessary to turn to one side and make a new track. It is level, hard and free from dust. By level, I mean generally level, for the Great Plains roll and frequently the ascent from a depression to the top of the roll is quite hill-like. From the top, the plain on every hand appeared as limitless and as level as the ocean, but in the depression one seems to be in the bottom of a basin.

Our ride was to be constant for 300 miles—night and day—with stops every fifteen miles for relays and three times per day for meals. For the first half of this distance we were regularly inspected by parties of Quantrill's men—rough-looking fellows, armed to the teeth, who would ride up and peer into the coach and leave us to go on unmolested. Of course we wondered why these fellows said nothing, made no attempt to relieve us of our property and, when Johnson said as much, Mr. Cottrill replied "that they were looking for Stuart, and as they did not find him thought we were not worth 'plucking.'" He then told us this story.

About a month previous Mr. Stuart was at a hotel in Independence, where he was paying off some of his staging bills, and one morning while at breakfast was surprised by a rapid discharge of firearms in the street, of the rush of frightened citizens into the hotel and a hasty fastening of doors and shutters. Going to a chamber window, he saw a body of Confederate cavalry riding through the streets, shooting right and left and pillaging the stores of the loyal people. The party was led by a slender man, with straw-colored hair which hung in lank locks over his shoulders and who spared no one whom he could get under the range of his pistols. This was too much for Stuart. He caught up his breech-loading carbine and, in spite of remonstrances, unfastened the front door, stepped out on the portico and drew a bead on the straw-colored head. The ruffian saw him and shouted to his men, at the same time leaning low in his saddle. The rifle went off, but killed no one. In his excitement Mr. Stuart had forgotten to calculate for a peculiarity of the weapon for over-shooting.

Just at this moment and as the guerrillas were closing up for a general shot at the man who had dared oppose them, a squad of Union cavalry made its appearance and the marauders "lit out." They were a band of Quantrill's, under his personal command. Not dreaming of further trouble, Mr. Stuart remained in Independence to complete his business. A week after the above occurrence, while again at breakfast, he was startled as before by a firing in the street, attended by the same circumstances. Going to a window he saw Quantrill, or the one whom the landlord called Quantrill and who proved to be the "yellow-haired," ride up before the hotel and demand that "the damned Yankee Stuart, in hiding there, be instantly surrendered or he'd make kindling wood of the establishment."

No answer being made to this, the party began shooting furiously at the windows, until not a pane or sash was left whole and the landlord and guests were in an agony of terror. At this juncture Mr. Stuart determined to surrender himself to save the others and, with this intention, unfastened the door to step out. By the rarest good fortune some Union cavalry showed themselves at this moment and, as the door opened, Mr. Stuart saw the Confederates turning to run. Bringing his rifle to his shoulder he fired—with better luck this time, for he brought down Quantrill's lieutenant.

After this Stuart left for Kansas City and for a number of weeks he received repeated warnings that Quantrill was scheming to waylay him on his journey to Santa Fé. It was well known that he was to travel over the line with Mr. Cottrill, to transfer the staging property and this was the reason we had been watched and overhauled all along the first few days of our journey. One morning we came into a little hamlet called Burlingame, where we were to change horses and get our breakfast. We were all in the washroom, trying to wake ourselves up with cold water, as well as remove the dust of travel, when the door of an adjoining bedroom opened and a tall, gentlemanly-looking man of distinguished mien came out, was instantly greeted by Mr. Cottrill and introduced to us as Mr. Stuart. To the question "How he came there?" he replied that he "had executed a flank movement on Quantrill by riding in a light carriage from Leavenworth, considerably to the north of the stage line." He had arranged relays previously and was thus enabled to make better time than we.

No serious adventure occurred to us after this until our arrival at Council Grove, unless I except a plunge into a rut at full speed at midnight, by which the right fore wheel dashed a hole in the side of the coach, demolished the front seat and left me and my seat-companion, Mr. Cottrill, to ride the rest of the night in the bottom of the coach.

At the time I arrived, Council Grove was but a stage ranche and the agency of the Caw Indians.[14] The tribe numbered but 1,000 and were lounging about the station, begging for whiskey and tobacco—adept in all the vices of the white man and possessing none of his virtues. The men were stalwart and fine looking, but very poorly dressed. Missionaries had in different times attempted to preach to them and instruct the children, but with poor success.

At the Grove we changed our horses for mules and, from this point to the end of the journey, were to use these animals only. An inspection of the coach, to see what had caused the accident during the night, revealed the fact that through long use the thoroughbraces had become so slack as to lower the coach body in dangerous proximity to the wheel. Mr. Cottrill suggested to the stage men that they had better tighten the braces. All of them were obliged to confess that they did not know how to make the repairs.

14. One early traveler along the Santa Fe Road described Council Grove as an "oasis" and "a most beautiful and fairy like place." Another account billed it as the "last place of any note on the great Santa Fe road, between Missouri and New Mexico." White settlers had built homes for themselves and accommodations for travelers prior to an 1846 treaty which created a reservation there for the Kaw people, who naturally considered it an "illegal town." Whites refused to leave and by 1860 lots were being advertised at "one of the best geographical positions in Kansas." The Caw/Kaw/Kansa people were originally from the Ohio Valley, but by 1800 the Kaw Indians had been driven away from the Missouri River onto land spread along the Kansas River. The Kansas-Nebraska Act of 1854 devastated these people, white squatters rushing to settle in Kansas "although not an acre of land within it was legally available for sale." By the following year whites had staked out the best lands at what would become the cities of Council Grove and Leavenworth. Chiefs visited with Presidents Franklin Pierce in 1855 and James Buchanan in 1857, the former delegation refusing to leave until rewarded with silver medals and a substantial cash payment as compensation for the white invasion. Although numbering only about 800 souls in 1860, nevertheless about seventy Kansa young men served in Company L, 9th Kansas Cavalry at a time when their families desperately needed them for the traditional fall hunt which provided food and buffalo robes for the winter. Remnants of the Kansa/Kaw nation, divided into separate bands by political infighting, were removed to Oklahoma in 1873. Bailey and Young, "Kansa," 471; *Times-Picayune*, June 28, 1840; *[Columbus, Ohio] Crisis*, February 19, 1862; *[Atchison, Kansas] Weekly Champion and Press*, April 21, 1860; Bailey and Young, "Kansa," 462–64, 472; Miner and Unrau, *End of Indian Kansas*, 102; Unrau, *Indians of Kansas*, 70; Unrau, *Kansa Indians*, 199; *New York Tribune*, June 20, 1857; *[Washington, D. C.] Daily Union*, July 19, 1855; *Cleveland Plain Dealer*, July 17, 1857.

It was worth looking on to see the ease and full knowledge of just how to do it with which Mr. Cottrill went at that coach and in half an hour had it all ready for the road.

The distance from Kansas City to the Grove is about 150 miles, over a level country with a rich soil, which produced abundantly wherever under cultivation. The grass grows luxuriantly three or four feet high, springing up green in the spring, drying and withering down in the fall. To a person who has never been upon the plains, a trip across them cannot be otherwise than interesting. Their appearance can hardly be imagined; to be appreciated they must be seen. As far as you can see, you behold a country as level as the ocean, with not an object to relieve the eye, and only an occasional roll to relieve the monotonous surface. Your breath seems to come more freely and deeper than in the crowded towns and cities, the heavens are bluer, the air purer and the sunshine brighter.

The route traveled is over the finest natural road in the world and day after day you roll along with no guide but the wheel-worn track that lies before you. Where the coaches or wagons meet on the plains, it seems like ships meeting at sea. Papers and items of news are exchanged, letters mailed, questions asked in relation to weather, how many days out, what Indians were met, etc., etc. As night approaches, the coach passes the encampments of the wagons and some person will run out for the news or to send letters. These camps are made by halting the wagons side by side, so that their wheels touch, forming an oval-shaped enclosure, open at the rear end, by leaving one wagon out. The tongues of the wagons point inward and, as soon as the ring is formed, the animals are loosened and go grazing upon the plain, in charge of two mounted men.

When it is necessary to hitch up, the animals are driven into the enclosure formed by the wagons, yoked or harnessed and attached to the wagons, when the whole thing dissolves into a string and takes the road. Should Indians attack while the wagons are in camp, the animals are driven into the ring and the entrance closed by placing the wagon left out into the same passage. Then the teamsters and herders make a fight from behind the wagons as a barricade. Should Indians appear suddenly while the train is in motion, it can form a ring with the tongues and animals inward and the wheels interlocked. A running fight may be made by forming the train into two lines, with the men between, firing from the wagons.

After the repairs were all made, our mules were "put to" and we resumed our journey. These mules were highly fed and groomed, with no labor but to go thirty miles per week, from one relay station to another, and return. They were frisky during the process of harnessing and had to be held by the head until we were all seated and the driver said, "Let them go." For the first two or three miles they went at a run, indulging in some mulish kickings and corvettes, the driver keeping his foot constantly on the brake, but after that they settled down to a swift trot of about nine miles an hour, which they kept up until we reached the next relay. In this manner we went on day and night until we reached Pawnee Fork, having made the drive of 300 miles in less than two days and two nights. All this time we had had no sleep, except what we caught in our seats.

Chapter 2

Across the Plains

Fort Larned, at the time I arrived there, was a small open post, garrisoned by two companies of infantry, under the command of a lieutenant.[1] The fort is situated upon the Pawnee Fork, a tributary of the Arkansas River, and the stage station is known to the plainsmen by the name of the stream and not the post. The water in the Fork is about twenty feet in width, from one to two in depth, with a fair current. The timber on this creek, like that of all the streams hereabouts, is scattered and ugly, except a few large cottonwoods at the fort. I mention this last fact in particular because Henry M. Stanley, the great African explorer, once wrote

1. In 1859 the Camp on Pawnee Creek was established upstream from the confluence of that stream and the Arkansas River to protect the mail and travelers on the Santa Fe Trail from marauding Indians. Re-named Camp Alert because of almost constant Indian alerts, the post was moved two and one-half miles upstream and named after Paymaster General Benjamin Franklin Larned on May 29, 1860. Fort Larned's storehouses, barracks, and officers' quarters were constructed of adobe with sod roofs. Although tasked with keeping Indians in check, infantrymen stationed there had little success in actually finding Indian raiders. The best that could be done was to established an escort system for wagon trains moving back and forth between Fort Larned and Fort Union, trains leaving each post on the first and fifteenth of the month. After the Civil War, Fort Larned was rebuilt with sandstone structures. The town of Larned grew up eight miles away with the construction of the Atchison, Topeka and Santa Fe Railroad. As with many other western installations, Fort Larned's importance lessened as the Indian threat diminished and it was transferred to the General Land Office in 1882. Oliva, *Fort Larned*, 1, 5–7. 9–12, 16–17, 20, 34, 61, 77.

letters from the plains and he occupied considerable space in one of them concerning the magnificent timber on the Pawnee Fork and the beautiful *elms* about the station.[2] As I have visited this post four times—twice before Stanley and twice since—being once stopped by a freshet on its banks for a week, I claim to know what grows there. This and a few other statements of the great traveler, which I know to be strained, have caused me to wonder if some of his African stories have no better foundation.

We arrived at Fort Larned just as night set in and drove directly to the stage company's station, but a few rods beyond the post, concluding not to visit the commandant before morning. Here we made our beds down upon the grass outside the station and indulged in a "good square sleep," a slumber only to be had under the clear, dewless skies of the Far West, where a generous supply of bed clothes is always comfortable, even in midsummer, and the air dry and bracing.

This expression "square sleep," with its companion phrase "square meal," are Westernisms, meaning a safe and undisturbed repose, in distinction from the restless slumbers of a journey or in the neighborhood of Indian alarms; and a good repast, regularly set out upon a table, with all the concomitants of a comfortable and social meal, from the irregular, uncomfortable and often badly cooked meals eaten from a blanket or a buffalo skin by the roadside.

Here I must introduce a story, although it is a digression, which always comes to my mind whenever I think of Fort Larned. The question is often asked me by friends, "Are the New Mexican women handsome?" The same question was put by Lieutenant Johnson, Dr. Nassau and me to Captain Nicodemus, as we rode along in the stage, and he frequently went into raptures over the

2. The son of an absent father and an uncaring mother, John Rowlands lived with his grandfather until his death caused the youth to be sent to a workhouse. John ran away as a teenager and landed in New Orleans in 1859, where he was befriended and unofficially adopted by the merchant Henry Stanley, taking his "father's" name. Captured at the battle of Shiloh while serving in an Arkansas regiment, Stanley switched sides and briefly served in the Union army. He later joined the Union navy but deserted to begin a journalism career that led him to report on Indian campaigns on the Great Plains. James Gordon Bennett of the *New York Herald* hired him to search for the missing Scottish explorer David Livingstone and in 1871, on the shores of Lake Tanganyika, Stanley met the object of his African search with the laconic inquiry, "Dr. Livingstone, I presume?" Additional explorations to the source of the Nile River and along the Congo River led to worldwide fame. After serving five years in Parliament, Stanley retired to a country home in Surrey and died in London on May 10, 1904. Bierman, *Dark Safari*, 5–6, 12, 24, 34–38, 48, 75–78, 111, 151–200, 346, 350, 354.

brunette beauties of Santa Fé and predicted our ready surrender to the flash of their jetty eyes upon our arrival there. He said at Pawnee Fork he should have an opportunity of showing us not only a Mexican *señorita*, but the handsomest one he had ever seen. Much we speculated over this prospective vision of dusky loveliness and frequent were the questions asked as to personal traits and the thousand details that go to make up the perfect woman, the captain never ceasing to respond and promise us a sight of something fine.

Morning found us all wonderfully refreshed by our sleep and in a position to appreciate and do ample justice to a breakfast of buffalo steak, fresh bread and butter and a cup of good coffee. Breakfast over, I said, "Now, captain, bring on your maid of the plains, the fair Carmelita."[3]

"I think," he replied, "that we had better go over to the post, call on the officers and leave Carmelita to get her eyes open before she receives us."

We acted upon this suggestion and went to the fort, where we passed an hour or two with the officers, looking over the barracks, storehouses and corral and then returned to the station. Here we learned that we were to resume our journey about noon, in two coaches, instead of one, and make but two changes of animals for about 267 miles. These two coaches were of the pattern known among stage men as "mud wagons," being carriages with canvas sides and tops, supported by wooden bows. There were three seats inside, but narrower than in the coach we had ridden in thus far. It was arranged that in one of the stages should be placed the mail bags, baggage, stores, bedding, etc., so disposed that Johnson and Nassau could ride lying down, for the former was still ailing and the doctor had been getting out of sorts with every day's travel west.

While we busily engaged in assisting to make the arrangements mentioned, Captain Nicodemus excused himself, and went to call on Carmelita, to prepare her for an introduction to his friends. Time passed away and we heard nothing from him and began to suspect that he had found the lady's society so delightful that he had forgotten all about us and his promise. At last we spied him at some distance away, sitting under a cottonwood tree, busy in

3. Carmelita cannot be positively identified.

packing a bundle. We immediately started for him and, when we were in speaking distance, Johnson said:

"Where is the Mexican girl?"

"In the house," was the reply, without looking up.

"Well, aren't we to see her?"

"Pshaw. You don't want to see her."

"You talk strangely and act strangely," said Doctor Nassau, "for a man who has been so fierce to present us to this girl that he has talked of little else for the last hundred miles."

"I think she does not care to see you."

"Did she say as much?" I asked.

"No, but I've concluded it would be rude to present so many strangers."

"Look here, captain," said Johnson, "no humbugging. There's some other reason and you might as well out with it, for you'll never have any peace till you do."

Here Nicodemus ceased his pretence to be busy with the package at his feet, stood up and faced us.

"Well, gentlemen, I hate to be obliged to confess it, but either that girl has grown almighty homely since I passed here a month ago or my life in New Mexico among so many homely women made me think her handsome by contrast. Then again my brief visits to Washington and Baltimore, where I saw hosts of beautiful women, may have had something to do with it, but one thing is certain—that girl isn't handsome now."

After some little urging, the captain took us into the station and into a room which did duty as a reception room, chiefly carpeted with buffalo and wolf skins, the walls ornamented with antlers of deer and antelope, the stuffed heads of a couple of buffalo and trophies of the chase generally. Here we found a wholesome-looking maid, with a dusky skin, black hair and deep black eyes, but with no special claim to beauty. She was easy enough in her manners, but the difficulty of making herself understood in English covered up whatever defects of education she had, which were not a few, doubtless, in her station in life.

We returned to the stages to find ten hardy little mules being attached to them, five to each. Two were harnessed to the pole and three abreast on the lead, by a simple but peculiar arrangement of the whiffletrees, while another simple device of the reins gave the

Captain William J. L. Nicodemus. Courtesy of Civil War Photos, United States Army Heritage and Education Center.

driver as much control of the five animals as he could have had of four. Mr. Cottrill explained that this was a common method of making up teams with the Mexicans and he had found by experience that five mules attached so near to the stage could draw as much as six strung out in spans. With hearty good-byes from our newly formed acquaintances of the fort and station, and a wave of the handkerchief from the "handsomest New Mexican girl in the country," we started out on this, the second stage of our journey. The mules now drawing us went into no ecstasies of speed as they took the road, like those of the relays of the previous 300 miles, but settled at once down to their work, as if they knew what was before them, for they were to go one-third of the 267 miles between Fort Larned and Bent's Old Fort before they could be relieved.

The method of driving, resting, etc., over what is, or was known, as the "long route" is briefly as follows. After the first night out, the mules were harnessed and the stages driven out of camp as early as three o'clock in the morning, continuing on the road until seven o'clock, when we halted, turned out the animals to graze and made preparations for breakfast. This over, we remained in camp until ten o'clock, reading, writing or swimming, if on the river, and sometimes making short excursions to get a shot at buffalo, deer or antelope. At ten we resumed the journey and drove until four, when we went into camp for dinner and turned out the mules to graze until seven, at which time we harnessed up for the last time and drove until ten o'clock. This being the last drive of the day, we usually ate a few cakes of hard bread, staked the mules out for the night, spread our bedding in the grass and slept until we were called in the morning.

The daily life in the coach may not be uninteresting. When we first drove out at three o'clock it was almost impossible to keep awake. We were constantly bumping our heads together or against the side of the coach, shaking ourselves awake only to fall asleep again and repeat the bumping. Occasionally a head would lean so far from the side of the stage that a sudden jerk would send a hat into the road and we would have to stop to pick it up. When the sun was fairly up we were always broad awake. After breakfast, while the trainsmen were harnessing and packing, some of us would take the road and make a walk of several miles before we would be overtaken and picked up. During the day we read, played cards, told stories, smoked or sang songs. Captain Nicodemus had a fine voice and loved singing. When on the Arkansas River we would go into the water for a swim every time we went into camp. Nicodemus was passionately fond of the water and he, Johnson and I were diving, splashing or swimming a great portion of the time.

We had not been out of the fort an hour before we saw a small herd of buffaloes, grazing a few miles to the northwest, taking no notice of us as we rolled along and finally passed them. It was the season when the cows were suckling their calves and we could see many of the little fellows scattered in the herd. At the stage station we had seen several which had been captured and became quite tame and were being fattened for veal. They were not unlike the domestic calf in size and shape, but were all of a light red color, in marked contrast with the dark bodies of their elders.

We did not go into camp the first night until about eleven, owing to a disappointment in not finding water at a point where the drivers had reason to expect it, which compelled us to go a considerable distance farther. On our morning drive to the breakfast camp, a kitchen cabinet was held for the division of labor in preparing meals. Barnum, a bright Connecticut man who drove the advance stage, was duly installed chief of the cuisine, Boomer, the conductor, and Jones, the driver of the second stage, assistants.[4] The rest of us were to make ourselves generally useful in any capacity which the cooks might direct. Captain Nicodemus and I were appointed collectors of fuel and whenever we went into camp for meals, if it was out of the region of trees or driftwood, he and I would each take a large gunny sack and scout the plains for *bois de vaches,* or buffalo chips. These having been bleached in the sun, many of them for years, they were free from any obnoxious odors and made a hot fire, like peat, upon which steak could be broiled to a turn.

We were not long in reaching camp after these arrangements were made and in due season the cooking was fairly under way.

4. Thomas J. Barnum, a descendant of the Connecticut Barnums, settled in Nebraska in 1857 but two years later headed for New Mexico. He became an early partner with Mahlon Cottrill in operating a stage and freight line between Kansas City and Santa Fe. By 1864 he was described as an "experienced stage superintendent" and "a man of wide experience in the vicissitudes of frontier life." Barnum amassed a fortune from his stage operations prior to his death in St. Louis on March 10, 1879. When his widow died in 1911, she left $100,000 to the archbishop of St. Louis. Barnum could have been the driver that Curtis remembered or it may have been a brother Lewis who went west to seek his fortune in 1862. *Otoe and Cass Counties* II, 915; *The Southwestern Reporter* 24: 780; *Waterloo Evening Courier*, February 16, 1911. Boomer and Jones cannot be positively identified.

The ham was sizzling on the coals, the tin coffee pot singing on one side of the fire and the luxuries, in the shape of butter, cheese and syrup, were produced from the stages. Coffee, the universal drink of the plainsmen, was brought out, but there was no mill for grinding it and for a moment all were in despair, until the doctor produced a small wedgewood mortar from his trunk and Johnson soon pounded enough for breakfast. Matters being now in an advanced state of progress, conductor Boomer ordered the table spread and the food placed upon it. The old hands, who had passed over the plains before, bustled about in obedience to this command, but the rest of us stood looking on with great curiosity.

We expected to see a regular crossed-legged camp table brought forth from some mysterious depth of the baggage stage and a respectable, if not very brilliant, lot of tin ware spread upon it, such as we had seen in our Eastern army life, but here disappointment met us at the very outset. Jones and Barnum came from the baggage coach, one bearing an old army blanket, which he spread upon the ground near the fire, for both table and cloth, while the other carried a dirty bag. By the time the blanket was spread—it smelt horsey, by the way—the second had untied the bag, which he turned upside down, and poured upon the ground a varied assortment of dishes, etc., which, being inventoried upon the spot, was found to consist of the following named articles, viz: twelve tin cups, ten tin plates, six spoons, seven knives, two forks, two tin canisters and two coffee pots. In addition to these were one frying pan and one stew pan, but as the cooks were not as careful of these, they were not kept in the bag. Out of respect to the visible disturbance in the faces of some of our party—the military part certainly—the articles selected for immediate use were taken to the spring and washed. We then sat down upon the grass about the blanket and fell to work in a manner hardly to be sanctioned anywhere but on the plains. The dearth of forks was supplied by Captain Nicodemus, who had in his baggage some mess articles which he had bought in the States to use in New Mexico.

During the forenoon of that day we drove over a perfectly level section of the plains for about twenty-five miles and for nearly the whole distance there were grazing, on our right, scattered herds of buffaloes. As we got opposite, each herd would seem to fancy that we were "heading" them, break into a canter and go loping monotonously along until they get in advance of us, when they would cross the road more than a hundred yards in advance of the leading stage. Occasionally a straggler would dash across so near that we would be tempted into taking a shot, generally without effect, as the motion of the stage prevented accurate aim.

Near the close of the drive one band of about fifty buffaloes showed that they were likely to cross quite near us and, as the road was perfectly level and hard as plank, Mr. Cottrill told Barnum to "whip up sharp and give Mr. Stuart a shot." Stuart clambered up to the driver's seat with his rifle and soon we were tearing along the road at the utmost speed of our mules. The buffaloes were on the curve and we on the chord, so that if we were not a match in speed we had a chance to come up to shooting distance before they crossed the road. At last the herd made a straight dash for the road, the driver put on the brake and pulled up the mules. Stuart said, "Sit still, inside," and presently we heard the crack of the rifle, simultaneously with which we all thrust our heads out of the coach in time to see a buffalo turn a somersault in the grass and lie still in death.

There is a heap of romance written about buffalo shooting, its dangers, etc. From some experience with both kinds of animals, I am prepared to say, and stick to it if necessary, that a herd of wild California cattle is much more dangerous than a herd of buffaloes. I have seen three horsemen dash into a herd of buffaloes, select one and actually drive it into camp to be killed, and I have seen California steers which nothing but the lasso or rifle could make tractable. The buffalo is but a big, lumbering fellow, which anyone can shoot without material danger, if well mounted and a good shot.

We camped at four o'clock and had some steak for dinner, as the result of Mr. Stuart's skill in shooting. Here we received our first alarm from Indians. Seeing a small herd of buffaloes feeding on the side of a ravine not far from camp, Johnson and myself started out with rifles to see what luck we might have. We went a considerable distance, but finding the herd was moving away and that there was no probability of coming up with it, we started to return. We had retraced our steps but a short distance, when Johnson exclaimed, "Look at the Indians!" and turning to the north I saw three mounted warriors standing upon a roll of the prairie. The cry of "Indians!" is always a startling one upon the plains, especially when you are a small party or a detachment away from your main body. The region of the scalp grows immediately sensitive and fearful visions of the probable method of your "taking off," should you fall into their hands, will always flit through your mind, for you will never for a moment doubt but that you will meet with death if they capture you. It is only the possible method that taxes your mind with its ghastly probabilities.

We did not delay to hold any consultations on the subject. We came to the mental conclusion, simultaneously, that camp was a good enough place for us and marched on, with all the haste we could and keep up the gait. We had no doubt but what we were a match for the three, but then what chances of scalping might be lurking behind that roll in the plain. We were marching as fast as was consistent with the reputation of a couple of army officers, when we noticed the Indians began to move towards us. Still disdaining to run, we lengthened our steps all we could and pushed on. Finding ourselves, after a little while, in the ravine, out of sight of the redskins, we took a "double quick" that resembled considerably a "run." Before we emerged from the cover we were in sight of camp, our pluck sensibly increased, our hats fitted our heads better and we resumed our walk with apparent confidence.

The Indians came into camp and proved to be three Caws, who had been in pursuit of buffaloes. After greeting all of us with a guttural "How" and shake of the hand, they began at once to beg for tobacco and whiskey, and were supplied with a pipe-full each of the former and a dram from the demijohns. They were not satisfied with one drink, but immediately asked for more and went through much gesticulation to show that their throats were in a parched condition. We gave them no more, however, and they soon departed.

From Fort Larned we had taken a diagonal route towards the southwest, in order to strike the Arkansas, up which river we were to continue until we reached Bent's Old Fort. All along this line of travel are United States posts, but we passed them during the night, with the exception of Forts Larned and Lyon. There are several features of the road worth mentioning, not spoken of by the ordinary traveler. The constant recurrence of the skeletons of oxen is one. This road has been for many long years the commercial route into New Mexico and, before the opening of the Texas route, into Northern Mexico. In a climate where flesh desiccates, but does not putrefy, the carcasses of buffaloes and oxen last a long time by the roadside before the skeleton shows through the fried hides and the bones last for years; hence this route is dotted with the bones of draught animals its entire length. On the buffalo range, the bleaching skeletons of the buffalo are a constant witness of the wanton destruction of this animal.

Another feature of the road is the line of sunflowers, or rosinweed, which springs up wherever a wheel breaks the surface of the ground, growing tall in the valleys and moist places, and dwarfed and stunted on elevated and dry localities. Where the bull buffalo has circled around his favorite cow, to keep off his jealous rivals, turning up the sod with his hoofs in circles the size of the circus ring, the sunflower for the rest of the year shows the scene of the bovine love passages by rearing its stem. Here is a chance for speculation concerning these seeds, which only need the disturbance of the soil to burst into life.

Still another feature is the presence of the gray wolf and coyote, hanging on the flanks of the buffalo herds and prowling about the camps of the trains in the night for bacon rinds, scraps and crumbs left by the fires; breaking into a reveille, with the first gray streak of dawn, of the most discordant howls, barks and growls imaginable, in all the tones which a dog chorus, composed of all the known dogs from the diminutive poodle to the Newfoundland, would produce, only worse. In our first camp after leaving Fort Larned we were startled by this morning serenade and the greenhorns of the party—among whom I was one—sprang from their blankets, seized their weapons and stood ready to fight the Indians whose war whoop they supposed they had just heard.

The prairie dog demands mention, as his habitations along the line are a constant and interesting feature. He is in no sense a dog. A gray squirrel, well fattened, with his tail cut off within three inches of his body and divested of most of its hair, would bear a close resemblance to the prairie dog, except in color, which is a tawny brown. For miles we would drive through their towns, each habitation having a mound of earth which had been thrown to the surface in excavating the burrow. The mounds are usually a foot and a half high and three feet in diameter, with the hole in the centre running downward at an angle of about forty degrees. As you approach the town you will see many of the inhabitants sitting up on their hind legs on the top of the mounds. As you come nearer, they fall upon all fours and stand in the entrance of their holes, barking—or, more properly, chirping—furiously. If you approach still nearer, the little fellows plunge into their burrows, out of sight. When you depart they again appear and are soon seen running about the town, evidently discussing your intrusion. They assemble in pairs and in groups and really appear to be holding conversation.

There are many tales told of how the rattlesnake and owl live on the most amiable terms with the prairie dog. Certainly the rattlesnake is always found in large numbers in the towns and the owl also is frequently met with, but they are doubtless there to eat the young dogs. I settled this question, so far as the snake is concerned, by ripping open one with a protuberant stomach and revealing the disfigured body of a prairie dog. As for the owl, I could not apply the test to him, but so good a mouser as he is known to be could be there for no good purpose.

In process of time we reached the Cimmaron crossing of the Arkansas River. This is where the Santa Fé trains cross to take what is known as "the Cimmaron route." A great portion of this road is dry during a considerable part of the year, so the stage company takes a longer route to ensure the passengers against suffering. The wagons are furnished with water kegs for the use of the men, while the oxen often have to go three days under the yoke without water.

At the crossing were encamped half a dozen trains, busily engaged in fording the river, which was exceedingly high and dangerous. All the wagons containing goods which could be injured had to be unloaded, the bodies filled with wood or boxes and barrels to the height of three feet and upon the top of this were piled the cases of perishable goods. When all was ready, the wagon would be driven into the river, amid the yells and vociferations of the Mexican drivers, and driven across, the oxen often disappearing from sight on the uneven bottom of the stream. But if one yoke went out of sight, the one in front had a foothold, so the unwieldy wagon went rising, falling and rolling to the farther shore. This river has been known to be so dry that travelers have been obliged to dig in its bed for water to drink.

On the opposite shore of the river was a large encampment of Kiowa, Cheyenne and Arapaho, a war party organized for the purpose of "lifting the hair of the Pawnees."[5] We were no sooner

5. The Cheyenne people originated in what is now Minnesota, but were pushed westward to the Black Hills and south onto the Great Plains by other groups like the Chippewa. The 1851 Treaty at Fort Laramie recognized two separate groups, one in the region of Wyoming, Colorado, and Nebraska and the other in Colorado and Kansas. Living a

halted than our camp was thronged with them, all begging and eying us with wistful gaze as we ate our breakfast. We condescended so far as to invite a couple of the chiefs "to squat" and dine with us, which they did without urging—carrying off all they could not eat. One of these chiefs, an Arapaho, was known as *El Cojo* (The Lame), from his left leg being stiff.[6] I had a fellow feeling for him—for what

---

nomadic lifestyle based on hunting bison, the Southern Cheyenne numbered some 1,800 people and the Northern Cheyenne about 3,000. Traditional hunting and trading bands were disrupted during their nineteenth-century warfare when war chiefs would surround themselves with followers and their families, thus severing old relationships and forming new family ties. On February 18, 1861, the Cheyenne and Arapaho signed a treaty at Fort Wise that sold most of their land except for a reservation in Colorado along the Arkansas River. In exchange, each nation was to receive $15,000 for fifteen years. The confederated nations of the Cheyenne, Arapaho, Kiowa, Comanche, and Prairie Apache had vowed to remain faithful to their Great Father in his defense of the Union. The Kiowa people, never numbering more than 1,400, originally lived on the northern Plains but gradually migrated south and by the end of the Civil War had been confined to a reservation in western Oklahoma and northern Texas. They lived by hunting bison and raiding, often in company with their long-time allies, the Comanches. One successful Kiowa raid was described as "a series of bold and revolting outrages." Over this sixteen-day period in New Mexico, the raiders "robbed the citizens of corn, stock, sheep, goats, horses, mules, furniture, and wearing apparel." One rancher at Bosque de los Pinos, the future territorial governor Henry Connelly, lost fifty mules and two horses to these Kiowa raiders, a loss estimated at $6000-$8,000. During the Civil War, the Kiowa generally supported the Union, but remained independent of control by Washington. Taking advantage of the absence of Southern soldiers on the frontier, they vowed to plunder Texas settlements and attack any Indian nations aligned with the Confederacy. The Arapaho people originally came from the northern Plains and during the Civil War were generally settled on two reservations, one in the Kansas/Oklahoma region and another centered around Sand Creek in Colorado. The Northern Arapaho numbered less than 700, while the Southern Arapaho slightly more than double that number. Subsistence for both groups centered on bison hunting with the result that they often left their reservation in search of the ever-dwindling bison herds. The Buffalo Dance was an important Arapaho ritual in which a woman represented a white cow and two young girls her calves. Forty other women dressed themselves to represent buffalo. When the dance concluded, a foot race ensued, the loser being pelted by "sticks, stones, dirt, or anything loose" by the assembled crowd. In addition to warring with the Pawnee, both the Cheyenne and Arapaho were bitter enemies of the Utes. The Pawnee people, originally four distinct groups living in northern Kansas and Nebraska, moved onto a reservation in 1859. They lived in earthen lodges organized into semi-permanent villages and supported by the cultivation of maize. The population in the mid-1850s was slightly under 5,000 but had declined to under 3,000 following the Civil War. In addition to primary hunts in summer and winter, the Pawnee constantly raided nearly every other Indian nation on the Plains. Following one encounter near Fort Larned between the Pawnee and their enemies, the Kiowa, Arapaho, and Cheyenne, one observer remarked: "The Pawnees have acquired the ill-will of the other tribes by their thieving qualities and by the recent commission of glaring outrages." Unafraid of other nations, the Pawnees exhibited their contempt for the Sioux and Cheyenne during the summer hunt in 1862. Although over 1,000 enemy lodges were encamped on prime Pawnee hunting grounds, they overcame two-to-one odds and brought in their customary supply of buffalo. For good measure, Pawnee warriors stole sixty horses from the Sioux camp. Moore, "Cheyenne," 159, 863–65, 867, 880; *San Francisco Bulletin*, October 14, 1862; *New York Times*, December 28, 1861; Levy, "Kiowa," 907–908, 920–21; *Daily National Intelligencer*, December 2, 1856; Hoig, *Kiowas*, 70; Fowler, "Arapaho," 840–42, 847, 857; *Rocky Mountain News*, June 12, 1861; Trenholm, *Arapahoes*, 167; Parks, "Pawnee," 515, 519–26, 543; *New York Tribune*, November 24, 1862; Hyde, *Pawnee Indians*, 257.

6. El Cojo (The Lame) was a war chief of the southern Arapaho in the 1840s, described by one white man as "the most infernal and meanest of the tribe." His fearsome reputation

reason my personal friends well know—and presented him with twenty Henry Clay buttons, a relic of the old Whig campaign of 1844.[7] He accepted them with Indian gravity and, retiring for a brief space, returned with them sewed on a double-breasted frock coat which he had taken from his wardrobe. Approaching me with an air of solemnity and gravity I never saw equaled, and taking me by the right hand, he gave me three slow and deliberate shakes, as slow as the time of a funeral march, pressing my hand with a firm grasp and looking me straight in the eye. Releasing my hand, he passed his arm through mine to the elbow and thus facing in opposite directions he pressed my arm firmly to his side, with our left arms he went through the same measured performance, then he touched our respective lame legs and said in Spanish, "*bueno, mucho Bueno*," in grave accent.

This demonstration on the part of *El Cojo*, I interpreted as meaning something very complimentary and as placing us decidedly above our fellows, on account of our common infirmity. By inquiry of a Mexican who could speak English, we learned that the chief was very brave and had received his injury in a fierce fight with the Utes.[8]

---

led to the rise of other chiefs more accommodating to white traders and settlers. Marginalized as a war chief, El Cojo and his followers tried to rehabilitate their image by claiming to buy horses rather than steal them. When this failed to win him more respect, El Cojo and his dwindling band joined the Comanche. Fowler, *Arapahoe Politics*, 25–26; Trenholm, *Arapahoes*, 124, 131.

7. One of the pre-eminent statesmen of the nineteenth century, Henry Clay's career included service as congressman, senator, secretary of state, and presidential contender. Clay won the Whig Party nomination for president in 1844 but lost in the general election to Democrat James K. Polk. Clay attempted another presidential campaign in 1848, but failed even to find backing in his native state of Kentucky. When Clay watched his party nominate Zachary Taylor, a military man with no qualifications for office, he refused to campaign for the nominee, effectively ending his national prominence. Henry Clay returned to the Senate in 1849 and died in Washington, D. C. on June 29, 1852. *Dictionary of American Biography* 4: 173–79.

8. During the early years of the nineteenth century the Ute people could be found throughout a territory that encompassed portions of Utah, Colorado, and New Mexico. Primarily foragers, the Utes subsisted by gathering, hunting, and fishing, supplemented by bison hunting after the Spanish had introduced the horse to North America. Chiefs of the Utes did not react favorably when summoned to Washington. The spokesman for one such delegation during the Civil War said, "You may give presents to the other Indians, but we don't want any of your presents. You want our lands because you know there is plenty of gold there, but all that you are willing to give is copper. Do you think we are fools? You talk sometimes as if you might whip us. You are now fighting with your own brothers, and you can't whip them. You would find it harder work to whip us." Despite these bold statements, the Utes were often called "Union Indians" because they refused to support the Confederacy. Their devotion to the Union was severely tested after the war when President Andrew Johnson outlawed Indian slavery, curtailing a lucrative and time-honored inistitution in the Ute nation. Callaway, Janetski, and Stewart, "Ute," 336–7, 340–45, 382; *Wisconsin Daily Patriot*, April 16, 1863; Simmons, *Ute Indians*, 113, 121.

Chapter 3

Along the Santa Fé Trail

Shortly after we left the Cimmaron crossing we came to the first relay station of the "long route." It was a rude house, built of cottonwood logs, standing a short distance to the right of the road. Since the last evening our company had been anticipating the "square meal" we were to get at Atlantic A. Moore's ranche and speculating as to what particular dainties would be set before us by the excellent housewife.[1] When we came in sight of the ranche, many miles across the prairie, and first recognized the house, corral and haystack, the drivers and conductor began wondering whether the mules would be driven up for the relay and their opinions varied with every roll in the plain, one declaring he could see the herd of mules in the corral, another that they were near the house and a third that he could see them grazing on

1. Atlantic A. Moore first passed through Kansas in 1858 when he and a brother were hired to drive army ambulances over the Santa Fe Trail. Upon their return, the brothers bought out a trading post at Cottonwood Crossing and claimed land that became commonly known as Moore's Ranche. Known to everyone as "Lank" Moore, Atlantic became the local postmaster in 1861. A founder of Marion County, Moore represented its citizens in the state legislature prior to moving to Arizona in 1882. An early resident of Yavapai County, Moore represented that county in the Arizona legislature while engaged in farming, mining, and the raising of livestock. He died on December 22, 1916, in Glendale, Arizona at the home of a son. *Kansas and Kansans* 3: 1205; "Legislature of 1868," 267; *Prescott Journal Miner*, December 30, 1916.

the plain, some distance from the station. The question was not definitely settled until we drove over the last roll, about five miles away, and a new section of the plain opened to the view, bringing out from the stage men a general chorus of disgust, "There they are!" The whole herd of some twenty mules was plainly visible two or three miles from the station.

When we drove up to the house a young woman came to the door and to the question "Where is Moore?" replied that he had gone in search of a stray cow, which had disappeared with her calf during the past night. To the next and, more important, question to most of us, "whether she could cook us a dinner," she replied in the affirmative. In a few moments we were out of the stage, the mules were unharnessed and turned loose and one of the stage drivers started off to drive in the distant herd. The time intervening between our arrival and the dinner hour we spent in various ways, writing, reading, walking or playing cards. As for myself, I entered the cabin and took a seat in the one large room that did duty as parlor, dining and reception room, where I found to my surprise a few copies of the *Atlantic Monthly*, Whittier's, Bryant's, and Holmes' poems, together with several novels, showing the presence of some person in the household of refined literary tastes. Who this person was did not long remain a mystery, for Mrs. Nancy Moore presently came in from the "lean to," in which was the kitchen, bearing in her hand a parcel which she had just received from the conductor and, handing it to me, said, "There is the last *Atlantic*."[2]

As Mrs. Moore walked backward and forward from kitchen to table, getting ready the "square meal," a young antelope followed her every step, with its nose touching the folds of her dress. I asked if the animal always did so and she replied that it never stopped following her, unless she tired of it and shut it up in its pen, when it would lie down and sleep. When her husband was absent she liked to have the little thing follow her—it did not seem so lonesome. I asked if she was not afraid of the Indians, living so utterly isolated and at their mercy. She answered that she was at first, but the continued peace had given her more confidence and she was not so much afraid now. Still she could not say she did not have many

2. Nancy Olive Waterman married Atlantic A. Moore in 1862 and bore the first white child, Ira A. Moore, in what would become Marion County, Kansas. She died at her son's home in Glendale, Arizona, on December 28, 1926. *Kansas and Kansans* 3: 1205.

alarms. She showed me the arrangements for barricading windows and doors, with the closet containing the weapons of defence, and said her husband had taught her the use of the rifle and revolver until she was a very respectable shot. As she grew animated in her conversation, she showed so much culture in her language and thought that I wondered how such a woman could have been brought to this remote stage station. I soon found myself following her back and forward with nearly the persistency of the antelope, listening to her remarks as she turned the buffalo steak on the gridiron or folded a napkin neatly into a goblet on the table.

Just before dinner was announced I heard our party outside greeting cheerily some newcomer and heard a new voice answer. "That is my husband," said Mrs. Moore and I went to the door to see the man who was mated to this intelligent woman. A tall man stood beside a mule from which he had just dismounted, the loop of the bridle rein hanging from his left arm, with a rifle in his right hand, the butt resting on the ground. He was clad in a neat buckskin suit, fringed along the seam of the legs, sleeves and about the neck, after the manner of many plainsmen, but, unlike the many, he wore spotless linen and a neat cravat. His features were regular, with an intelligent forehead, clear blue eyes and fair waving hair. Thrown across the back of the mule behind the saddle was a dead antelope and grazing but a short distance away was the cow and calf for which he had been searching. Leaning in the doorway, I was wondering who this man and this woman could be, evidently, from their manner of speech and habit, persons above the general type of plains people.

In a just audible tone I said to myself, "*Sed cos qui tandem*?" ("But who at length are you?") —quoting a phrase from the Æneid, not intending to be heard, when I was surprised by the ready reply, "*Si prima repetens ab origene pergam ante diem clauso compenet Vesper Olympo*" ("If I should begin at the beginning, night would be here before I closed.") So apt an answer showed me that the stranger was a classical man. I approached for an introduction and asked to be excused for my apparent pedantry, saying that the words came involuntarily to my lips. He laughingly answered that his supply of Latin was not very extensive. He had fitted for college, but never entered; had started for Colorado two years before, and stopped here upon an offer from the stage company to take their station, and rather liked the life for a change; should leave whenever the Indians showed signs of being troublesome or his wife should want to go.

I was once surprised beyond this in Arizona. A young man one day dismounted at my tent with dispatches and the mail from Fort Yuma and left his saddlebags while he went to dinner.[3] As I turned the mail out upon my table, a well-thumbed volume of Horace, a small Latin lexicon and a grammar fell out. When the mail rider returned, I asked whose books they were. He said they were his and proceeded to explain that he had been a sophomore in Michigan University, had got into a scrape, been suspended and rather than face his parents had run away.[4] Life in Arizona had given him a chance to reflect; he had written penitent letters to parents and faculty, had received favorable replies and was now getting up his studies with a view to re-entering college. Riding the mail route gave him good opportunities for "boning" at the rests, while his horse was grazing.

Dinner being announced, we sat down to a repast of the very "squarest" type. The linen was spotless and the snowy napkins were a touch beyond anything we had met with since leaving Kansas City. Our past few days' experience with the kitchen furniture heretofore enumerated and described, and the badly cooked food, made us appreciate this meal more than we otherwise should. As we got into the coach and drove away from this oasis in our culinary desert, driver Barnum exclaimed, as he flicked the ears of the off leader, "She's just the neatest outfit on the plains and them biscuit of hern just beat buffaler meat all holler."

This word "outfit," applied to Nancy Moore by the driver, needs a few words of explanation. When I first arrived at Kansas City

3. The original military post was established on a California bluff near where the Gila River emptied into the Colorado River, its purpose being to protect the influx of miners and immigrants headed for the gold fields. The first location was called Camp Calhoun, but this was moved in 1850 and Camp Yuma established. A second move to the site of an old Spanish mission occurred in 1851 when Fort Yuma was constructed from local trees chinked with mud. Briefly abandoned later that year because of the difficulty in supplying the post, Fort Yuma was re-occupied the following year. Situated to protect travelers from the Yuma and Mojave Indians, the fort gradually became a base for western explorations and an significant port during the development of steamboat traffic on the Colorado River. Rebuilt with adobe buildings during the last years of the Civil War, Fort Yuma became an important supply depot and the gateway to Arizona from California. The post was transferred to the Department of the Interior and the last troops left in 1883. Wharfield, *Fort Yuma*, 1–3, 17, 28, 48–53, 56, 63, 117, 133, 156, 176.

4. Curtis is referring to the University of Michigan in Ann Arbor, not *the* Michigan State University in East Lansing.

I noticed the word was in general use and that it was applied to everything. A pocket knife, a watch, a plug of tobacco, a wagon, a horse, a train, things the most homogeneous and heterogeneous I constantly heard called "outfits," and now I heard the term applied to a woman. I asked an explanation from my traveling companions and learned that from the custom of fitting-out parties at Kansas City, Leavenworth and the other points of departure for the various roads leading over the plains, the word "outfit" was first used for the complete stock of necessaries required for the journey and, in time, became a term for parts as well as the whole stock and was finally applied to everything. Certainly you never hear it anywhere else except on the plains or from the lips of a plainsman. If I hear the word in the East, used in the sense I have given, I know at once that the person using it has been on the plains or their border.

Our drive now was entirely along the northern side of the Arkansas River. Nothing can be more monotonous than was this portion of our journey. We rode along the bottom, as it is generally called, with the bluffs from one hundred yards to half a mile back from the riverbank, rising from ten to forty feet above it and extending back in a high, dry, uninteresting prairie, covered with a thick mat of buffalo grass. On the river bottom heavy grasses of the blue-joint and wheat varieties grow luxuriantly, mingled with various herbs and weeds. The river is frequently filled with low islands, covered with grass and rushes and nearly submerged. Along this portion of our drive, the artemisia is the characteristic plant, but I also observed two or three varieties of helianthus, thistle and geranium. The cactus began to appear in many varieties and we were beginning to be cautious of our footsteps, when out of the stage, for fear of a thrust from its keen spikes.

At one camp we attempted to vary the monotony by trying to capture some prairie dogs. One of their towns approached the banks of the river, so with buckets we began filling up a hole with water, having been told that the little animals would come out to escape drowning. Doctor Nassau and Lieutenant Johnson knelt on the side of a hole, with their eyes intently fastened in its depths and hands on the alert to grab the escaping dogs, while Captain Nicodemus and I ran back and forward from the river with the buckets. Our efforts brought out no dogs, but did raise a huge rattlesnake, which rushed out with head erect, sounding its rattles, to the utter demoralization of the doctor and lieutenant, the former declaring if that was the kind of game we were after he should retire from the hunt. We killed the snake and found that it had seventeen rattles.[5]

Our next relay was at old Fort Lyon, called before the war Fort Wise.[6] This post was under the command of Lieutenant James M. Warner, afterwards colonel of the 11th Vermont Infantry, in fact the order making Warner a colonel came on our coach.[7] We arrived in the evening and found the post was built of stone, situated in a low, damp flat by the riverside, a mist hanging over it, and smudges to keep off the mosquitoes burning before the windows and doors of the quarters. Lieutenant Warner met us at the door of the headquarters building and invited us to remain with him during the night. We accepted the invitation, passing a most agreeable evening, during which we learned of the appointment of our host to the colonelcy and also that we had brought an order changing the name of the fort from Wise to Lyon. The fort had been named after the governor of Virginia, but as he had gone over to the Confederacy it was determined to make a change. When bedtime came it was found that there were not mosquito bars enough to cover

5. It was a popular myth, perpetuated primarily by Reverend John G. Wood in *Illustrated Natural History* (1863), that a rattlesnake's age could be told by the number of rattles. One modern writer offers this observation: "No snake myth was ever more indelibly imbedded in the public consciousness, as may be seen by frequent newspaper reports down to the present day. And it is small wonder, for the great majority of the early accounts of the rattlesnake reiterated this entertaining myth, and there is something peculiarly satisfying in having so concrete a record of a creature's age." Klauber, *Rattlesnakes* 1: 277.

6. Constructed a mile upstream from Bent's New Fort under the supervision of Major John Sedgwick, 1st Cavalry, in 1860, this post was originally called Fort Fauntleroy but its name was soon changed to Fort Wise in honor of Virginia's governor, Henry A. Wise. Someone in the War Department finally realized that a Union fort should not be named after a man who was then a Confederate general so the post's designation was again changed, this time to Fort Lyon, after General Nathaniel Lyon who had been killed in the Battle of Wilson's Creek. This new name became effective on June 25, 1862. Troops stationed here during the Civil War escorted trains traveling from the Arkansas River to the Raton Pass on the Colorado-New Mexico border. This unhealthy site, which was prone to flooding, was abandoned on June 9, 1867. A new post, unimaginatively called Fort Lyon II, was built twenty miles upstream as a replacement. *Soldier and Brave*, 108–09; Frazer, *Forts*, 41–42.

7. James M. Warner graduated from West Point in 1860, was promoted second lieutenant in the 8th Infantry on February 28, 1861, and to first lieutenant on May 30, 1861. He was commissioned colonel of the 11th Vermont on September 1, 1862, and soon after the regiment was re-classified as 1st Vermont Heavy Artillery and assigned to the defense of Washington. Colonel Warner's regiment joined the Army of the Potomac for the 1864 campaign and he was badly wounded at Spotsylvania on May 18. He returned to duty in July and performed well in the Shenandoah Valley at the battles of Winchester, Fisher's Hill, and Cedar Creek. Brevetted a brigadier general, Warner resigned on February 13, 1866, and moved to Albany where he engaged in banking and life insurance. He died in New York City on March 16, 1897, while in a theater watching a performance of *The Geisha*. Cullum, *Biographical Register* 2: 519; Heitman, *Historical Register* 1: 1003; *Evening Star*, March 17, 1897; *Springfield Republican*, March 17, 1897.

the beds of all the officers, being one short, and here I found the first disadvantage of being the lowest in rank. I went to bed without a bar and passed a most uncomfortable night. Fort Lyon was a miserable post, in a fever and ague locality, abounding in things disagreeable, and the Government in 1867 moved the post to a better site, higher up the Arkansas and opposite the mouth of the Rio de las Animas Perdidas or Purgatoire River.

Next morning at sunrise we drove out of Fort Lyon and with but one adventure worth mentioning reached Bent's Old Fort. This adventure was the making of Johnson's bed, with a convenient knoll for a bolster; the knoll, after he had got fairly settled in his blankets, turning out to be an ant hill. We were all just beginning to drop into sleep, when Johnson dashed out of his blankets with a yell and began tearing off his clothing in insane haste. Our first thought was "Snakes!" and we were out about as quick as the man attacked, utterly bewildered by his exclamations and gyrations. The victim was laughed at when we came to understand the truth and he removed his bedding to a remote location in sullen silence. The ants had let go as suddenly as they had taken hold.

Bent's Old Fort is 3,671 feet above the level of the sea and was formerly an Indian trading station, occupied by Mr. William Bent.[8] It was partially destroyed by the owner, previous to abandoning it in 1849. The stage company purchased the property and partially restored it as a defensible station and depot of supplies. The fort originally enclosed over an acre of ground. A wall about sixteen feet high on the outside and four feet thick was built around this space, with a circular bastion on opposite corners, to defend the faces. Twenty-five feet inside of this wall a second one was built parallel to it, also entirely around the square. The inner wall was not so thick or so high as the outer, the interior of the fort being graded considerable higher than the ground outside. A roof was

8. William W. Bent, a member of the prominent Bent family of frontiersmen, made his first foray into the frontier in 1827 and two years later, in the winter of 1829–1830, saved the lives of two Cheyenne warriors thus beginning a lifelong relationship with that nation. An early trading post named Fort William was abandoned when Bent's Fort opened for business in 1835. This latter post became "the pre-eminent mercantile center for the southern Plains." Bent's Fort became an army supply depot during the Mexican War, but in 1849 he moved his trading operations thirty miles eastward where he built a new fort. Bent sold his trading business in 1856 and acted as an Indian agent for a year but resigned in 1860 in frustration. He spent his last years attempting to obtain payment from the government for goods supplied during the Mexican War. William Bent died on May 19, 1869, at his ranch on the Purgatoire River (Las Animas River) in Colorado. Thrapp, *Frontier Biography* 1: 99–100; *Oregonian*, June 30, 1869.

thrown across the twenty-five-foot space between the two walls, which space was divided into rooms of various sizes by transverse walls. The interior court was open to the sky. On the eastern side, midway between the corners, was a doorway, high and wide enough to admit a prairie wagon, in which were set huge plank doors. A dozen feet to the right of the doorway was a large window, through which trading was done with the Indians. All other doors and windows opened on the great interior court.

We stayed overnight at the fort and the next morning prepared to cross the Arkansas. The river was a quarter of a mile wide and rolling so furiously and so deep that the coach was taken across empty, drawn by a yoke of oxen. We watched the cattle, driven by a mounted driver, enter the water, go on a few steps, be taken off their feet and carried downstream until they caught a foothold again, struggle on again a few rods, to be swept away again, until they were a mile and a half down the river before they struck the opposite shore. From this point we were to drive to Santa Fé in one coach, making relays of from fifteen to twenty-five miles. The mules were driven across loose and caught up and harnessed on the other side.

At Bent's Fort I witnessed for the first time the method of catching up mules, which I afterwards found universally practiced in the army and in the West. Mules are very fond of the horse and this affection is taken advantage of to enable their owners to catch them without trouble. A gray or white mare of a tractable nature is turned out with the herd to graze. Her light color enables both the mules and the herders to see her and, in order to find her in the night, she wears a bell. Whenever it is desired to drive up the herd it is only necessary to catch and lead up the bell mare, when every mule will follow. When it was time to get the mules across the river, a small boy rode the bell mare over and all the mules followed. Five of these were caught and the mare with the rest returned to the north side.

There was a boat for the passengers to cross in, but Captain Nicodemus suggested to Johnson and me that we wade across. When the suggestion was made we were standing near the boat, with certain articles of personal baggage, which we were taking in our hands. I had my sword—which was too long for my trunk—and one of the demijohns. The demijohn had long since been relieved of its whiskey and was now used by me for taking along fresh water. When we were undressed for the wading, I found myself standing on the shore, with my clothing tied in a neat bundle in my left hand, the demijohn in my right, my boots held by the straps between my teeth, my sword under my left arm and my hat on my head. Captain Nicodemus and Lieutenant Johnson were equipped in pretty much the same way, except that the former had the lunch basket in place of the demijohn and the latter carried a rifle.

Nicodemus stepped into the water first, Johnson next and I followed. It took the utmost care in walking on the uneven bottom not to plunge headlong into the turbid current. The average depth was not more than three feet, but frequently I would put my foot into a hole which would bring the water suddenly up nearly to my shoulders. Stepping slowly along I had reached the middle of the river, Nicodemus had reached the bank and Johnson was four or five yards in advance of me, when the latter suddenly stumbled and lost his hat and, in attempting to catch it, fell and plunged out of sight. As he rose, still clinging to his "traps," I laughed and in opening my mouth to do so dropped my boots. Grabbing for them with my right hand I dropped the demijohn and throwing my left arm too far from my side my sword fell and sank. Amid this general disaster, I paused to take two objects in line on shore and two upstream in order that I might return for the sword and went on. The captain, who had seen all this from the bank, threw down his burdens, ran into the water and soon came back with the demijohn, boots and hat. As soon as I had deposited my clothing on the grass, I returned to the river and found my sword. The scabbard was wet, so I did not sheath the blade for several days after this accident, but when I did there was a little moisture still in the tip which rusted my sword point, so that I have a constant reminder of this exploit near me.

Johnson spread his wet garments on the bushes near the coach and spent the time in stalking round in Nicodemus's coat until they were dry. It was some time before the rest of the party joined us, so that the clothes were completely dried before we took our seats in the coach, with our old conductor still in charge, but with a new driver. After a drive of a couple of miles up the river, we struck off a little west of south for New Mexico.

The second day out we broke the tire of one of the hind wheels and, being a long distance from a blacksmith shop, had to devise means for holding the wheel together for the two or three days between us and Fort Union.[9] Straps which could be spared from the harness were wrapped around the wheel and by careful driving we managed to reach a station without accident, where we procured a green cow hide. This was placed in a brook and soaked soft, then cut into strips and wound round the tire and wheel rim. When it dried, it contracted and drew the wheel quite as closely together and as firmly as if the tire had been reset. Certainly we had no further trouble with the wheel and paid no further attention to it until we reached Fort Union.

Late in the evening we paused at Iron Springs long enough to fill our demijohn with the clear water. The brook running from the spring left in its bed a rich deposit of iron rust and the water had a decided metallic taste. Near where we left the Arkansas River we saw several umbrella-shaped demi-spheroids, coated with carbonate of lime in pyramidal crystals, resembling the bubbles of a huge boiling cauldron.

Much of our road ran along Timpas Creek, through a country which was beginning to break into hills, for we were fast nearing the Raton Mountains. The formation of the hills was distinct to the eye, first a stratum of limestone, ten feet thick, then hard sandstone, with ammonites and a variety of other shells, overlaying blue marl. From the sides of the hill protruded geodes, with crystallized limestone, and the ground was everywhere strewn with detached pieces of ferruginous sandstone. We began also to see for the first time, on the distant hillsides, the *piñon*, a stunted pine, and a dwarfed cedar.

At a distance of fifty-four miles from Bent's Old Fort, we halted and cooked a meal at Hole in the Rock, a large hole in a deep

9. In 1851 the site for Fort Union was chosen at a locality known as Los Pozos, a series of spring-fed pools in the valley of Wolf Creek upstream from its confluence with the Mora River. Originally built of pine logs with bricks for chimneys and fireplaces, Fort Union, located on leased acreage of the John Scolly Grant, was designed to protect the Santa Fe Trail but it soon developed into a vast supply depot for other western posts. By the Civil War the fort's buildings had rotted and were in a "dilapidated state," leading the army to move operations to a new site about one mile north. This new fort was protected by extensive earthworks in anticipation of the Confederate invasion of 1862. A third version of Fort Union was constructed near the earthen second fort and remained in service as an important supply depot until 1891 when the land and remaining buildings were returned to the original owners. Oliva, *Fort Union*, 50, 56, 58–61, 63, 68–69, 73, 253–54, 263, 317, 666–68.

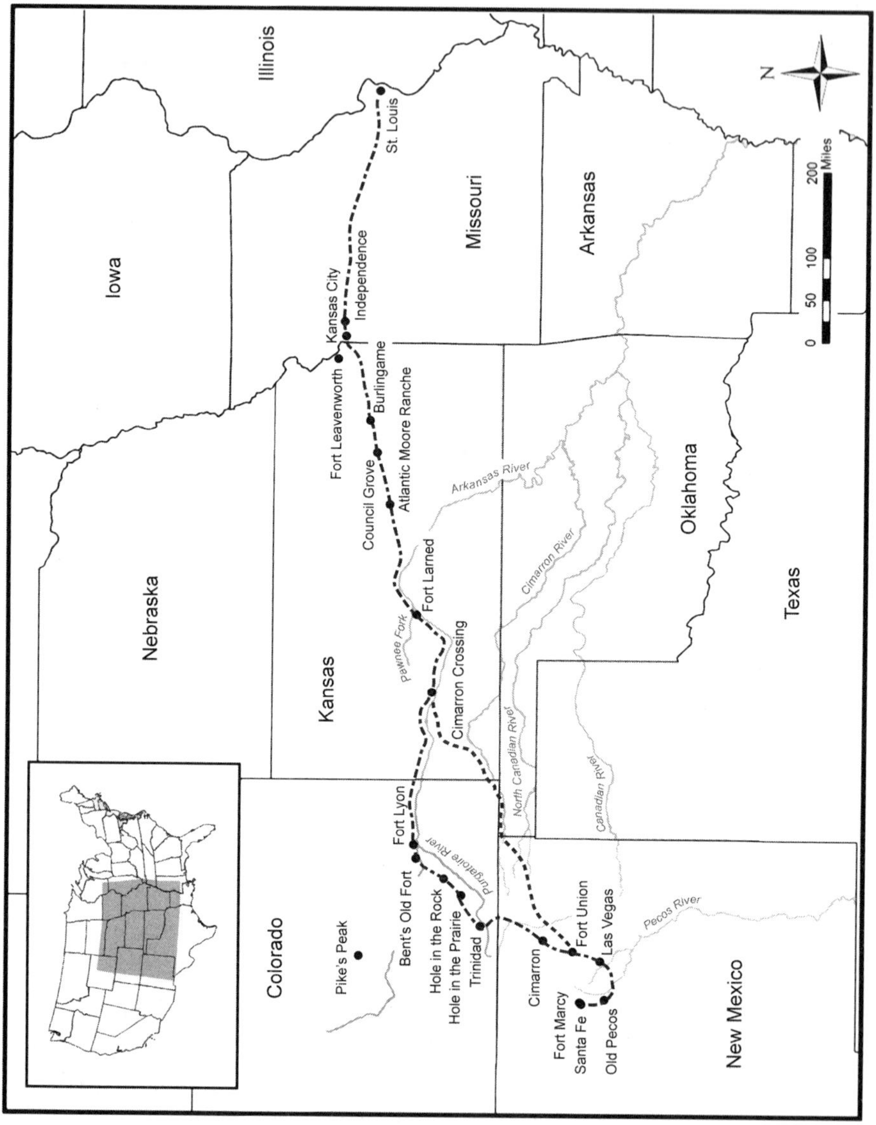

Santa Fe Trail

and ragged valley, filled with stagnant, though drinkable water. Here Stuart killed an antelope and Johnson a couple of black-tailed rabbits. All this day Doctor Nassau suffered much from pleurisy. We were now all crowded into one small coach and consequently not very comfortable. When the fit was on him the doctor was terribly out of humor and nothing would suit him. His ill-humor was contagious, too, and from being the pleasant, jolly company that we had been for the first part of the journey, we became gloomy and silent. Occasionally the doctor would burst out with a declaration that he could stand this misery no longer, get out a bottle of morphine, take a dose and while the effects of the sedative lasted he could be one of the most companionable fellows imaginable. Sunlight would reign in the coach until pleurisy asserted itself again, when we would once more be plunged in shadow.

Our next drive took us to Hole in the Prairie, a distance of fourteen and one-half miles. Here we picked up several petrified mushrooms and toadstools and a half-eaten ear of corn, the latter showing that the petrifaction was recent. A dead horse, with a dozen ravens and a wolf amicably feasting on its carcass lay but a short distance from where we halted.

A drive of twelve miles brought us to the town of Trinidad, at the entrance of the Raton Pass. The town is situated on the Purgatoire River, called by the mountain and plainsmen Picketwire, a corrupt pronunciation of the name. The river is a rapid flowing stream, a few yards in width, bordered by a generous growth of cottonwoods and locust trees. We stopped long enough to leave the mail and went on. We drove up the winding road, the scenery on either side being inexpressibly beautiful. The pine trees (*Pinus rigida*) began to attain a more respectable size, as we got into a country of more frequent rainfalls, but the *piñon* (*Pinus monophylla*) still outnumbered its tall relative. It bears a resinous nut, which is eaten as commonly by the Mexicans and Indians as the peanut by "Young America," affording abundant food, too, to the squirrels and wild turkeys with which the mountains abound.

Chapter 4

Into New Mexico

As we began the ascent of the Raton Pass, our attention was called to a bold mountain, which rose in severe majesty on our left, apparently not more than two miles away and nearly overhanging us. I say apparently because the mountain is really sixteen miles away and it is the exceeding rarity of the atmosphere which gives this impression of nearness. At the time I marched across the plains in 1866, we were in camp, to remain over Sunday, near Trinidad, and in the pleasant twilight of Saturday evening one of the ladies of our column, the wife of an officer, was sitting before our tent, making a ceremonial call upon Mrs. Curtis.[1] Mount Fisher, with its square, box-like summit, 1,500 feet above our heads, stood clearly defined against the moonlit sky and made a central point

1. Harriet Louise Hughes, a native of Holderness, New Hampshire, married Captain Curtis in that town on May 17, 1866. Immediately after their wedding the couple started for New Mexico and Harriet rode in an army ambulance from Fort Leavenworth to Fort Sumner, New Mexico. She shared all the assignments of her husband during his active service and while on assignment at various state military institutions. Following her husband's death in 1907, she moved back to New Hampshire and died on her farm at Ashland on January 24, 1924. Although her tombstone lists "Harriette" as her first name, her marriage record, death record, and census records indicate her first name as "Harriet," which is accepted as the official given name. "Harriette Louise Hughes Curtis," 171; *The Plymouth Record*, March 26, 1924; New Hampshire Marriage Records, 1637–1947; New Hampshire Death Records, 1654–1947.

of admiration for a good part of the conversation. In the enthusiasm over its beauty and what must be the sweep of vision from its summit, Mrs. D. proposed that on the morrow the ladies should make an excursion to its top. Mrs. Curtis at once assented, much to my surprise, for although I had been cheated myself several times during my first journey west, experience had made me a judge of distances and I did not reflect that these ladies were making the common mistake of newcomers. After listening some little time to the plans of the first speaker, who seemed fertile in the expedients necessary to make a pleasant excursion, I remarked, "I don't think you have provided food enough, Mrs. D."

"Why, captain, you don't suppose we are anacondas, do you? We shall be obliged to throw some away for the birds and squirrels," replied Mrs. D.

"Better lay in a little more," I said.

"What, for one day?"

"Four days."

"Four days!" in great surprise from both ladies.

"What do you suppose is the distance from here to the summit of that mountain?" I asked.

"About two miles," replied Mrs. D.

"It is seventeen to its base, and, by the route you would be obliged to take, twenty-one to the summit," I said.

Here there was a polite questioning of my word, as the evidence of their eyes was against me.

"Well," I explained, "you have only to wait for Monday's march. We go almost directly to the mountain, the road passes it to the right and you can see for yourselves. And even if it were but four miles, as you think, you have not taken into consideration the grizzlies, wolves and snakes of the region."

"Ugh!" in duet, followed by a prompt backing out from the proposed trip.

At this same camp our new officers first saw "water running uphill." This is an impression, of course, which everyone knows to be false, but it never fails to startle the newcomer at some time. At Trinidad one can see the valley of the Purgatoire River for many miles above and below the town, rapidly descending over its rocky bed to the valley of the Arkansas River. The *rancheros* have dug water ditches from the bed of the stream, high up the valley, following a water level along the hillsides, for purposes of irrigation, and as the ditch has runs parallel to the river for some miles and attains a great height above its bed, it seems to be running uphill.

But to resume my stage ride. The rocks of the pass were chiefly of a light sandstone, in strata not far from horizontal, and the road was covered with many fragments of volcanic rocks, of purplish brown color, porous and melting over a small fire. The road is well located, but, at the time we passed it, in a poor state of repair. There were no bridges over the many mountain brooks which broiled across the road and we made some ugly plunges and jerky up-rearings as we crossed them. Often the road sidled so we were obliged to get out and walk along the upper side, holding a rope from the top of the coach to prevent an upset. About halfway up we overtook an ox train of five wagons, one of which had upset, and the trader's goods lay scattered in confusion all along the bottom and sides of a deep ravine. Our conductor requested the wagon master to let us pass and, in order to do this, it was necessary for him to draw one wagon a little out of the road and then loosen the oxen from it. No sooner, however, were the oxen unhitched than the rotten log from which a Mexican had cocked the wheel was crushed by the 5,700-pound weight of goods in the wagon and the whole thing went crashing through the underbrush to bring up against a sturdy pine a little way down the mountainside.

We were not long in reaching the summit of the Raton, which at this point is said to be 7,500 feet above the sea. From the top we had a beautiful view of Pike's Peak, the Spanish Peaks, Wattahyah and the chain of mountains running south from the Wattahyah. To the east rose Fisher's Peak, of the Raton range, apparently as high above us as when we were at Trinidad. The top of this mountain from this point assumes a castellated appearance.

Another association with this pass comes so vividly to mind that I must be pardoned for mentioning it. In the dead of winter in 1867, when the pass was covered with snow and the frost hung in crystal festoons from the branches of the pines, I crossed this mountain again, on my way to command a station in Colorado. This time a baby had been added to the list of my personal baggage, so that an ambulance drawn by four mules held the valuable part of the household goods.[2] The body of the ambulance was filled with straw to half its depths, over this was thrown two thicknesses of buffalo robes, upon which wife and baby lay covered with bed clothes, the double curtains of the carriage fastened closely down on all four sides. Outside, the command plodded through snow and ice, taking two days to make the march through the mountains. Nights we had a comfortable fire in the tent, but the days were miserably uncomfortable.

But now our road through the mountains was strewn with flowers. Exhilarated by the mountain travel, the green foliage of the trees, the rich odor of the forest, all in such striking contrast to the desert behind us, this part of the journey was the most agreeable we had yet passed.

The descent of the mountains was made without difficulty and with considerable rapidity, relieved only by the sight of a grizzly bear looking down upon us from a height out of rifle shot. The same dangers attended the crossing of the streams which did on the northern side, dangers which were removed in 1865 by a turnpike company chartered by the Colorado Legislature. Soon after leaving the mountains we struck the Canadian River and halted at a relay station for a half hour's rest. The water in the river was clear and cool, flowing over a pebbly bottom, shaded by large cottonwood trees and willow thickets, which the wild hop vine clambered, covered with a luxuriant growth of the chaffy fruit. From this point the country opens out into an extensive plain and, from any of the neighboring heights, the valley of the Canadian and its tributaries, the Vermejo, the Poniente, the Cimarroncito, the Rayado and the

2. This baby would have been the couple's first child, Wardon A. Curtis, who was born on February 1, 1867. Curtis wrote numerous articles and plays while enrolled at the University of Wisconsin prior to his graduation with a bachelor's degree in 1889. One editor described his articles and books as "extravaganzas, and generally humorous." He would become an educator and writer of science fiction prior to his death on January 21, 1940, in Plymouth, New Hampshire. Wardon had consumed as many as two bottles per day of a "health" tonic sold under the name of Radiothor, which was actually water impregnated with radium. On November 4, 1964, his body was exhumed and removed to the Massachusetts Institute of Technology where scientists had begun to study the long-term effects of radiation poisoning. At one point, Wardon's body assayed at 7.9 micrograms (where 1 gram of radium is equivalent to 1 curie of radioactivity). A study in 1941 showed individuals with amounts between 1.2 and 23 micrograms were subject to ill effects. Known Radiothor drinkers suffered from anemia, skeletal damage including necrosis of the jaw and skull, kidney and bone marrow dysfunction, and abscess of the brain. *The Writer* 12: 43; *Wisconsin Cardinal*, December 17, 1892; New Hampshire Death and Disinterment Records, 1754–1947; *Omaha World Herald*, April 4, 1932; *The Tech*, November 12, 1958; "Radium—the Benchmark for Alpha Emitters," 226, 230–232; *Toxocological Profile for Radium*, 11–12.

Ocaté may be traced. These names, in order, mean the Red, the West, the Lost and the Slow Rivers.

On this plain we saw a herd of elk, or *wapiti*, and many antelope, in bands of ten or twenty, and hares were running in all directions. The cactus began to show itself in greater abundance and variety after leaving the mountains and we saw at the station the first horned frog.

With no marked adventure, we rode on until we reached Maxwell's ranche on the Little Cimarron. For a long distance before we reached this place we had heard from Mr. Stuart and Captain Nicodemus of the baronial manner in which Lucien B. Maxwell lived, the immense grant, forty miles square, which belonged to him, and the large number of laborers and animals he maintained upon the estate.[3] Mr. Stuart informed us that he would not be likely to invite us to dinner, but that we would be none the less welcome should we go to the house without an invitation—a point in etiquette which I found hard to understand. Nicodemus, however, when an opportunity presented itself, privately informed the military passengers that Maxwell was in a quarrel with the stage company and did not volunteer his hospitalities to the company or its passengers, but would be sure to extend us an invitation to his house and would probably include the others, as our fellow passengers. This turned out literally as predicted by the captain, for no sooner had we arrived at the Little Cimarron than Mr. Maxwell appeared and invited us to his house and made no exceptions in the party.

The house was a step-roofed *adobe* building, with a basement and one story. Along the front stretched a broad piazza, before which stood two brass six-pounders, looking down the valley. Extending to the rear about a hundred feet were two thick walls, being extensions of the side walls of the house, joining another house, of nearly the same dimensions, parallel to the first. A better description, perhaps, would be to take two houses of the same dimensions on the ground, facing the same way, placed one hundred feet apart,

3. Lucien B. Maxwell had accompanied Charles Fremont's first two expeditions on which he met the famous scout Kit Carson. Perhaps influenced by Carson, Maxwell settled in Taos in 1841 and three years later married a daughter of Carlos Beaubien, a marriage that led to him eventually gaining control of the vast Miranda-Beaubien Land Grant. This grant was at one time legally recognized as encompassing almost 1,800,000 acres, making him the largest landowner in the country. Being fairly well educated and proficient in Spanish, Maxwell created what essentially became a private American empire. By the time he died suddenly in Fort Sumner, New Mexico, Maxwell had lost much of his fortune and land. Keleher, *Maxwell Grant*, 25–29.

the front house elevated on a basement of six feet and the rear one without basement, then carry a wall from each end of the front edifice back to each end of the rear building and the general style of the establishment is before you. The two houses were each about fifty feet long by thirty deep. The front one contained the living rooms of the family and the rear one the kitchens, dining rooms and quarters of servants. The basement of the family building was excavated to some depth below the surface of the ground and used for a storeroom and cellar. Buildings and walls were painted white. Maxwell lived, as I remarked before, in baronial style, and when we sat down to dinner we found ourselves, with the family—consisting of Maxwell, his wife and daughter, a Roman Catholic priest, and a few relatives—sitting at a table of at least forty others, attaches and employees of the estate.

This valley was occupied by the Ute tribe of Indians, who at this time, and in fact every time I have passed through the valley, were in strong force there, their tepees being scattered throughout the valley. They are the vultures who have plucked the profits out of this estate for years, whose greed is never sated and whose demands this isolated family have never dared to deny. Mr. Maxwell has never refused hospitality to any human being, let his skin be of what shade it might. His immense herds of sheep and cattle, his flouring mills and other resources have enabled him to give apparently without stint or limit. But he has not lived there without fear, for he told me that much of his generosity to the Indians was to secure himself from attack and he only waited an opportunity to "turn the red beggars off the estate."

Most of my readers know of the discovery of gold in Northern New Mexico, the rapid building of the towns of Elizabeth, Virginia City and Cimarron. These discoveries were on the Maxwell estate and enabled the proprietor to sell out for several millions and remove to another place.

Mr. Maxwell's wife, formerly Maria de la Luz Beaubien, was Mexican and, of course, the interior of the house was arranged after the manner of Mexican residences.[4] The door from the piazza

4. Maria de la Luz Beaubien married Lucien Maxwell in Taos on June 3, 1844, and she managed the famous Maxwell Ranche until the couple moved to Fort Sumner in 1870. She was the mother of six children and three who did not survive infancy. Luz Maxwell died at Fort Sumner on July 13, 1900. *[Santa Fe] New Mexican*, July 20, 1900; Keleher, *Maxwell Grant*, 25, 30.

opened directly into the *sala* (reception room). This was richly carpeted, the walls were washed with gypsum and, to prevent it rubbing off on the clothing, rich damask was hung on the walls to the height of about five feet. All around the room ran what appeared to be a continuous settee or lounge, also covered by damask of a different shade from that on the wall. This settee is made of wool mattresses, two being folded once each and placed upon each other. The walls were adorned with pictures, most of them of a religious character, while an image of the Virgin at one end and a crucifix with a semblance of the Saviour at the other completed the ornaments. Two brass chandeliers, imported from the States, hung from the ceiling. The fireplace was in one corner, shaped like a horseshoe, curved upward, in which the wood was burned standing on end. There was a music room at one end of the *sala*, in which stood a Chickering grand piano, used by the daughter and only child of the household.

Here I must leave the thread of my story to tell an incident of the march before referred to, which is inseparably connected to Maxwell's ranche. When I passed through Fort Union on the way to Colorado, Mrs. Curtis became the guest of an officer's family at that post and on the morning we were to resume our march her friends persuaded her to remain until nearly night and then drive out, to overtake me at my next camp, a thing easy of accomplishment with a carriage holding only one woman, a baby, a servant, a driver and drawn by four mules. I gave my consent to the plan and went on to camp, about twenty miles from the fort. Here I passed away the afternoon, with little or no anxiety about the missing ones until night was approaching, then my eyes were constantly turning down the road in search of the expected ambulance. But time passed and there was no arrival until nine o'clock, when I heard the rattling of wheels, the rapid trot of animals and presently my ambulance came up to the tent. I approached, expecting to help wife and baby to the ground, when the driver said, "The captain's lady stayed behind. Here is a letter from her." I took the letter and learned that a paymaster had received orders to follow my command to Maxwell's and pay it before we should leave New Mexico. The friends at Fort Union had persuaded Mrs. Curtis to remain over until the next morning and then ride with him to overtake me at Maxwell's.

Next day we arrived at the Little Cimarron and went into camp about a mile beyond the ranche. The day wore away and no paymaster appeared. As evening approached, I spent the time chiefly in wandering back and forth from camp to house and return, generally miserable, and trying to persuade myself that no harm had come to wife or child. At midnight I gave it up and went to bed for an uneasy slumber, rising with the first gray dawn, to find there had been no arrival. When the soldiers resumed their march in the morning, I retained my private ambulance and driver, told Lieutenant John J. Lambert to continue the march to Fort Reynolds without me and that I would probably overtake him in a day or two.[5] It was my intention to wait at Maxwell's until afternoon and, if the lost ones did not then turn up, drive back to Fort Union in search of them.

I forgot to mention that on the previous day a violent windstorm had arisen about noon and had blown with terrific violence all night. Dust, sand and gravel filled the air out of doors and the weather was bitter cold. This had caused me to think, in addition to my other fears of what might have happened to the wife and child, that possibly the paymaster's ambulance had been overturned down some declivity by the hurricane.

Seeing my anxiety, Mr. Maxwell offered me the use of his light phæton and horses with which to drive back to Fort Union and about two o'clock I ordered up the team for a start. While sitting in the music room waiting for it, I heard the sound of wheels on the road and looking out saw an ambulance driving rapidly down from Fort Union. It was the paymaster with my wife, baby and servant.

We took dinner at Maxwell's, accepted from him a parting gift of a side of venison, got into our ambulance and the same evening

5. The Lambert family emigrated from Ireland in 1847 and settled in Dubuque, Iowa, where John soon learned the printing trade. He was commissioned first lieutenant in the 9th Iowa Cavalry on November 30, 1863, and promoted captain on May 6, 1865. After being mustered out on March 15, 1866, John sought a position in the Regular Army and was commissioned second lieutenant in the 5th Infantry on March 7, 1867. He served at Fort Reynolds as quartermaster and commissary until his resignation on March 31, 1872. In 1868 he purchased the *Chieftain*, the first newspaper in Pueblo, Colorado, and had his brother run the operation until he left the army. Lambert married in 1873 and retained editorship of the *Pueblo Chieftain* until his death in that city on January 5, 1916. Fort Reynolds was built along the Arkansas River in Colorado by Captain Simon Snyder, 5th Infantry, and officially established on July 3, 1867. Named for General John Reynolds who had been killed at Gettysburg, the garrison was charged with protecting the nearby settlers from Indian incursions. Rendered unnecessary following Indian pacification in the region, Fort Reynolds was abandoned on July 15, 1872. Mills, *Arkansas Valley*, 802; *Pueblo Indicator*, January 8, 1916; Frazer, *Forts*, 41.

overtook the soldiers in camp. As we rode along, my wife related her adventures in a voice hardly above a whisper, from a cold she had contracted. The major's team had left Fort Union at eight o'clock in the morning on the previous day and by mistake had taken the road leading from Fort Union to the Cimarron crossing of the Arkansas River instead of the one by the Raton Pass. They had encountered the storm at noon and suffered intensely from the searching cold. Not reaching Maxwell's in the time usually consumed in the journey, the party began to get anxious and, at nightfall, seeing an ox train camped by the roadside, drove out to it and asked where they were. Finding they were on the wrong road, the paymaster hired one of the Mexican drivers to guide the ambulance across the prairie to the Raton road.

The road was finally reached, but the night was so dark and the storm so cold and biting that it was unsafe to drive out of a walk. About nine o'clock a light was seen some distance ahead and the carriage drove slowly and wearily towards it, to find a rude Mexican hovel of two rooms, a little distance from the road. Here the major's party found a Lieutenant George J. Campbell and wife, who had left Fort Union a little later than they and had stopped on account of the storm.[6] The new arrivals soon aroused the Mexicans. The lieutenant and wife, who were just having their first nap, got up and assisted in doing the hospitable, Lieutenant Campbell giving up his bed to Mrs. Curtis, with his overcoat for a quilt and, retiring to the adjoining room, passed the time until morning sitting up with the other officer.

The ladies had a fire in their room, but as the stars could be seen through various holes in the roof it made no impression on the chilly atmosphere of the apartment. Night passed away at last and after a miserable breakfast of black coffee, eggs and cornbread the party resumed its journey. With the end of this adventure, I will go on with my stage ride.

The road to Fort Union ran along the edge of the mountain spurs and was bordered by much to please the eye of the close observer,

6. A native of Scotland, George J. Campbell served as private and artificer in the Dragoons and Engineers from January 13, 1851, to November 28, 1860. He served in the ranks of the 3rd Artillery from 1860 to 1864 when he was commissioned a second lieutenant in the 3rd Cavalry on May 18. Promoted to first lieutenant on January 7, 1866, he retired because of disability on July 29, 1868. Lieutenant Campbell died at Nunda, New York, on October 4, 1906. Heitman, *Historical Register* 1: 277; *Evening Star*, October 25, 1906.

but nothing of sufficient interest to the reader occurred during this portion of the journey.

As we crossed a ridge, nearly three miles away, Fort Union came in sight, a collection of rude *jacal* (shack) quarters, with the exception of a few buildings occupied by the military storekeeper and for the storage of ordnance supplies. This fort at the present day is one of the finest in the West. Its buildings are capacious and well built, with some pretensions to comfort and good taste in the arrangement of the rooms. It is the depot of supplies for New Mexico and Southern Colorado, the point from which army stores of all kinds are distributed to the other forts.

From the point where we first saw the post, the gleam of the sentinels' muskets could be plainly seen and shortly afterwards we could see figures moving about the parade. At last we drove up to a sutler's store, in which was the post office, and were soon busily engaged in exchanging greetings with the officers of the garrison, who were not slow in extending the hospitalities and making us feel at home.

Fort Union is 115 miles from Santa Fé and is situated in the valley of a small stream called the Mora. It was originally built without walls, stockades or breastworks, but during the Texas invasion of 1862, the object of which was the seizure of the stores and supplies here, some earthworks were thrown up nearby and several intrenchments on the ridge overlooking the fort from the west.

The invasion from Texas had found the territory almost destitute of troops to make a defence. The officers highest in rank had gone over to the Confederacy and for a short time it looked as if the territory must fall into the possession of the enemies of the Union. A rapid concentration of the few Regulars in the Far West, with the enlistment of volunteers in Colorado and New Mexico, enabled General Edward R. Canby to make a stand in the *cañon* twenty-five miles north of Santa Fé and deal such a blow to General Henry H. Sibley that he left the territory for Texas in hot haste.[7]

7. Henry H. Sibley graduated from West Point and was commissioned a second lieutenant in the 2nd Dragoons on July 1, 1838. Promoted to first lieutenant on March 8, 1840, he served as regimental adjutant until 1846. Promoted to captain on February 16, 1847, and major of the 1st Dragoons on May 13, 1861, Sibley resigned the same day. Commissioned colonel in the Confederate army on May 16, 1861, he was appointed a brigadier general on June 17, 1861. Following his unsuccessful invasion of New Mexico in 1862, Sibley's importance seemed to evaporate and he accomplished little during the remainder of the war. Sibley later spent several years in the Egyptian army and returned home to lecture about his overseas adventures, but he died virtually penniless in Fredericksburg, Virginia, on August 23, 1886. Heitman, *Historical Register* 1: 886; Warner, *Generals in Gray*, 276–77.

About three o'clock in the afternoon we left for Las Vegas, the first Mexican town on our road. Several passengers joined us at Fort Union, crowding us so that there was no longer any comfort to be had in the coach. Doctor Nassau was worse and in consequence crosser than he had been at any time before. From here to Santa Fé we were to drive, as we had during the early part of our trip in Kansas, day and night, with no pause longer than necessary to change animals.

We arrived at Las Vegas long after night, so that we could see nothing of the town. A few Americans live here and seem to control the trade. In company with *Padre* Donato, I once visited the dilapidated mud church which stands on one end of the *plaza*.[8] A cracked bell suspended from a beam laid across two supports hangs before the entrance. The form of the building is that of a cross, with an earthen floor, and void of seats or other accommodations for worshippers. In the nave is the altar, with a few rude and primitive decorations, and in rear of it are three daubs of paintings, one of which is intended to represent Christ nailed to the cross, while a rough wooden image of the Virgin Mary stood in the north transept.

8. This description of *Padre* Donato and the church is taken from W. W. H. Davis, *El Gringo; or, New Mexico and Her People*, published in 1857.

Chapter 5

Arrival in Santa Fé

When we drove up before the hotel at Las Vegas it was quite dark. By the light of the lamps, which streamed through the open windows and doorways across the *plaza*, we could perceive that we were in a narrow street with compact *adobe* buildings about us. Through one window, at the left of the house, we could look into a small room, in the centre of which stood a table, with piles of gold and silver upon it, while a mixed group of Mexicans and Americans were standing or sitting about playing Monte, with eyes directed eagerly towards the rapidly turning cards.[1] Through another window, more to the right, across the hotel office came the sharp click of billiard balls and from some hidden inner apartment came the music of a harp, playing the air of Mexico's favorite dances, *La Cuna* and *La Indita* (The Cradle and The Little Indian Girl). Most of our passengers were dozing and those awake showed no disposition to get out, for we had changed mules in another part of the town and our stop at the *fonda* (inn) was to be brief. But when the music of the dance saluted our ears, I heard the driver say in an undertone, "What's up? A dance?"

1. One person said of the ubiquitous gambling in the territory: "The natives of New Mexico are so addicted to the habit of 'Monte,' and other games, that is almost second nature with them." *Philadelphia Inquirer*, November 18, 1862.

"Don Ramon Vaca gives a *baile* (ball)," was answered by a man who stood leaning against a pillar of the piazza, but whose face I could not see.[2]

"Is Pablita there?"

"Yes, came with George."

"Dash him! I wish I hadn't got to go to Santa Fé. I'd fix him!"

"I'll drive for you and you can stay."

"But you don't know the road."

"Yes, I do, been over it twice. Besides, the mules know it."

"Well, slip up here quietly and say nothing to the old man. So George thinks he's got the inside track! I'll show him a trick! Good night. Look out for the nigh leader, she needs no touching."

"Good night, Bill. Hope you'll have good luck."

Sitting on the front seat, with my head near the speakers, I had been the only passenger who had heard this conversation and knew that a change of drivers had been made. I said nothing, for I thought one driver was as good as another and knew none of the difficulties of the road.

After a brief stop, a man approached from the hotel office, threw a leather bag under the driver's seat and we were off. The road ascended slightly as we left the town, but soon began to descend again into a narrow valley, which we followed for some four miles, when we turned abruptly to the right and passed a mountain ridge through a deep *cañon*. On the right a chain of serrated hills ran from northeast to southwest, while on the left the country opened into plains. The ridge appeared to have been cloven asunder by some great convulsion of nature and a beautiful road made through it, wide enough for four wagons to drive abreast. The sides of the *cañon* are formed of immense masses of rocks nearly perpendicular. The original formation was deposition in water, but there appears to have been a subsequent upheaval, as well as a subjection to intense heat, which has displaced the strata that now lies at an angle of 45°, with a dip towards the east. The ridge exhibits no other vegetation than a growth of scrubby pines and a few blades of grass among the rocks.

I made these observations at a later time, for at the period I am writing of nothing whatever could be seen. I could hear the low talking of the driver and conductor and soon learned that they

2. Don Ramon Vaca cannot be positively identified.

knew little or nothing about the road. Perhaps I was a little more interested in the conversation on account of what I had heard at the hotel and so kept awake from a sort of presentment "that something was going to happen," but it is certain that I was the only passenger awake and listening. Night wore on, our speed from a rapid trot had got down to a walk, and I heard the driver say, "Where the devil do you suppose we are?" "Dashed if I know," was the reply.

Upon hearing this I drew myself out of the cramped and crowded seat, squeezed through the window and swung myself up into the driver's seat. The stage lamps threw a yellow light upon the backs of the mules and into the road for half a furlong ahead, revealing the merest single-wheel track and scattering tufts of grass between. It needed no explanation that we were not on the Santa Fé road. To my question as to how we got off the road, it was explained that some miles back the nigh leader got to behaving badly and just as we came to a fork in the road the driver got out of patience and touched her with the whip. She immediately began jumping and kicking and as we came to the fork dashed down the left-hand road, probably forcing the other mules with her. Nothing was thought of it at the time and for a long time afterwards it seemed as if we were on the main traveled road, but as we went on the track kept growing less plain, until it seemed to have almost utterly disappeared.

I noticed that there was a deep ravine on the right and that the track often ran within a foot or two of the edge. I asked the driver if he did not think we had better turn back, but found him opposed to this. He said he knew by the mountaintops ahead that we were on the right general direction and that probably we should soon come to some Mexican cabin, where we could inquire and get set right. At this point we heard Doctor Nassau give out a series of growls over the situation, showing he had been a listener to a part of the conversation, waking up everybody, so that the growling was immediately general. When it became known that we had changed drivers and how the change was made, the growling was fiercer, if possible, than before, and I saw from Cottrill's manner that two discharges would be made out as soon as he got control of the line.

The driver and conductor relapsed into sullen silence and the mules dragged us slowly along until we suddenly came upon the edge of a declivity, at the bottom of which—but how far we could not see—we heard the rushing of water. The brake was put on and we started slowly down, but had gone but a few yards when the mules broke into a run and we went crashing over boulders and ridges into a creek containing a depth of twelve inches of water. The stage body, with its human load, was turned over, detached from the forward wheels, and thrown some ten feet to one side in the middle of the stream. The concussion seemed like a juvenile earthquake. As I was on the driver's seat, I took a plunge forward, landing face downward in the water, considerably jarred and wholly wet.

As soon as I could, I began looking for my companions and found them alive and kicking and scrambling out of the coach with all possible haste. All were more or less bruised. Johnson was the most seriously injured of any, the blood running in a stream from a gash in his head. Nassau had hung in some of the straps and escaped everything but a shaking up, still he swore more and louder than all the rest of the party together. In fact, the plunge had the curious effect of checking the growlings with most of the party, as soon as we had extricated ourselves and found no great damage done. Singularly enough, the coach had received no serious injuries in the running gear, the top was somewhat demoralized and there were minor breakages, not bad enough, however, to prevent our going on. The mules dashed off at the height of their speed, but the driver had managed to hold on to the reins and secure a footing on the forward axle in time to get them under control and returned to the creek.

This accident had detained us about an hour, when the coach was pronounced to be in a condition to enable us to go on. Johnson remarked, "There is only one thing lacking to make me perfectly happy."

"What is that?" asked Captain Nicodemus.

"To hear that George has disemboweled Bill and Pablita has danced on his grave."

"I don't know as I wish him such bad luck as that," said Mr. Cottrill, "but you may rest assured he'll never drive on this line again while I have control of it."

"Thanks," said the lieutenant, "you have no idea how that soothes my head."

Not long after this we heard the barking of dogs and presently saw a small house by the roadside. We stopped before it and our driver and conductor began shouting "*Hombre*!" after the manner of saluting strangers in Spanish countries, and at last we heard a sleepy voice answer, "*Quien llama*?" (Who calls?). Not being an adept in Spanish, I could not follow the conversation which ensued after the Mexican appeared and silenced his dogs with vigorous kicks, but I soon learned we were off the direct road about six miles, that by going a mile farther we would strike an excellent road and find no further trouble.

This proved true and after a slow drive of one mile, during which those of us who had received a wetting walked, to keep from taking cold, we reached a fine road and our mules broke into a sharp trot, bringing us into Tecolote just as day was dawning. We had consumed the entire night in what would have been a distance of thirteen miles had we stuck to the road. We stopped before a trader's station, in which was the post office, and after much exertion succeeded in rousing a salesman from his morning nap. He changed the mail and we drove on.

Six miles farther on, at Bernal Spring, we changed animals and took breakfast. The water of the spring is strongly impregnated with carbonate of soda and is neither palatable nor healthy. Almost overlooking the station was a mountain whose sides slope gradually up until within a few hundred feet of the top, where they become more perpendicular and rise up like walls of masonry, showing the natural layers of stone with perfect distinctness.

Our next drive was fourteen miles in length and brought us to the town of San José, on the Pecos River. The road approaches this town on a very high elevation, from which it first appears in sight deep down in a valley, but a circuitous and gradual descent brings one finally into the street. The Pecos is a rapid stream, with a considerable fall and a plentiful supply of water, well adapted for mill sites. I hear since I left the country that some woolen mills have been built at San José.

But a short distance beyond the town stand the ruins of an Indian pueblo—Old Pecos.[3] This town was in existence at the time

3. Pecos Pueblo, now Pecos National Historical Park, was constructed in the fourteenth century on a mesa eighteen miles southeast of Santa Fe and contained over 600 rooms in apartment-style dwellings that rose as high as five stories. Residents were agriculturalists and traded their produce with other natives until the arrival of Spanish colonists and

of the conquest of Mexico by Hernando Cortéz.[4] With the advent of the Spaniards the town gradually went into decay, until the inhabitants finally abandoned it and united themselves with Pueblo Pojoaque.[5] The most prominent feature of the ruins is the Roman Catholic Church, built by the missionaries a couple of centuries ago.[6] It is cruciform in shape, built of *adobes*, with a main entrance looking towards the southwest. All the woodwork shows evidence of having been fashioned by Europeans. In the rear of the church and covering a slope of the hill for two or three hundred yards are the ruins of the town. Large blocks of stone, some oblong and others square, and weighing a ton and upwards, lie about upon the surface of the ground, some of which show evidences of having been laid in water.

Pecos was, without doubt, originally a fortified town, occupying a promontory or rock somewhat in the shape of a foot. At the end of the short spur forming the terminus of the promontory are the remains of the *estufa*, with all its parts distinct, where was kept the sacred fire, which was never permitted to go out; at the other end are the remains of the church, both showing the distinctive marks

---

missionaries upset the economic equilibrium. Ravaged by disease and raids by Apaches and Comanches, Pecos Pueblo was a virtual ghost town by the time the Santa Fe Trail began to pump American goods into the Southwest. James Josiah Webb, the famous Santa Fe merchant, noted that the Pecos Indians had become so reduced in population that they could no longer maintain their irrigation system or perform community tasks. The last handful of survivors moved away in 1838 to join distant relatives at the Jemez Pueblo. Schroeder, "Pecos Pueblo," 430, 434; McManamon, Cordell, Lightfoot, and Milner, *Archaeology in America*, 190–92; Levine, *Our Prayers Are in This Place*, 52.

4. Hernando Cortéz participated in the successful conquest of Cuba that began in 1511. With permission from the Spanish governor of that colony, Cortéz set out seven years later to conquer the Aztec empire. He won over by might or diplomacy a number of native peoples who became important allies in his campaign to unseat the Aztec king, Montezuma. Cortéz treacherously captured Montezuma in 1519, but his men were forced from the city the following year when the king was killed. Cortéz laid siege to the Aztec capital in 1521, razed it to the ground and built Mexico City on the site. Appointed Governor and Captain General of New Spain following his conquest of the Aztec empire, he led other expeditions in the Caribbean until his final return to Spain in 1540. He died unheralded at Seville in 1547. Levy, *Conquistador*, 178, 182, 327–28; *Houghton Mifflin Dictionary*, 364.

5. Pojoaque Pueblo was a small settlement about sixteen miles north of Santa Fe. Having taken an active role in the Pueblo Revolt, residents of Pojoaque were decimated and driven from their homes when the Spanish reconquered the region. Some eventually returned only to see their best land gradually taken from them. Never a robust site after the Spanish arrival, the population dwindled to only 37 persons in 1860, living on over 13,000 acres, and by the early twentieth century the town had been abandoned. It has since been resettled by descendants of its original inhabitants. Lambert, "Pojoaque Pueblo," 324–25; *California Farmer and Journal of Useful Sciences*, June 19, 1863.

6. These ruins were those of the Mission of Our Lady of the Angels of Porciuncula which the Spanish had constructed in 1717. Ruins of the first church by that name, built in 1625 and destroyed during the Pueblo Revolt, can still be seen within the later structure. McManamon, Cordell, Lightfoot, and Milner, *Archaeology in America*, 192.

and emblems of the two religions. The fires from the *estufa* burned and sent their incense through the same altars from which were preached the religion of the Christian.

The next halt which we made was El Boca del Cañon. This *cañon* is a pass through the mountains, and appears to have been formed by nature expressly for a wagon road. It is about three miles in length and quite densely wooded with pine. In places it is only wide enough for one wagon. The sides are formed of ledges of rock, sometimes two or three hundred feet high, and almost perpendicular.

It was here that General Sibley and his Texans were repulsed in their advance upon Fort Union. As referred to elsewhere, Sibley had met with little or no resistance on his way up the Rio Grande. He had successfully occupied all the towns, including Santa Fé, up to this point. Here the advance column of Colorado Volunteers, under the command of the Methodist parson, Colonel John M. Chivington, and two companies of my regiment, met him.[7] The two forces encamped at the opposite entrances of the *cañon* for the night, expecting an engagement in the morning. The senior captain of the Regulars was William H. Lewis, the same who, as lieutenant colonel of the 19th Infantry, was killed by the Indians on the plains in 1878.[8] He was an officer whose skill in

7. John M. Chivington was a minister, outspoken abolitionist, and army officer, but is now best known for his implacable destruction of the American Indians. During the 1850s Chivington began to advocate force to advance God's will, a stance that soon grew to include Republican policies as well. His outspoken support for the Union resulted in his commission as major of the 1st Colorado. Following the Confederate withdrawal from New Mexico, in which he claimed an exaggerated role although Colonel John P. Slough actually commanded the Federal forces, Chivington was commissioned colonel of his regiment. In November of 1862 he assumed command of the Military District of Colorado where he contended against rebel guerrillas, Indians, and bandits. On November 29, 1864, he took his step into infamy when his hastily assembled force attacked a camp of peaceful Cheyennes on Sand Creek and killed several hundred Indians, including many women and children. Chivington resigned his commission on January 4, 1865, and, although he managed to survive several inquiries into his conduct at Sand Creek, his later life was doomed to failure. He died in Denver on October 4, 1894, after holding a series of minor local offices. Ball, *Soldiers West*, 149–68.

8. A native of Alabama, William H. Lewis was one of the few Southern officers to remain loyal to the United States during the Civil War. A graduate of West Point in 1849, he was commissioned second lieutenant in the 5th Infantry on October 7 of that year. Promoted to first lieutenant on March 3, 1855, and captain on May 7, 1861, Lewis spent the majority of his pre-war career in Texas and Utah with intervals chasing Seminole Indians in Florida and acting as instructor of tactics at West Point. The outbreak of war found him in New Mexico and he won two brevets during the Confederate invasion of 1862. Promoted to major of the 18th Infantry on July 14, 1864, Lewis later served at that rank in the 36th Infantry and 7th Infantry until his promotion to lieutenant colonel of the 19th Infantry on December 10, 1873. Lieutenant Colonel Lewis was mortally wounded in a fight with Cheyenne Indians in a canyon on Punished Woman's Fork on September 27, 1878. He died in an ambulance en route to Fort Wallace the following day and at the request of his family the remains were

the profession of arms was admitted by everyone. Gifted with rare good judgment, possessed of varied knowledge acquired by assiduous reading and study in his moments of leisure, his opinions on military matters were valued and desired. He never obtruded them. He never offered them unasked, but he always gave them fearlessly and freely when asked.

With a true soldier's eye, he saw that the vulnerable point of the Texas column lay in their supplies. A long way from their base, in a country not friendly to them, if their train could be destroyed, a fatal blow was dealt them and there could be no resource short of retreat. Captain Lewis being sent for by Colonel Chivington to advise on the situation, suggested that a force be sent to the rear of the Texans to destroy their train. The parson was a man of infinite pluck, but had no skill as a military chief. He could not see the use of the movement, but finally told the captain that he might take the two Regular companies and try his plan, but that he must be responsible for its failure should he not succeed. Captain Lewis accepted the situation. With his two companies he skirted the side of this three-mile *cañon*, hundreds of feet above the road, through the midnight darkness, a feat which cannot be fully appreciated unless its scene can be witnessed. Along an almost perpendicular mountainside the command crept slowly past the sleeping Texans, when a falling stone or stick would have revealed their intention and descended far in their rear. Just before daylight, the light of the burning train showed Colonel Chivington that the expedition had succeeded. A brief fight took place and the Texan invasion fell to pieces; the army surrendered.

The credit of this exploit was claimed by the minister with unblushing effrontery, but the authorities knew to whom belonged the praise and the highest military authority in this, and perhaps

---

sent to Sandy Hill, New York, for burial. Captain Joseph Rendlebrock gave this version of his demise: "His horse was shot in the thigh, and two old soldiers of Company B almost dragged him from it and begged him not to expose himself unnecessarily. He jumped to his feet, grabbed a carbine and fell into line with the skirmishers. The skirmishers rushed forward, Lewis with them, and when 100 yards from the enemy he, of all the rest, was struck by a ball. It severed the femoral artery of the left leg and felled him to the ground. He examined it as coolly as any man could, but said to Lieutenant [John W.] Martin of Company B, who was with him, 'I guess it's all over with me.' Then he took the buckskin strap from his revolver, and with his own hands tied his wound, putting the strap around his leg above the wound and using his revolver for a lever to tighten it. . . . But nothing could save him—he died in about four hours." Cullum, *Biographical Register* 2: 238; Heitman, *Historical Register* 1: 631; *New York Herald*, September 30, 1878; October 2, 1878, October 21, 1878; *Chicago Inter-Ocean*, October 3, 1878.

any other country, has been heard to declare "that Colonel Lewis was the best officer of his rank in the service."

As we passed along the road and emerged from the mountains, Nicodemus called our attention to a ranche on the right hand side and said that the owner was a man who a few years ago had won $30,000 at Faro.[9] He also said there was another man about the same distance out of Santa Fé, on the other side, who had won $40,000. I had occasion to know both of these men during my three years' service in New Mexico, having stayed at their houses frequently, and it may deter anyone who would like to win a few thousands at Faro to know that the "tiger" won it all back in a few years and both ranches have fallen into other hands.

On the 2nd day of July, 1862, we drove down the long declivity at the foot of which sits Santa Fé. The tinned spires of the churches were gleaming in the sunlight and the flag at Fort Marcy was plainly to be seen.[10] In a half hour's time we were driving along the narrow and dirty streets, curiously gazing at the gazers in the doors and windows of the low and shabby *adobe* houses. On the corner of the *plaza* we stopped before the *fonda* and disembarked from the Overland Stage. We were instantly surrounded by a number of officers stationed at the fort and department headquarters. They had come to welcome Captain Nicodemus, who was a member of General Canby's staff, was known to everybody and soon put us in the way of knowing everybody too.

Santa Fé, or as it is often written in Spanish, Santa Fé de San Francisco, was settled sometime between 1580 and 1600 and is in consequence the oldest town in the United States. Before it was settled by the Spaniards, an ancient capital of the Pueblo Indian

9. This ranch and stagecoach station was owned by Anthony P. Johnson, formerly a teamster at Fort Union. The site is now known as Cañoncito at Apache Canyon. Simmons, *Santa Fe Trail*, 197–98.

10. Located at Santa Fe, Fort Marcy originally had been constructed by General Stephen Kearny during the Mexican War. Located on a hill that overlooked the city, the post was named for Secretary of War William L. Marcy. There was not room enough for barracks in the fort, so soldiers lived in old Spanish buildings bordering the capital's plaza. Fort Marcy was briefly abandoned in 1851 by a department commander who declared the town to be a "sink of vice and extravagance." Re-occupied a few years later, Fort Marcy was evacuated when the Texans invaded New Mexico during the Civil War. Federal troops returned after the Texans withdrew from Santa Fe and Fort Marcy became headquarters for the Department of New Mexico. Following the Civil War, Fort Marcy's importance declined and it was abandoned and re-activated several times before its final abandonment on October 10, 1894. Thompson, *New Mexico Territory*, 51–52; Frazer, *Forts*, 100–01.

kingdom stood on nearly the same site.[11] In the vicinity of the town, fragments of painted pottery may still be found and on the road leading towards San Miguel the ruins of two old buildings still stand. The Indians continued to live here for many years after the Spaniards took possession of the country, but finally left the town to join some of the others in the valley of the Rio Grande.

The town is situated on both sides of a creek, sometimes called the Rio de la Santa Fé and sometimes the Rio Chico, about twenty miles east of the Rio Grande del Norte, into which the former stream empties to the southwest. The town lies at the western base of a spur of the Rocky Mountain chain, the summits of some of which are covered with snow for most of the year. It is laid out with considerable regularity, in the manner of all Spanish-built towns. In the centre is the *plaza*, or public square, about three acres in extent, from the four corners of which lead the principal streets, at right angles with each other. The *plaza* is the main thoroughfare and centre of trade, most of the stores and shops fronting upon it. The streets are of medium width and unpaved and, but for the *portales* (covered sidewalks), the foot passenger would suffer from the sun's rays or from rain in the rainy season. In the middle of the *plaza*, which is laid out in walks and fenced, stands a pagoda-shaped bandstand, built by the military authorities and of which I was architect when quartermaster at Fort Marcy. I also planned the walks and fences and planted the trees. Before this, the square was a barren sand waste.

The city had a population of about 6,000 souls, of whom, besides the military, scarcely 300 were American, the rest being Mexican, and was considered by the soldiery to be the best station in the Far West. Fort Marcy was, in fact, a part of the city and the parade ground cornered upon the *plaza* like two squares of the same color in a chess board. Our guard mountings and dress parades, at the request of the citizens, were generally held on the *plaza* and our regimental band played every evening on the band-stand in front of the Government palace. Balls and parties given by the ladies of the military and civil officials of the Government,

11. In referring to this Pueblo Indian kingdom, Curtis may be referencing either Tesuque Pueblo about nine miles north of Santa Fe or the much larger site of San Lázaro Pueblo, some twenty miles south of Santa Fe, which had been abandoned after the Pueblo Revolt of 1680. Edelman and Ortiz, "Tesuque Pueblo," 330; Schroeder, "Pueblos Abandoned in Historic Times," 247–48.

bailes and *fandangos* by the Mexicans, and the various amusements and advantages peculiar to a busy and populous town made life at Fort Marcy pleasant and much more to be desired than that at the secluded and isolated posts in the Indian country.

The public edifices in Santa Fé are few in number and of rude construction. The Government palace, a long, low *adobe* building, extends the entire north side of the *plaza*, and is occupied by the officers of the Territorial Government and is also made use of for purposes of legislation. About one square to the east of the plaza is the parochial church—or cathedral perhaps it should be called—as it is the church where the Roman Catholic bishop preaches, when not absent on episcopal duties. Perhaps no edifice in the territory so well exhibits the worth of the *adobe* for a building material. The church has a nave of fifty feet in length and forty in width, with a transept of seventy feet in length and forty in width. It has double towers and a chime of bells. There are no pews or seats inside and the congregation seat themselves on the floor, presenting the strange appearance of an audience rising when they kneel and sinking when they sit. The walls are adorned with many paintings, some of which are excellent, but the greater part of which are mere daubs. There are two other churches in the city, that of San Miguel and that of Nuestra Señora de Guadelupe and a Chapel of Santo Elizaro. An empty Protestant chapel stands near Fort Marcy.

Near the Church of San Miguel is a boys' school, in charge of a brotherhood, and on the north side of the river is a boarding and day school for girls, under the management of the Sisters of Charity. This building is two stories in height and was formerly used as a hotel. Like nearly all other houses, it has an interior open court.

North of the military post stands the unfinished capitol of the territory, which has cost already twice what it ought to when finally completed. It is built of stone and will be an imposing edifice when finished. Near it is the penitentiary, still incomplete, an institution much needed in this territory, which will not lack for tenants when ready to receive them. The city also contains one excellent hotel, two printing offices, which publish a newspaper each, some forty stores, numerous liquor saloons and *fandango* rooms.

All the buildings fronting on the *plaza* have *portales* extending their entire length, so that the pedestrian is sheltered, except when he crosses the streets at the corners. Under these *portales*, crouching against the walls of the buildings, the market women sit daily smoking the everlasting *cigarritos* and selling meats, fruits, vegetables and eggs. Before the sidewalks stand diminutive *burros*, loaded with billets of pine wood or grass brought from the mountains from ten to twenty miles away and for sale at six bits—seventy-five cents—per cord. The *burro* is used for all sorts of purposes. He carries the marketing of the peasant to town to be sold and bears his master home again; he carries the wife and children to church, or whithersoever they desire to go; and if the country belle wishes to ride into Santa Fé on a shopping excursion, she mounts the *burro* without saddle or bridle and ambles off to town. He is capable of long fasting and much fatigue; he bears the most cruel treatment with the resignation of a martyr and, after a hard day's work, will make a comfortable supper on thorns or cedar bushes, his happiness being complete if he has a heap of ashes to roll in. He serves innumerable purposes and fulfills not only all the duties of the horse and mule, but is used instead of all sorts of vehicles, from a coach to a wheelbarrow. He is the universal hackney of the country people, who, when they mount the *burro*, instead of sitting on the back, sit astride the rump, abaft the hips, and guide him with a sharpened stick.

On almost any day and especially on Sundays, cock-fighting may be seen going on near the *plaza* or in the neighboring streets.[12] This is the national and favorite amusement of the Mexican people. All classes indulge in it more or less, from the laborer in his blanket to the *caballero* (gentleman) in his broadcloth and the priesthood is not above participating in the elegant amusement. The Mexicans are born gamblers and there are numerous Monte banks in town. Sometimes three or four tables will be running in the same room. Monte is a betting game like Faro and is played with Spanish cards, which are considerably different from those in use in this country. The numbers run up from ones to eights only and the characters are cups, coins, swords and clubs, instead of diamonds, hearts, spades and clubs. Instead of a "Jack," they have a mounted horseman known as *El Caballo* (The Horse). The names of the denominations are, respectively, *copas* (cups), *oros* (coins), *espadas* (swords) and

12. Judge Joseph Gillett Knapp agreed with this assessment by Curtis, writing on April 3, 1863, from Mesilla: "To tell the truth Sunday in New Mexico is really a feast day, or holiday, not *holy day*—a day of galas and shows, of horse racing and cock fights." *Wisconsin Daily Patriot*, May 5, 1863.

bastos (clubs). With these cards immense sums of money have been lost and won and night turned into day by men and women through the fascination of the game. Women do not play the game as much as formerly.

A few years ago, quite a celebrated woman known as *Doña* Maria Gertrudis Barceló led the van in gambling in Santa Fé.[13] She was for years the most expert Monte dealer in the city and amassed a large fortune by the game. Her wealth gained her admission to the wealthiest circles of the town; she died in the odor of sanctity and was followed to the grave by a large concourse of mourning citizens. Her death took place in 1852 and she was buried with the highest honors of the church, at an expense of upward of $1,700 for spiritual services. It was my fortune to see this bill and obtain a copy of it, which I give for the delectation of my readers.

Dobles (tolling the bells)	$10.00
El sepulcro (the grave)	30.00
La cruz alta (the grand cross)	1.00
La capa (high mass vestments)	3.00
La agua bendita (holy water)	1.00
Los ciriales (candlesticks)	1.00
El incensario (vessels for incense)	1.00
Los posos (resting places)	30.00
El entirerro (the interment)	30.00
La misa (the mass)	20.00
El organo (the organ)	15.00
Los cantores (the singers)	16.00
El response del oratorio (response of the oratory)	10.00
Mas al diacono (deacon's fee, additional)	10.00
Los derechos del obispo (rites of the bishop)	1,000.00
	$1,178.00

13. Doña Maria Gertrudis Barceló, also known as the Gambling Queen of Santa Fe, married Don Manuel Antonio Sisneros in 1823, but retained her own name. Referred to by one author as "a courtesan, monte dealer, madam and an expert mule trader," she became adept at catering to the needs and desires of men traveling the Santa Fe Trail. She was an expert Monte dealer, card players noting that her hands moved as fast and smoothly as if she were knitting. Commonly known as *La Tules* (The Reed) due to her thin frame, she became one of the wealthiest persons in the territory with immense influence in financial, social, and political affairs. In the latter area can be included an actual affair with Governor Manuel Armijo and in the financial field a loan to General Stephen Kearny to pay his troops during the Mexican War. Described as both "colorful and controversial," *La Tules* was buried in Santa Fe on January 17, 1852. Williamson, *Frontier Gambling*, 244–48.

It will be seen that it was formerly an expensive matter to die and be buried in New Mexico. These charges are for the funeral services only and do not include the masses said for the repose of the dead. To the credit of the very worthy gentleman now at the head of the Catholic Church of New Mexico, Bishop John Baptiste Lamy, it is but just to say that these abuses of the Mexican church have been very generally corrected since he assumed the Episcopate.[14]

The town of Santa Fé is built literally of mud. To an Eastern reader, to say a house is made of mud is to suggest dampness, filth and disease. Few persons know that as fine a house can be built of mud in certain climates as of brick or wood. There are houses in Santa Fé rejoicing in marble mantles, soapstone fireplaces, calcined walls and all the modern conveniences which wealth can secure, whose walls are built of *adobes*. To build a house, it is only necessary to secure a small supply of running water near the chosen site, mix the earth, form the bricks, dry them and lay the walls and, after the house is finished, fill the hole from which the earth was taken with the rubbish. These houses, with but few exceptions, are of but one story in height. All houses of more than one story were built by Americans. The walls are very thick and the partitions between rooms are built like the outer walls and of the same thickness, consequently are cool in the summer and warm in the winter.

14. Educated at the Clermont and Mont-Ferrand Seminaries in France, John Baptist Lamy was ordained a priest in the Catholic Church in 1838 and came to America the following year. After Lamy had served eleven years in a series of Ohio and Kentucky churches, Pope Pius IX appointed him Bishop of Agathonica and ordered him to oversee the diocese in New Mexico Territory. He was a mixed blessing for his parishioners, condemning folk art in churches, but halting exorbitant charges for church services such as burials. During the Civil War period his bishopric contained over one hundred parishes with only about thirty priests to attend the faithful. Another half-dozen old Mexican priests ministered to the twenty Pueblo towns in the territory. In addition, Lamy oversaw the 130 male scholars being educated by the Christian Brothers Order and the female academy, 120 females being taught by the Sisters of Loretto. Elevated to archbishop in 1876, Lamy resigned that office in 1885 because of ill health and died in Santa Fe on February 13, 1888. One account gave the following estimate of "fees charged and collected" by the New Mexican clergy after meeting a resident of the territory: "He supposes that in the territory there are annually 5,000 baptisms, amounting to as many dollars; 3,000 marriages, at $8 each; 3,500 burials, at $6 each; offerings of the patron saints, and other matters relating to births and first fruits, amounting to $20,000; thus making a total of $70,000, without taking any account of the public parades and the arbitrary taxes which are under the control of each priest. To this sum must also be added the tithes of all the crops and increase of property, to be paid in kind or compensated for in money, and which swells the amount $100,000 more." Horgan, *Lamy of Santa Fe*, 26–32, 37–61, 70–71, 143–44, 251; *Denver Rocky Mountain News*, February 14, 1888; February 24, 1888; *San Francisco Bulletin*, September 13, 1864; *New York Evening Post*, December 27, 1862.

Nearly all houses are built in the form of a square, with an open *placeta* (courtyard) in the centre. In the front of the house there is a large double doorway which will, when open, admit a coach to the *placeta*. In the city this door is generally kept closed and is watched by a *portero* (gate keeper) who never admits a visitor unless satisfied that he is a friend. Around the courtyard is a continuous *portale* and often there are no doors from room to room, but one must pass along the *portale* in going from one part of the house to another. The outside of a true Mexican house is not attractive, rarely having any windows and but one door, which is wide enough to admit a carriage to the interior court. The roof is flat, with a slight parapet, and the water which collects upon it is carried off through wooden spouts, which extend about two feet outside the walls so that the pouring water shall not dissolve the *adobes*. The roof is made by laying *vigas* (beams) across and boards on top of them, and then covering all with about two feet of hard tamped earth. It rarely rains enough to penetrate the roof.

From the *portale* open the doors of the various rooms. The *sala* and the living rooms are on the side of the court next the street and the dining room, kitchen and servants' quarters are in the rear. Turning to the right and entering the first room, we find ourselves in the *sala*. This room is large enough for a dancing hall and is often used as such by this dancing people. From the ceiling hang candelabra made of tin or brass, according to the means of the family, and the walls are decorated with pictures, generally of saints, and looking glasses in large numbers. At the ends of the *sala* are either wooden images of the Saviour or the Virgin. The walls are snow white with a wash made of gypsum, which comes off upon everything that touches it and, to prevent this, strips of damask or calico are hung around the four sides from the floor to a height of five feet.

All around the sides of the room runs what appears to be a continuous sofa or settee, covered with damask, but which, when night approaches and the covering is taken off, turns out to be made of wool mattresses, folded once lengthwise and piled up in couples, with pillows, sheets and blankets tucked between the ends. These are laid on the floor for the guests to sleep on, for the Mexicans rarely use bedsteads. The common covering for the floor is a native woolen carpet, woven in white and black checks or stripes, very soft and thick. The ceiling is never plastered, but is often covered with white cotton tacked to the *vigas* or else the beams themselves, being left bare, are carved in fanciful designs and painted in colors. The fireplace is built in a corner and occupies but a small space. The mouth is shaped like a horseshoe, not generally more than two feet in height and the same is the width at the bottom. The back is slightly concave, instead of being a plain surface, and the circular hearth in front is raised a few inches above the floor. Andirons are unknown, the wood being placed on end against the back of the fireplace. Shovel and tongs are never seen.

There are rarely any chairs in a Mexican house. The favorite attitude of the Mexican women at their sewing and knitting is a sitting posture upon the floor, their backs resting against the walls or the mattresses before mentioned. Bureaus, stoves, etc. are never used. Kitchen utensils are meager in their appointment. They cook by open fires and generally in earthen vessels.

In one house in Bernalillo, where I passed the night when journeying on special service, the pitcher, wash bowl, soap dish and urinal were all of beaten silver. It is not uncommon in the wealthiest families to find many utensils of silver and so rudely fashioned that they seem to have been made by a blacksmith, the marks of the hammer being visible on the surface.

When the family enters to meet us, all embrace us, giving us a generous hug. This embrace, however, is made with as much fervor or laxity as handshaking is with us. A dear friend gets a fervent pressure, an indifferent acquaintance but a touch of the hands over the shoulder and under the arm. As we are Americans, chairs are offered us, but the ladies sit on the floor. The first act of hospitality is to offer us *cigarritos*, which one of the young ladies rapidly manufactures from tobacco, kept in a silver box, and a corn shuck. She lights it at the fire, takes the first one or two puffs herself and passes it to us. If the fingers are tapered and the lips sweet, even a non-smoker will not refuse the weed. Conversation never lags with the Mexican and we can have a pleasant time so long as we stay.

The national costume of the Mexican is disappearing in New Mexico and American ready-made clothing has come generally into use. The women, however, have not learned to use the bonnet or hat, although in other details of dress they follow the fashions. The female head is universally covered by the *rebozo* (shawl) which is a mantle of silk, linen or cotton, two yards long and one wide, with a deep fringe at the ends.

In New Mexico, courtship is carried on in a vastly different way. There young people have no moonlight walks and sentimental talks along the banks of a pleasant stream in summer; no strolls in the fields in springtime, to gather early flowers to present to each other as emblems of their own budding affection; no pleasant drives through shady groves, when the horse goes so slow and the afternoon is so warm it is impossible to return home before evening, when the moon will light the road. There are no pleasant evenings passed in each other's society, to study character and disposition, and when the eyes often speak volumes though the tongue is silent; no sweet good-byes at the doorstep away from ma's searching eyes, when a pressure of the hand is given and received in token of that affection which is as deep as it is silent. None of these little manœvrings are known to New Mexican wooers.

The old Spanish custom is adhered to and, in the first place, all proposals of marriage are made to the parents of the daughter. If a lad sees a *señorita* whom he fancies he should like to marry, he carries his troubles and desires to his father, who makes a formal application to the father of the girl and without delay asks the hand of the daughter in marriage for his son. The parents of the young lady then consider the merits of the young man and if they meet with their approval, the offer is generally accepted without consulting the wishes of the daughter, who like a dutiful child is expected to do just as her parents wish.

On the afternoon of our arrival, Lieutenant Johnson and I reported ourselves at headquarters to General Canby and he invited us to take dinner with him and his wife next day. We accepted the invitation and spent a few hours very agreeably at his quarters.

Next day, "the glorious Fourth," Johnson and I took seats in the coach for the lower Rio Grande. None of our late comrades were to go farther with us and Nassau and Nicodemus we never saw again. The former applied for sick leave and went back to the States on the return coach. Nicodemus joined his regiment on the Potomac but a few months afterward. Besides ourselves, there were but two other passengers—a quartermaster's clerk by the name of Bob Underhill

General Edward R. S. Canby. Courtesy of Massachusetts MOLLUS Civil War Photographs, United States Army Heritage and Education Center.

and Judge Richard H. Tompkins. [15] They were both about half drunk from the frequent parting cups they had taken with their hosts of friends in Santa Fé. The judge introduced himself to me in a novel manner. He had been sitting quietly on his seat by my side for half an hour without speaking, when I suddenly felt a keen thrust of some sharp instrument just above the knee of my lame leg. Jumping up, I saw the judge had pricked me with a pin.

"What do you mean, sir? I exclaimed.

"Nuthin', lieutenant, only want'er se'f (hick!) yer had a cork leg," replied he with drunken gravity, whereupon Johnson and Underhill laughed until I was obliged to join in and make friends with the inquisitive inebriate.

Our first stopping place was at Pino's ranche—Pino being the winner at Faro of the $40,000 before mentioned.[16] Here we took dinner, and then resumed our journey, stopping for the night at Algodones. Next day we entered the town of Albuquerque, the second in size in the territory.

15. Bob Underhill cannot be further identified. Judge Richard H. Tompkins first came to New Mexico in 1851 and was appointed clerk of the U. S. District Court. He served at U. S. Attorney in 1858 and 1860. Appointed territorial librarian in 1880, Tompkins died at Santa Fe on January 14, 1888. Hunt, *Kirby Benedict*, 190.

16. It is impossible to determine which member of the famous Pino family is described here.

Chapter 6

Albuquerque and the Rio Grande

The driver of the Rio Abajo coach was a stout young German, who united in himself the duties of conductor and driver. He carried an army bugle on the seat beside him, blowing a musical *tantara*, *tantara* as we entered each town, which had the effect of bringing out the inhabitants to see the coach arrive. This coach was drawn by six mules instead of five, as had been the custom from west of Pawnee Fork to Santa Fé.

We arrived in Albuquerque just before twelve o'clock and were told that we should go no farther before the next morning, welcome intelligence to us on many accounts, the principal one being that it would give us an opportunity to see this old town and make the acquaintance of the officers stationed there. Albuquerque was settled about 275 years ago, at the time the Spaniards first secured a foothold in the country, and was probably named after a duke of that name who was once viceroy of Mexico soon after the conquest.

The town is built of *adobe* around a square, in the centre of which stands an octagonal building of one story with a flagstaff running up through the centre. The building at the time I arrived there and, for some years afterwards, was occupied as a guardhouse by the garrison. On the north side of the *plaza* stood the parish church, inclosed by a fence, making a space all around the building of about twenty feet in width, which had been used as a graveyard until the ground was literally covered with remains. Skulls and bones lay strewn about and in one place I saw the hand of a child protruding from the earth. This sight made an impression upon me which has never been removed and I never think of Albuquerque without this unpleasant association of my visit to the church.

The hotel was on the southwest corner of the *plaza* and as I entered it my attention was first attracted by a contrivance for stirring the air and driving off the flies, which swarm here in myriads. Suspended from the ceiling of the dining room, about twenty feet apart, were several bits of scantling and stretched from one to the other were strips of cloth about six feet from the floor. The scantling being attached to the beams overhead by hinges, these huge fans were swung back and forward by a small boy who sat at the end of the room, operating them by a cord.

One of the officers of the New Mexican Volunteers, who was idling at the hotel, had a tame coyote which followed him about like a dog, but not with a dog's confidence and self-reliance. He looked menacing and acted so, lying down on his back and putting up his feet, with his tail tightly curled against his body, when approached by a stranger.

These were war times and Albuquerque was filled with soldiers, mostly New Mexicans, but there was one battery of Regular artillery. In the afternoon some of the officers of the battery invited Lieutenant Johnson and me to ride out to a ranche about four miles distant, to witness a Mexican sport called *coleada de toros* (bull tailing). A couple of saddle horses were brought round to us and in a short time we were galloping over the road in a cavalcade of officers and citizens for the scene of the sport, arriving there in about half an hour.

This ranche, about three years before, had been visited by the Navajos, who had killed many of the peons whom they found at work in the field and carried off several thousand head of sheep.[1]

1. The Navajo people, who refer to themselves as Diné, originally lived on the Colorado Plateau in the region of what is now called the Four Corners, where the boundaries of the states of Colorado, Utah, New Mexico, and Arizona now meet. Primarily sheepherders and agriculturalists, much of the Navajo territory had been appropriated by white settlers and other relocated Indian groups. Many Navajos had been captured and enslaved prior to the

Piles of stones dotted the scene of the raid, each mounted by a rude cross showing where the men were killed and scalped, each stone testifying to an Ave Maria or a Pater Noster which a friend had uttered before he threw it on the grave.

These Indians had swooped down upon the ranche one day entirely without warning. The men immediately fled, leaving the women and children to their fate. Those not carried away were violated and many were pierced with arrows and lances and left for dead. One of the women of the household told the story to me, through an interpreter, bitterly accusing the men of cowardice. She with her two grown daughters had managed to escape when the Indians first appeared and concealed themselves under a bridge which crossed a stream near at hand. Here they remained for some hours, but were finally discovered by a young chief who approached and stopped his horse on the bridge, saying in bad Spanish "that he wanted a Mexican wife and a few scalps." Dismounting, he thrust his lance under the bridge with a savage whoop. The point pierced the arm of the woman and caused her to shriek in pain. One by one he drew them from their hiding place.

"*Dios de mi alma*!" ("God of my soul!") said the poor woman. What a moment was this! For a moment they were surrounded by yelling savages, who brandished their weapons over them, but owing to some sudden diversion they were left alone, the Indians riding away and leaving them a chance to escape, of which they quickly availed themselves.

"*Ay de mi! Y los hombres*," she continued, "*quienes son esos hombres*?" ("Woe to me and to the men, who are not men, where are they?") "*Escondidos como los ratones*" ("Hidden in holes like mice"). "*Mire*!" (Look!") she suddenly exclaimed, pointing at the gay cavalcade of bull-tailers. "Look at these men, well armed and mounted, who are now so brave and fierce after the poor bulls. If twenty Navajos were to dash upon them, where

Fort Fauntleroy Massacre on September 22, 1861, when a dozen women and children were killed by soldiers. When General E. R. S. Canby was succeeded by General James Carlton, the new commander "targeted both the Mescalero Apaches and the Navajos for removal, isolation, and incarceration, and decided to place them together in one location to enforce a different future for both communities." Carleton tasked Colonel Kit Carson with subduing the Navajos during the years 1863 and 1864 with the result that more than 8,000 men, women and children had been concentrated on a reservation at Bosque Redondo near Fort Sumner in southeastern New Mexico. Brugge, "Navajo Prehistory," 490, 506–17, 527–30; Roessel, "Navajo History," 506–23; Witherspoon, "Navajo Social Organization," 524–35; Iverson, *Diné*, 48.

would they be? "*Vaya, vaya*! *Son cobardes*" ("Go, go! They are cowardly").

In a large corral, not far from the house, were about a dozen bulls. Round this were gathered the horsemen, all dressed in the picturesque costume of the country, now so fast disappearing, examining the animals as they were driven to and fro in the enclosure in order to get them excited for the coming sport. When all was ready, the bars were let down at the entrance of the corral and a bull driven out, who, seeing the country open before him, dashed off at the top of his speed. With a shout the horsemen pursued the flying animal, which, hearing the uproar behind him, redoubled his speed. Each spurs his horse to the utmost and strives to take the lead and be the first to reach the bull. In such a crowd, of course, it takes first rate horsemanship to avoid collisions and accidents and secure the lead. For some distance the party kept compactly together, enveloped in a cloud of dust that made them almost indistinguishable, while the bull could be plainly seen some hundred yards ahead.

The ladies of the ranche and vicinity were on the flat roof of the house, from which they could see every part of the field and urge on their respective favorites by gesture and word. Among the contestants was one lad, a child of the house, about fourteen years old, who sat his horse like a Comanche, swaying from side to side as the bull doubled and the cloud shut him from sight. This lad suddenly took the lead and the women screamed, "Viva Pepito! Viva!" waving their *rebozos* above their heads to encourage him. But two others are close behind him and presently are running neck and neck with him and the race for the lead and the first throw becomes very exciting. The men shout, the women wave their *rebozos* and cry out their names. "Alza!" "Bernado!" "*Por mi amor*, Jesu Maria!" "Viva Pepito!" they scream in intense excitement. The boy at last loses the lead and a tall, fine-looking Mexican, mounted upon a swift and powerful roan stallion, dashed ahead.

At this moment the quick eye of little Pepito saw that the bull had turned at an angle from his former course, but that the other horsemen had not noticed it on account of the dust that enveloped him. The lad checked his horse a single instant and then dashed out sharply to the right and cut off the bull. Shouts and vivas rent the air in appreciation of this manœuvre and the boy ranged up on the left quarter of the bull, bending down to seize the tail and secure it under his right leg for the purpose of throwing the animal to the ground. But here Pepito's strength failed him in a feat which required great power of muscle and, in trying to perform it, he was jerked out of his saddle and flung with considerable violence to the ground, stunned and senseless. Without paying any attention to the fallen lad, the cavalcade rushed on, the tall Mexican on the roan distancing all competitors. He dashed up to the bull, seized the tail in his right hand, throwing his right leg over it and, turning his horse suddenly to the left, upset the bull in full career, causing the huge animal to roll over and over in the dust, bellowing with pain and fright.

This exciting but dangerous sport exhibits the perfect horsemanship of the Mexicans to great advantage. Their firm and graceful seat excels that of the Americans and the perfect control which they exercise over their horses seems to make them almost a part of the animals they ride. The *coleada de toros* lasted as long as there was a bull left in the corral. Pepito sustained no permanent injuries, but before we returned to Albuquerque had recovered his breath and was receiving praise from every side for his superior horsemanship.

There is another game practiced by horsemen called *el gallo* (the cock). A rooster is made fast to a tree or a picket driven into the ground, the neck and head being well greased. The horsemen are ranged in line and start together, to strive and seize the fowl, burst the cord by which it is secured and ride away with the prize. The greased neck generally slips through the fingers of the first horseman and the bird falls a prey to one who has better luck, on account of the grease having been removed by those in advance. As soon as one is in possession, he rides off, pursued by the rest, whose object is to rescue the fowl. The game is a cruel one and the cock is generally torn limb from limb before the game closes, the scraps being presented by the fortunate possessors as a *gâge d'amour* to their mistresses.

In the evening there was to be a *baile* at the house of one of the *gente finos* (fine people), Anastascio Armijo's, and, as this was to be an aristocratic affair, there was considerable exertion made by our friends to secure invitations for Johnson and myself.[2]

2. Anastascio Armijo cannot be positively identified.

These were obtained through a brother officer and then my stage acquaintance, Judge Tompkins, came to see me and said that he could take me to an excellent family, friends of his, and perhaps we could get one of the young ladies to accompany me to the ball. I was delighted at the prospect of gaining admission to a Mexican house, a thing which I learned afterwards was not easy of attainment. In fact, it is exceedingly rare that one ever sees the ladies, even after he gains entrance.

By what special claim the judge secured the confidence of this family I do not know, nor what he could have said to them in my recommendation, but it is certain that I was at once admitted into the bosom of the family, introduced and embraced—after the manner of the country—by all, including two lovely girls of eighteen and twenty. I could not speak a word of Spanish, so sat silently smoking the *cigarritos* manufactured by the *señoritas* and which they lighted for me by taking the first puffs themselves, now and then asking and answering a question through the judge as interpreter. Why the judge should have selected me for this special favor, instead of Johnson, I was at a loss to guess, but think he was making reparation for sticking the pin into me.

After half an hour's talk by the judge and smoking by me, he announced that he could stay no longer and that he had made arrangements for me to accompany *Señorita* Teresa to the ball. He explained that there would probably be some elderly woman accompany us, according to the custom of the Latin races, and that I must not resent or notice this; that the family was really doing me a great honor in allowing me to escort one of the daughters, so contrary to the usual custom, and he hoped that I would do nothing to make them sorry for showing me so much confidence. Of course, at the time, I did not understand half of this and was almost ready to show resentment at the apparent insinuation lying in the caution, but now that I know the country and its customs so well, I wonder more and more at the favor done me on this occasion, a favor always repeated whenever I afterwards visited Albuquerque.

The judge left and I found myself alone with the two girls and without means of communicating with them save through the eyes. They produced pictures and books for my inspection and I smoked myself nearly sick in order to refuse nothing at their hands.

The time at last arrived for us to go to the dance and I expected to see the *señoritas* retire to effect some changes in their dresses, but no. They called for their things and proceeded to array themselves before me, even to the changing of their stockings and the clasping of their garters. This was a severe trial to me but probably was a *costumbre del pais* (custom of the country).

These girls were not brunettes, like the great majority of the Mejicanas, but were blondes, claiming to be of pure Castilian descent. This rare type of beauty is greatly admired among the Mexicans. Our red-headed or flaxen-haired officers always distanced all the others in the notice of the Mexican fair.

When the girls were ready, an old woman, who looked as old and wrinkled as one of Macbeth's witches, appeared, smoking a *cigarrito*, and showed that she was evidently the *dueña* who was to accompany us. The judge had told me I was to go with Teresa, but I found Inez took my right arm when the former took my left and we went from the door, all, including the *dueña* (mistress), smoking.

The party was select and all seemed to enjoy themselves very much. The Mexicans are graceful dancers, going into the poetry of motion with an enthusiasm that does not obtain among the more northern and colder-blooded races. At midnight, just as I was offering my arm to take my charges to supper, a message from the hotel arrived, saying that our driver had taken the whim to resume the journey at once and that if we wanted to go we must come to the coach immediately. I left the ladies a moment, in order to find the judge to act as an interpreter and explain the necessity which demanded my immediate departure. Many graceful things were said and I hurried away with Johnson to find the coach. We were both ready to scalp the driver, but could get no explanation from him in relation to his sudden determination to go on. In fact, we never knew.

The stage was soon on its way and this time the passengers had fallen off to Johnson and me. We disposed ourselves comfortably in opposite corners and soon fell asleep, not to wake until the notes of the driver's bugle announced the town of Peralta, eighteen miles from Albuquerque. We did not stay here long, but as soon as the mail was changed drove on, resuming our slumbers. We did not wake until the sun was well up in the sky.

The next stopping place was at Tomé, the county seat of Valencia, a town once very prosperous and possessing a large population, but now with barely 400 souls. The valley spread out several miles between mountains on both sides of the river. The soil is very productive and was formerly generally under cultivation, but the repeated raids of Navajos and Apaches frightened away the inhabitants until but a handful remain.[3] From being one of the most prosperous towns in the Rio Abajo and the scene of annual festivals, when hundreds of people flocked thither for purposes of religious worship and amusement, and fun and frolic was kept up for days in succession, it has sunk to be but a small place. The situation is rather picturesque and in this particular it will compare favorably with any Mexican town in the country.

We stopped at Tomé for a couple of hours, witnessing the gathering of the country people to a religious fête, to be held in the evening. The primitive ox carts were used by the women as coaches. These carts were boxes or frames, mounted on wheels which were cut from large cottonwoods and carved into a circular shape, with hubs all of the same piece. Over the tops of the carts were spread blankets to keep off the sun and underneath were huddled the women and children. The man of the family usually rode on the tongue of the vehicle, his time divided between belaboring his oxen and scratching his head, occasionally making a *cigarrito* by way of diversion. In one of the carts, a Paganini was playing the violin and the women were keeping time to the music by waving their bare arms and nodding their heads in cadence.

Later Johnson and I were standing before a wall trying to make out the meaning of a placard pasted thereon, when our attention was attracted by passing music. Turning, a strange sight presented itself. In a sort of sedan chair, borne by four men with uncovered heads, was seated what appeared to be a wax figure nearly as large

3. The Apache people were divided into seven distinct tribes that ranged over what are now the states of Colorado, Texas, Oklahoma, New Mexico, Arizona, and on into Mexico. When Curtis used the term "Apache" it is generally not known to which group he is specifically referring. Primarily foragers, acquiring most of their food through hunting and gathering, the Apaches acquired horses from the Spanish and became fierce warriors who struck terror first into the hearts of Mexicans and then the late-arriving Anglos. Outright warfare with the Americans was precipitated when Lieutenant George Bascom imprisoned Cochise and several other Chiricahua Indians. Cochise soon managed to escape, but when the other hostages were killed the resulting anger fueled twenty years of ferocious fighting with the U. S. Army. Opler, "Apachaean Culture Pattern," 368, 370; Ingstad, *Apache Indians*, xxvii.

as life, rather tawdrily dressed; following immediately behind were four priests, bearing tallow candles of a full yard in length. A motley rabble followed these, also bearing candles. Not to be lacking in respect, we pulled off our caps as the procession was passing and immediately a grave Mexican thrust candles into our hands and shouldered us into the procession. Before I could make up my mind what to do, Lieutenant Johnson said, "Let us go on and see what it's about." Accordingly, we marched on and entered a church where some kind of service was held, with a sermon in Spanish, but before it closed we left as it was time to take the coach. Our backs were adorned with tallow from the candles borne behind us, which spilled themselves at the jostling halts peculiar to the civilian procession.

The next place of any importance was Casa Colorado, where we entered upon a miniature desert of drifting sand. The sand was loose and there was not a vestige of grass or turf to hold it down. A strong west wind was blowing at the time and the sand drifted before it like snow on a winter's day. The particles were fine and dry and the atmosphere was so filled with them as almost to obscure the sun. The sand blew into our faces with force enough to be unpleasant, so that we were glad enough when the distance covered by this waste was passed.

That afternoon we reached La Joya in season for supper, the principal dish of which was *chili colorado*, a compound of red peppers and beef stewed together, flaming like the crater of Vesuvius, a dish of which the Mexicans are very fond and which Americans soon learn to like. The town, like Tomé, has been often raided by the Indians and our host showed us, with some pride, a bow, arrows and lance which he had taken from a Navajo he had killed in a fight the year before.

From La Joya to Parada, opposite Socorro, we met with no adventures worth recording. At this place we were to cross the Rio Grande upon a "dugout," too narrow to run the coach into and not large enough to take the mules. The usual method of crossing the rivers of the Far West is by fording and the roads nearly all lead to the fords. All the animals—oxen, sheep, horses, mules, donkeys and dogs—are used to this method and take to the water without giving trouble, the draught and riding animals never, to my knowledge, making serious objection. But at the time we reached Parada, the Rio Grande was swelled by the regular summer flood, caused by the melting snows in the Rocky Mountains.

At the shore of the river we unharnessed the mules and put the harnesses, trunks and mailbags into the boat and crossed, with two Mexicans rowing. Lieutenant Johnson, the driver and I each held the bridle reins of two mules, which swam alongside the boat, their heads only above the water. The swift current carried us down-river a long distance during our slow progress to the opposite side and we were nearly a mile below the point where we left the stage before we reached the western shore. After landing and assisting the driver in picketing the mules to graze, I walked up the river to watch the crossing of the coach, a thing not difficult, as the river was not far from 300 feet wide at this point.

The boatmen towed the boat slowly upstream until they were somewhat above the coach and then shot across, effecting a landing very near it. After placing the boat in position, with the stern to the shore, the coach was run down into the water astride of it and, as soon as the boat caught the weight, it was shoved off. It seemed to me to require some gymnastic ability on the part of the rowers to keep that top-heavy load from overturning into the river, particularly in a part of the stream where the current rolled in waves, and I could see the coach reel heavily, one way and the other, only to be checked by opposite movements on the part of the boatmen.

The coach fairly over, without accident, we again harnessed and in a few moments we were in the town of Socorro. This is quite a large place and of considerable importance in the territory. At the time I arrived there, a company of soldiers occupied it to protect the people against Indians. A rather novel disaster occurred to this town in the summer of 1864. At that time the Rio Grande rose much higher than it was ever know to before, so high that the water came into the streets of Socorro to a depth of two feet. As the buildings are all of *adobe*, the two feet below water became mud and the weight of the dry walls above gradually crushed each building slowly downward until the town was nothing but shapeless piles of mud, standing like islands in a lake. The military authorities furnished the inhabitants with tents and rations for some time afterwards. The town has since been rebuilt.

Chapter 7

Arrival at Fort Craig

The town of Socorro is situated on the west side of the Rio Grande Del Norte, upon a bluff overlooking the river. The meaning of the name is "succor" and is said to have been bestowed for the following reason. When the Pueblo Indians rose and drove the Spanish settlers out of the country in 1680, a party flying before their implacable enemies met a military force at this point, coming to their rescue, and in commemoration of the event, when the town came to be built, it was called Socorro.[1]

About three miles west of the town stands a mountain, Sierra Socorro, the summit of which has been computed as 2,700 feet above the plain. It is composed of a confused mass of volcanic rock. Viewed through a field glass, it appeared to be traversed by walls of reddish-colored basalt, seams of porphyritic lava and metamorphic sandstone. There is gold, galena and copper in this mountain, which has been mined with considerable success. A hot

1. This Indian uprising was the famous Pueblo Revolt of 1680. Led by Popé, who had been beaten by the Spanish for practicing witchcraft, the Pueblo Indians rose against their rulers, killing hundreds of settlers. Besieged in Santa Fe for several days, the Spanish eventually fought their way out of the city and abandoned the province of Nuevo Mexico. The united Pueblos repelled a Spanish invasion in 1681–82 and maintained their independence for twelve years until Diego de Vargas returned the province to Spanish rule in 1692. Simmons, "History of Pueblo-Spanish Relations," 186–87.

spring of some celebrity comes from the base of the mountain and falls into a pool some twenty feet long by fifteen wide and eighteen inches deep. The temperature of the water is about blood heat and it is believed to possess virtues which make it healing to the bather. The town of Socorro receives its water from this spring, the three miles from its source to the *plaza* cooling it to a drinkable temperature and affording the town better water than falls to the lot of most Mexican towns in the Rio Grande Valley, nearly all of them depending upon the murky river water for a supply. There are several warm springs in the Territory of New Mexico, some of which are medicinal in a high degree and, if in the States, would be a fortune to their owners. One in the neighborhood of Las Vegas has effected many remarkable cures of chronic rheumatism.

Our stage drove out of Socorro the next morning after our arrival and we were soon following the road along the western edge of the river bottom, occasionally passing a fine ranche or a hamlet, where we would stop to leave the mail or a package. At one ranche we heard a great noise from a gang of ten men, who were beating something in a huge trough, the perspiration from their naked bodies dripping into the substance at a great rate. Our coach halted for a few moments to give us an opportunity to see the process. Whatever the mess may have been—for I could not make it out—it was taken from the trough, after a time, boiled and transferred to a press, as primitive in its construction as anything used in the wine-making days of Noah. The hopper was the trunk of a scooped-out cottonwood tree. Into this was inserted a large plug of wood, upon which the lever rested about half way its length. Men, women and children were mounted upon each end, see-sawing with all their might and chattering like a lot of cockatoos. I suggested, as an improvement, that one end of the lever be confined and all the living weight be transferred to the other end. "No! No!" said the head men, "If that is done the fun of see-sawing will be over and I cannot get my work done."

At noon we stopped at a small hamlet to leave the mail and, as some part of the harness needed repairing, the driver told us we had time to get our dinner while it was in the hands of the *zapatero* (shoemaker). This was not the usual dining place for passengers, so we were obliged to prospect considerably before we found a place where the people were willing to furnish us something to eat.

We entered a miserable little *adobe* building, the door opening directly from the street into a room of about twelve feet square, with an earthen floor and walls of the same color. Troops of fleas were caracoling about the floor, while the flat odiferous bugs to which our New England women are such enemies, were sticking in patches on the walls. A dried-up old man, with a long grizzled beard and matted hair, which fell, guiltless of brush or comb, on his shoulders, came in to receive our orders for dinner. I requested him to get some water for washing and he seemed nearly struck dumb with surprise and backed out of the room with his eyes fixed on me with every expression of amazement. Presently he returned with a rude, earthen basin, but without towel or soap. Asking for these necessaries, he at first gasped at me in astonishment and then burst into immoderate laughter. "*Ay que hombre*! *Ave Maria Purissima lo que unloco es este*!" ("Oh what a man! What a madman is this!") "*Servilleta, pañuella, toalla, lo que el diablo quiere*?" ("Towel, napkin, handkerchief, what the devil does he want?"), repeating the different names I used to explain that I wanted a towel. "*Ha, ha, ha! Es medio-tonto, medio-tonto!*" ("Half-witted fellow"). "*Qué demonio! Quiere agua, quiere jabon, quiere toalla!*" ("What the devil! He wants water, towels, soap!"). "*Adios*! ("Good-bye!")

A meal of *tortillas* (a thin circular cake, about fifteen inches in diameter and about the thickness of blotting paper, made of Indian cornmeal, mixed in water and baked on hot stones or sheet iron), bean soup, eggs and *chili colorado* was in course of time placed before us and, without exercising any extra squeamishness, we partook of it heartily, paying fifty cents each for our entertainment, resumed our seats in the coach, which was now ready, and left this miserable hamlet.

Nothing further occurred worth mentioning until our arrival at Fort Craig. This fort stands on the right bank of the Rio Grande del Norte, on an elevated plateau, a couple hundred feet above the river. It commands the northern end of the route over the desert called the Jornada del Muerto.[2] A few miles south of the fort,

2. The noted Arizona historian Sharlot M. Hall wrote of the Jornada del Muerto:
We rode from daybreak; white and hot
The sun beat like a hammer-stroke
On molten iron; the blistered dust
Rose up in clouds to sere and choke;

the river makes a bend sharply to the right, sweeping a curve and not returning to its original parallel for ninety-five miles. A line drawn across this curve, like the string of a bow, is the road over the Jornada. The desert is about forty miles wide at the widest part, nearly a dead level and had no water its entire length, except what gathered in depressions after the rains. Since I crossed it, a man has succeeded in obtaining water by sinking a well eighty feet deep, about half way across, and the Government has granted him two sections of land as a reward. The Jornada is bounded on each side by a range of mountains. In the range between the desert and the river, a mountain or the peaks of several form the semblance of a man's face to the eye of a person standing in the vicinity of Fort Craig. The face is in profile, looking upward, and is a good likeness of a jolly friar with a double chin and slightly retrousse nose. This likeness probably gave the face and the range the name of Fray Cristobal.

Fort Craig was one of the few walled forts of the frontier. It was rectangular in shape, originally without bastions, and enclosed an area of about an acre. Since the Texan invasion, it had been strengthened by a few earthworks outside. The walls and quarters were of *adobe*, built for a garrison of four companies. At the time of my arrival, the 5th Infantry was stationed there, the entire regiment of 500 men being in the fort under the command of the senior captain present for duty, Henry R. Selden, a native of Bennington, Vermont.[3] This regiment, like most of the Regular regiments at the outbreak of the war, had been sadly decimated by the desertion of many of its officers to the Southern Confederacy. The story is an

---

But on we rode, gray-white as ghosts,
Bepowdered with that bitter snow,
The stinging breath of alkali
From the grim, crusted earth below.

Hall, *Cactus and Pine*, 35.

3. Henry R. Selden graduated from West Point and was commissioned second lieutenant in the 5th Infantry on March 25, 1846. Promoted to first lieutenant on September 8, 1847, he briefly served as regimental adjutant before receiving his commission as captain on October 18, 1855. His pre-war career included service on the Texas frontier, in Florida, and in Utah Territory. Sent to New Mexico in 1860, he served in that territory until commissioned major in the 13th Infantry on July 1, 1863, and colonel of the 1st New Mexico on April 25, 1864. Selden died of brain fever on February 2, 1865, while in command of Fort Union. His only heir was a son, Henry M. Selden, who had been living with a guardian in Vermont ever since his mother's death in 1854. His comrades said that he was "so cultivated; so pure in heart; so just in word and deed; so gentle; so kind; so brave; Colonel Henry R. Selden lived with us, was loved by us, and has passed away, and left not an enemy upon earth." Cullum, *Biographical Register* 2: 93; *Denver Rocky Mountain News*, March 25, 1865; Henry R. Selden Pension Records.

old one of the companies of the 7th Infantry at Fort Fillmore, whose officers all deserted but one second lieutenant; how on the morning when the Texan advance made its appearance and the officers surrendered without a blow, the loyal non-commissioned officers and privates fell into line and with tears in their eyes begged for an officer to lead them against the enemy; how, when the second lieutenant attempted to do so, he was hindered by the other officers; and how the buglers and drummers broke up their instruments, the color sergeant concealed the flags and declared they should never be surrendered.[4] The lieutenant afterwards marched the regiment up the Rio Grande to Fort Union.

While my regiment did not have an experience quite so unfortunate, it had lost many of its officers and, at the time I joined, several companies were under the command of first sergeants, appointed by order of General Canby to be acting second lieutenants, which appointments were afterwards confirmed by the President. These men were selected for their loyalty and firmness during these days of trial and have proved themselves to be excellent and brave officers.

I have neglected to mention that a large party of young officers, recent appointments from civil life, was in camp near Socorro when I passed there, but I had no opportunity to call on them. They had been appointed to the Regular Army and sent to Fort Columbus, New York Harbor, where they had been drilled first like private soldiers, afterwards as officers and when considered proficient had been ordered to join their regiment.[5] They had marched across

4. Fort Fillmore was located on the left bank of the Rio Grande some six miles south of Mesilla. Established on September 23, 1851, by Lieutenant Colonel Dixon S. Miles, 3rd Infantry, the post was named for President Millard Fillmore. Fort Fillmore was never a high priority of the War Department. One inspection in 1859 revealed that ten of the horses being used by the 1st Dragoons and the Regiment of Mounted Rifles were old veterans of the Mexican War. Originally constructed to control the Apaches, the Federal garrison abandoned the fort to Confederate invaders on July 26, 1861, and later surrendered. Fort Fillmore was abandoned by the Confederates a year later and re-occupied by California troops, but they were soon transferred to Mesilla and Fort Fillmore fell into disrepair, never to be used for military purposes again. Thompson, *Texas and New Mexico*, 58–59; 67–68; *Soldier and Brave*, 226; Frazer, *Forts*, 99.

5. Fort Jay had been built on Governor's Island in New York Harbor, but was demolished in 1806. Fort Columbus was constructed as a masonry post on the site in 1808 and was capable of mounting about 100 guns that could command shipping in the East River. A battery of the 1st Artillery was stationed there on April 18, 1837, and Fort Columbus remained an artillery post until November 15, 1852. On that date the fort became what was termed "the great recruiting depot of the army" where most new recruits were introduced to military drill and discipline. On January 20, 1904 the name of the installation was again designated as Fort Jay. There was speculation that the name had originally been changed

the plains with a small escort of recruits. My Norwich University education and Johnson's Volunteer service had enabled us to join immediately.

Upon my arrival at the fort, I reported to Captain Selden, who received me cordially and said that I would be assigned to his company, F, which I would command while he continued as regimental commander and the first lieutenant as adjutant. I joined his mess, which consisted of himself and the adjutant, Lieutenant Allen L. Anderson.[6]

Young hunters always have the "buck ague" when they first get in shooting distance of deer and young officers—even the regular-bred West Pointers—have a nervous dread of first giving a command to "Old Regulars." I had drilled companies, had handled on the parade a regiment of a thousand men in every evolution of the tactics and I had been under fire, but when I first stood up before these grizzled veterans—for the men of the 5th Infantry were old soldiers in both senses when I joined—and saw their imperturbable faces turned towards me, bodies fixed as straight as arrows, the old first sergeant, with his twenty-five years' service chevrons on his sleeve, looking like what I had idealized an "old guardsman" to be, I grew fearfully nervous. My first command was a wrong one and not a man moved. My Volunteer soldiers had always obeyed me if they knew what I meant, even if I gave a wrong command, but these men stood like posts. Nettled at what I thought was unnecessary punctilio, I gave the same order, louder and sharper, and still not a man moved. I began to grow moist; I walked slowly up and down to collect my thoughts; I glanced towards the officers' quarters and saw one of the old sergeants, who was acting as an officer, make a quick motion

---

by political opponents following the treaty with England negotiated by John Jay in 1794. Smith, *Governor's Island*, 55, 68, 77, 106, 132.

6. Allen L. Anderson graduated from West Point in 1859 and received a commission as second lieutenant in the 5th Infantry on September 5, 1859. Advanced to first lieutenant on May 14, 1861, he served as regimental adjutant from December 31, 1861, to December 3, 1863, when he was promoted to captain. Commissioned colonel of the 8th California on March 7, 1865, he served in that rank until mustered out of Volunteer service on November 10, 1865. Anderson remained in the army as a captain, although he received brevets to major, lieutenant colonel, and brigadier general for his war service. He resigned on January 7, 1867, and worked as a civil engineer until his death at Santa Barbara, California, on June 9, 1910. A colleague wrote of Colonel Anderson: "He was a talented man, of exemplary habits and rare scholarly attainments." His father was colonel of the 93rd Ohio and briefly served as governor of Ohio in 1865. Robert Anderson of Fort Sumter fame was an uncle. Heitman, *Historical Register* 1: 163; Cullum, *Biographical Register* 2: 490; Hunt, *Brigadier Generals*, 14; *Thirty-ninth Reunion*, 420.

as if performing the *carry*. I saw it in a flash—I had been giving a command to *march* while my men were at an *order*. This is perhaps a trivial thing to mention, but as I said before, all new officers have a somewhat similar experience and this was mine and the last where I ever felt piqued or nervous.

In a few days all the new officers had arrived and been assigned to companies. None of them were from West Point and I soon gathered from conversation at our mess that the old officers were somewhat anxious about the character and ability of the new appointees. I will here mention that some months afterward I heard Anderson say to Captain Selden, while we were at dinner, "I was very anxious when the new lieutenants arrived for fear we had got a poor lot of sticks, but I believe that there is not a bad one among them."

"Thank you," said I, "I suppose a tenth of that compliment belongs to me."

"You are welcome to it. Generally we of the Point look with dislike upon civil appointments which come in to hold some of us out of promotion and frequently the men are the dissipated sons of congressmen or their friends. But the war, or something, has improved them, for we have got a lot of good fellows, who know their business."

On the 15th of July we moved into camp on the south side of the post and down on the river side, leaving the fort in charge of a battalion of Colorado Volunteers. While in camp, we held daily drills and occasional reviews. At the reviews the men were in uniform, but at drills and off duty they were a motley looking set. When the war broke out, New Mexico was supplied with clothing, camp and garrison equipage for but a small number of men. With the rapid concentration of troops from Utah and Colorado, pretty much everything was exhausted. The ready-made clothing stores of the Jews in every town and village had been required to turn in their stocks for the use of the army and every variety of garments, outer and inner, caps and hats, shoes and boots, had found their way into the quartermaster's storehouse. Our battalion, formed for drill, was the queerest-looking military assemblage I ever saw, unless I except the "flood-wood" and "string beaners" of the old militia days. Nothing but their "set up" and step showed the soldier.

It was while in this camp that I had that experience which falls to the lot of every newcomer. There was an order that no whiskey or other intoxicating drink should be sold to an enlisted man without a written order from his company commander. At this time the company had not been formally turned over to me, so that I did not have authority to sign such an order. I was standing before my tent, about four o'clock in the afternoon, when a private approached me from the company and, after a respectful salute, handed me a slip of paper. Reading it, I found it was an order on the post sutler to sell Private Thomas Cleary a quart of whiskey, with a line left blank for my signature and on the next line my rank, all in due form for me to sign.[7] After examining it, I said, "Is it customary for the officers to sign these?"

"O yis sir-r," replied the man. "It was my intintion to tak' it t' the commanding officer, but he is out of camp and I thought may be the liftinent would do as well."

Of course I signed after this and the man went for his whiskey.

A little later, another man came with an order for a quart more and an hour after another, slightly unsteady in his gait, came towards me, but when within a short distance he suddenly paused, crushed the paper into the palm of his hand and turned in another direction.

"Halt, sir!" said a loud voice just behind me and turning I saw Captain Selden.

The soldier halted.

"Come here," said the captain and the man approached.

"Hand me that paper!" The man gave it to him.

"You rascal!" thundered the captain. "You know no one is to give these orders but myself. I ought to send you to the guardhouse!"

"Two other men have had orders today," said the man.

"Who signed them?" asked the captain, evidently, as I thought, ready to scalp anyone who had done so. I looked towards the man from behind the captain and slightly shook my head.

"I don't know," said the soldier.

7. Thomas Cleary enlisted in the 5th Infantry as a private on June 14, 1855. He re-enlisted on April 14, 1860, and again on July 31, 1864. After being transferred to the 14th and 32nd Infantry, Cleary was discharged on July 31, 1867, as a corporal. He was last located at Fort Yates in Dakota Territory in 1890. Thomas Cleary Military Service Records, 1890 Veterans Census.

"Go to your quarters and don't let me catch you at this trick again." Then turning to me, the captain asked in a mild tone, "How many orders have you signed, Mr. Curtis?"

"Two."

"For how much?"

"A quart each."

"I ought to have cautioned you. That is an old soldier's trick upon new officers. I was so fond of displaying my autograph when I first joined that I got a whole company drunk before I was overhauled. Send all men to me, hereafter, who ask you to sign such orders."

Upon comparing notes with the other nine new officers, I found only one had been wise enough not to sign an order when presented to him, while a newly arrived assistant surgeon had signed for ten quarts. Luckily for the others, they had the benefit of my experience, so escaped further trouble.[8]

One afternoon I was lying on my bed, with the tent door open, looking out upon the regimental parade, watching Captain David H. Brotherton's dog steal corn for the captain's pony, when the adjutant entered, said we were ordered down the river to the Mexican line and that I must get my company ready to march next morning, July 21st.[9] I immediately started for the company, gave the order and returned to watch the dog. The dog's name was Grouse. He was a fine setter of rare intelligence and very fond of the pony. He often wandered far away on the plain with him, lying down to see him graze or following him if he moved away. Today there was a pile of sacks of corn-on-the-ear before the tent of Captain Selden, one of the sacks was broken open and the ears scattered about. Grouse would stealthily approach, with all the air of a thief,

8. One teetotaler explained the prevalence of alcohol at Fort Craig: "Go where you may, wherever soldiers are found, and I guarantee that a whiskey barrel is not very far distant." He further explained: "It is considered here a soldier's privilege to get drunk occasionally, especially on pay day." *[Sacramento] Weekly Rescue*, July 1, 1864.

9. David H. Brotherton graduated from West Point in 1854 and was commissioned second lieutenant in the 5th Infantry on March 3, 1855. Promoted to first lieutenant on August 22, 1859, and captain on September 25, 1861, Brotherton served in the typical pre-war rotation of duty on the frontier, in Florida and in Utah Territory. Promoted to major on March 20, 1879, he was transferred to the 7th Infantry on December 18, 1879, and while in command at Fort Buford accepted the surrender of Sitting Bull on July 20, 1881. Promoted to lieutenant colonel of the 25th Infantry on July 3, 1883, Brotherton retired on August 14, 1884, and died at Waynesboro, Pennsylvania on September 17, 1889. Cullum, *Biographical Register* 2: 390–91; Heitman, *Historical Register* 1: 250; *Philadelphia Inquirer*, September 26, 1889.

starting and shrinking at every sound, abstract an ear of corn, then run off and place it before the pony's nose and sit down to see him eat it. This dog was killed by a pack of wolves that very night.

At the mess table at supper, the route of our march was discussed. It had been learned that the route over the Jornada del Muerto was perfectly dry and that it would be useless to attempt a march that way without water tanks. The road on the west side of the river, around the bend, was covered by water for a great portion of the way and we should be under the necessity of slowly making our way over the broken foothills back of the river bottom. This march was particularly dreaded on this account, for it would be attended by constant and weary labor for a long way.

The command was to consist of our regiment, a battery of artillery and four companies of cavalry. We were to follow up the Texan retreat and occupy the lower country until a California regiment should arrive, when we were to return up country.

Chapter 8

On the March

Our orders were to leave on the 21st of July, but owing to a delay in the arrival of a clothing train from the north, we did not get away until the 23rd, at seven o'clock in the forenoon. It had been originally intended that we should march over the Jornada, but a messenger who had been dispatched on the 19th by the commanding officer of the column, Colonel Marshall S. Howe, returned with the information that there was no water in the depressions of the plain, so we were compelled to take the route along the west side of the river.[1]

Our column consisted of the 5th Infantry, a small body of cavalry and a company of cavalry acting as artillery, having four twelve-pounders in charge. We had the usual complement of wagons for the companies, a quartermaster's train of fifty wagons and a large

1. Marshall S. Howe attended West Point from 1823 to 1827 but did not graduate. He was a deputy sheriff in Maine when commissioned a first lieutenant in the 2nd Dragoons on June 11, 1836. Howe was promoted to captain on January 1, 1839; major on July 13, 1848; and lieutenant colonel on June 14, 1858. Commissioned colonel of the 3rd Cavalry on September 28, 1861, Howe served throughout the Civil War and retired on August 31, 1866. He spent the last years of his life overseeing government property at Harrodsburg, Kentucky, and died in that city on December 8, 1878. A son, Lieutenant Albion Howe, was killed in action with Modoc Indians at the Lava Beds, California. Heitman, *Historical Register* 1: 547–48; *Portland Daily Press*, May 1, 1873; December 14, 1878; *Breckenridge News*, December 18, 1878.

contractor's train, containing supplies for the California troops which were shortly to arrive in the lower country. The contractor accompanied us for protection from the Indians.

Had the river not been exceedingly high, our march would have been over a level road through the river bottoms, having no disadvantage except that it was longer than the one over the desert. The overflow had covered a great portion of the road and this compelled us to climb over the spurs and ravines of the foothills. Almost our first adventure was the upsetting of five wagons on a side hill and the scattering of the contents down the declivity for a hundred yards. It was no small job to gather up this stuff, repair the wagons and move on again.

The first day's march was but twelve miles in length and ended at a *bosque* (forest) on a point of land around which flowed the river. Here I had leisure to notice our command as it entered the *bosque* and proceeded to pitch tents. I was astonished to see how many infantry soldiers were mounted on ponies, mules and donkeys. This was so different from what I had seen in the East that I inquired of Anderson the reason. He said it cost nothing in this country to keep these animals and, as long as their possession did not interfere with the men's duties, but few commanders objected to their owning them. When a long march took place, however, it was generally ordered that they should dispose of all animals. This matter had been discussed, when orders were received for us to march and it had been thought a positive advantage that some of our men should be mounted. At least two-thirds of the infantry officers were owners of horses, but I was one of those obliged to walk.

All of the companies owned dogs and one captain, Samuel Archer, had twenty, his personal property.[2] He was an eccentric character, a promotion from the ranks for gallantry in the Mexican War, generally esteemed and respected by both officers and men. It was a curious sight to see him with his pack of dogs crossing the parade, dogs of all sizes from a noble Staghound down to a Skye

2. Samuel Archer enlisted as a private in the 5th Infantry on May 5, 1845, and received promotions to corporal and sergeant prior to being commissioned a brevet second lieutenant on June 28, 1848. Elevated to second lieutenant on January 30, 1849, and first lieutenant on March 3, 1855, Archer acted as regimental adjutant for three years until commissioned captain on March 27, 1861. Promoted to major of the 3rd Infantry on March 30, 1864, Archer was supposed to have drowned on April 9, 1866. Heitman, *Historical Register* 1: 168.

terrier. In his quarters there was always an extra bed for the dogs which could not find accommodation on his own.

Very few of the company dogs were not of the best blood. Indeed, it was rare to find a thorough mongrel or cur in the regiment. One company, K, possessed a pet bear, which rode in the feed trough of a wagon during the marches and was staked out near the cook tent when in camp. He was captured in Utah and marched with the regiment for two years.

One of the regular and constant recurring incidents of the march was the pursuit of hares by the dogs. The country abounded with them and much larger game too, if we could have had time to hunt it. The greyhounds would be trotting along in the most dejected manner by the side of their companies, when one of the spaniels or other small dogs, who kept up a constant scouting in the bushes, would give voice and instantly, from every part of the column, there would be a concentration of dogs running with intense canine excitement towards the game. Presently the hare would be seen springing rapidly away from the road with every dog in pursuit—the fox hounds baying deeply and the curs barking furiously, but the pointers, setters and greyhounds silent. The greyhounds were always the last to pursue, but they were always the dogs to kill the game and a shaggy little retriever of Captain Archer's was sure to bring it to his master.

At our first camp, a guard of two companies was detailed with three lieutenants as officers of the guard. I was one of the three. As the ground enclosed was large, it was determined to make a "running guard" of it, letting each relief stand through one-third of the time. We drew lots for the reliefs and the second fell to me. This gave me an opportunity to sleep through the first and last thirds of the night. The lieutenant in charge of the third and last relief slept the entire night, neglecting to get up when I roused him. The *bosque* was full of snakes, chiefly rattlesnakes. This made visiting and inspecting sentinels not a very agreeable duty.

The next day the guard followed in rear of the train and I had an opportunity of witnessing the difficulties in getting the wagons over the hills. It was a cruel sight to see the whipping, straining and falling of the mules, in the prolonged effort to bring the heavily laden wagons up through the sand and over the boulders, the wheels often

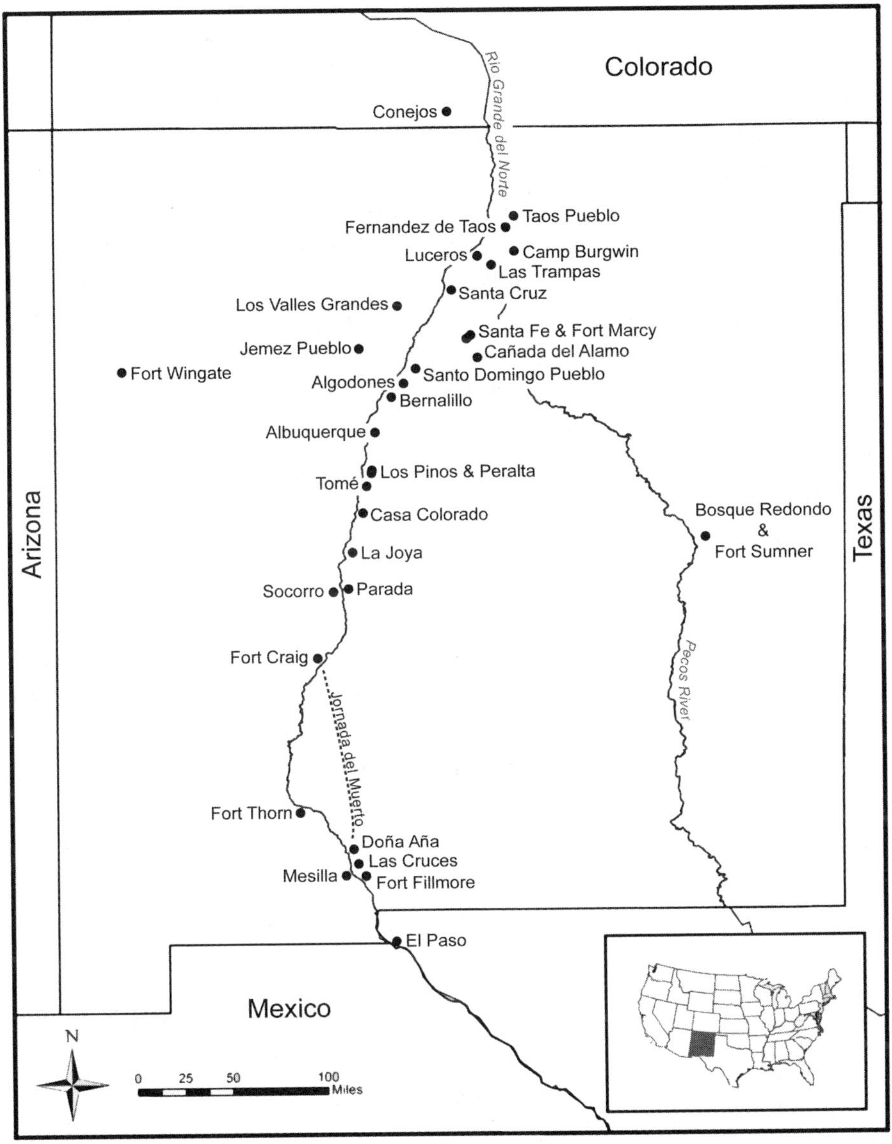

New Mexico Territory

sinking to the hubs in sand. I sat on a stone at the top of one hill for three hours, watching the train get up a declivity of a quarter of a mile in length, wagon masters and teamsters shouting, jumping and swearing like devils, plying the blacksnake and mercilessly pelting the mules with small stones.

As we were marching along after the train had reached the top of the hill, I noticed a little white terrier lying under the leaves of a soapweed. I called Lieutenant Samuel L. Barr's attention to him and he said it was a dog belonging to a fifer of his company and asked me to hand it up to him.[3] Barr was mounted and I was on foot. I took the little fellow up and passed him to the lieutenant. In doing so, I discovered that he was lame and, in examining his foot, found a long cactus thorn thrust into it. This I drew out with tweezers. As we marched along, Barr said the dog's name was "Billy," that he had been picked up in Utah by our fifer and had accompanied him ever since. The man was fond of it and on "dry marches" would often put his hat on the ground to give the dog a drink from the dent in top. Billy had been in several actions with the Texans, in one of which he received a wound from a sabre across the back and in another a bullet in the left side, which could be felt with the hand. He was, in fact, a battle-scarred veteran and honored as such by the command.

I will dispose of Billy at this point by saying that he was in the command that marched to Arizona in 1864. His master, Joseph Cain, had been discharged from the service and accompanied me as a servant to San Francisco and New York.[4] In some of his walks about the former city, Billy was lost. The night before I sailed for Panama, I was walking from the Presidio to town and in the outskirts met Billy, evidently on his way to the post. I spoke to him and he began to approach me, but a passing team came between us, frightened him away and, although I called for some time, I saw nothing more of him. I wrote a letter that evening to the

3. Samuel L. Barr was commissioned second lieutenant in the 5th Infantry on October 24, 1861. Promoted to first lieutenant on April 30, 1863, and captain on October 31, 1866, Barr was mustered out on January 1, 1871. Charles Curtis said of his comrade, "He was an excellent officer and popular in his regiment." After leaving the army, Barr went to school and received a medical degree. In 1884 he was the attending physician for the Canadian Pacific Railway. He bought a drug store in Cavour, South Dakota, began to practice medicine and became active in veterans organizations. Doctor Barr died at Washington, D. C. on October 10, 1892, after having visited the capital with other representatives of the G. A. R. He had just eaten a hearty dinner and lighted a cigar when he fell over in the arms of his cousin. He is buried in Arlington National Cemetery not far from the grave of his friend, Charles Curtis. Heitman, *Historical Register* 1: 194; *Army and Navy Journal* (October 22, 1892) 30: 142; *The National Tribune*, October 20, 1892; *Boston Journal*, October 11, 1892.

4. Joseph Cane enlisted as a musician in the 5th Infantry on November 1, 1857, under the name Joseph Caine. He re-enlisted, under the name Joseph Cain, on September 10, 1862, the same year in which this Irish native became a naturalized American citizen. He was discharged on September 10, 1865, at Fort Whipple upon the expiration of his service. Cane was admitted to the New York State Soldiers and Sailors Home in Bath, New York, on January 16, 1916. He died there on October 11, 1920. Since Captain Curtis knew Cane as "Joseph Cain" during his enlistment, that spelling has been retained in the narrative. Register of Enlistments; 1920 Census, New York, Steuben County, Bath; Historical Register of National Homes.

commanding officer at the Presidio, who had before promotion been a captain of A Company in the 5th Regiment and knew the dog well, telling him that Billy had probably gone to his post. Shortly after I reached New York, I received a letter from the major, stating that the dog had turned up, reported to him and he had attached him to a company of the 9th Regiment, the soldiers accepting him with honor on account of his record and scars.

About noon we took the guard to the river for water. At the place where we halted, there was a broad flat of sand, across which the men marched without any difficulty, but which gave way beneath Barr's pony and, but for the vigorous application of spur and the consequent rapid taking of hoofs, would have swallowed the horse, if not the rider.

At three in the afternoon we arrived at a large cottonwood grove, known as the *Bosque Bonita* (Beautiful Forest) or Adobe Wall. The last name is given on account of a rare formation of sandstone, closely resembling *adobe*, which is about ten feet in thickness, rising fifty feet above the surface of the earth and is one hundred feet long. The *bosque* covered at least ten acres, with a dense undergrowth of willows and cane grass, in which ran myriads of snakes of every variety. As I approached the line of officers' tents, I noticed a long and dense line of dead snakes, with their heads all turned in the direction I was walking. Following the serpentine trail, I found it ran through my tent to a large hole which entered the hillside just below my pillow. My tent had been pitched after the command reached the *bosque*, the sides looped up and the bed "made down."

As I stood surveying the line of snakes, which seemed to grow wider and thicker until it reached the hole, looking (if I looked as I felt) generally disgusted, the practical joker of the regiment, Captain Henry B. Bristol, approached and said, "We killed all we could, Curtis, but the bulk of them got down the hole."[5] Of course I knew this was a practical joke, but still I could not make up

5. Through the influence of Lewis Cass, a family friend, Henry B. Bristol received a commission as second lieutenant in the 5th Infantry on May 15, 1857. Promoted to first lieutenant on May 13, 1861, and captain on June 1, 1862, Bristol received brevets to major and lieutenant colonel for his service in New Mexico. The citation for the latter award noted "his untiring zeal and energy in controlling the Navajo tribe of Indians at the Bosque Redondo and for his praiseworthy efforts in advancing their condition from that of savages to that of civilized men." Bristol retired on March 20, 1879, and died in New York City on May 10, 1904. Heitman, *Historical Register* 1: 246; *New York Times*, May 12, 1904.

my mind to sleep with my head near that wolf hole, snakes or no snakes. I sent my servant for a detail to gather up the reptiles and move my tent. I afterwards learned that the whole thing was a trick of Bristol's invention. Knowing my aversion to snakes, he had sent men to pick up all they could and arranged them in the manner described.

Our next march took us through the town of Cañada del Alamo, where we procured for our private mess some chickens, onions and *tortillas*. We camped in a *bosque* two miles below the town and had been there but a few moments when a mounted express arrived from Santa Fé with orders for all but four companies of infantry to return up the Rio Grande. I belonged to one of the companies which were to turn back, but this did not prevent Colonel Howe from detailing me to go below as quartermaster. A rather laughable circumstance was connected with this detail, which my army friends who were acquainted with the late colonel will not fail to appreciate. He sent for me and in his terse, sharp way, said that "he had made me quartermaster and commissary of the command going below, in order that I might ride, that I was lame and ought not to be compelled to march on foot, but should have a good horse and be comfortable." When I had receipted for the stores and the command was fairly on the road, I received a note from Colonel Howe that no horses could be spared for my use. I immediately went to see him, and reminded him of what he had said.

"Can't give you a horse—need 'em up country—infantry officer no business to ride," was all the reply I got. Accordingly, I set out alone to overtake the command, which was some miles in advance. Once up with the train, however, I was master of the situation and immediately ordered the wagon master to saddle and bridle a spare mule for me. So presently I was riding, not on a horse, but on a pot-bellied, diminutive, buckskin-colored mule, with zebra stripes on her flanks and quarters.

My experience in receipting for this train and its contents was similar to what often happens to green officers. I had no knowledge of the somewhat complicated methods, accounts and responsibilities to the quartermaster and commissary departments and was about as well fitted to do the business belonging to them as a newly graduated college student would be to take the place of cashier in a national bank.[6] My only resource was to wait upon the officer commanding the companies going down the river and ask for a sergeant who had at some time acted as quartermaster sergeant or clerk. After some consultation with the lieutenant in command of Company A, a sergeant who had acted in both capacities was ordered to report to me.

I trust it will not be considered unbecoming of an officer if I acknowledge that for some months I was really the pupil of this intelligent sergeant, Thomas M. Granville, in the care of the stores for which I receipted.[7] His very first suggestion relieved me from I know not how much trouble. All the stores were in wagons and the invoices purported to be a correct enumeration of each and every article, weight, bulk and kind. I was about to sign the receipts which had been prepared for me, without question as to the accuracy, placing blind confidence in the integrity of the officer who was making the transfer, when the sergeant asked to speak to me alone. Walking to one side with him, Granville showed me a letter which he had written addressed to the commanding officer, asking for a board of survey to verify the invoices, explaining that the request would probably be denied, but the fact that I had applied for a board and been denied, would save me from the responsibility of any deficiency which might arise when I should unload the train at Las Cruces.

This suggestion of the sergeant was of the greatest service to me and gave me ample protection when my official correspondence opened with the auditors of the Treasury. When we unloaded,

6. Quartermasters and commissaries dealt with tremendous amounts of supplies and rations. Just for example, one advertisement for sealed bids to supply Fort Craig, south of Albuquerque on the Rio Grande, called for bidders to deliver 500,000 pounds of flour and 2,500 head of cattle for the period from September 1, 1862, through August 31, 1863. Vast piles of rations and supplies meant that officers were responsible for huge sums of money. Mismanagement of government funds could lead to an officer's dismissal. *Denver Rocky Mountain News*, July 7, 1862.

7. Thomas M. Granville enlisted in the 5th Infantry as a private on April 22, 1858, and was promoted sergeant on October 8, 1859. Shortly after the war began, Granville wrote directly to Secretary of State William H. Seward in an effort to receive an officer's commission. Shortly afterwards he was recommended for promotion to second lieutenant by Captain Henry Bristol, his company commander. The following month another recommendation was made by the post commander at Fort Union, endorsed by all the officers then at the post. Another letter to Secretary Seward was ignored and Granville was discharged on April 22, 1863. He moved to California, but eventually ended in Washington, D. C. where he died on July 9, 1882. U. S. Army, Register of Enlistments, 1798–1914; Letters Received by the Commission Branch of the Adjutant General's Office, 1863–1870, Thomas M. Granville, June 8, 1863; *Sacramento Daily Union*, August 11, 1875; U. S. Headstone Applications for Military Veterans, 1925–1963.

I found I had receipted for 1,500 pounds more hard bread than I had received, 100 more pounds of candles and many other things. In fact, my predecessor had attempted to shift all the responsibility of his own deficiencies upon me and this letter had prevented me from falling into the trap. I have told this story at the risk of getting prosy, simply to show what responsibilities are often suddenly thrust upon young officers. It is a frequent custom to take the youngest officer for this duty and all are not so fortunate as I was in getting a reliable sergeant to help them through, but involve themselves in serious debt with the Government in their attempts to master the intricacies of their duty.

Years afterwards, when I had become thorough master of the quartermaster and commissary systems, I met Granville perched on a high stool in one of the best banks in San Francisco. I did not recognize him in his fashionable civilian garb, but the words "Cañada del Alamo" made me look again and I recognized my old quartermaster sergeant. He was out of the army, in a good situation and did not hesitate to speak plainly about our experience. He said that he had not liked the detail when it was first offered him, but, seeing how verdant I was, he concluded to assist me. The detail had been left at his option to accept or reject.

I had a herd of 64 beeves and 400 head of sheep and goats, which were driven along by three Mexican herders and three butchers. By taking the cut-offs over the country, although they traveled much slower than the command, they always reached camp as soon as the rear guard.

In riding along beside the contractor's train, I noticed a novel method of marking the oxen or ornamenting them, I am not sure which. A piece of skin two inches wide was stripped down the forehead of the ox about six inches and left hanging. The scar healed over and the pendant skin remained alive, with hair on each side. These hairy tassels swayed from side to side as the oxen toiled beneath the yoke.

About ten o'clock in the forenoon, we reached Fort Thorn, an old United States post that had been abandoned three years before on account of the fever and ague which prevailed there.[8] The men

8. Formally established in 1853 Fort Thorn was one of the few frontier posts not named for a West Point graduate, honoring Lieutenant Herman Thorn, 2nd U. S. Infantry, who died on October 16, 1849, while crossing the Rio Colorado in New Mexico Territory. Fort Thorn was situated eighty-five miles south of Fort Craig on the west side of the Rio Grande

and officers were constantly ill and, at the time it was dismantled and abandoned, there was not a man of its garrison of two companies who did not have the shakes. The post is walled, with a broad entrance in the north and south walls, through which the road passes. All the buildings looked entire and the flagstaff stood in the center of the parade, as if the post was still occupied.

When the Texans entered the country, the Confederate newspapers spoke of their having taken Fort Thorn. They did occupy the post for a few weeks and raised their flag on the old staff, but, finding the Union soldiers were willing they should remain there and enjoy the fever and ague to their heart's content, they moved out.

Our train was to take us as far as San Diego Crossing, where we were to meet a train from Las Cruces and transfer our stores over the river on boats. The train was to return to Fort Craig under the escort of a squadron of Colorado cavalry, which was encamped a few miles above the crossing. As we passed their camp, they told us that a party of Apaches had swum the river the night before and stolen several of their horses. Thinking the river a sufficient guard against approach from that side, no sentinels had been posted there.

Next night, the 30th, the contractor's train, but one day's march behind us, was attacked and thirteen draught animals killed. They had been unable to keep up with our rate of marching and our commander was unwilling to wait for them.

On the morning of the 31st, we reached the crossing, which is quite deep and narrow, and found but one boat, a miserable contrivance of poor boards, caulked with shreds of soldiers' clothing. It would not hold the weight of six men and leaked like a sieve. We went into camp on the shore and I had the boat drawn out of the water, and turned over for repairs. With bits of blankets, candles and cracker boxes, we caulked and patched the craft so that it kept out water and got everything ready for crossing. During the night

---

del Norte in what proved to be a decidedly unhealthy location. A surgeon would report in 1856: "The month of July last, seventy-eight men out of ninety (ninety composed the entire command) were sick with remittent fever." An Apache sub-agency was located there prior to the abandonment of the fort in 1859. There was a brief skirmish near the old fort in 1861 between Union and Confederate troops, and General Sibley used the location as a staging point for his invasion of New Mexico Territory in 1862. Briefly re-occupied by California troops after Sibley's defeat, Fort Thorn was then abandoned permanently. Stanley, *Fort Thorn*, 3–5, 7, 14–14, 17–19.

I was aroused by the discharge of three muskets in rapid succession and the falling in of the men and general detaching of parties to the flanks and vulnerable points. Two more shots were fired and nothing further occurred during the night. It proved to have been an attempt on our herd by the Apaches. No one was hurt.

Early in the morning, the slow process of transferring our stores to the eastern bank of the river began. I watched it for a portion of the forenoon and then, taking my revolver, a canteen and a few crackers, I crossed the river and started for San Diego Mountain, which stood above five miles from the river, commanding the crossing and southern entrance to the Jornada del Muerto.

It may seem singular that a man should dare to go on such a trip when he knew from the three recent demonstrations of the Indians upon the Volunteers, contractors and ourselves that they must be in force in the immediate vicinity of the crossing. I cannot account for my foolhardiness, but place it among the inexplicable eccentricities which distinguish the newly arrived lieutenant. I went on without a thought of danger and at this time I shiver to think of it.

San Diego is a table mountain, some 2,000 feet above the river, with very precipitous sides and the last thirty feet a mass of perpendicular sandstone. The day was exceedingly warm and I was forced to sit down often and rest. The way was pathless, over huge boulders, amid mesquite bushes and endless varieties of cacti, the tornillo, the fouquieria, the agaves and yuccas, all furnished with terrific spikes and thorns, and even the grasses armed with stinging barbs.

When I arrived at the perpendicular wall, I skirted it for some time before I could find a place sufficiently ragged and seamed with cracks to give me a chance to climb upward. Finding such a place at last, I climbed slowly and carefully to the top. Arriving there, I found a perfect flat of some four acres upon which were many evidences that Indians had camped there frequently, while the charred embers and scraps of food at one place showed that a party had been there very recently.

With my field glass, I stood and looked around the country for a long time. The Rio Grande del Norte, like a silver thread woven irregularly into a green carpet, wound its course through the country north and south for a hundred miles, while outside the green on either hand, stretched the brown, arid sands of the desert. Far to the north were the Fray Cristobal Mountains and at the same distance south, the Sierra de los Organos, so called from their resemblance to the pipes of an organ. There are good silver mines in the last range. At my feet, by the riverside were the white tents of the command and creeping slowly along from the north was the contractor's train, which had been attacked. To the south, I could see a long line of dust rising from a deep ravine, showing the approach of the train from Las Cruces.

My sightseeing over, I started to return. Hungry and tired I had a difficult task before me and at one time grew so ill that I was forced to lie down a long time before I recovered sufficient strength to go on. I did not reach camp until after sunset and found a party of soldiers under a sergeant just starting out to "look for my dead body." I got laughed at by my fellow lieutenants for a romantic youth and received a caution from the commanding officer not to try such an experiment again, unless I was tired of living.

Chapter 9

Encounter with Apaches

After my arrival in camp, I learned from the commanding officer that the train which I had seen on the Jornada, from the top of San Diego Mountain, belonged to *Señor* Estevan Ochoa, a Mexican contractor, that the stores in the train were to be transferred to me at Las Cruces and that it would be best for me to be present when they should arrive there.[1] I learned from our wagon master that Ochoa would probably encamp on the west side of the mountain and that, if I could ride out there in the morning, I could probably get him to come into our camp with his ambulance for myself and baggage. Accordingly, next morning I took Wagon Master Black's mule and started.[2] As I got into the saddle, Black asked me if I did not want his spurs. Having noticed

1. Estevan Ochoa spent his youth in Kansas City where he learned the English language and learned the rudiments of the freighting and mercantile trades. He started his own business in Mesilla and soon had built up a profitable operation in southern New Mexico. He expanded into what would become the Arizona Territory and became a wealthy man in Tucson. Devoted to the Union, Ochoa gave up his fortune when the rebel forces came in 1862. When Union forces drove off the invaders, Ochoa returned to Tucson and resumed his lucrative trading network and his company became one of the largest freight businesses in Arizona, in addition to running its own stage line. He lost most of his fortune with the coming of the railroad, but held several political offices before his death in Las Cruces on October 27, 1888. Farish, *History of Arizona* 2: 206.

2. Wagon Master Black cannot be positively identified.

during the journey that his mule was an unusually lively one and often distanced the ponies in the occasional races of the march, I thought I should not need them and replied no.

I had not learned mule nature thoroughly at that time or I should have known better than to trust myself on one without something to quicken his sluggish spirits. The mule was a splendid animal of his kind. He was about the size of a cavalry horse, with more points of resemblance to his equine ancestor than to the asinine. In rate of speed, as I have mentioned above, he could distance many of the horses.

For the first half mile he went at a good rate, until he missed the prick of the spurs. As soon as he learned that my heels were not armed, he deliberately fell into a prosy walk. And here is one of the greatest differences between the mule and horse. A horse of any spirit will respond readily, even when weary, to the voice of his rider and show a desire to do his best at all times. But a mule, even when fresh from the stable, generally needs the whip or spur to quicken his gait when speed is required. Let him once know that these persuaders are absent and he will take his own gait and his own time.

The mule I was now riding was a mule. That is saying enough. I kicked my heels against his pachydermatous sides until my legs ached and it made no difference in his pace. I rode up to a mesquite bush and broke off a stout limb with which I belabored him with unceasing assiduity, searching for the tenderest places in his anatomy, but only succeeded in getting a dull trot out of him. Soon my cudgel was worn out and the beast fell back into his walk.

My road lay up a ravine on the north side of the mountain and I often thought what possible chance I should have for escape if an Apache should show himself near me. After a ride of some seven miles, I reached the level of the Jornada to find that the train had left and was far distant in the south. There was nothing else to be done but to attempt to overtake it, traveling as it was at a good walking gait and my mule not doing much better. I tried half a dozen devices to accelerate the animal's speed, but nothing seemed to reach his senses until I plucked a cactus, armed with many thorns, and fastened it on the end of a cord made from my pocket handkerchief, divided into three strips and tied together. With this I could strike a blow taking effect on the animal's belly and succeeded in producing a respectable canter.

When I overtook the train, I found *Señor* Ochoa had gone on to Las Cruces with his ambulance. So I had made my trip for nothing and was obliged to return to the crossing. I could not go on with this train because the mule I was riding was to return upriver with his owner. Besides, all my baggage was behind.

It was well along in the afternoon when I overtook the train and I concluded it must be some dozen miles back to camp. My route from the crossing had been almost directly east until I reached the road on the Jornada del Muerto, there I turned south and rode constantly in that direction until I reached the train. My ride back would be straight to the crossing, along the hypotenuse of the triangle. As I glanced at the fast-sinking sun, the thought of Indians came unbidden to my mind and what chance I should have in a race with them if I was to depend upon the *vis inertiæ* contained in that mule's skin. The thought suggested the possibility of borrowing a pair of spurs. I asked the Mexican wagon master if he would lend me a pair until I could reach Las Cruces and return them. He answered by going to a wagon, halting it and taking from the front box a pair of immense Mexican mule spurs, with steels two inches long. He fastened these on my heels and told me "it gave him pleasure to be able to serve me and that I could leave them at the house of *Señor* Ochoa in Las Cruces when I should arrive there."

Starting back, I did not at first try my spurs, enjoying in anticipation the surprise I was going to give that hybrid. I coaxed him for some time, but, so far from getting him to trot or canter, he began to show a decided antipathy to leaving the train at all. Then I plunged the spurs into him! I reveled in speed—we dashed over the plain as if a hundred Indians were in our rear seeking my scalp. A looker-on would have thought the mule never walked a step in his life when he could avoid it, that his natural gait was a "tearing gallop." But the reflection came that I might need the animal's best powers before I reached camp and that a less rapid rate of speed would best subserve this end. I therefore came down to an easy amble in the direction of the crossing.

As I glanced over the plain, I saw nothing like life, except the train toiling on to the south. There were no ravines or clumps near the road behind which an enemy might lie concealed, but far to the right and apparently half way to the crossing from where I left the train, a spur of San Diego Mountain came down, gradually sloping to the level of the plain. What might be behind that spur gave me some uneasiness. I looked carefully to my revolver to see that the caps were all right and examined my carbine and ammunition.

If anyone wonders why I should be so anxious on this day, when the very day before I had been so careless of my life, I will explain that the last evening after my return from the mountain the old Indian campaigners had related stories of hair-breadth escapes from the redskins, until I began to fully realize the risk I had run. It was very plainly impressed upon me that the three recent demonstrations showed conclusively that Indians were lurking in the vicinity, ready to pounce upon stragglers or run down upon our herd should a chance offer.

My eyes were constantly turned in the direction of the mountain. At times I was sure that I could see a head peering above the ridge, but so undefined that I concluded it was but an effect produced by my strained vision. I kept up the brisk canter to which I had brought the mule, without pressing him too hard, and looked earnestly in the direction of camp to see if any parties were on the road and coming near me. Nothing in sight. The sun was getting lower and lower until it nearly touched the horizon and the distance was fast closing between me and the spur. At last, when I was nearly opposite, I suddenly saw three heads appear above it and presently, as they skirted the spur to gain the open plain, I could see that the heads belonged to three mounted Indians. I did not wait to be positive about this, but dashed the spurs into the mule and sent him flying along the road. He had beaten time and again the grain-fed ponies of the regimental officers with the six-foot wagon master on his back. Could he not now, with a lighter weight, beat these grass-fed ponies of the Indians?

The spur from behind which the Indians started was nearly a mile off the road, so that, if I continued on my present route, it was if we started at the opposite extremities of the base of a triangle to see who could reach the apex first. There was no hope for me to turn off to the left, for there I should soon become involved in the swamps and chaparral of the river banks; neither could I turn back, with much hope of success, to overtake the train of Ochoa. There was only the possibility of distancing the Indians in the race for the crossing, with the certainty that for the first two miles we were all the time closing upon each other.

My eyes were constantly riveted on the Apaches, I could see them wave their arms above their heads and soon I could hear their blood-curdling war whoops. The prospect was not inspiriting and my hair began to feel light on my head in anticipation of the encircling scalping knife. Still, mingling with my dread, was the determination to sell my life at as high a price as possible and, with this resolve, I pulled my cartridge pouch round in front and unslung my rifled carbine. As I did this, I could not help regretting that I was not a crack shot with some chance of hitting an Indian if I fired at him. Standing upon my feet upon the solid ground, perfectly cool, I was a poor marksman. How could I expect, upon this galloping animal pressing forward at the top of its speed, to make an effective shot at an enemy also moving at a high rate of speed? I would not have bet anything on my chances.

Dashing along the road, I ascended a slight roll in the plain and beheld about five miles ahead the white tents of the command. The thought was instantly suggested, could they hear a shot at that distance? Without further reflection, I fired my carbine in the air, loaded it and fired it twice more. Just as I was busily loading it again, an arrow fled past me in front, grazing my jacket sleeve. Glancing to the right, I saw that one Indian was within a hundred yards of me and the two others a little behind. I also noticed that my mule was really gaining perceptibly, but still the distance was narrowing and I knew that in a few moments more the Indian could shoot with great certainty of hitting. I raised my carbine, took deliberate aim at the leading Indian and fired. Simultaneously with the explosion, the pony of the second Indian fell headlong, the pony of the third Indian fell over him and I had unhorsed two of my enemies. The first Indian suddenly reined up and went back. Next, he and the one whose pony was not killed resumed the chase, but in the two or three seconds delay, I had put so much distance between us that they almost immediately gave it up and halted to send two harmless arrows after me. My first thought was, "Thank God for being a poor shot!" My bad shooting had brought the whole pursuit to a close much more effectually than would a good shot at the leader, which, if it had done what I intended, would have killed him and still left two pursuers.

A short distance farther and I met a party of mounted soldiers coming out. My shots had been heard and they were coming to my aid. It was quite dark when I got into camp and I was greeted with heartfelt congratulations by my friends. My "crack shot" was unmercifully quizzed, but all agreed that it was a good one for me.

I had left in the morning shortly after breakfast and, without being out of the saddle but once when I plucked the cactus, I had ridden without ceasing until seven in the evening. I had been angry enough to cut my mule's throat a dozen times that day, but now I felt that if I owned him no price could buy him. The poor fellow came in for a good share of admiration and his master, the wagon master, gave him an extra dressing and feed, accompanied by many endearing epithets of praise.

A train had arrived from Las Cruces shortly after I left camp in the morning, was now loaded and ready to start next day at reveille. It consisted of but eleven wagons and could therefore take but a small portion of the freight. I received orders from the commandant before I went to bed to accompany these wagons and send them back as soon as discharged, with Ochoa's train, and such other means of transportation as I could find. The command was to remain at the crossing to protect the stores until they could be shipped.

Next morning, I left with the train, mounted on my Zebra, and accompanied by my clerk and sergeant, with an escort of twenty men to guard the train. Our march the first day was about twenty miles to Robledo, where formerly had been a village, now abandoned and fallen into mere heaps of earth on account of the marauding Apaches.

Next morning we entered the town of Doña Aña. As I rode across the *acequia* (irrigation ditch), just above the town, I met a Government express rider to whom I gave letters for Fort Craig and the States. The expressman was accompanied by a Mexican with a led horse, going for a priest to bury a man who had been killed by the Indians the previous evening at the very entrance of the streets. The place was a fair sample of the common Mexican town and needs no description. I passed through it without calling at house or store and pushed on rapidly to Las Cruces. The distance between the two towns was inconsiderable, with many houses along the road giving security from the Indians, so I rode on alone to the close of my journey and reported to Lieutenant Colonel Edward E. Eyre, of the California Column, which had recently arrived.[3] In fact, it was the news of this arrival which had caused all but four companies of our force to turn back at Cañada del Alamo. The train of Ochoa was being unloaded under the eye of a board of survey and, after directing my sergeant and clerk to see that everything was properly stored, I went to look for permanent quarters.

I found two companies of Regular cavalry in town and went in search of the officers for some information in regard to rooms and messing arrangements. I found the captain of one of the companies occupying pleasant rooms, with many conveniences, which he said I could probably secure as soon as he left. He said that he had received orders to start for Santa Fé with the two companies as soon as our battalion should reach Las Cruces.

I took dinner with Major George W. Howland and then went with him to secure the rooms, which I was not long in doing on reasonable terms.[4] I then hunted up *Señor* Ochoa, delivered the borrowed spurs and engaged his twenty-five wagons to return to San Diego Crossing with the eleven Government wagons to bring up the rest of the stores. I also hired about twenty two-wheeled Mexican carts, drawn by one yoke of oxen each, to go for the same purpose.

3. Edward E. Eyre first came to California across the plains in 1849. He settled in Sacramento and became involved in the mining business. Eyre was commissioned major of the 1st California Cavalry on August 24, 1861, and was promoted to lieutenant colonel on November 1, 1861. He resigned on November 30, 1862, and settled in San Francisco. An astute businessman, Eyre made a fortune in the stock market and his family became a fixture in San Francisco society. He was president of the Germania Lead Works when he died in that city on January 15, 1899. *California Men*, 87; *California Adjutant General*, 41; *Sacramento Daily Union*, January 17, 1899; *San Francisco Call*, January 16, 1899.

4. George W. Howland graduated last in his class at West Point in 1848 and was commissioned a second lieutenant in the Mounted Rifles on June 30, 1851. Promoted to first lieutenant on March 3, 1855, and captain on May 14, 1861, he was transferred to the 3rd Cavalry on August 3, 1861. Brevetted to major for actions at Valverde, New Mexico, Howland was promoted to major of the 2nd Cavalry on December 1, 1866. He retired on April 8, 1869, and was appointed postmaster at Santa Fe. Howland lost that position soon after and worked as a clerk until his death in Santa Fe on December 21, 1886. Cullum, *Biographical Register* 2: 226; *Newport Mercury*, December 25, 1869; *Daily New Mexican*, December 22, 1886; December 23, 1886.

Chapter 10

Las Cruces and Mesilla

I had arrived at Las Cruces on the 3rd of August, five days in advance of the command to which I was attached, which gave me considerable leisure to look about the town and form acquaintances before my fellow officers arrived. The town was distant from the Rio Grande about a mile and a half at the time of which I am writing, but I learn the river, after the eccentric manner of western streams, has since changed its course and now flows close beside it.

There is but one principal street in the town, running north and south, with houses set closely together for a half a mile. In fact, the street is nothing more than the regular mail road down the river, with a village clustered upon it at this point. A few cross streets branch out in the densest part, mere culs de sac, and it is the only Mexican town I ever saw in which there was no *plaza*, a simple widening of the street before the parish church answering in place of one.

The street sloped gradually downward from the southern terminus of the village to the northern. The best families of the place were clustered about the church and courthouse in the upper part and the more common people were in the lower. I noticed almost immediately upon my entrance to the town a marked distinction between the people and those I had met above the Jornada. At the time I did not know that this distinction has been noticed by nearly all travelers in the country, that the inhabitants of the Rio Arriba and the Rio Abajo are marked by many different traits, all in favor of the Rio Abajo. Such, however, is the fact, more and more observable as one approaches Mexico. The gentlemen were distinguished by a more generous hospitality and a nearer approach to the high Spanish manner which I had learned from books to attribute to the Spaniard. The ladies were more beautiful as a class, much better read and more tastily dressed than those north of the Jornada. The houses were much better furnished, with more articles peculiarly Spanish, and richer in material and design. One thing, however, disturbed me somewhat and that was the great fondness displayed for mirrors. In my sleeping apartment were twenty-five of these articles upon one wall, a large one in the center and the other twenty-four of all sizes and designs ranged on each side and above it.

The two companies of the 3rd Cavalry were located at the upper end of the town and hence in the best quarters. When the 5th Infantry arrived, the officers and men were obliged to take quarters in the lower town. The ladies of the upper town gave a ball on the first Sunday evening after my arrival, to the officers of the 3rd, and the next Sunday the women of the lower town gave a ball to the 5th. Both of these affairs were "tip-top" and the officers of the two regiments went to them without distinction. It was my first experience of a Sunday party, but I found it the universal custom in the Southern territory and Mexico to keep holy the first half of Sunday and take the rest of the day for pleasure and fun. At the first ball I saw more handsome ladies collected than I had ever before seen in one gathering in the country. Rich jewelry, of native gold and native workmanship, gleamed on well-rounded necks and arms, only rivaled in brilliancy by the eyes of the wearers. The dresses were of the costliest fabrics, not always of the most recent fashion, but where the centre of fashion was so far distant, only the newcomers saw the difference.

At the ball in the lower town, the hall was less elegant, the dresses less fine, the jewelry not so abundant and costly, but the beauty of the women was just as attractive, while there was decidedly less reserve and more freedom from restraint than at the *gente finos* assembly. Both affairs were unique, and worth studying. The last one had a bit of spice in it which made a more lasting impression than the first. Two *señoritas* quarreled over receiving the attentions of our blonde Lieutenant Barr, spat in each other's faces, clawed down their respective headdresses and finally drew two gleaming stilettos upon each other. A ring was immediately cleared and the friends of the fair and fiery combatants began urging on their favorites to fight. But before anything serious could take place, the officers interfered and bore the pugnacious beauties out at opposite doors, kicking and screaming vengeance against each other, when the dancing went on as if it had never been interrupted.

The fair hair and mustache, blue eyes and light complexion of Lieutenant Barr made him the most attractive of men in the eyes of the Mexicans. Whispers of "*Mire el guëro*" ("Look at the blonde one") followed him wherever he went. The *guëro* is always a favorite with Mexican women, the same as in our country the olive-colored foreigner, with dark hair and beard, is thought so much of by our fair country women. Barr's landlady used to exhibit him like a curiosity to all her callers. She would lift his hair on her fingers, call their attention to its fineness and tendency to curl and taking him by the mustaches would say, "*Mirar sus bigotes, son rubios tambien*" (Look at his mustaches, they are blonde too).

I must here mention that on the days previous to the two balls, I saw crowds of women bathing in the *acequia*, under the windows in the rear of my quarters, "in the garb of Eve," tumbling and splashing in the water, enjoying themselves like ducks in a puddle. They seemed in no manner disturbed by the passersby, who walked along the bank of the ditch, but laughed and joked in perfect innocence, with no apparent consciousness that they were doing anything uncommon. The Mexican passersby appeared to take it as a matter of course. If a stray officer or soldier would stop and look on, immediately something in his manner would strike the bathers, they would huddle away from him and keep immersed to the neck until he passed on.

In this connection I must tell of a bathing adventure of my own. At the call for reveille every morning, it was my custom to rise and, with towel and soap, repair to the *acequia* for a bath before dressing for breakfast. The place which I selected for this purpose was a brisk five minutes' walk from my quarters, where the ditch widened into a large pool, about four feet deep, concealed by a long unoccupied building on one side and a dense wood on the other. Here I would lay aside my clothing, take a brief swim and return to my room. One morning, as I was standing in the water near the bank, busily applying soap, I noticed, some distance away, a woman approaching me, bearing upon her head a large earthen water pot. I saw that she was evidently coming to the *acequia* for water. Not being quite as "innocent" as the damsels I have mentioned above, I retired to the middle of the pool and sank on my knees to obscure my nakedness. My evident modesty, however, did not convey to the damsel any idea that I desired her to go elsewhere, but she came directly to the shore of the ditch, exactly in front of me.

Here she lowered her *tinaja* (earthen jar) to the ground, dipped with a gourd a few quarts of water into it and proceeded to wash it out, her eyes fixed calmly on me. She was a young woman of about twenty, evidently a servant or of one of the humbler families at the lower end of the street. She said nothing, but kept rinsing that *tinaja* until I was sure it was clean. The water was cold and the air was cool at this hour of the morning. I began to wish she would hurry away, when to my great disgust she took off her shoes and stockings and washed her feet. After this was done she let down her hair, washed that all out, combed, braided and put it up. By this time my teeth began to chatter badly and I was glad to see she was beginning, although leisurely, to dip water into the *tinaja*.

At last the pot was filled. She placed a little cushion upon her head, stooped and raised the vessel, with its five or six gallons of water, slowly up to the top of her head. As she attempted to place it on the cushion, she accidentally knocked it off and it fell to her feet. Without any hesitation, she said in Spanish, "If you please, sir, will you pick up my pad?" I walked quickly out of the water, raised the pad and placed it on her head. "Many thanks, sir" she said, and turning, walked away without looking round again.

I hurried on my clothes and walked briskly up and down the street for half an hour, striving to restore a little warmth to my chilled limbs. Next day and afterwards, I went farther away for a bathing place, where I was safe from interruption from female water carriers.

On the 4th of August, in company with the post surgeon, Doctor Sylvester Rankin, I rode to Mesilla, a large town on the opposite side of the river and nearly opposite Las Cruces.[1] A ride of a mile and a half, most of the way through a forest of cottonwood with thick undergrowth, brought us to the river. There was no bridge or boat there, but an excellent ford nearly half a mile broad. My mule was not very tall and I was fearful lest she should be swept away or the water flow over her back. I shook my feet out of the stirrups, coiled and extended my legs on the mule's neck, grasped firmly the pommel of the saddle and, "accoutered as I was, I plunged in." The water swept strongly against Zebra's sides, often nearly overwhelming her in its murky current, but she pushed unsteadily on and at last took me safely out on the other side, on a broad and sandy beach, but a few rods from the first houses of the town.

Mesilla—the name means a small table, or sideboard—is a large and prosperous town, the point of departure of the southern Overland Stage route, and shortly to be one of the principal stations on the Southern Pacific Railroad. At the time I first saw it, it had the only kiln-burned brick house in the territory, three steam gristmills and some other small manufactories. Its trade was considerable with the surrounding country and the agricultural excellence of the valley near it was noted throughout New Mexico. It has a large and well laid-out *plaza*, shaded by several cottonwoods, on the northern side of which stands a large church.

After looking over the town for some time, the doctor took me to the house of a Colonel Samuel J. Jones, where he had been invited to dinner, assuring me that I would be perfectly welcome, as his friend.[2] This Jones is a character who formerly figured as a

1. A graduate of Buffalo Medical College in 1857, Sylvester Rankin practiced in that city for a short time before moving westward to Kansas, Colorado, and New Mexico. He joined the army as an assistant surgeon in the 2nd New Mexico and put his knowledge to use after the battle at Valverde, New Mexico. Rankin served until July of 1865 when he crossed into Mexico and became a surgeon in Emperor Maximilian's army. Following the ouster of Maximilian, he practiced medicine in various parts of that country until he settled in Victoria City in 1876. In the early hours of May 22, 1881, Doctor Rankin was ruthlessly murdered by a dagger thrust into his heart. Rankin's murderers snatched his gold ring, sleeve buttons, pocketbook, handkerchief, and hat before disappearing in the darkness. The killers, criminals named Miranda and Gonzales, were quickly identified, tried, sentenced, and hung. *New York Times*, June 8, 1881; *Cincinnati Daily Gazette*, June 9, 1881.

2. Samuel J. Jones was a notorious character during the pre-Civil War days in Kansas. He first arrived in Kansas in 1854 and the following year led a pro-slavery mob at Bloomington, being rewarded with the appointment of county sheriff. Jones made several newsworthy arrests of Free Soilers, but was ambushed in retaliation. Out for vengeance, he organized a posse that

sheriff at Leavenworth in the old "bleeding Kansas days," being heartily abused by the *New York Tribune* as a violent "raw-headed-and-bloody-bones" Democrat. The readers of the papers during the Lecompton Constitution and Sharps' rifle days in Kansas could rarely glance at a column of Kansas news without seeing some mention made of Sheriff Jones, either in praise or censure, according as the paper was Democratic or Republican. As the papers from which I imbibed my political nourishment were of the latter stripe, I had formed a decided opinion that Jones was a heavy, coarse, brutal fellow, who reveled in the gore of abolitionists and took every occasion to harass them. What my opinion is now, let the account of my visit show.

When the doctor and I entered the house of Colonel Jones, we were shown into a cozy sitting room by an Indian servant and in a few moments an elegant lady entered, to whom my friend presented me, introducing her as Mrs. Jones. We entered into a pleasant conversation, during which I saw from her accent that she was a Virginian, a guess which was afterwards confirmed by her. After we had spent about a half hour in chat, I heard a light step in the hall, through the open door, and presently a gentleman of fine appearance, easy carriage and cultivated manners entered. I did not for one instant suspect this could be Jones and was nearly astonished out of my equanimity when Rankin introduced him as the colonel.

It is hard to describe the struggle which went on in my mind during the rest of the afternoon, in the vain effort to reconcile the *Tribune's* statement with the evident character of the polished gentleman before me. I could not keep it out of my mind and fear that I may have been almost rude in the way I watched his every movement.

After dinner we were walking in the flower garden and I said, "Colonel, you are a far different looking man from what I expected to see."

"You used to read the Republican papers, lieutenant?"

"Always. They did not make you out a saint."

---

almost destroyed the town of Lawrence. Jones resigned in 1857 when the governor refused to authorize the use of balls and chains to restrain his political opponents. Shortly thereafter he moved to Mesilla where he lived the rest of his life, however a stroke left him paralyzed and incapable of speech for the last ten years. Jones died in Mesilla on December 10, 1883. Blackmar, *Kansas* 2: 37; *Rio Grande Republican*, January 5, 1884.

"No. I have met many gentlemen who got their impressions of me from the newspapers, some of them quite laughable."

"Tell Curtis the one about the old gentleman at the Planter's Hotel," said the doctor.

We went into an arbor at the end of the garden, a servant brought in a watermelon, apricots, peaches and some other fruits of the estate and, while the doctor and I discussed these, Jones told us the story.

It was during the height of the Kansas troubles that he was staying at the Planter's Hotel in Leavenworth for a few days, for the purpose of transacting some business connected with his office of sheriff. One day, when the hotel was very much crowded and every available room was taken, Sheriff Jones entered the office just as a gentlemanly stranger, with overcoat over his arm and handbag in his hand, approached the desk to register. Before he could do so, however, the clerk told him that it would be impossible to furnish him with a room, for everything was taken or engaged, for some time to come. The stranger showed so much distress and looked so tired, that Jones approached and said, "Sir, if you have no objection to sharing my room with me, there is a cot-bedstead you can occupy, if you please."

The stranger gladly accepted, registered his name and was presented to Mr. Jones as Mr. H. When dinner was called, they went to the table together and, as they partook of the edibles, talked politics in a quiet way without excitement or personalities, each evidently favorably impressed with the other, although they could not agree. At supper, they again met, during the evening they went to a concert and afterwards sat in the reading room for a long time, discussing the situation. When bedtime arrived, they went to the bar for a "night-cap" and ascended to their room together. Once in bed, they continued their talk for some time longer, still on the political situation, until Mr. H dropped asleep.

Next morning they came down for their "eye opener" and breakfast together and afterwards entered the office to secure the morning's papers. Each sat reading silently until some ten minutes had elapsed, when Mr. H. looked up to the hotel clerk and said, "I notice by my paper that Sheriff Jones is in town. Do you know him?"

"Very well, indeed," replied the clerk.

"I wish, should opportunity offer, you would point him out to me."

"Certainly," said the clerk, "No better time than now. This chamber-mate of yours is the sheriff."

"What! This gentleman!" exclaimed Mr. H., bounding from his chair as if he had received a prod from a bayonet.

"Yes, sir, this gentleman and no other," said the imperturbable clerk, evidently enjoying the scene. "You have been intimately associating since your arrival with the genuine Sheriff Jones, notorious and blood-thirsty as he is reported."

Mr. H. sank back quietly into his chair, trying to resume his paper and look unconscious, but it was of no use. Presently he arose and extended his hand to Jones, who arose also. "I beg your pardon, Mr. Jones. It is not necessary for anyone to tell me you are a gentleman. I know it! I had read so much about you and believed it, that I expected to see a six-foot, broad-shouldered, red-faced, brutal-looking man, going about like the giant Blunderbore, in search of victims.[3] Why, before I met you, if I had had my choice to sleep in the same room with Sheriff Jones or the incarnate fiend, I should have chosen the fiend."

This ends the story, with only the addition that these two men were still friends at the time of my visit and I was shown many little gifts which ornamented the centre table and bookshelves from Mr. H. I have met Colonel Jones several times since, in New York, Washington and St. Louis. When the Texans invaded New Mexico, by his personal interventions, he saved many Union people in Mesilla from loss of property and I am happy to say the favor was reciprocated when the return Union wave swept back over this region.

After my return to Las Cruces, duties were heaped upon me. In the midst of turning over stores to the commissary of the California Column, I was ordered on court martial duty and had hardly taken my seat for the trial of prisoners, when an order came from General James H. Carleton making me confiscating officer of the property of Don Rafael Armijo, who had joined the Texans in their invasion and had left the country with them upon their defeat and consequent retreat.[4]

3. Blunderbore was the name of the giant killed by Jack in the traditional English fairy tale, "Jack the Giant Killer." Rose, *Giants*, 53.

4. A native New Englander with deep-seated religious beliefs, James Henry Carleton's first military experience came as a lieutenant in the Aroostock War of 1838-1839. Receiving a direct commission into the 1st Dragoons in the latter year, Carleton spent nearly

General James H. Carleton. Courtesy of Massachusetts MOLLUS Civil War Photographs, United States Army Heritage and Education Center.

When the court adjourned at night, I went to Mesilla, the scene of my confiscating labors, and reported to the general. I received full instructions and went to the store of Armijo on the *plaza*. This store was about a hundred feet long, with three sets of doors in the front, the counter running the entire length of the building. In the north end were dry goods and millinery, the goods running through groceries, hardware, wooden ware and general stock to the southern end. In the rear were two courtyards, surrounded by storerooms filled with all sorts of goods saleable in the territory.

A sergeant, named Le Roy, was detailed as an assistant, and a Portuguese as an interpreter.[5] The business agent of the Armijos, who had been in the guardhouse ever since the arrival of the Union troops, was turned over to me and I was ordered not to allow him out of my sight or the sergeant's at any time. I was to sleep in the store in any convenient place I could find and the agent was to sleep between me and the sergeant. In accordance with these instructions, a wide bed was made under the colonnade of an interior court and each night found the sergeant, the agent and me sleeping in a row, the agent chained to my right ankle by locked clasps, the key of which was hidden in a place known only to Sergeant Le Roy and myself. In the morning, the sergeant would go for the key and release us, for we were both prisoners, so far as personal freedom was concerned, during the night.

---

all of his military service on the western frontier. A diligent reporter for Eastern newspapers, he sent off the first account of the battle of Buena Vista to be published. Carleton gained valuable experience when he served with Kit Carson in the New Mexico campaign in 1851. As a captain and brevet major he led the detachment that buried the dead of the Mountain Meadow massacre and wrote a report on the affair. Commissioned colonel of the 1st California Infantry in 1861 and brigadier general in 1862, Carleton led California Volunteers into New Mexico Territory where he succeeded General Canby. He is remembered for his "surrender or die" campaign against the Apaches and Navajos that resulted in portions of these nations being confined at Bosque Redondo for several years. Brevetted major general for his war service, James Carleton died on January 7, 1873, in San Antonio. He was so popular in California that one editor wrote that he had graduated first in his class at West Point, although he had never attended that school. Rafael Armijo and his brother Manuel, a three-time governor of the territory, had a reputation for dishonesty prior to the war although they operated several trading operations containing merchandise estimated to be worth hundreds of thousands of dollars. The brothers became Confederate sympathizers and sold supplies to the invaders from Texas, accepting Southern bonds in exchange. The Confederacy reneged on these bonds and the U. S. government confiscated all of the property of the disloyal Armijos. Rafael and Manuel were also indicted for treason, although these charges were eventually dismissed in 1867. Rafael Armijo died in Albuquerque in 1887. Kane, "James H. Carleton," 122–25, 127, 132–37, 141–42; *San Francisco Bulletin*, January 8, 1873; Moorhead, *New Mexico's Royal Road*, 110; Keleher, *Turmoil in New Mexico*, 203–4; Tittman, "Exploitation of Treason," 137–38.

5. Sergeant Le Roy seems to be a pseudonym since the U. S. Army Register of Enlistments does not list anyone by that last name serving with the units then in New Mexico.

I secured board at the house of a Mexican merchant, *Señor* Antonio Barella.[6] The sergeant went home with the agent to his meals. My duties were to take a complete account of the stock in both Spanish and English, giving the cost prices only. I was also to keep a sharp watch for other goods belonging to the Armijo estate, said to be concealed somewhere in the town. Each morning a guard from the California Volunteers of a non-commissioned officer and ten men reported to me, for the purpose of guarding the property and keeping out interlopers. This guard was very inefficient in one respect and gave me much trouble. They were Volunteers recently raised and could not be made to understand that I, as a second lieutenant, had any right to keep out the captains, majors, etc., who were continually demanding entrance and obtaining it, too. I got tired of instructing a new guard every morning and getting slight obedience to my orders and made application to the general in command for a permanent detail from the Regulars. The request was granted and one afternoon a detachment of the 5th Infantry arrived, taking up quarters in a remote corner of my extensive establishment.

It did me good next morning to take a station from which I could watch the sentinel at the door, a grizzled Irish veteran, to see what success my bores would have in passing him. There were several attempts made by lieutenants and captains, but these turned away without a word at the sentinel's sharp "Halt! You can't go in there, 'gainst orders!" But after a time my greatest bore, a major, who used to come in and loaf half a day at a time, pulling down the goods from the counters where they had been invoiced, mixing them with those which had not and often helping himself to tobacco, liquor and little knickknacks, came along. When the sentinel halted him, he pushed on superciliously, affecting to brush the sentinel away by a lordly wave of the hand. The next thing he knew, he received an admonitory thrust of a bayonet in the abdomen. Stepping back, he exclaimed, "Let me pass! I have business in there!"

"Have ye the liftinent's permission?" asked old George Hoey.[7]

"No. I don't need it."

6. Antonio Barella cannot be further identified. The surname could possibly be Barela.

7. George Hoey enlisted in the 5th Infantry as a private on November 25, 1856, and re-enlisted on September 29, 1861. He was discharged from the 5th Infantry on September 29, 1864, to re-enlist as a veteran volunteer in the 1st California Cavalry. Hoey was mustered out on September 10, 1866. Curtis said that he was the shortest man in the company and he measured 5' 6 ½". George Hoey Military Service Records; *Records of California Men*, 103.

"Ye'll not get in here till ye have it, sir. Thim's me orders."

This ended the conversation and the major passed on. He never forgave me for this and never spoke to me afterwards, when he could avoid it. I never grieved over his silence, however.

One day, as I sat at the door of the Armijo store, about four o'clock in the afternoon, I heard a rapid discharge of firearms in a side street and started to see what was the trouble. As I passed along the front of the building, the sergeant of the guard said, "It is nothing but a Mexican funeral, sir. It will pass here on the way to church." I returned to my chair and sat down. Presently, the head of the procession appeared round the corner, consisting of half a dozen musicians, playing violins, guitars and a small harp. Next came four young girls clad in white, with wreaths of flowers about their heads, bearing a small coffin on a bier, and behind them walked the mourners. Lastly came a crowd of men and boys armed with shotguns, rifles, muskets and pistols of every variety of pattern, loading and firing as fast as possible. I followed the procession at a respectful distance and entered the church with it. The parish priest was absent and the people all knelt for a few moments in silent prayer before the altar, with the lidless coffin on the floor in their midst. When opportunity offered, I looked into the coffin. It was a child, a girl. Her breast was covered with flowers, a few toys and her little hands were crossed over a picture of the Virgin Mary.

Chapter 11

New Mexico Stories

My duties as confiscating officer ran smoothly along, after the change in the guard before mentioned, giving me occasional opportunities of spending an hour or two in visiting newly made acquaintances and rambling in the suburbs of the town. In one of these calls I entered the house of the parish priest, Father Abeytia, and found the reverend gentleman discussing a whiskey toddy and somewhat under the influence of his potations.[1] He received me hospitably and ordered up a refection of *vino del pais* (wine of the country) and ginger snaps. The quarters of the priest were in an extension of the transept of the church, with a small door opening into the interior. While we sat chatting, a party of men and women opened the door and informed the priest that they were ready.

"Wait, then, till I am ready," he replied and resumed his conversation with me.

Presently the door opened again and a woman said, "Please come now *Padre*, the baby is beginning to cry."

"Let it cry then! I'll come when I get ready!" was the angry reply.

1. Father Abeytia cannot be positively identified.

"What is wanted of you?" I ventured to ask.

"It is a christening."

"Why not go through the ceremony and then come back here?" I suggested.

"So I will, if the lieutenant will wait."

"I will go with you and witness the service, if you will permit me."

"Certainly, I shall be pleased to have you."

The priest rose rather unsteadily to his feet and made such difficulty in getting into his vestments that I offered my assistance and he accepted it. When he was arrayed, we entered the church, where we found quite an assembly of ladies and gentlemen gathered before the baptismal font, with a newly born babe waiting the arrival of the priest.

The ceremony was concluded in a few moments and at its close I was invited, by the father of the child, to attend the christening party at his house, in company with *Padre* Abeytia. We found the house on the north side of the *plaza*, under the shade of several huge cottonwoods, and were conducted to the *sala*, where refreshments were set out in profusion. Before partaking of these, each guest marched through the chamber of the mother of the baby, who was bolstered up on pillows in bed, paying her some compliment, expressing kind wishes and immediately leaving. She was a handsome young woman, married the year before, and the sponsors of the child were her old friends and schoolmates.

After half an hour, I returned with the priest to his rooms and sat down to spend the evening. He was a genial gentleman, a first rate talker and told me the following tale of Indian warfare, suggested by the remark that the mother of the recently baptized child was the daughter of a very brave man, "lame in the leg like you."

The priest spoke English well and fluently. I ought here to say that I never saw him under the influence of liquor before or afterwards. Nor do I desire to convey the impression that the priests of the Roman Catholic Church in New Mexico are generally a dissipated class of men. I found them, with rare exceptions, temperate men and always God-fearing and hard working in their pastorates.

But to the priest's story.[2] In a ranche, situated in the valley of a small tributary of the Rio Grande del Norte, about half way

2. *New York Herald*, September 11, 1848.

between Mesilla and El Paso, lived a Mexican family by the name of Orteza, the head of which, a sturdy old sexagenarian, was known as El Coxo (Game Leg) through all the region round about. The family were *vaqueros*, or cattle herders, and consisted of eight strapping sons, any one of whom could *colear* a bull or at the game of *el gallo* tear from its stake the unhappy fowl and bear it safe from the pursuit of competitors to the feet of his admiring lady love more successfully than any other *ranchero* in the *tierra afuera* (broad country).

The third and handsomest son, a lad of twenty, named Escamilla, five feet eleven in his *zapatos* (shoes), straight and lithesome as a reed, always bore the palm of superiority in horsemanship and all manly sports. He had received something of an education at the Mexican city of Queretaro, where were located the best schools of the Mexican Republic, and was a courteous and polished young gentleman. His city breeding had given him a taste for dress and he quite dazzled the eyes of the handsome *señoritas* of the neighboring ranches when he first returned home and attended a big "bull tailing" dressed in the latest fashion of the cities. In the very first passage of arms, he succeeded in overturning three immense bulls by the tail with consummate dexterity and won enthusiastic *vivas* from the maidens who graced by their presence the exciting sport.

Not far behind Escamilla and almost rivaling him in quickness and good looks was his next older brother, Juan Maria, a man who in the eye of the more experienced *vaqueros* far excelled his brother in manliness of appearance, quite equaled him in horsemanship, lacking only the finesse which the latter had obtained in the polished circles of Queretarian society and the education of the schools. Juan might also be less skilled in some of the feats acquired by his brother in the trials of horsemanship in the pursuit of the wilder and more active bulls of the *tierra caliente* (warm country).

Previous to the arrival of Escamilla, Juan Maria had been the first at *el gallo* and bull-tailing and had always laid the trophies of the sport at the feet of one Ysabel Mora, called, from the *hacienda* where she lived, Ysabel de la Cadena, a handsome young girl of seventeen, the toast of the country for miles around and celebrated by the *cantadores* (folk singers) at the last fair held in El Paso "*la moza mas guapa de la tierra afuera*" (the most sprightly lass in the broad lands).

It so happened that the last year Ysabel had made her first appearance at a function, at this *el gallo* she was wooed and in a measure won by the presentation of the remains of the gallant rooster at the hands of Juan Maria. As his offering was so well received, Juan thereafter began to look upon Ysabel as his sweetheart and she, nothing loath at having the properest lad in the valley at her feet, permitted his attentions and apparently returned his love.

With the return of Escamilla from school, however, with his dandy manners and superior education, the tide of love was diverted from Juan Maria to his brother, who, far from respecting the feelings of his elder, took every means, even verging upon the dishonorable, to supplant him in the affections of Ysabel. The frank and noble-hearted Juan, far from resenting this treatment, quietly gave way to his more favored brother, the affair was concluded between the *señorita* and Escamilla and a day appointed for the marriage ceremony. The wedding was to take place at the *hacienda* of the bride's father, where, in honor of the occasion, a grand festival was to be held, at which all the *rancheros* for forty miles around were to be present, including, of course, El Coxo and his stalwart sons, the brothers of the bridegroom.

Three days before the day appointed for the wedding, El Coxo and his sons, mounted on horses, a cross between the mustang and the American, made their appearance at the Hacienda de la Cadena, exacting a buzz of admiration from the collected guests.

The bulls to be used in the sports of the next day were grazing on a plain some miles distant from the *hacienda*. To collect these, El Coxo and all his sons, except Escamilla, attended by the father of the bride, rode out, leaving the other *rancheros* to complete a large corral for containing the animals until wanted for the sport.

The day was closing and the sun was fast sinking behind the serrated peaks of the mountain range to the west of the valley, tingeing their summits with a golden flood of light, while the sandy, mesquite-covered plain beneath lay cold and gray under the deep shadow of the *sierra* (mountain range). The shrill cry of the quail was heard as it called together the bevy for the night; hares limped out of their thick covers and sought their feeding grounds;

overhead the melancholy cry of the *grulias* (cranes) sounded feebly in the aerial distance of their flight. The lowing of the cattle resounded from the banks of the *arroyo* (stream), where the herdsmen were driving them to water; the laborers were quitting their *milpas* (maize fields) and already seeking their homes, where, at the doors, the women with naked arms were pounding corn on the *metate* (grinding stone), in preparation for the evening meal; and the universal quiet, the soft and subdued beams of the sinking sun, which shed a chastened light over the whole landscape, proclaimed that the day was drawing to a close and that man and beast were seeking their well-earned rest after their daily toil.

Escamilla and Ysabel, careless of the beauty of the scene and hour, were strolling along, conscious of nothing save their own enraptured thoughts and the aerial castles, which probably both were building, of future happiness and love. As they sauntered onward, a little cloud of dust arose from the chaparral in front of them and, in the distance, but seemingly in another direction, they heard the shouts of the returning *vaqueros* and the thundering tread of the bulls they were driving to the corral. In advance of these was seen one horseman, trotting quickly on towards the *hacienda*. Nevertheless, the cloud of dust before them rolled rapidly onward and presently several horsemen emerged from it, galloping toward them in the road.

"Here come the bull fighters," exclaimed the girl, withdrawing her waist from the encircling arm of Escamilla, "Let us return."

"I think they are my father and brothers," answered he and he continued, "Yes, there are eight, look!"

But what did Ysabel see, as, with eyes almost starting from her head and spellbound with sudden fear, she gazes toward the advancing horsemen, who are now turning a bend in the wood and are within a few hundred yards of them!

Escamilla follows the direction of her eyes and one look congealed the heart of the trembling coward. A band of mounted Apaches are upon them. Naked to the waist and painted in all the horrible designs of Indian war, with brandished spears they rush on. Heedless of the helpless maid and leaving her to her fate, the cowardly lover turned and fled, shouting, as he ran, the dreaded signal of "*Los barbaros*! *Los barbaros*!" ("The barbarians! The barbarians!")

A horseman met him—it was Juan Maria, who, having lassoed a little antelope on the plains, was returning in advance of his party to present it to the false Ysabel. The exclamations of the frightened Escamilla and one glance down the road showed him the peril of the poor girl. Throwing down the antelope which he was bearing in his arms, he dashed the spurs furiously into his horse and galloped like the wind to the rescue. No heart of hare was this brave lad, but made of the mettle that dares anything for honor and for his fellow man! He flew down the road, but already the savages were upon Ysabel, with a whoop of blood-thirsty joy. She, covering her face with her hands, shrieks to her old lover to save her, "*Salvame, a Juan Maria, por Dios, salvame*!" (Save me, Juan Maria, for God's sake, save me!") At that moment the lance of the foremost Indian pierced her heart and in another her reeking scalp was brandished exultingly aloft by the murderous savage.

His triumph, however, was brief. The clatter of a galloping horse thunders over the ground and causes him to turn his head. Almost bounding through the air, his lasso describing circle after circle above his head, until released from his hand it uncoils and, with unerring precision, falls about the neck of the Apache. Instantly, Juan's horse comes to a dead stop, his feet braced rigidly forward, and the Indian falls heavily to the ground with a broken neck.

But the odds are fearfully against the brave Mexican youth, who is armed with nothing but a small rusty sword, carried for cutting a way through the chaparral and not for defence. But with this poor weapon he attacks the nearest Indian and cleaves his head by a sturdy stroke, causing him to drop dead from his horse. The others, keeping at a distance, assailed him with arrows and already he was pierced with many bleeding wounds. Still the gallant fellow fights bravely against the odds until he hears the loud *vivas* of his father and six brothers, as they come like a whirlwind to join the fight. At the very moment when they closed, an arrow, discharged at but a few paces distance, buried itself to the feathers in his breast and his brothers reach the spot only to see him fall from his horse and die.

At this juncture forty more Apaches joined their friends and a fierce combat ensued between El Coxo and his sons, who fought with desperate valor to avenge the death of Juan Maria and poor fickle Ysabel. Half a dozen Indians bit the dust and two more of the brothers were bleeding on the ground, when the *rancheros*, who had been engaged in repairing the corral, came up in force and compelled the Indians to retreat. As night was coming on, no pursuit was made.

On the ground lay the still-quivering body of the girl and the two Indians near her who were killed by Juan Maria. One of them had his neck broken and his brains dashed out by the jerk to the ground he had received from the lasso. In his hand was still clutched the raven scalp-lock of the girl. Juan Maria was quite dead, pierced with twenty bleeding wounds; two of his brothers were dangerously wounded; and six Indians, besides those killed by Juan Maria, fell by the avenging arms of El Coxo and his sons.

The bodies of Ysabel and Juan Maria were borne by the *rancheros* to the *hacienda* and both were buried next day, side by side, at the very hour when the wedding was to have taken place. Escamilla, ashamed of his cowardice, soon after disappeared and was never again heard of.

The traveler, in passing the Hacienda de la Cadena, can see, about three hundred yards from the gate, two wooden crosses roughly hewn out of pine logs. On one side, a rudely cut inscription invites the passerby to bestow:

Un Ave Maria y un Pater Noster
Por el alma Ysabel Mora,
Qui á los manos de los barbaros cayo muerta,
El dia 11 de Octubre, el áno 1845,
En la flor de su juventud y hermosra.
One Ave Maria and one Pater Noster
For the repose of the soul of Ysabel Mora,
Who fell by the hands of the Indians
On the 11th of October, of the year of 1845,
And in the flower in her youth and beauty.

On the other:

Aqui jace Juan Maria Orteza,
Vecino de Cardena
Matado por los barbaros,
El dia 11 Octubre, del ano 1845.
Ora por et Christiano, por Dios.

Here lies Juan Maria Orteza,
Native of Cardena,
Killed by the Indians
On the 11th of October, of the year of 1845
Christian, for the sake of God, pray for him.

A goodly pile of stones thrown against the foot of the two crosses shows that many an Ave Maria and Pater Noster has been said in accordance with the injunction contained in the inscription. It is a custom of the country to cast a stone on a grave when a prayer is uttered.

The story closed, I thanked the priest and returned to my quarters to chain the agent to my leg and go to sleep.

Chapter 12

Across the Jornada Del Muerto

One day, when I was nearly through with my work on the Armijo property, I found I was in need of some writing paper to carry on the accounting, so I walked across the *plaza* to a variety store, kept by a Frenchman, to procure some. As I entered the door, I found no one present but the proprietor and he was standing on a stool behind the counter, directly opposite the door, busily occupied in arranging articles on the shelves. He did not hear me enter and, as I was not in a hurry, I stood waiting for him to turn. After a few moments, he turned his head and saw me standing in the middle of the floor, glancing along the closely-stocked walls. He sprang down with such evident perturbation that I looked with some curiosity at him before I mentioned what I wanted. When I asked for paper, he showed so much relief that my suspicion that something was wrong was strengthened.

I had previously received orders to look for goods supposed to be concealed in some part of the town by Armijo's agent before the Union forces had arrived. I had searched as closely as possible and not aroused suspicion of my design, but with no success up to this time. The singular actions of the Frenchman at once suggested the idea that I must be on the track of the hidden stores. After my package of paper was made up, I said, "If you have no objection, sir, I should like to look through your rooms."

"Why, lieutenant, I have nothing concealed," he answered in a fidgety manner, his very reply corroborating my suspicions and determining me in not making any further attempt to disguise the motives for my search.

"You are doubtless aware," I said, "that a considerable portion of the most valuable stores of the Armijo property is thought to be concealed somewhere in town. I think it best for me to look for it here."

"Certainly, certainly sir, it will give much pleasure to show you round, but I can assure you there is nothing concealed on my premises," he replied.

"Then I shall give you no offence if I perform my duty."

I went to the door, beckoned to the sergeant at the entrance of the Armijo store, and, when he came over, asked him to go round to the rear entrance of the Frenchman's place and remain there until I should relieve him, allowing no one to enter or depart. I then began my search. The building was built around a court and contained a large number of rooms, which I searched minutely and without success, the Frenchman keeping close to me and never ceasing to protest that there were no goods concealed on his premises. Notwithstanding these assertions of innocence, the man's very earnestness made me the more positive that the goods were somewhere in the building. But where, was the question. As I asked myself this question, I was standing before a doorway in which no door was hung, the aperture being filled with old rubbish, consisting of boxes, stovepipe, bagging and trash generally. I had passed this doorway half a dozen times, but its very appearance had disarmed suspicion. Stepping up to it now, I seized a length of stovepipe, drew it towards me and down fell most of the stuff crammed in the space, revealing a tier of bales in the room beyond.

My attendant, as soon as he saw the discovery was made, hastily requested that I would remain here a few moments until he could go for some Mexican gentlemen and hurried away. In a few moments, he returned with three of the principal Mexicans of Mesilla and I was invited to a conference in an inner room. There a proposition was made to me that I should go back to my store, say nothing and that during the night the goods I had discovered should be run over the line into Mexico. I was assured that the secret was now my own and that I was perfectly safe to agree to their proposition, as no one would be the wiser for it. Various sums were offered me, up to $20,000 in gold. I suppose I might assume a high grade of virtue and tell my friends that I rejected all these overtures with scorn, but I must confess the proposition had its charms and that it took a severe wrench to get myself out of the toils of this temptation and safe across the *plaza*.

I placed a guard over the goods, next day had them brought to my place of business, examined and entered on my returns. They consisted of rich silk goods of various patterns and designs and were worth much more than the price offered me for my silence.

During my confiscating labors, I boarded at the house, as before mentioned, of *Señor* Barella. The family consisted of the father and four sons, two of whom had been educated in New England and spoke English as well as I did. There was a daughter, whom I caught a glimpse of at the christening described and again as I passed from my bedroom to breakfast one morning, but she never came to meals and all my efforts to meet her were of no avail. I had no Judge Tompkins to vouch for me here, as in Albuquerque. The girl was very handsome and I sent her bonbons without stint, which she acknowledged by sending me various little dainties in the culinary art, but my duties ended without my having been able to speak to her. I mention this in corroboration of what I have already said in regard to the seclusion of the women in New Mexico. At the table, three times each day, I met the male members of the family only, no woman, save the Indian girl who waited at the table, showing herself.

On the 28th of August, I returned to Las Cruces to rejoin my command, having been absent since the 12th. A wagon came over to Mesilla for the guard and the baggage. This day was impressed on my mind by an accident which befell me as I rode my mule Zebra slowly through the woods on the Las Cruces side. I had tied a bundle to the saddle just behind my left thigh, which contained a pair of stiffly-starched white pantaloons. The string fastening the package gave way and the pantaloons leaped like a Jack-in-the-box into the air, causing my mule to deposit me on the top of my head in the middle of the road. I do not know how long I lay there senseless, but I was picked up by a party of strolling soldiers and taken to my quarters, where I fully recovered before the next morning.

The next day after my return, I arrayed myself in a white linen suit, the day being very sultry, and started from my quarters to visit the officers at the lower end of the street. This was about two in the afternoon. At ten in the morning, we had noticed a fearful thunderstorm raging about the summit of Sierra de los Organos, fifteen miles to the east of us, but not a drop had descended upon Las Cruces, nor had a cloud hovered over it. As I walked down the road, my attention was attracted by a series of shouts and screams from men and women on the western outskirts of the town, but I could not make out what was said. As I approached the lower level, a voluminous stream of water dashed across the road, suddenly swelling into a deep and broad torrent, which rapidly gullied a bed through the street. I paused on the brink, thinking I had better turn back, but at this juncture two lieutenants, on the *plaza* of a house opposite, began bantering me to try the leap and, as an inducement, displayed a basket of grapes and a watermelon. I went back a few paces, ran and sprang across, succeeding in striking fairly on the other side, but the treacherous bank gave way under my feet and I went down into the roily stream all over. My friends lent me a couple of hands each and drew me out, but alas for my white linen suit. It was the color of chocolate and very unambitious in its set.

The *arroyo* continued to run for half an hour and then suddenly subsided. I returned to my quarters for a change of clothing, an object of interest to many dark eyes as I passed up the street. I think I never attracted so much attention before. This *arroyo* was the result of the great rainfall fifteen miles distant and had cut its own pathway from the mountain to the river.

Orders were received on the 28th for us to get ready for the march up the river to rejoin our regiment at Fort Craig. As quartermaster, I had to get the transportation ready. Accordingly, I rode to Mesilla to see what wagons our California friends could spare us. I found they had two large water tanks, capable of holding 900 gallons each, which had been used in crossing the Gila Desert, and ten wagons which we could have. I reported this to Captain Joseph Updegraff and he at once determined to take the tanks and march over the Jornada del Muerto.[1]

1. Joseph Updegraff enlisted as a private in the 3rd Artillery on March 9, 1846, and was transferred to the 5th Infantry where he was promoted to corporal and sergeant. He received a brevet commission as second lieutenant on June 28, 1848, and to that full rank on October 7, 1848. Updegraff was advanced to first lieutenant on December 31, 1854, and

These tanks resembled in general dimension and color the body of an army wagon, without the canvas top. They were made of cedar, with a canvas hose in the rear, for drawing water. As the ten wagons were not enough to take the baggage and supplies of our four companies, I succeeded in getting the surplus articles into a Mexican train which was to leave the day after we did.

On the 30th we left Las Cruces at nine o'clock in the morning, camping at Robledo on the Rio Grande, the last encampment before reaching the Jornada. Here our two water tanks were filled and on the following day, after a few miles hard pulling up a difficult ascent, we struck the level of the desert. Our first camp on the desert was north of San Diego Mountain, where the plain broke off sharply towards the river, which was four miles distant. We did not use any water from the tanks at this place, but drove the herd of mules and other animals to the river, sending water kegs by the drivers and a detail of soldiers mounted on mules for a supply for our use.

Next morning found us rolling over the hard and level road of the Jornada. This road is as smooth as a cement floor for ninety-five miles, not a perfect level, as it slightly undulates and at certain points has quite deep depressions, in which water collects in the rainy season and makes this route the favorite one during a brief portion of the year. The Mexican traders pass over it at all seasons without much difficulty, following the method well-known to plainsmen and army men. Suppose, for instance, a train is bound southward, heavily loaded; it will camp on the river at the northern end of the Jornada until about four o'clock in the afternoon, when it will start out, drive twenty-four miles and go into camp until the same hour of the second day. Driving the same distance on the evening of the second day will bring the train to the centre of the plain, where the herd can be driven, grazing as it goes, to a spring six miles off the road, remaining near it until time to get back to the wagons and resume the journey. The fourth drive is a dry one and the fifth brings the train to the point where we first encamped, where the animals can be driven four miles to the river. The next drive brings it to Robledo and the desert is passed. Going

captain on February 25, 1861. He was promoted major of the 9th Infantry on December 1, 1863, and died at San Francisco on June 19, 1866. Heitman, *Historical Register* 1: 978; *1866 Official Register*, 100.

north, with an empty train, the distance may be made in three days. Water for the trainsmen is carried in ten gallon kegs, which hang under the rear axles.

Our course this route is attended with great danger during Indian hostilities, as the savages can look down from the mountains, which border the Jornada its whole length, upon the toiling trains and watch their opportunity for a descent. The places where the animals have to be driven so far from the train for water are the favorite points of attack, particularly the one in the middle of the desert, where the spring is in a rugged country, well adapted to concealment.

During the Navajo war, the Government established a small fort at this central watering place, for the protection of travelers and merchants, breaking it up when the campaign closed.

All along the road are scattered little heaps of stones, usually surmounted with a rude wooden cross, made of fragments of boxes from the passing trains, marking the spot where some traveler met his death either by thirst, starvation or Indian arrows. Occasionally, a group of these heaps, covering a considerable tract, would indicate the scene of a desperate struggle with the Indians. Journey of the Dead is an appropriate name for this desert and every few miles we would pass some locality of which a blood-curdling story would be told. One, on our second day, where a heap of rocks, a natural formation, stood close beside the road, was shown to me as a point where a lieutenant had met his death by carelessly riding in advance of his train. Arrived opposite the rocks, a Navajo had dashed out between him and the wagons. The lieutenant dismounted, got behind his horse and began firing. The Indian also dismounted and stood behind his pony as a shelter. When the sixth shot had been fired, the Indian mounted, rode up to the officer, killed and scalped him and galloped away, waving his gory trophy defiantly at the infantry guard of the train![2]

The regulations governing the issue of water to our men and animals were that each man should receive three quarts daily and

2. Curtis was probably referring to the death of Lieutenant Ludam A. Bargie of the 1st New Mexico Cavalry. He was killed on June 16, 1863, near Point of Rocks on the Jornada. Bargie's body was mutilated by the Apaches who cut out his heart and carried off his head. Bargie's body was recovered and buried at Las Cruces, although later removed to Washington, D. C. The pile of stones that Curtis saw may have been for the express mail carrier who was killed on that same day. *Condition of Indian Tribes*, appendix 119, 249; *Sacramento Daily Union*, August 19, 1863.

each horse and mule one pail full. The scene at the rear of the tanks when the water was being drawn was a curious one. The men were present with all kinds of vessels to receive their allowance and mingled with them were the animals, thrusting their noses eagerly through them towards the water, yielding their places only upon being severely belabored and constantly renewing their attempt.

Our animals suffered more from thirst than those of the Mexican trains, on account of the difference in our methods of traveling. We left camp at three o'clock in the morning, mostly marching until noon, the men moving slowly during the first hours, quickening their pace with daylight and lagging as the heat increased towards noon. The dogs of the men and officers were the greatest sufferers for want of water and were frequent sharers of their masters' allowance.

Scattered over the plain were many palm trees, with shaggy sides made from the dying leaves which clung closely to the trunk, making them as combustible as a pile of pine shavings. In the dark hours of the early morning, it was a frequent amusement of some of the younger officers to set fire to these trees, so that our line of march was often lighted by a dozen columns of fire.

I rode my mule Zebra, but I had such a miserable saddle that the girth cut against her forelegs until there were deep gashes under the shoulder. To prevent further mutilation, after I discovered the state of things, I used to leave the girths very loose, getting my servant to hold down one side of the saddle while I mounted on the other. As we went at a walk, there was no particular danger of a fall from a loose saddle, but whenever the command halted for a rest, I would start to dismount in the usual way and no sooner would my weight rest in the left stirrup than the saddle would slide quickly under the mule's belly. I would fall on my back and present a tableau of a sprawling officer, clinging to a bridle rein, at the other end of which was a kicking and frantic mule. My servant would run up and turn the saddle; I would arise, receive the pleasantries of my comrades and get ready for next time. That these falls occurred pretty often may be gathered from this circumstance. One of the acting lieutenants, William Mills, used to walk some distance in advance of the command, sometimes getting nearly a mile ahead.[3]

3. William Mills enlisted as a private in the 5th Infantry on October 28, 1858, and was promoted through the ranks to first sergeant prior to receiving a commission as first

We soon noticed that whenever the column halted, he halted also and without looking round. At camp, Barr asked him how he knew the command halted, when he was often too far away to hear the command. "Oh," he replied, "I always hear Curtis drop."

Company K's bear came to the end of its existence on the third day of the march. It rode in the feedbox, behind the wagon in which the men's knapsacks and haversacks were stored. In one of the haversacks was a loaf of bread and some bacon, which the bear smelled through the tailboard of the wagon and determined to make its own. It rose on its hind legs, reached over the rear of the wagon, and fished out the tempting haversack. As the bear drew the haversack out of the wagon, it fell into the road. The bear immediately jumped down after it and the chain with which the animal was fastened to the wagon being short, its weight snapped it and left it free.

There were two or three men in the company who dared approach the bear and they were in advance, with the main body. All the wagons passed and no one dared attempt securing it. At last the rear guard came up and some of the men approached Bruin with a view of reclaiming it, but a warning growl made them keep a proper distance and leave it alone with the contents of the haversack. Next evening, while we were in camp, a Mexican train passed us about six o'clock and on the side of the wagon top we saw fastened a fresh bear skin and four quarters of bear meat. Upon inquiring of *Señor* Ochoa, for it was his train, we learned that he came upon the bear during the first hour after leaving his last camp and, finding that he had either got to leave or kill it, he chose to put a ball through it and get some fresh meat. No one regretted the bear's death; it had long been a bore and was tolerated simply because it had been so long in the company.

The third day, we reached the centre of the desert at eleven o'clock and camped near the depression where water gathered in the rainy season, now a sandy and verdureless region, with nothing to cast a shadow except an occasional soapweed about two feet high. As soon as we arrived, our animals were turned loose and the

---

lieutenant in the 16th Infantry on February 19, 1863. Wounded at Chickamauga, Mills served for a time on the staff of General George H. Thomas. Promoted to captain on February 13, 1866, he was transferred to the 2nd Infantry on April 17, 1869. One report said of Mills, "He was a rugged looking man, a correct type of the army officer." One of the oldest captains in the service, Mills led his troops on the long trek from Fort Omaha to the Pine Ridge Agency in South Dakota where he died on December 30, 1890. *Omaha World Herald*, December 31, 1890; *General Orders, 1891,* 54.

herders began driving them slowly along to the water springs, six miles distant, taking the kegs with them for a supply for the men. The day was fearfully sultry and soldiers and officers crept under the wagons for a shade, filling every available space and still leaving many out in the sun, for we were marching without tents. I took my saddle and blanket and perching the former on a soapweed, spread the latter over all, constructing a shade beneath which I could draw my head and breast and leave the rest of my body in the sun. In this position I dropped into an uneasy slumber of perhaps an hour and was awakened by a loud shout from the commanding officer, hearing his last words, "I am astonished, sir, to see that you do not know any better than that! You might frighten a sensitive person into insanity!" Crawling out of my shade, I saw standing near me a foolish-looking lieutenant with a huge, dead rattlesnake in his hand, which he had evidently intended to draw over my face when interrupted by the captain. Some desire to emulate Bristol's joke at the *adobe* wall had led him to try the snake on me.

At this camp, one of the men's horses was bitten by a rattlesnake and died from the effects. A soldier, asleep in the sun and somewhat under the influence of some whiskey which he had stolen from the doctor's medical stores, was fly-blown in the nostrils and the next day sneezed fat maggots from his nose. The doctor did not know how to treat the case, but our veteran captain, who had served in Texas and had seen many such cases, suggested an injection of calomel, which soon effected a cure.

When we were on the last day's march before reaching the river and two days from Fort Craig, Captain Updegraff detailed me to ride ahead, with the news of our approach. Lieutenant George McDermott, however, requested me to allow him to go in my stead and the captain allowed the exchange.[4] McDermott took my mule and started, leaving me his horse. One reason for detailing me was because my mule was in a very fresh condition, evidently not suffering from the short supply of water, while the horses were generally used up.

4. George McDermott enlisted in the 5th Infantry as a private on November 8, 1850, re-enlisted on September 8, 1855, as a sergeant and re-enlisted again on July 8, 1860, as a first sergeant. He was discharged on January 4, 1863, to accept a commission as second lieutenant in that regiment. Promoted to first lieutenant on July 14, 1864, McDermott died in Washington, D. C. on June 21, 1878. George McDermott Military Service Records; Heitman, *Historical Register* 1: 662; Headstones Provided for Deceased Union Civil War Veterans, 1879–1903.

McDermott's horse was a huge fellow and the saddle was so wide that it soon gave me a strain in my groin, so that I was laid up for some weeks after I arrived at Fort Craig. I rode much of the time with both legs on the same side of the saddle, but there were so many occasions where it was necessary for me to ride in the ordinary way and the pace of the horse was so hard, that I got badly used up before I reached the fort.

When we reached the river, the animals were loosed and all plunged into the stream for a "good square drink." My horse went into the water and out eleven times in ten minutes, each time apparently drinking a barrel of water, but as he could not hold so much, I suppose he was simply nosing the grateful fluid.

Upon our arrival at Fort Craig, we learned that the other companies of the 5th Infantry were at Peralta, several days march up the river. I was detailed September 4th as Assistant Adjutant General of the Southern District of New Mexico, performing the duties while upon sick report until the 11th, when, by the advice of the surgeon, I applied for permission to join my company at Peralta. The surgeon had been ordered to the States and I could ride with him and receive his care.

Chapter 13

From Peralta to Fort Marcy

I arrived at Peralta on or about the 16th of September and found the portion of the 5th Infantry which had turned back at Cañon Alamosa, July 26th, encamped in a large *bosque* near the river. The report was current that an order was out for the regiment to go to the States and that, as soon as the companies from below should join, we were to take up the line of march. This news was received with enthusiasm by officers and men, for all looked upon the East as the scene of great battles and great opportunities. Our regiment had among its officers some of the best military men of the army, men who only wanted the chance to attain prominence and reap the rewards of gallant service and fine abilities. How often at the time, and many times since, have I heard the regret expressed that Henry Selden, William Lewis, David Brotherton, Samuel Archer and others could not have had the fortune to take a part in the campaigns of the East. No one seemed to doubt but they would have attained eminence. At this time, it is known that the regiment was really ordered east, but the general commanding our department was loath to lose his only body of Regulars. Accordingly, he kept us in camp at Peralta while he sent his remonstrances to

Washington and, at last, assured a revocation of the order. Of this we knew nothing for many long months.

About a week after my arrival, Captain Updegraff, with his battalion, marched into camp and we all moved into another section of the *bosque*, where we were told we should remain all winter. This camp was shaded by immense cottonwoods, the ground was perfectly level and the grass was velvety and like that of a well-kept lawn. Every morning after guard mounting, company drill was held for an hour and a half and in the afternoon battalion drill for the same length of time. It was the game season and our Nimrods, with the fine dogs of the command, were out every day scouring the country for geese, ducks, quail, partridges and sandhill cranes.

The fall was beautiful beyond description; not a cloud flecked the sky the whole time; the air was delightful through the days and the evenings were just cool enough to make the campfires in front of the officers' line of tents enjoyable. There we used to sit on our camp stools to a late hour, listening to the tales of the seniors and the songs of the juniors, or speculating on our chances should the regiment go east, or perhaps reviewing the latest items of news from the scene of war and predicting the next intelligence.

Referring again to the shooting of game, I must tell of Bristol's exploit. This officer was the regimental joker, the man who always kept the mess tables in a roar and spent a great part of his time in planning and playing practical jokes. Like most men of his kind, he could never appreciate a joke at his own expense, getting angry invariably at the first scent of any fun poked at himself. One day Bristol concluded he would go out shooting and for some three hours the notes of preparation which he sounded would have got a whole regiment into the field. Guns, ammunition, pouches, hunting suit, lunch, liquor flask were all collected; inspections and selections were made; the propriety of taking a pack mule to bring in the game was canvassed; all the dogs of the command were paraded before his tent, their merits discussed, and two of them, a spaniel and setter, selected.

Everybody in camp got excited over the preparations and no one doubted but something extraordinary was to be done. At last Bristol left. The day went on until evening like all other days, but just as the sun was going down, our jester returned and flung down before the campfire in front of his tent half a dozen ducks, which to my eye looked suspiciously like tame birds from some rancheman's yard.

"Aren't those domestic ducks, Bristol?" I asked.

"Domestic grandmother!" he exclaimed. "No! I laid for those fellows two hours before I got a shot, in a pond five miles from here, and I took the whole of them with both barrels. There were several others wounded, but these were all the dogs brought out."

While he was still going on at some length in describing his day's adventures, a rancheman, riding on a raw-boned pacer, came into camp, approached the group who were listening to the captain, dismounted and, holding the extreme end of the lariat in his left hand, advanced to Bristol and laid the right on his shoulder. The man was a German in all his features and his words immediately corroborated the impression.

"Vot vor you kills mine ducks, hey? Vat vor you sneaks come round mine bond and shoots all mine leedle ducks, hey?"

"Kill your ducks!" exclaimed the astonished captain. "These are wild ducks."

"Vild ducks! So is mine horse vat stands dare vild," shouted the irate German. "I zee you creep, creep, c-r-e-e-p ze bond-side 'long. I go round to vatch. I hear ze bang, bang. I zee ze tam togs zwin ze ducks out ze vater. Ah, mine boor leedle ducks," poking them with his feet in a most disconsolate manner. "It is too vicked, ain't it?"

By this time, most of the officers had gathered round the campfire, the oldsters laughing immoderately, and teased the crestfallen joker unmercifully. The youngsters enjoyed the situation hugely, but said nothing, having a wholesome dread of Bristol's resources in the way of retaliation. After a few moments, the captain took the irate rancheman to one side and purchased his silence. What became of the ducks I never knew, for they did not appear on the mess table and none of us dared stir up Bristol's anger by saying "ducks."

As fall advanced and the days grew cooler, water began to ooze up through the surface of the ground and gradually encroach upon the camp, until it was found necessary to move. When this was decided, it was also determined to go into regular winter quarters and, in order to carry out this plan, the whole command was sent into a bottom, near the river bank, to cut *terruños* (turfs). Each company was in the charge of an officer and was armed with axes and spades. Long parallel lines, eighteen inches apart, were cut through the thick clayey turf and then cross lines were cut nine inches apart, the pieces were then loosened and raised by the shovels and piled in long tiers, four feet high. Each *terron* averaged six inches in thickness. It took four days continuous and hard labor for the men to cut and pile enough of these turfs for the purpose for which they were intended. When enough were cut, they were hauled to the ground selected for our winter camp.

The camp had been laid out in streets and all the sites of the men's and officers' tents indicated by stakes set up in the ground. The men's huts were built first and were of the same size on the ground as an ordinary wall tent. The walls were built of *terrones* in the height of six feet, laid in mortar made of the earth in the vicinity and a wall tent was pitched on top for a roof. In the back end of each hut was a wide, open fireplace and in front was a wooden door, hung on hinges. No windows were necessary, as the canvas roof admitted the light.

The officers' huts were built of the same material, but were circular in shape and the roof was made by pitching a Sibley tent on the wall. To give this steadiness, no centre pole was used, but three stout spars were stood up like a tripod, the feet outside the hut and the upper ends meeting and lashed together over the centre. The top of the Sibley tent was suspended beneath the centre of the tripod. These huts were fifteen feet in diameter, with a fireplace and door like the men's. The *terruños* and the mortar, in which they were laid, were so strongly impregnated with alkali that the huts, when finished and dry, looked as if covered with frost.

The floors were made by pouring in water, digging up the surface and mixing it to the consistency of mud, adding enough other earth to raise the whole a foot higher than the outside surface. This mud was smoothed to a perfect level and when dry made a hard and solid floor.

When everything was completed, we got our furniture into our houses, erected our penates, built a fire upon our hearths and settled ourselves for a comfortable winter. Young officers are not unlike college boys in their sports and tendency to mischief, so we had some rich times in these circular huts. One lieutenant invited us all into his tent to witness a circus—the shape of the hut suggesting the idea, I suppose—and we were surprised to find ringmaster, clown and pretty much everything but the horses in the arena.

Navajo captives at Bosque Redondo. Courtesy Palace of the Governors Photo Archives (NMHA/DCA), Negative # 028534.

But alas for our prospective comfort. On the 9th of November, an order came for A Company to go to the Bosque Redondo on the Rio Pecos and D and F Companies to Santa Fé. All the time we had been engaged in establishing this winter camp, I had overheard the men under my supervision growling and saying we would never occupy the quarters after they were built. By inquiry, I learned that it is an old superstition of soldiers that if they are set to work to build quarters, plant a garden or do anything for their comfort, they will go away and someone else will come and enjoy the fruits of their labor. Although this has often proved true, I have known many instances where it did not. In this particular case, it was true, in a degree, for three companies left, after living but a short time in the quarters, but the others remained until spring.

The breaking up of our winter camp was not our greatest disappointment; the order showed us conclusively that our chance of going east was at an end, for this time at least. So long as we remained together, we knew there was a chance; as soon as we separated, we knew our chance was over.

We left Peralta early on the morning after receiving our order, with the regimental band. All the officers were mounted and some of us very badly. Zebra had been left at Fort Craig, so that I had to make other arrangements for this march. The horse which I secured must have belonged to the same stock which produced the steed of Don Quixote, the Knight de la Mancha, but anything was preferable to walking for I had not entirely recovered from my ride over the Jornada. Lieutenant Benjamin Taylor, Jr., of D Company, was as poorly mounted as myself and bestrode a horse whose architectural anatomy was quite equal to mine.[1] From some bond of sympathy between our animals and a desire on our part to contrast their merits, we rode together.

Our first halt was at Albuquerque, where, it is perhaps needless for me to say, I lost no time in calling upon the young Mexican ladies to whom I had been introduced by Judge Tompkins. A *baile* had been arranged for us by the officers of the garrison and all the officers attended it, as a matter of course.

1. Benjamin Taylor, Jr. enlisted in the 1st Connecticut Artillery on May 22, 1861, and was a sergeant when he was commissioned a second lieutenant on March 1, 1862. He received an appointment as second lieutenant in the 5th Infantry on February 19, 1862. Promoted to first lieutenant on December 1, 1863, Taylor resigned on September 28, 1865. He died in Glastonbury, Connecticut, on January 24, 1873. Heitman, *Historical Register* 1: 945; *Hartford Daily Courant*, January 25, 1873; Benjamin Taylor, Jr. Pension Records.

We were to march at reveille next morning. I went to the stable as soon as I was awake, to look after Rosinante, but found nothing but the bridle, saddle and lariat. That gallant steed was missing. While I was commiserating myself at the prospect of marching on foot, Lieutenant Taylor came up with the intelligence that his horse was gone also. We sent men to look through the streets, corrals and grazing places, taking part in the search ourselves, but the hour approached for us to leave and, when the bugle sounded the "Fall in," I joined the column without my horse. Taylor got permission to remain behind with our servants, to look for the beasts, and overtake us at the next encampment.

I set out on foot. Several of the men, who owned horses and mules, offered them to me, but I would not accept them, preferring to walk to compelling them to do so. After I had marched about ten miles, Captain Selden, the regimental commander, came back and informed me that he had a horse along which he was taking to the department commander at Santa Fé and that I might ride him if I could find a saddle and bridle. This I was not long in doing among the teamsters of our train and was soon mounted on a good horse.

That night we encamped at the town of Bernalillo, on the estate of Don Juliano Perea, a *rico* (rich person) of the territory.[2] About sundown, Lieutenant Taylor appeared, riding my horse, and soon after the two servants came in mounted on the other. The animals had been found two miles out of Albuquerque, in the herd of a *ranchero*.

The rainy season was now fairly upon us. There had been an occasional drizzle while we were working at our winter quarters and during our march to Bernalillo, but now the sky was completely obscured with clouds and showed every appearance of a storm. The soldiers, accustomed to rainless skies, turned in without pitching their tents, making down their beds between the rows of what had been a large cornfield. I looked out of my tent after I had extinguished my lamp, preparatory to going to bed and stood for a moment looking at the long lines of campfires, glowing in the misty darkness, around which a few soldiers still stood smoking their evening pipes. The rain was already beginning to fall and its patter could be heard upon the tent as I closed and tied the entrance.

2. When Curtis refers to Juliano Perea he probably means Julian Perea, "one of the wealthiest merchants and ranchers in New Mexico." Moorhead, *New Mexico's Royal Road*, 109; Bernalillo County, 1860 Census.

Next morning, I awoke at reveille to find our campground flooded with water. The soil had turned into a thick and pasty mud, which stuck in heavy clods to the feet. Blankets and tents were saturated with water, the men were wet to the skin, the horses and mules were humped with the wet and cold. In fact, everything was in a high degree dreary and cheerless. Only by great effort could fire enough be procured to make coffee for the men before we took the road. The breakfast was of hardtack and uncooked bacon. I continued to ride the general's horse and turned mine over to my servant. At the town of Algodones we halted for a short rest and purchased wood for our next encampment. The people hospitably opened their houses for the men and officers to warm themselves at the fires.

We continued our march after half an hour's halt and camped for the night opposite the Indian pueblo of San Felipe.[3] This town is on the western shore of the Rio Grande, on a narrow belt of land between the river and a cliff which overhangs the town from a height of nearly 200 feet. The space between cliff and river widens gradually into a large, arable interval below the town, which is highly cultivated by the Indians. Up the river, the space narrows until the perpendicular wall of the height is flush with the river. On the top of the cliff at this point are the ruins of an old pueblo, a tower of which stands on the extreme point, evidently a lookout. It had not ceased to rain all day and where our tents were pitched, the rain froze upon them as it fell.

We bought three beeves of the Indians soon after reaching camp and butchered them before supper. The dry wood, procured at Algodones and drawn in the wagons out of the rain, made good fires and steak was soon sizzling along the whole line.

Next day I was officer of the day and marched behind with the guard. The rain of the previous day had changed into a fine snow and the wind now sharp and cold from the north. It was too cold to ride on horseback and I walked most of the day, leading my horse by the lariat. A short distance above San Felipe, we turned

3. San Felipe Pueblo was originally at the top of a mesa located six miles north of the confluence of the Jemez and Rio Grande Rivers., but early in the eighteenth century the inhabitants moved to the bottom where they built the Katishtya Pueblo, a structure two stories high, accessible only by ladders. Residents relied on agriculture and the pasturing of animals for their subsistence. The pueblo's population in 1860 was estimated to be 360 and their land claim was almost 35,000 acres. Strong, "San Felipe Pueblo," 390, 393–95; *California Farmer and Journal of Useful Sciences*, June 19, 1863; White, *Pueblo of San Filipe*, 10.

away from the river for Santa Fé and began the more rapid ascent that leads to that place. In my notebook I find I indulged in some speculations when I reached the top of the hill, from which the last glimpse of the Rio Grande may be had, as to whether I should ever see that muddy stream again. "I am not sorry to have seen it, but I should be sorry to see it again," is the sentence which closed the entry of the 16th day of November. In the light of the fact that I have crossed the stream seven times since, seeing it for the last time as I marched to the west on my way to Arizona and the Pacific, that entry is rather amusing.

Twenty-five miles of marching in the bitter cold brought us at last to the ranche of Don Miguel Pino, where I found the officers had ordered a supper to be prepared for us in the house.[4] This supper was particularly acceptable after the cold march, so I retired to my mattress in my tent tranquil and contented and slept entirely oblivious of the fierce gale which leveled quite a number of tents in the command. I knew nothing of the night's disasters until reveille. As officer of the day, I ought to have made the rounds after midnight, but sleep was too much for me and I was obliged to confess myself delinquent in the morning.

With daylight the weather moderated, although it continued to snow all day. The snow, however, was soft and feathery, only annoying because it balled the animals' feet. In a country where there were no fences or telegraph poles along the roadsides, it was exceedingly difficult to keep in the track after the snow had gotten deep. The adjutant had to march in advance, with a pocket compass and a detail of men, to "feel out" the road for us. The animals, in their desire to avoid marching into the wind, always showed a tendency to turn gradually away from it if left to themselves and only by the greatest and constant effort were we kept from wandering over the plains.

4. A member of the prominent Pino family of New Mexico, Miguel Pino was commissioned colonel of the 2nd New Mexico on August 19, 1861, and was mustered out on May 31, 1862. Pino served in the legislature and as a judge after leaving military service. An obituary captured his spirit: "He knew the disadvantages under which his countrymen had been born and circumstances had placed them, and was ever keenly alive to wrongs and oppression, whenever inflicted upon the poorest of his native countrymen, by any one, born and educated under more favorable circumstances. This was natural to his proud and lofty nature, and a high merit in his character." Pino died in Santa Fe on June 20, 1867. Miguel E. Pino Military Service Records; *Daily Alta California*, March 25, 1864; *Santa Fe Weekly* Gazette, June 29, 1867.

It is a custom of troops when entering a garrison or large town to halt a considerable distance from it, get out the full dress, burnish the arms and equipment and make a showy entrance. We had talked this over as we marched up the river and were somewhat disappointed that the snowstorm had prevented our display. We were actually in the streets of Santa Fé before we knew it; the snow was so thick we had not been able to see a house until we were close upon it. We plodded along the streets and through the *plaza* spiritless and dejected, our footsteps and the wheels of our train so muffled in the snow that no one turned out to see us and no one saw us except an occasional street passer.

Arriving at Fort Marcy, we found there were ample quarters for the men, but only enough for half of the officers had been repaired since they were burned out by the Texans at the time of their retreat. Captain Selden took quarters on the public *plaza* and the regimental quartermaster and lieutenants of F Company, which included me, found quarters near the post in the house of *Padre* José Manuel Gallegos, a priest of the Roman Catholic Church who had been excommunicated for "keeping a woman" and raising a family of four children.[5] This former priest was a man of excellent abilities and had been to the United States Congress twice and to the Territorial Legislature several times, but I think there is little doubt but what he was a scamp. It does not look well for the morals of New Mexico that this unworthy priest could always be elected by a large majority whenever put in nomination for an office. He was not recognized by the clergy and it can be said to their credit they always opposed him.

The *Padre*, as he was always called in Santa Fé, received us with Spanish courtesy and gave us excellent rooms in his extensive house, which with the court extended over a couple of acres.

5. Padre José Manuel Gallegos had studied for the priesthood at Durango College and was ordained in 1840. Assigned to Albuquerque, Gallegos became immensely popular in the community, but proved to be a rather atypical priest. He liked to drink, gamble, smoke cigars, and ostentatiously ride around the city as he courted politicians, army officers, and traders. He even set tongues wagging when he took in a woman with three children who had previously been a mistress for several Mexican officers. Shortly after Bishop Lamy arrived in New Mexico, he replaced Gallegos who then turned to politics. In 1853 he was elected territorial delegate to the U. S. Congress although he could not speak English and rules prevented his use of an interpreter during floor debates. Gallegos moved to Santa Fe in 1857 and died there on April 21, 1875, "the most universally known man in the Territory." Bryan, *Albuquerque*, 59–61.

Our life during the winter of 1863 was very pleasant. The civil authorities and the military were many of them married and a few had daughters of the society age. There were also a few American traders with families. These, with some of the best Mexican families and those of the Jewish merchants, made up a mixed society, to be sure, but an exceedingly pleasant one, nevertheless, and where the prevailing language was English. The ordinary *bailes* and *fandangos* were of almost nightly occurrence, notably so immediately after payday, when the soldiers were flush and anxious to get rid of their money.[6] A theater was opened in a large hall, the actors were from the California Volunteers and the Regulars, the lady actors being the wives of the soldiers, with a drummer boy in petticoats, now and then, in a subordinate part. An ordnance sergeant had married a wife to whom all the officers instinctively raised their hats and she was the "leading lady" in the troupe. The scenery was painted in a highly artistic manner by a sergeant of my company and the whole thing was placed under the direction of Lieutenant Taylor.

6. One New Mexican correspondent described how soldiers' pay was accepted: "Small change is exceedingly scarce in these parts. It is difficult to obtain gold or silver coin in exchange for Treasury notes or 'green-backs.' In fact, the Mexican people have been so unaccustomed to the use of paper money—it never having circulated here before—that they are extremely cautious about taking it. The Israelite merchants partake of the same feeling, and so the 'poor soldiers' are fleeced on every occasion, when they present a $5, $10, or $20 bill in payment of articles which their necessities may require." *Philadelphia Inquirer,* November 18, 1862.

Chapter 14

Quartermaster Duty

Duty at Santa Fé was mostly local guard duty with the usual drills, varied occasionally by escort service to some distant post or a dash after Indians who had made a raid upon some herdsman's flock. During the time I was in the city, I saw none of the shooting and stabbing which is said to have distinguished its hot-blooded and jealous inhabitants. Under martial law, a provost guard, detailed from the infantry companies, patrolled the streets night and day to keep order, searching all strangers who entered the *bailes*, *fandangos* and gambling places for concealed weapons, so that no New England village could be more quiet or peaceful than this Mexican city. Formerly, a pistol shot or a dirk thrust had been the most frequent cause of death among the male population and such occurrences caused less remark in the community than pugilistic encounters in the Eastern States and were far less likely to be followed by legal punishment. I saw but one quarrel at a *fandango*, those fruitful places for starting quarrels, and that was a fist fight between a gambler and a Jew over a Mexican girl, unless I except the attempt on the part of one *señorita* to stab another, through jealousy, at a dance on the previous Christmas Eve.

Shortly after my arrival at Fort Marcy, I was made quartermaster of the post and in this capacity had the rebuilding of the officers' quarters and the corral assigned me by the quartermaster of the department. The *adobes* used for the purpose were obtained by demolishing several old buildings on the military reserve and a few belonging to the civil authority, which were given us if we would tear them down. The principal of these last was the old *palacio de justicia* (courthouse), which stood at the south-eastern angle of the *plaza*, partially obstructing one of the streets leading out of that corner. It was formerly an old commissary storehouse belonging to the Mexican military garrison, was about one hundred feet long, twenty-five feet wide and one story high. At the west end of the governor's palace was a small building known as the *calabozo* (municipal lockup), where culprits for minor offences were confined or prisoners on trial at the courthouse were kept during the sitting of court. This building also was torn down. How old it was no one knew. It was standing in 1692.

It is difficult for persons living in a changeable climate to understand how a simple mud building can last nearly 200 years in a good state of repair. A kiln-burned brick house will begin to show seams and cracks long before this time, if it is so fortunate as to last so long. The *adobe* of which the New Mexican house is built is made of the very earth upon which the house stands. The mud is made by running a stream of water on to the ground, shaping the *adobes* (eighteen inches long, nine wide and four thick) and laying them in the wall with the same kind of mud of which they are made. The *adobes* taken from the *calabozo* had hardened so that they rang like bricks when struck with a trowel.

From these old buildings, the corral walls, storehouses, shops, stables and granaries were all built, the entire labor being performed by the men of the infantry companies. On the ground from which many of the buildings were removed, the commanding officer directed a post garden to be laid out, appointing me in charge and Private Hoey as gardener, with permission to detail extra help during the weeding and hoeing seasons. The space cleared consisted of about four acres in the very heart of the town, the fort being on one side of it and the public square on the other. A close board fence about eight feet high was erected all around the garden, leaving but one entrance, on the side of the fort.

All agricultural operations in New Mexico depend upon irrigation for their success. A water ditch flowed along the north side of the garden, between it and the rear of the soldiers' quarters. From this, we turned on water enough to saturate the soil so that it could be plowed and harrowed, for no impression can be made on the earth in New Mexico in a dry state, and in a few days all the seed was in the ground.

In a short time, all the plants were up and Hoey called on me to get the water turned into the ditch for our use. Accordingly, I called upon the *maestro de las acequias* (master of the water ditches) and asked that the water be furnished us for an hour the next day. With great politeness, he assured me that the water was entirely at my service and should be sent down at the time desired. I gave no more thought to the subject, thinking that, as the man had promised, the water would come, so kept busy with other concerns until two days had elapsed, when Hoey again called upon me and complained that the plants were perishing in the parched earth for want of water. I went again to the *maestro*, was again received with the greatest deference and assured that the water should come on the morrow.

Next day the water did come and Hoey began watering the garden, but right in the midst of his operations a farmer from below the town made his appearance, said the water belonged to him on that day and that I was infringing the law by taking it. Remembering the promise of the *maestro*, I told Hoey to go on with his work and the result was a constable put in his appearance and threatened me with arrest if I continued to break the water law. Hoey had by this time flooded that portion of the garden which most needed water, so I promised to obey the law and withdrew, cautioning Hoey on no account to touch the water again unless he knew positively that it belonged to me. That very afternoon, he put a big stone in the ditch, checking the flow so that at least a third of the water turned aside into the garden. The farmer caught him at the theft and I was obliged to put Hoey in the guardhouse. Along in the evening I let him out again, for I could but sympathize with the fellow in his difficulties and admire the interest he showed in the garden. That very night, as I returned from a *fandango* after one o'clock, I heard voices in the garden and, walking up to the fence, peeped through a wide crack and saw the persistent

Hoey and another soldier industriously irrigating the soil. I walked up to the ditch and found a small stream of water had been turned out of it. I could not make up my mind to arrest the culprit, but went to my quarters and never let him know I saw him at his thieving practices.

Before I tell my further adventures at gardening, I must explain some of the laws governing the supply of water. The Chico River flows nearly through the centre of Santa Fé, running from the mountain range, ten miles distant on the east, downward to the Rio Grande, twenty-five miles distant on the west. About a mile above the town, two ditches lead out of the river and run parallel to its course on each side for several miles below the town. On our side of the river, there was but two-sevenths as much land under cultivation as upon the other, giving us, in consequence, the supply of water for but two days in the week and sending the whole down on the other side during the other five. In the very driest days of midsummer, the whole body of water would be turned from the river into the *acequias* and would not more than fill a ditch a foot deep and three feet wide. The supply of water was regulated by law, each landholder along the river being entitled to a certain share, according to the number of acres under cultivation. The labor of irrigating the land went on day and night all summer.

As our land was a new piece, newly brought under cultivation, and as we were Regulars, "with no rights the country was bound to respect," we had not been put on the water list. Of course, all this time I was ignorant of the existence of any rules and did not suppose but there was plenty of water for everybody, every day in the week. After Hoey's midnight irrigation, the *rancheros* kept a watch on the *acequia* so that he could not take the water and it was not long before he was after me with complaints that the vegetables were drying up again. I called on the *maestro* three times, eliciting many promises as usual, with the usual non-fulfillment. After the third promise, getting vexed at the situation, I took twelve men, armed with muskets, and marched them up the *acequia*. Wherever a small ditch turned out of the main one, I placed a man on guard. At the head, I turned in the whole current and placed a man to see that it ran in as long as I should want it and then went back to the post.

The water ran gurgling, babbling, purling and sparkling—and all the rest of the pretty expressions popular to the field—all the afternoon and Hoey and his aide, with spade and hoe, guided it along the withering rows and beds of vegetables, until everything had been watered finely. Then I took off my guard and sat down on the piazza of the quarters to contemplate the result of my labors. In the midst of my felicitations, a constable appeared with a writ for my arrest in Spanish. I could not read it, so went with him to the *plaza* to find an American merchant who could interpret it to me.

Finding the merchant, he read the document and I learned from it that I had smashed half a dozen Territorial laws into smithers. I had stolen water, diverted water, wasted water and done everything to water but drink it. I had abused, maltreated and endangered the life of the truthful old Januarius, who presided over the water works, and finally I had headed an armed insurrection. I began to feel as if hanging was entirely too good for me, when Don Simon Delgado, the *alcalde* (justice of the peace) before whom I had been cited, appeared and, before proceeding to try and sentence me, asked how I came to break the law.[1] I told him the whole story, from beginning to end, when the old fellow was gracious enough to laugh heartily at my mistakes and difficulties and tell me if I would pay the constable for his trouble, he would tear up the writ and let me off, confident that I would not repeat the offence. Of course I agreed to this and I had the satisfaction of learning soon after that a new *maestro de las acequias* was appointed, the authorities having learned a thing or two about him in connection with my adventure. I had no further difficulty about water and we had an excellent garden.

In my office I employed Sergeant Samuel L. Compston and Private Raymond Landy as quartermaster sergeant and quartermaster clerk.[2] The latter was known throughout the regiment as

1. Described as "a noble type of the fine old Spanish gentleman," Simon Delgado belonged to one of the territory's most prominent families. A prosperous rancher and businessman, he also served in the legislature. A newspaper notice said of Delgado: "He was a man upon whom you could depend at any and all times, and no one, even his political enemies, ever spoke of him without saying 'Don Simon is a good man.'" He died in Santa Fe on June 19, 1867. *Denver Rocky Mountain News*, April 5, 1864; *Daily Alta California*, March 25, 1864; *Santa Fe Weekly Gazette*, June 29, 1867.

2. Samuel L. Compston enlisted on August 30, 1856, as a private in the 5th Infantry and rose through the ranks to become quartermaster sergeant of the regiment, a position he held when promoted to second lieutenant on March 19, 1863. Compston died of disease at Fort Stanton, New Mexico, on October 31, 1863. A native of Newfoundland, at the age of nineteen Raymond Landy enlisted in the 5th Infantry on October 27, 1854,

a man of excellent abilities and education, evidently a scholar, and he had been once or twice told by Captain Selden that, if he would be temperate in his habits, his name should be sent in for a commission. But the man's intemperate habits were so thoroughly established that he could not overcome them. During the year that he was in my office, he would remain sober until my papers were finished and dispatched on the 20th of the month. On the next morning he would start off on a big drunk which would last until he was placed in the guardhouse, where he would remain until it was necessary to complete the papers of the next month and he would be released only to repeat the same line of conduct every month in the year. This man ended his life in a tragic manner, as I shall shortly relate.

Sergeant Compston soon showed himself a man of superior education by the manner in which he carried on the correspondence of the office. He took this entirely out of my hands, so that I was obliged to give simple directions only, and he would draught a letter perfect in every way, to which I had only to add my signature. Owing to the strict formalities of military usage, there can be no intimate intercourse between officer and man. For this reason there had never been any conversation between the sergeant and me, except of a strictly official character. I had made up my mind as to his ability from his letters and gentlemanly manner.

One evening, as I sat on the portal of the officers' quarters, Sergeant Compston approached me and asked if he might consult me in regard to a matter personal to himself. I replied in the affirmative and he then asked me if I thought it would be any use for him to apply for a commission in the New Mexican Volunteers. I replied that I thought he had much better apply for a commission in the Regulars. When I said this, he turned quickly upon his heel and walked rapidly away. This was not intended to show me disrespect, as the reader has probably seen, but was caused by the man's first thought of how utterly hopeless was such a proposition so far as he was concerned; that is, from his standpoint, for no one but himself knew the bitter disappointment of his youth, disappointments with which I afterward became well acquainted.

---

and reenlisted on September 1, 1859. He was murdered in Santa Fe on October 17, 1863, by Sergeant John L. Kennedy. Heitman, *Historical Register* 1: 319; *Albuquerque Weekly Press*, November 10, 1863; U. S. Army, Register of Enlistments, 1798–1914; *Rocky Mountain News*, December 16, 1863.

Perhaps a month went by and I heard nothing more of the sergeant's application for a commission, either in the Volunteers or Regulars. Thinking I might have discouraged him, in some way unknown to myself, I one day asked him why he did not make out his application for a commission in the Regulars. He replied that there was no hope for him in that direction. I answered, "An application can do you no harm and might do you much good. It can make you no worse off, certainly."

Next day he handed me an application written upon a sheet of foolscap, giving a history of his army records to date. Some experience had taught me that an application may be too lengthy. Accordingly, I handed back the paper, saying, "Put that all on one page." This remark seems to have been considered as a rebuff to the sergeant, for I heard nothing from him for nearly a month more, when I again gave him a hint that he had better forward his application without delay.

When I entered my office on the afternoon of the next day, I found the application lying on my table condensed to less than a page. I recommended it strongly, took it to the regimental and department commanders and secured their favorable endorsements, forwarding it to Washington the same day.[3]

Eighteen days after the application left, the non-commissioned officers of the garrison gave a ball at El Progresso Hall and Sergeant Compston attended. During the evening, a private soldier of my company, through jealousy of some attention the sergeant bestowed upon a Mexican girl, struck him and in consequence got knocked heels over head.[4] Burning with jealousy and a desire for revenge, the private went to the quarters for his musket to shoot the sergeant. On his way back to the ballroom, he met my clerk Landy, on one

3. The recommendation for Samuel Compston's promotion stated that he was "an honest, intelligent, and respectable man, an excellent non-comd officer and one who is thoroughly conversant with all the details of the service." However, this glowing recommendation was written on December 17, 1862, by First Lieutenant Martin Mullins, Company E, 5th Infantry, not Second Lieutenant Charles Curtis of Company F. Mullins's letter was endorsed by Captain Henry Selden, then commanding the regiment, and General James Carleton, commanding the District of New Mexico. Letters Received by the Adjutant General, Lieutenant Martin Mullins, December 17, 1862.

4. Sergeant John L. Kennedy was in his third enlistment in the 5th Infantry when he murdered Raymond Landy in Santa Fe on October 17, 1863. Kennedy was quickly apprehended and tried by a court martial, but inexplicably found not guilty. He rejoined his company at Los Valles Grandes and was discharged from there on December 14, 1863, by special order. U. S. Army, Registers of Enlistments, 1798–1914; *Rocky Mountain News*, December 16, 1863.

of his periodical sprees and, mistaking him for Compston, shot him dead and fled. I was in bed when the report of the killing was made, but I got up at once, turned out the command for inspection and then reported to the commanding officer. A picket was at once established entirely around Santa Fé and next day each house was searched until the murderer was found.

As I was standing near the coffin of the murdered Landy on the following afternoon (I was officer of the day and had the details of the funeral to attend to in the absence of the adjutant), Sergeant Compston was standing opposite, looking sadly at his old comrade and fellow clerk. At this moment, an orderly handed me a letter from the War Department, which I at once broke open and found to contain the appointment of Sergeant Samuel L. Compston to be a second lieutenant of the 5th Infantry. I handed it to the sergeant over the coffin of the dead drunkard, who had ended his days in such perfect keeping with his life. Could there be a more striking instance of what bad habits and good habits can bring men to, than was presented at that moment? A few days afterwards, I was still more forcibly struck with this reflection. In examining the effects of the late Private Landy, an old crumpled piece of parchment was found in the bottom of his knapsack, which, upon examination proved to be his degree of Bachelor of Arts from Princeton College. That very day, as I stood in a room of the officers' quarters, seeing Lieutenant Compston on his knees before his trunk, unpacking his effects, he suddenly threw a diploma towards me, saying, "Read that."

I read it and found it was a degree of Bachelor of Arts from Edinburgh University, Scotland. "Why did you never show this before?" I asked.

"It would hardly do for an enlisted man to show a degree to his comrades," was the reply, "and certainly not to the officers."

I leave the homily which might be preached from the lives of these two men to the readers. One thing was very clear to my mind. I had now neither sergeant nor clerk in my office and must look for a new detail.

In time I became possessed of all the chief points of interest in the history of Lieutenant Compston. He was the son of a prominent Presbyterian Doctor of Divinity in Londonderry, Ireland, a man not unknown in this country; had been sent to college, but his wildness had angered his father; and he had finally run away to America. He arrived during the financial depression of 1857 and, after trying various means to gain a living, enlisted in the fall of that year for five years in the 5th Infantry.

Santa Fé had been a fearful place in years past and recently, up to the days of the war, when the suspension of the writ of *habeas corpus* and other war measures had placed military law in the ascendant.[5] During our occupancy of the city, a provost marshal had been appointed and a provost guard, consisting of a sergeant and twelve men, patrolled the town day and night, armed with revolvers and policemen's "billies." No man was allowed to travel in the department without a pass, which he was obliged to show whenever he passed a military post. Every stranger who entered the city was required to report at the Provost Marshal's office, register his name and leave his arms on deposit until he should leave town. Whenever a *fandango* was held, the provost guard stood at the doors and searched all suspicious characters for weapons. The consequence of all these measures was that Santa Fé and New Mexico generally, from being a lawless, cut-throat community, became as quiet as Vermont.

But notwithstanding the fact that good order prevailed and that most persons were congratulating themselves that a strong hand held the reins, there were a few individuals who complained of red tape, the system of espionage, the lack of individual freedom, etc. and notable among these was Judge Joseph G. Knapp, an associate justice of the United States Court, who held court in the Third District of New Mexico, at Mesilla.[6] This gentleman let no

5. A New Yorker serving in the 1st Colorado shared an unflattering portrait of the New Mexicans at this time: "The native inhabitants are a low, indolent, cowardly and degraded race, they are far below the native Indians, both morally, intellectually and physically. It is nothing but one grand lazar house, a great festering sore, combining all the vices of the old Spaniards and the Indians with which they have become amalgamated without retaining any of their virtues. You may think this is over drawn but it is not. I think it would be as hard to find one virtuous woman in New Mexico as it was to find five righteous in Sodom and Gomorrah." *Jamestown Journal*, August 15, 1862.

6. J. Gillett Knapp graduated from Hobart College and moved to Wisconsin in 1835 to begin a career in the law. A colleague recalled that he "lacked judgment and discrimination" and "was also without tact and judgment in the trial of cases." Despite these shortcomings, he won a political appointment as U. S. District Judge for New Mexico Territory in 1862. As noted by Curtis, Judge Knapp believed that military authority was always subordinate to judicial authority, even during wartime. His colleague explained that at one point "he refused to state his name or business, and the commander ordered that he be tied up by the thumbs until he complied. Upon being released he felt that such an indignity to a high judicial officer should not be allowed to pass unnoticed and unpunished, and so instead of going to his destination to hold court, he went on to Washington to lay the matter before the president, and demanded

Judge J. Gillet Knapp. Courtesy Wisconsin Historical Society.

opportunity pass to attack the military rules of General Carleton and boast that "he should travel when he pleased and where he pleased, and without a pass from any military satrap."

One day in the summer of my first year in Santa Fé, Lieutenant John B. Randolph, a Virginian, was officer of the day and in visiting

that the military authorities be reprimanded, and the commanding general removed, but it resulted in his own removal instead." Knapp moved to Limona, Florida, in 1876, where he became a noted writer and agriculturalist, and died there on July 2, 1888. *Wisconsin State Horticultural Society*, 322–24; *Report of Wisconsin State Bar*, 147–49; *Springfield Republican*, July 21, 1888.

the guardhouse at noon he found a well-dressed gentleman confined there and learned that he had been brought up by the provost guard a short time before.[7] Mr. Randolph asked what the stranger's name was and learned that he would give none. In fact, he had been confined for refusing to report to the provost marshal and give his name. Mr. Randolph turned to the stranger and asked, "What is your name"

"I refuse to give it," was the answer.

"I must have it, to complete my register of prisoners," said the lieutenant.

"That is nothing to me," replied the stranger with great self-sufficiency. "I positively refuse to give my name to anyone under compulsion."

"You do?"

"I do!"

"Sergeant Cunningham, take that man over to the flagstaff, tie him up by the thumbs and raise him gently on his toes until he finds his name," said the imperturbable Randolph.[8]

"You dare not tie me up, sir!" exclaimed the stranger. "If you knew my name, you would not dare to commit such an indignity."

"Precisely. Give me your name and I will do nothing further. Refuse and I shall tie you up."

"I refuse."

"Do your duty, sergeant."

The sergeant took the prisoner to the flagstaff, tied a drum cord tightly round the thumbs below the middle joint, passed the string through a staple driven into the staff seven feet from the ground and proceeded to draw the stranger slowly upward. It did not take long before he yielded and consented to tell his name. As soon as he was released, he pulled a handful of letters from his pocket and

7. John B. Randolph enlisted as a private in the 3rd Battalion, District of Columbia Volunteers on April 15, 1861, and served three months. On August 5, 1861, he was commissioned second lieutenant in the 5th Infantry and was advanced to first lieutenant on October 26, 1861. Randolph resigned on April 30, 1863, but served as a sergeant in the Marine Corps from July 20, 1864, to November of 1866. He also served as a sergeant in the general service from September 13, 1873, to January 1, 1875. Lieutenant Randolph died on May 14, 1930, in Walter Reed Hospital in Washington, D. C. Heitman, *Historical Register* 1: 815; John B. Randolph Pension Records.

8. William Cunningham enlisted as a private in the 5th Infantry on October 25, 1858, and re-enlisted as a sergeant on August 27, 1863. He mustered out on August 23, 1868, as a first sergeant. Sergeant Cunningham was described by Edmund Wells as "a man of fairness and considerable good judgment and horse sense." William Cunningham Military Service Records; Wells, *Argonaut Tales*, 283–84.

displayed them before the astonished gaze of Randolph. The name which the lieutenant saw on the envelopes was Judge Joseph G. Knapp, Associate Justice, United States Supreme Court, Territory of New Mexico.

A few moments afterwards, an excited lieutenant dashed into my room, exclaiming, "By Jove, Curtis, I'm in for it now! My commission is not worth its weight in shucks."

To my question what ailed him, he replied, "I've just tied up Judge Knapp, of the United States Court!"

Of course, this affair soon flew all over town. As soon as the provost marshal learned the name of the prisoner, he was released and allowed to leave town without a pass. In process of time, a letter appeared in the *New York Tribune* detailing the whole affair and the President was also informed of the deep disgrace put upon one of his appointees, but nothing came of it to our great astonishment and Randolph's intense relief. It was not until a long time afterwards, that General Carleton informed us that President Abe Lincoln enjoyed the whole thing heartily and said the judge so thoroughly deserved all he got that he should take no notice of the lieutenant's infraction of regulations. A few months afterwards, the judge resigned his office and went to the States.

Of course, the lieutenant had not the shadow of a right to tie up the judge or even an enlisted man and there was probably not another officer in the territory who would have done it, but it was poetical justice after all, fully deserved.

Chapter 15

Romantic Entanglements

During the summer, there occurred an episode in my life exceedingly rare for a New Englander and one which gave me much anxiety at the time. My conduct in the affair can scarcely be defended in this part of the country, where blood runs coolly and where in the rare occasion when it is suddenly raised above temperate, the feelings find vent in superlative epithets or very rarely in fisticuffs. I will let the incidents reveal themselves in the regular current of the narrative.

At the time when I was for a few days Acting Assistant Adjutant General of the Southern District of New Mexico, at Fort Craig, a man by the name of Bentley, a private of the California Column, reported to me on his way to Santa Fé, where he expected to be made an aide-de-camp on the staff of General Carleton.[1] The history of this man had come to my ears while I was confiscating officer at Mesilla. One morning he was posted as sentinel at the door of the store and Sergeant Le Roy, who was my assistant, pointed him out to me, relating at considerable length a great portion of the man's history. It is not necessary for me to enter into the details of this history, further than to say that the portion which made

1. Bentley is a pseudonym and cannot be further identified.

the greatest impression upon me, arousing my indignation and fixing the man's features indelibly in my mind, was the story of his marriage to an estimable California girl, his cruel abuse of her and final desertion.

When I arrived in Santa Fé, I found Bentley dressed in the uniform of a lieutenant and established at headquarters as aide-de-camp. He met me and claimed acquaintance, but I could not treat him with the cordiality which I should have bestowed had I never heard Sergeant Le Roy's story. There was a mean streak in the man, which developed itself in many ways. He was servile and humble to the commanding general and, for a long time, a spy upon the acts of the youngsters of the 5th Infantry. At first when he came to our quarters, we treated him with the same hospitality which we bestowed upon any of our friends, acting with perfect freedom of speech and manner in his presence. It was not long, however, before one and another of us were sent for by the general and lectured on account of our peccadillos or for our free speech. We were for a long time at a loss to know which of the staff officers were reporting us, for all visited at the post, but after a time we cornered the matter down to Bentley. We treated him gentlemanly, however, after our discovery, simply excluding him from our confidence and keeping our skeletons in our closets while he was with us.

During the winter just passed, Bentley had been a regular attendant at all the parties given by the American ladies and had shown marked attention to the daughter of a Territorial judge. In March, it was rumored that he was to go to Fort Bliss, at the southern end of the territory, to stay there in the position of quartermaster and the rumor soon became an established fact.[2] The night before his

2. Colonel Alexander Doniphan's command was the first American army unit to occupy El Paso del Norte, an important pass between two mountain ranges along the Rio Grande near what is now El Paso, Texas. He remained from December of 1846 until the following February when his command marched off to reinforce Saltillo. Originally in the New Mexico territory ceded to the United States after the Mexican War, the area was transferred to Texas in 1850. The American installation was originally known as the Post Opposite El Paso, but after several years of neglect the post was re-established in 1854 as Fort Bliss, named for William W. S. Bliss, General Zachary Taylor's chief of staff who had died in 1853. The southern gateway to New Mexico Territory, Fort Bliss was used as a rendezvous for the Navajo Campaign of 1859. The garrison surrendered to Texas forces in 1861 and became the assembly point for the Confederate invasion of New Mexico. Re-occupied by California troops after the Confederate withdrawal, Regular troops relieved the Californians in 1865. The garrison was transferred one mile northeast to Camp Concordia in 1868 and the site of old Fort Bliss was washed away by the Rio Grande. The name Fort Bliss was re-introduced later at a different site and that installation is still an important army post today. McMaster, *Musket, Saber, and Missile*, 9–12, 16–19, 22, 25–28.

departure, a grand ball was given at the house of the judge, where we all enjoyed ourselves highly. Next evening I was sitting in the *fonda* billiard room, when Lieutenant Byers of the staff took a seat beside me and asked, "How did you enjoy the ball?"[3]

"As well as a non-dancing man can enjoy a party where the chief enjoyment is in the dance," I replied.

"Do you know why the ball was given?" he continued.

"No, if there was any special reason."

"There was."

"Well, what was it, if it is not a secret?"

"It was in honor of the engagement of Bentley and Miss Vose."[4]

"You do not mean to say that is true?"

"Yes, the judge told the general so and we were all notified at headquarters and went in a body to congratulate Bentley."

"The contemptible sneak and spy!" I exclaimed. "He has a wife in Stockton, California, whom he abused, cheated of her fortune, shamefully abandoned and now he dares propose to marry Miss Vose."

This ended the conversation, for in my indignation I arose and walked away, probably leaving Lieutenant Byers somewhat astonished.

Notwithstanding that I soon after learned the ball had, without doubt, been given in honor of the engagement, I said nothing more about Bentley's previous marriage, reflecting that possibly Sergeant Le Roy's tale might have been false and that I should only make unnecessary trouble if I said anything more about it. Time passed along and one afternoon I waked up from a *siesta* to find an open letter lying on the bed table beside me, addressed to myself. This letter was insulting to me, insinuating that I had circulated an idle tale about him, that he should take an early opportunity of making settlement with me, etc., etc.

Taking this in my hand, I went at once to General Carleton's headquarters. Entering, I stood just inside the door and asked, "Who received this letter?" No one replied. I again demanded, "Who received this letter?"

"I did not," said the adjutant general, Captain Benjamin C. Cutler, advancing toward me.[5] "Neither did I write to Bentley."

3. Lieutenant Byers is a pseudonym and cannot be further identified.

4. Miss Vose is a pseudonym and cannot be further identified.

5. Benjamin C. Cutler was commissioned first lieutenant and adjutant of the 1st California on August 15, 1861. He served in that capacity until August 6, 1862, when he was promoted

I saw by the captain's manner that he at least was not concerned in reporting my remark to Bentley, but all the other aides-de-camp sat at their desks industriously writing and never once raised their heads. Stepping to the door, I called, "Orderly!"

"Sir," replied the orderly, a soldier of my company detailed permanently at headquarters, entering and standing at attention.

"Did you bring this letter to my room?"

"Yes, sir."

"Who sent you?"

"Lieutenant Byers."

"That's all. You may go."

I then turned to Lieutenant Byers and said, "Next to a man who will do what I have good reason to believe your friend Bentley did, I class the contemptible sneak who bears tales" and turning on my heel, walked back to my quarters. Of course, I was very much excited and somewhat intemperate in my language, but it would be difficult even now to persuade me that Byers did not deserve all he got.

That evening all the aides called upon me and asked me where I got my information concerning Bentley. I told them all the circumstances. When I got through, they assured me that I was mistaken and went into much narration of what they called facts to show that Sergeant Le Roy's story was a tissue of falsehoods from beginning to end.

Of course, after all this, there was but one gentlemanly course for me to pursue and that was to write to Lieutenant Bentley and apologize. This I did at some length, telling him under what circumstances I heard the story, how I had never mentioned it but once and that was to his friend Lieutenant Byers; that if the story was current in Santa Fé, Byers must have repeated it, for I had not told it to my most intimate friend; and had only been betrayed into my exclamation by sudden feeling when I learned of the engagement between himself and Miss Vose.

---

captain and appointed assistant adjutant general of New Mexico Territory by General Carleton. Brevetted major for his war service, Cutler mustered out of service on January 20, 1866. He remained in New Mexico and was appointed surveyor general of the territory shortly before his death on October 18, 1868, in Albuquerque. Cutler was buried in the Masonic Cemetery, but in 1895 the bodies there were dug up and re-interred in the National Cemetery in Santa Fe. Heitman, *Historical Register* 1: 349; Pettis, *California Column*, 37; *New York Herald*, October 20, 1868; *[Santa Fe] Daily New Mexican*, October 21, 1868; *Brooklyn Daily Eagle*, November 16, 1868; *Albuquerque Daily Citizen*, May 21, 1895.

About a month after this, Lieutenant Randolph, of the 5th Infantry, went down to Fort Bliss in command of an escort to a paymaster and while there Lieutenant Bentley produced a copy of his letter to me and my apology, representing me as having done him an injury and then not being man enough to maintain my position, that I had backed out by attempting a weak apology, etc., etc. Of course, this was all detailed to me when Randolph returned and all our officers were fighting angry. I went downtown and hunted up an experienced duelist, Judge Joab Houghton, a man who had been principal in three duels and second in five.[6] Between us we made out the necessary documents for the judge to serve on Bentley in order to bring about a meeting. As I left the judge's office at the conclusion of our meeting, he said, "Curtis, I'll pay for all the coffins in this case," from which I inferred he did not believe Bentley would not come to time.

He never did. I remained in New Mexico and Arizona until the fall of 1865 and never met Bentley after he left Santa Fé. In justice to myself, I caused inquiries to be made at Stockton and found that the abandoned wife was still living and that no divorce had been applied for or granted to either party. As soon as the facts were all gathered, the engagement came to an end and the staff officers took an early occasion to set them right with me. From Bentley I heard, in many ways, he was "determined to shoot me on sight, no matter where he should meet me." This threat was so often repeated and accompanied with such oaths, that I really was alarmed for my safety and never neglected to keep a revolver near at hand during the time I served where I was likely to meet Bentley.

In order to please the inhabitants of Santa Fé and make a parade before the windows of department headquarters, we used to hold guard mounting and dress parade on the city *plaza*, instead of the military square. The regimental band was first-class and the men of the garrison well-drilled, so that these ceremonies were showy

6. A civil engineer by profession, Joab Houghton came to New Mexico in 1845 and the following year was appointed U. S. Consul at Santa Fe. A prominent trader, he was appointed a judge by General Stephen W. Kearny and served from 1846 to 1852. Although obviously unqualified for his judgeship, Houghton was nevertheless appointed U. S. district attorney in 1862. He was appointed judge of the third district in 1865, leading one editor to complain that "those not bred in the law should not be entrusted with its administration." Removed from his position in 1869, Judge Houghton opened a law office in Santa Fe and remained in that city until 1876. He removed to Las Vegas, New Mexico, and died there on January 31, 1876. Twitchell, *Leading Facts* 2: 272–73.

and attractive. Our left rested on the Governor's Palace, in front of which, nearly opposite its centre, was a sundial. At this sundial the old and new officers of the day used to meet a few moments before the details marched on. One morning, as Lieutenant Watson stood alone at the sundial, his attention was attracted to a window of the palace, where stood a beautiful young girl, a relative of the governor, a child of an American father and Mexican mother.[7] When the lieutenant looked up, she moved away from the window. Next morning she stood in the same place again and again moved away when the lieutenant looked in her direction. This sort of thing occurred every time Watson went on as officer of the day, until one morning he threw a kiss to the young lady. Startled at his audacity, she did not return again to the window, but some mornings after, when the lieutenant again threw a kiss, she stood to one side of the window but left a hand in sight, making a motion of throwing a kiss in return. It was not long after this before matters progressed so far that billets were dropped into the parlor windows by the lieutenant as he passed along the portal and soon he received answers.

A short time before this romance began, I had attended the anniversary exercises of the boarding school of the Roman Catholic Sisterhood and seen the young lady, whose identity I will conceal under the name of Rafaela, graduate. The school building contained an interior court about 300 feet square, with a colonnade or piazza running entirely around it. It was one story high on three sides of the court, but two stories high on the side next to the street. The entrance was sufficiently broad to admit a coach and directly above it, on the inside, was a space or gallery in which sat a brass band and orchestra, composed of priests and members of monastic brotherhood. Directly opposite the entrance, a stage was erected under the piazza, for the literary exercises. The whole courtyard and the space under the colonnade was filled with sisters, upon which were assembled the first families of the territory to see their daughters graduate.

The exercises were not unlike those of any seminary in the East. The young ladies were dressed in the conventional white, with pink or blue bows and sashes, and I was surprised to see how many of them were blondes. The custom of secluding the unmarried girls in the Latin countries prevents one's knowing how much beauty there

7. Lieutenant Watson is a pseudonym and cannot be further identified.

may be concealed about him. The women one ordinarily meets in the streets of the Mexican town are the dusky descendants of the Spanish and Indian connections and it is only at church or upon some occasion like this that one sees the Castilianos.

Among the brightest misses of the graduating class was the fair-haired and blue-eyed Rafaela. She came very near me during the distribution of the prizes. It was the custom, as each scholar received a prize from Bishop Lamy, for her to come down from the stage, seek her parents or guardian and place the prize in his or her hands, with a low bow, and again receive it, accompanied by some complimentary phrase. His Excellency, Governor Henry Connelly, sat near me, and when *Señorita* Rafaela took her prize, she came to him and placed it in his hands.[8] It was a sight worth witnessing, and one which I shall not soon forget, to see the chivalrous manner in which Governor Connelly returned the prize and to hear the graceful compliment which he bestowed on the blushing girl before him.

The exercises lasted through the afternoon and consisted of the usual stereotyped essays, themes, dialogues and musical and instrumental selections. An English dialogue afforded me much amusement and I sat wondering whether the French dialogues of our American seminaries would puzzle a listening Frenchman as much as this English dialogue did me. Of course, the listening Mexicans applauded this particular thing vociferously, for the same reason that the weak witticisms of the Latin salutatory of the college boy elicit more applause than the better things of the English oration. Everybody wants everybody else to think he understands the language. When the exercises closed, I had expected to see the young ladies of the school in the parlors and recitation rooms, but with the last note of the Nunc Dimittis, the young ladies were quickly enveloped into obscuring cloaks and *rebozos*, hurried

8. Henry Connelly graduated from the Medical School at Transylvania University in 1828 and headed west, settling in Chihuahua, Mexico, as a businessman. In 1848 Dr. Connelly moved to Santa Fe and remained there the rest of his life. He served several terms on the territorial council prior to being appointed governor of New Mexico Territory by President Lincoln on September 4, 1861. Connelly left office on July 16, 1866, and died in Santa Fe on August 12. One editor offered the following eulogy: "Although he had lived upon the frontier for a large part of his life he was ever as polished and urbane as though moving in the most refined society. He was a well read and observant man, and both in public and private life greatly respected and beloved." Twichell, *Military Occupation of New Mexico*, 365–66; *San Francisco Bulletin*, September 21, 1866; *Weekly Champion and Press*, August 30, 1866; *Weekly Journal Miner*, October 13, 1866.

into waiting family carriages and snatched from our view. In all the parlors I met but one scholar, an intelligent American girl, who possessed all the ease of manner with thorough capability of taking care of herself.

The throwing of kisses and exchanging of billets-doux soon reached a proposal of marriage on the part of Lieutenant Watson and an acceptance on the part of Rafaela. A formal application to the governor met with his approval, but the Catholic mother of the girl would not consent to a Protestant alliance, meeting the proposal by shutting up the indiscreet damsel and making the young man miserable for a few weeks. But it was not long before several of the governor's household were found who were willing to carry letters, a brisk correspondence ensued and soon plans were made for an elopement. The night was selected and came. The damsel leaped from a window into the arms of her waiting lover and both hurried away to find an *alcalde* who would marry them under civil process.

Watson knew it would be a hopeless thing to ask a priest to unite them and he was not quite sure of the Mexican *alcalde*. However, delays were certainly dangerous in this case, so the lieutenant beat at the door of a justice of the peace until he raised him, got admission to the house and asked the sleepy official to marry them. The *alcalde* bustled about, got a lamp and approached the couple, but when his eyes fell upon the half-terrified Rafaela, he refused to begin the ceremony and started at once for the palace to inform *La Señora* of her daughter's escapade. Finding they were betrayed, the young couple fled to another *alcalde*, with the same result and a third one with no better success. Finally, at their wits end, they went to the house of Chief Justice Kirby Benedict of the Supreme Court.[9] The handsome old judge, six feet tall in his stockings, met the young couple in his parlor with his unfastened suspenders

9. Kirby Benedict, shortly after attaining adulthood, moved to Illinois and began a law career during which he became friends with Abraham Lincoln and Stephen Douglas. He was appointed an associate justice of the New Mexico Territory Supreme Court by President Franklin Pierce in 1853. Five years later he became chief justice and served in that capacity until 1866 when he failed to be re-appointed. Benedict resumed the practice of law but had become "very irritable and morose" after being passed over for another term in the Supreme Court. He could not get along with judges who had previously been underlings and his attitude, fueled by alcohol, resulted in him being suspended from the bar in 1871. Humiliated by the court's refusal to reinstate him, Benedict died on February 27, 1874, while walking in Santa Fe. Twichell, *Leading Facts of New Mexican History* 2: 393–94; Hunt, *Kirby Benedict*, 223–24.

hanging below his dressing gown, took in the situation at once and, amid the beating and pounding upon his windows and doors of three *alcaldes*, the mother and governor, pronounced the excited young people man and wife.

The knockers were admitted. *La Señora* stormed and raved, the governor pretended to look severe and scold, but squeezed the lieutenant's hand cordially on the sly and kissed Rafaela. *La Señora* put her arm about the frightened girl, assuring her that this kind of a marriage was no marriage at all and bore her off home. Next day the governor, judge and others succeeded in convincing the mother that the marriage was legal, that there was no use in opposing the wishes of the young couple, who were determined to call it a marriage anyway, and that the best thing she could do would be to make a virtue of necessity. Accordingly, *La Señora* told the daughter if she would remain quietly at home until suitable preparations could be made and not see the lieutenant, she should be married at the cathedral by the bishop. This was assented to and, on a beautiful Sunday in June, the young couple was married according to the rites of the church, with bridesmaids and groomsmen, and much glitter of military accessories.

Chapter 16

En Route to Conejos

Although we had a fine garden, with a great variety of vegetables, many unknown to this northern climate, still the one universal vegetable without which no meal seems complete, the potato, was absent. This root does not grow in New Mexico and, in fact, anywhere in the valleys of Colorado, New Mexico or Arizona, owing to the presence of alkali in the soil. On the elevated divides and mountainsides of Colorado, where the alkali has been leeched from the soil, the potato grows profitably. I ought, perhaps, to qualify my statement that the potato does not grow in New Mexico, for it really does grow very rank as regards tops, but has no roots. In certain parts of Colorado, the first year's crop will be good, but to insure a good one the second year, fresh seed must be obtained from a country where there is no alkali.

Owing to this want of potatoes, of course, it followed that the price was exceedingly high at times. During the war, they never went below seven dollars per hundred weight and I once knew them to reach nineteen dollars. At the time of which I am writing, the report reached our department commissary of subsistence that potatoes could be purchased at Conejos, in Colorado Territory, for seven dollars per hundred weight. The report having become generally circulated among the officers, it was determined to dispatch a lieutenant, with a detail of men and four wagons, to make a purchase of a supply for the command and headquarters. There was considerable anxiety on the part of the lieutenants to secure this detail, as it would give an opportunity of traveling through the northern section of New Mexico and visiting the town of Fernandez de Taos, next to Santa Fé the most important town in the territory.

I did not for a moment suppose there was a possibility that I could secure the duty, as I was busy in constructing the Government buildings and engaged in several other matters which demanded my close attention. Still I wanted to go and regretted that my chances of doing so were few. One day I called upon Captain Amos F. Garrison, the commissary of subsistence, and in the course of our talk he mentioned that he should like to send me for the potatoes.[1] Upon my signifying a willingness to go, he said he would call on General Carleton at once and secure me the detail.

"Then you would be sure to prevent me from going," said I.

"Why so?" asked the captain.

"Have you been so long at headquarters that you have not found out that men are more likely to get what they don't want than what they do?" I continued, "If you can, in your application for an officer to go on this duty, manage to give the general to understand that you have proposed it to me and that I have declared positively that I do not desire to go, in fact that it would be a great inconvenience to me, I think there can be no doubt but I shall be sent."

"But could I do so conscientiously?"

"Do I understand that you want me to go?"

"Yes."

"Well, I don't want to. It would complicate my business seriously if I should go away at this time and, while I am very much obliged to you for the compliment, I must respectfully decline."

The captain stood looking at me for a moment as if perplexed, then a twinkle in his eye showed that he comprehended my meaning and he disappeared through the door to the general's room. In a few

1. Already a veteran of the Seminole War, Amos F. Garrison was appointed a captain in the commissary department on June 26, 1846, and served during the Mexican War until he was discharged on November 30, 1848. He again served as a captain in the commissary department from August 7, 1861, until he was mustered out on January 10, 1866. Garrison was brevetted major for his wartime service in the subsistence department. He died on August 5, 1877, at Hermosilla, Mexico, while serving as vice-consul at Guaymas. Heitman, *Historical Register* 1: 448; *Philadelphia Inquirer*, September 3, 1877.

moments he returned laughing and said, "Well, old fellow, you can pack your traps, for you are going."

"Thanks. I knew he would send me if he thought I did not care to make the trip."

I had not been in my quarters but a few moments when an orderly appeared with a special order detailing me to go to Conejos, Colorado, a distance of 108 miles by the traveled road, to purchase several hundred weight of potatoes and to take such detail, not exceeding ten men, from my company, as I saw fit. I was further instructed to go as fast as possible, without unnecessary delays, and not to pay more than seven dollars per hundred weight for the potatoes. To enable me to be absent the time necessary for making the journey, Lieutenant Taylor was authorized to sign my name to such papers as would require signing during my absence and to overlook my business, but without my responsibility.

Suspecting that the next men in my company subject to detail on detached service were a hard set, I called at the orderly room to look at the list. As I surmised, the first four names for detail were four of the worst men in the company. Not wishing to fight my way to Conejos and back with a lot of dissipated men, I ordered the first sergeant to skip those names and detail Corporal Coffey and four other soldiers whom I selected.[2] The report of the change was soon known throughout the barracks and, in the course of half an hour, the sergeant waited upon me with a request from the four men who had been set aside, that I would grant them an interview. I did so and, presently, four men—two Irishmen, a German, and an American—entered and stood at attention. They were soldierly-looking fellows, excellent at drill and superior in a fight. Their pugnacious qualities, exaggerated by their bibulous propensities in fact, were what had given them their worst reputation.

McGreevy, one of the Irishmen, was spokesman.[3] In a respectful and soldierly manner, he represented for himself and fellows

2. John Coffey enlisted in the 5th Infantry as a private on April 29, 1858, and re-enlisted on March 29, 1863. He deserted on May 11, 1866, and surrendered on February 6, 1868. He was transferred to the 9th Infantry and 12th Infantry and, after making up his time, Coffey was discharged on December 16, 1869, at Camp Cady. John Coffey Military Service Records.

3. Thomas McGreevy enlisted in the 5th Infantry on July 11, 1860, as a private. He was discharged on July 11, 1865, at the expiration of his enlistment and apparently remained in New Mexico as he resided in Roswell during the 1890 Veterans Census. McGreevy spent his last days at the United States Soldiers Home in Washington, D. C. and died there on January 13, 1909. Register of Enlistments; Thomas McGreevy Pension Records; 1890 Veterans Census; U S. Veterans Gravesites 1775–2006; *[DC] Evening Star*, January 16, 1909.

that they had not been on a detached service for a long time, having already been several times set aside by officers, and that they were very anxious to go on this trip, that if I would consent to take them, they would promise to behave properly and give me no trouble. Asking them individually if they would each promise me what McGreevy had proposed and they assenting, I sent word to the sergeant to change the detail to include Privates McGreevy, John Sands, Bergen and Timmons, retaining Corporal Coffey.[4] This made my party, including the four teamsters and me, consist of ten. The route was not a dangerous one and there was little use for the men, except as a night guard over the animals whenever we should camp by the roadside and to assist should there be any breakdowns or other casualties.

On a pleasant day in October, I left Santa Fé at daybreak, the men of the escort riding in the first wagon and myself mounted on a horse which I had borrowed of the officer commanding the California Cavalry. Our day's drive took us in a general northwesterly direction to the valley of the Rio Grande del Norte, through the Indian towns of Tesuque, Cuyamungue and Pojoaque to the Mexican town of Santa Cruz. Much of the distance of the country was rugged and the hills were covered with a scanty growth of pine trees, which clung with the greatest tenacity to the barren soil. The road was composed of a loose and deep sand, through which it was impossible to travel faster than a walk. Along the roadside were frequent rude crosses, surrounded by heaps of stones, marking the places where solitary travelers had been waylaid and murdered, while a large space covered by these tumuli pointed out the scene of a struggle in the Revolution of 1837.

4. John Sands enlisted in the 5th Infantry on April 6, 1858. Apparently having second thoughts, he deserted on May 13 but was apprehended four days later. Sands eventually embraced army life for he re-enlisted on February 10, 1863. Wounded in the shoulder in an encounter with Apaches on January 24, 1865, he was treated in the hospital at Fort Whipple by Doctor Coues, who described the progress of his case in the *Medical and Surgical Reporter*. Unaccountably, Coues noted the man's initials as "G. S." in his report. John Sands died as the result of his wound at Fort Whipple on February 22, 1865. John Bergen enlisted in the 5th Infantry as a private on May 10, 1858, and re-enlisted May 29, 1863. Standing exactly six feet, Bergen was the tallest man in his company. He was transferred to the 14th Infantry shortly before his death from fever on November 16, 1866, at Fort Goodwin, Arizona Territory. Patrick Timmons enlisted as a private in the 5th Infantry on September 17, 1851. He deserted on February 24, 1855, and was apprehended on April 2 of that year. Timmons re-enlisted on September 13, 1856, and again on July 13, 1861, and was discharged on July 13, 1864, upon the expiration of his enlistment. He died on August 17, 1897, at West Orange, New Jersey. Register of Enlistments; Hayden Arizona Pioneer Biographies; Coues, "Some Notes on Arrow-Wounds," 323–24; Final Statement, John Bergen; Patrick Timmons Military Service Records; New Jersey Deaths and Burials, 1798–1971.

At Pojoaque Creek, I halted the wagons for a short time to give the animals a chance to graze and the men to take a lunch. To the right of the road, as we left the place, I observed some interesting sandstone formations, which in the distance looked not unlike a town; some resembled broken columns, single and in rows, ruined porticos and fallen pilasters. One locality, from its resemblance to a half-ruined building, had received the name of The Church, three sides were still standing, while the fourth, looking toward the south, had fallen. Here the sand hills sink down into the valley and the Rio Grande comes in sight, a beautiful and clear, but not a broad, stream.

We arrived in Santa Cruz about three o'clock in the afternoon and went to the house of *Señor* José Duran, the only Mexican I ever met who acknowledged himself to be a Protestant.[5] He showed me a Spanish translation of an Episcopal Prayer Book and claimed to be a regular communicant of the church. He was a fine-looking and intelligent gentleman. Santa Cruz has a population of about 300. A small *adobe* church stands on the *plaza* and a priest resides in an adjoining house to minister at the altar. I called upon the Reverend Father and passed a pleasant evening listening to his account of the conspicuous part this little village had played in the history of New Mexico. It was always the rallying place for the northern Indians in the various rebellions and several severe battles have been fought in this place.

Next morning, we resumed our journey, passing through the Indian towns of San Juan and Nambé.[6] At the latter place we found the Indians had executed two of their number the day before for witchcraft, an offence against the civil law for which the authorities were tried in Santa Fé sometime afterwards. At Luceros, about ten miles from Santa Cruz, I was invited to dine with an American gentleman by the name of Barker and let the wagons go on in charge of the corporal, while I remained to avail myself of American hospitality.[7] The dinner was excellent and what made

5. Senor José Duran cannot be positively identified.

6. San Juan Pueblo was located near the confluence of the Rio Grande and Rio Chama Rivers. These Indians, whose population in 1860 numbered 341, were primarily agriculturalists and claimed over 17,000 acres. This pueblo was significant because after 1862 the Spanish and Mexican priests were replaced by French priests. Nambé Pueblo, located about fifteen miles north of Santa Fe, was one of the smaller pueblos whose population had declined to 103 in 1860. They subsisted on agriculture and grazing over 13,000 acres. Ortiz, "San Juan Pueblo," 278, 282, 288–90, 293; Speirs, "Nambe Pueblo," 317–18; *California Farmer and Journal of Useful Sciences*, June 19, 1863.

7. Barker cannot be positively identified.

it in marked contrast to the dinners of the territory was the presence of the host's wife and two daughters. A short time after dinner I galloped after my wagons, overtaking them at the little town of La Joya. Here the road, which for the last ten miles had been following a northeasterly direction along the eastern bank of the river, turned a right angle around a spur of mountain, pursuing a southeasterly course to the little hamlet of Las Trampas, where it again resumed its general northeasterly course. Pushing rapidly through this place, we ascended a mountain range, densely timbered, over a rough road, which kept us down to a slow walk, and night began to fall before we turned the summit. Once over this, however, I rode on in advance, in search of a camping place, determined to halt at the first water. Mile after mile had been passed over without finding water and it had become so dark in the forest that I could barely see the road, when I suddenly emerged from the wood into a lovely valley. On my left I noticed a large house, with simple outbuildings, so, concluding the comforts of a house were preferable to those of camp, especially as the sky promised rain, I rode up to the door and rapped. After considerable delay, a female voice asked, "*Quien es*?" ("Who is it?")

"*Amigo*" ("Friend"), I replied.

"*Qui quieres*?" ("What do you want?") came next.

I explained who I was and what I wanted, then the voice replied that the man of the house was absent in Taos and that she could not possibly entertain strangers under the circumstances.

I was riding away from the door, when I looked over my shoulder and saw three female heads looking after me from the window. Presently the door opened and I was called back. Dismounting and entering the house, I found an elderly woman standing in the reception room, with two beautiful young women, evidently her daughters, and I was told that I could stay. A large outer room was shown me for my men and a corral for my wagons and animals. After securing these, I went out to the roadside with a lantern to stop the wagons. They seemed to be a long time in coming and it began to rain quite freely before they came in sight. I conducted the wagons to the stables and soon had the men in their room, with a roaring fire on the hearth.

My hostess and her daughters soon prepared me a good supper and did me the honor, upon my invitation, to sit down and eat it with me, a favor they would not have shown me had *El Señor* been at home. It was explained that he had been called to court in Taos and that his four laborers had all been summoned as witnesses. This had left the ladies entirely alone, with only such assistance as the men of a neighboring ranche, three miles away, could render night and morning. I had arrived half an hour after these friendly neighbors had left.

The name of the ranche was Ojo Zarco Clear Spring, situated near the headwaters of a tributary to the Rio Grande, called El Embudo and was forty miles from my last camping place. I passed as pleasant an evening as possible with the ladies, where conversation was somewhat difficult on account of my imperfect knowledge of Spanish. We smoked *cigarritos* without limit and played *Malilla* (Spanish whist) until bedtime.[8]

I have already mentioned that there are no bedsteads in a Mexican house and how the divan or settee, which runs around their rooms, is composed of *colchónes* (mattresses) which are unfolded and spread upon the floor when night comes. When I signified a desire to go to bed, all the ladies busied themselves in getting out two *colchónes* for my use, placing one upon the other, preparing sheets, pillow cases, blankets, etc. After everything was ready, I began to get impatient for the women to go and leave me to my slumbers and, in order to hasten matters, divested myself of coat and boots and lay down on the outside of the bed. Still they smoked on and showed no signs of leaving. At last, getting desperate, I plunged under the blankets and removed my garments beneath, drawing them out and placing them on the outside of the bed. So far as I was concerned, I was ready for sleep.

Presently the mother and daughters got out three more *colchónes*, made three beds in the corner diagonally opposite me, two beds being placed side by side in the corner, and the third being placed along the foot of the other two. These women betrayed no squeamishness in undressing before me, hardly looking at me through the whole performance, and finally disposed themselves, the two girls in the corner and the mother in the bed at the foot of the girls.

8. Doctor Elliott Coues commented on these two popular pastimes, complaining that the New Mexicans "have only just energy enough to bask by day in the sun rolling cigarettes, and cheat each other at cards by night." Coues, *Birds of the Northwest*, 108.

A little after sunrise next morning, I bade adieu to my kind entertainers, paid my bill and resumed my journey. All the region between La Joya and the Taos Valley is exceedingly mountainous and woody. The road, therefore, ran over a very wild region. Five miles from Ojo Zarco we passed Chamisal, six miles farther Llano, two miles farther Peñasco and six miles farther still Las Piedras. All of these places, with the exception of the last, were simply ranches, taking their names from some feature of the locality. Las Piedras stood at a point where the road began the ascent of the U. S. Mountains, the town being 7,452 feet above the level of the ocean and the highest point of the mountain road 10,734; this ascent and descent into the valley of Frijole Creek being made in a distance of twelve miles.

We paused at Las Piedras for half an hour to look up fresh meat and eggs for our noonday halt, the men exchanging their bacon and soap for mutton, onions, *chili* and eggs, getting in return a much greater bulk than they gave. Up to this time, I had had no reason to regret that I took with me the quartette of hard-heads. They had passed through all of the towns without visiting the groggeries and had behaved exceedingly well. Shortly after I got into the mountain road and was riding along in advance of the wagons, I heard Sands singing, at the top of his voice, an original song which he had composed on the Battle of Valverde, a song which gave the singer as much difficulty in adapting its measure to the cadence of the tune to which he sang it, as the soldier finds in trying to keep step to a marching tune over a corduroy road. The song was followed by boisterous laughter, general and noisy conversation, sure precursors of a drunk.

Hoping that the men had only got a small quantity of liquor, the effects of which would soon wear off, I rode a considerable distance ahead, that I might hear nothing and so have an excuse for not interfering. The road wound torturously upon the mountainside, through dense forests of pine, spruce and hemlock and the wagons crept slowly along, compelling me occasionally to stop, dismount and wait for them to come in sight. At one of these halts, just as the wagons could be seen turning a bend in the road far below, my attention was attracted by the teamster of the first wagon swinging his hat and beckoning to me. I at once mounted and rode back. As I came within earshot of the wagons, I heard yells, curses and shrieks of pain. Coming up to the front and looking in, I saw my four men were rolling over in the bottom of the wagon, evidently bound together in a knot of arms and legs, gouging, biting and scratching like the cats of Kilkenny. Stopping the wagons, I called for Corporal Coffey and he emerged sober and in his right mind from the rear wagon. We got into the wagon where the social recreation was going on and soon deposited the malcontents over the tail-board into the road. They staggered to the side of the way and sat down in a row on the grass, a frowsy, bloody, seedy and generally dilapidated-looking squad, noisily remonstrating in hic-coughy tones against the liquor being spilled, for I had ordered the corporal to inspect the canteens and pour out all the liquor he found in them. The canteens of each of the four had been filled with whiskey and two were still full when I turned the men out of the wagon.

I ordered the teamster to drive on, intending to leave the drunken men where they were, to sober off, confident that they would follow as soon as they were able and hungry. The wagons had hardly started when McGreevy, the steadiest one on his legs, made a dash at the first wagon, leaped into it and, almost as if he had not paused an instant, tumbled headlong into the road from the rear. Picking himself up with drunken gravity, he went back and took a seat with his comrades. As he did so, I saw he held something concealed under his coat, but, supposing it might from its bulk be only a canteen, I took no further notice of him and we were soon out of sight.

We toiled on to the summit of the roadway and soon began the descent, the mules going at a trot nearly all the way down, the road emerging from the forest into a beautiful open valley, through which flows the Frijole, near the ruins of old Camp Burgwin.[9] The roofless walls and towering chimneys of this old dragoon station still stand in a valley which, at the time I saw it, contained but one habitation in a distance of fifteen miles of it. I rode on with a view

9. Cantonment Burgwin, its name suggesting a post less permanent than a fort, was established in 1852 some ten miles southeast of Taos on the wagon road from Santa Fe to Colorado. Named to honor Captain John H. K. Burgwin who had died in 1847 in the army's attack on Taos Pueblo, the cantonment was seemingly at the end of the world since there were no civilians within miles of the post. A palisade of upright logs surrounded a plaza flanked by barracks, storerooms, and other buildings. A succession of units and commanders shuttled in and out of Cantonment Burgwin during the 1850s as the army attempted to pacify local Apaches. Its buildings deteriorating and the Indians having been driven away, the post was officially closed on May 18, 1860. Murphy, "Cantonment Burgwin," 5–26.

of inspecting the valley for houses, for I had determined not to halt for my men to come up until I should find a house. I felt quite sure they would be compelled to follow me if they had no means of procuring food, but I was not sure that they would do so if they came up to a house where food could be had, especially if whiskey could be obtained also.

Some six miles below Camp Burgwin I saw, half a mile to the right of the road, a wooden house, built quite like a New England cottage, clap-boarded, shingled, painted and with red chimneys. Riding up to it, I found three Mexican women sitting in a large room, on one side of which was a suspicious-looking buffet, suggestive of *aguardiente* (liquor). In answer to my questions, I learned that the house was owned by an American, who was now absent in the mountains. I told the Mexican wife of the absent proprietor about the men I had left behind and hoped she would not sell them any liquor when they came up. She immediately declared, *por Dios* (by God), that she had not a drop in the house. Not placing much dependence in this assertion, after a little time had elapsed, I asked, "*No tiene aguardiente por me*?" ("Have you no liquor for me?")

"*Si señor. Yo tengo poquito por mi madre por medicina*" ("Yes, sir. I have a little medicine for my mother"), she answered, at the same time opening the buffet and disclosing to view a goodly array of decanters and bottles, filling four shelves. I could not help thinking that the mother was a pretty sick woman if she required such a quantity of the inebriating fluid. The sight of so much liquor led me to decide to remain until the men should come along, for I felt sure they would make a disturbance here and perhaps remain for some time. I went out to the road and, when the wagons passed, told the corporal to drive down the valley some distance, halt at the first place where the train would be out of sight of the house and wait for me. I then returned to the house, led my horse behind it, securing him near a small stack of hay, to wait for the men.

Two long hours passed slowly away before I saw anything of the loiterers. At last, when my patience was nearly exhausted, I saw four heads appear above a ridge a mile away and stop long enough to take a look down the valley, to see if the wagons were in sight. Convinced that the way was clear, the heads gradually put on bodies and presently I saw the four men fully revealed, making rapid strides for the house. I waited until they were within a few rods of me and then stepped out into sight, telling them to pass on and they would find the wagons halted for them around the first bend. Three of the soldiers started off without a word and were quickly out of sight, under the edge of the hill upon which the cottage stood. The fourth stood sullenly kicking the small stones on the ground with his toes and holding under his left arm something concealed, for it was McGreevy, the man who leaped into the wagon at the time I left the party on the mountain. He was now perfectly sober, so far as his gait showed anything, but sullen and angry from the after effects of his intemperance. I approached him and said, "What have you got under your coat, sir?"

"Bread, by God!" was the answer, accompanied by a snatch which brought into sight a large flat loaf, which he tossed into the air and dexterously caught on his toe, dividing it into a dozen fragments, which flew in every direction.

"Go on to the wagon!" I ordered.

"Not till I've taken the consate out uv yez, sir. It's man and man now and I'll just tach ye to lav us boys hilpliss on the road whilst ye rode on at your aize," stripping off his coat and, without a moment's delay, pitching into me with his fists.

I am no John C. Heenan and labor under the additional disadvantage of being a cripple, so would have been justified in law had I taken the revolver by my side and shot the mutinous fellow dead, but I could not make up my mind to do that.[10] I assumed the defensive according to the code taught in my father's barn by a peripatetic boxing master in my boyhood, a code I had had little occasion to practice. The fellow came at me with a tremendous blow, but a parry sent it harmless over my head, while a "left," put in under the right eye, sent him to the grass. I believe I was justified, for the reasons I have given, in jumping on the man and giving

10. John C. Heenan was a famous boxer of the 1850s and 1860s although his fame rested on three bouts which resulted in two losses and one draw. A young blacksmith from Benicia, California, Heenan first came to prominence in 1858 when he lost a match to John Morrissey, the reigning American champion. His next fight was against Tom Sayers, the English champion. On April 17, 1860, this bout was declared a draw after the British crowd rushed the ring in the thirty-seventh round. The "Benicia Boy" took on the new English champion, Tom King, on December 10, 1863. Defeated again, Heenan became a hanger-on in the boxing world and by 1870 had developed symptoms of consumption. In 1873 he headed west for his health but died on October 25 at Green River, Wyoming Territory, aged thirty-nine. *New York Herald*, October 27, 1873; November 2, 1873; *Philadelphia Inquirer*, March 6, 1910.

him a severe mauling before he recovered from the astonishment I had inflicted upon his senses by knocking him down. He was a big fellow and I knew he would show me no mercy if he once got hold of me. Accordingly, I bruised his anatomy out of all shape or recognition, eliciting a cry for quarter, upon which I let him up and he snatched his coat and ran down the valley after the wagons.

Mounting my horse, I followed McGreevy until I came up with the rest of my party, behind a bend by the roadside. It was already late in the afternoon, owing to the delay caused by my drunken escort, and I ordered the teamsters to get as much speed out of the mules as possible. When I entered the Taos Valley, at Francisco Ranchos, I could just discern the town of Don Fernandez de Taos—or Taos, as it is usually called—in the gathering twilight, resting against the dark background, six miles across an uneven valley. Halfway across I rode on alone, to make arrangements for housing men and animals. I cantered rapidly along, but night gathered so fast that I could see nothing of the road after a short time and had to depend upon the horse to keep the track.

The barking of dogs and appearance of lights showed me at last that I was getting into the town and presently I found myself riding up a street, with a long, brilliantly-lighted house on my right, from which came the sound of jingling glasses and other notes of festive preparations. I dismounted and found my way to the door, intending to ask the way to the military agent, but no one answered my knock, so I walked in through a spacious hall, across elegant parlors, in the direction of the jingling glasses. Presently I found myself in a small room, where stood at an elegant sideboard, a gentleman and lady evidently busily engaged in preparing for a ball, instructing servants, etc. I wore no insignia of rank and was, withal, a rough and dusty-looking customer to the surprised lady and gentleman. To introduce myself, I offered my card and asked my question. The gentleman at once accompanied me to the door, pointed out the agent's, then said, "that he was giving a little ball in honor of the court officials, who were holding court in town, and that he would consider it a favor if I would honor his humble abode with my distinguished presence" and all the other Spanish compliments which fall so easily from the Castilian tongue.

I went to the agent's, established my men comfortably, ate supper, got ready and went to the ball.

Chapter 17

No Potatoes, But a New Assignment

The name Taos was originally applied to the country lying about the valley and headwaters of a stream of that name, a tributary of the Rio Grande del Norte, but has long since, by universal custom, come to belong to the town of Don Fernandez. It is situated at the junction of two forks of the Rio de Taos and five miles from the western base of the Rocky Mountain range. Five miles to the southeast, at the point where I entered the valley by the road down the Frijole, is a town called Francisco Ranchos, or Ranchos de Taos, whilst at about the same distance to the northeast is the celebrated Indian pueblo of Taos.[1] This village is interesting as a curious relic of the Aztecan age. One of the forks of the Taos River, as it

1. Taos Pueblo was located some seventy miles north of Santa Fe on a plateau of the Sangre de Christo Mountains. The pueblo had buildings up to five stories high which were only accessible by ladders. Its mountainous location meant that the Indians relied more on hunting and gathering than most other pueblos which were generally agricultural. Population in 1860 was 363 on an acreage of over 17,000 acres. The pueblo's relatively isolated location contributed to its residents becoming leaders in the revolts of 1680 against the Spanish and 1847 against the Americans. During the latter revolt, Governor Charles Bent was murdered. While avenging Bent's death, the U. S. Army pursued some 300 rebels into the San Geronimo Church in Taos. After a desperate stand, the Indians were driven out and the church destroyed. As they fled, the rebels "suddenly saw the walls of the San Geronimo collapse. They took this as an omen and surrendered." The ruins are still visible today. Bodine, "Taos Pueblo," 255–56, 259–60; *California Farmer and Journal of Useful Sciences*, June 19, 1863; Keegan, *Taos Pueblo*, 29.

issues from the mountains, makes a delightful nook, in which the Indians have placed their town, consisting of two large buildings, one on each side of the stream. These buildings are made of *adobe*, about 400 feet long and from 150 to 200 feet wide, rising by successive steps until an irregular pyramidal building, five stories high presents an almost impregnable tower. If five boxes, each one smaller than the other, were piled up, the largest at the bottom, the next smaller on top and so on to the smallest, an idea may be obtained of the appearance of the pueblo buildings.

This town has always been impregnable against the assault of the marauding tribes of the plains and mountains. The Spaniards, too, have never been able to effect a lodgment and have only succeeded in bringing these Indians to terms by a regular siege. The pueblo has always been and still is the leading community among the Indians. It has furnished the great leaders in all the rebellions against the whites and made the best and pluckiest resistance.

In the Mexican War, on the 19th of January, 1847, the Mexicans and Pueblo Indians of the three towns of the Taos Valley rose and murdered Governor Charles Bent and six other persons.[2] They then marched with a force of several hundred towards Santa Fé, gathering reinforcements as they advanced. The military commander at Santa Fé, Colonel Sterling Price, learning of the movement, marched a strong force over the same road over which I traveled from Santa Fé and found the enemy strongly posted in the little hamlet of La Cañada, on the opposite side of the stream from Santa Cruz.[3] The Indians and Mexicans were charged at the point of the

2. Charles Bent was the oldest of the four Bent brothers who became famous in the Colorado and New Mexico territories. By 1823 Charles, along with brother William, was employed by the American Fur Company as a trader in the Sioux country. In 1828 the two brothers along with Ceran St. Vrain formed their own company and began construction of what become known as Bent's Fort. Four years later Charles moved to New Mexico to superintend business operations at that end of the Santa Fe Trail. Appointed governor of the territory by General Stephen Kearny in 1846, Charles Bent was killed on Taos on January 19, 1847, in an uprising of the local Mexicans and Indians. *Dictionary of American Biography* 2: 205.

3. Sterling Price briefly attended Hampden-Sidney College and prepared for a law career, but gave up his initial plans to become a successful tobacco planter in Missouri. After four years in the state legislature and a term in Congress, Price was commissioned colonel of the 2nd Missouri on August 12, 1846. Promoted to brigadier general on July 20, 1847, he was honorably discharged after putting down the Pueblo Revolt of that year. Price served as governor of Missouri from 1853 to 1857 and commanded that state's secessionist militia during the first months of the Civil War. Commissioned a major general in the Confederate army in 1862, Price, referred to as "Old Pap" by his men, never achieved notable success on the battlefield. He fled to Mexico with other ex-pats after the war, but returned to Missouri the next year and died in St. Louis on September 29, 1867. Castel, *General Sterling Price*, 3–6, 14–15, 82, 273–78, 280, 283; Heitman, *Historical Register* 1: 807.

bayonet, when they left for Taos, leaving a large number of dead on the field.

At the crossing of the Embudo, another skirmish took place, with a small loss on both sides. The Mexicans and Indians fled back to their valley and the troops pursued them over the mountains, through two feet of snow, to the walls of the pueblo, where the enemy fancied themselves secure. In times past many bloody sieges and lengthened resistance to Spaniard, Mexican and Indian had taken place here. Built of a material almost impregnable to shot, having no entrance except by movable ladders to the top of the first story, each story smaller than the one below, irregular in its plan and the whole judiciously pierced with loopholes for defence, the combination presented a system of fortification peculiarly sui generis.

The attack began on the afternoon of the 3rd of February and continued until the middle of the forenoon of the 5th. A few artillery pieces had so broken the walls that the Indians saw the fruitlessness of further resistance and surrendered. Three hundred Indians were killed and fifty Americans, including Captain John H. K. Burgwin of the Dragoons, for whom the cantonment previously referred to was named.[4]

The valley of Taos is one of the most productive in the Territory of New Mexico and yields a large amount of grain. It is mountain-locked on every side. The name of the first settler is said to have been Pando, who was for some time the only settler in the valley. It is related of him that in order to secure the friendship of the hostile Indians by whom he was surrounded, he promised his daughter, still a child, to one of the chiefs in marriage. When Juanita reached the marriageable age and let her Indian lover come to claim her, she did not fancy his dusky skin and aboriginal accomplishments, so refused to marry him. This rebuff not only incensed the chief, but his whole tribe also, and they made a descent upon Pando's ranche, killing him and all his peons, and carrying the maiden

4. John H. K. Burgwin graduated from West Point in 1830 and received a brevet appointment to second lieutenant in the 2nd Infantry on July 1, 1830. He was not commissioned second lieutenant in the 1st Dragoons until March 4, 1833, but promotion came more rapidly to first lieutenant on June 30, 1835, and captain on July 31, 1837. Burgwin's entire career was spent on the frontier. During the Mexican War he was mortally wounded on February 4, 1847, in the assault on Taos Pueblo, New Mexico. Following his death at that place on February 7, one of his fellow officers said that "the army did not furnish a better specimen of the combination of the gentleman with the officer." Heitman, *Historical Register* 1: 263; *Daily Union*, April 19, 1847.

away captive to their home south of the Arkansas River, for they were Comanches.[5] She lived with these Indians several years, was sold to the Pawnees, and again sold to a St. Louis trader, at which city she died many years ago.

To return to the thread of my narrative. I found the military agent to be a Mr. Ceran St. Vrain, a large trader in merchandise, and an extensive land holder who held title to nearly a hundred miles square.[6] Rooms were given me in the storehouse and I took my meals at St. Vrain's house.

Soon after my set-to with McGreevy, I had made up my mind that as soon as I reached Taos I would turn over my four troublesome men to the county jailer for safe keeping until I should return from Conejos and I mentioned as much to Corporal Coffey. He probably told the men, for I soon saw from their demeanor they were dreading something. Besides, they were exceedingly attentive to me and anticipated all my wishes before I could express them. Even the bruised and battered McGreevy, who could scarcely look out of his eyes, and whose "under lip hung under his chin," let no opportunity pass to conciliate me. Accordingly, long before I reached Taos, I concluded to give them full liberty and see what would come of it.

5. The Comanche people originated in the northern Plains, but quickly adapted to using the horse and eventually migrated to the southern Plains where they roamed over what are currently the states of Kansas, Colorado, Texas, Oklahoma, and New Mexico. The Comanches were primarily bison hunters although many were pushed onto reservations when Texas was admitted as a state. At the time of the Mexican War, the various Comanche peoples totaled an estimated 14,000. The Confederacy attempted to harness this manpower, promising "to furnish each warrior with a flintlock rifle and ammunition, as well as rations of sugar, coffee, salt, soap, and vinegar" in addition to bulls, cows, calves, and hogs for warriors' families. Confederate authorities reneged on the promise of rifles due to a shortage in the Southern armies. Confederate treaties with the Comanches had little impact on the frontier and by 1863 a delegation from that nation had signed a treaty of perpetual friendship with the Federal government. Kavanagh, "Comanche," 886–89, 901; Kavanagh, *Comanches*, 388–89, 394–95.

6. Ceran de Hault de Lassus de St. Vrain was of French descent and used his family money to purchase goods to supply fur traders in Taos. He made his first of many trips between St. Louis and Taos in 1824. St. Vrain briefly attempted life as a fur trapper, but quickly realized his future lay in the business end of the venture. He formed a commercial relationship with Charles and William Bent and became a partner in the construction and management of Bent's Fort. Prior to the Mexican War St. Vrain, by now a Mexican citizen, and a partner were awarded what would become known as the Las Animas Land Grant, four million acres that straddled the Mountain Route of the Santa Fe Trail. He raised a company of volunteers that assisted in the Pueblo Revolt of 1847 and was commissioned colonel of the 1st New Mexico Cavalry, but declined the latter appointment because of his age. St. Vrain spent his later years milling flour for the army and freighting both military and civilian goods throughout New Mexico and Colorado. He died in Mora, New Mexico, on October 28, 1870. Wetherington, *Ceran St. Vrain*, 15, 18–22, 25, 30, 35, 39, 60–61, 85–86.

Judge Kirby Benedict. Courtesy Palace of the Governors Photo Archives (NMHA/DCA), Negative # 006997.

At the supper table I met Judge Benedict, United States Marshal Abraham Cutler and half a dozen lawyers from Santa Fé and learned from them that nearly the whole New Mexican Bar was in town, in attendance upon Circuit Court.[7] All were invited to the ball at the house where I had stumbled upon an invitation and most of the conversation of the table was upon that subject. Supper disposed of, we made our toilets and started for the scene of festivity. As I passed the corral where my wagons were parked, I looked in for a moment, to see if my men were quiet and found them all fast asleep under the wagons. Arrived at the *baile*, I found myself in a parlor where were assembled all the lovers of the dance and jollity that the town of Don Fernandez afforded, including the court, the bar and the *genta fine*. The floor was already filled with merry dancers and four musicians were dealing out an exhilarating compound of catgut, brass and rosin. Not being a dancer, I had ample opportunity to watch the rest. The occasion was not unlike all the others I had attended in the territory. All New Mexicans are exceedingly fond of dancing, passing through the measures of the quadrille and the mazes of the voluptuous waltz with an ease and evident delight very apparent in every feature of face and limb. Some of the musicians play with considerable skill and, at times, I have listened to performers who would have been considered respectable anywhere.

Besides the dancing, there were many other games going on in the various rooms surrounding the *sala*, the principal of which was Whist. A couple of priests, a lawyer, a doctor, a Jew and a Mexican *alcalde* played about the best game I ever saw. They were a jolly set and took their wines and toddies regularly at the deals, with no interruption, except when the priests were absent for half an hour at some midnight church service, until four in the morning, leaving the table "as steady as mills," when the last game left one of the *padres* and the Jew winners, by half a score.

7. Abraham Cutler had a history as a strong anti-slavery advocate in Kansas during the 1850s, so when Senator James Lane from that state nominated him, President Lincoln dutifully offered him the nomination of United States Marshal. After reaching New Mexico, Cutler took his oath of office on April 16, 1862. One of his primary jobs was the confiscation of property and goods of Southern sympathizers, for which informants would be rewarded with a percentage. Cutler and his cronies would fake information, then the marshal would confiscate property, charge exorbitant fees and purchase, along with friends, much of the condemned property for pennies on the dollar. Cutler left office early in 1866, but lawsuits over his high-handed enforcement and peculation continued for over five years. Ball, *United States Marshals*, 35–39; *Weekly Journal Miner*, February 11, 1871.

Next day I found it necessary to have some repairs made to a wagon and the mules shod, so concluded to remain over a part of the next day. My men behaved well, notwithstanding the temptations of the city, and on my return from the *baile* I found them still sleeping under the wagons. During the time of the repairs, I wandered about the town viewing the sights, making my first call at the courthouse. I found the courtroom about forty feet long, fifteen wide and eight high. There were neither boards nor carpet to hide the earthen floor, which was damp and cold. On the south side were two windows, about two feet square each, without glass, being covered instead with cotton cloth tacked to the frames, which answered the double purpose of shutting out both light and dust.

Three chairs and three old benches afforded the only means of sitting for bar, officers, witnesses, jurors, lookers-on and those who were not fortunate in the scramble for seats had the pleasure of leaning against the wall or sitting on the floor. The roof was none of the tightest and the sky could be seen through the chinks and crannies. At the west end was the crowning glory of the room, decidedly the most ornamental feature in the establishment. A small nook, some eight feet by four, was partitioned off for the judge. The front was trimmed with a few yards of florid calico and, as a matter of comfort, a couple of boards were laid down for a floor. The little place which held His Honor much resembled a sentry box, but was inferior in point of equipment. A small pine table in front was used by the clerk, marshal and lawyers.

The county jail, that necessary adjunct to the courthouse, where prisoners are lodged and fed at the public expense, was a small room at the east end of the building. Prisoners confined there were about as safe as if picketed out on the *plaza*. At the time I saw it, the jail door was fastened with a buckskin string.

The manners of the Far Western court are rather free and easy. The proceedings are not unlike courts generally, unless I except the regular presence of an interpreter who is sworn to render all that is said into both Spanish and English. All the lawyers and officials understand the two languages and use them as occasion requires. If the jury is Mexican, it must be addressed in Spanish, while, when speaking to His Honor, the same lawyer will drop into English. During the trial I saw one lawyer arise and ask the judge for permission to smoke in court, leave was granted and the gentleman smoked a regular clay pipe through the proceedings.

Taos was the home of the celebrated Kit Carson.[8] I had met Carson in Santa Fé, where he was for some time acting as president of a general court martial. He was colonel of the New Mexican Volunteer Cavalry. His character has been highly drawn by the writers of cheap novels and his physique and costume magnified by the wood engravers who embellish such prints. In reality, Colonel Carson was a small-sized, modest-looking person, five feet seven inches in height, moderately thick-set and, like all men whose life is chiefly spent in the saddle, slightly bow-legged. In conversation he was a mild and soft-spoken man, with a voice quite like that of a woman. He had brown eyes and dark hair, with a face tanned by long exposure to the sun and wind of the mountains and plains. He dressed plainly, or in his colonel's uniform, and his whole appearance was entirely different from what I had been led to expect from the tales I had read of him.

On the afternoon of the next day after my arrival at Taos, the mules having been shod and the wagons repaired, I resumed my journey and stopped at the house of the military agent at Arroyo Hondo, six miles from Taos. The following day, I drove to Rio Colorado, a distance of fifteen miles, over an exceedingly tortuous and rough road. At this place I lodged with an old French mountaineer by the name of Charles H. Beaubien, a man covered with scars, and having his arms so stiffened by numerous breaks and batterings that he could not touch his mouth with his hands.[9]

8. Although unable to read or write, Christopher "Kit" Carson would prove adept at communicating in Spanish and Indian sign language. An extensive knowledge of the western territories gained in trapping and trading led to his being hired as a guide and hunter for the expeditions of John C. Fremont in the 1840s. Fremont's reports, combined with exaggerated press accounts, led to Carson becoming a reincarnation of James Fenimore Cooper's frontier character Natty Bumppo. Commissioned lieutenant colonel, then colonel, of the 1st New Mexico Infantry in 1861, he retained that rank when several regiments were consolidated into the 1st New Mexico Cavalry in 1862. Carson is most noted for his successful campaigns against the Apaches and Navajos which resulted in the majority of these nations being penned up at Bosque Redondo. Brevetted a brigadier general in 1865, Kit Carson died at Fort Lyon, Colorado on May 23, 1868. Remley, *Kit Carson*, 3–6, 206–209, 217–29, 262.

9. A native of Canada, Charles Hippolyte Trotier Beaubien came to New Mexico in 1822 where he ingratiated himself with Mexican officials including Governor Manuel Armijo who gave Beaubien and his partner, Guadalupe Miranda, an immense grant estimated to extend over one million acres. In 1846 following a number of years of litigation, Beaubien bought out his partner and in the same year was appointed a judge by General Stephen Kearny despite having no legal training. Beaubien virtually retired in 1851 and allowed his family to run his vast estate and business interests. He never again left Taos and died there on February 10, 1864. *Denver Rocky Mountain News*, February 9, 1908; Hafen, *French Fur Traders*, 29–41; *Minutes of the New Mexico Bar*, 24–26.

It was a curious sight to see him place a glass of whiskey in his crossed arms, tip back his head, raise the liquor up to a convenient height and send the burning liquid down his ever-craving gullet. Perhaps it was even more curious to see him raise a two gallon keg and drink out of the bung, but I am not certain.

My march after leaving Rio Colorado was through timbered country for a great part of the way, ending at Costilla, a distance of twenty-five miles. Costilla is the last town before entering Colorado Territory; in fact a few of the houses at the north end are in Colorado. From Costilla I drove the following day to Conejos, a distance of thirty miles in a direction a little south of northwest. I crossed the Rio Grande at Colonas Ferry, on a boat worked by a warp. Here I met an immense train loaded with potatoes on its way to Denver and learned that a gentleman of that place had made a "corner" in those vegetables and forced the price up to fifteen dollars per hundred weight. Of course, this ended my journey, for my orders were not to pay over seven dollars. I went on to Conejos, where there was a military garrison of Colorado cavalry, to draw rations and forage for my return trip.

My drive back to Santa Fé was over the same road, without incident worth alluding to, unless I mention that in one place I saved fifteen miles by driving my wagons along the side of a declivity with my men holding on to a rope, which led over the top of the wagons, to keep them from overturning. A day's work of a dozen men would have made an excellent road of this and saved the distance I have mentioned, but there is not energy enough in the country to do so much.

Arrived at Santa Fé, I reported my want of success, thanked Captain Garrison for his kindness in assisting me to take so pleasant a trip and resumed the routine of my duties. The day after my return, McGreevy called upon me and with an anxious visage asked if he was to be tried by court martial for his performance on the road.

"Why do you think you will be tried?" I asked.

"Because I behaved shamefully, sir," was the reply.

"How came you to break your promise to me?"

"We thought the Liftinent meant we wor not to dhrink in the towns and that he wouldn't moind a bit of a spray when we got into the mountains, where there was no one to say us."

"Does it take four canteens of whiskey for a quiet spree for four men?" I asked, remembering that their difficulties began before they finished the first.

"The four of us went to four different places for a canteen full, sir, thinking won of us at laste would get some and, begorra, we all got it!" said McGreevy, a suggestion of a smile creeping about the corners of his mouth and a twinkle in his bruised eyes.

"Don't you think I punished you enough on the Frijole?" I asked.

"Not as much as I deserved, sir, but I shud be willin' to call it quits, if it's all the same to the Liftinent," answered the culprit, a little Irish policy showing itself in the reply.

"Very well, McGreevy, I have no intention of punishing you further. The whole thing was a breach of faith, as well as discipline, on the part of you men, and could be punished, but I have no present desire to give you your deserts."

"Thank you, sir. I'll inform the rest of what you say" and he left me with an elaborate salute. I will add here that McGreevy followed me in my marches to Los Valles Grandes and Arizona and was always an excellent soldier, always taking pains to do me a favor when opportunity offered. I discharged him at Fort Whipple, Arizona and have not seen him since.[10] When I handed him his discharge, he became quite tearful and assured me that "I was one of the best friends he ever had."

In Santa Fé there was a wealthy American farmer, a rancheman, who owned one of the finest estates in the country, the houses and outbuildings of which were close within the city limits, on the southeast side, being arranged with great taste, surrounded by vegetable and flower gardens, with nothing neglected to make the grounds attractive and a pleasant place of resort to the citizens and officers. The gentleman, whom I shall call Mr. Brown, was not legally married to the woman who presided over his domestic affairs, but was the mother of his five children.[11] While this essential

10. Fort Whipple was originally laid out in the Chino Valley near the Verde River in Arizona Territory as protection for the new territorial capital. Both the capital and fort were moved the following spring about twenty miles south to the vicinity of Granite Creek. Named for General Amiel Whipple who had surveyed the region in 1853 and died of wounds received at Chancellorsville, the fort was established by Major Edward Willis, 1st California on May 18, 1864. The main purpose of the post was to protect the rich mining region from hostile Apaches. Closures and name changes marked the fort's history until the 1920s when the army transferred the property to the Public Health Service. *Soldier and Brave*, 74; Frazer, *Forts*, 14–15.

11. Mr. Brown is a pseudonym and cannot be identified.

link of the matrimonial chain was missing, it made little or no difference to the free and easy livers of a country where marital morals were low, but it did make a great difference with the wives of the officers. Mr. Brown's eldest child, Genie, was a young lady of nineteen years, who possessed all the education, accomplishments and refinement which a five years' course of study at the Sisters' Seminary in Santa Fé and a year at a St. Louis school could give her.[12] To these were added grace of person and remarkable beauty of the brunette type. To most of the balls and parties of Santa Fé, Miss Genie was sure of an invitation, but it was no uncommon occurrence to see our ladies, during the dancing, refuse to touch her hand during the swings and changes and generally hold themselves aloof. This conduct always irritated the youngsters and I have no doubt that Miss Brown received more general and marked attention from them on this very account than for any other reason. I shall not soon forget how, when the rude and coarse wife of a court official thrust her aside, causing her to step back into her train and fall against the piano senseless, a dozen young officers leaped to catch her and almost quarreled about who should take her home. Only one lady stirred to help her, the wife of a grizzled colonel of cavalry, every inch a lady, and our favorite from that time.

We were all in the habit of calling at Brown's repeatedly, alone and in squads. The fine rooms, well-selected library, the elegant musical instruments, the fine singing and playing of Miss Genie and her excellent powers of conversation and entertainment were the attractions. Not one breath of suspicion against her character was ever uttered; the purest girl that ever lived never received higher respect than this girl did from us. Only because of the father and mother's relations did the ladies *taboo* her.

One Sunday evening, near the close of my second year in Santa Fé, I asked Lieutenant Randolph to attend *tattoo* for me, so that I might make a call at the Brown's. When I reached the house and was admitted, I found the young lady sitting on a sofa, looking somewhat sad, and, although I was greeted cheerfully enough, there was something in her voice and manner which seemed to indicate that she was in no mood for receiving callers. Accordingly, I determined to make my call as brief as politeness would allow and with this

12. Miss Genie cannot be identified.

intent kept my cap in my hand, dropping the remark that I was passing, and just looked in for a moment, etc.

I had sat but two or three moments when General Carleton was announced and entered. As he came in, I rose to go, but received a look and motion from Miss Genie which meant "don't go." I sat down. The conversation ran along generally and I was not long in discovering that the general desired me to leave, indicating it by asking me if it was not time I was going to *tattoo* and similar remarks, at each of which I glanced at our fair entertainer and saw that she wanted me to stay. It was a regular game of "freeze out," where rank did not count, and a blank shoulder strap might be preferred to one enclosing a couple of stars.

At last the general, after an hour and a half's stay, rose to go. Miss Brown accompanied him to the door and, after seeing him fairly outside, returned, made me a curtsy and said, "Thanks."

"Not at all," I replied. "I have enjoyed the evening hugely. It isn't every day I can outrank a major general. I suppose you have no further use for my services?"

"I cannot explain my conduct," answered the young lady. "I do not like the man who has just left and do not like to be alone with him."

Leaving, I went back to my quarters and sat down to write a letter at half past eleven. As I wrote along, I accidentally dropped a blot on the sheet and exclaimed aloud, "Confound my luck!" At that moment Captain Selden walked through the door which had been left ajar, saying, "You'll confound the luck worse than that, young man, when you read this order" and handed me a sheet of paper. Turning it, I read an order for me to take my company and leave for Los Valles Grandes next morning at reveille to relieve a company of California Volunteers who were watching a trail into the Navajo country. At first I was amazed and then, as the ridiculousness of the whole matter burst upon me, I burst into laughter.

"Well, Curtis," said the captain, "you are the only man I know of who can greet a piece of ostracism like that with a laugh."

As soon as I could speak, I told all the incidents of the evening and when I finished we closed the door and both laughed, the captain breaking in occasionally with mock bits of advice and finally telling me "that a second lieutenant that did not know any better than to 'freeze out' a major general, deserved anything that might befall him."

That the reader may fully appreciate how unreasonably angry the general must have been, I will say, in the first place, that his headquarters were always closed on Sundays and that he had to go to his office late at night in order to write it. It was fresh, in his own handwriting and signed, not by his adjutant general, but by himself. In the second place, I was commissary and quartermaster of the post, with property enough to occupy me four days in turning over to my successor, if I worked hard all the time.

I went down to the company at midnight and turned the men out to pack for the march. When the first call for reveille sounded, I was ready to draw out, but at this juncture another order came revoking the first in a measure and giving me five days more in Santa Fé. Accordingly, the company was obliged to go into quarters again for a few days. During the day the general called to see me and with great affability assured me that he could not do a young officer a greater favor than to send him to Los Valles Grandes. "The country is full of game," said he. "The trout fill the brooks in myriads and the scenery and surroundings are beyond comparison. Even the isolation, Mr. Curtis, will have its advantages to one of your studious turn."

All very pleasant, but I had much rather have stayed in Santa Fé. Upon such slight things as a major general's temper does a second lieutenant's fate often depend.

Chapter 18

Indian Attack at Los Valles Grandes

I was the only officer with my company—the others being in the Army of the Potomac, holding colonelcies of Volunteers—and the number of men, through the various casualties incident to our campaign against the Texans, had become reduced to thirty-five.[1] Ten of those were general prisoners in the guardhouse, five wearing ball and chain, confined for various infractions of discipline, to which there were peculiar temptations in a Mexican town.

With this company and a baggage and supply train of six rickety and coverless wagons, I left the City of Holy Faith at reveille on the 24th of October, 1863, en route for my new station. The march of four days, with its camping and marching adventures, its winding through hills and down streams, its halts in two Indian villages, its fording of the Rio Grande del Norte, its ascent and descent of the Jemez Mountains, a spur of the Rocky Mountains, would of itself make a sketch much longer than the one to which I am linked.

1. Lieutenant Curtis and Company F left Santa Fe on October 24, 1863, and arrived on October 27, after a journey of fifty-two miles. On October 31, the regimental muster roll records that Company F consisted of thirty-two enlisted men present for duty and three present but under arrest. Fourteen men were absent—eight on detached service, three on leave and three absent without leave. Return of the 5th Regiment for the Month of October, 1863, U. S. Returns for Regular Army Infantry Regiments, 1821–1916.

On the morning of the fourth day, we entered the timber at the foot of the Jemez range and began our ascent. The woods were filled with wild turkey and mountain grouse and our company hunters and sportsmen laid in a good stock for the first meal in our new home. It took us from early morning until noon to reach the summit. What with constant halts to aid the tired mules up the steep places, to fill up sloughs with earth, stones and logs, to pry mired wheels up to firm ground and to mend broken harnesses and wagons, we were half a day in going over a distance which could have been accomplished by the soldiers alone in a few hours. The trees changed with our ascent from giant pines to dwarf pines, from dwarf pines to hemlock, from hemlock to aspen, and lastly from aspen to fir before we reached the top and paused for the straggling wagons and men to arrive. We were not on the extreme summit of the range, for from this place, the highest point of the road, the mountains towered upward to the right and left many hundred yards farther.

Our downward march on the western slope was through the same kind of forest, but rapidly and without rest, so that we reached the opening where the forest frayed out into the great valley in just two hours from the time we started. From the limit of the forest I caught my first view of Los Valles Grandes. The valley was fourteen miles long and of a nearly uniform width of eight miles. It was almost literally surrounded by mountains. In fact, there was no other wagon road out of it, save that by which I entered, but at the southern extremity there was a precipitous *cañon*, which let out a stream of water which rose in the valley and to the west there was another *cañon* called La Puerta, impassable for wagons, which led into Los Valles del San Antonio. The valley, on the edge of which I now stood, was lower in the centre than at the edges, not unlike a saucer, and perfectly treeless, except that opposite me a point jutted out from the mountains like a cape into the sea for about two miles and was covered densely with towering pines. Waving grass covered the whole valley.

From where we left the timber to the Volunteer encampment, the distance was just six miles and nearly all the way downhill. The encampment was at the end of the timbered point, a little to the south, and was on a little flat, enclosed by a horseshoe-shaped ridge, the cabins facing and looking out of this open side.

About a hundred yards in front of the cabins flowed a stream of pure water, about sixteen feet wide and about three feet deep, which rose from forty-two springs not a rifle's shot distance north. Across the round side of the horseshoe were strung sixteen small cabins, a kitchen, a stable and a storehouse. Up to the ridge, behind the cabins, overlooking all, was the guardhouse, in front of which paced the sentinel, and behind and a little north of the guardhouse, less than half a mile distant, was the wooded point. At the brook in front of the cabins I met the Volunteer officer.[2] He was so anxious to leave this place of exile that he told me, almost immediately after passing the first civilities, that if I had no objection he would load up the wagons as fast as I unloaded them and make his march towards Santa Fé that afternoon. In fact, he had been packed and ready to start any day during the last fortnight. I raised no objection, but on the contrary, was very glad of an opportunity to get into quarters at once.

At the first glance at the camp and its surroundings, I did not like the military situation. It seemed too open to surprise, the adjacent forest crept up too near its flank and the solitary sentinel did not have a range of vision to the rear of fifty yards. He was not on the summit of the ridge by about that distance and could see nothing to the west of it. I expressed my opinion of the situation to the Volunteer, but he remarked, "Pshaw! I haven't seen an Indian for the year I have been here and I don't believe there is one in the country." This statement did not satisfy me and, in posting the sentinel detailed from my company, I placed him where he could see the country to our rear. A fortunate move for me, as the sequel will show.

For the rest of the evening we were kept busy in getting into our huts and making ourselves comfortable. Each cabin would hold

2. This officer was Second Lieutenant Philip A. J. Russell of the 1st California. In August of 1863 First Lieutenant Erastus W. Wood had been sent to Las Valles Grandes with orders to "kill every Navajo or Apache Indian who attempts to go through that noted thoroughfare," although women and children were to be captured. Russell was advised that the department commander "desires you make the huts that you are building for your men as substantial and as comfortable as you possibly can, and lay up a good supply of wood, and if possible have a supply of hay cut and stacked up for, say, eighteen government animals, in case your own party or any other party of troops are obliged to remain during the winter at Las Valles, and, for say, what ten beef cattle would consume in four months." When Wood turned the camp over to Lieutenant Russell a few days later, the new commander was cautioned that "you must be sure to be on your guard against surprise, and teach parties of your men detached from the main body to be vigilant all the time." Russell was also ordered to construct a storehouse large enough to contain supplies needed by forty men for three months, as well as to build an oven. *Condition of Indian Tribes*, 131–33, 239.

about two men conveniently and seemed to have been built on no general system, but each after the taste of its individual occupants. Many were built of pine logs, neatly hewed on the inside, but streaked with pitch drawn out by the fire, so that it was defiling to lean against the wall. Others were built of quaking asp, a kind of poplar, and all had neat, open stone fireplaces and chimneys on the back side. As the adjacent forest of hard pine furnished a bountiful supply of fuel, there was no objection to so many fires and, in the dearth of occupation in this isolated place, labor of some kind was absolutely necessary. I thought plenty of wood chopping would keep the men out of mischief.

My own cabin, built by my predecessor, was about the shabbiest one of the lot. It was in the extreme right of the row, far from stable and kitchen, and was built of quaking asp, about ten feet long, eight feet wide and five feet high. How in the world its first occupant got into it without creeping on all fours was an enigma to me, for he measured six feet one inch in his stockings. Although I rejoice in a much lesser altitude, I could not think of bumping my head against the rafters, so I had the earthen floor dug out two feet below its original level before I moved in and entered my house by two downward steps. This house I occupied one month, when I moved into a more spacious one which I had built and which rejoiced in a glass window, a cheap carpet and many other minor luxuries, besides a tolerably well supplied bookshelf. My first cabin had no windows, but its ample fireplace, with its flue draft and its numerous chinks, furnished plenty of fresh air. The door was made of boards hewn from the log with an ax, swung on wooden hinges and was fastened by a wooden latch, raised by a leather string.

The next day after our arrival in the valley was spent in perfecting arrangements for our comfort; in filling beds with hay and cutting the hay for the same; splitting logs for firewood and repairing the cabins, which had been sadly neglected and broken after the Volunteers found they were not to remain in them a second winter. We found plenty to do on this day and were not looking sharp for Indians.

Ten head of beef cattle had been turned over to me and I had placed a soldier in charge of them, with orders to herd them in the valley immediately in front of our encampment and all day long I had from time to time noticed them grazing, not a thousand yards distant. About noon a Mexican hunter and his son had ridden into camp, the former on a mule and the latter on a *burro*, and their animals were also grazing with my cattle. About four o'clock in the afternoon, I had found time to take a book and sit down in my cabin before the open door for a little literary relaxation. I had hardly become interested when I heard a shouting out in the valley. Running to the centre of the parade, I saw my herder running at the top of his speed for camp, waving his hat and yelling at the top of his voice. Simultaneously, a war whoop resounded through the valley and I saw that half a dozen redskins had captured the ten beeves, mule and *burro* and were making down the valley.[3]

Before I had hardly taken in this part of the situation, a shot from my sentinel on the ridge and a shout of "Indians!" accompanied by the thundering clatter of a thousand hoofs, told me that the cattle stealing was but a small part of the program now enacting. A shout to my men to "Turn out!"—to "Fall in!" in rear of the guardhouse—to a corporal to bring a box of ammunition and a pickax to open it—to the men, when fallen in, to take distance right and left as skirmishers—to commence firing—was said and done in about the time it takes to write it. From my line, I could see not a hundred yards distant, about 300 Indians coming down upon us like a whirlwind. As soon as they saw we were getting into line, 300 throats gave vent to such discordant yells as rent the air to tatters and lint. They gesticulated, swung their arms and did everything to inspire terror, but while I was a new man at this business, it was an old story to my men, who were old Indian campaigners and looked and acted coolly.

I had my prisoners on the line with the rest, the five with ball and chain loading and firing as calmly as if they were leg-free, and my Mexican guests took a hand also. In fact, I believe the first Indian whose war whoop was stopped by a bullet got his quietus from old Valencia.[4] Four Indians tumbled from their saddles and two ponies fell headlong, when the charge halted, broke right and left and swept around the encampment to keep out of rifle shot in front. A cheer from the men and a general handshaking of congratulation at their escape from a well-planned attack and

3. This Indian raid occurred on November 4, 1863. *Condition of Indian Tribes*, appendix, 254.

4. José María Valencia of Cañoncito, New Mexico.

we returned to our cabins to complete arrangements for whatever might next occur. As soon as the Indians were out of shot, I ordered the chains cut from the five prisoners and returned them all to duty.

In my wood yard was a pile of logs, many of them four feet in diameter and all about twenty feet long. These we drew by hand, for we had no animals, to the different flanks of the camp, on the ridges, and built breastworks. While engaged in superintending this, I took an occasional look through my field glass at the Indians. They had assembled about a mile to the south and seemed to be holding a council of war. Presently four Indians separated from the party, collected the cattle which were feeding near and drove them up in front of my camp just out of rifle shot. Here they drove them back and forward several times, evidently challenging me to come and take them.

As I have remarked elsewhere, Indian fighting was new to me and I was not sure that I had better make any attempt to recapture my herd. To do so I must divide my command, retaining enough to prevent the main body of Indians from taking the camp. I was positive also that there was no possibility of foot soldiers overtaking the mounted Indians in charge of the herd. In fact, the whole thing was being done to draw me out of the camp, precisely what they had intended in the first place, but in which they had failed. The military reader has, of course, seen some time ago that the Indians captured my herd, letting the soldier in charge escape and alarm the garrison, and whooped to attract our attention in another direction, while the main body should charge in and seize the camp. What would have been the result had my sentinel been walking where the California sentinel used to walk and from which point the charging column could not have been seen until within a hundred yards of the camp, I hardly dare think. It is highly probable that the Navajos would have ridden out of Los Valles Grandes with thirty-eight fresh scalps.

That evening the Navajos built a fire on the opposite side of the valley and about midnight I took fifteen men and made a reconnaissance towards it. Approaching it I found the Indians had gone, but had left the hides, heads and hoofs of the ten beeves as the only evidence of their having been there. There is little danger in making a night advance on the mounted Indians of the West, for they rarely operate without their ponies and ponies are worthless in night attacks.

Life at Los Valles Grandes was somewhat monotonous socially, as I rarely received visits from the outside world, the nearest hamlet being sixteen miles away and officers of the army having but rare occasions for visiting this outpost.[5] The mail arrived from Santa Fé every Saturday afternoon, about four o'clock, in the saddlebags of two cavalrymen, who brought us all the popular magazines and papers, as well as our letters. As the hour approached for their arrival, nearly every man off duty would be lounging about the parade ground with his eyes turned anxiously towards the northeastern side of the valley, where the mountain road broke from the wood into the valley. There was a black stump standing a few rods out of the wood and when the cavalrymen appeared, it always seemed as if the stump divided into three parts, two moving down the slope into the valley and one standing still. Two specks came swiftly down the grassy road until they were hidden by the northern ridge which enclosed our encampment. I cannot convey to you any idea of the pleasurable sensation it was to me to see those two soldiers and their fine horses burst into sight again around the point of the ridge and come galloping into the parade. One must be exiled in a similar manner to appreciate the full value of the mail. Sometimes the mail failed to come on Saturday, owing to some accident or delay on the regular line beyond Santa Fé, and then, indeed, were we in the dismal dumps until it appeared.

After the men had dismounted and were busily engaged in getting the packages out of the saddlebags, one would be answering my rapid questions as to news and the other would be surrounded by my men, answering theirs. It was in war times and the express riders often had news a day or two later than the newspapers.

Life in the valley, to my men, seemed to be pleasant. The duty was light and there were no temptations to dissipation or to be out of quarters at night. Men who had been very troublesome in Santa Fé—where there was no limit to the quantity of whiskey

5. Referring to "the hills of Navajo," another soldier confessed: "Let me say that an eternal loneliness rests amongst them. Their utter desolation saddens the beholder and a prolonged existence here would cause humanity to retrograde into a savage state." He then proceeded to enumerate the reasons for his pessimistic outlook: "No books, no literary pursuits, little social pleasure, and no exercise." *Denver Rocky Mountain News*, April 8, 1864.

obtainable—under the enforced temperate habits of our encampment developed many excellent traits and gave no trouble whatever. Their evenings were spent over papers and books, with which they were well supplied, and quiet games and their days in hunting or scouting.

There were two posts, but, except at the guardhouse, sentinels did not walk post during the daytime. After the new guard was mounted at eight o'clock in the morning, the old guard, numbering six men and a non-commissioned officer, a limited number of volunteers from the men not on duty and Valencia, who was employed as guide, went on a scout until three o'clock or later. This scout was for the purpose of looking up Indian signs, but the men were allowed to shoot game and rarely returned without a deer or a few turkeys and grouse. We were in the midst of a game region. Ducks swam in the brook before our cabins and every few mornings some nearly breathless soldier would arouse me before reveille for permission to shoot them. Deer grazed in herds in sight of Sentinel No. 1 and turkeys and grouse were everywhere to be met with in the woods. There were no fish in our brook, but six miles away, in the valley of San Antonio, there was a stream literally swarming with trout. I have set a gunny sack in a small tributary of this brook, with the mouth held open with sticks and, going upstream and beating the water with a willow branch, have driven the trout into the bag until it was a living mass of flapping, shining fish.

Bears, panthers, wildcats and wolves, both the gray and coyote, were frequently met with and our Mexican hunters, Valencia and son, were constantly employed by the soldiers in tanning the skins of those animals. The wolves were very easily taken by poisoning the offal of the deer and beef cattle. I have found as many as seven gray wolves lying around the poisoned flesh in the morning and the scouting party has brought in five more the same day, which had died in various parts of the valley.

During the time my wagons were absent to convey the Volunteers to Santa Fé, I had no means of communication with headquarters between mails, except by sending men on foot. Knowing the celerity with which Indians and Mexicans make long marches, I dispatched Valencia and his son to Santa Fé at eleven o'clock on the night of the Navajo attack, with a full account of the same. The distance by cut-offs known to them was eighty-two miles and they handed my letter to the department commander at half past three o'clock on the afternoon of the next day, having traveled at the rate of five miles an hour.

In my letter to the commanding general, I said that the Navajos had taken the road to Pena Blanca, where they must cross the Rio Grande and, being now well-rationed with my beef for a campaign, would probably operate in the neighborhood of Gallesteo, crossing the Santa Fé and Rio Grande road near Pino's ranche and that if a cavalry force was sent immediately down the road, it stood a good chance to intercept them. For reasons best known to him, however, the general sent the cavalry to me, where there was no further use for it and the Navajos did precisely what I supposed they would do—ran off several thousand sheep from the grazing lands of Gallesteo. Had the cavalry been sent to the point indicated in my letter, nothing but egregious carelessness could have prevented their meeting with the Indians.

I was very glad to see the three California officers who came with the command and for the two days which they spent with me, in order to rest their horses after a forced march, we fished in the valley of San Antonio. We took a number of men with us, detailed some to guard and graze the horses, while the rest fished. In passing, I will say that I have often gone to this brook alone, armed with a rifle and two revolvers, and caught fish with the loops of the lariat over my left elbow, the horse cropping grass at the other end and looking over my shoulder for Indians between the nibbles and bites. I did this after I had discovered a path over the mountain practicable for traveling on horseback. I always came and returned by La Puerta, reserving the path for an escape in case of an attack. In the open valley I had little to fear, as my horse was very fleet and there was no chance of an ambuscade.

Chapter 19

Pueblos and Navajos

After two days the cavalry left the valley and on the same day my wagons returned from Santa Fé, loaded with commissary and quartermaster stores for our use. They also brought instructions for all but one wagon and one set of mules to be sent back. Six mules and a wagon were thought to be sufficient for hauling wood for a small force like mine.

Now that the reader has become somewhat familiarized with my surroundings and manner of living, I must relate a second Indian affair, which occurred about the middle of November, but little over a month after I took command of the camp. I had become familiar with all my surroundings within a radius of twelve miles and was quite competent to act as guide over any trail or pathway within the limits of my command. My new cabin had been completed, I had moved in and, for a bachelor, was very comfortable.

Valencia was employed as a spy and guide and was, in addition to this, frequently sent out hunting for the kitchen. One morning he had left camp before reveille, in order to reach Los Vallecitos, four miles south of Great Valley, before sunrise. He had been gone about an hour and I was enjoying breakfast in my most comfortable manner, i.e., reading and eating too, when I heard rapid footsteps approaching my door and presently Valencia tumbled into the room without knocking and with exhausted breath gasped, "*Muchos Navajos, Teniente, muchos Navajos*" (Many Navajos, Lieutenant, many Navajos).

To my questions where and how many, he replied that he had been pursued from the southern bounds of the valley by a mounted party of about fifty Navajos who were now just over the ridge to the south of the camp. Giving a hasty order to the first sergeant to get the men under arms without delay and without noise, I took my field glass and went to the crest of the hill to inspect. Lying down, I looked through the top of the grass and saw that a party of fifty-three Indians were halted, as if in consultation, about two miles to the south and they were in full war costume, painted and feathered to the scalp. Evidently, by their conduct, they were unaware of the existence of a camp of soldiers near them and, after a brief talk, resumed their march in the direction of La Puerta.

I returned to the parade and sent for the mule team, which had gone for fuel; as soon as it arrived, had the six antiquated hybrids saddled with pack saddles; and, as we had no others, packed two men into each. With these I sent two cavalrymen who had arrived with the mail the night before, giving each one a "blacksnake" with which to spur the flagging zeal of the mules and bring my men, by the mountain path before mentioned, to the other end of the Puerta before the Indians. My orders to this novel "cavalry" were to get beyond the Indians and to meet them in the *cañon*, but on no account to fire unless the Indians showed fight, to leave their mules picketed at the entrance and so dispose themselves as to impress the Indians with the idea that there were more soldiers in front of them than fourteen. I would follow up close behind the Navajos and between us I thought we could capture them without much bloodshed.

After the "cavalry" had left, I kept my men out of sight, until I saw that the Indians were well into the *cañon* and supposed the horsemen were well on their way to their destination, then I rapidly closed into the *cañon* and waited. After a time, I saw the Indians rise into sight on a slope a mile away and it was plain that they had perceived me following in their rear, for they broke into a trot and shouted back what was doubtless intended for opprobrious epithets, for the gestures accompanying them were certainly of a "sarcastic" character, to say the least. But a few moments more elapsed, when the Indians showed evident confusion. Then they rode at a gallop to the north side of the *cañon*, evidently looking for a place of escape. Failing to find one, they next rode furiously to the south side, where they met with no better success, halted and consulted. After a brief conference, one of their number rode out and showed a white flag. Upon this, I rode up and made signs for them to dismount and lay down their weapons. They did so and retired from their ponies and weapons long enough for my men to secure them.

I was certainly very much surprised at such a bloodless victory and could account for it in no way. The Navajos are a brave tribe and do not generally surrender without some show of fighting. However, I could congratulate myself over the success of my strategy, shook hands with the chief and began my return march to camp. We had marched but a short distance when I heard one of the veterans of my company, Private Cleary, say to a comrade, Private Hoey, "Do ye moind the cut o' that chap's hair, Mike?"

"Indade I do, Tom."

"He's no Navajo."

"Not a bit of it."

I had a great respect for the opinion of these old soldiers, for they had campaigned against Indians in Texas, Utah, Colorado and New Mexico long before I had ever seen a redskin, so without appearing to notice their remarks, I approached the chief and said, interrogatively, "Apache?"

A shake of the head.

"Ute?"

Another shake.

"Navajo?"

"*Si, Señor*," and a bow of the head.

It seems the chief could speak Spanish, but I was not up in that tongue at that time, so could not talk with him. I was, however, satisfied that my prisoners were Navajos, notwithstanding the undertoned growling of Private Cleary, who had again observed to his Irish companion, "Mike, did ye iver see Navajos with blankets like thim?"

"Niver," quickly answered the affirmative Hoey.

When within a mile of camp, we met Valencia, who had not been with us since we left the post. As soon as he came up to the

Indians, there seemed to be an immediate and mutual recognition between them. He and the old chief met and embraced, with a "*Como lo va, compadre*?" ("How do you do, friend?"). After a few more salutations, Valencia approached in a somewhat shamefaced manner, saying, "*Teniente, los Indios son Pueblos*" (Lieutenant, these Indians are Pueblos).

The reader will understand the joke, when I tell him that many of the principal towns in New Mexico are inhabited by Indians, a relic of the civilization which Cortéz found when he entered Mexico. These Indians constitute the best part of the inhabitants of the country; are temperate, frugal and industrious. They are also very brave and in the Mexican War, when General Stephen W. Kearny made a conquest of the Territory of New Mexico, they made the best and most desperate stand in its defence against our troops and in our Civil War many of them enlisted in the Volunteer regiments raised in the Territories of Colorado and New Mexico.[1] They dress in their towns in the Indian style, generally, and when at war paint and disfigure themselves like any other Indians, so that a green soldier would not see any difference between them and other tribes, but to the experienced eye there are many points of difference.

The party of Pueblos which I had captured was from the town of Santo Domingo and was in pursuit of a party of Navajos, who had stolen fourteen of their cows the night previous.[2] When they

1. Brevet Major General Stephen W. Kearny died in St. Louis on October 31, 1848. His thirty-six-year military career started on March 12, 1812, with a commission as first lieutenant in the 13th Infantry. Captured at Queenstown, Kearny was exchanged and promoted to captain in 1813. The good will of General Winfield Scott led to his retention in the postwar downsizing as a captain in the 2nd Infantry. In 1825, now assigned to the 1st Infantry, Kearny participated in the expedition to the Yellowstone country. He assisted in the construction of Jefferson Barracks and won promotion to major of the 3rd Infantry. In March of 1833 Kearny became lieutenant colonel of the 1st Dragoons and two years later was elevated to colonel. He led his dragoons on numerous Indian campaigns and expeditions until assigned to command an invasion of New Mexico with the rank of brigadier general. He annexed that territory to the United States in August of 1846 and by the end of the year had also overseen the capitulation of California. Kearny spent most of 1847 quarreling with and testifying against John C. Fremont and was brevetted major general just months before his death. Hutton, *Soldiers West*, 43–61.

2. Santo Domingo Pueblo was located approximately thirty miles southwest of Santa Fe. Although it shared the same misfortunes as other Pueblo peoples, such as disease, slavery, and attacks from neighbors, the Santo Domingo people remained one of the largest pueblos although the physical buildings were only two stories high. The Santo Domingo people remained influential in the territory long after their participation in the revolt of 1680. Lieutenant Amiel Whipple was greeted hospitably during his visit in 1853 and toured the entire settlement, including the interior of the kiva, but could add no new details to what others had experienced. By 1860 their population had dwindled to just 261 people, although they still claimed 75,000 acres. Lange, "Santo Domingo Pueblo," 379–81; White, *Pueblo Indians*, 20; *California Farmer and Journal of Useful Sciences*, June 19, 1863.

saw Valencia, they pursued him with the intention of asking him if he had seen any signs of Navajos in the valley. Seeing that he was frightened and disappeared, they gave up the pursuit and resumed their march.

My appearance and demonstration had astonished them beyond measure. When I put the questions, "Apache?" "Ute?" "Navajo?" the chief thought I was asking if he was in pursuit of these tribes and so answered "No" to the first two and "Yes" to the last. Of course, my fellow officers at Santa Fé had their laugh at my brilliant strategy, its successful capture and peaceful result.

A week after my captives had left Los Valles Grandes, at the close of a fruitless hunt after the cattle thieves, a gentleman rode up to my cabin about nightfall, mounted upon a mustang and accompanied by a Mexican guide mounted on a mule. The gentleman introduced himself as Theodore H. Dodd, United States Agent for the Navajo tribe of Indians.[3] He handed me a letter of introduction from the department commander, which stated that Dodd was on his way to the Indian town of Jemez to prevent the massacre of a number of Navajo women and children who were living there and authorized me to furnish him all the aid in my power.[4]

Dodd explained, after he had dismounted and entered my cabin, that the Navajos, being at war with the Government, many of their principal men had left their wives and children, together with a few old men, in the town of Jemez for safety. The party of Santo Domingo Indians who had been captured by me had returned home very much vexed at their want of success in not

3. Theodore H. Dodd was commissioned captain in the 2nd Colorado on December 14, 1861, and promoted to lieutenant colonel on February 21, 1862. When the 2nd and 3rd Colorado were combined to form the 2nd Colorado Cavalry in 1863, Dodd continued as lieutenant colonel in the new regiment. Mustered out after the expiration of his three-year enlistment, he unsuccessfully lobbied for an appointment as sutler at Fort Union. Appointed agent for the Navajo Indians at Bosque Redondo, he arrived there on June 25, 1865, although his paperwork was delayed. Dodd died there on January 16, 1869, of a paralytic stroke shortly after being wounded in the arm by an arrow. Theodore H. Dodd Pension Records; Letters Received by the Commission Branch, February 20, 1865; *Condition of Indian Tribes*, appendix, 233; *Daily New Mexican*, January 23, 1869.

4. Jemez Pueblo was on the Jemez River about twenty-five miles northwest of Bernalillo. The Jemez people frequently resided with Navajo groups, occupying several village sites until coalescing into the Jemez Pueblo in the early eighteenth century. They relied on herding, supplemented by hunting and trading. The U. S. Congress confirmed the old Spanish land grant to the "Pueblo of Jemez" in 1858. Two years later the Jemez residents numbered 650 and laid claim to an area of more than 17,000 acres. A patent covering this land was signed by President Abraham Lincoln in 1864. Sando, "Jemez Pueblo," 418–19, 422–23, 426–27; *California Farmer and Journal of Useful Sciences*, June 19, 1863; Sando, *Nee Hemish*, 19.

overtaking and recapturing the cows stolen from them and, learning through a Jemez Indian that these women and children were at Jemez, they had determined to wreak vengeance upon the Navajos by killing them. Upon my expressing some surprise that the Jemez Indians should permit such a grave outrage of the laws of hospitality where they outnumbered by several hundreds the Domingians, Dodd further explained that the peculiar situation of Jemez, in an advanced position towards the Navajo country, had made it to their advantage to be upon good terms with these predatory nomads and that they had not dared to refuse protection to the women and children sent to them. The Domingians had told the Jemez Indians that, if they interfered to prevent the slaughter of the Navajos, they would be considered by the military authorities as allies of that tribe and treated accordingly.

After some consultation, I told Dodd that I could mount six men only, unless I put two in a saddle, as I had in my recent strategic manœuvre, but that would necessitate slow traveling, unless we started at once. He said there was no necessity for us to start before morning and he thought we had better take all the men we could, even if we marched at a walk. I told him that it was not likely that fight would be made against us, but that I would put two men on each of the two largest mules, which would give us eight men besides ourselves.

Before going to bed, I instructed the guard to call the cooks at three o'clock, so that we could get breakfast and be on the road shortly after four. I still had nothing but pack saddles for my men to ride on, but by folding the blankets in a peculiar manner, placing them in the saddles and looping the packing straps to answer as stirrups, they could be made tolerably comfortable.

As my guest was agent for the Navajo tribe, I learned much of those Indians during the evening, before bedtime. They are different from the wild tribes of the plains and the village Indians of New Mexico. They own large herds of sheep and ponies and cultivate the soil to a considerable extent, but have no fixed habitations. They are a fine looking race. The men do not disdain labor, like their red brethren of the plains, but are industrious and frugal.

Next morning we were called at fifteen minutes before four, had finished our breakfast and were ready for the march at half past. My camp was to be left in charge of the sergeant for the next three days

Colonel Christopher "Kit" Carson. Courtesy of Massachusetts MOLLUS Civil War Photographs, United States Army Heritage and Education Center.

and I did not anticipate any danger to it, because the Navajos had recently been severely whipped by the New Mexican Volunteers under Colonel Kit Carson. There were several regiments of New Mexican Volunteers raised during the late war, which were largely officered by old sergeants of the Regular Army, some Mexicans and a few scouts. The celebrated Kit Carson was colonel of the 1st New Mexican Cavalry.

I appointed the Mexican guide *arriero* (muleteer) and gave him a wagon whip with which to mend the pace of the mules, should it be necessary, for my men were not supplied with spurs and a mule's hide is proof against withes or cudgels. Our singular cavalcade took up its march along the stream to the southern end of the valley, where we crossed it to the east and entered the timber. This stream and the one in the valley, six miles to the west, unite and form the Jemez River. The timber was of pine and the trees were of giant size. The road wound about through valleys and over hills for four or five miles. At one place it passed along the side of a precipice with but half dozen feet between it and the brink. A valley of a few hundred acres lay 200 feet below us, filled with red sandstone columns, the tops of a few of which were even with our path. The walls of the precipice were often worn into many fantastic shapes by the action of the weather for ages and here and there arches as well as the columns could be seen, which seemed almost the work of art, so irregular and symmetrical were the outlines.

The explanation of the origin of these sandstone columns and the many other similar shafts found in the Rocky Mountain country is very simple. They are formed by the erosion or cutting of running water, which separates them from the mound or bluff. The disintegration or wearing of the sides proceeds more rapidly than the top, so that they become gradually narrowed down to slender shafts, without becoming diminished in height. Many of the monuments had a cap of black stone on their tops, jutting a little outside the red sandstone on all sides, which often gave them a certain quaint resemblance to human forms. They are beautiful monuments of the gentle but persistent action of the weather in that climate.

A ride of four hours and the pine trees gradually began to dwarf and in an hour more had sunk to *piñons*, a tree bearing the same relation to the pine that the scrub oak does to the oak. The *piñon* grows where it rarely rains and attains the size of, and looks at a distance, very much like an apple tree. At the end of the fifth hour, we stood on the edge of a plain and 2,000 feet down a slope of forty-five degrees flowed the Jemez River toward the east. The valley of the river was simply a *cañon* through a plain, for directly across from where we stood, the plain continued to the south. The path crept down the side of the *cañon* by innumerable zig-zags to the bottom and ended close by the riverbank, amid a dozen hot springs, so hot that I have frequently boiled eggs in them.

Permitting the soldiers to ride on down the valley, I remained behind for a short time, in order to examine the springs and explore their surroundings. Near the point where we struck the river a somewhat dilapidated building stood. It was built of the trunks of *piñons* and cedars, set up in the ground, with the chinks filled with mud. The house was about fifty feet long and had formerly been occupied by invalids who came to the *aguas termales* (hot springs) to be benefited by their healing properties. The house had been abandoned since the Indian troubles, but some weeks afterwards, when I sent some sick soldiers there, the people flocked in and filled it up again.

The manner of bathing was by digging a long trench in the ground near a spring, about seven feet long and three wide. The water was turned in until the hole was full, when it was allowed to cool for some time, in order not to scald the bather. There was a small gateway at the foot to empty the bath. To screen the bather, willow branches were framed over the trench and covered with blankets.

In the river opposite the springs was an island about a hundred feet long; the stream on each side of it was about twenty feet wide and twelve inches deep. In winter, I have seen fragments of ice floating down on the southern side of the island, while the water on the northern side was above flood.

About the springs were incrustations of pure sulphur; sulphur that would burn when lighted with a match.

A half mile above the springs stood the ruins of a church, the tower of which was imbedded in the hillside up to the belfry, so that I found no difficulty in stepping into the belfry windows from the ground. The hill had evidently slid down upon the church and caused its abandonment. The walls of the building were of stone laid in mud and, although the roof, doors and windows had all disappeared, were nearly as perfect as when first built. Covering nearly two acres about the church were the ruins of other buildings. This had been a station out of a Jesuit Indian mission over two centuries ago.[5]

The beams in the church tower, which had supported the bells, were still sound. They had originally been about two feet square, as could be seen by the apertures in the wall in which they had been set, but they had withered, if that word can be thus used, to the size of my arm. They had the ring of sound wood and cut like it, but from outside influences had worn away without rotting.

After a half hour's exploration, I remounted and, after a six-mile canter, overtook my command at the town of Cañoncito. This town is built around a *plaza* of about an acre and is really one continuous building, open at one corner only. It is flat-roofed and one story high, built of *adobe*. The entrance is wide enough to admit a wagon and in case of an attack can be closed. There were a few stables and *jacals* outside, but no residences. About thirty families occupied the town.

From Cañoncito to Jemez the distance was four miles and we pressed on, as we had been doing since morning, with all the speed we could get out of the mules without breaking them down. As Jemez came to view across the broad bottomlands and the end of our journey approached, our anxiety increased lest we should be too late to accomplish our purpose. The men in the pack saddles were suffering from their constrained and awkward positions, while the poor mules required frequent reminding from the "blacksnake" that they must mend their gait.

The last two miles of our march lay through the cultivated lands of the town. Every few furlongs we splashed through the *acequias* by which the land was irrigated and on each side stood fields of still-ungathered corn, with yellow pumpkins and gourds scattered through the rows. The low town was but a mile away and the tinned spire of a church, peering above the houses, flashed in the rays of the afternoon sun full in our sight, when we suddenly became conscious of a murmur in the air. Ordering a halt, I listened. In a moment there came the unmistakable war whoop

5. This church cannot be positively identified.

of a band of Indians and we knew that the Santo Domingians were ahead of us. Telling the men to come as fast as possible, Dodd and I put spurs to our horses and dashed ahead. We flew over the ground, past the corn, across the *acequias* and through a long, narrow street into the town. Dashing around a corner, amid the most hideous din conceivable, we came into the *plaza*, the outskirts of which, and the surrounding roofs, were covered with the Jemez Indians, men, women and children as spectators. Riding round some object in the centre of the square were some 150 mounted Indians, painted and hideously ornamented, as only the American Indian can paint and ornament. Pressing through this ring, I burst into the centre and behold, alas! every one of the poor creatures whom we had ridden so long and so hard to save, dead. Dead and mangled most horribly.

But I cannot dwell upon this scene. I went back to meet my men and took them by a side street to the house of the priest, *Padre* Gutierrez, where we were furnished with quarters and stabling.[6] The priest told me that the Indians from Santo Domingo had arrived about half an hour before we had and, although he had made every exertion to rouse his people to protect the Navajos, he had failed and they had been butchered in cold blood before the eyes of the inhabitants.

After resting awhile, I went back to the *plaza* on foot to see what was going on, for the whooping still continued unabated. The first object that caught my eye through the cloud of dust which enveloped everything was a fierce pair of buffalo horns, overlopped with shaggy hair. The sturdy form of a naked Indian soon revealed itself beneath the horns, with shield and lance, dashing at full speed around the square on a white pony, which, like his own body, was painted all the colors of the rainbow. Then, in single file, his followers came on, painted to the eyes, their own heads and their horses covered with all the strange equipment that the brute creation could afford in the way of horns, skulls, tails, feathers and claws. As they passed me, they fired a volley over the heads of the crowd, dropped into a walk until their ponies recovered breath, when off they went at full speed to the opposite side of the *plaza*, where they went through a mimic fight with lances, muskets, and bows and arrows. Sometimes a fellow would stoop almost to the earth to

6. Padre Gutierrez cannot by positively identified.

shoot under his horse's belly, at full speed, or to shield himself from an impending blow.

Returning to the priest's, I sent word by him that unless the Santo Domingo Indians left immediately for their town, I should fire upon them and authorize the Jemez Indians to do the same. It is needless to say that they were not long in leaving.

The bodies of the thirty-one Navajos were buried on a hill close by the town that evening.[7]

7. Since Theodore Dodd had not been appointed Navajo agent until 1863, this expedition could not have occurred as Curtis described it. His description of the affair was obviously based upon the following incident that occurred on September 27, 1863: "Lieutenant P. A. J. Russell, 1st infantry California volunteers, with four mounted men and a party of Pueblo Indians, started from Valles Grande on the trail of a band of Navajos who had stolen a lot of stock from the Pueblos. The trail was followed into the town of Jemez, where the party recaptured one hundred and twenty five head of sheep and two horses. Killed eight Navajos and took twenty women and children prisoners." *Condition of Indian Tribes*, appendix, 252.

Chapter 20

Indians of New Mexico

It seems to me absolutely necessary to give some account of the Indians of New Mexico, together with a brief history of the early settlement of the country. There is hardly any question discussed by our newspapers of which they are so conspicuously ignorant as of the Indian question. All Indians are alike to them—Comanche, Sioux, Navajo and Pueblo—while in reality there is almost as much difference between them as between a Malay and a Chinaman.[1] I once read in one of the great New York dailies that the "Isleta Indians had been successfully put upon a reservation by the Government, and that they had over a thousand acres under cultivation, and fully solved the practicability of placing the Indians upon reservations, and compelling them to abandon the wild and marauding life of the plains."

1. "Sioux" is a generic term used to describe various related tribes of the northern Plains. The term has its origins in the Ojibwa language and therefore reflects a name given to them by outsiders. Siouxan groups fall into three main divisions—Santee, Yankton, and Yanktoni—which are further subdivided into bands. When Curtis uses the generic term, it is unclear to whom he might specifically be referring. The Federal government began "an aggressive military policy" against the Sioux and other Plains Indians during the 1860s. This policy included the construction of new forts to protect immigrant routes and the pursuit and defeat of non-compliant groups (renegades to the government) who refused to live on established reservations. Tensions remained high for several decades, resulting in military victories for both Indians and whites. DeMallie, "Sioux Until 1850," 718–19; Gibbon, *The Sioux*, 6.

Now the fact is, when Francisco Vasquez Coronado entered New Mexico in 1541, he found this same town of Isleta standing precisely where it stands today, with its regularly built houses of four and five stories in height and the inhabitants living by the cultivation of the soil precisely as they do today.[2] To be sure, they were destitute of the horse, ox, sheep and goat, which were introduced by the Spaniard and for a beast of burden possessed only the dog. But they had large flocks of turkeys, the feathers of which they worked into robes, the wild buffalo furnished them with ample clothing and bedding and they wove the hair of the dogs into blankets.

The discovery of New Mexico is a romance in itself. We all are acquainted with the acts of the Puritan fathers and the dates of their settlements, but I will venture to say that few know that the Mexican town of Santa Fé, in the very interior of the country beyond the Great Plains, in the Rocky Mountains, not an easy place to reach even at the present day, was settled in 1543, seventy-seven years before the landing at Plymouth Rock.

On June 17, 1527 Panfilo de Narvaez sailed from San Lacar de Barrameda with five ships and 600 men, intending to land in Florida and move north in search of El Dorado and gold and silver mines.[3] The force of Narvaez landed near Tampa Bay in Florida on the 28th of February, 1528. They were fully mounted and were

2. Don Francisco Vasquez Coronado led an expedition into what is now the American Southwest in search of the fictitious seven cities of Cibola. Governor Coronado left New Galicia, a province of New Spain, in 1540 with a small army of *conquistadores* and Indian slaves, but found only mud-brick pueblos instead of cities of gold. Their first stop was a Zuni pueblo, where the Spanish suggestion of submission was rebuffed violently, a scene that was to be repeated during the expedition. The *entrada* added to the geographical knowledge of the region, including the discovery of the Grand Canyon, but Coronado returned to Mexico with nothing of substance beyond a few semi-precious stones. The Isleta Pueblo was located on the Rio Grande about fifteen miles south of Albuquerque, although it was composed of several smaller villages that had changed location and composition over time. The residents numbered 440 in 1860 and 786 in 1864, claiming over 110,000 acres, and relied on agriculture for subsistence. The Indians from Isleta seemed to be in constant conflict with the Navajos. Isleta differed from other Pueblo groups in that it did not have a strong Kachina cult for its young men although there were Kachina chiefs among the elders. *Dictionary of American History* 2: 61; Flint, *Documents of the Corondao Expedition*, 2-3. Ellis, "Isleta Pueblo," 351, 355; *Rocky Mountain News*, October 21, 1863; December 2, 1863; November 29, 1865; Goldfrank, *Isleta Paintings*, 7.

3. Panfilo de Narvaez was a conquistador and civil official in Cuba before receiving a commission from the Spanish crown to conquer and settle Florida. After landing in Florida, Narvaez dispatched his ships and began an ill-advised overland march in search of treasure. Stranded without tools or supplies, Narvaez and his men built rude boats and attempted to reach Mexico by sea, but the commander of the expedition was lost in November of 1528. *Dictionary of American History* 13: 382–83.

accompanied by many priests. They pushed on at once into the country and are supposed to have penetrated as far north as the upper boundary of Georgia, where they had several fierce battles with the Apalachians, which proved so disastrous to the Spaniards that they returned to the coast at Apalachee Bay and built five vessels in which to sail to the Spanish settlements in Mexico. They built these boats without tools of any kind, except their swords and such as they could manufacture from their stirrups, spurs, etc. The boats were smeared with resin obtained from the pines and rigged with cords made from the palmettos and the manes and tails of horses. During the time they were occupied in building the boats, they subsisted almost entirely on horse flesh, killing one horse every three days.

From the time the Spaniards landed at Tampa Bay until they embarked at Apalachee Bay, they had marched 1,400 miles. The boats were five in number, thirty-one feet long and about fifty men were placed in each. They embarked on the 22nd of September, killing their last horse before sailing. Out of the 600 men who left Spain, but 250 were now left.

They sailed along the coast with numberless adventures and hardships and, in crossing the mouth of the Mississippi River, the boats were separated. Two only kept together, the others were never heard of again. Alvar Nuñez Cabeza de Vaca, in command of these two crews, landed on an island on the coast of Louisiana or Texas and went into winter quarters.[4] During the winter all died but Cabeza de Vaca, a Spaniard named Dorantes and a negro. These three men lived with the coast Indians six years before they could effect their escape. Then they began a journey into the interior, crossing the Great Plains into New Mexico. They found that country densely populated by a people living in houses and large towns. They were everywhere received with cordiality by the inhabitants, who looked upon them as gods or superior beings. Gifts were lavished upon them and the sick and ailing were brought to them to be cured. They were very fortunate in

4. Alvar Nuñez Cabeza de Vaca was appointed treasurer of the Narvaez expedition in 1527. After being captured by Indians along the Texas coast the following year, Cabeza de Vaca and a dwindling band of comrades remained with various Indian tribes until 1535. In that year they began an overland trek across Texas and Mexico that ended in Mexico City. A report of his travels led to the Coronado expedition of 1540. *Dictionary of American History* 13: 593–94.

making many cures and so attained to great eminence in the opinion of the Indians.

Vaca pursued his journey down the Gila River into New Spain and to the City of Mexico, where he arrived in the spring of 1536. He sailed for Portugal on the 10th of April and arrived in Lisbon August 9, 1537, having been gone ten years, six of which he was a prisoner and four a wanderer over the plains. These wanderings, which have been minutely written out in Spanish, are intensely interesting and form a book of several hundred pages.

Thus New Mexico was discovered. Its further explorations were effected by Francisco Vasquez Coronado, Governor of New Spain, who with an army of 800 men, marched from Culiacan on the Pacific Coast, north and northwest, by way of the Colorado River and Colorado Chiquito River, through the Indian town of Zuni into New Mexico, arriving on the Rio Grande in 1541.[5] He found the country densely populated and had some fierce battles with the natives. He made no attempt at colonization, but returned to Mexico the following year. Santa Fé was occupied by the Spaniards for some time, about 1543, but permanent settlement was not made until 1680. The town was in existence and occupied by Indians when New Mexico was discovered.

At the present day there are but twenty-six villages of Pueblo Indians in New Mexico. They have abandoned many of their former towns on account of diminishing population and have united with their neighbors. These twenty-six villages are principally situated in the valley of the Rio Grande and their whole population does not now exceed 12,000. Formerly there were four distinct nations, speaking as many languages, namely the Piros, Teguas, Queres and Tagnos.[6] Each village is distinct from

5. Zuni Pueblo was located on the Zuni River and contained 1,300 inhabitants in 1860. These people filed no claim that year, their territory ranged to the Zuni Mountains and encompassed several smaller, associated villages. These Indians were ruled by a governor elected by a popular vote that was usually won by the pueblo's most wealthy resident. Primarily peaceful agriculturalists, Zunis occasionally engaged in conflicts with other Indians. Although a few men owned old muskets, most armed themselves with bows and arrows, along with stout oak clubs used to kill wounded foes since they never took prisoners. Zuni agriculturalists kept up a substantial trade by supplying U. S. forts with thousands of dollars' worth of corn, thereby keeping the Indian economy in a "thriving condition." Following the Civil War, interaction with army officers, such as Charles Curtis, declined as the Zunis became important traders with the Navajos and Apaches. Woodbury, "Indian Town of Zuni," 467, 472; *Rocky Mountain News*, April 27, 1864; Crampton, *Zunis of Cibola*, 114–15.

6. Modern linguistic scholarship has identified Curtis's Piros as Tiwa, Teguas as Tewa, Queres as Keresean, and Tagnos as Tanoan. A fifth linguistic group not identified by Curtis is Towa. Eggan, "Pueblos: Introduction," 234–35.

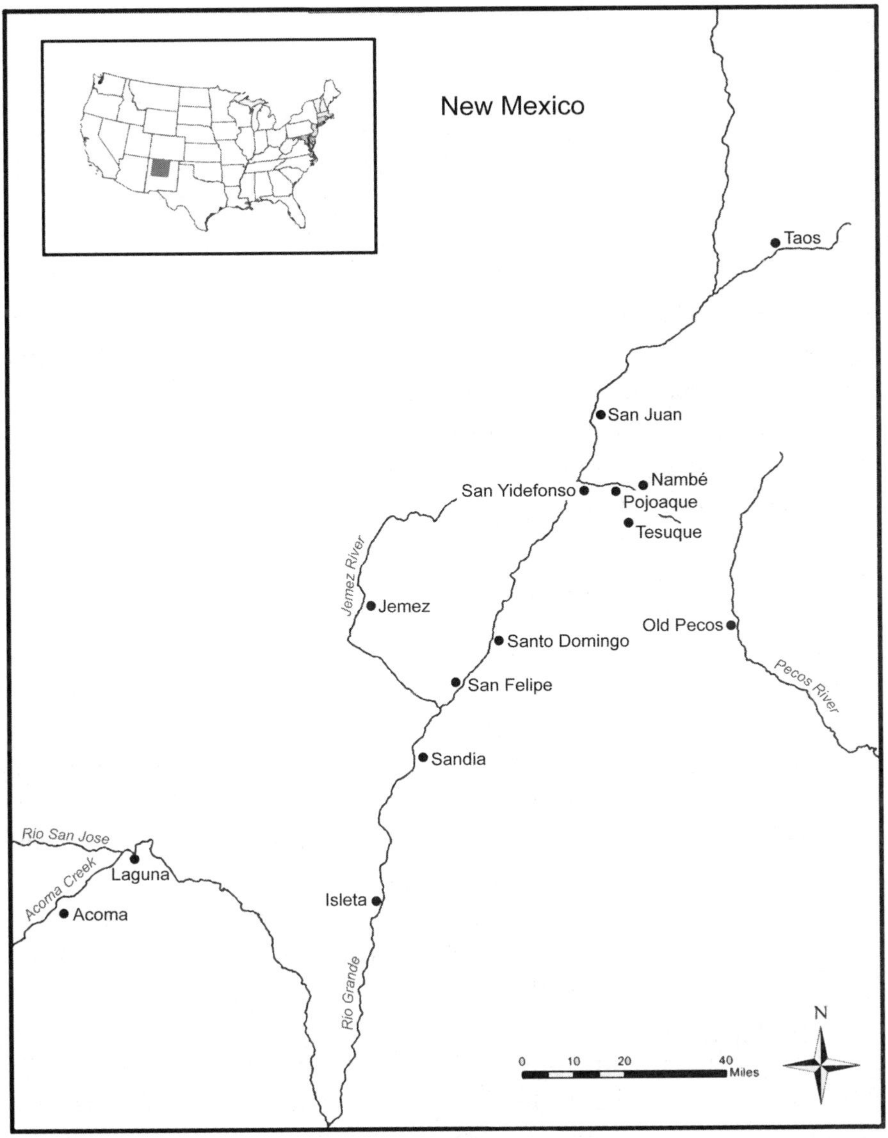

New Mexico Pueblos.

its neighbor and has no common bond with the others. They are ruled by a governor, an *alcalde*, a constable and a council of wise men. They also have a war captain, who has full powers in time of war, but has no authority in time of peace. They have generally embraced the Christian religion and have churches in all their towns. They are a quiet and orderly people generally and form the best part of the population of New Mexico.

They dress in cloth of their own manufacture, woolen in winter and cotton in summer.

One of the best samples of a Pueblo Indian village, as it existed at the time of the invasion of Coronado, is that of Taos, situated seventy-five miles north of Santa Fé and which I visited while stationed at Los Valles Grandes. It consists principally of two large *adobe* buildings, between 300 and 400 feet long and about 150 feet wide at the base, situated upon opposite sides of a small creek. They are six stories high and resemble a large box set on the ground, with a smaller one on top of it, another still smaller on top of that and so on to the sixth and smallest, thus forming a terraced structured from top to bottom.

Each story is divided into numerous little compartments, the outer tiers of rooms being lighted by small windows in the sides, while those in the interior are dark and are usually used for store-rooms. To enter the building you ascend the first story on ladders and go down into the lower rooms through trap doors. All the other stories open outward, with regular doors. There are no inside stair-cases, but all communication between story and story is by ladders on the outside.

In every Indian village there is a room partly, and sometimes almost wholly, constructed under ground, in which councils are held and in which certain heathen rites, from which the priests have not been fully able to wean them, are practiced. This room is called the *estufa*, is esteemed a consecrated place and reserved as such.[7] A fire is kept burning in the *estufa* night and day, guarded by a child and an old man. The Indians say that Montezuma kindled the fire, that he will come again from the east and restore the power and prestige of his people.[8]

Their towns were formerly built upon heights, that they might the more readily be defended against the marauding tribes. The present town of Jemez is in a valley, but the ruins of the old town are on a neighboring height.

The ruins of Acoma, which I once visited, are on a rock which rises in a plain to the height of 200 feet.[9] Its top is perfectly level

7. The *estufa* as described by Curtis is now generally referred to as a *kiva*.

8. Montezuma, the last Aztec emperor, played a prominent role in the myths of the Pueblo people. This passage encapsulates two separate themes of the Montezuma myth, one of keeping a fire constantly burning and one of a promised return from the east. Parmentier, "The Mythological Triangle," 617–20.

9. The Acoma people lived about sixty miles west of Albuquerque in several villages, the largest of which sat on top of a mesa and was accessible only by ladders. Curtis could be

and embraces several acres, on which the town was built and there is but one pathway to the top, which wound along one side, in many places only wide enough for one person. The bare and moccasined feet of the Indian had worn steps in the solid rock. Up this height in time of danger the flocks and herds had been driven and I noticed in the corral the manure had accumulated to a depth of eight feet.

The interior of the houses are neat and comfortable. The rooms are usually about fifteen by ten feet. In one corner is the open fireplace, in which the wood stands on end. The walls are of *adobe*, the ceilings of heavy timber. Skins, warlike weapons, instruments of husbandry, trophies of the chase and war, blankets and clothing hang on the walls or are folded on shelves. Along one side of the room runs a bin, against the sides of which rest long, gravestone-shaped stones, just at the angle a washboard leans in the tub. A woman on her knees leans over the upper end of the slab with a small piece of stone—about seven inches long, five wide, and one and a half thick—in her hands and rubs Indian corn upon and down upon the slab until it becomes meal, when it is deposited in earthen pots. I have seen six of these mills running in one room. The men do the outdoor work and the women the indoor. The hair of the unmarried women is gathered in large knots on their temples, while the married women comb theirs back. They are neat, often pretty and much more chaste than their Mexican sisters.

A word or two about the Navajo and I must close. The customs of this tribe appear to be a cross between the Indians of the Plains and the Pueblos. They are a fine-looking race, tall, well-shaped and brave. They own large herds of ponies and sheep and occupy the country west of the Rio Grande and east of the Colorado. They weave beautiful blankets, some of which, large enough to cover a double bed, have been sold for $200 each. I have seen the men

---

referring to ruins located along some dry riverbeds about fifteen miles from Acoma Pueblo. The population in 1860 was 523. In 1857 the Acoma won a case against the Laguna people in the Supreme Court restoring their ownership of a painting of Saint Joseph given to them by the king of Spain in 1629. The Acoma and Laguna people engaged in a lengthy land dispute with boundaries being ignored by both sides, a situation exacerbated when the Federal government built Fort Wingate on Acoma land. A delegation of Acoma governors journeyed to Washington in 1863 to meet President Lincoln, who presented them with engraved silver canes, which the Pueblos understood to be recognition of their sovereignty. Garcia-Mason, "Acoma Pueblo," 450, 454, 458–59; Minge, *Acoma*, 60–61.

sitting beside the women who were weaving, knitting stockings, for the men of this tribe do not disdain to work and women of property are admitted to their councils and have a vote.[10]

The Navajo is purely nomadic and cannot be induced to live in fixed habitations. They stand up stout rails so that their tops touch and the lower ends reach the outlines of a circle about fifteen feet in diameter, cover the rails with twigs and the twigs with straw and then throw on dirt until the hut looks like a mound. A hole is left in the top to let out the smoke and a low door in one side. In winter, an entry of earth is built before the door, through which the visitor must crawl on hands and knees. When a death occurs in a hut, it is immediately pulled down and a new one erected elsewhere.

When I was stationed at Fort Sumner, the Navajos were employed by the quartermaster in building houses. One of them got to be so proficient in making and laying brick, that after he had finished working for the Government, he built himself a "white man's house," of one story, fourteen by twelve feet. He made a front and back door and immediately behind the last he erected a regular Navajo hut, so that his house, the interior of which was perfectly bare, was, after all, only an entry to his habitation. Visitors to the Navajos were always taken to see this house and the Indian seemed quite proud of it. One day, while examining his shotgun, it was accidentally discharged and killed his only son, a lad of fourteen. After the funeral, he demolished the hut and began upon the house and it took long and tedious argument on the part of the officers to convince him that as the death did not occur in the house, it might be spared.[11] He finally allowed himself

10. The Navajo were strongly matrilineal and status depended upon relationships with the mother. Residential groups were centered around a head mother, who had the largest sheep herd and most land for her group, and she decided in which group an individual would live. Each person had a right to speak for herself or himself, so no person could impose their will on the larger group, which would act only upon reaching a unanimous agreement. Although the Navajo women could not "vote" in the sense that Curtis meant, the factors listed could have given him the impression that women were allowed to vote on important issues. Witherspoon, "Navajo Social Organization," 524–28, 533.

11. The Navajo had a strong aversion to death and, when a person died, the survivors felt compelled to abandon and destroy the home. One author has remarked, "Even to look upon the bodies of the dead animals, except those killed for food, is a peril." This practice was undoubtedly due to the Navajo fear of ghosts which were thought to be the "malignant" part of the deceased. Ghosts would remain with their earthly groups, becoming offended by even minor cultural offenses and creating mischief, such as chasing people, pulling their clothes, or throwing dirt at them. Lamphere, *To Run After Them*, 77; Kluckhohn, *The Navajo*, 126–27.

to be convinced, sealed up the back door, cut a new door on one side and built a new hut.

Thus the reader can see why the Navajo, who understands how to spin, knit, weave, cultivate the soil, etc., as well as the Pueblo, cannot live in fixed towns. His superstition connected with death—that the spirits of the dead always haunt their old habitations—leads him to destroy his house when death invades it. He is not as peaceably inclined as the Pueblo Indian, but has been for years the terror of the Mexican and has occasionally pounced upon the herds of the Pueblos.

The entire Navajo tribe was conquered and brought upon a reservation at Fort Sumner, during the war. General Carleton found himself, at the close of the Texan invasion, in possession of several regiments of Volunteers and one of Regulars and he used them in conquering this tribe.[12] The Navajo war lasted four years and upwards of 2,000 men were engaged in its prosecution. The reservation system was faithfully tried with them. They are a people well acquainted with agricultural pursuits and in this respect, of course, have the advantage of the Comanche, Sioux, Cheyenne, etc., yet the experiment failed and after four long years' trial, they were sent back to their own country and rehabilitated with all of which they had been despoiled.

12. On August 6, 1863, General Carleton set down his thoughts on campaigning against Indians in New Mexico: "The troops must be kept after the Indians, not in big bodies, with military noises and smokes, and the gleam of arms by day, and fires, and talk, and comfortable sleeps by night; but in small parties moving stealthily to their haunts and lying patiently in wait for them; or by following their tracks day after day with a fixedness of purpose that never gives up. In this way, as large a command as that at [Fort] Craig ought not to be run over or hooted at by a few naked Indians armed with bows and arrows. Some flour, bacon, a little coffee, and sugar, thrown on a pack-mule, with the men carrying, say, two or three days' rations in their haversacks, and it will surprise the country what a few resolute men can do." *Condition of Indian Tribes*, appendix, 124.

Chapter 21

Lost in the Wilderness

The next morning after the massacre at the Indian pueblo of Jemez, I rose to an early breakfast and at seven o'clock, with *Padre* Gutierrez as cicerone, started out to pay a visit to the head chief of the town. Arriving in front of a two-story house, we mounted the ladder to a terrace or second floor and entered a small room, the ceiling of which was so low that a tall man could not stand upright. The floor was covered with four cowhides for a carpet, stiff and un-tanned. On the walls were exhibited a few colored prints of saints, a rude wooden image of the Saviour and a large wooden crucifix. In one corner was the bed of the chief, even more imperishable in its character than the carpet. A space large enough for two persons was built up out of *adobe* in the corner, covered with bull hide and upon this solid couch the chief and his wife slept after the fatigues of the day.

We had not been long seated when a delegation of the head men of the village came in to pay their respects. They were fine-looking men physically, but all needed an application of soap and water. Each wore a white and black striped blanket, held about the waist by a sash of red woolen stuff, leggings, moccasins of buck-skin and their faces were adorned with many singular devices in paint. After shaking hands with us, they all sat on the floor, made themselves *cigarritos* and smoked in silence, never speaking unless addressed.

After a little conversation with the Indians, with the *padre* as interpreter, I was invited by the chief "to see the house." I was conducted into an inner room, which was about thirty feet long and fifteen wide, where were four women on one side grinding corn. One woman simply broke the grain, the next made it a little finer and the two last reduced it to flour. At the farther end of the room was a moccasin-maker, mending and making those foot coverings. In one corner was a small fireplace, in which smoldered a few coals, of no use except to light the everlasting *cigarritos*. Tobacco and corn husks were offered us by a dusky maiden and upon my confessing that I could not make one and further that I could not smoke, I created considerable astonishment. She was not to be daunted, however, but made a *cigarrito*, lighted it, taking a few puffs first herself, and then handed it to me. Of course, my gallantry would not allow me to refuse such an offer, so I took it, amid the musical laughter of the soft-voiced Indian women, and smoked it to the stub.

As I had but little time, I refused an invitation to explore the pueblo further and returned to the priest's house, where I examined my mules and found most of them needed a day in the stable before it would be practicable to undertake to return with them. I was determined, however, to return myself at once, as my presence was necessary at Los Valles Grandes. Finding one of the mules, a new leader in the team, was quite as fresh as when she started, I directed Corporal Linstock to mount her and accompany me.[1] Just as I was about to start, the *padre* told me there was a nearer route to Los Valles Grandes than the one by which I came, which would take me into Los Vallecitos with a saving of five miles. He gave me such explicit directions and they made the road so clear, that I determined to try it.

At half past nine, A. M., I started out of Jemez. The old road by Cañoncito was a curve; the one I now took was the cord to the bow. It ran up a valley filled with deserted ranches for ten miles; at the end of that distance we entered a deserted town, in which not a single inhabitant remained. It had formerly contained about

1. Corporal Linstock is a pseudonym and he cannot be positively identified.

500 souls, but the Indian troubles had scattered them to other and more populous towns for security. All the buildings were in good condition and ready for re-occupation whenever the householders should feel safe to return. A mile beyond this town our road, which had now become a bridle path, entered the timber and ran along the eastern side of a brook. It was somewhere on this stream that I lost the road. I never knew where, as I never went over it again, but without doubt I neglected to cross to the western side at a point where I remember seeing the road divide. The *padre* had said nothing about a fork, so I kept on the direct road up the stream.

We trotted on for some hours, my horse ahead and the mule close behind, until I saw that the road gradually began to disappear and I thought sufficient time had elapsed for us to enter Los Vallecitos, if we were on the right track. Perplexed and somewhat alarmed, at last I dismounted and ascended a hill, or rather a mountain, on my left, to see if I could get the lay of the land or see any familiar signs. After long and tedious exertions, I stood on the top, but here arose another difficulty—the summit of the mountain was covered so densely with trees that it was impossible to see anything. Upon the very highest point stood a dead pine, with limbs from base to top. Up this I climbed and was rewarded when I reached the top by being able to look off without obstruction. About thirty miles east I could see the Rio Grande, running north and south for many miles. To the northwest, where my post must be, I could see nothing but ridge upon ridge, covered with an apparently interminable forest. I saw that if I continued my present route northward until I passed the mountain, leaving it on my left hand, I could probably turn to the west and somewhere come into the road I had lost or the old one by which I went to Jemez. Certainly I could not help crossing one of them if I traveled west.

I descended the tree and mountain and found the corporal and animals waiting where I had left them. Mounting, we continued north until we had passed the mountain and here, as I had anticipated, was a path running west. The forest was somewhat open and the grass rank, so that the path had been cut by the hoofs of animals through the turf, showing a long black line in advance.

Overjoyed at our good fortune, I was pursuing the journey at a tolerably rapid rate, when I was astonished to find a tree of about ten inches in diameter growing in the very center of the path. This was conclusive evidence that my road had not been traveled for many years and in no part of our country but in the Far West could a path have remained so long without being "grassed over." Every plainsman knows that old roads on the plains and in the Rocky Mountains do not disappear for a long time after they are abandoned. To the experienced eye, however, it is not difficult to tell the old road from the new. My eye not being experienced, I had to run upon a ten-inch quaking asp before I found my route was an old and abandoned one.

We were all the time ascending and the change in the trees and grasses showed that we were getting up into a cold region. Neither the corporal nor I were provided with blankets. He had a greatcoat, but I had simply a military cape. The road grew rough and the trees closer, so that we were obliged to walk our animals and, to add further to our discomfort, it began to grow dark. We were pushing on in silence, when the corporal startled me with the exclamation, "Lieutenant, there's a grizzly!" He had hardly got the words out of his mouth, when his mule bolted with a snort to one side and left the corporal on his back on the ground. Luckily, he held the end of the lariat in his hand and, with rare presence of mind, took a turn round a sapling before the mule had run away its full length. It brought her up very suddenly. My horse was frightened, but behaved tolerably well. In the dim twilight I could see an object on our right which certainly looked as big as a grizzly and did not look as if he intended to fight or move away. The corporal asked, "Shall I shoot him?"

"No. If he has a mind to let us alone, we shall be better off to follow his example. Keep still. Go to your mule's head and try to soothe her. If the bear sees we are not after him, he will probably leave."

The corporal did as he was told, succeeded in quieting the nervous animal somewhat and, after about five minutes watching, we had the satisfaction of seeing the bear quietly disappear in the woods and we resumed our journey.

It had now grown quite dark, but to our joy we saw the moon was rising. The trees had become spruce and hemlock and a frost was gathering on the grass. Still up we mounted and with every mile it seemed to grow colder. At last we broke from the forest into a little opening and found we stood upon the summit of the range. The moon shone fully upon the summit and we dismounted to reconnoitre. Crossing the opening, I looked down the western side of the mountain. The path pitched into a ravine overhung with giant and dense hemlocks, much larger that anything we had seen on the opposite slope, and, as the moon was behind us, we saw that we should, after a few steps, be in Egyptian darkness.

I concluded it was impracticable to go on and began to search my pockets for a match. Not finding any, I asked the corporal for one and he, although a smoker, had none. Here was a dilemma. Freezing cold and no blankets, it would be impossible to stay all night without a fire, except at great discomfort.

I took some cotton batting from the lining of my cap, picked it up fine, sprinkled a few grains of powder in it from a cartridge, gathered dry twigs from a dead spruce, carefully placed the cotton on the twigs and discharged my revolver over it. It blew the cotton out of existence and left me no fire. While I was doing this, the corporal stood looking down the dark ravine. Abandoning all hope of making a fire, I approached a tree and saw a large Catholic cross had been cut in the bark.

"Corporal, here's a cross cut in the tree," I said.

"Yes, sir," answered the corporal, still gazing down the ravine. "I suppose whoever made it thought it was about time to be making a cross when he reached this place."

At last the corporal approached me and said if I was willing to try it, he would lead the way down and we would push on. I assented and we started on foot, with the bridle reins over our arms, for it was impossible to ride down the steep pathway. It was a fearful path, every few rods huge trunks of trees lay across the ravine, sometimes sufficiently high for us to pass under them, but more often so low that we were obliged to climb up the side of the ravine to outflank them. Underbrush and stones tripped our feet in the darkness and our perplexed animals hung back in their bridles and kept us straining to get them along.

Two hours of this passed and we suddenly emerged from the wood into a grassy plot and the moon, just clearing the top of the mountain which we had descended, bathed everything in silvery light. The babbling of a brook some distance ahead of us alone broke the silence and we stood still awhile letting our animals graze while we speculated as to our whereabouts. Beyond us rose another mountain range and, as nothing looked familiar from our present standpoint, we feared we had another rough journey before us. We walked slowly down the slope to the brook, and—hurrah! here was our old road from Los Valles Grandes to Jemez. We were only about seven miles from home.

After our animals had taken a long drink from the brook, we mounted and broke into a canter for home. Neither horse nor mule needed the spur, each seemed to understand, and visions of a warm stable and good provender were a sufficient spur to their heels.

In a short time we reached the foot of the valley and far away we could see the light at the guardhouse. The clatter of our animals' hoofs rang along the valley and our spirits rose to such a degree that I hummed and whistled tunes as we flew along, after the manner of the traveler when near his journey's end. At last came the welcome "Who goes there?" of the sentinel and, after the necessary delay for the sergeant of the guard to identify us, we entered the post.

Sending my horse to the stable by my servant, I entered the cabin and consulted my watch. It was half past two. We had been seventeen hours on the road, enduring fatigue and hunger. Had we not missed the road, we ought to have been back at four o'clock the previous afternoon or a little later had we come by the old road. But we were alive and the grizzly hadn't eaten us.

On the afternoon of the day following my return to Los Valles Grandes, the detachment arrived without accident, having traveled over the "cut-off" that caused me so much trouble, but which they found no difficulty in following.

Chapter 22

Winter Quarters

The fall was now getting far advanced and although the weather was still fine and likely to remain so until the last of December, I determined to make preparations for cold weather, partly for the sake of giving my men occupation and more for the sake of their comfort and my own. The daily scouting, in which I often took part in order to be personally acquainted with my surroundings, and the cutting and hauling of wood for our sixteen fires was about the only fatigue duty required of my men. Discontent and mutiny is more apt to grow out of the idleness than hard work, so I began organizing regular labor with a view to keeping the men constantly occupied.

As my own cabin was the poorest of the lot and partly under ground, I determined to build me a new one and build it sufficiently large to afford quarters for another officer, should one come. Work was begun upon this at once. Two square cabins, sixteen by sixteen feet, were carried up eight feet, built of pine logs and situated ten feet apart. A roof was thrown over both huts and the space between, making them one building with a passage through the centre. Windows and doors were sawed through the logs, the former looking out upon the parade and the latter opening upon the passage. Inside of the rooms, the logs were dressed smooth by means of an adze and in the corner of each a stone chimney and fireplace was built. Earth was thrown into the cabins to raise the floor about a foot above the ground, made into mortar and smoothed level with a trowel. When dry, this made an excellent floor and in my own cabin I laid a carpet. Next, in order to give the sentinel a greater range of vision over the valley, I erected a lookout station on the ridge south of the camp. In locating this camp, the department commander had directed that it should be concealed, a precaution of no use against the ever-watchful Indian. If it had any primary advantage, this was lost as soon as the Navajo discovered its location and then its situation in a depression was a serious disadvantage.

The lookout was constructed of four logs set upright, with a platform on top and a ladder running up inside the frame. The height from ground to platform was fifty-one feet. On this the sentinel walked during the daytime in warm weather.

This lookout proved of essential service to me before winter set in. Early one morning, the sentinel discovered a party of Indians creeping along the skirts of the forest on the eastern side of the valley, barely distinguishable in the remaining light, evidently seeking the trail leading out of the valley through which the raiders had disappeared with my beef. The distance between me and the trail being less than between the Indians and that point, I determined to intercept them. Accordingly, I quickly mounted six men on the mules and rode across the valley. At the same time I dispatched a foot party to cut off the retreat. My plan succeeded and I soon captured without bloodshed a dozen Navajos with twenty-three ponies and four *burros*. In fact, it was the gray hair of these diminutive asses that first attracted the sentinel's notice. The Indians were sent to the reservation at Bosque Redondo and the animals were returned to their owners.[1]

1. The reservation at Bosque Redondo was located on the Pecos River in eastern New Mexico and was used to hold nearly 9,000 Navajo and Mescalero Apaches beginning in 1862. In an attempt to remove the Navajo people from their homeland, General James Carleton ordered Colonel Christopher Carson to conduct a "scorched earth" campaign against them in 1863 and 1864. After many Navajo had been killed or captured, the survivors endured a mass relocation to Bosque Redondo in what is now known as "The Long Walk." Confining them in virtually unspeakable conditions, the Federal government attempted to make farmers out of the Indians, but many died of starvation prior to a treaty in 1868 that allowed the Navajo to return home. The attempt to teach the Indians white farming techniques proved an abject failure. Roessel, "Navajo History," 510–15.

None of my men had had any experience in felling trees or in loading logs. Here my State of Maine experience came into play, for although not an expert in the handicraft of the backwoodsman, still I had learned enough by observation to instruct my men in felling and loading the logs and in getting them into the walls of the cabin. We also made a coal kiln and burned a quantity of charcoal for our blacksmith shop, but not without losing our first stock. Drawing the kiln one afternoon and not completely extinguishing the fire, we found next morning, when the horse cart went into the wood for a load of coal, that where the previous evening had been a black pyramid, there was now only a bed of white ashes. Our next attempt was a success.

Our stable was constructed of logs and the hay, cut in the summer by the Volunteers, was stacked on top for a roof. I cut a large quantity more of the dead meadow grass of the valley, to be used as bedding for the men and animals and for fodder should we use up the other. The forest was full of dead pines, perfectly sound and seasoned, which had been killed by camping parties building fires against them. These were felled and drawn into camp, sawed, split and piled for winter. Being the hard or pitch pine, the wood made an excellent and cheerful fire.

Game was so plentiful that we had not killed the cattle sent us and a herd of about twenty head of steers and cows had accumulated. Some of the cows gave milk, so we had enough of that luxury and even made some butter. We had hunted turkeys and killed and taken them by the wholesale, until turkey meat was a drug. One man had captured, early in the fall, a hen turkey with fifteen young ones just out of the shell. The old one had been confined in a coop and the brood allowed to run. They were not long in getting tame and seemed to prefer camp to wood life.

The fall passed away and December up to the 15th, when there came a snowstorm, which left us with about twelve inches of snow. There had been a few flurries of snow before this, which stayed but a few hours, and they have always remained associated with the extraordinary good luck of the scouting parties in shooting grouse. During the falling of the snow, the grouse huddle about the trunks of the trees and stand with their heads beneath their wings. The greenest sportsman cannot help knocking over a few, under the circumstances.

With the conviction that snow had come to remain all winter, I determined to have a sled and bobsled made for drawing the logs out of the wood and, when I sent my team to Santa Fé for supplies, I asked for some old wagon tires for shoeing the runners. There was not a man in the company who had ever seen a sled of any description, so my New England experience was again of use. I made drawings for the carpenter and blacksmith and personally superintended the making of the sled. It was completed the day before Christmas and, on the morning of that holiday, the men asked my permission to take a sleigh ride, which was cheerfully granted. A wagon body was stripped of the cover and placed on the sled and seats laid across and covered with blankets, flags were fastened to the corners and various devices in ornamentation were attached to the sled. The four leading mules were attached and about fifteen men, with the laundress and her three children, took seats and the team started. The snow was light, the surface of the valley level and the sled went smoothly and swiftly down the brook, amid the shouts and laughter of the soldiers. After riding a distance of about two miles, the sled returned and took another load and the whole forenoon was passed in this amusement.

During the time I had been in the valley, I had not only done all the duties of commanding officer, adjutant, quartermaster, commissary and company commander, but I had also been post surgeon. The medicines which I dispensed were specifics and were prepared for me by the surgeon at Santa Fé. In the fall, two cases had got beyond my powers of treatment, and I applied for a doctor. On the 20th day of January, the long-expected and anxiously-waited for doctor arrived. As Doctor Sylvester Rankin dismounted from his pony, he remarked, “This is the coldest place I have seen in New Mexico in fifteen years.” He was not far wrong in this. On the other side of the mountain, only five miles away, there was no snow all winter, while in our valley I doubt if any New England winter was ever colder than this proved to be before it was over.

Of course, the arrival of the doctor broke the monotony of my life somewhat. He moved into the adjoining room of the double cabin, but was rarely there except to sleep, spending his days and eating his meals in my room. From having had no one to talk with for several months, I must have inflicted an extra amount of talk upon him for some time after his arrival.

Soon the coldness of the weather increased and the snow gradually got so deep that there was no chance of getting out of the valley with either wagon or sled. By constant use, we kept the wood road open for some time and continued to increase our pile of fuel by daily additions, but after a while a big storm made that impossible and all work ceased. The cattle could no longer graze, so all but four were butchered and the frozen meat hung up in the storehouse. The hay disappeared rapidly, until there was left but a scant covering on the stable and one night, in a violent gale, the wind stripped off what remained and left the animals exposed. We had no thermometer in camp to indicate the weather and I can only judge of the severity of the cold by our experience. It was so cold that the sentinel, let him wrap himself ever so carefully, could not walk his post twenty minutes without freezing nose, ears or fingers. The cold was always accompanied by a searching wind against which no amount of clothing seemed a protection. Sentinels relieved each other every fifteen minutes, until I concluded to take them off and let Jack Frost stand guard. There certainly was no danger of attack from Indians in such weather.

On the morning after the wind blew the hay off the stable, I went out with a number of men to nail canvas on the walls and over the tops, to protect the suffering animals. We froze the ends of our fingers in about five minutes. I was forced to divide the party into two reliefs, one to be warming themselves while the other was working. A cow and her newly-born calf died while we were doing our best to save them by wrapping them in straw and blankets. On the following day, the wind increased to a hurricane and stripped the canvas from the stables in shreds, carrying it away entirely. I put the mules into the guardhouse, the doctor's pony and my horse into our private kitchen and butchered the remaining cows. For over a week this weather continued. There was not a cloud in the sky, nothing but flying snow, which flew from the summit of the ridge behind us high over our heads and through which we got occasional glimpses of a cold, brazen sun. No duty could be done and we attempted none.

Now the wisdom of providing plenty of fuel was shown, for the men rarely left their cabins, except to get wood or bring their rations from the kitchen. All the cabins were roofed with earth, the walls plastered with mud inside and banked with turf on three sides. They were comfortable with their open fires and there was no chance for suffering if the occupants did not go out of doors.

Hungry gray wolves and coyotes prowled nightly about our parade, searching for the scraps from the kitchen and the offal of the slaughtered cattle, mingling their howling, barking, snarling and wrangling with the roaring of the storm. Some strychnine was put in incisions made in the carcasses of the cow and calf and next morning several gray wolves lay dead by the side of the bait, within the limits of our camp. The skins of these wolves were tanned for me by Valencia and stitched into a robe which for years did duty as a bed cover or a mat in my western marches.

About the 1st of February, the Indian corn for the horses and mules was nearly gone and I made application to the quartermaster at Santa Fé for a supply. After the usual delay peculiar to the routine of some offices, I received orders to purchase corn in the Indian town of Jemez and not to pay over a certain price for it delivered. As soon as I received this order, I had my doubts whether anyone could be found to deliver grain at Los Valles Grandes for the same price for which it could be delivered at Santa Fé. At the latter place the ranche men could draw their grain to market in wagons and in large quantities. From Jemez to the valley there was no wagon road. This would necessitate the use of a pack train, a much more expensive means of transportation, and now that we had three feet of snow on the ground, it was doubtful whether a pack train would come at any price.

Besides, we must first reach Jemez in order to make the arrangements for purchase and transportation. This was a serious undertaking. From the top of our lookout, the valley presented one sheet of snow, nowhere less than two feet deep and in many places three times that depth. Something, however, must be done or the animals would starve. Past experience had led me to doubt the practicability of representing the difficulties of the case at Santa Fé, for either the authorities could not or would not see the situation we were in. Because there was no snow from Santa Fé to the eastern slope of the mountains, a distance of seventy-five miles, they could not see why, only five miles farther, on the other slope, there should be a complete blockade. This was all the more surprising to me because my men were often obliged to tramp a path through the valley and over the mountain to let the express riders in and it could not be possible these men would not corroborate my reports at headquarters.[2]

I called in my spy and guide, Valencia, and his son, and examined them as to the possibility of reaching Jemez and packing corn to the camp. They said that provided it did not storm, it could be done, but doubted whether I should be able to get the Pueblos to transport the corn at any price. The terrors of a winter in the valleys were well known and wholesomely feared. To my question whether he thought we could get out of the valley on the trail to Jemez, he shrugged his shoulders and uttered a despondent "*Quien sabe*?" ("Who knows?") and gazed vacantly in the fire for a moment. Presently he added that if the weather continued fair, we could break through and return and, as the winter had got so far advanced, he thought there was more of a chance we should have no more storms until March.

I determined that the attempt to reach Jemez should be made and was considering whether to go myself or send a sergeant in command, when Doctor Rankin surprised me by requesting that I allow him to go. Perhaps I need not explain that the army surgeon is not subject to detail in line duty or any duty outside of his province as a medical man, except on courts martial and boards. But in this case, I was glad to avail myself of the services of an intelligent and educated man, who had been fifteen years in the country. I accepted the offer and made a detail of a corporal and four men, including the two Mexicans. The doctor was to ride his own pony, the corporal my horse, the two men two of the mules and the Mexicans to go on foot, with permission to mount any of the other four mules which were taken along, should they choose. I sent all the animals so that some grain might be brought back should the doctor fail in getting a pack train to bring a sufficient supply. The detachment was to take four days' rations, and a few cooking utensils.

Next morning at six o'clock, in a bitter atmosphere, the party assembled before the door of my cabin. The hair of the animals was already covered with frost and the breath of animals and men

2. Curtis was not accurate in assuming that Los Valles Grandes was the only location to experience extreme weather that winter. On November 22, 1863, Santa Fe had six inches of snow, followed by bitterly cold temperatures. At Fort Wingate one soldier complained that the cold "was so intense that hardy resolute men groaned with the pain from it." He reported that men's "feet, hands, ears, and noses were frozen" and overheard Colonel Carson say that the cold was "more intense and the sufferings greater than any known to his great experience." *Rocky Mountain News*, December 16, 1863; *Albuquerque Weekly Press*, February 23, 1864.

ascended in clouds. All were provided with blankets and wraps and started off confident of making their way through. It was still quite dark and after a few moments I lost sight of the party and entered my cabin. After it became light, I went out and looked down the valley and to my surprise the detail was not more than two miles away. The animals floundered and staggered along and every now and then all the men would dismount and tread a path through a drift for the animals. It was noon before the party disappeared in the timber at the foot of the valley. Had I had a horse or mule left, I should have sent after and recalled the men and I was exceedingly surprised at their pluck and perseverance in pushing on.

I sat down to while away the afternoon in reading and writing, but could not keep my mind off the detail and was disturbed by fears that it might have been bad policy to send them even to obey a peremptory order. However, as evening descended and there were no signs of their return, I came to the conclusion that they had reached the *cañon* of the Jemez River and their worst difficulties were over. I played a game or two of Solitaire and about ten o'clock went to bed. I had slept perhaps an hour when I was aroused by a furious knocking at my door and a voice shouting, "For God's sake, open the door quick!" Jumping hastily out of bed, I threw a billet of pitch pine upon the glowing coals and opened the door. The pine burst into a brilliant blaze and by its light the doctor staggered into the room, in the centre of a frost cloud, himself grizzled from head to foot in frost. Without stopping to dress, I began getting him out of his wraps, overcoat, boots and stockings. With the first glance at his face I saw that his nose and ears were frozen and, upon further examination, found the first joints of his fingers and toes were in the same condition. I then began dressing and asking questions.

"Where are the men?"

"Out there," he shivered, rather than replied.

"All of them?"

"All but the damned Mexicans."

"Where are they?"

"Don't know. Left them on the road."

"Any of the men frozen?"

"Yes, all of them, more or less. Think Corporal Portfire is the worst."[3]

3. Corporal Portfire is a pseudonym and he cannot be positively identified.

By this time I was dressed and out of the quarters, looking up the men. I found the company awake and kind comrades were working over the frozen men, while others were rubbing down and caring for the animals. I got out the doctor's medicine chest, and, under his instructions, administered the proper remedies and liniments. Corporal Portfire's nose, ears and cheeks were badly frozen and nearly the whole of one foot, but neither his hands nor the other foot. The two privates, Hoey and Cleary, had escaped with only their ears and noses frozen.

As I superintended the work over the men, I examined them in regard to their trip and the loss of the Mexicans. It seems all went well after they got into the timber, until three o'clock, when they had reached within a mile of the descent of the *cañon*. Here a dispute arose between the doctor and the Mexicans about the way. There were two ridges ahead and the Mexicans said the proper road led along the left, while the doctor insisted that the right must be equally practicable and ended by taking it. He led on until he reached the *cañon* and, after wasting an hour in vain search for a place of descent, gave it up and announced his intention to return to camp. His excuse for this was that it was getting late and but half the distance to Jemez had been traversed. This was correct, but the road, after reaching the bottom of the *cañon*, would have been better and he could have got on more rapidly. Besides, there was a good house, unoccupied, at the hot springs, at the bottom of the *cañon*, where he could have sheltered both men and animals.

After the detail turned back, no notice was taken of the Mexicans for some time, until Hoey called attention to the fact that they were missing and then the doctor considered it too dangerous to attempt to go back for them. Of course, I felt disturbed on account of the loss of these men, but could see how foolhardy would be any attempt at rescuing them under the circumstances. I slept none for the rest of the night, but sat up administering medicine to the doctor and men.

Next day at noon the sentinel reported two objects coming up the valley. Taking my field glass and going to the top of the ridge, I made them out to be the two Mexicans, following the path to the post. They made very slow progress and the young man was leading his father. Every few steps the old man would fall and, after some exertion, be raised to his feet by the son and come painfully on. I returned quickly to the parade and dispatched two men, with four mules, blankets and whiskey to help the Mexicans to camp, but too late to save the life of our old guide, hunter and scout. He was badly frozen and so thoroughly chilled that there was no chance of recovery. The son was but little frozen, not worse than the soldiers of the doctor's party. It appeared that after they found themselves deserted by the doctor, they followed the trail back to Los Vallecitos, to a spring on the western side in the edge of the timber. Close by the side of the spring a granite boulder rises perpendicularly twenty feet. In the southern face of the rock is a slight cavity and before this the Mexicans built a fire and passed the night without blankets or covering of any kind. Their sufferings must have been fearful. As soon as it was daylight, they began their return to camp.

Valencia died three days after his return and was buried on the height by the lookout station and the following May I erected a plain, wooden cross over his grave, with the following inscription in Spanish:

Aqui yace José María Valencia,
Vecino de Cañoncito,
Morido de frio, el dia 5 de Febrero,
Del ano 1864.
Ora por el, Christiano, por Dios.

(Here lies José María Valencia,
A native of Cañoncito,
Who died of cold on the 5th of February,
Of the year of 1864.
Pray for him, Christian, for God's sake.)

Chapter 23

Return to Jemez

The second day after the failure of the doctor to reach Jemez, I started with the same number of soldiers, but without a guide, to try my luck in getting through the snow and finding grain. I had the advantage over the doctor of having my road broken open for the worst part of the route and there had been no wind or fall of snow to fill it. I met with no difficulty until I reached the point where the first party wandered away from the true path. Here two feet of snow covered every vestige of the trail and it was not without considerable search that I found the point where the descent of the *cañon* began. The path downward was a zig-zag, through a dense forest of *piñons* and junipers and so steep that we were forced to dismount and lead the mules. One mule, led by Corporal Linstock, slid off the path and went down to the next zig-zag with an avalanche of snow, taking the corporal with him and scratching him badly through the trailing and snow-clad branches of the trees. The mule came out right side up and nothing broken and no other adventure occurred to us in the descent. When we emerged from the wood at the bottom of the *cañon*, the sky was filled with the steam from the hot springs, as if a score of locomotives were at work there on an up-grade. We entered the house at the springs and prepared our lunch. We warmed ourselves thoroughly by sitting on the hot rocks about the springs and warmed our food by setting our camp kettles, with our rations in them, in the boiling sulphur water. We rested for half an hour and resumed our journey.

Down the valley of the river the snow was not over a foot deep and there was now no further need of dismounting and breaking paths. Still we could not go faster than a walk and evening had come long before we reached the village of Cañoncito. We were all painfully conscious that we had fingers and toes and the complaints of the men were frequent and emphatic. The distance seemed to grow longer as the evening advanced, while the air grew colder and it was with great pleasure that I saw the first light from the distant town. We reached Cañoncito about half-past eight and soon secured quarters for the men and stables for the animals. The men were provided with rations for four days and I had lunch for supper and breakfast, after which I expected to buy what I should need.

Valencia's family lived in Cañoncito and they were deeply distressed at the report I brought of his illness. A second son of his started next morning for the valleys, with some little home comforts for his father and to assist in taking care of him. The old man had been a distinguished hunter and Indian fighter and was held in high esteem by his countrymen. He had kept us constantly supplied with game at Los Valles Grandes and during the winter had killed five bears. One day he brought me in the scalp, weapons and trinkets of a Navajo warrior. He reported that he found the Indian lurking in the woods in the vicinity of our camp and, while the red man watched us, the Mexican watched him and ended by dropping him with an arrow.[1] Valencia always carried a bow and arrows, as well as rifle, saying "that it was well to be able sometimes to take a silent shot," a wise precaution in an Indian country, where the very "grass has ears." I kept the scalp hanging over my mantle-piece for a long time and gave it away at last to a Pueblo Indian, who tanned me a dozen skins in return for it, a bargain of his own making.

Numerous were the anecdotes of Valencia to which I listened during my first evening at Cañoncito and, if all the tales were true,

1. This encounter apparently occurred on November 9, 1863. *Condition of Indian Tribes*, appendix, 254.

he was a brave and generous Mexican and so, indeed, I always found him.

Next morning, at sunrise, we left Cañoncito for Jemez, now but seven miles distant. We were not long in reaching the town and I immediately called upon my friend, *Padre* Gutierrez, as the man most likely to know the state of the corn market, as well as the possibility of my getting a pack train to go to Los Valles Grandes. I found the priest at his breakfast, with a comely and dusky "niece" setting vis-a-vis at the table. Upon my entrance the maiden started to withdraw, but at my earnest entreaty, the priest condescended to bid her remain in her seat and pour me a cup of his excellent coffee. Like all Mexican girls, she was not loath to remain in the presence of the *gringo*. She had only started out of respect to the wishes of the priest, for the Mexican man is not as indulgent with his women as the American, for one may be the guest of a Mexican family for weeks and never meet a lady at meals and but rarely catch a glimpse of one about the house. If none of the men are about, *las señoritas* are not indisposed to give a foreigner a glimpse of their black eyes, olive complexions and well-turned ankles, but when *el hombre de la casa* (the man of the house) is present, she shows but one eye through the folds of her *rebozo* and is the pink of retiring modesty.

When I told the priest that the object of my trip was to purchase corn, he replied that there was plenty to be had for the price named. When I said it must be delivered at the valleys for that price, he shrugged his shoulders and said the Indians would not go there for any price whatever. And to corroborate his statement, he sent a servant for three of the principal men of the town, when we examined them briefly on the subject. They were willing to sell corn, but obstinately refused to go to the valleys. To explain their refusal, the priest related many disastrous adventures in the valleys in times past and, before he concluded, I ceased to wonder at the Indians' reluctance to take a pack train into the snows of that region.

Finding I could get no corn delivered at my camp, I purchased enough to load my animals, even putting a very considerable amount on the mules upon which the men were mounted, intending to feed from this portion on our return march. At noon I started on my return, intending to pass the night at Cañoncito.

Jemez Pueblo. Courtesy of Ben Wittick, Palace of the Governors Photo Archive (NMHA/DCA), Negative #031251.

At three o'clock I arrived at that place and secured the same quarters for my men which they had occupied the night before, but I was obliged to take rooms with a *Señor* José Cordova, as a sudden sickness in my former host's family prevented their entertaining me.[2] In the new place, I found an elderly couple, with a large family of boys and girls, ranging from young man and womanhood to infancy.

During the last hours of the afternoon, I wandered about the village, making calls and searching for objects of interest, and with the approach of evening returned to my quarters with an excellent appetite. The last of my private lunch had been consumed at breakfast and I had purchased nothing at Jemez, expecting to find plenty to eat at Cañoncito. My anxiety may be imagined, therefore, when I found, upon inquiry, that there was nothing to eat in the village but *frijoles*. Over my head in the *sala* were roosting two cocks, tied by the legs to opposite ends of a roost, and I proposed that one of them should be killed for my supper. But this proposition was received with high disfavor. My host said nothing short of *cinco pesos* (five dollars) would buy one of those cocks. They were the crack gamecocks of the town and had cleaned out everything in Jemez at the last Saturday's cock fight. "*Como claro mis cuervos del gallo, el compañero fino*!" (How clear my cock crows, the fine fellow!) said old Cordova, gazing fondly at the red cock on the right hand end of the roost.

"*Valgame Dios*! *Lo que es un hermoso pájaro de esta mina*!" (Good God! What a handsome bird is this of mine!) replied the eldest son, admiring with equal fondness a yellow-capped cock on the other or left-hand end of the roost.

I saw that I was not likely to eat either of these cherished fowls and upon inquiry learned that there was not another fowl in the place. This brought me back to the question of beans. I found there was a quantity of bean soup left from dinner which could be warmed for supper. I asked the women if they could make me some *tortillas*. A piece of the hot *tortilla* is torn off and bent into the shape of a spoon; with this the person dips up some bean soup and eats spoon and all. It makes a very palatable dish. In answer to my question, I found there was no corn in town. I then asked if a quantity of my corn could not be ground and cooked without much

2. Jose Cordova cannot be further identified.

delay. This was assented to and shortly afterward a young Cordova went to the corporal with my order for corn and in a few moments more I heard from an adjoining room the grating of the hand mills reducing it to meal.

In process of time, a bowl of bean soup and a stack of hot *tortillas* were set before me on the table and I was not slow in doing them ample justice. Before leaving the table, I gave orders for a similar provision for breakfast and added thereto a quantity of coffee, generously given me by the soldiers out of their scant ration and which I gratefully accepted.

Supper over, the women of the family spread mattresses and blankets over the floor and in a few minutes all were in bed, fifteen in all including myself, in a space of hardly more than that number of square feet. All, myself joining, smoked *cigarritos* and talked incessantly. Every few moments, the rival cocks on the roost over our heads would set up an ear-splitting crow, which invariably called forth loud ejaculations of praise from their respective owners.

Next morning I breakfasted on *frijoles* and *tortillas*, paid for my lodging and went out to overlook the packing of my animals. When the packing was completed, I noticed that two sacks, capable of holding two bushels of corn each, were empty.

"Where is the corn that was in these sacks, corporal?" I asked.

"That's what the lieutenant ate for his supper and breakfast," answered the corporal.

"Do you mean to say that those Mexicans pretended to use all that corn for my two meals?"

"That's what the young greaser said when he brought back the empty sacks, sir."

It was no use to scold and I knew from experience remonstrances with the Mexicans would be of no use, so I concluded to mount and go on. This story soon got out among the officers and I was often unmercifully quizzed about my capacity for eating forage.

Our march from Cañoncito to the valleys was devoid of interest. The cold weather continued to hold, but there was no wind and our path remained open. This experience in corn buying convinced the quartermaster at Santa Fé that my reports about the snow were based on fact and I soon after received a large amount directly from the depot.

The last of February and the first of March were windy and unpleasant enough, but the cold weather was broken and the temperature of the wind was such as to rapidly melt the snow and soon bring the earth to view throughout the extent of the valley. The grass grew green and luxuriant with great rapidity and one day a flock of 7,000 head of sheep made its appearance from Peña Blanca, in charge of two men, a boy and four shepherd dogs. This had been a favorite summer herding place for sheep and cattle, until the Navajo difficulties had made it dangerous to graze them in the valley. The presence of the soldiers made it safe again, so the flocks and herds made their appearance with the first verdure. As soon as the flocks arrived, we purchased a few sheep, but found the animals so thin that they were little better than skeletons. It was marvelous, however, to see with what rapidity they gained in flesh after their arrival.

Every flock of sheep in New Mexico has a number of goats in it, to enable the shepherds to drive it with the greater ease. The goats always lead the flock wherever it goes and are never given to making sudden rushes or turning backwards to no apparent reason, like sheep. They move steadily on, are easily turned in any direction and the sheep follow them as faithfully as a herd of mules will follow the gray mare. The goats of the flock were milked and the milk brought to our camp each night for sale to the soldiers.

Soon after the arrival of the sheep, a herd of neat cattle entered the valley and took up their station on the western side, the sheep being on the eastern. The herders of the cattle soon began bringing in cow's milk for sale and the doctor, who had never bought any goat's milk but always declared it impossible for him to drink it, now became a constant buyer. In fact, I had never sat down to a bowl of goat's milk and bread without drawing upon myself the whole battery of the doctor's wit and sarcasm. He declared the milk smelt "goaty" and was strong in taste, that it injured his appetite for me to have it at the supper table. When he began to have cow's milk, he became even more abusive and was always insisting that I should change milks. Perhaps had he said less I should have changed, but his constant fault-finding and abuse of a very sweet and palatable article of food made me a regular and constant purchaser of *la leche de cabra* (goat milk).

After standing the doctor's nonsense a considerable length of time, I thought it best to put an end to it and took a very easy and effectual method to close his mouth on the subject for all time. One evening I took a walk along the side of the brook toward the southern end of the valley and, as soon as I had the ridge between me and the camp, I sat down on the grass and awaited the approach of the milkmen, who always reached the parade by the same path and at about the same time. The sheep herder arrived first and I stopped him until the cattle herder appeared. When both men were with me, I proposed that they should exchange vessels and then proceed as usual. I gave each of them a small bribe to be sure they should carry out my instructions and then returned to camp, directing them not to come in until I had been home at least ten minutes.

I returned to my cabin and found a plate of hard bread and two snow-white bowls on the table, awaiting the arrival of the milk, and the doctor getting impatient at the delay of the herders. At last they came and, of course, the doctor bought goat's milk and I bought cow's milk, the doctor all the time keeping up a running fire of abuse of my milk and praise of his own, trying to persuade me to take part of his and throw mine away.

"Do you really think there is any difference, doctor?" I asked.

"Difference?" he replied, in great disdain, "I can tell the difference two rods away."

"Do you believe this spoonful has a different odor from that you hold in your hand?" I said, proferring him a spoonful of cow's milk.

"Go away! Don't put it near me! I'd as like take an emetic! Now, this milk," he continued, taking a big spoonful from his own bowl, "is the only fit milk for a Christian and a white man to eat. That may do for greasers and heathen or a man whose taste has been vitiated by association with them, but I had rather take calomel and jalap." And so the conversation rattled on until the doctor had reached the bottom of his bowl of bread and milk and had drained the last drop. After he had lighted his pipe and the obnoxious lacteal fluid had got well settled in his stomach, I opened the conversation by asking:

"Doctor, do you believe if I were to place goat's milk in your bowl tomorrow evening, and you did not know it, that you could perceive the substitution?"

"Certainly. I should detect it the first sniff."

"Well, suppose the man who generally brings you milk should be hired to bring you goat's milk, are you sure you could detect the cheat?"

"Detect it, man! Have I a nose? Can I smell a stench? It would be impossible to cheat me."

"Still, old fellow, you put away about a quart of goat's milk for supper this evening, as I can swear, for I hired the men to exchange milk before they came into the camp."

The doctor jumped up so suddenly that he overthrew his chair and disappeared into his own room. For two days he stayed away from my room and I saw nothing of him, but on the second he came in with a sickly smile and said, "Lieutenant, that was a rough joke, but, after reflection, I believe I deserved it. Say quits?"

"Of course, doctor. You made my stomach qualmy for some time, by your original and disagreeable comparisons of objectionable things to my food, but on the whole I cherish no grudge and hereafter I shall take cow's milk with you, for I must acknowledge that is the best."

"Do you know," replied the doctor, "I thought when I tasted that milk that night there was something peculiar about it, but you looked so sober I never suspected a swap?"

One day the small boy who came into the valley with the sheep herders came into camp crying bitterly and in a high state of excitement. Upon examination, I found he was a Navajo, who had been taken prisoner in infancy by the Mexicans. He had been fearfully punished by the herders, his back was covered with the scars of old whippings and bloody with the last one from which he had run away. He claimed my protection from his pursuers, who were not slow in following and claiming him, and I did not refuse it. I showed the Mexicans an order of the Government directing officers of the army to take all Navajo prisoners found in the hands of white people and send them by the first opportunity to the Fort Sumner reservation. This did not satisfy the herders, but they had to submit. The boy had been baptized by his Christian captors by the name of Antonio and clad in the garments of civilization.[3] He appeared to be a very bright and intelligent boy and went to work cheerfully about my quarters and the doctor's, doing all the

3. Antonio cannot be further identified.

housework, assisting the cook, blacking the boots, etc. He lived with me during the remainder of my stay in the valley and was turned over to his tribe about the last of June of the same year. I tried hard to get permission to keep him, but the commander-in-chief was unyielding and I sent him away sobbing bitterly. From babyhood he had lived among the Mexicans and had forgotten the language and customs of his tribe and, as he often expressed it, "wanted to be an American." Three years afterward, when I was stationed at the reservation, I one day attended an Indian pony race and as I walked along the track I saw a young Indian, clad in the light and airy "breech-cloth," lying flat on his stomach in the sand, resting his chin in his two hands. He was looking up at me with a smile. I recognized Antonio.

"Are you Antonio?" I asked in Spanish.

"Yes, sir," he answered, without changing his position.

"Do you want to live with me now?"

"No, sir."

"Don't you want to be an American?"

"No. I like my own people best."

This rapid conversion of Antonio from the ways of civilization to those of savage life was not the rule, however. There were a large number of cabins at Fort Sumner which had been occupied by the troops before the permanent quarters were erected. In these there lived at least thirty young women, who had been taken prisoners when children from the Navajos and Apaches. Most of them had been brought up as servants in the wealthiest Mexican families and a few had been partially educated. These young women could not be induced to adopt the ways of their tribe, but lived isolated, doing the laundry work of the officers and men.

In this connection I will relate an incident which occurred while I was stationed on the Fort Sumner reservation. The garrison of this post consisted of six companies of infantry and two of cavalry, whose duty it was to keep the Navajo and Apache Indians from leaving, see that they worked upon their land and did their best to support themselves. The fort was under the command of a lieutenant colonel and there were six other officers who held higher rank than I. But by one of those singular combinations of circumstances to which the military service is subject, all of these officers were detailed away on special duty at other posts and I found myself, a lieutenant, in command of this great post for two weeks.

During this time a Roman Catholic priest, from Anton Chico, came to my quarters one day, leading by the hand a little boy about six years of age, whose features were unmistakably Indian. But a short distance behind the priest and boy were three Indians, two women and a man. The priest stated that the child had been taken prisoner when but a year old, during a raid of the Mexicans into the Navajo country, and that he had taken him to bring up, out of pity, with a hope that at some future time he night be fitted to do missionary work among his people. The child had been gently nurtured in the priest's household and taught to read, which he did with unusual facility for one of his age, as I can witness.

About a week before, the two Indian women present had appeared at Anton Chico and asked permission to examine the child, one of them claiming to be his mother and detailing with great accuracy all the particulars as to the time and place of the raid and capture. She said if the child was hers, it would have a mark of a peculiar description on his left hip. The priest caused the child to be stripped and the mark was found. Being fully convinced that the child belonged to the woman, he told her to take him away. But here a new difficulty arose—the child flew into the arms of the priest, clung to him tenaciously, cried and begged frantically that he should not be given to his mother. On her side, the mother knelt on the floor, tried gently and tenderly to draw her child to her and besought, in soft tones and with constantly falling tears, that her child would come to her, using mingled Spanish and Indian terms, but the child would not leave the priest or even look at her.

Perplexed and desirous of doing the best thing for the child, the priest came to the fort to consult the commanding officer. He being absent and I being the acting commander, the party brought their difficulty to me. I saw at a glance, by the way the boy clung to the priest and the constant upward glance of his eyes to the priest's face, where his trust and affection was placed and I could see that all this affection and trust was returned by this childless man. Evidently five years of constant care and instruction of this little Indian boy had made him very dear to the poor priest. But on the other hand was the mother. Clad in her bizarre and graceful Indian costume, she sat on the floor at our feet, constantly making efforts

Indian mother pleading for her child. Sketch from *Harper's Young People.*

to attract the attention of her child, proffering him a pair of exquisitely embroidered moccasins and strings of beautiful shells and beads, plucking gently at his garments and in soft accents begging him to look at her. The child only answered by pushing her hand away and persistently looking in another direction.

Here was a dilemma for me. The child's welfare, if an education and the refinements of civilization are an advantage, seemed to dictate that he should be given to the priest and, as all his childish love and confidence was placed in him, it seemed manifestly the best course. On the other hand was the mother. How could I again take away the child, who had once been torn ruthlessly from her breast and so unexpectedly restored to her? Besides, there was my own experience with Antonio, where the authorities insisted, as they should in all such cases, that he should be turned over to his tribe. I shirked the responsibility. I told the priest that I would keep the boy in my own charge until the commanding officer's return and refer the matter to him. This was assented to and, after a short conversation with the *padre*, the boy turned cheerfully to me and signified his willingness to stay.

As my quarters were not very roomy, I detailed a soldier, Private James Evans, to sleep in a tent in my back yard and take charge of the boy, telling him not to let him go out of his sight.[4] This back yard was surrounded by an *adobe* wall, nine feet high, with a single door in the front wall and a double door in the back. These doors were always closed and locked at night.

Every day, for four days, the mother called on her son and never ceased her efforts to win his attention, but he would have nothing to say to her. Nights the child slept in the tent and in the same bed with Evans. On the morning of the fifth day, the child was missing. He had been stolen by the Indians, had made no sound and was not missed until reveille awoke the soldier.

I never saw the child again to recognize him. The priest came back on the sixth day after his first visit and sadly listened to the details of the stealing of his protégé. There was a choke in his voice and tears in his eyes, as he bade me, "*Adios, Señor Teniente, es como deberia ser*" (Good-bye, lieutenant, it is as it ought to be).

4. A native of South Wales, James Evans came to America in 1860 and began working in the iron industry in Pennsylvania. One year later he enlisted in the 41st Ohio on September 8, 1861, and was in the battles of Shiloh, Perryville, Stone's River, and Chickamauga. Wounded and captured in the last engagement, Evans was confined in several rebel prisons, including Andersonville, prior to being exchanged in December of 1864. Mustered out on January 30, 1865, he enlisted in the 5th Infantry on May 1, 1866, and served with Charles Curtis at Fort Sumner until he received his discharge in May 1869. Later that year he was hired at Norwich University and was employed there until 1901. Evans died at Northfield, Vermont, on January 8, 1904. Ellis, *Norwich University (1911)* 2: 85–86; Kimberly, *Forty-first Ohio*, 196; *Saint Albans Daily Messenger*, January 8, 1904.

Chapter 24

Good-Bye to Los Valles Grandes

To return to Los Valles Grandes. With spring I began the construction of new quarters for my men, intending to make them one building, with a hollow court and bastions for defence in case of attack. It was to have two large rooms for dormitories, with two fireplaces in each, a kitchen and bakery. By the middle of May the building was finished. At this time another officer, Lieutenant Samuel L. Barr arrived, to be permanently attached to the company. He brought the intelligence that the Navajos had generally surrendered and that as there was no further use for us in the valley, we should probably soon be ordered elsewhere.

But it seems headquarters had other plans, for soon plows, harrows, hoes, shovels, etc., arrived in the valley, with two extra mule teams, and we were ordered to get the ground ready for planting and raising potatoes. We were to hang up the musket and bayonet and "take down the shovel and the hoe." I was ordered to take a wagon and a detail of five men and go to Conejos in southern Colorado, a distance of 125 miles, and buy forty bushels of seed potatoes. As with my first trip to Conejos, my orders explicitly stated that I should not pay over seven dollars per hundred weight for them.

I found upon my arrival at Conejos that a Denver man had again just bought all the potatoes in the market at fifteen dollars per hundred weight, so I was again forced to turn back with an empty wagon. Arriving again at Los Valles Grandes, I reported my want of success to the department commander and an express immediately returned with orders for us to break up the camp and return to Santa Fé, to fit out for Arizona.

The weather for the last three weeks of our stay in the valleys had been exceedingly variable. Every morning and until noon, the sky would be clear and the air balmy with the odor of new vegetation and the myriads of flowers. But with the afternoon usually came rain and hail, accompanied by thunder and lightning, which often appeared to strike on the mountaintops around us and kept up a constant and terrific cannonade.

On the morning of June 9th, eight months after our entrance, we left Los Valles Grandes. We did not regret the leaving—a soldier rarely does that—for the excitement of new scenes and the march have their attractions which quite balance the fatigues. Again a few of the old veterans grumbled their conviction that "they knew when we began to build new quarters we should not stay to occupy them." It remains a common belief among soldiers that if new quarters are built, fine gardens made, ice stored or something done for their future comfort and pleasure, they will leave the post or camp before they can enjoy it.

The forenoon was consumed in climbing the inner slope of the mountain and by one o'clock we were descending the outer slope, in the thick timber. The regular daily thunderstorm now broke upon us and hailstones fell thick and large, driving the animals frantic as they cut into hair and hide. It was impossible to hold the mules or guide them in any way and we were forced to clear them from the wagons and harness and fasten as many as possible to the trees. Quite a number broke away in spite of us and went back at the top of their speed to their old stable in the valleys, among them the doctor's pony and my horse. When the storm was over, we had mules enough left to draw our wagons to the camp at the bottom of the descent and we sent back a couple of mounted men to bring back the animals who had deserted.

Next day we marched through a drizzling rain nearly all day long, the mud cleaving to the feet of the men in heavy clods and everyone soaked to the skin. At four o'clock in the afternoon, the sky cleared and we camped on the edge of a perpendicular cliff, with a face 1,000 high from foot to crest.

Strolling to the edge of the precipice, after all the camping arrangements had been completed, I detached a large stone which overhung the valley below, in order to witness the effect of the fall. It fell shear about 300 feet, when it struck a horizontal projection with a downward slope and, bounding far out from the face of the cliff, went to the bottom with a crash that awoke a hundred sleeping echoes in the valley. This experiment of mine had attracted the attention of the men and presently they scattered along the edge of the precipice, with shovels, picks and crowbars, and—all thought of the fatigues of the day forgotten—loosened boulder after boulder, some of them immense fellows, and sent them bounding and thundering to the bottom until the earth fairly trembled with the shocks. When this amusement ceased, a party of Utes appeared and wandered about the campfires, picking up the scraps of food which were scattered around or stood, with the imperturbable gravity of the American Indian, witnessing the display of some soldier's trinkets who was vainly endeavoring to awaken some interest in his possessions. Barr, the doctor and I stood back witnessing the soldier's failure, when the doctor said, "I believe I've got something that will astonish those redskins. Here!" he shouted, "Come here."

The Indians came up to the doctor's tent and he went inside a minute. Presently he appeared with a Spencer carbine and a seven-shooter revolver and handed them over to the Utes. If there is anything that will interest an Indian it is firearms, but probably these men had seen similar weapons before, for they betrayed no emotion, but simply passed them back with a chorus of grunts. The doctor was vexed and began chewing tobacco at a great rate, spitting furiously and scolding all the time. Presently he got a piece of tobacco under the plating of his false teeth and, to remove it, he raised his hand and took out the whole of his upper teeth. Instantly every Indian fled back precipitately ten feet and all began jabbering and gesticulating excitedly. The doctor saw the point at once. Without showing any emotion whatever, he replaced his teeth, and, taking a bite from his plug, retired to his tent to put away his pistol and carbine. He certainly had succeeded in astonishing the Indians beyond their gravity this time and in a way he had never thought of.

After some animated discussion, during which all the Indians about the camp had collected in one group in front of the officers' tents, the chief advanced to the doctor's tent and asked in Spanish, "if the Big Medicine would let his red brothers see him take out his teeth again." The doctor came out and gratified them by popping his teeth out and in several times and then returned to his tent. I suppose no Indians were ever more astonished than these.

The next day we were down in the Rio Grande del Norte Valley, in the country where it rarely rains. At noon we reached the river opposite the Indian pueblo of San Yidefonso.[1] There was but one boat for crossing and that was not wide enough to run a wagon on. Consequently we were obliged to unload everything for transportation to the other side and then run the empty wagons, one at a time, into the water and float the boat beneath them between the wheels. It made a cumbersome and top-heavy load and had to be rowed over with the greatest care. To get the mules over, we mounted naked Indians on the doctor's gray pony and my horse and sent them across. The horses waded in, followed by the entire herd of mules, and when beyond their depths, all swam directly for the other shore and were soon seen shaking the water from their hair, rolling in the sand or cropping the grass.

The crossing took place about fifty yards above a fall in the river. It took us about five hours to cross all the baggage, the wagons and mules. The last trip but one, the boat took over most of the men and the laundress, with her tubs, traps and children. The laundress was timid and had been very much concerned all the morning for fear the boat would go over the falls, especially as her husband, Corporal Rounds, was in charge of the rowing party.[2] As the boat left with her on board, the three men who

1. San Ildefonso Pueblo was located near the east bank of the Rio Grande some twenty-two miles northwest of Santa Fe. The population in 1860 was 154 and agriculture was the main source of subsistence on the 17,000 acres claimed by the residents. San Ildefonso participated in the 1680 revolt, but when the Spanish returned twelve years later they took shelter on an impregnable mesa north of the village. After repulsing three Spanish attempts to overcome them, the remaining villagers surrendered in 1694 and returned to San Ildefonso. Not content under Spanish rule, particularly with the arrival of smallpox and other European diseases, in 1696 residents locked two priests inside their church and burnt the structure. San Ildefonso contained two unequal moieties—Summer, the largest, and Winter, both of which were perennial foes of the Navajo. Edelman, "Pueblo San Ildefonso," 308, 312, 315; Curtis, *North American Indian*, 30–31, 36; Whitman, *Pueblo Indians*, 4–5.

2. Corporal Rounds is a pseudonym and he cannot be positively identified.

remained behind with me kept chaffing her with, "Good-bye, Mary! I'm sorry to see the last of yez, darlint! Why didn't ye leave a lock of hair before leavin' us forever?" etc., etc. The boat moved steadily on until it had reached a considerable distance from the shore, when an oar snapped suddenly and the blade floated away on the current. There was but one oar left and immediately nearly every person in the boat seemed to be demoralized. I shouted the military command, "Attention!" and instantly every man stood at an "order arms" and silent. I then called, "Corporal, is there a man in the boat who can scull?"

An instant's delay and the answer came, "No, sir."

"Take the oar, corporal, and see if you can reach bottom."

The corporal took the oar and thrust it down its entire length and his arm to the shoulder and the reply came, "No, sir."

The boat had begun to get considerable headway towards the falls and the men were showing symptoms of uneasiness, while the laundress was clasping her children in her arms and weeping silently. I again called, "Steady men. Don't get excited and we will save you all!"

At my feet lay the doctor's saddle and my own and coiled to the pommel of each was a lariat of about fifty feet in length, made of rawhide and, by the merest accident, there was also a picket rope on the shore. I instantly seized a lariat and began uncoiling it and the men with me, catching the idea, uncoiled the other ropes. I then attached the lariats to the picket rope, one at each end, so that the heavy iron pins of the joined ropes were at the ends. Hastily coiling one end and holding it loosely in my left hand, I ran down the shore to where the boat was now floating swiftly towards the falls. I waded into the water to my thighs and then threw the iron pin towards the boat, letting the coil spin out of my left hand. The pin went straight into the boat and was caught by the corporal and belayed. I then ran to the shore end of the rope and drove the other pin into the earth to its head. Instantly there was a fearful strain upon it and I feared the rope would part. We seized the rope, twitched the pin from the ground, and drove it in again a few feet nearer the shore, the three men drawing hard all the time on the boat while I drove the pin. Again it stretched so hard that we repeated the process and this time saw that the speed of the boat had somewhat slackened and that she was slowly swinging into the shore. In a few moments all danger was over and the men were disembarked. The boat had stopped within ten feet of the brink of the falls.

As soon as Lieutenant Barr from the other side saw that all were safe, he sent an Indian to swim over with another oar and, in a short time, we all stood on the eastern bank of the river. What might have happened had those saddles and the ropes been carried across on one of the first trips instead of the last trip of the boat is fearful to think.

We camped for the night at San Yidefonso and during the latter part of the afternoon visited the *estufa* and church. The chief of the pueblo extended us the hospitalities of the place and showed us a grazing ground for our mules, insisting on furnishing a guard for them from his own people, which we cheerfully accepted. The church was built of *adobe* and cruciform in shape. It had two towers with belfries, but the bells were not in them. Two upright posts, ten feet apart, with a beam across their tops, stood in front of the church door and the three bells of different sizes hung to the beam. To ring them, a cord was attached to each tongue, hanging down to the ground. Three naked Indian boys kept up a tremendous clangor, at Matins, by swinging these tongues with all their might. The *vigas* of the church roof were carved in all sorts of fanciful designs and gaudily painted.

Above and around the altar were images of saints, some of fair proportions and others of Lilliputian dimensions, but in very good preservation. There were many paintings, but of no high degree of merit. On many, the hand of time had made severe ravages, the canvas being badly decayed and the figures faded into faint and undefined shapes. They looked old and bad enough to sell for specimens of the "Old Masters" in the New York market, if properly christened. The most curious object was a banner made of cowhide, exceedingly old, upon which was painted, in profile, a singular figure, armed with shield, sword, visor and lance, riding furiously over a host of prostrate enemies, whose countenances betrayed the greatest astonishment.

Next morning we left San Yidefonso and in two days more my company arrived at Santa Fé after eight months' life at a camp where there was no chance for dissipation and the men found themselves plunged into the fast life of the New Mexican capital, with eight months' pay in their pockets. No one but the Regular officer, who has had an experience of this thing on the frontier, knows the extreme difficulty of keeping up discipline immediately after payday. Each one of these men had at least $100 placed in his hands by the paymaster the morning after our arrival and the news of this payment was not long in reaching the ears of the keepers of the *fandango* saloons and the *señoritas* who attend them. A big dance was immediately announced at El Progresso Saloon and invitations were showered upon the soldiers. Permission was given to every man to attend, except those detailed for guard, and we prepared ourselves to see as little of the consequent drunkenness and rowdyism as possible with a show of keeping up discipline, until the money should be gone.

The second day after our arrival in Santa Fé was a National Thanksgiving, appointed by the President, and great preparations had been made by the military and civil authorities to see it properly celebrated.[3] Our order to break up camp at the valleys had directed us to proceed to Santa Fé and prepare for the march to Arizona. Nothing whatever had been said of the possible duration of our stay there, a rumor only having reached us, through a staff officer, that we were at liberty to stay a week. The reader can, therefore, judge of our surprise when, about eleven o'clock on the day when the whole town was given over to enjoyment and the celebration of the Thanksgiving, an order was placed in my hands for me to get my company ready to leave town at two o'clock the same day.

Barr and I went to the quartermaster to find how many men were fit to load the wagons and make preparations for the road. It was the day after the soldiers' *fandango* and the holiday was in full blast, so we found but a dozen men, including the guard, in a marching condition. A corporal with a file of the guard was sent round the city to find the men and get them together, while the rest were set to work loading our camp and garrison equipage and personal effects. I was the owner of about 300 volumes, mostly novels, but among them was a copy of Xenophon's *Anabasis*, a Horace, a few French works and some mathematical textbooks,

3. Not to be confused with the well-known national holiday celebrated today, the Thanksgiving mentioned by Curtis was a singular one proclaimed by Lincoln on May 9, 1864 as a "common thanksgiving and prayer to Allmighty God" for recent Union victories. Curtis celebrated this in June due to the delay in receiving the news.

which I kept along that I might not entirely rust out of a knowledge of what I had once learned. As I was going literally into the wilderness, I was very anxious to take these books with me and placed them among the first articles loaded, in the inner end of the officers' wagon. When the loading was completed, there were still left upon the parade ground enough articles to fill one more wagon. Accordingly, I applied to the department commander for another, stating my desire to take my books along. He replied by sending my regimental commander to oversee the reloading of the wagons and with orders to leave out all superfluous baggage. The result was that my 300 books were thrown into the parade and I never saw them again.

I should not have mentioned this incident of the books but for an after occurrence, which showed how whimsical was the decision in regard to not allowing me the extra wagon. A few days after our arrival at Los Pinos, a hundred miles south of Santa Fé, the commanding officer of the Arizona column, Captain Allen L. Anderson, joined us, having ridden as the sole passenger in an ambulance drawn by four mules from Santa Fé, while his trunk came in an army wagon drawn by six mules, with nothing else in the wagon. I was not averse to sacrificing my personal property in any exigency of the service which rightfully demanded it, but I have never recovered from the vexation I felt to see a solitary man and his trunk enter Los Pinos with an ambulance and army wagon to draw them, while, for lack of a wagon, my books had been unceremoniously dumped on the Fort Marcy parade, to become the property of anyone who cared to pick them up. And even had there been a necessity in the case, why not have them put in Captain Anderson's wagon? *Quien sabe*! (Who knows!)

Our loading completed, Barr and I, with fifteen men and three wagons, left Santa Fé, never to see it again, at three o'clock in the afternoon. We left a sergeant behind to bring up the other twenty men when they should be in a condition to travel, having no doubt but they would overtake us within two days. Ordinarily, I should not have left in such a condition, but my experience had been such that I was very willing to turn my back on Santa Fé.

We camped the first night at the ranche of Don Miguel Pino, eighteen miles on our road, and next morning pushed rapidly on to the Rio Grande and camped at Algodones. As we were forming

Captain Allen L. Anderson. Courtesy of Massachusetts MOLLUS Civil War Photographs, United States Army Heritage and Education Center.

for the march the next morning, our twenty absent men came in sight, soon joined us and made the regular day's march with no apparent distress.

I ought, perhaps, to say that had we had any inkling we were to leave Santa Fé so soon, we could have taken measures to prevent any disorder or straggling, in ways well-known to the officer. But looking on our stay as certain for a week at least, we could not object to granting the men some latitude, especially as it was on a national holiday.

From Santa Fé to the Rio Grande, a distance of twenty-five miles, there was no settlement or house, except that where we passed our first night. At the point where we struck the river, we could see the Indian pueblo of San Felipe, situated on the west bank, under a high bluff which extends for several miles along the stream. Nestling under the precipice, with its double-towered church and overspreading cottonwoods, the town is very picturesque. On top of the bluff, a little north of the present town, about 200 feet above the water, are seen the ruins of the old pueblo, where the Indians lived in the more warlike days of the past. The valley is cultivated by irrigation and is very fruitful.

Our second camp, as I before mentioned, was at the town of Algodones. The translation of this name is "cotton for inkstands," but why so-called I never learned. We left Algodones about six in the morning and shortly afterwards passed through the village of Bernalillo, owned and principally inhabited by the Perea family, who trace their descent directly from Spain and boast of a sprinkling of blue eyes and blonde hair among their sons and daughters. They are very wealthy and have a private chapel and a family chaplain, their family and dependents making a large congregation. The Pereas have introduced to some extent American implements of husbandry, the plantation is under excellent cultivation and the *acequias* in fine condition.

The vine-growing region of New Mexico begins at Bernalillo and extends down the valley of the Rio Grande to some distance below El Paso in old Mexico. Throughout this extent, grapes of a superior quality are cultivated. The flavor of the grapes fresh from the vine is excellent and they are thought by good judges to be equal to those of the Mediterranean. I have no means of arriving at the quantity of wine made each year in New Mexico, but it doubtlessly reaches several thousand gallons. It is chiefly used for home consumption.

The mode of cultivating the grape is different from that pursued in the United States, except California. The vine is not trailed on frames, but is kept trimmed close to the ground. In the spring, the branches which have grown out the previous year are cut off close to the parent stock, which is rarely more than three feet high. They are set out from cuttings and begin to bear the third year after planting. In the fall, before the cold weather sets in in the more northern country, the main stock is covered with earth.

The country constantly improved in appearance as we journeyed southward. The hills receded farther from the river, more land appeared to be cultivated and the mode of farming was more improved than that in the northern portion of the territory. The old plow of the days of Elisha and the bar lashed across the horns of the oxen for yokes were frequently seen, but the latest patents were in use upon the best ranches.

As we passed through the Indian town of Sandia, the women brought fresh vegetables to sell, in baskets borne upon their heads.[4] We bought onions, beets, turnips and eggs of them. Next we passed the village of Los Ranchos, which extends along the road for nearly half a mile and soon after leaving it caught sight of the church steeples of Albuquerque, four miles to the south. As we neared the town, some of the officers connected with the garrison rode out to meet us and extended us a warm greeting. They announced that there was to be an officers' *baile* for us and a *fandango* for the soldiers on the evening of our arrival. Entering the town, the men were assigned quarters in empty barracks and Barr and I were the guests of the officers.

Albuquerque is not as pleasant a place of residence as Santa Fé nor has it as fine buildings, but it has many attractions and the Mexican society there is fine. High winds prevail in the spring

4. Sandia Pueblo was located about fifteen miles north of Albuquerque on the east bank of the Rio Grande. The Spanish burned the village following the 1680 revolt and it was not permanently reoccupied until 1748 by refugees from various pueblos in the region. The population had declined from an estimated 3,000 in 1680 to only 217 in 1860. The eighteenth century saw the Sandia people exposed to smallpox epidemics and frequent raids by the Apache, Comanche, and Ute. Transfer of power to the Mexican and United States governments exposed the residents to fraud and sales of their ancestral lands, which had been reduced to 24,000 acres in 1860. Brandt, "Sandia Pueblo," 343, 345, 349–50; Pritzker, *Native American Encyclopedia*, 68–69.

and fall, when the sun is often obscured by the clouds of dust. In summer, flies and mosquitoes in untold billions swarm day and night through the streets and houses and give man and beast no single instant of peace. The difference of altitude between this place and Santa Fé is nearly 3,000 feet. At the time I passed through there, the army depot for the Rio Abajo was at Albuquerque and my orders were to get my outfit for Arizona of the depot quartermaster. But I was not long in finding Lieutenant Barnacle had taken as his motto, "How not to do it" instead of "How to do it," so I took the responsibility of going on to Los Pinos, where there was an officer of another stamp and, if it should be necessary for me to render an explanation for my course, I had no doubt of my ability to do it.[5]

5. Lieutenant Barnacle is a pseudonym and he cannot be positively identified. Records for Fort Craig for the month of July 1864 list Captain Heman Miller, U. S. Volunteers, as assistant quartermaster of the post and depot, while Alexander B. Johnston, 1st California Cavalry, is listed as assistant commissary of subsistence of the post and depot. Since Captain Miller was a native of Vermont, it is most likely that Curtis butted heads with Lieutenant Johnston. Heitman, *Historical Register* 1: 710; *Official Records*, ser. 1, 41, pt. 4, 380; *California Men*, 245. First Lieutenant Nelson Thomasson was the Acting Assistant Quartermaster and Acting Commissary of Subsistence at Los Pinos. This post, located near the village of Peralta, was created as a replacement for the depot at Albuquerque, eighteen miles to the north, that had been destroyed during the Confederate occupation. Bordered by the Rio Grande on the west, Los Pinos depot occupied buildings on some seven thousand acres owned by Governor Henry Connelly and his family. Initially established in May of 1862, construction on the depot was halted when the new department commander, General James Carleton, learned that the post was on private property. Miller, "Los Pinos," 1; Thompson, *New Mexico Territory*, 111–12.

Chapter 25

Departure from Albuquerque

On the afternoon of our arrival in Albuquerque, I took a long walk alone, around the streets and far into the suburbs. As I turned around a garden wall about a mile from the *plaza*, I came upon a bevy of women and girls in the garb of Eve before the fall, tumbling and splashing in an *acequia*, in a grove of cottonwoods. At the first glance, I supposed them to be a lot of boys and advanced nearer than in strict politeness I ought. I had heard stories about the *señoritas* of New Mexico bathing in a nude state on St. John's Day, believing that to go into the water on that day gained them certain benefits for the ensuing year; but I had learned that in towns where Americans had settled, the custom had died out. These women before me seemed in no way disconcerted by the presence near them of men of their own nationality, but laughed and joked, splashed and plunged, in apparent innocence and unconscious of perpetrating any impropriety. But no sooner had the bathers caught sight of me than they instantly sank into the water up to their necks. I paused on the brink of the pool and looked at the group of heads whose eyes were fixed on me reprovingly.

At last, the one nearest me said, "*Usted no tienen verguenza, señor*?" ("Are you not ashamed?").

"Why should I be ashamed?" I asked.

"Because you are an American," answered another.

"Ought not you to be the ones ashamed?" I asked.

"*Lo que un cinico becario*! ("What a shameless fellow!"). "*Salpique el, muchachas*!" ("Splash him, girls!"). Before I could beat a retreat, I was wet from head to foot and was obliged to hasten back to my quarters for dry clothing.

About nine o'clock in the evening, Barr and I started for the dance, which was held in the house of a private citizen on the east side of the *plaza*. In the *sala* we found about fifty couples, Mexicans and Americans, the latter including most of the officers of the garrison. On the continuous sofas, made of mattresses as before described and running round the room on a banquette, sat the dusky maids of the country, clad in their best, and nearly all of them smoking *cigarritos*.

> "Catalinas, and Pablas, and fair Inesillas,
> In pretty lace veils and becoming *mantillas*,
> Eviras, Antonias, and Carmelas, and Floras,
> And dark-eyed Jacinthas, and sweet Isadoras.
> Are crowding the seats and smoking as coolly as
> Though it was one of their common *tertulias*."

Most of the *señoritas* were dressed in high-colored silks, cut in the prevailing fashion, and they wore about their necks large and rich necklaces, beaten in curious designs from the native gold by the Mexican *plateros* (silversmiths). Over their shoulders they now wore their *rebozos*, the occasion allowing them to be dropped from their heads and no longer to enviously conceal their charms from appreciative eyes. At one end of the *sala* sat a group of four musicians, playing respectively a violin, harp, clarinet and guitar. In a small room at the end, opposite the musicians, a temporary counter had been put up, on which was sold *vino del pais*, *aguardients* and *dulces* (native wine, liquor and candies). From the sale of these articles the expenses of the dance were paid.

At last, the band broke out with the air so familiar to army ears and which always opens the Mexican dance, suggested at once by the words

> Old Johnnie Greer is a *bueno comandante*,
> He lives in Albuquerque in a '*dobe* shanty.

and the gentlemen rushed for their partners. The etiquette of the Mexican ballroom is very accommodating and introductions are not necessary in order to secure a partner. A gentleman who does not speak Spanish need only approach a women who is disengaged, crook his elbow and she is in for the dance. As each *señorita* took the arm of her partner, she deposited her *rebozo* on her seat and sometimes flung away her *cigarrito*, but not always, and often I could see the bright flash or the curling smoke of the cigar in the mazes of the dance. When the gentlemen conducted their partners to their seats, they invariably raised the *rebozo* and the girl turned her back to have it placed upon her shoulders.

At a certain part of the evening, *improvisadores* would go around the room singing, to the tune to which the dancers were dancing, some original doggerel in which the peculiarities of most of those present were touched off, raising choruses of laughter. I need not mention, perhaps, that *Teniente Cojo* (the Lame Lieutenant) got his full share.[1] One verse, referring to an episode in the career of one of the lieutenants of the post was repeatedly encored. Its chorus was the concluding words of the indignant beauty to the presumptuous suitor, and his meek reply.

Soy Mejicana
De este pais.
Yo, un soldado
Ay de mi.

A Mexican girl
Of this country am I,
And I a poor soldier—
Woe is me.

There are some customs at Easter at these dances which prevail in no other section of our country. The young women are provided with *cascaras de huevo* (eggshells) filled with eau de cologne and other sweet-smelling articles, which they break over the heads of their friends as a matter of fun and the operation is looked upon as a capital joke. There is a twin custom that you may kiss the fair assailants, provided you can catch them and inflict the penalty

1. The rumor on the frontier was that Curtis "at Bull Run got shot in the knee which made him lame." Wells, *Argonaut Tales*, 306.

before they reach their seat, not an easy task with your eyes smarting from their cologne bath.

Before I left Albuquerque, I purchased a considerable quantity of provisions for our mess and replenished our crockery. I copy the following from a notebook now lying before me:

Bought at Albuquerque, N. M., June 18, 1864, of Strachan & Co.

6 tumblers	$3.75
3 dinner plates	2.25
4 soup plates	3.00
1 pitcher	4.50
1 salt dish	.50
1 dozen knives and forks (steel)	5.00
1 dozen cans corn	27.00
1 ½ dozen cans tomatoes	20.00
1 dozen cans peaches	24.00
1 ½ dozen cans preserves	20.00

The reader might wonder why we did not go without corn, tomatoes, peaches and preserves when they cost so much. Well, sometimes we "had company" and wanted to treat them in a civilized manner. Besides, it was necessary to be provided with anti-scorbutics.

At Los Pinos I found a train of 80 wagons loaded with quartermaster and commissary stores for Fort Whipple, Arizona, 12 luggage wagons which carried the company and troop property, 300 beef cattle and 800 head of sheep. To draw these 92 wagons and furnish mounts for wagon masters, herders and other train men took 560 mules. Add to these the 163 horses of the cavalry and officers and it will be seen what constant vigilance against surprise was required through an almost unknown region, over desert and fertile plains, through barren and forest-clad defiles or along the cottonwood-fringed banks of running streams. This march was to be for fully 500 miles through a hostile Indian region, where the Navajo and Apache ranged, and we were cautioned from departmental headquarters to hold ourselves in constant readiness to repel attack.

Upon the arrival of Captain Anderson from Santa Fé, I was immediately appointed acting quartermaster of the column and receipted to various quartermasters for the mules, wagons and all the various articles belonging to a train, besides all the camp

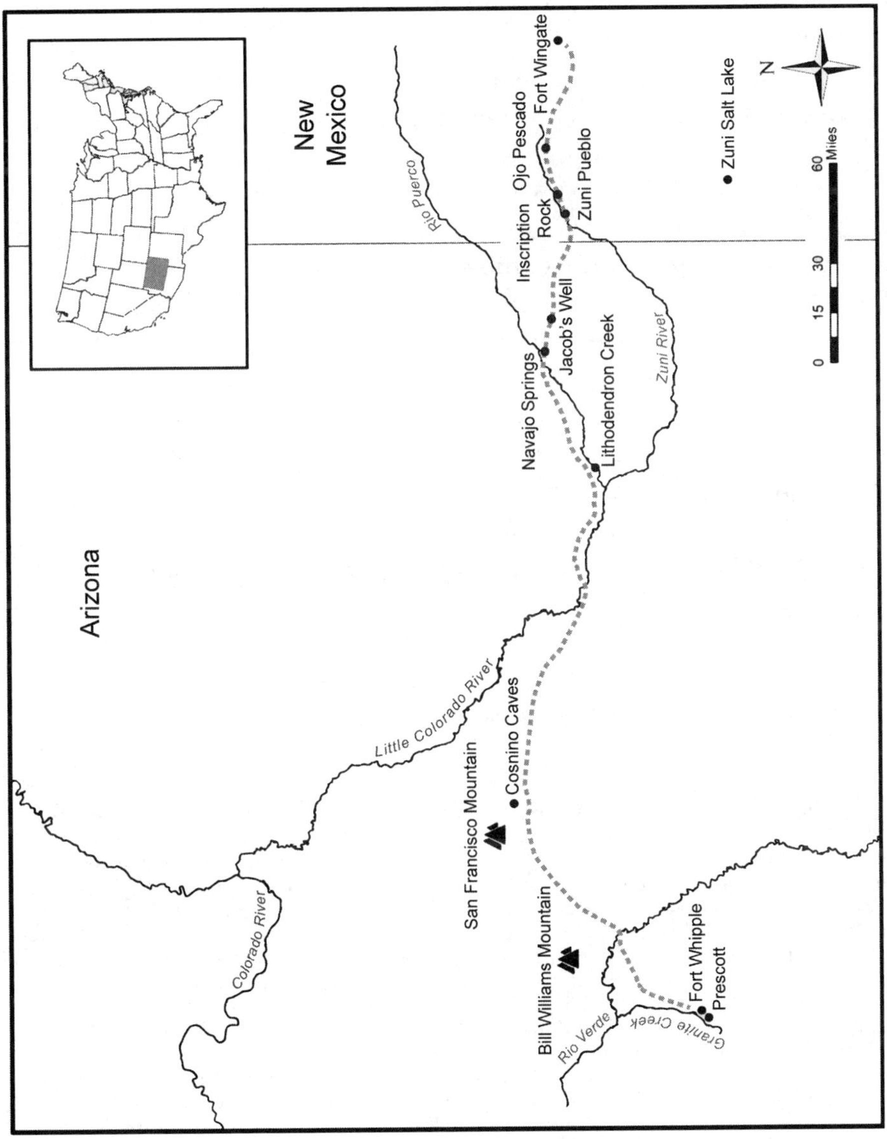

From Fort Wingate to Fort Whipple.

and garrison equipage of the command. In my second capacity, as acting commissary of subsistence, I receipted for all the articles of subsistence in the train, including the cattle and sheep. By this act, I became individually responsible to the Government for all this property and gave no bonds for the honest performance of my duties.

Our command was to consist of the company which had been stationed at Los Valles Grandes and a company of Kit Carson's New Mexican cavalry, which was to join us when we should reach Fort Wingate.[2] Our officers for this march consisted of Captain Allen L. Anderson, commanding officer; Doctor Elliott Coues, assistant surgeon; Doctor Cimex, acting assistant surgeon; Major Cyrus C. Clark, paymaster; Lieutenant Samuel L. Barr, commanding company; and myself, quartermaster, etc.[3] All of these officers were to be stationed in Arizona, except Major Clark, who was to return after paying the troops in that territory. Of these gentlemen, all excepting Barr and myself, who were not likely to have much leisure, were prepared to make collections and researches in aid of some branch of natural history or science. Captain Anderson selected mineralogy and geology as his branch; Doctor

2. Fort Wingate was established near the town of San Rafael, New Mexico, on October 22, 1862, by Lieutenant Colonel J. Francisco Chaves, 1st New Mexico. Named for Captain Benjamin Wingate, 5th Infantry, who was mortally wounded at the Battle of Valverde, the fort served as the base of operations for Colonel Kit Carson's campaign against the Navajos in 1863 and 1864. Detachments from the post also protected miners and settlers heading for the Arizona gold mines. When the Navajos were allowed to return to their homeland, the garrison was transferred to another site near the new Navajo Reservation. *Soldier and Brave*, 234–35; Frazer, *Forts*, 108.

3. Elliott Coues was one of America's most noted ornithologists. Coues enlisted as a medical cadet in 1862, received a medical degree from Columbian College in 1863 and was appointed an assistant surgeon in the Union Army in 1864. He collected specimens wherever his assignments took him until his resignation in 1881. Coues's field work led to numerous publications, now classics, in which birds of the western United States were first introduced to the world. He spent seven years contributing some 40,000 definitions on biological sciences to *The Century Dictionary*. After a brief foray into theosophy, Coues spent his last years editing books on Western travel, supplying much new material and copious notes. He died on December 25, 1899, after an operation at Johns Hopkins Hospital in Baltimore. Doctor Cimex is a pseudonym and he cannot be positively identified. Curtis's disdain for the doctor is obvious from the pseudonym he was given—*Cimex* is the genus for the common bedbug. Cyrus C. Clark received a commission as captain in the 1st Connecticut Artillery on May 22, 1861, and was promoted major of the 14th Connecticut on August 4, 1862. Seriously wounded in the side by a shell at the battle of Fredericksburg, he was honorably discharged on February 28, 1863. Appointed additional paymaster of Volunteers with the rank of major on February 27, 1863, Clark mustered out on November 1, 1865. He became a physician after the war and his last years were spent in and out of National Soldiers Homes. Major Clark died on July 14, 1923, at the National Home for Disabled Volunteer Soldiers at Hampton, Virginia. *Dictionary of American History* 4: 465–66; *New York Tribune*, December 27, 1899. Heitman, *Historical Register* 1: 303; Page, *Fourteenth Connecticut*, 95, 102; Hampton Soldiers Home Records.

Coues, who was already a distinguished ornithologist, took ornithology; Doctor Cimex, entomology; and Major Clark declared for botany. Great preparations went on in the way of arranging apparatus for stuffing birds; boards and cases for impaling bugs, beetles, spiders, and creeping things generally; presses for pressing leaves, grasses and ferns; and boxes to hold minerals and geological specimens.

The commanding officer was a man of about thirty, tall and slim, with blue eyes and brown hair. He was an excellent engineer, having planned and overseen the erection of many of the important posts in New Mexico. He was conscientious to a fault and a Christian gentleman throughout. Major Clark was a handsome man of about thirty-five, dark-featured, of medium height, with black hair and eyes. He had been a lieutenant colonel of a Connecticut regiment, had been fearfully wounded in the hip at Chancellorsville by a fragment of a shell and upon his recovery had been made a paymaster. Barr was a descendant of the Delaware Swedes. He had light hair, moustache and eyebrows and light blue eyes. As an officer he was severe and somewhat of a martinet with his men, but an excellent drillmaster, and a brave fellow. Doctor Cimex was a negative character, and needs no description, as he did nothing worth noticing, merely filled a place in the tent and at the mess table.

Doctor Elliott Coues was at that time still some months short of being twenty-two years old, and had but recently been commissioned an assistant surgeon in the army. He was a man of good features and figure, a little above medium height, with light brown hair and no beard or moustache, and of a complexion bronzed in his calling of field ornithologist. In his conversation we gathered that he had served as a medical cadet in the Army of the Potomac for some time before he was advanced to his present rank and that he had hunted and collected birds in Labrador. He also remarked with pardonable pride that he had been sent as surgeon in charge of our column at the request of the Smithsonian Institution that he might "shoot up the country between the Rio Grande and the Rio Colorado," and that as soon as he should report he had done so he was to be relieved and ordered to Washington. Doctor Coues was a sentimental young man, entertaining a good opinion of himself and decidedly opposed to receiving advice on any subject whatever, believing it to be a reflection upon his intelligence if anyone cautioned him against the pitfalls and caltrops of the country.

Clad in a corduroy suit of many pockets and having numerous sacks and pouches attached to his saddle, Coues regularly rode out of column every morning astride of his buckskin-colored mule, which he had named "Jenny Lind" on account of her musical bray. He usually brought in all his pockets and pouches filled with the trophies of his search, and when he sat upon the ground and proceeded to skin, stuff and label his specimens he was never without an interested group of officers and men about him. To anyone interested to learn the art of preparing the specimens he became an earnest and painstaking instructor. In time pretty much every person in the command was contributing something to the doctor's packing cases.[4]

Los Pinos is not a town, but the Chaves estate or rather the buildings of the estate. The *peon* quarters were large enough to hold two full companies of soldiers, the residence afforded ample accommodation for a dozen officers and the offices and storerooms. There was a Roman Catholic chapel for the use of the family, but the military authorities had desecrated it by using it for a commissary storehouse. Bacon and sugar were piled upon the chancel and altar; flour, vinegar, soap and salt filled the body of the house; and whiskey was issued in the priest's robing room. High above all this looked down the sacred paintings and wooden image of the Virgin.

The Chaves family had not lived here since the Battle of Los Pinos, when the house had received considerable injury and a twelve-pounder shot had dropped down from the wall, where it had struck into the piano. They had moved to Santa Fé and the Government had rented the estate for a military post.

4. Doctor Coues was ready to escape New Mexico and shared his thoughts with a friend: "Santa Fé is a wretched place in my way of thinking. If here, I should either be sick with ennui,—or become dissipated and loaferish,—neither of which I propose to do. I have got a tangible, definite object in view big enough to claim all my time and energies and I intend to let it do so." Dall, *Baird*, 365.

Chapter 26

Headed for Fort Wingate

On Friday, June 23rd, all our preparations having been completed, we pulled out of Los Pinos at sunrise and took our way to the river, about a mile and a half distant. There was a large ferryboat at the crossing, owned by the Government and operated by two soldiers. The boat was sufficiently large to take four loaded wagons on board at each trip, besides other freight of a considerable amount. The mules and oxen were made to swim across and by three o'clock everything was over but the company and the sheep. We had held some discussion as to how these sheep were to be got over and were about equally divided between the boat and swimming, when Captain Anderson decided the matter by ordering me to try them at a swim. Accordingly, the sheep were driven upstream about half a mile and driven into the water, but instead of going across, they swam directly downstream on the swift current and, as soon as they found themselves below their drivers, they landed. Again they were driven up and the men of the company were strung along the riverbank like skirmishers, to prevent them from landing. The sheep again took the water, the men yelled and hooted and slung sticks and stones to frighten them into going across, but in spite of the most frantic demonstration they swam down the current and again landed.

Next we tried to get them into the boat and with this view surrounded them by the company in one rank, curved like a horseshoe, with the flanks resting on the river, the sheep in the centre and the boat at the opening. Gradually we decreased the curve, arresting the few adventurous bucks who tried a dash between our legs, and at last had the whole flock huddled and jammed into the boat. The boat was operated by a warp and in order to start it, a man must be at each end. To get to the outer end and not startle the sheep was a difficult thing to do. One of the boatmen waded toward the bow in the water, his head concealed beneath the side. When he reached the prow, he raised his head above the gunwales and, presto! every sheep was in the river in an instant and in a moment more were on land.

Again we repeated the driving, got the flock on board and again they jumped out. We tried it once more, leaving the ferryman in the bow, standing upright. The soldiers waded into the water and stood on each side of the boat to keep the sheep from springing out. All worked well and the boat started. When it had got about fifty feet from the landing, twenty-five sheep went over the side and reached the shore, but the rest stayed on board and were safely landed on the other side. I re-transferred the twenty-five left behind to the Los Pinos commissary and left them.

We halted for the night at the town of Los Lunas, but two miles from Los Pinos in a direct line, for we had consumed most of the day in crossing the river and it was not considered practicable to push on farther that day. In Los Lunas was stationed a company of New Mexican cavalry and the officers "did the hospitable" by getting up a *baile*, at which we met all the *gente finos* of the town. It was in this place that the year before I had witnessed a celebration of Good Friday. Passion Week had been observed with unusual fervor and culminated on *Viernes Santo*, or Good Friday, with a procession of the priesthood and people. At the head of the procession was borne a large wooden cross, upon which was fixed a wooden image of our Saviour and which was carried by several bareheaded men. The women, representing virgins bearing candles in their hands, surrounded the cross. Through the length of the procession, there were images of the Virgin Mary, Mary Magdalene and St. John.

In the afternoon a second procession appeared, headed by a man on horseback intended to represent a Roman centurion, surrounded by a guard armed with spears, about as hard a looking crowd of greasers as I ever saw. Two Mexicans led the horse and, in order to make him appear spirited, pricked him constantly with thorns carried in their hands. Behind the guard came an open coffin, in which what was purported to be the dead body of Christ. A number of priests and choirboys surrounded the coffin and chanted sacred hymns. In the evening, there was an exhibition of fireworks and Judas Iscariot was blown up amid uproarious *vivas*.

The *baile* went off pleasantly and I left for my tent about eleven o'clock. When I entered the door and struck a light, I was surprised to find my camp bed occupied by a six-footer in the uniform of an officer. Upon examining him more closely, I found he was under the influence of liquor and wet to the skin. All efforts to awake him were unavailing, so I procured lodging elsewhere. In the morning, I found my unwelcome guest was a scion of a Virginia family, who held a commission in the Volunteers. He had left Los Pinos at ten the evening before to ride to Los Lunas. As the ferryboat was not running, he attempted to swim his horse over the river. When part way over, he fell off, but was fortunate enough to catch hold of the animal's tail. In this way he was towed to the shore, where the horse clambered up the bank and made for his stable and the wet and half-drunken lieutenant walked into town, when he blundered into my tent and bed.

Next morning, June 24th, we broke camp at five thirty and marched to the Rio Puerco, or Dirty River, a distance of fifteen miles. The current in the river was a mere thread and exceedingly dirty, yet we had to use the water for lack of better. Next day we marched twelve miles to the valley of the San José. Different portions of this stream are called by different names—Rio Gallo, Rio de la Laguna and Rio Rito. We camped at El Alamo, sometimes called Sheep Springs. The water issues from beneath a sandstone ledge, but is neither palatable nor abundant. The mules and horses were driven three miles to the river for water, but the sheep and cattle went without.

Our next march was about twelve miles and ended at the ruined Mexican town of Rita. The town had been deserted several years before, possibly on account of Indian depredations. Some suggest the want of water as the cause, for the stream that now flows by the foot of the hill upon which the ruins stand is narrow and, a short distance below, sinks beneath the surface. The *mesa* is of black lava, fifty feet high. A mile above Rita, I visited the ruins of Rancho Colorado, situated on the top of a red sandstone bluff, 150 feet high. The houses were of stone and very much dilapidated. There were sheep folds on the bluff, in which the manure had accumulated to a depth of ten feet, and the single pathway on which the flocks had been driven was worn a foot into the sandstone.

On four thirty o'clock on the morning of the 27th, we left Rita and continued our way westward. We ascended the valley, crossed the stream and followed the road over a chain of hills about 250 feet above the valley. A short distance north, the river was crowded into a *cañon*, above which a valley opened and revealed the Indian pueblo of Laguna.[1] The town stands upon a rocky eminence rising from the river and the crowded houses, with terraced stories, seemed actually piled upon one another. The river flows at the foot and irrigates a large and well-cultivated valley. This is a town which was in existence and, in most particulars not different, when Coronado's expedition visited it in 1540. It contains 1,000 persons.

In the centre of the town is a small *plaza*, not much more than a court, upon which the buildings face and to which two straggling and narrow alleys lead. Nearby stands a half-ruined Catholic church, in which a priest occasionally holds service. The church and its small court have been used for a cemetery until it is no longer possible to dig a grave without unearthing the bones of previously buried bodies. These are thrown into a little enclosure adjoining the church, where there is now an immense heap of bones and skulls. One of our amateur naturalists abstracted a skull and took it to the train.

Expressing a desire to see the inner life of the pueblo, an Indian who could talk excellent Spanish volunteered to act as guide,

1. Laguna Pueblo likely referred to the main village of a total of six inhabited by the Laguna people. Now referred to as Old Laguna, it was located on the San Jose River about forty-two miles west of Albuquerque where the residents practiced agriculture. Spanish explorers discovered a beautiful lake west of the village and called it Laguna, from the Spanish describing a depression in the earth filled with water. Refugees from the re-introduction of Spanish rule founded Laguna Pueblo which was officially recognized in 1698. A population of 927 in 1860 claimed a total of some 45,000 acres. When their Navajo enemies were removed to Bosque Redondo during the Civil War, the Laguna people spread out into their vacant territory. Ellis, "Laguna Pueblo," 438, 441–43; Pritzker, *Native American Encyclopedia*, 43–44; Dutton and Marmon, *Laguna Calendar*, 6.

and I was conducted up a ladder to a terrace and into the room of the chief of the town. We found His Eminence practicing an art which has recently become popular—the ceramic. He was painting an immense *tinaja* with some startling and impossible things in nature. Grouped about the room were a dozen Indians occupied in various ways, but none rose or noticed our arrival, except by the usual guttural salutation, but continued their work. Upon being presented to the chief and expressing a desire to see the Indian god kept in the *estufa*, he laid aside his brushes and paint and led the way to the terrace and down the ladder.

We crossed the court to another building, ascended a ladder to the terrace and then descended to the lower story inside, where all was dark as night. Following my leader by sound and not sight, we penetrated to the centre of the building, through several rooms and at last entered one in which was a dim light. Here we found a dried-up old Indian, entirely naked except a small cotton cloth about his loins and moccasins upon his feet. Some conference was held between the chief and the semi-desiccated Indian and the interpreter was required to question us as to our nationality. It appeared that Mexicans were not allowed to see the god, while no objection was ever made to Americans. Everything having been made satisfactory, the naked man went into an adjoining room, presently returned with an object in his arms, wrapped up in a blanket, and placed it carefully on the floor. He then uncovered it and an object was disclosed to view that looked like nothing I had ever seen before. It was made of leather and was about ten inches long and the same in diameter. One side was painted red and the other green and upon the green side was a rude semblance of a man's face. All the Indians knelt devoutly around this image and seemed to hold it in great veneration.[2] Thanking the chief and paying my conductor, I hastily sought the outer air and, mounting my horse, dashed after the train which had been moving all the time I was exploring the pueblo.

The road from Laguna to the Mexican town of Cuvero runs for twelve miles over a broad plain, with a table mountain on the right. A stranger, in passing over this section of the road, would never dream, from any evidence of his eyes, that there was a town for many long miles. Yet when you turn the western end of the

2. Curtis here refers to a kachina, an ancestral spirit distinctive to each pueblo.

mountain, you find a Mexican village of about seventy families, situated upon a sandstone ledge, on one side of which is a narrow fissure from whence gushes a rill of clear, cold water. Below this trickling stream are small cavities in the rock, from which the town draws its supply. By the side of the fountain stands a singular column of sandstone, about fifteen feet high, somewhat in the shape of an urn, with a hole worn at the base so as to admit of a passage through it.

Passing through the town, we encamped about twenty-five yards beyond the last house, on a broad plain with a westerly dip. The officers of the command occupied but one tent, a Sibley. This kind of tent sits on the ground like an inverted funnel. Its diameter is about fifteen feet across the bottom. Around the tent and close under the sides, our beds were spread upon the ground. Usually we ate our meals outside, by the cook tent, for the location of the tent was generally selected in a shade, but if the sun poured down without obstruction, we ate inside. On this occasion we had our dinner set in the tent shortly after midday. Our table was circular and the tent pole ran down through the centre. The half dozen of us drew our chairs about the table and began eating. Scattered about the tent were the rolls of bedding, valises, trunks, etc.

We had eaten but a few minutes when a few raindrops were heard on the canvas, in a couple of minutes more it was coming down in torrents and the water began running under the tent and threatening to wet our bedding and baggage. I left the table, took my chair, piled all my personal property on it and returned to eat standing. All of my messmates followed my example and for a few minutes more we stood around the table trying to finish the meal. The rain was so heavy and came down with such violence that the air inside the tent was in a haze with mist and our table and food damp with it. Presently the water began running through the tent ankle-deep and we concluded to adjourn. This we did precipitately and took refuge in a shed about twenty-five yards away, from which we could witness the scene. The plain, as far as we could see, seemed one lake of running water about six inches deep. It ran through all the tents of the men and had borne away many loose articles. The men, like their officers, had run out of their tents and sought shelter where they could find it, many of them climbing into the tops of the wagons.

The rain lasted about half an hour, then the sky cleared and before night the earth was so dry that by putting down a good layer of straw, no inconvenience was felt from the dampness. These sudden rainfalls are peculiar to this Western country. The traveler encamped on the bank of a nearly dry riverbed, with not a cloud in the sky, will be surprised to see a sudden rush of water come roaring down the stream filling the banks full and, in a few hours after, the riverbed is as dry as before. There had been a big shower far up the river. It has become a rule in the army to always cross a stream before going into camp, if you intend to camp in the vicinity of it. This is sometimes departed from, but I have personally known of two instances where neglect of this rule has caused much difficulty.

Our next march took us within a few miles of Mount Taylor, an eminence of volcanic origin, which rests upon sedimentary strata, whose horizontality is still undisturbed. We journeyed over a smooth road for a few miles and then came again into the valley of the Rio San José, called here the Rio Gallo, whose current was now pure and full, flowing impetuously over a bed of lava. Following the valley of the Gallo for eleven miles, we camped at what is known among Americans as the "Hay Camp," for here hay is cut in the broad valleys for some of the military posts. For the whole length of this valley a sinuous streak of black lava skirted our road. It looks as if it had flowed along a half fluid current, spreading out broad and thick in the depressions and running in narrow threads down the slopes, cracked and broken across in places after it cooled.

Near this camp is a deep gully, down which it was difficult to make the descent. We visited a spring of water which gushed out from under a perpendicular wall of rock, about a hundred feet high. The gully was enclosed by this wall upon all sides but one and Indian hieroglyphics were scattered over the entire surface.

June 29th we marched into Fort Wingate, a post occupied by two companies of New Mexican cavalry, commanded by Lieutenant Colonel José Francisco Chaves.[3] Here we found a first lieutenant

3. José Francisco Chaves belonged to one of New Mexico's most prosperous and influential families. Relative of a New Mexico governor, Chaves was educated at St. Louis University and the New York College of Physicians and Surgeons. Following the death of his father, his mother married Dr. Henry Connelly, who would serve as governor during the Civil War. His step-father appointed him a major in the 1st New Mexico, but he was promoted to lieutenant colonel on September 20, 1861, and later served at that rank in the 1st New Mexico Cavalry. He was stationed in New Mexico and detailed to lead the escort for the new

of our regiment acting as quartermaster and he soon made us all comfortable in quarters. This was one of the forts planned by Captain Anderson and he took great pleasure in showing us the details of his work. We remained at Fort Wingate until the afternoon of July 1st and this gave us ample opportunity to see what kind of soldiers the Mexicans make. So far as the drills went and good behavior in garrison, I never saw better troops. Their officers, as I have previously mentioned, were largely selected from the non-commissioned officers of the Regular service, generally from the cavalry arm, and these officers had secured as good discipline and soldierly carriage as distinguishes any Regular regiment of cavalry. Like the Bedouin Arabs, the Mexican is literally born to the saddle and these men are perfectly at home in it. The buglers at Fort Wingate excelled any I ever heard. The Regular service never picks up any Mexicans, although it is more largely composed of foreigners than natives. Whether this is from any unwillingness of the Mexican to enlist or because the recruiting officers do not want them, I have never learned.

At the Battle of Valverde, near Fort Craig on the Rio Grande, there were engaged 2,500 Texans against about 5,000 Union troops. Of the Union forces, three regiments were Mexicans and these ran away at the first fire. Their greenness, of course, must be taken into consideration, but their hereditary terror of *Los Texanos* went far to inspire them with fear. Soon after the battle, all but the cavalry regiment were mustered out and their places filled by Volunteers from California and Colorado.

The day following our arrival at Fort Wingate, the officers of the garrison gave us a dinner, at which were present, beside the officers, quite a number of citizens, including a priest and the sutler. One laughable incident of the dinner was connected with Barr and me. He and I used on extraordinary occasions to amuse the company by delivering a comical speech, I doing the talking and he making the gestures. I would take my place at the end of the table with bottle, glass, spectacles, jackknife, handkerchief, etc. before me. Barr would stand behind me, passing his arms under mine, while I concealed mine behind me. Of course, the chief

territorial officers of Arizona where he served until mustered out in 1865. He later served in a variety of political offices including delegate to Congress and in the state legislature for numerous terms. Chaves was murdered on November 26, 1904, at Pinos Wells, New Mexico. Keleher, *Turmoil in New Mexico*, 480–81.

fun of the thing was in the absurd gestures he made, causing me to appear to use all the articles arranged before me at all sorts of improper places in the speech. The thing was received with uproarious applause by the whole party, except the Mexican priest and a Mexican trader who sat beside him. They sat and looked on with perfect gravity, a look of disdain, if anything, on their countenances. When all was over, the priest turned to Captain Anderson and asked, "What was that man saying?"

"He was making a speech," replied the captain.

"Is that the way Americans make speeches? I thought he was drunk or crazy."

From this, it appeared that the Mexicans had not seen that two persons were concerned in delivering the speech. The matter was explained to them and, when they took in at a glance all the absurdity, not only of the performance but of their own obtuseness, they laughed louder and longer than anyone else had before them and were amply assisted by the rest of the party.

Chapter 27

Inscription Rock

At one o'clock P. M. we resumed our march and left Fort Wingate. From that post to our destination was 318 8/10 miles and for the whole route we did not expect to meet a civilized being or see a white man's habitation. The distance had been accurately measured by nearly every Government train that passed over the road and we had an odometer attached to the wheel of one of our wagons for the purpose of measuring it again. We were furnished with printed schedules of all the camping places on the road, the distances between them and whether wood, water and grass could be found at them—wood for cooking, grass for grazing and water for drinking. Upon consulting this schedule, if we found there was no wood at the next camping place, we put all we could upon the train before we left camp or at some place on the road where there was plenty. If there was no water at the next place, we filled all the kegs and barrels with which we were supplied for our own use and let the animals go without.

Our marches rarely exceeded fifteen miles per day and often they were not half as long. This was on account of our heavily loaded train, which could not move a great distance per day unless the road was very smooth. Usually the command, which now included the cavalry which had joined us at Fort Wingate, pushed on ahead when we broke camp in the morning and we rarely saw it again until we reached the next camp. A rear guard was detailed and placed under my orders daily, to protect the train. When our next stopping place was to be at a "dry camp" (i.e. where there was no water), we usually left in the afternoon, completing the march along in the evening, and left the dry camp early the next morning. This is precisely what we did on the day we left Fort Wingate. Our camp for that night was to be on the open plain, where there was no wood or water. Accordingly, all the animals were driven to water the last thing before starting and then we pushed on.

At Fort Wingate quite a number of emigrants for the gold regions of Arizona joined us—parties of men with six-mule teams, some with spans and one fellow with a pair of donkeys. There was also one of those wandering families of American Arabs, who never appear to stay long anywhere, consisting of father and mother, one boy of eighteen years and five daughters.

Late in the evening we reached the dry camp and pitched our tents. The horses and mules were turned loose and could be heard rolling in the grass or whinnying and braying for their corn ration. Campfires flashed up in the grass in twenty different places and soon the rattling of tin ware and the hissing of frying bacon could be heard in preparation for supper. Supper over, we retired to our tent, where the doctors had emptied their pouches of the slain birds and bugs of the day's collection and our other amateurs had gathered their specimens together and all were comparing notes. A brief conversation on the incidents of the day and all turned in. As elsewhere mentioned, we all slept in the tent. This statement, however, does not include Colonel Chaves, who commanded the cavalry. He slept in the open air, outside the tent. This officer held the rank of lieutenant colonel in Kit Carson's regiment, but was under special instructions to do certain duties on the road and exercised no authority over the Regular company or the train. Soon after we were in bed the increased braying and stamping of the mules, the rattling of halter chains, the shouts and cursing of the drivers and wagon masters showed the mules were being led up to the wagons to receive their supply of corn. And as we were dropping off to sleep came that sound so familiar to so many of my old soldier readers, the low murmuring of many voices in the adjacent tents; the champing of corn by about 500 horses and mules; the rattling of halter chains upon the feed boxes; the occasional squeal of a mule; the stamping of feet; the steady tramp of the sentinels; and the marching on and off of the relief.

In the morning our servants always called us about half an hour before breakfast. This was to give the men an opportunity to pack our bedding, strike the tent and get everything into the wagon. After we had eaten, the mess chest was hastily packed—usually without washing the dishes, that being left until we reached the next camp—and we were ready to start. For some reason or other, our ornithologist never could see why we were called a half hour before breakfast, "to stand gaping round a fire before the meal was ready, when we had so little time for sleeping; he could not see why we should not improve every minute of the time, and it was barbarous to waste time in such a manner, etc., etc." The doctor had very early shown us that he could take no advice or brook any suggestions, so we wasted no breath in explanations, but simply wondered why a man of his intelligence could not see why we got up at the time we did.

On the 2nd of July we camped at Agua Fria. This is a permanent spring, whose waters gush from a broken bed of lava, flow about half a mile and then hide themselves again among the volcanic rocks. This was the last stream on our route whose waters flow into the Atlantic Ocean. Its source is near the summit of the Sierra Madre, 7,700 feet above the level of the sea. Colonel Chaves had brought along a few bottles of champagne from Fort Wingate and these he placed in the spring, to cool during the night. Next morning it was nearly ice cold and made an excellent drink. Another drink not so nice was taken here by some of the men. Doctor Coues had a ten gallon keg of alcohol in which he occasionally put a lizard, snake, horned frog or other reptile.[1] This keg rode in the front end of our wagon and was often left there all night. The old topers of our company were not long in snuffing the alcohol and, without making any inquiries into its uses, they determined to steal a quantity of it. This they did on the night of our encampment at Agua Fria. Next day the men were sick and some of their comrades told them they had been drinking distilled rattlesnake juice. This gave them such a fright that they came round and confessed and submitted to a

1. Doctor Coues verified this statement when he stated: "Have a keg full of rattlesnakes, *Phrynosomas* [horned lizards] and several saurians of all sorts." Dall, *Baird*, 366.

violent emetic with great resignation. The doctor's keg was never again molested.

At the Agua Fria camp was the ruins of an old stockade mail station, which had been burned some years before by the Indians. Some of the charred logs remained and the chimneys stood as they were built. Formerly what was known as the Butterfield Overland Stage Line had passed this way and over a portion of our route, but the roughness of the road, with the dangers from Indians, had caused it to be abandoned. Over the same route had been surveyed one of the proposed railroads to the Pacific, generally known as the 35th Parallel Route. It was the favorite route of the Southern people before the late war and I believe is generally considered by army men as the most practicable and least difficult of construction. Certainly to me, who has passed over two of the others, this will always seem the best. It is out of the range of snow and presents few great difficulties in engineering compared with any of the others. To be sure, my judgment is made up simply from observation. From the stage station our road wound up a gradual height of about 200 feet and we stood on the backbone of the continent. On our left the water flowed to the Atlantic, on our right to the Pacific. Far to the north and south rose the mountains of the Sierra Madre chain, which was here broken down into a pass of the height mentioned. The pass was filled with large pines for about half a mile each side of the summit and then all trees disappeared.

On the Pacific slope for the first time! It was a new sensation to find ourselves moving on a down grade towards the ocean and we began to speculate upon the possibility of seeing the western ocean before we should return east. But as our regiment, with the exception of our company, was in New Mexico, we did not think it probable we should ever get so far away from headquarters. A very gradual slope, averaging for eight miles fifty feet per mile, led us to a wide valley in which we found El Moro, or The Moor, called by the Americans Inscription Rock.[2] This rock is about

2. Inscription Rock, now known as El Morro National Monument, is a 200-foot sandstone butte that towers over the ancient trail from Zuni to Acoma in New Mexico. A pool of water at its base made for an important stopping point for ancient and modern travelers alike. Indians inscribed petroglyphs on the sandstone, followed in turn by Spanish conquistadors and missionaries and American soldiers, traders, and emigrants, all of whom carved their own names in the sandstone. Hundreds of these inscriptions are still visible. The first English transcriptions were made by Lieutenant James H. Simpson in 1849. Julyan, *Place Names of New Mexico*, 119; Simpson, *Journal*, 104–7.

200 feet high and juts out from the mountainside, in which its rear is embedded, about 1,000 feet. Approaching its northeast corner by our road, it appeared as clear cut and rectangular as a cathedral or castle. It is composed of white sandstone of a yellowish tinge and the summit is broken so as to present at a distance the appearance of turrets, like a Moorish castle, from which its name is derived. Under the eastern side there is a natural cave in which was a pool of rainwater, which our animals drank, but which we did not touch. The sides of the rock are perpendicular, smooth as a tombstone and cut in the surface, about the entire eastern and northern faces as high as a man can reach, are innumerable inscriptions, in every style of art from the finished letters of some wandering sign painter or gravestone cutter to the rude lettering of some poor fellows who had turned their letters J and S the wrong way.

Among the most ancient inscriptions which are dated are the following, of which I give a free translation:

"In the year 1641 Bartelemo Rontelo passed this place."

"In the year 1716, upon the 16th of August, Don Felix Martinez, Governor and Captain General of the kingdom, passed this place to conquer the Moquis."

"On the 28th of September, 1737, the worshipful Doctor Don Martin De Elisario Coctron, Bishop of Durango, arrived here, and left for Zuni on the 29th."

"Juan Garcia de la Rivas, the first elected Alcalde of Santa Fé, Aug. 26, 1710, by the hand of Bartolo Fernandez Moro."

July 14th, 1736. Inspector General Juan Paez Huriador passed this place, and Corporal Joseph Armenta, Antonio Sanduval Martinez, F. Gnapo, Alonzo Barala, Marcus Duran, Francisco Barsla, Louis Paoheen, Antonio de Salas, and Roque Gomez."

"Governor and Captain General (could not decipher the name) of New Mexico, for our lord, the king, passed this place on his return from Zuni, July 29th, 1620, and put them in peace, at their request, asking the favor to become subjects of his majesty, and anew give their allegiance; all which they did by free act, knowing it prudent, as well as Christian (rest of inscription unintelligible)."

"Passed this place with dispatch (name not decipherable) April 16, 1606."

"Passed this place Sergeant Major and Captain Juan Archuleta, and the traveler Diego Martin Barba and Second Lieutenant Juan Yuez Jatapo, in the year 1636."

There were several other inscriptions besides those, which bore indistinct dates, but were undoubtedly very old. Our party also made one discovery, which settled a long-disputed question among the historians of Mexico in regard to the route followed by Coronado in 1540, when he entered New Mexico. As we were walking along the northern and eastern faces of El Moro, copying the quaint inscriptions and Indian hieroglyphics into our notebooks, Doctor Coues stumbled and fell into a cactus which grew against the side of the rock and reached a height of eight or ten feet. The doctor's fall lacerated him somewhat, but our pity for him was lost in amazement at seeing the name CORONADO staring us in the face from the rock where the branches had been swung aside by his fall. In a few moments we had cut away the cactus with our knives and had laid the whole inscription bare. It gave quite a detailed account of the object of Coronado's expedition, its composition, etc.[3]

Wishing to see the ruins said to be on top of El Moro, I started in company with Doctor Coues for the summit. To gain this we walked along the eastern face until we reached the hillside and, climbing up until we were on a level with the top, we walked out upon it. In the centre of the top we found a deep pit, apparently running down to a depth nearly equal to the distance from the top to the plain, outside. In this pit were growing half a dozen pines whose topmost branches just reached the level on which we stood. On the southern side of the pit and on a rise in the surface overlooking it lay the ruins of a large building, which had been constructed of stone. In some places the walls, when not concealed by rubbish, bore evidence of having been built with considerable skill. In a few places they still remain to a height of six or eight feet, vertical, straight and smooth. The masonry was well done, the stones being of uniform size, about fourteen inches in length, and six in width. The layers were horizontal and each successive

3. Curtis and his colleagues were convinced that they were following in the footsteps of Coronado. When they discovered old Spanish inscriptions that were barely legible in places, the Americans (who had no background in the Spanish language) excitedly claimed to have found Coronado's name. It was more wishful thinking than scholarly observation. A transcription of the earliest recorded inscription reads: "Through here passed the Adelantado Don Juan de Oñate from the discovery of the South Sea on the 16th day of April, year 1605." Pérez de Villagrá, *Historia de la Nueva México 1610*, xl.

Ruins atop Inscription Rock. Courtesy of National Archives.

stratum, with some appearance of regularity, broke joints with that below. Scattered about, in great profusion on every side, were fragments of pottery. Arrowheads of obsidian were also in the ruin.[4] Upon the opposite side of the gorge was a second ruin, very similar to the one described, but not parallel to it.

The question of course arose how could the people have subsisted who formerly lived here? Not a drop of living water is within the valley or for many miles away. It is possible that if the cavity which I have mentioned as containing rainwater was excavated and the sediment cleared out, it might prove to be a spring, but that could not have furnished irrigation for the valley. One theory is that the inhabitants were pastoral people, who kept their flocks in the valley, and for safety from the predatory Indians lived on the top of this rock.

4. Obsidian is a volcanic glass that is widely available in the southwest and fairly uniform in composition compared to other types of stone used to manufacture arrowheads. Because of its unique properties, obsidian was and still is a preferred raw material for flintknappers. Whittaker, *Flintknapping*, 69.

While the doctor and I were sitting and speculating about the pueblo and its former inhabitants, Colonel Chaves and Lieutenant Barr appeared from a trip they had taken to the north end of the rock and boasted that they had been farther than any man had ever been before. From some feats of Barr's and mine in the climbing line at Los Valles Grandes, I did not believe he had been farther than I could go and so ventured to remark that I believed I could beat them.

"I'll bet you a hundred dollars you can't," said the colonel.

"I can't go so much as that," said Barr, "but I'll bet you five, you can't."

"Perhaps I ought not to try it, but I shall, although I cannot accept the wager, for I never bet," I replied.

"Never mind whether you take the bet or not," said the colonel, "if you go farther than we did, the money is yours."

"Same with mine," added Barr.

This being a downright challenge, I rose to take a view of the situation. Barr and the colonel returned to camp and Doctor Coues accompanied me. The top of El Moro is cut up into all sorts of rugged heaps and masses. We climbed up difficult heights, slid down difficult slopes and at last stood on the brink of a perpendicular descent to a platform about fifteen feet below. Here we found the initials of the colonel and Barr cut in the sandstone and correctly concluded that they had been no farther than this point. I walked along the brink of the descent until I came to an angle or corner, like the corner of a room, and concluded that I could go down the angle by holding onto the rough sides with hands and knees. Once down, I could see no obstacle to my going to the very northeastern corner of the rock and looking down upon the camp and perhaps convince the bettors I could beat them, by ocular demonstration. I attempted it and got down without difficulty, the doctor sitting down above and witnessing the descent.

Now I must introduce an old companion that I have reluctantly kept out of sight hitherto, as I thought she could be of little or no interest to the reader—my setter dog Victoriana, called Vic for short.[5] She had been my constant companion at Los Valles Grandes,

5. Prior to Curtis's departure from Santa Fe, he had been presented by Lieutenant Ovenshine with a six-month-old setter, a gift from a lady friend named Victoriana for whom the dog was promptly named. Everyone, however, called her Vic. Curtis recalled how he passed the time training Vic at the isolated Los Valles Grandes camp: "She was taught

had accompanied me on all the trips I have related and was with me now. She was a beauty, white and liver colored, with mottled paws and muzzle, and a tail snowy white and as flowing as the plume of a hussar. As I reached the bottom, Vic began running along the edge of the declivity, whining with anxiety, winking her eyes and ears as she caught my eye. Knowing that if she leaped down I should have great difficulty in getting her back again, I ordered her away and threw stones at her to enforce the order. She disappeared from sight and I passed on. I was walking through a natural arch when Vic dashed by me like a flash. She had made the leap.

I walked a considerable distance and actually succeeded in getting into one of the turrets and looking down upon the camp. I threw down stones to attract attention and had the satisfaction of knowing that Chaves and Barr saw me. After some time spent in sightseeing, I thought it time to make my return. When I reached the perpendicular wall, I found Coues had gone, probably and very properly tired of waiting for me. And now came the difficult problem for solution and the one which compelled me to introduce Vic—how was I to get my dog up that fifteen feet of perpendicular wall? I made diligent search along the whole width of El Moro to see if there was any other way of getting up or any place where I could throw the dog up, but I could find none. Returning to the wall I seized Vic by the hind legs, swung her round my head and sent her gyrating through the air to the top, where she landed somehow among the rocks. In a moment she was back at the edge, with bloody nose, making motions as if she intended to jump down. I threw stones at her, scolded her terrifically, so as to keep her back, and then began climbing.

---

to bring my slippers when she saw me remove my boots, shut a door if I shivered, carry messages to the first sergeant, my servant and the cook, lead my horse from the stable to the cabin, and do many other things. I practiced her at long distances, and succeeded in sending her from a valley where I was fishing to camp, a distance of six miles." This training would save Curtis's life one day when he, a sergeant, and Vic were trapped by Navajos inside a dilapidated cabin nine miles from the Los Valles Grandes camp. The two men could keep the Indians at bay by firing from windows, but the attackers switched plans. They cut the limbs from a log about four feet in diameter and began slowly rolling it toward the cabin, like a portable breastwork. Curtis attached a note to Vic's collar and sent her off to get reinforcements. Three hours later, after covering eighteen miles round trip, Vic brought a message that a squad of mounted soldiers were on their way. Luckily, the Navajos had been delayed by numerous rocks that covered the ground, forcing them to dig under the log to remove these obstructions while they remained under cover. After being rescued, Curtis recorded the result: "For this Vic was presented with a silver collar by the company. Ten silver dollars were put in it, and as much more paid for making it." *Virginia [Minnesota] Enterprise*, July 5, 1895.

I put my back in the angle and, with the palms of my hands and my knees resting against the rough surface, began the tiresome and slow task of ascent. After much effort, I was about half way up, when down came Vic. There was nothing for it but to go down again and get her. It was almost sunset, would be dark soon and I could not afford much delay. I was tempted to go to the edge next the camp and call for a rope, but that would turn my victory into defeat, I should be laughed at whenever El Moro should be mentioned and the story of my climbing be made a campfire yarn for my discomfiture. After considerable difficulty I again caught Vic, gave her a good cuffing and again threw her to the top. This time she stayed and, after a long and tedious climb, I got up too. Then I effected a reconciliation with Vic and we went to camp conversing after our manner and playing with sticks and stones. When I entered camp I told my adventures, but I never claimed the $105 and never received them. My reputation as a climbist, however, stood high ever after.

Next morning—the Ever Glorious Fourth—a big jorum of punch was manufactured under the direction of Captain Anderson and generally circulated among the officers and men, in honor of the day. There was, however, a small amount of punch per man and we did not all of us partake of it. Before leaving camp my attention was called to various groups of Indian hieroglyphics upon the rock, which, from the effects of the weather and comparison of the most ancient of Spanish inscriptions, seemed to antedate them all.

Chapter 28

Sightseeing and a Captive Boy

As we left the camp, we passed over a slight ridge and rolled down a long and beautiful valley whose bed was lava, now covered almost entirely with a grassy soil, and after a march of fourteen miles reached the Ojo Pescado. This spring bursts from a broken point of the lava bed and forms a very beautiful stream which abounds in a fine fish peculiar to the Rio Gila and its tributaries. A circular wall formerly enclosed the spring, but it has, from various causes, been much broken. Nearby are the ruins of several pueblos which are so old that the present Pueblo Indians do not have any traditions concerning them. Some think they formed a part of the seven towns which Coronado visited in 1540 and which no one is able to identify with any existing pueblos.[1] A deserted town of more modern date stands below. This is occasionally occupied by the Zuni Indians, when they come to cultivate their well-watered

1. Although it is generally accepted that Coronado never found the fabled seven cities of gold that he sought, it has been argued that he did indeed find seven cities. For example, in 1874 Doctor Oscar Loew published an account of the Moqui Indians of Arizona in which he claimed that Coronado visited their seven towns which were situated atop four different mesas. In 1881 Lieutenant John G. Bourke, aide-de-camp to General George Crook, stated positively: "In my opinion, the seven (7) cities of Cibola alluded to in the narrative of Fray Marco de Niza and of Coronado are the Moqui Villages, in north-eastern Arizona." Other writers have argued for other locations in the past and continue to do so. Loew, "The Moquis Indians," 351–52; Hale, "Coronado's Discovery," 242.

valley. The older pueblos were circular in form and measured about 750 feet in circumference. The walls, like those upon El Moro, had been built of stone. Pottery of a beautiful polish, with checks, bands and stripes upon it, was found in fragments upon all sides. None of the pottery of the most ancient Indian villages ever contained representations of animals or human beings upon its surface. The more modern pottery of the present Pueblos is often in the shape of some animal or has the painting of one upon it. We amused ourselves at the Ojo Pescado in trying to match the fragments, often with curious success. I put together nearly complete, a wide-mouthed jug or pitcher with a frog-shaped handle and a beautiful butterfly upon the side.[2] This of course must have been of new manufacture. We visited still another ancient pueblo, by a footpath which led to another break in the lava bed, where a clear and abundant spring leaped into the sunlight and life. This, like the spring already mentioned, had been walled. A cliff of lava rises twenty feet above the spring and on the summit is the pueblo, strongly walled about. We searched for hieroglyphics on the opposite side of the valley with some success. They were out on the sandstone bluffs.

Our next march took us to the junction of the Rio Pescado with the Rio Nutria, or Otter River, but incorrectly translated in our schedule Beaver River, where we went into camp at 10:15 A. M. Here we first met with the Zuni Indians, who had large plantations of corn throughout the valleys of these streams. And here also we met with three of the celebrated Zuni albinos.[3] There has always been a tradition among the white settlers of the country—for the Indians invariably deny it—that a colony of Welsh miners once penetrated into this country and fell into the hands of the Zuni Indians, who murdered the men and married the women.

2. Curtis is here describing what was probably a water pot. The Zuni people placed images of frogs, toads, tadpoles and mythological horned water serpents on jars so that they might be filled with water. Tadpoles, frogs and dragonflies also appeared to symbolize summer rains and the ponds they formed. Creatures and insects that lived near water were painted and carved into rocks near the pueblos to ensure the annual rainfall. Young, *Signs from the Ancestors*, 126; Rodee and Ostler, *Zuni Pottery*, 15.

3. Very few southwestern Indian groups have albinos; those that have a concentration of albinos are the Hopi, Zuni, and Jemez. The frequency of this occurrence is roughly 1 in 200. Sometime in the past there may have been a cultural preference for the trait and hence its persistence both historically and in modern communities. One contemporary writer noted of the Zuni albinos: "The origin of these people is a mystery, and tradition does not enlighten us on the subject. However, they do not intermarry among the Zunians, although in other respects they live in harmony with them. They are very white, and have white hair and weak eyes, and a Scandinavian cast of countenance." Woolf, "Albinism Among Indians," 23–35; *Rocky Mountain News*, April 27, 1864.

Zuni Indian with Albino Zuni. Courtesy of Library of Congress.

What has given some force to this story is the presence of a few English words, or what sounds like English, in the Zuni vocabulary. For instance, *eat-a* signifies to eat, and *eat-on-a-way* means eaten enough. Again, the expression "Look ye!" so common in the mouth of Shakespeare's Captain Fluellen, is used by the Zunis to express admiration or astonishment.[4] But Welsh or no Welsh,

4. Captain Fluellen's comment appears in William Shakespeare's *Henry V*, Act 2, Scene 2. *Oxford Shakespeare*, 603.

there has always been since the Zuni pueblo was first known, and still is, a number of perfectly white people among them. They are spoken of by all travelers over that route and are generally called albinos. Those that I saw at the junction and others met with at the village itself were simply white people, with blue eyes and brown or blonde hair, nothing more or less. In dress, speech and manners they were Indians, otherwise they were as fair as the purest Anglo Saxon. A law compels these white Indians to marry among themselves and forbids them to marry with their more dusky fellow townsmen. This accounts for the long preservation of the white features which otherwise would have long since disappeared beneath the bronze tide of Indian blood.

Our camp was where the river entered a gorge, twelve miles from our last encampment at Ojo Pescado. We had seen no timber since we left Agua Fria, but used for fuel the *piñons* and scrub cedars from the *mesa* slopes along the road.

Upon the brow of the northern *mesa*, which terminates in cliffs of metamorphic rock, stand what are called the ranchos of Zuni. They resemble in structure and appearance the deserted town of Ojo Pescado. They are used simply as watch stations or shelters for the shepherds and their flocks. The view is extensive, overlooking the tablelands in every direction. At a distance of about five miles to the west can be seen the town of Zuni, rising on a mound in the centre of a valley. Below the ranchos are numerous patches of well-cultivated soil, irrigated by the water from numerous springs. A few hundred yards above is a spring held sacred by the Indians. It is circular in shape, about a dozen feet in width and very deep. An *adobe* wall of about four feet in height encloses it; upon the top of which were arranged a row of inverted glazed jars. These water pots are the votive offerings of the tribe to the spirit of the spring, which are made every year in March, when the spring is cleaned out. There is a belief that if anyone takes away one of these pots he will be struck by lightning. This terrible threat, however, did not prevent Major Clark from taking one away under his cloak and lightning has not yet blasted him, but then it may finally. Great pains have been taken in the decoration of these offerings and they were generally covered with painted frogs, tadpoles, turtles, rattlesnakes and butterflies. In the depths of the pure waters could be seen many earthen images of reptiles and creeping things.

At early dawn on the 6th of July we left camp at the junction of the Pescado and Beaver Creeks and, after a march of about six miles, passed the pueblo of Zuni to the right. While the train moved slowly on, I rode into the town for the purpose of examining it and learning anything about it worthy of interest. The first impression the visitor receives, and the strongest, is the entire self-dependence of their people. If all the rest of the human family were destroyed and they were the sole survivors, I doubt if the Indians of Zuni would miss their lost brethren for some time or be any loser by the casualty. Their tools, their arms, their clothing and all articles of utility seemed, with rare exceptions, to be of their own manufacture. When offered money for any article, they did not seem to desire it, but proposed an exchange instead, usually for tobacco or some article of food.

The town is compactly built, most of the houses being full five stories in height, and stands on an eminence in the middle of an extensive plain, which is cultivated without irrigation to any great extent. The ground is naturally very moist and this, with occasional rains, seems to be sufficient for raising corn and grain. There was little to distinguish Zuni from the pueblos I have already mentioned, except the presence of tame eagles perched upon the high walls or circling in the air overhead. Every traveler who has passed over this route and has written anything about Zuni has mentioned these eagles.[5] When I climbed to the top of the central and highest building of the pueblo, I saw three of them perched near us and asked the guide how they were tamed. He replied that they were taken from the nest when very small, brought to the village, reared and that they never left afterward.[6] There had always been eagles there and should the people be without them, disaster would be sure to follow. I saw several more of the white Indians and here I must remark that when Father Marco de Niza visited Zuni in 1559, 319 years ago, he says, "The first man I saw come out of the town was a *white man of fair complexion*."

5. One of the first American travelers to encounter these Zuni eagles was Doctor Samuel Woodhouse, who wrote in 1851: "Since I have been here I have seen several [bald] eagles & [sharp-shinned] hawks [*Haliaeetus leucocephalus* and *Accipiter striatus*] caged on the roofs of the houses or else a rope attached to one leg & a stone to the other [end]. They are walking about." Wallace and Hevly, *From Texas to San Diego*, 89.

6. These "tame" eagles were removed from their nests when young and raised by the Zuni, as well as the Hopi. The eagles were not pets, but were raised for their feathers which were periodically harvested in elaborate rituals. Stevenson, "The Zuni Indians," 114.

On a high *mesa*, some distance from the modern pueblo, stand the ruins of what is generally known as "Old Zuni."[7] There is a tradition among the Indians that a great flood once entered this valley from the west and utterly submerged the country. The people saved themselves by flying to the *mesa* and built the town now crowning the hill. To appease the angry spirit that had brought this deluge upon the country, a young man and maiden were thrown from the *mesa* into the sea, which then subsided, leaving the two persons sacrificed as statues of stone, standing there to this day in the plain. After this, the people returned to the valley and rebuilt their first town. Zuni contains 2,000 people.[8]

Doctor Coues, Major Clark and I visited the ruins upon the *mesa* and found an Indian priest going through certain ceremonies. An oval basin had been scooped from the earth, seven feet in length. Near one end stood a vertical column four feet high, neatly trimmed with colored feathers, and a circular network of cords. Placed at the other extremity of the basin was a cedar post of about the same height and quaintly carved. A forest of feathered sticks surrounded the basin and strings of shells and beads were hung along their tops. The Indian seemed to be just finishing his worship as we approached and closed by blowing from a long tube four puffs of a white powder towards the four cardinal points of the compass. The powder, upon examination, proved to be *pinole* (ground parched corn). The Indian told us he had been "praying for the tribe's daily bread."[9] Doctor Coues rode off alone, after we

7. Curtis seems to be referring to what is now known as Dowa Yalanne, a thousand-foot mesa about three miles southeast of Zuni Pueblo. A Zuni myth associates the mesa with the home of the gods, where lightning, thunder, and rain were made. Julyan, *Place Names of New Mexico*, 113.

8. A writer from Fort Canby explained the relationship between the Zuni people and the white soldiers and settlers: "Colonel Kit Carson leaves to-morrow for Moqui, and will scour the country in the vicinity of the San Francisco country. He has fifty Zuni Indians with him—the best spies and guides in the world; and as hardy and daring as the Bedouins of the desert. These Indians are from the city of Zuni, and, while inured to the hardships and customs of savage life, are far advanced in civilization. They are good agriculturalists, profess the Catholic religion, and are celebrated for their bravery and hospitality. The Navajo is their natural foe, and they look on Americans as their friends and allies." *Philadelphia Inquirer*, January 2, 1864.

9. The Zuni viewed their world as a continuum from the Raw to the Cooked, humans being the Cooked (or Daylight) People and offerings being made to the Raw People. Their rituals included offerings of tobacco smoke, cornmeal (sometimes mixed with other substances like shell or turquoise) or small amounts of cooked food. Willow sticks, with carved faces adorned with paint and feathers, stood in as substitutes for the Daylight People. Rituals were performed for a variety of reasons, including long life and riches, so the claim by Curtis that this ceremony was for daily bread would be consistent with Zuni tradition. Tedlock, "Zuni Religion," 499–508.

had seen the ruins, after his daily practice in bird shooting, and left the major and myself to overtake the train.

Our next camp was at Arch Spring, about twelve miles from our last resting place. When we reached the spring, we found a long and narrow cornfield stretching between it and us. It extended for several miles along the roadside and we found that our only way to reach water was to go through this field. As quartermaster, it devolved upon me to make some arrangements with the Indians for permission to pass through their corn. After considerable dickering, they agreed to let me cut a path twenty feet wide through the field, provided I would pay a certain sum per bushel for the grain which would have grown upon the space if it had been left to ripen. To get at an estimate, I called in the emigrants who had had experience in raising corn and soon got at the probable amount. This I paid for in shelled corn out of the train, because the Indians would not take money. The spring was walled up with *adobe* on three sides and arched over the top. We found the water as thick as Indian meal gruel, with a red mud. To drink it left a grit between the teeth and it felt pasty between the tongue and the roof of the mouth. The animals were driven through our narrow road with great difficulty and it took the constant attention of an extra guard and any number of Indians to keep them out of the corn during the night.

Next morning, Doctor Coues made an unusually big fuss at being called a half hour before breakfast and declared his intention to have his own way hereafter and sleep the full time. He had got in late the last evening, with a pouch full of dead birds, and he was very tired and cross. As soon as his breakfast was done, he mounted his buff-colored mule, Jenny Lind, and went off with shotgun and pouch for another days' collection. The march for the day began in the afternoon, for the next camp was to be a dry one. The march was nine miles in length and terminated near a hillside, where was plenty of wood and grass, but no water. The cooks were called at three o'clock in the morning and we were on the road before four. The doctor, as he had threatened, did not get up when called and all the rest of us combined to make him miserable. His legs were scratched with cactus thorns. Spanish bayonets were thrust into his thighs, his ears were tickled with cane grass tufts and water finally brought him profanely to his feet. Our march was this day twenty miles long, over a generally level country, but towards the last sloping considerably towards the west.

Late in the afternoon, we arrived at a Hole in the Plain, known variously by the Indians, Mexicans and Americans, as Wah-nuk-ai tin-ai-e, Ojo Redondo and Jacob's Well. This spring is a curiosity. In the midst of the plain is a conical pit, about 300 feet wide at the top, and 125 feet deep. At the bottom lies a pool of water, very green and unpalatable when we were there, some thirty yards in diameter and apparently quite deep. It is bordered by a fringe of rushes. A spiral pathway winds downward to the water. Navajo trails lead from it in various directions. The grazing was excellent, but there was no wood. As soon as we arrived, we took the precaution to get up sufficient water for the command before allowing the animals to go down to drink. It was a curious sight to stand on the brink of this well and see the 500 mules, 100 horses, 300 beeves and 800 sheep go circling down its sides and up again. The water tasted of about a dozen distinct nasty things, I should judge from the observations of the members of our mess, when we, from the sheerest necessity, reluctantly took a drink of it. The cattle waded into it and one emigrant's sore-backed *burro* fell into it and was with great difficulty extricated by the soldiers. I should have been sorry to have followed our command and camped at the well the day after.[10]

In this spring are specimens of the Axolotl, so well known in the lake about the City of Mexico. One of our men fished in the spring and caught one about ten inches long. Its appearance at first suggests the idea that it is a fish with legs. Like many enigmatical animals, it has been bandied about considerably in the course of investigation and, according to recent observations, it is not considered an adult batrachian with perpetual gills, but is in its preliminary or tadpole stage. To be sure, the mature animal

10. Doctor Coues recorded his impression of Jacob's Well: "It is an enormous hole in the ground, right in the midst of a bare, flat plain; one might pass within a hundred yards and never suspect anything about it. The margin is nearly circular, and abruptly defined; the sides very steep—almost perpendicular in most places; but a path, evidently worn by men and animals, descends spirally, winding nearly half way around before reaching the bottom. It is, in fact, a great funnel, a hundred yards wide at the brim, and about half as deep; and at the bottom there is a puddle of green, slimy water. Tradition goes, of course, that this is a 'bottomless pit;' and as the water had not perceptibly diminished after all our party and five hundred mules and cattle had had their fill, the story may go for what it is worth. The water is bad enough—warm, and probably muddy, though the mud is not visible, owing to the rich green color of the dubious liquid." Coues, "Journal Extract," 8.

has not yet been seen, but naturalists think this argues nothing, as there have been similar cases known before, where the adult was not found until some years after the *larvœ* was discovered. The Axolotl has gills three in number on each side, furnished with fringes. It can accustom itself to live on land, in which case the gills gradually disappear.[11]

Just before sunset, a couple of mounted Navajos rode into camp and reported that the band to which they belonged had recently surrendered and were awaiting the transportation of their effects to the Bosque Redondo Reservation. When the two Indians arrived in camp, besides the two ponies upon which they were mounted, they had three others, two of which were driven by two boys mounted upon the third. These two boys were in a nude state and their bodies entirely covered, face and all, in a wash of gypsum to prevent sunburn. While the Navajos were talking with us, the boys remained apart, holding the ponies, and when one of the animals got fractious, we overheard the largest boy, apparently about fifteen years old, exclaim in excellent Spanish, "*Lo que caballo*! *Queria pegar jugar me un truco petardo*!" ("What a horse! He wanted to play me a trick!").

Instantly, Colonel Chaves turned towards the boys, and, walking towards them, asked, "*Como se llama, muchacho*?" ("What is your name, boy?")

"*Manuel Romero, Señor*."[12]

"*Cuanto tiempo han estado aqui*? (How long have you been here?)

"*Dos anos, Señor*" (Two years, Sir).

"*Que edad tienen tu*? (How old are you?)

"*Tengo quince anos, Señor*" (I am fifteen, Sir).

"Where were you taken?"

"At Pena Blanca, where I was herding sheep for Don Simon Baca."[13]

11. The axolotl was of great interest to scientists worldwide during the period when Curtis wrote his narrative. One British scientific journal explained that the axolotl could be found on the high plateaus of the Rocky Mountains from Montana to Mexico City, although most common in the latter region and generally associated with that place. This strange amphibian was described in the following manner: "The animal is ten or twelve inches long, fish-like in form, but with four legs, a long tail like that of a salamander, and a tuft of gills on each side of the large, flattish head." "The Axolotl," 64.

12. Manuel Romero cannot be further identified.

13. This man was Simon Delgado y Baca, the latter name being his mother's surname. He was also commonly known as Simon Delgado.

"Then you are the son of *Señora* Romero, of Pena Blanca."

"Yes, sir."

"Ah, the poor mother," said the colonel sadly, "she has thought you dead all this time. Get yourself ready to go with me. I will take you with me to the end of my march and bring you back to your mother on my return."

The boy smiled at the words "get yourself ready" and looked down over his naked body with tearful commiseration.

"That other boy is an Indian, is he not?" asked the colonel.

"Yes, sir, a Pai-Ute."[14]

While this conversation was going on, most of us had gathered about the speakers and presently the Navajos objected to losing their slave. It was briefly explained to them, with Manuel as interpreter, that it was our duty to take the boy and then they asked that we give them two sacks of flour in exchange. It was an interesting sight to see this graceful naked boy standing between the Indians and the officers, acting as interpreter in a matter in which so much of his future happiness depended, for he was by no means sure in his own mind that this was the end of his captivity. His face had something of the imperturbable gravity of the Indian as he translated, careful to give no offence to the Navajos and always speaking in the first person when he spoke for them. For instance, he said, when they proposed to take two sacks of flour in exchange, "We say we want two sacks of flour for me."

Colonel Chaves, in order to terminate everything pleasantly, gave the flour and in a few moments afterwards the Navajos left the camp. As they mounted and broke into a gallop, Manuel stood looking calmly on, but when he fully realized that he was free, a deep sob broke from him and, dropping down upon the ground, he burst in a torrent of tears. Then our men, with that generosity which always distinguishes the soldier and sailor, began bringing

14. Curtis must have been referring to the Southern Paiute, one of three major groups of Paiute people. The Southern Paiute consisted of sixteen sub-groups that moved across the Arizona-New Mexico area. They interacted with the Utes, sometimes as antagonists but often collaborating on matters of subsistence and trade. Traditional subsistence consisted of foraging and the hunting of small game due to the absence of large mammals. The Southern Paiute adapted slowly to agriculture due to their nomadic wanderings and the fact that their social units were small, often only single families. Paiutes reacted to frequent slave raids by neighboring nations with a "defensive response," wherein they "abandoned their homes, fires, and stores at the approach of any mounted party." Spanish and American observers considered these tactics to be cowardly, but the Paiutes thought them prudent in the face of danger. Kelly and Fowler, "Southern Paiute," 368–71, 380, 387; Leland, "Population," 608–19; Knack, *Boundaries Between*, 45.

out articles of wearing apparel until, if Manuel had accepted all the pantaloons, drawers, shirts, caps, stockings, shoes, etc., that were offered him, he would have needed a modern belle's "Saratoga" to hold them all. But here Captain Anderson stepped forward and interfered, thanking the men for this evidence of their generosity and telling them the boy should be fitted out from the quartermaster's stores and, turning to me, ordered him supplied.

In a few moments more, Manuel was seen bounding down the spiral pathway to the water at the bottom of the well, in order, as he expressed it, "to wash off the Indian before putting on white man's clothing." During all this interpreting and trading, none of us had given a thought to the Pai-Ute boy or noticed that when the Navajos left he was not with them. It was not until Manuel had dressed himself in his new clothing that we had a suspicion the Indian boy had remained with us. As Manuel was walking along behind an army wagon, admiring his new habiliments, he heard a snickering in the wagon. He gave a whoop of joyful surprise that drew our attention in his direction and presently we saw him draw the grinning and struggling Pai-Ute boy out of the wagon. Poor little fellow! He could not bear to lose his old companion, Manuel, so he had concealed himself in the wagon and the Indians had not looked for him, probably thinking the rule that had applied to one boy applied to both. Captain Anderson adopted the little Indian, named him Bob, and furnished him with suitable clothing.[15]

15. Bob cannot be further identified. It was not unusual for soldiers to "adopt" Indian children. About the time of Captain Anderson's promotion to colonel of the 8th California, the *Wilmington Journal* carried an article about a Sergeant Flynn who had just returned from service on the Rio Grande. Some soldiers had mistakenly killed a mother and daughter, but Flynn discovered a six-year-old Apache boy survived. The sergeant named the boy Edward, although his comrades shortened that to Ned, and took him home. The Apache boy was described as having "agreeable features, with little of the coarse, angular characteristics that often mark the face of the pure aborigine." *San Francisco Bulletin*, January 26, 1865.

Chapter 29

Coues and Consequences

From the two Navajos we had learned there was plenty of excellent water at Navajo Springs, seven miles from Jacob's Well. As we had now been two days without good water, drinking just as little of the miserable stuff as we possibly could get along with, Captain Anderson declared his intention of going only to Navajo Springs next day and remaining there until the following day, in order to rest and enjoy the water of these springs. When Doctor Coues heard the captain say this, he exclaimed:

"Oh, captain! then don't let us hurry away from here in the morning, but take a good night's rest."

"Are you very tired?" asked the captain.

"Haven't had a square sleep since I left Los Pinos."

"Do you need more than the rest of us?"

"Guess not, but blast me if I can see why, when we have only ten or twelve miles to go in the march and it only takes about five hours to make the longest one, we should deprive our natural sleep in order to start before daylight."

"You haven't been able to find out the reason?"

"No. I can't see it."

"Well, doctor, you see if you can't study it out tonight. I will give orders to have breakfast at eight o'clock tomorrow morning, and give you plenty of time for study."

We were all glad to hear this, for we were in need of rest. Those who marched on foot were pretty well used up. Perhaps I need not tell the reader why we made our early starts and short marches, but I will venture to do so, presuming there are some like the doctor, intelligent but inexperienced. One reason was because the weather was hot and both men and animals could stand the fatigue better in the cool part of the day. Another was that the draught and saddle animals were tied up nights and, in order to give them plenty of time for grazing, they should reach camp early. There are minor reasons, but these are the principal.

We went to bed in good season and nothing happened during the night to disturb us. The night, like all nights in the Far West, was cool and enabled us to enjoy the luxury of a couple of blankets, with the greater luxury of a sound and healthy sleep.[1] Morning came and no servants looked in to wake us and no rattling drum or brazen bugle sounded their notes of reveille at the first peep of day, but we were left to turn over at daylight and court renewed slumber in a new position. But even a sweet sleep must have its end and, after several fruitless efforts to secure a few moments more of the delightful unconsciousness, I gave it up and rose to a sitting posture. As I glanced around the tent, I found all were awake but Doctor Coues and one after another rose up, as I had done, and were stretching their limbs and rubbing their eyes preparatory to making a further rise and dressing. Before anyone had spoken, I said, "H'sh. Don't speak so as to wake the doctor. Let us give him one good sleep."

"But he will lose his breakfast, if he does not rise with us," said Anderson.

"Let him lose it, then," whispered Barr. "He deserves a little discipline and the loss of a breakfast is what will cure him."

The captain was a little reluctant to have a practical joke played upon the doctor, but the united persuasions of all the occupants of

1. On July 8, 1864, Doctor Coues explained the unique nature of the weather: "Last night we shivered under blankets, and blew our numb fingers this morning. By ten o'clock it was hot; at eleven, hotter; twelve, it was as hot as—it could be. The cold nights stiffen our bones, and the hot days blister our noses, crack our lips and bring our eye-balls to a stand-still." Coues, "Journal Extracts," 8.

the tent at last prevailed and he consented to withdraw and leave the slumbering "sawbones" to the tender mercies of the rest of us. We soon informed our servants that they were to enter the tent and pack our baggage and bedding without disturbing the doctor. They managed this successfully, removing all but the sleeper and his bed and storing everything in the wagon without his even so much as winking. When breakfast was called, we sat down and ate and the doctor slept. After breakfast, a sergeant and a half dozen men came to take down the tent and load it and they were instructed to get the pins out of the ground by working them with their hands and on no account to strike a blow with an ax or mallet. In the meantime, the whole command had breakfasted, the sheep and cattle had already started on the road in advance, according to custom the mules had been attached to the wagons and all were ready for a start. Even the doctor's mule had been saddled ready for mounting and was held by his servant near the tent. Nothing remained to be done but to strike the officers' tent and load it, for us to be on the road.

This joke had in some way been circulated among the men, so that there was an unusual silence in the whole command. The company stood in line at an "In place, rest," and the teamsters stood with whips in hand, ready to drive out at the word "March," but the central point of vision for all eyes was our tent. The detail succeeded in pulling all the tent pins without making a noise, lifted the tent bodily and carried it to one side, revealing the doctor asleep, flat on his breast, with a pillow drawn closely over his head. It was eight o'clock and the midsummer sun was pouring its fervent rays upon the doctor's naked legs, for, with the increasing warmth of the morning, he had kicked off the bed clothes. The heat disturbed him and he turned slowly over. The sun flashed in his eyes. He opened them and sat up. In an instant he took in the whole situation and leaped to his feet, crying, "Where in hell are my breeches?" His pantaloons and clothing were at once taken to him by his servant, his bedding was rolled up and thrown into the wagon and we were off, leaving him to complete his toilet, mount his mule and come on when he should get ready. It may be needless for me to add that, after this, when the servants called us in the morning, the doctor was the first man to get out of his blankets.

The road from Jacob's Well to Navajo Springs is a gentle down grade all the way and, the intervening seven miles being quickly passed over, we found ourselves in a broad basin, in which in the winter months the water gathers from the fifteen springs and forms a pool, but which was now dry and parched. In fact, upon examination, we found the springs were brim full, but that there was no overflow. These springs were of the depth and general dimensions of flour barrels set into the ground, end up. Their tops were even with the ground and their locality was readily distinguished from a distance, by a little grassy ring about their mouths. Interspersed with the water springs were half a dozen mud springs, which were easily distinguishable from the others by being rounded up about two feet above the earth and very green on their grassy slopes. Our wagon master, who had been here before, had cautioned us against allowing our animals to crop the grass on the sides of the mud springs, saying that, if they once put their hoofs over the inside margin of the grassy ring, they were gone and it would cost much trouble to extricate them. Accordingly, I sent word throughout the train and among the emigrants that care should be taken to prevent all animals from getting into the mud springs.

We had not been in camp half an hour before we discovered that the supply of water was not adequate to our needs. The thirsty animals and men exhausted the springs in a few minutes and they did not fill again or filled so slowly that we could not see the flow. The question at once arose whether we should turn back to Jacob's Well or push on. It was now eleven o'clock and if we were to go on there must be no delay. In our interview with the Navajos, they had said that they had come by way of Puerco Creek and that there was plenty of water in it. To insure against mistakes, Captain Anderson called up Manuel, examined him on the subject and he reported that, when he crossed the Rio Puerco three days before, water was flowing in its bed. The captain gave orders for the command to be ready to start at twelve.

Doctor Coues, crestfallen and ashamed at the result of his attempt to get a good square sleep at Ojo Redondo, did not show himself in camp until eleven o'clock. Soon after his arrival, he unsaddled his mule and started to picket her out to graze, leading her by a lariat about fifty feet long, he at one end and she at the other. Seeing her heading for a mud spring, I called out to the doctor to be careful and was entering into an explanation of my caution when he interrupted me with a burst of anger and some incoherent remarks about minding my own business, etc. Without turning his head, he walked on towards the outskirts of camp, his mule following until near a mud hole, when she began cropping the grass on its border and at the same time walking up the slope towards the treacherous centre. There could be but one result if the mule was not stopped, but how could I deal with such a man as this willful doctor? It really seemed as if he needed another lesson and I quietly stood still that he might receive it. There was considerable slack rope between man and beast, so that the short pause of the mule at the grass was not telegraphed to the doctor. But when she put her hoofs over the margin and took a plunge into the bowels of the earth, completely disappearing from sight, the rope was jerked violently from his hands and he turned round to see the catastrophe realized, against which he had been kindly cautioned. As soon as he saw what had happened, he began bawling, "Oh my mule, Curtis! Oh poor Jenny Lind! She's gone! She's gone!"

Without paying any attention to the frantic doctor, I ran quickly to the margin of the mud spring and, seizing the lariat, pulled with the assistance of a passing soldier the head of the mule above the mud. As soon as her muzzle appeared above the surface, she gave such a snort and blow as covered me with mud from head to foot. In a few moments, we were surrounded with soldiers and emigrants and all went to work to extricate the hybrid from her predicament. Wagon tongues, tail boards, commissary boxes, etc. were soon laid around so as to make a safe platform on the borders of the spring. A rope was got down under the buttocks of the animal, with a squad of men at each end, another was got under the forelegs and at the word "Pull!" all pulled together and the mule came floundering and stumbling out, head foremost, scattering mud over everybody near her. All the officers were too much vexed to notice the doctor, even to scold him, but when, a few moments later, he insisted on taking some water from the only spring in which a drop was left to wash his mule, he waked up Anderson and got such a going over as only your mild, unprofaned men can give when aroused. His whole line of conduct from the Rio Grande to this place was gone over and held up for his instruction and admiration in a masterly manner and it did him lots of good.

When the time approached for us to leave camp, Captain Anderson ordered me to take ten cavalrymen, each provided with a long-handled mining shovel, and proceed to the Rio Puerco, where, if I found no water on the surface of the creek, I was to dig down to the bedrock for it. It often happens in these western streams that after no water can be seen running between the banks, it may be found running through the loose sand if a hole is opened down to the bedrock. Miners have often opened a trench across such a river and put in a compact clay dam, through which the water cannot ooze, and this has forced the water to the surface. We rode very rapidly over the five and a half miles lying between Navajo Springs and the Rio Puerco of the West, as it is called to distinguish it from the other Rio Puerco which we crossed soon after leaving the Rio Grande. We descended into the valley of the river and found its bed apparently as dry as the desert of Sahara. Dismounting, we sank ten holes across the bed from shore to shore, about five feet deep, striking the underlying ledge at that depth, but very little water flowed into the holes, so little that I at once saw we should not be able to camp there.

I sent back one man to tell the captain that I had gone on to Carrizo Creek and enable him, if he concluded to turn back, to send me word. The distance from the Puerco to the Carrizo, over a sharp intervening ridge, was seven miles and the river, when I reached it, seemed to be but a reproduction of the first, dry and unpromising. I opened a row of holes across the bed, but with no better fortune than in the previous case, so I sent back another man with a message for Captain Anderson and pushed on to Lithodendron Creek, thirteen miles farther. Here I found about an acre of water in the bed of the stream under a cliff, thick and pasty with red mud, and but a miserable quencher of our intolerable thirst, but it was water and better than none. Accordingly, I sent word back to the command and sat myself down to wait for it.

The drive and march on this day had been exceedingly unfortunate. Instead of starting in the cool of the day, as had been our custom heretofore, we had been betrayed by several combining circumstances into staying until eight o'clock in the morning. Our first march to Navajo Springs, where we expected to remain nearly twenty-four hours, had been easy on account of its downward slope, but the next three stages to the Puerco, the Carrizo and the Lithodendron Creeks, with their dividing ridges, making about thirty-two miles in all off a hot day in July, had been severe in the extreme.

The reader will recollect also that we had had no good water since we left the last camp before passing through Zuni. At Arch Spring it had been a muddy gruel, at Jacob's Well an alkaline tincture of decaying vegetable matter, at Navajo Springs the water was impregnated with alkali, as at Jacob's Well, and but little more palatable at the Rio Puerco and Carrizo Creek, the little water which we found was thick with red earth. Our condition and that of the animals was pitiful. The thirty-two miles was not a difficult march to make, had the situation of the road been known beforehand. In that case, we could have left Jacob's Well as early as three o'clock in the morning and marched to Carrizo Creek. At Navajo Springs, we could have filled the water kegs of the command for cooking at camp and after a halt of a few hours completed the march to Lithodendron Creek without distress. Or we could have left Jacob's Well at three in the afternoon and made a dry camp at Carrizo Creek, completing the march next morning. But to go over the same distance in the heat of the day, distracted by expectations of finding water and disappointments at not finding it, is in itself a sore trial to the tired soldier with an empty canteen.

To pass away the time until the command should arrive, I concluded to visit and examine the petrifactions which have given the name to the creek. During the afternoon, as I passed over the divide, I had noticed sections of petrified trees, but was in too much haste to examine them. The valley of the Lithodendron, from bluff to bluff, seemed to be about a mile wide, and the bluffs forty feet high. There were ruins of stone houses near the pool of water and considerable quantities of broken pottery, some of which seemed very ancient. Some of the walls were below the present surface of the country. In a deposit of red marl, on the west side of the creek, was quite a forest of prostrate and petrified trees. I measured one which was over one hundred feet in length and nine feet in diameter at the butt. The stump upon which it grew was close by and showed evidences of having been charred by fire before it turned to stone. The trees were, without doubt, originally pine and the limbs, bark and gum could be distinctly identified. The soil now produces no trees of any kind, even the stunted pine and cedar being absent.

The afternoon passed and eight o'clock arrived before any evidence of the approaching train showed itself. At precisely five minutes after eight, the bray of a mule was heard far up the road on the ridge between Carrizo and Lithodendron Creeks and I knew the command was near. In half an hour more, the first sergeant of the infantry company, with five men, approached the border of the shoal warm, muddy water and stooping, they filled their quart cups and drank the contents at one eager and continuous draught. These five men were all who appeared for some time and two hours passed away before the last man straggled wearily in and drank his share of the filthy water. The mule teams were as slow in getting in and many of the wagons were drawn by half their complement of mules; the other half having given out, had been unharnessed and attached to the rear of the wagon.

We spent a miserable night at Lithodendron Creek. There was no wood or grass and the tired and hungry mules wandered back and forward from the water to the wagons all night, never ceasing to bray their discontent. Few of the men slept and I know none of the officers did. We tried it, gave it up and sat up till morning, talking and trying to check our fevered thirst with the miserable water. The sheep and cattle did not suffer much. They had not worked and a day without water was of little account to them.

Our next march was to be sixteen miles in length, and would terminate at the Colorado Chiquito, a living stream of as pure water as any in New England. Of course, we were impatient to reach it and as soon as the eastern sky showed the first streaks of day, we began making preparations to resume our march. The first half of the distance was all uphill and our wagon master had grave fears that our weak and hungry mules would hardly be able to get the heavy, loaded wagons to the summit. But to stay here was to make matters worse and so we drove out. To our great satisfaction, nothing happened to delay us. The night's rest, even without forage, seemed to have recuperated the mules' strength and they pulled patiently and slowly on. Once on the backbone of the divide, the wagons ran almost of their own weight down the descent of eight miles to the river.

Relieved of all anxiety concerning the train, I galloped forward and joined the officers at the head of the cavalry, all eagerly pushing on with but one absorbing idea—water! At last, as we turned around a bluff, we caught sight of the long green line of cottonwoods, which in this country always indicates the river courses, and our impatience and thirst increased and our speed as well. We broke into an easy canter and the double line of horsemen went clattering down the curves of the road towards the river, the horses full as eager as the men. At last we reached the timber, burst through the underbrush, went pell-mell down the steep bank, the horses plunged into the river up their bellies and all dismounted to our thighs in the water. Oh, the refreshing powers of water! It never tasted so good before and never but once afterward.

Chapter 30

Colorado Chiquito and a Porcupine

Just after I left the train to join the cavalry in front and while I was still some distance behind, I noticed a slightly defined path—where the wagon road swept round a curve to the right—which, like the cord of a bow, ran from point to point of the curve and cut off a good part of the distance, so I determined to take it. Dashing into it and putting spurs to my horse, I was fast overtaking the cavalry, when my attention was called to a small white object lying in the pathway directly ahead. Curbing my horse to a walk, I saw that it was a small cotton bag, with a string tied around the middle and something in each end. I dismounted, picked up the bag and opened it. In the first end was a fresh loaf of white bread, from which a good slice had recently been cut, and when I opened the second division, I found a couple of pounds of fine black tea. Here was a discovery! Who had been along here so recently and with what object, so far from any settlement, in the heart of an Indian infested country? I examined the pathway to see what tracks had recently been made and which way they pointed and soon found the tracks of an iron-shod horse turned in the same direction we were going. I remounted and, fastening the bag to my saddle, galloped on, concluding that some party of emigrants to the Arizona gold mines had recently passed over the road and one of their number had dropped the tea and lunch. Still this conclusion did not fully satisfy me, but thirst and a desire to reach the river and quench it soon drove all other thoughts out of my head and I dashed on at the top of my horse's speed, joining the cavalry about a mile before they reached the river. So intent was I about the water that I never mentioned the bag, but plunged headlong and recklessly down the bank with the rest and dismounted into the stream. We drank enough, and much more than enough, and our animals did likewise. In fact, we were obliged to force both ourselves and horses away from the river.

As we rode two and two up from the riverbed, through the bushes, we saw on a slight elevation before us, over which the road passed, the chimney of a burned mail station. While we were looking at it, two horsemen rose into sight from the opposite slope of the hill and stood clearly defined against the sky. Seeing us, they suddenly halted. They were too far away for us to see faces or discern features. We could only see that they wore civilized clothes and that it resembled the military in cut and color. As soon as Captain Anderson saw them, he exclaimed, "See those Indians!"

"They are not dressed like Indians," said Colonel Chaves.

"No, but Indians have captured our trains and stolen our clothing," answered Anderson. "If those fellows run, I shall know they are Indians."

The captain had hardly finished this sentence when the two men on the hill wheeled suddenly and disappeared. Instantly the captain gave the command "Forward!" and away went the cavalry with a rush up the hill. I did not join the pursuit, for what reason it is hard to say. I know I said audibly to myself, "Those are not Indians" and heard the voice of Colonel Chaves behind me quickly reply, "Of course they are not." He and I were the only two who did not join in the pursuit, he from some intuitive impression that the men were not Indians and I from some conclusion I had drawn from my bag of bread and tea, for somehow I felt that those men were in search of the lost bag.

Chaves and I rode to the top of the hill and halted to see the chase. Before us the road ran in a slight curve to the right for four miles, when it turned to the left and disappeared behind the cottonwoods that fringed the river. About two miles ahead on the road were two horsemen flying on the wings of fear and highly excited horseflesh and behind them were two other horsemen, not a whit slower in their speed and eagerness to annihilate space. Behind them, all along the road, given out by their exertion, was the rest of the cavalry, in all stages of exhaustion. The poor animals had been for days without grain, the last day without grass and had just drank at least a barrel of water each and here they were attempting to make a cavalry charge!

The pursuers were a couple of sergeants who were well-mounted and, as afterwards appeared, had kept concealed in their company wagon a small quantity of corn which they surreptitiously dealt out to their equine favorites. This had enabled them to outstrip all others. As Chaves and I stood looking at the race and saw it finally disappear behind the timber, Captain Anderson rode back to us and expressed his regret to the colonel at having sent his men off on this chase. He had become convinced, almost as soon as the men started, that he had made a mistake, but not in season to stop the pursuit. He directed me to bring the train down the river to a point where he would select a camp and he and the colonel rode one way, while I turned back to meet the train in the other.

When the wagons reached the river, the animals were so crazy for water that I ordered the teamsters to unharness everything and let all go to drink. It was with the greatest difficulty that the mules could be restrained long enough to get their harnesses off and, as fast as they were loosed from the wagons, they shot like stones from catapults in the direction of the river. At one moment the mules, oxen and sheep were all in the stream at once, filling themselves with the cooling water. When they came up the bank, they all fell so ravenously upon the abundant green grass that I rode on to overtake Captain Anderson and ask his consent to let the animals graze for an hour before coming into camp. I found him about two miles below the chimney, sitting under a broad cottonwood, where he had selected a camping place, and proffered my request. He readily assented and I returned to the train.

At the end of an hour and a half, we were all in camp on the Colorado Chiquito and the captain imparted the welcome intelligence that we were not to stir out of this place for two days, but remain to rest and graze the animals. After we had been in camp about an hour, I was surprised to receive a visit from Lieutenant

Charles M. Hubbell of the New Mexican cavalry.[1] I had met this officer at Los Lunas the year before but had no idea that he was in this part of the country. In a few words he explained that about a month before he had established some *jacal* quarters, by order of the department commander, two miles below where we were encamped and had been there since with twenty-five men. A week before he had sent a man to Fort Wingate with letters and told him to be sure and buy two pounds of tea for his use. The man had made the round trip and had returned that very morning but without the tea, having lost it somewhere on the road. However, he was so positive that he had the tea when but a few miles from camp that the lieutenant had started back to look for it, accompanied by a soldier. When they arrived at the chimney, they were surprised to see the heads of a large number of men riding up through the bush from the river. Believing the Apaches had turned their position, the lieutenant wheeled about and fled for camp, never once looking behind him till he arrived at his quarters, and there learned that his pursuers were men of his own regiment. At the close of this tale, I produced the bag containing the loaf and tea.

The valley of the Colorado Chiquito is very broad and fertile and the banks of the river are bordered with cottonwoods and mesquites of a small growth. This river was named Rio de Lino by Coronado in 1540, on account of the abundance of wild flax in its valley. There was evidence of former cultivation and we traced the line of ancient *acequias* throughout the valley. The soil seemed admirably fitted for raising Indian corn or cotton. The stream is rapid, its waters fresh and clear and sufficient for the irrigation of a considerable portion of the lowlands that border it. Its sinuous course through the bottoms is marked by cottonwoods for many miles. The gravelly plains that bound the river bottoms are thinly covered with grama grass. Great quantities of broken pottery abound and there is no lack of evidence that this country had once been thickly populated. Some of the pottery seems to have been worn as by a flood and the patterns were generally unlike

1. Charles M. Hubbell was commissioned a first lieutenant in the 4th New Mexico on November 18, 1861, and his company subsequently became part of the 5th New Mexico. In the reorganization of the New Mexico troops, Hubbell received a commission as second lieutenant in the 1st New Mexico Cavalry effective August 1, 1862. He was promoted to first lieutenant following the death of Ludam A Bargie on June 16, 1863, and captain on March 25, 1865. Hubbell mustered out on September 11, 1866, and died on December 29, 1908. Charles M. Hubbell Military Service and Pension Records.

any we had before seen. Arrowheads of jasper were frequently found entire.

At the time I passed through the valley of the Colorado Chiquito, nothing was known of the lower part of its course or at what point it entered the Colorado, its mouth being hidden somewhere in the great unexplored *cañon* of that river, 300 miles of which had not been explored. Major John Wesley Powell, in his recent exploration of the Great Cañon, has mentioned the discovery of what he supposes to be the mouth of the Colorado Chiquito.[2] This valley was within the limits of the Navajo country and we frequently fell in with representatives of this nomadic people, wandering about to graze their herds or cultivate their favorite fields. Manuel acted as our interpreter and they always professed the best intentions and friendly feeling.

We arrived at Colorado Chiquito July 10th and the afternoon of the 11th Colonel Chaves and his men left to carry out the principal object of their march. This was to try and find a new road to Fort Whipple from the valley where we now were, which should avoid the rough route over the lava beds and scoria about the foot of San Francisco Mountain and through the fearful descents and ascents of Hell and Rattlesnake Cañons. If the colonel should find a practicable road, he was to pursue it to the end of the journey, making full details for the guidance of future military expedition, but, if he failed, he was to rejoin us before we should leave the river. We all wished him Godspeed as he mounted and rode away and we watched him until his column disappeared on the plain far to the south.

After two days' rest, on the 13th of July, at four thirty in the morning, we left our first camp on the river and marched down its course towards the west. It was so torturous in its flow that the road did not follow its banks, but took a straight line over the

2. John Wesley Powell repudiated his parents' plans for him to enter the ministry and instead chose to follow what he called the "outdoor sciences." After dropping out of three different colleges, Powell became a teacher and principal, spending school vacations floating the length of both the Ohio and Mississippi Rivers. Commissioned a lieutenant in the 20th Illinois, he raised men for a battery in the 2nd Illinois Light Artillery and became its captain. After losing an arm at the battle of Shiloh, Powell returned and served through the remainder of the war as a major. A series of explorations and surveys in the Rocky Mountains and on the Colorado River cemented his reputation as one of America's premier scientists and explorers. When he became too old to be in the field, Powell served as director of both the Bureau of Ethnography and the United States Geological Survey. Major John Wesley Powell died on September 23, 1902, at his family vacation home in Maine. Worster, *River Running West*, 60–61, 75–79, 81, 85–94, 135–51, 199–202, 360–65, 394–95, 569.

country, so that often the line of cottonwoods, which indicated the whereabouts of the river, were many miles to the southward. I find no mention in my notebook of any incident worth mentioning until we reached our third camp on the river, on the 15th, the day we crossed to the south side. Here a provoking incident occurred. Before leaving Los Lunas, I had purchased, for the use of our mess, a complete set of chinaware to be used on swell occasions after our arrival in Arizona; here we expected to exchange courtesies with the civil authorities of the Territorial Government. In bringing the china to camp, I ordered Private Hoey, who was acting as cook, on no account to open the box in which it was packed until we reached Fort Whipple, but to use our common dishes on the road. Hoey faithfully observed this injunction until we reached Jacob's Well, when he ventured to produce a butter dish to replace an old one, broken that day. Of course we all saw it and knew it was contrary to orders that it was on the table, but then it looked nice and how could we object. Next day another article appeared, the next still another and by the time we reached the camp after crossing the river, all our precious china was in use. At this juncture, Hoey's crony and factotum, Cleary, came up to the cook tent for a coal to light his pipe and to chat a while. After lighting, he leaned back against the tray and spilled everything crashing to the ground. I was looking on, but I philosophically turned away, while the compunctious Hoey bewailed his folly in getting out the china and his carelessness in not taking better precautions against breaking it. *Sic transit gloria murrhini*! (Thus passes the glory of cups!)

The weather was oppressively warm all the way down the river and, as we marched across the bends, a mirage was a daily sight. Lakes with wooded headlands, islands with rugged heights and towns in deep and picturesque bays tantalized us with visions which reminded us of scenes at our far distant homes, for we were all too well posted to be deceived into believing the rippling surface before us, moved by the summer breezes, was veritable water. Still, it was hard sometimes to believe ourselves deceived, so closely did the mirage resemble water and so near to us did it often appear. One day I was riding in Major Clark's ambulance, for a change and the sake of the shade, when the major remarked, "There is a brook over there on the left."

"It looks like it certainly," I replied, "but I think it is a mirage."

"It can't be. See! There is Anderson's dog trotting on the other side and you can see his reflection in the water."

"That's the very reason I believe it to be a mirage. If it were water, 'Nap' would be wading in it."

Anderson's dog was a cross between a New Foundland and a setter and retained all the fondness for water of the first-named strain. His name was Napoleon, which had been curtailed to the first syllable for convenience. When Major Clark called my attention to him, he was about 200 yards in advance, on the left side of the road, trotting along with open mouth and parched tongue hanging over his lower jaw, evidently very uncomfortable in the sweltering sun. At his side seemed to be a brook of about five feet in width, placid as a mirror, and in its surface was reflected the revered image of Nap's white and shaggy head. Notwithstanding my confident assertion of my belief in the mirage, I rode on half expecting the apparent brook would turn out to be a real brook. But as the distance diminished, its well-defined banks grew filmy and at last disappeared and left only the hot barren sand and the uncomfortable dog.

On the 16th, while in camp, I visited a salt marsh where a party of Navajos was gathering salt from the grass upon which it had crystallized.[3] They gathered it in baskets, which exhibited much correct taste in their construction and were woven so closely as to be watertight, as I found by experiment. Many of the baskets were large enough to hold three bushels. They were made of slips of light-colored reed, one-twentieth of an inch wide, ornamented with a black edge, a row of small figures a little below the edge and low down a circle of engrailed lines.

As we were marching along the river on the 16th, we saw a big dust cloud rising far to the south and concluded that Colonel Chaves was returning from his expedition to find the new road.

3. Collecting salt was referred to as "going to my mother's house," the mother referred to being Zuni Salt Lake in New Mexico, the traditional salt-gathering location forty-five miles south of Zuni Pueblo used by many native groups in the Southwest. Navajo salt gathering operations involved an experienced leader who led the party in ritual sweatbaths and the assembly of white clothing and food. Salt was scooped up by hand, dried and placed into baskets. When the animals would be fully loaded, everyone would take a purifying bath and no one would then be allowed back in the water. Upon leaving for home, salt gatherers were not allowed to look back at the lake or misfortune or death could befall the offender. Hill, *Navajo Salt Gathering*, 6–15.

After some time had passed, we saw a moving column rise on a roll in the plain and, taking a look through a field glass, recognized our old comrade and his dusky men rapidly closing the distance towards us. Before we reached the camp, Chaves joined us and reported the route he had inspected impracticable for wagons.

Early in the morning of the 15th, one of the rear guard killed a porcupine of a rare species, unknown until the survey for a railroad over this route in 1853-1854, and I advised him to keep it until we reached camp, for our ornithologist to add to his zoological collection. Accordingly, the man slung the hedgehog over his shoulder, packed him to camp and next day, soon after reveille, he took the animal to Doctor Coues. The doctor threw him into the top of our wagon and when we got to camp carefully took off the skin and stuffed it. It was a custom for most of us, after reaching camp and completing the camping arrangements, to throw down a blanket beneath some shady tree and sleep during the preparation of dinner. On this day, Colonel Chaves and I prepared our couches under two little cottonwoods which stood side by side, with our pillows resting against the trunks. It did not take us long to fall asleep and I slept soundly for about an hour, when I woke up and was immediately conscious of an odor of carrion near me. Glancing towards the colonel, I saw him sniffling and looking all round his locality, as if in search of the offensive object. I began to search also and we raised our blankets, looking carefully under them and all about our vicinity, but could find nothing.

"Where can that stench come from, lieutenant?" asked the colonel.

"That's more than I know," I replied. "At first I thought it must be near, but I think now it is blown here from some distance."

"But there is no breeze."

"True, but as we cannot find it and it evidently is not about us, I'm going to lie down again."

Suiting the action to the last words, I stretched out on my blanket and, as my head settled into my pillow at the foot of the tree, my eyes followed the trunk upward. About seven feet above the ground hung the flayed carcass of the porcupine.

"Colonel, look there!" I exclaimed, pointing to the beast.

"*Valgame Dios*!" ("Good God!") "Why is there no place to throw tainted meat but it must be hung over a gentleman's head?"

"Oh-h-h-h, doctor!" I shouted, knowing Coues was nearby.

"What do you want?" he replied, from his tent.

"Why didn't you throw that carrion away and not play such a wretched joke as to hang it over my head?"

"Carrion! Jokes! We are going to have that for dinner!"

"Great Jove!" and I was out of my blanket and sniffing the carcass in close proximity, to be sure that I could not be mistaken. "Doctor, it certainly is badly tainted."

"No it isn't," replied the doctor, approaching. "I skinned it and I ought to know. I've often heard that hedgehog is good eating and Captain Anderson and I are going to have this cooked."

"But it smells badly. That soldier killed it yesterday morning, carried it all day in a hot sun and today, since we started, it has been in the top of a wagon, sweltering in its skin and not disemboweled."

"I don't care if it has," replied Coues. "It is going to be cooked!"

Upon this, I gathered up my bedding and left for another resting place and in a moment after I saw the colonel doing likewise.

When dinner was called, I approached with some misgivings, but there was no porcupine on the table and, in answer to my question about it, I learned that Hoey had not yet finished cooking it and also, that as some of us objected to it, it would not be placed on the dinner table, but on a side table by the cook tent. Dinner went on and the hissing of the frying quill-pig could be heard distinctly from the cook fire. At last Hoey said it was done and Anderson left the table to taste it. I was seated in full view of the cook tent, while the doctor, being on the opposite side of the table, was back towards it. Anderson approached the dish on the side table which contained the experimental fricassee, speared a piece with his fork, raised it to his nose, daintily smelled it and threw it on the ground with a very visible expression of disgust. At this juncture, the doctor called out, "Say, Anderson, is it good?"

Catching the captain's eye, I signaled "Don't tell him."

"Some persons might like it," replied the captain, returning to our table, "but I don't."

The doctor now rose with an air of considerable importance, approached the side table with an elevated sense of proprietorship and, gathering a number of pieces of the porcupine flesh upon his fork, plunged them into his mouth without hesitation. But he had hardly shut his teeth together, when a sudden set took place in his features, while a pallor crept over his face and in a moment more he emptied his stomach of all he had previously eaten. This was a second lesson resulting from his obstinacy and no one was polite enough not to laugh at him.

Our march continued down the river without incident until the 18th of July, when we reached our last camping place on the river.

Chapter 31

Troubles with Coues and Indians

At five o'clock on the 19th of July, we left our last camp on the Little Colorado, and struck off to the southwest, in the direction of San Francisco Mountain, whose towering summit had for many days stood as a landmark before us. Our route for a long distance was over a flat tableland, from which wide tracts had been eroded to a moderate depth, leaving exposed lines of low bluffs and isolated fragments of the removed stratum. The whole surrounding country seemed one of utter desolation, destitute of tree, shrub and grass. The sun's rays were thrown back in a yellow glare and the road was hot and dusty. Fragments of black lava lay in heaps on every side, mingled with scoria, for this is a volcanic country and the huge mountain before us once belched fire, smoke and melted stones. The mountainsides are streaked with cooled rivers of lava and about its base are half a dozen gaping craters, in the summits of hills but a few hundred feet high.

As evening approached and the sun sank behind the mountain range, the air seemed to suddenly cool and at the same time the road became as suddenly worse. It ran here through a few square miles of fragments of lava, graded in size from a pebble to pieces two feet in diameter. The wagons went crashing and rattling over the obstacles at a fearful rate, rising on the larger stones two feet above the roadbed, to come down with a fearful jar upon the next one in front. I remained behind with the wagon master, anxious for the safety of the wagons and their contents, and expressed myself to him as generally disgusted with the character of the road, using somewhat forcible language. "You'd better keep your withering expletives a few days longer, lieutenant," said he, "this is a turnpike to what we are coming to." Not knowing what might be in store for me, I took his advice and a little while after, when two wagons broke completely down—one severing an axle, and another crashing a wheel—I said nothing in comment, but ordered the contents of one wagon distributed through the train. A wheel from the wagon which had a broken axle repaired the one with a broken wheel and all the remaining parts of the unloaded wagon were put on the train to repair further breakages. At this point then, I left but an axle and a wheel. When I arrived at Fort Whipple, I had two less wagons than I started with and those I left were distributed in broken fragments over hundreds of miles of road.

We reached camp at ten o'clock and found the company collected by the roadside, on a patch of greasewood bushes, a shrub resembling in size the currant bush, from which they had built big, flashing fires which could only be kept going by constantly collecting the greasewood and frequently piling it on the fire. By this intermittent blaze, we managed to cook our food and keep warm until bedtime. Once in bed, we became aware of the presence of scorpions, spiders, centipedes and rattlesnakes, which had emerged from their retreat to enjoy the evening air and many of us were too nervous to sleep. Doctor Cimex was for a while in his glory, collecting bugs, beetles and hideous and poisonous insects generally. Huge velvety tarantulas, long, sinuous and repulsive centipedes, brown and black-clawed scorpions were chloroformed and impaled in great numbers. The lights in our tent seemed to attract all the many-legged and many-winged things to us and the prospect of going to sleep was not pleasant, even to tired and sleepy men.[1]

1. A discharged soldier shared similar observations of Arizona wildlife: "A wild, parched desert; coyotes, Indians, rattlesnakes, wolves, scorpions, and tarantulas are the general products. Every portion seems at war with civilization. Not a blade of grass without a thorn, not a well of water without snakes and wolves; the very anathema pronounced against Adam seems to be verified in Arizona; the curse is fixed there." *California Farmer and Journal of Useful Sciences*, August 8, 1865.

At last, Chaves advised us to take our beds outside the tent. He said the snakes by this time had crawled away, as they always do from a camp, and that the insects would not molest us if we got away from the fires and light. Accordingly, we selected sleeping places on small patches of grass which we succeeded in finding among the greasewood bushes and were soon settled for sleep.

It was a very cold night to follow such a sultry day so I pulled up my blankets close about my chin and settled down into the mattress for a comfortable snooze. Just as I was losing consciousness, I was roused by a sudden yell near me and springing up I saw Doctor Cimex in the dim light reflected by the guard tent fire, dancing a frantic and furious jig, tearing at his clothing with both hands, and stripping off article after article in the greatest haste, flinging them about him in reckless disorder and all the time uttering the wildest expletives of mingled profanity, pain and distress. I shouted to the sergeant of the guard to bring a lantern and hastened to the now-naked doctor. When the lantern came, we found the doctor's bed literally alive with red ants. He had selected a fine knoll for a bolster, placed his pillow against it and turned in. This knoll turned out to be an anthill and the brave inhabitants had resented the invasion by issuing in force and ejecting the intruder. The doctor moved his bed and the ants immediately left.

Going back to my own bed, I took the lantern and looked into it. A centipede six inches long glided under a fold of the blanket and disappeared. Ugh-h-h! Could I get into that bed again? No, sir! I determined to sit up and walked down into the wagoners' camp among the supply wagons. There I found the wagon master, with half a dozen teamsters, sitting around a fire built of pine knots, which they had brought in the wagons from some previous camp, playing cards. They invited me to join, but I declined and sat looking on. The wagon master told me if I would like a snooze out of the way of the insects, I could get it by crawling up into the top of the wagon, nearest on the right, where I would find a bed and blankets at my service. I accepted the invitation, found the bed and slept "like a brick" until reveille at three o'clock.

This had been a dry camp and very unpleasant. In the morning we found some of our mules had strayed and we were obliged to wait until they were found. They had started back to the river for water and were not overtaken until they got there. At this camp

I did a favor to the father of the young women whom I mentioned earlier. During the delay of hunting for the mules, I visited the camp of the emigrants and stopped by the wagon in which the mother and daughters rode, to talk with them. During my stay, my attention was called to something the old man was doing to the feet of his oxen. He seemed to be making a kind of boot out of rawhide and tying them on, over the hoofs of the oxen. It was explained to me that the oxen had worn their hoofs through to the quick on the flinty roads and could not draw much longer unless something was done for them. I at once told the man to turn his oxen into the Government herd of loose cattle and take up an equal number of fresh ones to draw his wagons. He did this and we went on.

The stray mules had been led away by Barr's pony. The herd had been allowed to graze, our corn having long since been fed out. It was, in fact, absolutely necessary that the animals should be turned out nights that they might be fit for the road the next day. Some of the most lively mules had been hobbled and all the horses had been "staked out," but during the night something had frightened the pony—probably a snake—and he had snapped the lariat and taken the road to the river, accompanied by about fifty of the mules. The clatter of the galloping hoofs was heard by me from the start and I descended from my bed in the wagon to find the wagon master and three or four assistants already saddling for pursuit. The night was dark and windy and the animals could only be followed by sound. They were brought back about ten o'clock A. M.

While the mules were being attached to the train, a party of Navajos appeared on the outskirts of the camp, well-mounted and with apparent warlike intentions. They were painted in their fiercest style and decorated with many ornaments acquired in the chase of the grizzly, the puma and other wild and dangerous beasts and their headdresses and shields were resplendent in colored feathers. They had come up from a southerly direction, so knew nothing of our fugitive mules or they would doubtless have tried to secure them. We threw our cavalry out in the direction of the party and showed a white flag in token of our desire to speak with them. This was at first received with considerable derision, as was shown by contemptuous gestures and a grand display of arms in a threatening manner, accompanied by ear-splitting whoops and yells. The Indians numbered about 200. Captain Anderson, accompanied by the Mexican boy Manuel, as interpreter, rode out in front of the cavalry about a hundred yards and stopped. Presently the chief of the savages advanced to meet the captain, but paused when a distance of twenty-five paces intervened. He asked, "What do you want?"

"I want to know whether you are our friends or enemies," said the captain.

"We are friends and we want to come in and talk with our white brother."

"I cannot let you come in with your whole band, but you may bring twelve of your chief men to this spot and I will meet you with my chief men."

Upon this, the chief departed towards his band and presently returned with twelve others, while, at a call from Anderson, the seven officers, the wagon master and an assistant, with two of the emigrants, moved out to meet them. The conversation which followed was chiefly in answer to questions put by the Indians in regard to the reservation at Fort Sumner, what was being done there by their brethren who had already surrendered and what would be done with the present party should they surrender. They said they were a band which had hitherto maintained its independence, but they had been so closely hunted recently they were thinking of giving up. When they first saw us, they thought us a body of troops in search of them. Anderson assured them that he was moving through the country for a very different purpose; at the same time he advised them, at some length, against the folly of holding out longer; that there could be but one result and that was final defeat and great loss of life, if they persisted; and protection and subsistence if they would surrender. The chief promised to consider the advice of his white brother and then proceeded to caution us against the Apaches, who, he assured us, were on the warpath in great numbers and would dispute our march through their country.

A good shaking of hands now took place, some tobacco was distributed, and the interview broke up, the Indians moving off to the northeast and we resuming our march to the southwest. This camp had been fearfully disagreeable, with its bogs and snakes, its ants, its stampede and other troubles and we were glad to get once more on our way.

For some time past I had been greatly concerned for the safety of the train. We were in the midst of hostile Indians and liable any moment to an attack. Our command always marched off in the morning after breakfast and we did not often see it again until night. My guard was but a handful of men, struggling behind a train which often extended for two miles along the road and one end of it, in the rough country, was often invisible from the other. Doctor Coues's double-barreled shotgun was always startling us in all sorts of places and at all hours of the day. In a country where the report of firearms usually signaled danger or mischief, this constant banging of the ornithological fusee kept the wagon master and myself tearing along the line of wagons from one end to the other, many times a day. On the morning of the interview with the Navajos, I had asked Captain Anderson to order Coues to stop firing on the march, until we should get out of the present dangerous country. I told him there would be plenty of opportunities for the doctor to shoot birds when we were all together in camp or after we got over the San Francisco foothills. I drew a vivid picture of our embarrassment in the rear, owing to the firing, and also asked for an increase of the guard. All these requests were granted and positive orders were given to both the military and emigrants on no account to fire, except in case of danger from Indians, and that whenever a report should be heard, it was to be considered a signal for the train to halt and everybody to close up on its centre.

I was pleased with the success of my request and rode along the train with more cheerfulness than I had felt for many days. The road, after leaving the dry camp, crossed a valley and broke into a thin forest of stunted cedars and *piñons*, which were gradually succeeded by pines along the mountain slope on our right. Within the next few miles we rose in regular steps upon wave after wave of volcanic rock and then entered a system of conical peaks, beautifully regular. One among these had a broken crest and a stream of lava which had once poured from it had been arrested and cooled in its serpentine course. Its summit was about 500 feet above the plain and a well-beaten Indian trail wound up its side, but we had not the time to examine it or learn for what purpose it was made. The pines increased in size and numbers as we went on, tall, straight and sound, from one to two feet in diameter, and from sixty to one hundred feet high. It is a species of yellow pine, called by our botanist *Pinus brachyptera*.[2]

As our train was slowly and laboriously toiling up the waves of lava just mentioned, with the forest on the right and the extinct volcanoes on the left, I was startled by two reports of firearms, which sounded strangely like the doctor's shotgun. But remembering the strict orders of Anderson about firing, I concluded that it must mean danger, immediately halted the train and rode forward to see what was the trouble. About 500 paces in front of the train, I came upon Anderson and Coues, dismounted in the road, going into ecstasies over a pair of birds which the latter had just shot. While I was looking on in amazement at the captain's conduct in thus ignoring his own order, the cavalry, headed by Chaves, came charging back from the front, with carbines unslung. Presently the infantry appeared at a double-quick from the same direction and for five minutes there were constant arrivals from the rear, with a great cracking of whips and shouting among teamsters as they hurried to park the wagons. There was no need of explanation, we could all see it. Captain Anderson simply remarked, "They were such beautiful specimens I could not help permitting the doctor to shoot them," and went forward with the command.

I returned to my train, started it and rode along at the head of it for an hour, when Wagon Master W. H. Moore came up.[3] "Don't you think we had better get even with the captain?" he asked.

"For what?" I asked.

"For the scare he gave us."

"How can we get even?"

"Well, the captain said when he gave his order this morning that you should have authority to give the wagon men and emigrants permission to fire if you thought best. Now, my men have not fired

2. Southwestern Ponderosa Pine.

3. William H. Moore arrived in New Mexico in 1848 and soon opened a trading post at Tecolote on the Santa Fe Trail. He traded with the Indians and Mexicans while supplying U. S. posts, especially Fort Union. In the 1850s he partnered with Burton Reese but by the Civil War he was in business with William C. Mitchell, both of whom had received appointments as sutlers. Moore made a fortune from his sutler building, said to be "built like a fort," at Fort Union. Two years after the war Moore's assets totaled nearly $200,000 but that fortune gradually declined due to political interference and a changing economic situation on the frontier. He died at Watrous, New Mexico, on May 6, 1890. Miller, "Perils of a Post Sutler," 9–13, 17.

their revolvers since they left Fort Wingate and I think they should be discharged and reloaded."

"All right, I give the permission," I replied. "But first send a man ahead to let Barr into the secret. I don't want those poor foot soldiers running their legs off to play a joke on Anderson. The whole thing verges on the insubordinate, but I'll take the risk."

Everything was arranged in course of half an hour and the wagon master had assembled five of his assistants on a height commanding the country for a long distance ahead. At the word, they began firing as fast as they could cock and pull trigger. In a few moments all the command in advance, except the infantry, came tearing back like mad, the captain in advance, pale with excitement. Of course he saw nothing was the matter as soon as he saw me and when he learned that I had given permission to the wagon men to fire, he opened upon me a battery of words which sometimes hit hard. However, I could take jaw, if I only escaped worse usage and, besides, I felt confident there would be no more firing, which was indeed the fact, and when the captain cooled down he was kind enough to say my "fusillade was a rough joke, but he guessed he deserved it."

The day's march ended at Cosnino Caves, at the eastern foot of San Francisco Mountain.[4] This mountain is a huge volcanic pile with several conical peaks near the centre, elevated to the height of at least a mile above its base. From the east, its axis appears to extend from northeast to southwest about ten miles, where it is terminated by a gigantic mass of granite. Its steep slopes are streaked with lava and its ridges are covered with dense forests of pine and spruce. Near our camp, a dry bed of what must have been a considerable stream in the rainy season broke through a ridge of granite some fifty feet high, making a passage of twenty feet in width, with perpendicular walls a couple of hundred feet long. This crevice was very deep and contained many thousand gallons of rainwater, sweet to the taste, but full of insects which traversed its crystal depths in jerky zig-zags. I strained my water through a napkin before drinking it, but Colonel Chaves and Doctor Coues drank theirs al fresco. The latter said there was more nourishment

4. The Cosnino Caves, apparently named by Lieutenant Amiel Whipple in 1853, were named for a generic term applied to several groups of Yuman Indians who lived in the area, especially the Walapai, Havasupai, and Yavapai. McGuire, "Walapai," 36.

in the unstrained fluid, while a drop of whiskey killed all insect life and added to the nourishing properties.

Just before dinner, Barr and I went in search of the Cosnino Caves. We found them to be oven-shaped excavations beneath the lava crust of the mountain, generally one cave of ten feet in diameter, from which radiated several smaller ones. The cavities were regular and covered with a vitreous substance, hard brownish-black, like iron. They had been artificially plastered and there were many fragments of pottery scattered about. The caves had evidently not been inhabited for a long period, except perhaps by an occasional visitor. The entrances to several had been choked by heaps of disintegrated rock. They are called Cosnino Caves after the tribe of Indians which roams over this region of the country.

While climbing from cave to cave, I had picked up a small specimen of detached lava, about three inches in width and one in thickness. It had first attracted my attention from its having a hole an eighth of an inch in diameter through its centre and because it was creased as a seamstress's wax becomes by use in waxing thread. About the same time, Barr found a flower, which we both recognized as a new discovery. He broke off the stalk near the ground and, taking my bit of lava, thrust the stem into the hole. When we returned to camp, the flower was taken in as a contribution to Major Clark's collection and was not removed from the stone, but placed on the dinner table beside the major's plate. When we were called to dinner, the major approached his plate and, seeing the flower, picked up the piece of lava containing it caressingly, after the manner of naturalists and examining it closely broke into raptures over it. I regret that my knowledge of botanical terms will not admit of my going into the details of what the major said of this plant. To his eyes, it was a flower actually growing out of a porous stone and he gave us an excellent lecture about it and its family, holding the lava in his left hand and touching the leaves and petals lightly with the tips of the fingers of his right. While he was still going on and all were listening with deep interest, Barr reached out for the flower as if desiring to examine it and it was handed to him. Taking the stone out of the major's hand, he seized the stalk of the flower and pulled it out of the hole. This drew a good laugh upon our botanist and forced him into a new classification of the plant, not much different from the first, I am happy to say in his

Major Cyrus C. Clark. Courtesy of Massachusetts MOLLUS Civil War Photographs, United States Army Heritage and Education Center.

defence, for, upon going to the caves after dinner, several more of the same flower were found and they were really growing out of the fine crevices in the lava.

Our next march took us to a dry camp, which we reached at five o'clock P. M., after a two hours' march. At half past four the following morning, July 22nd, we left for San Francisco Spring, but found the spring dry and were obliged to push on to Volunteer Spring, where we arrived at six in the evening, after a long and tiresome day's drag. The whole distance was thirty-two miles over a hilly country and through forests of pine. Volunteer Spring was in a thick pine wood and was named after a column of California Volunteers who had been obliged to camp here nearly a month on account of the loss of their draught animals by the Apaches. They were traveling in the same direction we were and had camped for the night in the timber, herding their mules into an open space a little south of the encampment. Not having met with any Indians on the march, the officers did not realize any danger and, in consequence, were careless in the disposition of the guards and in the night the Indians took nearly every hoof. The train was a large one, consisting of over a hundred wagons, loaded with stores for Fort Whipple, and there was also a large herd of beef cattle.

After a fruitless attempt to recapture their herd of mules, the Californians found they could go no farther until animals procured from Fort Whipple should arrive to draw their wagons, so they went regularly into camp and sent an express to the fort for assistance. Fort Whipple was but a small post and its whole number of mules but barely sufficient to draw twenty wagons and the distance required five days to go each way, so it took a long time to get the Volunteers out of their predicament.

When we arrived at Volunteer Spring, we found plenty of evidences that a large command had been encamped there for some time. Arrangements for butchering and cooking and an oven for baking were still in good condition. I went to the opening, where we should be obliged to herd our beasts, to see what measures were best for their security. It was about thirty acres in extent and covered with luxurious grass. On all sides it was surrounded by forests.

We hobbled as many mules as we possibly could and staked out all the saddle animals. We posted a chain of sentinels entirely round the ground, putting three men on a post. The sentinels were not to walk, but two men to sleep while the third watched. This is the best method in an Indian country, where the moving soldier would only attract the enemy and an Indian arrow could give him a silent death. None of us undressed when we went to bed. I placed my carbine and revolver near my pillow and my boots where I could jump into them without delay.

It was, perhaps, about midnight when the clatter of 2,000 hoofs, making the ground tremble like an earthquake, aroused me and I got into my boots and, giving Anderson a good shaking, rushed out in the direction of the herd. As I was running through the timber but half awake, the cracking of a couple of muskets struck my ear and presently a third and a moment after a fourth. Then all was still as death, not even a mule's hoof striking the ground for a few moments. Pushing on, I heard voices and going towards them came upon my wagon master and assistants and, in their company, made the rounds of sentinels and found they had killed three Indians. It seems the redskins had planned a stampede and, creeping into the opening to carry it out, had come upon our silent sentinels and got their exit. The mules had smelt them and got uneasy, simply—there had been no stampede.

As I turned back to camp, I met Anderson and the other officers and reported. Confident that there would be no further trouble, we went to bed and slept soundly until morning. When we left camp next day, we left the dead Indians as they fell, knowing their comrades would come back and bury them as soon as we were out of sight.

Chapter 32

Arrival at Fort Whipple

We left Volunteer Spring at 4:30 A. M., on the morning of July 23rd, the road still running through the pine forest, over the hills and across the ravines radiating from the base of San Francisco Mountain, making the task of dragging the wagons over the rough country very difficult. Our bacon wagons had given us a great deal of trouble ever since we left the river. The warm weather had tried out much of the lard and it had penetrated every portion of the running gear, until there was no longer any adhesion of the parts and the iron straps and braces had to meet all the strains. These were constantly snapping and every device possible to the ingenuity of the wagon master was used to repair damages. Chains, ropes and straps were used without stint to bind the dislocated parts and poles were cut from the roadside trees to strengthen them. The articles which broke beyond repair were replaced by the parts which we had retained of the first broken wagon and one other.

In order to give me a quick communication with the command, in case of danger from the Indians or other contingency, a couple of cavalrymen had been detailed daily, ever since we entered the wooded country, to accompany me and act as messengers.

About eleven o'clock in the forenoon, as we were riding down a long slope in the road, a deep ravine opened on our left and we could see for a couple of miles a straight vista between the trees. A huge grizzly bear appeared from the timber of the ravine, crossing from the southern to the northern side, and he paused for a moment and looked sullenly at us. One of the Mexican soldiers asked me to allow him a shot and, as I felt safer with so many soldiers about me than I did when I met the grizzly mentioned in my Los Valles Grandes experience, I gave my consent. The Mexican stopped his horse, drew his rifled carbine to his shoulder, fired from the saddle and the bear fell heavily to the ground. I rode down the ravine to examine the game and found he had been shot through the heart. We put the carcass into a wagon, to be skinned and dressed when we should reach camp, and rode on. We had gone but a few miles farther when the same man called my attention to a second bear, up a hillside, standing on his hind legs, plucking the berries from a juniper bush with his forepaws and cramming them into his mouth. I again gave permission to fire and this bear, which proved to be a cinnamon, also fell dead at the first shot. I ought to have mentioned that when I gave the first permission, I sent a message forward to Captain Anderson, telling him we intended to fire, so that he would not return to the train thinking us attacked.

When we arrived in camp at Cañon Springs, the two bears were dressed and the meat distributed among the soldiers, a generous piece of both grizzly and cinnamon being sent to us, to which we did ample justice and found the flesh tender and juicy. The skins were stitched to the canvas cover of the wagon, one on each side, and remained there until we arrived at Fort Whipple, when both were tanned and became the property of Major Clark and Captain Anderson, the former getting the grizzly and the latter the cinnamon.

Next day we journeyed nine and a half miles to Bear Springs, over very much the same kind of country we had been going through for the last three days. On this march the infantry company killed a grizzly. The bear was seen quietly ascending a hill near the roadside and half the company rushed after the grim monster. He seemed unconscious of pursuit until the men were close upon him. Then he began to run, but the steep hill retarded his progress and a volley of balls made his fur fly in all directions from different parts of his hide. Twice he turned as if to show fight, showing all of his teeth and giving utterance to a threatening growl, but the crowd of eager pursuers was so large and the firing so hot, that he continued his flight to the top of the hill, where he fell dead, riddled with bullets. Upon examination, it was found that he had been hit in twenty-five places and that but one bullet had reached a vital spot. It was very evident that our Regulars had no skilled marksmen among them. This bear was also eaten, but the flesh proved strong in flavor when roasted or broiled, but made excellent soup. The skin was treated like the others and became the property of Barr. During this march the privilege to fire was again restored to Doctor Coues and others, as it was thought we were fairly out of the dangerous country.

From Bear Springs to Turkey Spring was our next march and the distance was but four miles and a half. A faint idea of some of the difficulties of this march may be obtained when I say that we left Bear Springs at four o'clock in the morning and arrived at Turkey Spring camp at half-past seven in the evening. The road was heaped with boulders of granite and I found the wagon master's assertion, on a former piece of rough road, that "it was a turnpike to what we were coming to" was literally correct. Wagons had in several instances to be unloaded and the contents carried by hand over the rocks. The bacon wagons gave out continually and we were obliged to get out a small traveling forge and repair the chains and bolts that were constantly breaking.

While all this hard work was being done by train men and soldiers, Coues and Clark were out shooting and they succeeded in bringing in a deer and a dozen turkeys. These were cooked and they disappeared before our hungry men, at a late supper, like the morning mist before the summer sun.

After leaving Turkey Spring, the road was very bad for a short distance and then it gradually grew better, all the time descending from the San Francisco slopes into a broad valley. As soon as I saw there was likely to be no further trouble with the train, I started off for the front to overtake the command. I had proceeded but a few miles when it began to rain and soon the water was coming down in torrents. I drew my cape closely about my neck and galloped on down the muddy road, in which the water flowed as in a brook. Soon the rain changed to hail and, the wind being in my face, I held my arm across my forehead to shield my face from the cutting ice. The thunder crashed terrifically overhead and the sky seemed filled with lightning, flash and crash coming simultaneously so that I was by no means at ease. At last I reached the plain and was fast leaving the timber, when a bolt of lightning struck on a pine but twenty feet on my right, cleaving it from top to bottom and causing my horse to bound several feet to one side. Busied with screening my face from the hail, I was not looking out for jumps, so got unseated and fell in a heap in the mud and water of the road. Blinded by the flash, stunned by the report and jarred by the fall, some minutes elapsed before I was able to get up and take in the situation. The road all about me was filled with the shattered branches of the pine and I was wet to the skin. My horse was grazing but a few rods away and I rose painfully and, making my way to him, succeeded in mounting and resuming my journey. In another hour I reached camp and my tent and got into dry clothing.

That evening when I went to dinner I found all the officers at the table before me. As I took my seat, Captain Anderson, who sat at the head of the table, said, "Curtis, take a piece of duck?"

I was just on the point of extending my plate, when I paused to answer a question of Colonel Chaves, on my left, and in the interim Barr remarked, "This is the best duck I ever ate."

"Yes," assented Coues, "I never shot a finer duck than this."

This repetition of the word *duck* awakened a slight suspicion in my mind that there was something wrong or, at least, mysterious about the fowl, so I said, with no shade of suspicion in voice or countenance, "I will take some of the beef," whereupon there was a general chorus in praise of the *duck*, which corroborated me in my suspicions and I insisted on taking beef. Looking at the plates around the table, I saw they all contained pieces of the so-called duck, but no one was eating it. "Now," said I, "as you have failed in the joke, tell me what this fricassee is made of."

"Joke!" exclaimed Coues. "That's a duck I shot today."

"Then why don't you eat it? I never knew this mess to refuse duck before and none of you have touched this."

"I'll tell you," said the honest Anderson. "The doctor wanted to get even with you for that Jacob's Well affair, so he had a large hawk cooked for your benefit. How came you to suspect?"

"That is my secret. If I should tell, you would beat me next time. It smells nice and I am going to taste it." I took a piece, smelled it, tasted it and pronounced it good. The rest did the same and the result was we picked the bones of that hawk clean. So much for the doctor's "getting even."

Our camp was on the brink of a *cañon* known by the Mexicans as Cañon Diablo and by the Americans as Hell Cañon, a distinction without a difference. This *cañon* extended for many miles through the plain, about 200 feet deep and 400 wide, with perpendicular sides except near our camp. Here there was a break in the wall, giving a slope to the bottom of about thirty-five degrees on both sides. Early the next morning we made our preparations for crossing. Both hind wheels of each wagon were locked and a pair of "wheel mules" was attached by a chain to the hind axle to hold back. In this manner all the wagons of our train were taken to the bottom of the *cañon*. To draw them up the opposite side twelve mules were required and on some of the wagons twenty. The emigrants used various methods of descent, one wagon being held back by two mounted horsemen with ropes attached to the axle and the other ends to the pommels of the saddles. Their horses had been trained to lasso cattle and understood bracing their feet and standing firm. They went down the slope, sliding on their braced-out feet, but when within a third of the distance to the bottom the girth of one saddle broke and the rider went swiftly over the horse's neck, to tumble heels over head down the hill while the horse flew rapidly back to the plains above. The whole day was passed in crossing and we camped the following night but 400 yards from the camp of the previous night.

From Hell Cañon we marched without adventure worth mentioning to Fort Whipple in two days. The road was generally level and the country grassy. We found the fort a fort in name only, there being neither cabin nor corral, only a collection of tents in which were quartered two companies of California Volunteers. These companies were awaiting our coming to be mustered out of the service and return to their homes. Soon after our arrival on July 29th, Major Clark paid off all the troops and returned to New Mexico in company with Colonel Chaves. The rest of us remained at Fort Whipple without breaking our mess for almost a year.

In the winter of 1863 the governor, secretary, judges and other officials of the newly organized Territory of Arizona, together with a considerable retinue of retainers, hangers-on and adventurers arrived in New Mexico, on their way to Arizona to establish the Territorial Government. At that time the only settlements in the new territory were along its southern border and the most considerable town was Tucson. All north of the overland route, between Mesilla, through Tucson, down the Gila to California, was almost entirely unexplored and unknown to the white man, being inhabited only by the Apache and Navajo Indians. Enough, however, was known of the country to cause the belief to be generally held that it abounded in gold and silver mines and a few marvelous tales were told of their great richness, finding plenty of believers, who only waited for military occupancy to enter and develop the treasure-bearing region.

First Arizona Territory Officials. Sitting (left to right): Judge Joseph P. Allyn, Governor John N. Goodwin, Secretary Richard C. McCormick; Standing (left to right): Governor's Secretary Henry W. Fleury, U.S. Marshal Milton B. Duffield, District Attorney Almon Gage. Courtesy of Sharlot Hall Museum Library & Archives / SHM Photographs / PO-1321P.

The governor and party therefore paused in Santa Fé for some time to consult as to the manner and means of establishing the Territorial Government and where it was best to locate the capital. The department commander had received orders from Washington to afford all the aid in his power to the Arizona officials, to give them a large military escort and establish a military post wherever the capital should be located.

The choice seemed to be between two plans. The first was to go to the already established town of Tucson, where there were good buildings and a large population and where speculators, looking upon that place as sure to be fixed upon, had already "gobbled up" all the best sites for houses and ranches in the town and vicinity. The second was to enter the territory from the north and establish a new town in a new region, upon land to which no one had a claim. The last plan had the advantage of giving the Territorial officials a chance to do the "gobbling" and they were not slow to adopt it. In a new country they would be the first arrivals and could locate everything to their own advantage, besides opening up prospects in an entirely new mining region.

Accordingly, with a powerful escort and a large train, bearing all the military supplies and material for establishing a Government fort and the civil appliances necessary to establish the Territorial Government, including a printing press, types, compositors and editor, the new governor and party took up their line of march. They traveled over the road which I have already described (known as the Lieutenant Whipple route of 1853) to Antelope Springs, on the southern slope of the San Francisco Mountains, where it turns southwest (over the Lieutenant John G. Parke route of 1851) to near the southern foot of Bill Williams Mountain.[1] At this point,

1. Amiel W. Whipple graduated from West Point in 1841 and began a distinguished career in the Corps of Topographical Engineers. Commissioned second lieutenant on July 1, 1841, first lieutenant on April 24, 1851, and captain on July 1, 1855, Whipple was promoted to major on September 9, 1861. His topographical duties included work on the boundaries with Canada and Mexico, as well as the survey of a potential railroad route to California through Arizona Territory. Commissioned brigadier general on April 14, 1862, Whipple received brevets for service at Second Bull Run, Fredericksburg, and Chancellorsville. Mortally wounded at the latter battle on May 4, 1863, he died at Washington, D. C. on May 7, 1863, and was elevated to major general on the day of his death. Fort Whipple in Arizona Territory was named for him. John G. Parke graduated from West Point second in the class of 1849 and was assigned to the Corps of Topographical Engineers. Promoted to second lieutenant on April 18, 1854, and first lieutenant on July 1, 1856, he was commissioned captain on September 9, 1861. Promoted to brigadier general on November 23, 1861, and to major general on July 18, 1862, Parke spent several years serving under General Ambrose Burnside, often as his chief of staff. Following Burnside's removal in 1864, Parke became commander of the Ninth Corps.

known as Lockwood Spring, the party turned nearly due south and marched over a road of their own discovery and making through Turkey, Rattlesnake and Hell Cañons, to a point on the Rio Verde where they proceeded to lay out a town.

The ceremonies attending the founding were unlike those of the Spanish race, who had founded all the other towns in New Mexico and Arizona, so there was no erection of crosses, pouring of holy water and saying of masses by a surpliced priest, while all reverently bowed the knee. But champagne popped, punches were brewed and drank and, amid much hilarity and speech-making, the corner-stone of the governor's house was laid. But before the walls were fairly ready for a roof, the hunting and prospecting parties reported upon several better locations and, after a more careful and considerate investigation, it was consequently determined to re-locate the capital upon its present site. This is twenty-five miles south of the first settlement, in a valley which is of the nature of a cul de sac, for the traveler must retrace his steps five miles down the valley if he desires to pursue his journey after visiting the town if he travels on wheels, but pack animals can get through the mountains.

The second ceremony of locating the capital was quiet and orderly, the liquid stimulants which had been laid in at Santa Fé for that purpose, having been exhausted in the abortive settlement on the Rio Verde. The new location was on a tributary of the last named stream, called Granite Creek, hardly more than a brook for a great part of the year, often sinking entirely out of sight beneath the sandy places and reappearing where the bed was of ledge or clay.

The town was called Prescott, after the author of *The Conquest of Mexico*.[2] The valley in which it is situated is beautiful,

---

He received four brevets for his war service and remained in the army, reaching the postwar rank of colonel and superintending West Point until his retirement on July 2, 1889. General Parke died in Washington, D. C. on December 16, 1900. Heitman, *Historical Register* 1: 768, 1025; Eicher, *Civil War High Commands*, 416, 564.

2. William Hickling Prescott, prominent American historian, graduated from Harvard in 1814 but an accident during a food fight in his junior year left him blind in one eye. Periodic inflammation in his other eye left him at times completely blind. While convalescing in Europe, Prescott purchased a noctograph, an implement that allowed him to write legibly. He began work on *History of the Conquest of Mexico* in 1839 and the three-volume work was published in 1843. Prescott followed that success with his two-volume *History of the Conquest of Peru* in 1847. These and other works melded history and literature to make his subjects more accessible to the reading public. Prescott's research in archival material and full documentation of sources set a new standard in historiography, while his topics challenged his countrymen to look outside the nation's boundaries. Prescott was still involved with publishing his latest book when he died at Boston on January 28, 1859. Gardiner, *William Hickling Prescott*, ix, 21, 24–25, 37–38, 249, 269, 272.

the surrounding mountains being well wooded with pine and spruce. Evidences of a former Aztec town appear all through the vicinity, long lines of stone foundation showing themselves above the ground in several places.[3] The town has many advantages, owing to its central position in the territory and in the midst of a fine mining region.

To dispose of Prescott finally, I will say that it grew very rapidly to be a considerable town and the first Legislature was held there between September 26 and November 10, 1864. Almost the first bill introduced was one removing the capital to Tucson and, as a majority of the representatives were from the southern part of the territory, after a hard fight they carried the measure. Governor John N. Goodwin vetoed it and the capital remained through 1866.[4] The bill was again introduced and a new governor, Richard C. McCormick, approved it and the capital moved to Tucson where it remained for ten years.[5] However, the rapid settlement of Prescott and the adjacent farming and mining country soon brought the balance of power back again and the capital returned to stay.[6]

3. What is now known as the Aztec empire never extended as far as Prescott, yet early settlers were convinced that the old remains had been left by those people. No less a personage than Governor A. P. K. Safford expressed the jumbled anthropological wisdom of the 1860s: "The old Aztec ruins that you find all over the country, prove that this country was once occupied by them, the extensive ruins of large houses, of forts, and ditches for irrigation, prove that they were an intelligent and industrious people, but they have all passed away before the ravages of the Apaches, and no record nor a living soul is left to tell the story of their suffering, nothing save those silent, broken walls remain to tell us that such a people ever lived." *Weekly Journal Miner*, December 4, 1869.

4. After graduating from Dartmouth College in 1844, John N. Goodwin began to practice law in his hometown of Berwick, Maine. Elected to Congress in 1860, he completed his term and was appointed chief justice of the Arizona Territory, but shortly thereafter was appointed governor after the first appointee died prior to taking office. While serving as governor, Goodwin simultaneously served as the territorial delegate to Congress. Following his term, Governor Goodwin moved permanently to New York City where he again practiced law. He visited Paraiso Springs in Monterey County, California, for health reasons and died there on April 29, 1887. Keen, "Arizona Governors," 7–8.

5. Richard C. McCormick worked as a correspondent for the *New York Evening Post*, covering both the Crimean War and the first months of the Civil War. When President Lincoln established the Department of Agriculture in 1862, McCormick was appointed the chief clerk. Appointed secretary of the Arizona Territory in 1863, he often acted as governor during John Goodwin's term and was elected the territory's second governor in 1866. His newspaper, *The Miner*, published in Prescott upon his arrival, was the first published in Arizona. After serving three terms as Congressional delegate, McCormick served as assistant secretary of the U. S. Treasury in 1877 and Commissioner of the Paris Exposition of 1878. Elected to Congress in 1894, McCormick spent the last years of his life supervising his many mining ventures and died on June 2, 1901, at Jamaica, Long Island. Keen, "Arizona's Governors," 8; *New York Times*, June 3, 1901.

6. Curtis was mistaken about the peripatetic state capital. Although first officially established at Prescott in 1864, the capital moved to Tucson in 1867, came back to Prescott in 1877 and finally found a permanent home at Phoenix in 1889.

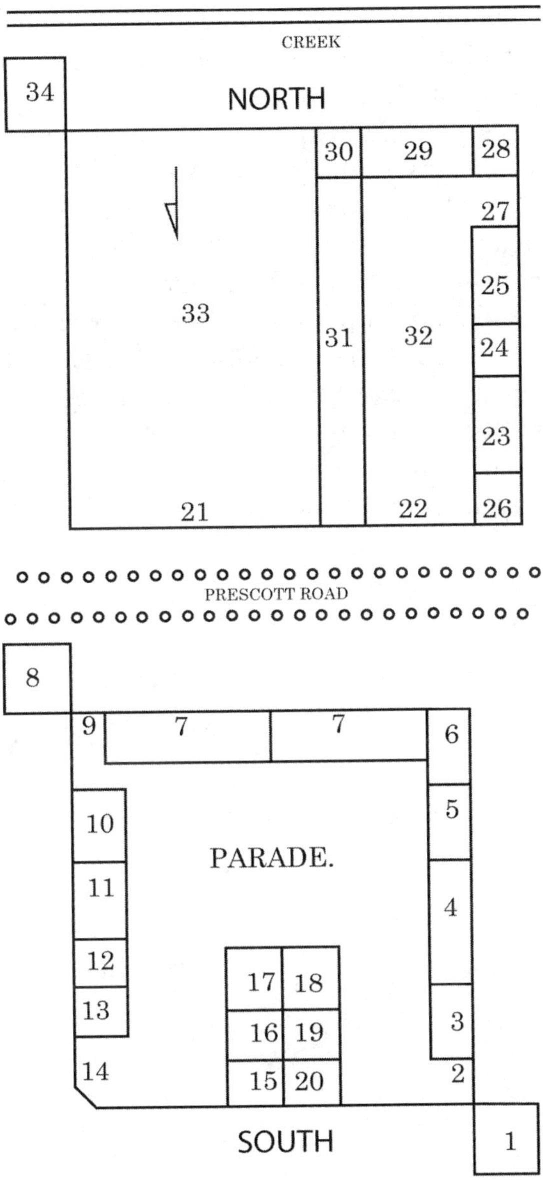

EXPLANATION.

1. Block-house used as ordnance store-room.
2. Secret gate.
3. Quarter-master and Commissary office.
4, 5, 6. Quarter-master and Commissary store-rooms.
7. Company quarters.
8. Block-house used as Company property room.
9. Passage from interior to store-room.
10. First Sergeants' room.
11. Company property room.
12. Sergeant Major and clerk's room.
13. Adjutant's office.
14. Great gates.
15, 16, 17, 18, 19, 20. Officers' quarters.
21, 22. Gates.
23. Quarter-master men's quarters.
24. Quarter-master men's kitchen.
25. Grain room.
26. Corral master's room.
27. Secret gate.
28, 29. Harness maker and carpenter's shops.
30. Store-room.
31. Stables.
32. Open yard.
33. Cattle yard.
34. Block-house used as blacksmith's shop.

Plan of Fort Whipple based on original by Lieutenant Curtis.

Two miles north of the town site and down the creek a location for the fort was chosen and the name of Whipple selected for it, in honor of Amiel W. Whipple who had explored the 35th Parallel Rout in 1853 and died ten years later of wounds received at the Battle of Chancellorsville. The place was a tableland at the foot of a mountain, perfectly level, overlooking the creek from a miniature bluff about thirty-five feet high. At the foot of the bluff there was a space between it and the creek about 200 feet wide, upon which a large corral for cattle, mules and horses was erected and this was all that had been built at the time of my arrival, July 29, 1864. Beneath the foot of the bluff ran the only wagon road out of Prescott. Soon after we were fairly established in tents on the tableland where the post was to be established, I received orders to purchase material for rebuilding the corral and building the fort.[7]

7. Edmund Wells described the newly constructed corral: "To the north of the fort and on the flat below, under cover of the rifles and fort armament, were the Post corrals, large stockade enclosures with buildings stabling the cavalry and Post service horses, and mules, army wagons, ambulances, and scouting equipments. The cattle and sheep herds were kept in a separate corral, and all under constant guard by posted sentinels." Writing from Fort Whipple on August 1, Doctor Coues explained that his new station was a fort in name only. He needed several days to get his hospital in order, then "I shall get settled in my tent,—we have nothing else to live in." Wells, *Argonaut Tales*, 314.; Dall, *Baird*, 366.

Chapter 33

Building a Fort

As Fort Whipple was to be my home for nearly two years and the point from which all our operations against Indians were fitted out, I have thought it best to give an outline of it. In a council called by the commanding officer in relation to the plans of construction, all the officers except him had voted to build an open post or barracks, but he had a fancy for building a defensible fort and dwelt largely upon the dangers to be expected from the Indians about us, while we were such a small command, so far from any means of reinforcements.

My experience at Los Valles Grandes, where with only thirty-five men I had successfully resisted a surprise made by 300 Navajos, in a camp capable of maintaining no defence whatever from any natural or artificial advantages, being nothing but a row of small cabins concealed under a ridge, had led me to feel little respect for Indian prowess or skill in war. But the commanding officer decided for the closed stockade and ordered me as quartermaster to purchase the material. This meant simply the cutting and hauling of the logs, for all the timberlands still remained the property of the Government.

The military reader will at once perceive that Fort Whipple had several grave defects—defects which are all the more inexcusable when it is known that Captain Anderson, who planned it, was a graduate of West Point and ought to have been posted thoroughly in the subject of the construction of defensible posts. After the fort was finished, it was discovered that there were no kitchens for officers or men and we were shortly after obliged to add on sections for that purpose, one behind the officers' quarters and the other outside of the company quarters, on the side towards the corral, thus effectually destroying the line of defence on two sides. Another defect was the absence of any hospital arrangements, while the gravest fault was the absence of water and all chances of obtaining it should we ever be shut in by an enemy. The fear of any dangerous enemy, however, left the brain of the commanding officer long before the first year was out and several buildings began to be put up outside of the wall.

The direction from the fort across the corral is towards the north, the road at this point making a bend and running due east and west. East of the fort about thirty yards and a little towards the rear stood the hospital and, at a corresponding distance on the west side and exactly opposite the hospital, stood the sutler's store. Both of these buildings were built of the same material and in the same manner as the fort. The roofs were steep and shingled, as there were more frequent rains here than in New Mexico on account of the mountainous character of the country.

The population of Prescott at the time of our arrival was in a very destitute condition. The Apaches were so troublesome that the mines and ranches had been generally deserted and the miners and farmers had gathered into the town for protection, at a great risk of starving.[1] Owing to the long distance to any source of supplies and the danger attending transportation, the commonest necessaries commanded extravagant prices. A bag of flour containing one hundred pounds was worth $60 in gold and the same weight in bacon was worth $70. Our quarters were constantly overrun with hungry-looking men who were hoping

1. Less than a year later conditions had not improved, as noted in a letter from Prescott: "This is no country for a white man. It is the hardest country I ever got into. There are some good quart lodes here, but it will cost more than they are worth to work them. There is no money here, and only about fifteen hundred inhabitants in the Territory, and the Indians are so troublesome that it is not safe for less than ten men to go out together. There is but little farming land, very little timber and less water." The letter writer concluded by telling his friends in Colorado, "If you know of any body coming here, tell them to stay at home." *Denver Rocky Mountain News*, June 26, 1865.

for an invitation to eat with us and I am happy to say they did not often hope in vain. This being the situation of affairs, I determined in my capacity of quartermaster to let the work out for building the fort in such a way as to be of general advantage to the community. It was determined to build a stockade. Logs were to be cut twelve feet long, not less than ten inches in diameter at the smallest end, the ends to be squared. Trenches were to be dug four feet deep along the line for the walls and partitions and the logs set up in them close together. Upon the top end of the logs was to be pinned a string piece and slot-holes for muskets were to be pieced between the logs of the outer walls, six feet from the ground. A shelf was constructed for the men to stand on when they fired, about two feet from the ground.[2]

I advertised for bids from responsible parties to supply me with the logs for the fort, but when I found the average price, instead of letting the job to one or more individuals who would hire the work done at a lesser rate so as to make a profit, I divided the logs into lots of fifties and hired the work done, letting no one man cut more than fifty and paying the contractor's price. This gave me considerable trouble, but it sent the money to the right place.

It would be interesting to know who all the men were who cut logs for me. A Baptist missionary, the son of an English baron, a scion of one of the best New York families, a lawyer and a doctor, to my certain knowledge, cut fifty logs each for my post and a great many men whom I never saw before or afterward.

While the fort was being built, we lived in tents scattered around under the cedar trees on the flat. My tent was framed of scantling and covered with wagon sheets, having a regular door, which, although made of canvas, turned upon hinges. The size of the tent

2. Many years later Edmund Wells remembered the plan of Fort Whipple: "The south side of the enclosure was devoted to officers' quarters and administration offices; the east side to quartermaster and commissary supply stores and ammunition magazine; the north and west sides were built into quarters and barracks for the soldiers. In the southwest corner of the enclosure, was the office of the Post Adjutant who had charge of a pair of large heavy lumber gates closing the gateway and main entrance into the fort; they swung out on the south front to the large level plot used for the parade ground. In the center of the enclosure a flagpole stood from the top of which the Stars and Stripes unfurled daily to the play of the mountain winds; at the foot of the pole stood a mountain howitzer mounted and ready for action at all times, the only field piece at the fort. Across the parade grounds to the south were the sutler's store and a line of stockade log houses occupied by citizens employed at the fort. The Post hospital was on the outside of the enclosure, close by under the complete view of the Post sentinel as he walked his beat day and night on guard." Wells, *Argonaut Tales*, 313–14.

was about ten by twelve feet and in the rear of it was pitched a wall tent, opening into the larger, which I used as a bedroom. In the front part were a centre table, a few chairs and a stove. In the wall tent, at the head of my bed stood my iron safe in which I often had a considerable amount of money, to be used in the construction of the post and for other purposes.

For some unexplained reason, in the establishment of the cordon of sentinels I was left outside. My tent stood fifty feet out of the general group of tents and the line of sentinels was so arranged that "No. 4's beat" was behind my tent about four rods. Why no better care was taken of the Government funds, even if my life was not worth looking after, I do not know. I slept with a sharp knife under my pillow with which to rip down the rear of the wall tent in the direction of the sentinel should I have dangerous visitors and I kept the key of the safe in a place known only to myself, so that if I succeeded in getting out, no one could get off with the safe before I gave the alarm. I also, when there was no moon, had another contrivance by which I could be awakened should the door be opened in the night, a contrivance which worked well as I often had a chance to prove when friends visited me after I had gone to bed.

The men's quarters were finished first and they moved into the post, then the officers' quarters, mine the last. I had been much interested in building the fort and several of my suggestions were adopted. The secret gates marked in the plan "2" and "27" were my invention. A thick log was sawed off close down to the grass and hung on hinges on the inside, so that it would turn out of the wall and make an aperture sufficiently broad to allow a person to pass through. These were used when the great gates were closed for the night. I constructed the great gates of logs, binding them on the inside by cross-ties and diagonal-ties and hanging them upon numerous hinges made of army wagon tires. A log was set in the ground for the centre of the gates to rest upon when shut and two were arranged so that they would sustain their weight when open. Big braces were planted against them nights, the feet resting against logs set in the ground with their heads just above the surface.

The chinks in all the walls which composed the sides of quarters or storerooms were plastered up, inside and out, with mud. Fire-places and chimneys were built of stone, laid in mud. Floors were made by filling the inside of the rooms with earth to a height of one foot above the outside surface, mixing the whole into a mud and then smoothing it to a water level to dry. When dry a carpet or mats could be laid and the floors proved very hard as well as comfortable.[3]

As quartermaster and commissary, I was at the head of more men than the commanding officer nominally, though, of course, all were under him. I had eighty civilians in the quartermaster's department as teamsters, herders, mechanics, clerks, etc., and five in the commissary. I had a flock of 2,000 sheep, which had been taken from the Navajos, 300 beef cattle, 200 mules and 30 horses. In a starving community, where prices ranged so exceedingly high, every man seemed to be on the steal and it was with the utmost difficulty I could find trustworthy men to put in charge of property. A regular system of theft from my flock and herd was established when they were grazing day times and it took considerable ingenuity to ferret it out and bring the culprits to justice. A herder could get more money for a sheep than I paid wages in a month. The temptation was too great for ordinary natures.

We found upon our arrival at Fort Whipple one troop of California cavalry and one company of California infantry. Both of these organizations were somewhat depleted, having been in the service nearly three years, with but three months more to serve. Reenlistment of such as were willing to join a veteran organization was completed by the time our train was unloaded and we were established in camp and these veterans took our train back to New Mexico. The men who were unwilling to reenlist were sent to more southern posts and consolidated with other portions of their regiment, to serve the remainder of their time. Later, as mustering officer, I mustered out most of these men.

One of the first incidents worthy of mention which occurred to us after our California comrades had left was connected with the mail. We were nearer the California coast than to New Mexico and had a weekly connection with it—when the Indians did not scalp the mail carrier—while with Santa Fé we kept up only a monthly communication for the purpose of carrying our army reports and returns and even this was taken off when we

3. While Curtis took pride in his construction of Fort Whipple, some of the construction seemed sub-standard. A letter written from Prescott on November 12, 1865, noted of the fort: "The quarters are being re-roofed, the old roofs being worthless." *San Francisco Bulletin*, November 27, 1865.

were transferred to the Department of the Pacific, to which we geographically belonged.[4]

The mail carrier was a citizen employed by the civil and military authorities to carry the mail from Prescott to La Paz, a distance of 170 miles, from which place a coach ran to San Bernardino, California. A portion of the carrier's route lay through mountain paths, forests, *cañons* and ravines, affording rare places for Indian ambuscades, consequently it was not an infrequent occurrence for the mail rider not to arrive at Prescott on the appointed day; and for the military party sent out to look for him to find a cold, stark body lying supinely in the road, a fringe of Apache arrows shot into the abdomen, with their feathered shafts radiating outward and upward; the stony eyes glaring at the cloudless sky, and a pool of dried blood which had welled from the life wound by one side. The scalp would be invariably taken and often the body mutilated almost beyond recognition, every scrap of clothing, the mail bag and all accoutrements taken away and the letters and papers torn and scattered on every hand. The letters were usually simply opened and scattered, while the picture papers were always torn to shreds.

During our first month at Fort Whipple, one of these painful incidents occurred.[5] In the absence of any postmaster, or regular mail facilities in the new territory, the mail was made up at my office. The man who had been carrying the mail for some time was named George Ferrin.[6] He had been an old sergeant in the 2nd Dragoons and had served on the frontier until he had grown grizzled. He was about forty-eight years old, six feet high and of the finest proportions. The shape of his shoulders, breast, thigh and calf was something to admire. The poise of his head above

4. Mail sent from Fort Whipple to New York, via Santa Fe, took about forty-five days to arrive with the same length of time to return. When Lieutenant Curtis awarded a new contract to the firm of Robertson & Parrish shortly after his arrival, he announced that the express riders would also carry civilian mail. The *Arizona Miner* responded by saying "it is proper to give credit to Quartermaster Curtis for the prompt and cordial manner in which he arranged for forwarding the letters of our citizens. His action will not be forgotten." *Arizona Miner*, August 24, 1864.

5. The incident alluded to by Curtis involved William Bottsford, an express messenger working for L. Dukes & Co. He had arrived in Prescott from the Colorado River settlements on July 26 and began his return trip on August 1. When near Granite Mountain, Bottsford was fired upon by a band of Apaches. He escaped despite having an arrow in his back, the wound being treated by Acting Assistant Surgeon Thaddeus P. Seeley. Upon hearing of the attack, Captain Anderson sent out a party of cavalry but their search was unsuccessful. *Arizona Miner*, August 10, 1864.

6. George Ferrin cannot be positively identified.

Two Apache Hunters. Courtesy of Smithsonian Institution.

a well-formed and muscular neck was not the result of military drill, it was natural. A long moustache, turned right and left, like a hawk's wings, entirely concealed his mouth and his brave gray eyes looked out above cheeks bronzed by years of exposure to prairie and mountain winds. His face was regular, the nose well shaped, and his expression was of that imperturbable character peculiar to the well-instructed and disciplined soldier.

When he reported to me the last time I ever saw him alive, he sat on a California horse—a cross between the mustang and the American—in a Mexican saddle, richly upholstered with silver ornaments. A neat jacket, buttoned to the throat, covered the upper man; black buckskin pantaloons cut to the shape of the leg and ornamented along the outer seams from hip to ankle with minute silver buttons the lower. Buff leather leggings encased his legs below the knee and on his head he wore the army slouch hat. A black leather belt about the waist sustained two ivory-handled Colt's revolvers, an ammunition pouch and a hunting knife. Across his lap he carried a Spencer carbine, sure for seven successive shots without refilling the magazine in the breech.

Dismounting before the door, he entered the office, his spurred heels jingling as he strode over the *adobe* floor and reported himself ready for the mail. After making up the bundle and packing it in the saddlebags, I asked him how long he had been mail rider.

"About two months, sir," he replied.

"Then you have made about sixteen round trips?" I asked.

"Eighteen in all, sir."

"Have you met any Indians on the route?"

"Yes, three times in the mountains beyond Skull Valley, but never in the plain on the other side, nor on this side."

"Did you ever exchange shots?"

"Once, as I was going through a *cañon* with a greaser whom I picked up on the road, a shot from the sagebrush went through my hat. I dismounted, gave my horse to the Mexican and walked backward through the pass," he said quietly.

"Did any Indian show himself?" I asked.

"Yes, one redskin raised his head a little too high above the greasewood and my carbine raised him a few feet higher."

"What do you mean by that?"

"An Indian always jumps up when he gets his death wound. That fellow leaped up like his kind, that's all."

"Don't you think they will get you finally?"

"It is getting a little skittish, I must allow, and I've concluded to make this my last trip. When I went out before, I kept hid in Skull Valley through the day and rode through the mountains in the night. I'm thinking the route is getting too dangerous for one man to ride it alone."

Poor Ferrin! He little thought as he bade me a gruff "Good-bye," sprang into his saddle and galloped away that this was the last trip he would make anywhere in this life. I stood in the door of my office for a moment watching the receding horseman, his figure rising and falling gracefully with the motion of his horse.

A week went by and the day arrived upon which the mail was due. On that day, beside the commanding officer, I was the only officer in the garrison for duty, Barr having gone to Wickenburg in command of an escort to a pack train. We did not get particularly anxious when we found Ferrin did not arrive on the fixed day, but when the afternoon of the next day came without bringing him, Captain Anderson ordered me to take ten men, mount them on saddle mules and go to meet the mail rider or learn what had become of him. We took four days' rations and started. I rode my own horse in preference to a mule and soon placed myself on the trail through the mountains. The first section of the ride was through the Granite Mountain range, which lies to the west of Prescott, not generally considered dangerous, probably on account of its nearness to Prescott and the existence of settlements in Skull Valley on the other side, making this portion of the trail much traveled.

If I possessed the ability to describe scenery, I might give a glowing account of the forest through which we passed—the rugged granite cliffs which often overhung the path, the dizzy heights along which we threaded our way, looking down a thousand feet sheer to some silver-threaded stream which wound its way through the *cañon* far below and the sudden opening in the most unexpected manner of vistas of broad valley as we turned around an angle of the mountains. But I cannot do it. I can only say that the grandeur of all the Far Western scenery is beyond my power to portray. The memory of it dwells in my mind vividly and I can never forget the slightest feature, though I fear I shall never be able to describe it.

Chapter 34

The Missing Mail Carrier

Night was upon us when we entered Skull Valley and rode up to the door of the newly constructed log dwelling of Joseph Ehle.[1] This man had accompanied us from New Mexico to Arizona with his family, consisting, besides his wife, of one son and five daughters. He evidently belonged to that class of men who are called "rolling stones." From the various conversations held with the family as we marched along, we found he had lived in nearly every western state between New York and Colorado. He was evidently of German extraction, so that his girls and boy were not of that lank and cadaverous physique which generally distinguishes the white nomad of the West. On the contrary, the young women were plump, buxom and, on the whole, the three oldest girls most of us thought, before we saw the last of them,

1. Joseph Ehle was a native of New York, but moved to Canada as a boy. At the age of twenty-one he settled in Iowa where he married Margaret Williams. From there his wanderings took Ehle to California, Oregon, Colorado, and finally to Prescott where he built a log home and a gristmill. The Ehle family were said to have brought the first sewing machine, honey bees, and chickens to Prescott. They also carried along the region's first house cat, one of whose kittens was sold to a local miner for an ounce of gold dust. In 1865 he moved temporarily to Skull Valley and kept a government station, but returned to Prescott in 1866. At the time of his death on November 27, 1912, in Los Angeles at the age of ninety-nine, Joseph Ehle was reputed to be the oldest Mason in the world, both in age and service to the fraternity. Farish, *History of Arizona* 3: 207–10; McClintock, *Arizona* 2: 321.

were pretty nice looking. Probably the absence of all contrast had something to do with it.

The oldest girl was twenty and the youngest twelve years old. Their education was not of a high order, nor their language of the most grammatical, but in the absence of a better type of femininity they received much attention from the gentlemen of our command and were much esteemed. Indeed, they were fully deserving of our respect, for they respected themselves. One of them—Olive, the beauty of the family—quite charmed one of our officers and he entertained serious thoughts of proposing that she should be sent away to school to be educated, that he might marry her. What would have come of this, no one can say or how far he had gone toward having his proposition accepted.

At the door of the Ehle ranche we stopped and I was at once surrounded by the whole family, who greeted me with all the cordiality of old and dear friends. Dismounting, I accepted their hospitality for the night, soon had my men comfortably disposed in an outbuilding and the animals in the corral. Supper was generously served to us all and made doubly appetizing by being prepared jointly by all the pretty girls, a circumstance not frequent in my New Mexican and Arizona experience. I shall never forget that meal during life. I sat at a small round table in the centre of a large room, the walls and ceiling of which were of hewn pine logs, a large open fireplace was immediately in front of me and the heap of pitch pine fagots burning in the midst cast a brilliant light to the remotest corner. The walls were hung with garments, domestic articles, cooking utensils, firearms, trophies of the chase and many other things. The furniture was made in the rudest manner from lumber which had been carved and planed into shape by no better tools than the axe, knife and shave. The walls were pierced with loopholes for muskets and windows and doors provided with the means of barricading against attack.

I ate and talked and laughed and that expresses but imperfectly how that meal was disposed of with a circle of girls about me watching for an opportunity to wait upon me, talking all the time. Asking questions about absent friends of the long march and recalling its ludicrous events, kept us in a whirlwind of excitement through the whole meal. The perfect freedom from restraint and lack of conventionalism which ran through the whole evening's entertainment until bedtime made it especially delightful.

When the time for sleep arrived, the five girls took me by the hand in turns, wished me good-bye, for I was to leave before they should rise in the morning, and lighting a tallow-dip climbed a ladder in the corner to the garret above, where, after much laughing and some screaming, they were soon asleep.

I have not mentioned the mother all this time, simply because she sat in the chimney corner smoking and, after greeting me on my entrance with a word and nod, had not spoken ever since. She sat in a straight-backed, sheepskin-covered chair, leaning forward, her right elbow on her right knee, the hand sustaining the elbow of the left arm, the fingers of the left hand holding a long-stemmed pipe between her lips, slowly removing it as she puffed out the smoke and as slowly replacing it as the smoke rose above her forehead and was drawn into the chimney by the strong draft of her fire. When the girlish fun in the garret had entirely subsided, Margaret Ehle slowly rose, knocked the ashes from her pipe and, placing it carefully on a shelf, turned to me and asked, "Whar' ye goin', Leftenunt?"

I explained as briefly as possible the object of my trip.

"That Ferrin's a fool," came next with slow deliberation.

'Why so?" I asked.

"Any feller that'll go gallupin' through that Injin hole at the risk of his life every week aint got sense, you needn't tell me!"

"It takes a brave man to do that sort of thing," I said.

"Brave, mebbe, but dreffful reckless. You'll never see 'im agin in this life. I dreamed o' seein' him ridin' a white horse the night after he went by here and that's a sure sign," nodding her head in an emphatic manner that forbade contradiction.

"I hope it's not as bad as you predict," I replied, "and that he is simply delayed."

"You'll find him skelped up thar in the *cañon*, now you mind me," still keeping up her nodding.

I found as the conversation went on that Mr. Ehle agreed with his wife, although he did not base his reasons upon the flimsy fabric of a dream. He said the Apaches had been growing more troublesome recently and that they had threatened especially to have the scalp of Ferrin before long. This report had been brought in by a friendly Mojave, with whom the Apaches were at peace.

Next morning I started long before sunrise and after a few hour's ride reached the point where the road turns out of Skull Valley into the *cañon*. The road from this point to La Paz is a wagon road and ascends for about a mile at a very steep grade, through an irregular formation of granite boulders, well calculated to afford concealment to any lurking foe. I dismounted my men at the foot of the hill and sent two of them about 300 yards in advance, then started six more and left the remaining two to follow 300 yards behind. All the animals were kept by the central or main body. In this manner we marched slowly to the top of the hill, looking about carefully for any evidence of a conflict between the mail carrier and Indians.

We reached the summit and halted, closing up the command. From this point we could see far down into the *cañon* ahead of us. Presently one of the men said, "Do you see those two vultures settling down in the *cañon*?" I looked to the point indicated and saw the vultures, then adjusting my field glass I looked along the road in that direction and presently my eyes fell upon the body of a man stretched across the road.

"There's a dead man in the road below, men," I said. "Mount and follow me." We rode quickly down to where the body lay. As we approached, I saw that it was entirely without clothing, lying flat upon its back, the face turned upward. At first I thought this could not be Ferrin, for the head was bald, but soon I saw what I had taken for a bald crown was the bleached skull of a scalpless head. The softer parts of the body were studded with the long shafts of the Apache arrow, which stood up like a bunch of cane grass. All about the body for many yards were scattered fragments of letters and papers. The road was filled with the tracks of moccasined feet and the tracks of a white man's shoes. A horse's track coming from the direction of La Paz came up to the spot and then turned into the sagebrush to the south.

Yes, this was Ferrin. He had ridden with the mail for the last time. His breast which had faced many a foe and bore several honorable scars had received no wound in this encounter. There were three ugly wounds in his back, but we all knew that they were not received in flight, but from a cowardly, ignoble foe, who dared not face him.

"Look round in the brush, men," said I, "and see if there is any evidence that Ferrin sold his life dearly."

"He was the lad for that, Liftinint," answered Private Cleary, who was one of my party. "He kilt a few of the raskils, if he had half a chance."

Diligent search was made through the sagebrush and surrounding rocks for a long time without success, but, at last, one man called out that the earth had been disturbed where he was. Going to him, I called all the men to see the place, so that if they should find similar ones in their search they would know what they meant. The spot indicated showed no difference from the hard, baked soil about it, save that it had been disturbed slightly and showed the traces of a sweeping or brushing done with a branch. Taking a bayonet from one of the men, I carefully scraped away the sand, little by little, going deeper and deeper, until a red tinge showed itself in the sand and soon I laid bare the evidence that some person or animal must have bled to death in this place.

"Ah, Ferrin, me b'y, 'twas yer dead finger pulled that trigger!" exclaimed Cleary. "B'ys there's more of 'em! George never went without plinty o' company!"

The search was resumed and soon we had indisputable evidence that five Apaches had met their death. On the back side of a rock, some distance from the road, there was a stain of blood from the top to the bottom, a distance of twenty feet. The struggle must have been fearful and there was no means of knowing more of it than now lay at our feet.

We scooped a grave beside the road with our bayonets and sword and, putting a noose made from a piece of a lariat over one wrist, for the body was too far gone to be touched, dragged all that remained of the dead dragoon to his last resting place. I read the burial service from a pocket prayer book which I had taken along from the presentiment that I should have a use for it, while the men stood around with uncovered heads. We then filled the grave and built a pyramid of loose stone over it.

Hastily collecting the scattered mail, we remounted and rode back to Skull Valley, without taking any precaution against attack. We stopped at the Ehle ranche to tell the family of the mail rider's death and left all the girls in tears. The old woman paused in her monotonous taking of her pipe stem from her mouth and replacing it, to say, "Didn't I tell yer?" and resumed her smoking, without showing any apparent emotion further than a slight choking, possibly caused by the smoke.

We arrived at Fort Whipple at dusk and gave out notice that the mail would be distributed to the public at Prescott on the next day at three o'clock P. M. That night my sergeant and clerk spent a great part of the night in piecing the torn letters together and trying to learn for whom they were intended. The next day at the proper hour most of them were distributed, affording considerable amusement to the crowd.

Many of the letters were signed with initials, or nicknames, or not at all and such letters usually bore no date and no address, except a pet or nickname. The sergeant stood up like an auctioneer and would read aloud from the letter in his hand until someone, recognizing a friend's language, would shout for him to stop, as that letter was for him. Love letters, business letters and home letters were all treated in this way and often some queer things would come into the possession of the crowd, causing roars of laughter when the owner called for his letter.[2]

2. Carrying the mail continued to be a dangerous proposition in Arizona. On May 29, 1865, Doctor Coues explained: "'Mail,' in the abstract, is the same the world over, I suppose; in the concrete, however, it varies with circumstances. Here it means a couple of men, with as many donkeys, carrying the precious little packets on one side of huge leathern panniers, and bacon and beans on the other. Civilized mails come to grief sometimes by running off the track; our mails in a different way. Thus the last one, due a week ago, came in yesterday in a fragmentary condition. A hundred Apaches had attacked it in a *cañon* about twenty miles from here, killed one of the men, wounded the other badly, and stampeded the donkeys. We sent out a strong party, and they gathered up the fragments; nor were they the traditional 'twelve basketsful,' hardly twelve handfuls." "Letters, Extracts," 536.

Chapter 35

Horse Flesh

Doctor Coues's mule, which had borne him faithfully from Albuquerque to Prescott, both on the direct marches and in his lateral ramblings along the route in search of ornithological specimens, was the property of Uncle Sam and so at the end of the journey was turned over to Wagon Master Moore, to be sent back with his train to New Mexico. This left our doctor on foot. He was entitled to ride, by virtue of his commission, but there was no horse market in Arizona and not enough horses at the fort to mount the cavalry. This state of affairs made it necessary for the doctor, in order to continue his bird shooting, to borrow horses of his fellow officers, and we, who were owners of animals, found that the doctor knew as little of the endurance of a horse, or his needs, as he did of a Peruvian llama. He invariably overworked them and brought them back in such a condition, boasting of the speed with which he had passed from some point to the post, that we began remonstrating with him and laying down conditions when we lent him our steeds. But it was all to no purpose. He continued to ride about the country at a furious gait and the finer and more sensitive the beast, the worse he was used. At last, we jointly agreed to lend him no more horses.

At first this made the doctor sullen and he went about by himself, apparently very much vexed at our course. Then we began to see him in the company of ranchemen and miners, looking over various seedy quadrupeds—mules and horses—evidently with the intention of buying. One day, after this had been going on for something more than a week, he was seen, quite early in the morning, to ride off with a rancheman, who lived twenty-five miles away. We saw nothing of him until evening, when we were all sitting under the shade of the cedars and pines enjoying an after-supper smoke. The quiet was suddenly broken by the clattering of galloping hoofs in the road under the bluff and presently the doctor appeared in sight, dashing furiously up the western slope, mounted upon a buckskin-colored horse, whose breast, sides and flanks were reeking in froth and sweat. As the doctor came into sight, he gave a whoop that would have rivaled an Apache and, rising in his stirrups, swung his hat wildly about his head. He rode close up to where we were seated and, pulling his horse up suddenly from full sped to a full stop, exclaimed, "There is a horse that belongs to me, by Jove, and I mean to ride him to suit myself! I'll show you fellows that a horse does not need so much dashed coddling as you pretend!"

The horse was a fine specimen of the cross between the mustang and American, already mentioned by me as being the kind furnished the California cavalry, a hardy animal, capable of enduring great fatigue and making long journeys upon scant forage. The doctor had paid a good price and got a good horse, but we all were ready to predict that the quality of goodness would soon disappear under the peculiar treatment which the doctor was likely to give him.

As our stables were yet unbuilt, we kept our horses near our tents. Feedboxes were nailed to the trunks of trees or placed between two standing near together. A staple or hook was driven into the tree to which to fasten the horse. Each officer did much toward taking care of his own horse, the servants doing the dirty work and the police part, which came round every morning, taking away all the refuse accumulations of these open air stables. The doctor's horse was provided for in this manner and, as his tent was near all the others, we were the witnesses of his eccentric treatment of "Buckskin." He would come in nearly every evening with the animal in the condition I have mentioned, tie him, all puffing and heated, to the tree where the feedbox had been previously supplied with Indian corn and leave him to fill himself at his leisure. We pitied the horse enough to remonstrate with his owner and assure him that such treatment would certainly result in a founder. Our answer was equivalent to a "mind your own business."

I will here anticipate the thread of my story to say that in September we had a nightly frost and most lovely days. One evening, after sunset, when the weather had begun to be quite chilly, the doctor tied Buckskin to his tree, in a fine perspiration, to eat his forage, leaving him unblanketed through the night. The next morning, when a soldier who used to water our animals unfastened the doctor's horse, he was dead lame. To the conversation that ensued we were all listeners through the thin canvas walls of our tents and soon gathered to witness the result of the doctor's folly. The horse was almost unable to put one forward foot before the other and it was necessary, in order to get him down the bluff to the creek for water, to back him down.

This was a salutary lesson to the doctor. He would not take advice, but when once taught by experience the folly of some line of conduct, he was never known to repeat it. Buckskin, by good treatment, recovered the use of his limbs and remained in the doctor's possession while he stayed in Arizona. He was never ridden uselessly hard after the occurrence above mentioned and great care was exercised in properly feeding and covering him.

While I was still living in my tent, I came into possession of a horse that has a history. The circumstances connected with my purchase and the eventful history of "Two Bits" during my ownership I propose to relate.

My servant at Fort Whipple was Joseph Cain, the fifer of F Company. He was a handsome Irishman of a fine figure and a soldierly demeanor and the best servant I ever had. The manner in which he took care of my tent and its contents was above criticism. He would come into my quarters every morning before reveille, so silently as not to arouse me, take my clothing outside for a polishing and brushing, return them to the room and place each article on a chair by the bedside in the order in which I should take them when dressing. On certain days of the week when I rose from my bed, I would find a bath of the proper temperature prepared and fresh linen substituted for what had been thrown off the previous

Assistant Surgeon Elliott Coues. Photograph from *Bird Lore*.

evening, all this being done without my hearing a footfall or the slightest noise.

The man was strictly honest, picking up any stray articles of value which he might find when putting the tent in order and placing them in some conspicuous place where I would find them upon my return. In one instance he saved me from a serious loss. I had been paying off my quartermaster employees and, in returning the packages of greenbacks to the safe, I accidentally left a package of one hundred dollar bills, amounting to $1,500, on the table. I left the post to visit the log cutters in the woods and did not return for three hours. When I entered the tent, I found Cain waiting for me. He handed me the package, with the remark that he "thought he had better stay by it until my return."

When the New Mexican Cavalry arrived at Fort Whipple, they "turned in" sixteen horses, which had been condemned by a Board of Survey as "useless and recommended to be sold." Examination of these veteran steeds showed them to be generally decrepit and worn out. They were thin in flesh, sore-backed and some of them were unable to rise in their stalls.

I ordered an auction held for the sale of these horses on a certain afternoon and employed an auctioneer to knock them off to the highest bidder. The day before the sale was to take place, I was sitting in my tent writing when Cain entered and asked, "Would the liftinent like to buy a foin horse?"

"No, Cain," I replied. "I have one horse that is good enough for my use and I cannot afford the expense of a second."

"You can buy this one for a song, sor."

"How much?"

"If the liftinent will let me have five dollars, I'll buy him the bist horse in the post."

"The best horse in the post for five dollars! Cain, you are talking nonsense," I replied and turned to my writing as if I had disposed finally of the question of purchase. But Cain seemed to have set his mind on buying a horse and was ready with something more in support of his project.

"If the liftinent will buy the horse, he'll not be sorry. I've known the baste for tin years—from the time I jined as a music b'y at Fort Craig."

"He must be very old, then?" I asked.

"Nobody knows his age, sor. He's a viteran, but he's a foin horse all the same. The liftinent shall have no care of him if he'll buy him."

"But I shall have to buy his grain and hay."

"Not a bit of it, sor. There's a surplus in the corral and the wagon master'll let me have all I want if the liftinent says so."

More to please a valued and trustworthy servant than with the hope of securing a good horse—in fact, I did not expect to get a horse at all—I gave the five dollars to Cain and he retired.

I did not attend the sale nor did I know what disposition was made of the horses. I merely noticed that the money account had increased seventy-five dollars by its means, showing plainly enough that the value of the sixteen horses averaged but a little over four dollars each. Over a month went by and I had entirely forgotten that I had given Cain five dollars with which to purchase a horse, when one day, as I was again writing in my tent, I heard the rapid clatter of a horse's hoofs approaching and presently the animal stopped in front of my quarters. After the delay necessary to secure the horse to a neighboring tree, there was a knock on the canvas door and to my "Come in," Cain's face showed itself, wreathed in smiles.

"Will the liftinent please come out and see his horse," he said and he immediately withdrew. The fact that I had invested five dollars in horseflesh was at once recalled and I went outside, with considerable curiosity to witness the result.

I found Cain in charge of a fine, large bay horse, in good flesh, smooth as satin and bright-eyed as a colt. He led him about for me to examine his points. The most prominent features which struck my eye were a pair of handsome, well-pointed ears; a forehand fine and long, rising boldly above the withers; a mane and tail thinly haired; a small, lean head; the hollows about the eyes showing the age which the eyes did not; withers high; loins short and straight; flanks and ribs full and round; haunches strong and elastic; legs clean; and feet well-shaped. No doubt there were many other points which a good horseman would have perceived, but I, not being an expert, could only see that the horse before me was a good specimen of his kind.

"You don't mean to tell me that is the horse that you bought for five dollars, Cain?"

"Four dollars and forty cints, sor. I bought the halter for the sixty that was lift."

"But I don't see how such a horse could be had for that money. Is this really one of those broken-down hacks I sold at auction?"

"Not a bit else, sor."

"Tell me how you made a new horse out of an old one."

Cain's story, rendered into proper English, was nearly as follows. He was one day at the corral and saw a stable man kicking and pounding an old horse to make him stand up. The animal would make attempts to rise, but each time would fall back through weakness. Cain approached and recognized an old acquaintance from certain saddle marks and a peculiar shaped spot in the forehead. From some knowledge of horseflesh, picked up in a stable during a wandering life before his enlistment, the soldier perceived that the horse was not diseased, but simply low from ill treatment and neglect. He at once determined to get me to buy the horse at the auction.

I asked the horse's name and learned it was Two Bits. This information naturally begot the second question, where did he get such a name? I found Cain was well posted upon this point and he shortly put me in possession of Two Bit's history. The horse had first belonged to the Mounted Rifles Regiment and was with them at Fort Craig, New Mexico, in 1859. On the Fourth of July of that year, the officers and civilians of the post and vicinity got up a horse race, with an entrance fee of $30 and a purse of $300 to be awarded the horse running 800 yards in the best time, the race to be open to all American horses. On the day of the race, the first sergeants of the Rifles waited upon the officers in charge and asked to be allowed to enter a company horse for the stakes, they, the sergeants, to pay the entrance fee. After some discussion, the officers granted their request.

At two o'clock in the afternoon of the Fourth, the horses were assembled at the straightaway course on the plain to the west of the fort, Two Bits being present and ridden by the boy fifer, Joe Cain, of F Company, 5th Infantry. The officers walked around the company horse, commenting upon his points, and Major George W. Howland seemed to utter the general sentiment when he said that he "would not give two bits for that horse's chance to win." A bit is a Southwestern term for twelve and a half cents.

The race came off and the tenderly cared for and gaily caparisoned horses of the officers and civilians and the plainly decked out pet of the soldiers burst down the track in line to arrive scattered and blown at the goal, with the company horse three lengths ahead of all. From that day on, the victor was called Two Bits.

With the breaking out of the late Civil War, all the mounted regiments were made cavalry. This wiped out of existence the two dragoon regiments and the rifle regiment, the latter being re-christened the 3rd Cavalry and ordered from New Mexico to the States. Before leaving, the horses were turned over to the New Mexican Volunteer Cavalry and so Two Bits met his old rider of the Fort Craig race at Fort Whipple. Cain had recognized his old friend and, knowing that he could not own a horse, he did the next best thing—he made me his owner. This gave him the care of his favorite and a chance for an occasional ride.

We had not been long at Fort Whipple before a race was got up at Prescott and great excitement in consequence prevailed among the owners of fast horses. The purse was to be for $250 and the entrance fee $25. The race was to be a running race for saddle horses and the distance 800 yards. A few days after the announcement of the details, Cain proposed that I enter Two Bits, assuring me that I was sure to win the purse if I would do so. Not being a betting man, I refused and consequently plunged the fifer in deep despair. For several days he went about silently, showing in his manner that he was disappointed and dejected. At last I took pity on the fellow and one morning when he came in after breakfast, to put the tent in order, I said, "You do not suppose, Cain, that old horse would stand any chance in a race, do you?"

"He would just that, sor," he answered with emphasis.

"But he is very old. He must be twenty-seven at the least."

"Yis, sor, and he grows faster as he gits older."

"Your love for the horse misleads you, Cain," I replied, smiling at the earnestness of the man. "I admit that he is easy and free under the saddle and the best horse I ever rode, but it is not reasonable to expect him to beat younger horses at his age and after all the ill-treatment he has undergone."

"I wish the liftinent would let me try him, that's all."

"I'll let you, Cain, as you desire it so much."

"Thank you, sor, and you'll win the money," said Cain, his face breaking into sunshine.

"No. I don't want the money. I will pay the entrance fee as a reward to you for procuring me Two Bits. You are not likely to win the purse, but if you do it is yours."

This arranged, the horse was taken out daily and run over a piece of the road near the fort until the day for the race came. I shall not attempt to describe the struggle. It came out like the old one at Fort Craig several years before, amid the thundering cheers of the soldiers who were present and who looked upon the triumph of the horse as that of a comrade. Cain rode back into the post richer by $250 than when he went out in the morning, surrounded by an admiring crowd of bluecoats, who caressed and praised Two Bits at every step.

Next morning at reveille I found my clothing where I had left it upon going to bed and my boots unpolished. After breakfast, no Cain appeared to put the quarters in order and, upon inquiry, I learned he was in the guardhouse, with a goodly number of the infantry and cavalry who had helped spend the winnings of Two Bits for the sutler's whiskey and eatables at a symposium held in the corral. When fully sober, all were released without further punishment and returned to duty. Of the $250, Cain brought me $57 after his release, for safe keeping. All the rest had vanished like the dust kicked up by the horse on the course when he won the race.

I rode Two Bits on nearly all my business trips, pleasure excursions and Indian hunts. Some months after I became the owner of Two Bits, we were obliged to put on a fortnightly military express between Fort Whipple and Fort Wingate, this section being a link in a continuous line from the Pacific coast to Santa Fé and thence by stage line to the East. This express consisted of but one man, who rode the entire route without relay. At first the riders went and came regularly with no adventure, but at the last there would be occasional breaks and investigation would show that the express had been captured by the Indians. The service finally became so dangerous that it was with the greatest difficulty I could find men who were willing to ride the express, even for the large pay given. At last, matters reached such a desperate state that a whole fortnight elapsed after the time when the express should have started and I had not succeeded in finding anyone who dared undertake the trip. I was on the point of asking for a detail of soldiers from the cavalry troop, of sufficient strength to protect itself over the route, when a private of the New Mexican Company entered my office and said he had come to offer to ride the express.

This man's name was James C. Sutherland, an Ohioan by birth, who for some unexplained reason had enlisted in the New Mexican troop.[1] He was not at home among his outlandish comrades and was

1. James C. Sutherland enlisted as a private in the 4th New Mexico on November 18, 1861, and served in that regiment until it was consolidated into the 1st New Mexico Cavalry on May 10, 1862. Promoted to corporal on January 1, 1862, and sergeant on August 9, 1862, he was reduced to the ranks on September 21, 1862. Sutherland had a brief stint as a lance

generally placed on some special duty which separated him from them. He was about five feet seven inches in height, of a compact and sinewy frame, showing great strength and endurance. He had light hair, closely cropped, with a closely shaven face; his face was sun-burned, but where his skin was not exposed it was very fair; his eye was gray and looked cool and determined. What were Sutherland's antecedents we never knew. A mystery hung about him and we were all convinced from his speech and occasional remarks which he dropped that he was a man of superior cultivation, while a sundial which he constructed and placed in our parade ground showed that he was a man of some scientific knowledge.

Sutherland entered my office and said that he would ride the express for the pay offered, upon condition that he would use my horse Two Bits.

"Why Two Bits?" I asked.

"Because he is fleet and he is capable of great endurance, two very necessary qualities for a horse in an Indian country," was the reply.

"But he is my private property and I do not wish to spare him on such service. I will give you your choice of all the horses in the corral, but I cannot spare Two Bits."

"Then I do not care to go, sir," answered Sutherland. "I have turned the matter over in my head for some time and thought I would go if I could procure Two Bits. He has several qualities possessed by no other horse here—he never whinnies in the presence of Indians and he will never run away from his rider if turned loose to graze. I fully considered these peculiarities before I offered my services. The risk is too great with any other horse."

Upon saying this, Sutherland withdrew. I consulted with the post commander about the offer and finally, upon much urging, gave my consent to let Two Bits go. Two days afterwards, the express left for the long ride to Fort Wingate. The horse carried, beside his rider and his ten days' rations, the mailbag weighing fifteen pounds, a carbine, two revolvers, an overcoat and three blankets.

---

corporal in 1863 but generally served as a private until mustered out on November 30, 1864. Although due $100 in bounty money, Sutherland left a trail of debt, including the army for loss of clothing and ordnance and the sutlers at Forts Canby and Sumner. His debts totaled almost $150. His military records indicate that he had been detailed as an express rider and one letter dated Fort Canby referred to "the daring and fearless express rider Sutherland." James C. Sutherland Military Service Records; *Rocky Mountain News*, March 30, 1864.

The rest of the story was related to me nearly two years afterwards by Sutherland, at Fort Sumner, New Mexico, where he was engaged as interpreter to the Navajo Indians. I cannot make the tale as interesting as he did, but must tell it in my own language.

The first three days of Sutherland's ride were through a section of country not considered dangerous. He rode day and night, dividing his time so that the horse could graze at stated periods and, where he felt secure, he slept while the horse fed. On the fourth day he entered upon a portion of the route over which the Navajos roamed and he was obliged to be constantly on the lookout, not daring to sleep much and pursuing his journey chiefly under the cover of darkness.

About noon on the fifth day he found himself descending from a mountain range to the borders of a plain, which stretched for ten miles away to a hill beyond. Just before reaching the plain, the road descended into a ravine, from which it rose over a low ridge to descend again to the plain. Over this ridge the road divided into two, joining again when they touched the plain. One of these roads had been rendered impassable for wagons by gullying, but was passable for horsemen. In the ravine Sutherland dismounted, in order to stretch his legs, and walked along behind Two Bits, leaving the horse to choose between the two roads. He took the old one, walking slowly up the crest, his rider but a few paces behind.

When the horse arrived so near the crest of the ridge that he could look over to the plain beyond, he suddenly stopped, his ears pointed forward, his eyes and nostrils distended to their utmost, as if he perceived some object to inspire fear. Sutherland sprang quickly forward and placed himself where he could look over the ridge. Just on the edge of the plain, where the new road descended from the ridge, behind a boulder which would have concealed them from any person passing that way, but fully in sight of anyone passing on the old road, were two Indians, crouched low. They were watching with all their eyes for the express rider whom they had probably seen descending from the mountains and whom they were sure would come over the ridge by the usually traveled road.

Sutherland unslung his carbine, moved the pistols in his belt more to the front and dashed down the road upon the plain. The Indians, who were about 300 yards away, turned and, seeing that they were discovered, dashed round a spur of the boulder, immediately afterward appearing mounted on two ponies and gave chase.

The pursued and pursuers started even on the edge of the plain for the race across it, but 300 feet apart. Two Bits threw himself into the task of running away from the mustangs, with all the elasticity and grace which had distinguished him for years on the race course and had always led to victory. He soon distanced his pursuers and settled down to a gait which his rider was in hopes he might hold until the Indians should give up the chase. This, however, soon proved impossible. Two Bits was old, he was heavy-laden, he was fatigued by a long journey and he had eaten nothing but grass for five days. This want of grain is a serious want with the American horse, a want which the Indian horse, never grain-fed, does not share with him.

Sutherland, as he sped along the road skirted with cactus and Spanish bayonet, could hear the clatter of the mustangs' feet, beating a monotonous accompaniment to the shrill staccato of the war whoop, which their riders unceasingly yelled. For the first two or three miles the American horse seemed to gain perceptibly; then came a mile that the pursued and pursuers held relatively the same position; after that Sutherland could see that the Indians were gradually gaining upon him and at last an arrow which whizzed past his ear showed that they were within shooting distance.

Whatever else he may have been, Sutherland was not a crack marksman. He turned in his saddle and fired shot after shot at the Indians, as his horse galloped wearily on, with no result except to make the redskins crouch lower in their saddles and prevent their returning the fire. At last his carbine cartridges were exhausted and, throwing the useless weapon into the road, he drew a revolver. The Indians had now got nearly up to him and about thirty paces to his right, when a lucky shot took one in the arm, breaking it and causing him to fall from his pony, which ran far away to one side and began to graze. The other Indian did not abandon the chase when his comrade fell, but kept on as before. He at last came up to a neck and neck race with Sutherland and, beginning to hold the white man's skill with his revolver in contempt, he gradually closed the space between them until scarce ten paces divided the horses. The Indian evidently intended to draw the last shot from his opponent and then finish him at his leisure. At this moment Sutherland was struck with a brilliant idea. He turned Two Bits quickly to the right, held his revolver nearly to the mustang's neck and fired. The pony plunged headlong in the road, flinging the rider a double somersault into a Spanish bayonet, where he instantly picked himself up and sent an arrow after the flying expressman, giving him an ugly wound in the shoulder.

Sutherland was now safe so far as the two Indians were concerned, but he soon found that Two Bits was nearly used up. The old horse began to show signs of exhaustion and soon dropped into a slow walk. Night was approaching and the mountains beyond the plain were still far away. To ease the horse, the rider dismounted, but the loss of blood soon compelled him to mount again and ride wearily and anxiously on. At last, in the deepening twilight, Sutherland saw a bright fire in the far distance on the mountainside above the plain. In the hope that it was the fire of a white man, he headed his horse for it.

Two Bits traveled so slowly that hours elapsed before he brought his rider near the fire. At last, the rattle of halter chains over feedboxes reached the ear of the expressman and he knew that the bright blaze came from the campfire of a Government train. With the welcome sound he grew faint and fell from his horse into the road senseless. Two Bits kept on into the camp, approached the campfire, around which sat our old friend Wagon Master Moore and his assistants, staggered, fell and died.

The appearance of a horse, saddled and bridled, a mailbag strapped on his back, his saddle covered with blood, his sudden fall and death, startled the whole camp into activity. Horses and mules were quickly saddled and lanterns were soon hurrying down the road. The seekers had not far to go before they came upon Sutherland, lying apparently dead in the road. He was taken into camp, tenderly cared for, and the next day taken to Fort Wingate, the place for which Moore's train was bound.[2]

2. In a paper read before the Wisconsin Commandery, Military Order of the Loyal Legion of the United States, on May 15, 1903, Curtis retold the story of Two Bits. In that version, which has some additional details, Curtis stated that Quartermaster Sergeant Charles Porter, rather than James Sutherland, had ridden Two Bits. This was a correction of the 1880 version in which Curtis said he had obtained the story from Sutherland in 1867. He probably assumed that Sutherland had been the rider, but later realized that it had actually been Sergeant Porter. At the conclusion of his 1903 account, Curtis included a suitable postscript to the Two Bits narrative: "Was Two-Bits left to be food for the coyotes? No! The train escort was composed of infantry soldiers, some of whom had been stationed at Fort Craig at the time of the first horserace mentioned in this paper; and after listening to Porter's account of his journey they gave the gallant old steed a soldier's burial with three volleys, and erected a pyramid of stones above his grave." It became a tradition among the soldiers that all who passed by would dismount and add another stone to the pyramid over the horse's grave, their way of honoring Two Bits and his final sacrifice. Curtis, "A Cavalry Veteran," 32, 50.

Chapter 36

A Bad Day Fishing

The Apache was on the warpath and we were constantly making expeditions about the country to rescue some besieged ranchemen, act as escort to a train or pursue a successful raiding party to recapture stolen property. Still we ventured out frequently on pleasure trips, going distances over mountains and through valleys for the purpose of hunting and fishing, never neglecting to make ourselves thoroughly acquainted with the country passed over, so that our knowledge might be available in case of necessity. Doctor Coues pursued his search for birds during the two years he was in the country, with but few interruptions and, although he wandered over a great part of the country alone, escaped any serious scares from the Indians. It seems almost unaccountable that this should be so when hostilities never ceased during the whole time we were at Fort Whipple and bloody fights were of frequent occurrence. He fired his doublebarreled shot gun many times a day, but for some reason or other the Apache never heard it or, if he did, never looked up the doctor.[1]

1. Doctor Coues related his experiences with the Indians who glided virtually unchecked throughout the country: "For some years after the Territorial government was established, it was at the risk of life that one went out of sight of Prescott or Fort Whipple alone or with a small party. The Apaches lurked behind every rock, and hid in every bush; or, failing that,

One day in the fall of the same year of my arrival at Fort Whipple, Governor Goodwin called at my quarters and asked me to be one of a party to go fishing and shooting on the Rio Verde the following day. It was proposed to be gone several days. We were to go directly north, to the site of old Prescott, now known as Postle's ranche, stay all night and next day go down the valley of the Rio Verde, which here crosses the Santa Fé road, and for a distance of about twenty miles runs nearly due west, where it resumes its general southeastern course. The river was said to abound in fish, which were always eager for the bait.

The next day, about two o'clock in the afternoon, I took a small wagon which my carpenters had made from a wrecked ambulance, but which contained little of the former vehicle beside the wheels and axles and, attaching to it two diminutive mules scarcely larger than their parent ass, the doctor and I took a seat and started.

At the corral we found the governor, Lieutenant Barr, a lawyer named Henry Fleury and a man named Ralph Henri, who was known to be an excellent shot and distinguished for nothing else in many respects being a mere child, entirely dependent upon others for the common necessaries of life, having no capacity for taking care of himself.[2] But he was without exception the best shot with a rifle that I ever saw.

The governor and the other members of the party were in a large, covered spring wagon, in which were placed our provisions, fishing tackle and the other necessaries for the journey. I took the lead, started and for about half an hour found no difficulty in keeping up a good rate of speed. But the spirit of a mule soon flags and,

---

under cover of every three blades of grass—a trick they did to perfection—and reddened with blood every trail that led to the capital or the post. People were killed and stock was run off within a few hundred paces of both these places, and more than one pitched battle came off within ear-shot. A regular part of my business for two years was the extraction of Apache arrow-heads." Coues, *Zebulon Pike* 2: 747.

2. Henry Fleury left his home in Jamaica, New York, in the summer of 1863 to join the territorial officers of Arizona on their journey to establish the first government there. Upon reaching Arizona, Fleury acted as private secretary for Governor Goodwin and Secretary McCormick, filling the offices of both men in their absence. Like most government officials, he also became involved in mining and owned the Thunderbolt Quartz Mill on Lynx Creek. A wealthy man due to sound investments, Fleury eventually lost his fortune by vouching for friends in their business deals. Justice of the Peace during his entire stay in Arizona, Fleury was appointed a probate judge in 1870. After the legislature moved to new quarters, he bought the old building and lived there until his death in Prescott on September 3, 1895. Ralph Henri cannot be positively identified and may be a pseudonym. *New York Evening Post*, September 1, 1863; *Weekly Journal Miner*, August 28, 1869; April 9, 1870; September 4, 1895.

after wearying my arm with belaboring the hybrids for another half hour, I fell behind the governor's wagon, which was drawn by horses, and found my animals good at following, if not at leading. They required no further whipping for the rest of the journey.

Our road passed down a beautiful valley, on one side of which, for eight miles, ran the Red Rocks. Below that, the country opened into a broad valley, skirted at long distances on each side by mountains. At two places our wheels ran over walls which just appeared above the surface of the ground and which could be traced for acres around in regular squares, the foundations of the houses of a former people, whose history we shall probably never know.

About six o'clock in the evening we arrived at Postle's.[3] This was a single *adobe* building, standing among the rugged chimneys and debris of the first settlement of the Arizona officials. Postle had been shrewd enough to secure this place for a ranche, by far the best for many leagues around. A constantly flowing stream of pure water, which fell over a natural fall of about fifteen feet to a plain below of indefinite extent, had first attracted the officials to the locality for their capital. In the hands of the rancheman a dam had been made on the fall and a ditch taken out of the stream, leading half a mile away at right angles to it, from which small streams led over the plain, for irrigating purposes. A space of several hundred acres was as green as a New England farm, except where the Indian corn had recently been stacked and the potatoes dug.

Postle was a short, thick-set Englishman, of whose antecedents I have no knowledge. He had as a partner a man named Jack Brown, a tall, lank fellow with swarthy complexion, jet black eyes and hair, who looked as if there was no end of fight in him.[4]

3. A native of England, Robert Postle was a grocer in Tucson before the Civil War. Commissioned a second lieutenant in the 1st New Mexico Cavalry on February 7, 1863, he was promoted to first lieutenant on September 4, 1863. Placed under arrest for allegedly cheating a fellow officer in a horse race, Postle was court martialed and dismissed from the service on December 31, 1863. A letter stating that "he has been Guilty of Conduct which must forever debar him from possessing the character of Gentleman" was signed by Colonel Christopher Carson and all the officers of the regiment. After a stint at running the Postle & Brown ranch, he received a commission as captain in the 1st Arizona but apparently never served in that capacity when he could not find enough recruits to fill his company. Postle was naturalized in 1865, spent the remainder of his days on his ranch and died there on April 9, 1871. Robert Postle Military Service Records; *Prescott Daily Courier*, March 20, 2001; McClintock, *Arizona* 1: 194; *Daily Alta California*, November 16, 1865.

4. In a notice dated August 15, 1864, Robert Postle and J. M. Brown announced that they "have this day taken up and squatted on that tract of land situated at and near the old site of Fort Whipple, consisting of about five hundred acres." The *Arizona Miner* published their notice and commented that they were presently "cutting some two hundred tons of

These men had come from New Mexico in company with us, had seized upon this ranche soon after their arrival and I learn are still there. The peculiar manner in which all their mules were marked had first attracted my attention. All Government stock is branded on the left fore-shoulder with the capital letters, "U. S." If the ingenious reader will draw these letters on a piece of paper, close the top of the "U" so that it will look something like an "O," then draw a perpendicular line on the left side of the "O," beginning even with the top and extending it a little below, the result will be a respectable "P." Next, with the "S," draw a line from the upper extremity diagonally to the lower extremity and you have a kind of "&." To these letters add a letter "B," and you have a "P & B," standing for Postle and Brown. I have no doubt how these men got their stock.

We passed the night at the ranche, eating a supper cooked by Jack, the principal dish of which was jerked beef, pounded fine with a hammer and fried with a little pork. Jerked beef is simply dried beef. The ox being butchered, the flesh is cut from the bones in strips, dipped into a weak brine, plentifully sprinkled with pepper and hung over a line to dry. When hard as sole leather, it is stored. It is taken on long marches where fresh meat cannot be carried and may be eaten without cooking, with bread or hardtack. Soon after my arrival at Fort Whipple, I had forty head of beef jerked by order of Captain Anderson.[5] As I ate the beef at Postle's, I could not help wondering whether it did not come from the post. Very likely it came in after the "P & B" manner. I have already mentioned how Government property slipped away in Arizona.

The evening was passed in card playing and conversation and at an early hour we retired to our mattresses, which were spread

---

hay" and planned on planting 200 acres of grain the following year. The ranch, isolated midway between Prescott and the Verde Valley, was fortified with stone-walled corrals. On September 13, 1866, the two partners, "by mutual consent," dissolved their partnership with all debts to be paid by Postle. *Arizona Miner*, September 21, 1864; September 26, 1866; McClintock, *Arizona* 1: 189.

5. Doctor Coues described the operation of jerking beef at Fort Whipple: "We had a large herd of cattle, one or more of which were daily slaughtered for the supply of the garrison; and early in the fall it was deemed advisable to 'jerk' all the beef that remained on the hoof, since, in this state, it was always liable to be stolen by Apaches, and winter fodder was procurable only in limited quantity. The shambles were located in a grove of cottonwood near the fort, and day after day the meat hung drying in thin strips festooned upon ropes stretched between the trees, while bones and offal covered the ground at a little distance. These were high times for the Buzzards, Ravens, wolves, and all the dogs of the neighborhood; the place became a rendezvous for holding high carnival." Coues, *Northwest Birds*, 382.

Robert Postle. Courtesy of Yavapai Cowbelles.

beneath the sky a little way from the wall of the cabin. The next morning we took an early breakfast and, shouldering our rifles, fishing rods, knapsacks and blankets, started for the valley of the Rio Verde. Our party, all told, consisted of Governor Goodwin, Lieutenant Barr, Doctor Coues, Mr. Fleury, Bob Postle, Ralph Henri, Pauline Weaver and me.[6]

Pauline Weaver was an old trapper and hunter, who had a great reputation in the West. The various towns of Weaver in the Pacific states and territories are named after him. At the time I knew him, he must have been nearly eighty years old. He belonged to that class of men of which Carson, Boone and Pfeiffer were well known representatives and had wandered along, just in advance of the march of civilization, like James Fenimore Cooper's Leatherstocking, through the whole region from Kentucky to the Pacific and from the British line on the north to the Mexican line on the south.[7] His name was Paul, but the Mexicans had made Paulino

6. Powell Weaver, whose name eventually became Pauline as noted by Curtis, left his home state of Tennessee at an early age and became a trapper for the Hudson Bay Company. He came to the Southwest about 1830 and for decades became engaged as a guide, trapper, and prospector. One of his contemporaries offered a description of the old frontiersman: "In stature he was over six feet in height, broad-shouldered and straight as an arrow. His eyes were black, nose on the aquiline order, and large mouth. His mingled black and gray hair fell in straggling locks to his shoulders, and his black grizzled beard flowed well down his broad chest. His features were strong and prominent and his deep bass voice had the blast of a fog horn, or as though coming from a deep cavern." Pauline was still on the army payroll as a guide when he died on June 21, 1867, at the age of sixty-nine. Originally buried at Camp Lincoln on the Verde River, Weaver's remains were transferred to the Presidio National Cemetery in San Francisco in 1892 but were moved again in 1929 to Prescott. Numerous geographical features in the Southwest bear his name. Hayden Arizona Pioneer Biographies, Arizona State University; Wells, *Argonaut Tales*, 268.

7. Daniel Boone, the pioneer and Indian fighter, made his first exploration of the Kentucky wilderness in 1769. He returned six years later as an agent of the Transylvania Company and erected a fort at what would become known as Boonesborough. Boone was the consummate frontiersman. During his lifetime he was a businessman, militia officer, explorer, debtor, farmer, trader in ginseng, furs, and slaves, hunter, Indian agent, justice of the peace, legislator, landowner, trapper, and surveyor. Always willing to take a chance on the next best thing, he found himself constantly in debt but always managed to claw his way back to begin another downwards spiral. His life story encapsulated the story of the American frontier. Daniel Boone died on September 20, 1820, near what is now Marthasville, Missouri. Albert H. Pfeiffer was commissioned captain in the 1st New Mexico on July 6, 1861. Upon the consolidation of the New Mexico regiments, he became captain in the 1st New Mexico Cavalry on June 26, 1862. Promoted to major on March 31, 1865, Pfeiffer was brevetted lieutenant colonel effective as of March 31, 1865. He remained in the service and was mustered in as captain in the New Mexico Battalion on October 8, 1866, and was mustered out on October 31, 1867. Wounded twice by Indians during his service, he became a national celebrity for eluding an Apache ambush while bathing in some hot springs about six miles from Fort McRae. Despite being wounded by two arrows, Pfeiffer managed to escape although his wife and another woman were killed, along with several of the escort. He spent the remainder of his life seeking revenge for the murder of his wife, but died in bed on April 6, 1881, near Del Norte, Colorado. Morgan, *Boone*, 20–21, 39–40, 109–10, 249–51, 302–304, 378–79, 429; Albert H. Pfeiffer Military Records; *Indianapolis Sentinel*, June 2, 1881.

out of it and the name Pauline had superseded the others. He did not wear the traditional hunter's garb in which many novel writers garb their Nimrods and adventurers of the Far West, but wore the slop-shop clothing of the trader. His arms were of the modern type, the rifle being a Henry breechloader and his two ivory-handled, silver-mounted revolvers of the Colt pattern. In figure, Weaver was about five feet eleven inches in height, with no superfluous flesh, still erect in spite of age, but rheumatism had given him a slight limp. His eyesight seemed as strong as ever for long distances and his aim was perfect.

Our walk from Postle's to the Rio Verde was about two miles. Where we struck it, the river entered a *cañon* from the plain, at this point gathering its current from several tributaries before it entered between perpendicular walls which enclose its course for fifteen miles. The space between the walls of the *cañon* was about 200 yards wide; the river ran in the centre of this and was, on an average, not more than fifty feet broad. This left a broad shelving border between the shore and the wall on each side, except where the winding course of the stream approached one wall and made the space on that side narrower and the opposite side wider. The *cañon* itself wound along through the plain somewhat deviously and was nowhere more than 150 feet high. Along the banks of the river grew dense fringes of willow bushes, while between them and the walls was here and there a black walnut tree.

We entered this walled valley of the Rio Verde, following a well-beaten path on the right or western side. Looking along the crest on either side, I said to Postle, "This seems to be a good place for Indians."

"Not a very good place, sir. They do not care to be confined to this space in a fight and if they attack us from the height it must be a fight at long range."

"That is true, but it would be an awkward trap to be caught in, down in this gully, striving to make our way out with a lot of Apaches on the plain above."

"Yes, but you'll not see them there. I've not seen an Indian about my place for a year."

We now passed on for a little more than a mile, where we selected a camping place close under the western wall, at the very foot of which a beautiful spring rose and sent a crystal thread of water to join the river a hundred yards away. Along this little stream grew the willows and but a few yards on the north side was a huge black walnut, beneath which we threw down our packs containing our bedding and provisions.

It was agreed that we should all return to this place promptly at five o'clock in the afternoon and that until that time we should go wherever we pleased, either hunting, fishing or searching for specimens, geological or botanical.

For myself, not being a good shot, I selected a line and hook and began looking up bait with which to lure the fish. By moving over stones and rotten wood, grub worms and bugs were found in sufficient quantities to fill my bait box and, after a short search, I found a break in the willow border, where I could stand and throw in my line.

The Rio Verde, so far as I have explored it, which has been about twenty miles below Postle's—opportunity having been given in various hunts after Indians—seems to be a regular succession of beaver dams, one dam flowing into another. Weaver, who was an old trapper of "Ahmeek," said he had trapped this river twenty years before and found it as I have described it.[8] The Indians had prevented any trapping since that time.

As I stood on the turfed bank of the stream, the water was about two feet below my feet, the thick, matted grass overhanging the surface. The water was perfectly clear and of an average depth of about six feet. All over the bottom could be seen numberless suckers, a fish which needs no description. These lay lazily on the bottom, rarely stirring, and, as I found by experience, perfectly indifferent to the bait which I moved temptingly to their noses. About two feet above the suckers was a fish which kept moving rapidly about, seizing the bait with a dash resembling that of the trout, but possessing none of the timidity of that beautiful fish. I had seen this fish but once before. On our march to Arizona, on the Rio Pescado, near Zuni, I saw the first specimen. There appear to be two varieties of the genus, known as *Gila robusta* and the *Gila elegans*, from the river where it is found and its tributaries.[9]

The fish literally swarmed in the river. One had no occasion to move about in order to catch a mess. Finding them so plenty

8. Ojibwe term for beaver.
9. The Roundtail Chub and Bonytail Chub.

and so willing to bite, I did not catch above two dozen before I went back to our camping place, exchanged my line for a rifle and started to explore the valley. I found little to interest me outside of the beaver dams. Confined between the walls which bound the narrow valley of the stream, one could see in a space of half a mile all that there was of interest. I stood on a dam for a long time, examining its construction and the marks of the teeth which had cut off the trunks of trees and bushes used to construct it. There were no houses in the dams and the beavers must have made their homes in the banks. Several slides bordered the edge. While I was fishing, I had seen several of the little animals pass my line beneath the surface and as I walked along the banks I occasionally got a glimpse of one, through the willows, swimming along the river.

Some distance below our camp, I fell in with Doctor Coues and Henri. The former had already secured a dozen birds to add to his collection and the latter held in his hand three ducks. Examining these, I saw they were each killed by a single bullet. I asked Henri if he had shot them with his rifle. He answered in the affirmative. In fact, he had no other weapon.

"He is the best shot I ever saw," said the doctor. "Show Curtis a bit of your skill. Kill that jay on the wing."

Almost as soon as I raised my eyes to see a bird fly from the branch of a walnut tree a couple of dozen yards off, Henri's rifle cracked and the bird fell to the ground. Henri sent his dog for it and when he returned the ball had hit it just back of the head.

I joined Henri and continued my way down the river. After a short time we came to a place where the river broadened out into quite a little lake. My companion said we should probably find some ducks here. We crept carefully along behind the fringe of willows until we came to a thin place in the foliage and Henri, peering through, reported that there were six ducks in a little bay on the other side. I looked and saw some ducks alternately diving and swimming, about fifty yards away.

"If the lieutenant would like to try a shot, I'll wait for him," said Henri.

"But I shall only scare them," I replied. "I shall kill none."

"Well, I shall get just as many whether you shoot or not. I can always get one with a rifle."

This was true, if I was to judge from his success with the jay. Accordingly, I began to get ready for a shot. I sought out a place where I could lie at length, rest my rifle over a rock and take deliberate aim. Henri stood a few feet away, concealed by the willows, with his rifle resting easily over his shoulder while he watched my preparations. At last I got ready, aimed long and carefully and fired. Every duck rose into the air. There was another report and one fell directly into the water. Presently one of the others began to behave oddly and in a moment more fell to the earth some distance beyond the other bank. The dog plunged into the river and shortly brought in both ducks. Henri's was shot through the head and mine was hit back of the wings and near the top of the body.

At five o'clock we met at our camping place, according to arrangement. Weaver and Henri built a fire and began making preparations for supper. I had brought in a good string of fish. Governor Goodwin and Doctor Coues had a number of quail and Weaver produced a duck and two geese. There was certainly no lack of provision.[10] The want of shotguns was the great drawback in securing small game, for there were but two weapons of this kind in the party, the doctor and governor having those. Postle had shot nothing. He had been exploring the valley in search of a mill site combining water power and some chance of getting in and out of the *cañon* with wagons. He had met with no success, however.

With so many cooks and assistants, it did not take long to spread on the grass a meal fit for a king and one which did not go begging for appreciative eaters. We were all of us ravenously hungry with our long day's walk and exercise since an early breakfast, a fast broken only with a biscuit or two carried in the pocket when we left camp.

After supper, the smokers smoked and all chatted for a while. A quartette set down to a game of Euchre and by the firelight, assisted by the full moon, played far into the night. With bedtime most of us placed our bedding on the turf beneath the walnut and found no difficulty in going to sleep and sleeping soundly until

10. Edmund Wells offered a description of the Rio Verde at this period: "The river was lined by banks covered with tangled and heavy growths of willows and vines, cottonwood, ash, and other trees, furnishing shelter and retreat for the many wild animals infesting the neighboring mountains, and the myriads of wild fowl which flocked the secluded spots angling for the abundant fish swarming the shallower waters of the river." Wells, *Argonaut Tales*, 289.

morning. During the early part of the night, we were serenaded by a party of coyotes that had scented our supper and approached to the edge of the cliff above our heads. The sound of the water falling over the dams was the sweetest of music to our ears, music which no one can appreciate until he has lived long in a country where the sound of the falling rain and the murmuring of brooks is rarely heard. The beaver played all night, sliding down their slides and slapping their flat tails on the water so that they could be heard for a long distance.

With the gray of dawn most of us were up. The fire was replenished, the fowl not eaten the previous evening was soon broiling on the coals under the supervision of Henri and Weaver and the rest of us went down to the river for a plunge and wash. A noisy and boyish frolic of a quarter of an hour in the Rio Verde put our blood in a glow and brought us back to the campfire with the best of appetites. In a few moments we were once more gathered about our food under the branches of the walnut and had nearly completed the meal when—swish! swish! swish! came three arrows down through the branches of the tree. Probably the branches and leaves destroyed their direction, for none of them hit anyone in the party. I need not say that we were on our feet instantly and with one impulse ran back to the face of the cliff. Two more arrows came down as we ran, one going through the left shoulder of Postle's coat, merely grazing the skin, the other touching the rim of the governor's hat.

Once against the wall we were for the time being safe. The crest of the cliff at this point hung over its base and there was no point along the top which commanded us. We were in a bad predicament, however, for all the arms but Henri's, which happened to be leaning against the wall were out under the tree where we had been sitting for breakfast.

I began to look about us for some means of reaching our weapons, but could think of none that would not expose the person going for them to the fire of the Indians. At last, I asked Henri if he was willing to undertake to cross to the opposite side of the river, from which he could command the height above us and which his unerring aim would soon clear of enemies. My plan was this. The spring, as before mentioned, rose at the very foot of the cliff, the stream running directly to the river at right angles with both river and wall. This stream was bordered with the bush willows. By walking in its bed, Henri could reach the river unseen. Over there he could follow the bank down by wading along the shore to the beaver dam half a mile below, along the top of which he could cross to the opposite side. Once there we could secure our arms and make other arrangements for getting out of our unpleasant predicament. Henri agreed to the proposition as soon as made and in a few moments was threading his way through the willows. To divert the Indians' attention from him, we rigged up a dummy out of our clothes and pushed it out into sight, drawing instantly half a dozen arrows, one rifle shot and any amount of war whoops.

From where we stood we could see Henri work his way along until he reached the river when he was lost to sight. From that time we waited an hour and a half in the greatest suspense. The Indians above us kept up their yelling most of the time and, finding they could not reach us with their arms, they began rolling stones over the edge of the cliff. These would strike the ground but a few feet in front of us, sending splinters, gravel and mud into our faces as they struck.

At last, just one hour and thirty-five minutes after he left, we heard the ring of Henri's rifle and simultaneously a big rock and an Indian fell down the cliff together, the redskin clinging to the rock and describing circles in the air as they came down. A dull, sickening thud on the ground and we saw the Indian had fallen underneath, with an immense boulder on his stomach, pinning him to the earth.

We did not stop long to contemplate the sickening spectacle, but gathering our arms and baggage together prepared to leave. Before starting I sent Barr, Postle and Coues to join Henri on the other side. By keeping close to our wall we could command the crest of the cliff opposite. The party on the other side could command the crest over our heads. In this way we were absolutely safe from attack by a small party and, in fact, we saw nothing more of our red enemy, but retraced our steps to Postle's without further adventure.

Arriving at the ranche, Henri reported that he saw at least fifty Indians on the cliff above our heads. Some of them were busy in rolling a stone to the edge and the idea struck him to shoot one just as the stone was balancing to the fall. With what success we have seen.

We returned to the fort the same day, well pleased with our excursion.

Chapter 37

Cash and Carrying on

My sojourn in Arizona was during the darkest period of the war, when the lack of marked success by the Northern army depressed our finances to the lowest point they ever reached. Although so far away from the struggle, we felt every fluctuation as readily as did those much nearer the scene of strife. The Pacific states and territories maintained a gold basis throughout the war and when people there talked dollars and cents they meant coin. Arizona belonged to the Pacific slope, hence the same distinction between coin and paper was maintained there as at San Francisco. The officers and soldiers were paid in greenbacks, the quartermaster and commissary employees were paid, by special order, "in gold or its equivalent."[1] As I had no gold, I calculated the difference between hard money and paper as quoted in Wall Street and made the payments upon that basis. My pay as a first lieutenant amounted in greenbacks to $110 per month and $41.25 in coin. My clerk was paid $125 in "gold or its equivalent," which made in greenbacks about $333, a decided advantage to the clerk over the officer who employed him, especially as the

1. A notice in the *Arizona Miner* on October 5, 1864, noted: "Messrs. Bowers, Sutlers at Fort Whipple, take and have constantly taken, greenbacks at 50 cents on the dollar." *Arizona Miner*, October 5, 1864.

clerk was furnished with rations by Government, while the officer purchased his.

This made it necessary for the officers to study the most rigid economy, for only the plainest articles of food could be purchased of the commissary and butter, cheese, milk, potatoes and other vegetables we could not afford. Butter was worth three dollars per pound, cheese in the same proportion, milk twenty-five cents per quart in summer and one dollar in winter and potatoes often fifteen dollars per one hundred weight, all these prices being in coin.[2]

The men working for the Government were looked upon by the other Arizonans as exceedingly fortunate. They had regular and stated pay. The others, owing to the Indian hostilities which prevented them from carrying on the mines, were generally destitute and often at their wits end where to get anything to eat. Prices were so exorbitant that my employees were under severe temptation to steal from the Government to sell to the civilians. My large flock of sheep, which furnished us with much of our fresh meat, was regularly preyed upon. An officer could buy a sheep for one dollar in greenbacks of the Government; the civilians could get one for sixty cents in the market and for something less from my herder. I seemed to be surrounded by thieves, without an honest man to redeem them. The very cook of one mess was getting rich by selling the bacon, sugar, candles, soap and salt through the kitchen door. I used to prowl about the post at all times of night to waylay the kleptomaniacs who used darkness to conceal their operations.

One night I slipped out through the secret way near the ordnance storeroom and walked softly along the outer wall which formed one side of the commissary storehouse. Hearing a slight noise a short distance in advance, I halted to take an observation. In the starlight I could see a man standing on a ladder raised against the wall, running his naked right arm into one of the slots made for musketry, scooping out handfuls of flour from the pile

2. Charles Curtis was not the only man to complain about the Arizona economy. Writing from Prescott on February 1, 1865, George Sands complained: "The little money now in the country is rapidly going out to California, to pay for provisions. California is swindling us seriously, charging high prices, and demanding gold for payment." Sands then enumerated some of the current prices: "flour from 36 to 40 dollars per hundred; bacon, sugar and coffee, 1.00 to 1.25 per pound; beans 40 to 60 cts.; board $21 per week; hay $60 per ton; pine lumber $50 to 60 per m." *Denver Rocky Mountain News*, June 10, 1865.

of sacks inside and depositing it in a bag which he held in his left hand. I recognized a lawyer in town and, not wishing to arrest him, I drew my revolver and fired a shot a few inches above his head. He dropped to the ground so suddenly that for an instant I thought I had killed him, but the thought was barely formed when the man sprang to his feet and fled down the bluff like a gazelle. Next day I sent Cain to his quarters with the bag which he had left filled with flour. He called upon me at once and told a pitiful story of privation and suffering.

On another night, I went to the corral, the stables of which were not yet finished. To accommodate the horses and mules, a long picket rope was stretched along the outside of the wall next the creek and to this the animals were tied. The sentinel who guarded the corral had orders to search around it continuously a considerable distance, which left the side where the animals were picketed unguarded for a space of about seven minutes from the time he left the western corner until he again appeared at the eastern. I was in constant fear of a raid upon the stock by the Indians or horse thieves, so periodically demanded an increase of the guard in order to make my record sure in case of accidents. The request was always denied on the score of the large amount of duty required of the garrison for escorts and other detached service.

As I approached the corral at the front side, I met the sentinel on his round. I passed him and walked along in the direction from which he had just come. As I turned the corner, I heard a voice say, "Cut as many mule halters as you can, never mind the horses." I stooped so as to be concealed by the bodies of the mules and, passing round behind them, presented my revolver at the head of a ruffian who had just cut loose half a dozen mules, ordering him in a whisper to come with me and be silent. I walked backwards to the place where the other horse thief was, but before he had demanded impatiently of his comrade, "If he was ready to light out?" I secured the two without much difficulty. Number two drew a revolver and would have fired had not the sentinel luckily appeared and caused him to change his mind. I disarmed them and left them in charge of the sentinel, while I examined the picket line to see how many mules were loose. I found each man had cut the halters of six. Crossing the creek, which was but a few inches deep, I found two horses tied to the cottonwood trees on the opposite side, saddled and bridled. These belonged to the thieves and were to be used to drive off the mules when once loosed. I sent the men to the guardhouse.

On still another night, I found two men in my cattle yard killing sheep, intending to carry them off on their backs. These men were also secured, nothing further happened by which I lost any stock and I was soon made doubly secure by getting the corral finished and in securing the services of two honest men in charge.

These two men were from Portland, Maine and had both been first mates of ships. They did me excellent service as corral master and wagon master during the rest of my stay in Arizona, relieving me of all further anxiety about the corral and its contents and enabling me to sleep soundly nights.

The sutler's store was made a regular place of assemblage for a large number of the idle miners adrift in the neighborhood. It was a much better stocked store than any in Prescott and therefore was frequented by the successful as well as the unsuccessful seeker for gold. Every evening found the large back room filled with choice spirits, mostly made up of miners, but largely composed of traders, ranchemen, hunters and the officers of the garrison. The chief amusement was in card playing and the games were usually Don Sancho Pedro, Whiskey Poker and Freeze Out. There was little or no gambling. Men cannot gamble without money and as the majority was generally "hard up," there was no call for it. Whiskey and other stimulants were furnished liberally by the sutler and this fact, doubtlessly, was a chief attraction to many of those who gathered here with the approach of evening.[3]

I was not a frequent visitor at the sutler's store. I had chanced to be present when a Jew trader opened his stock of goods in Prescott and, seeing a large number of the Tauchnitz edition of *British Authors*, I purchased the whole lot before anyone else had

3. Herbert Bowers emigrated to California during the Gold Rush and originally commenced mining, but eventually engaged in banking at Nevada City in that state. He moved to the Prescott area and began placer mining in 1863. The following spring Herbert and his brother Nathan formed a partnership that won the appointment to sell sutler supplies at Fort Whipple. In 1867 the brothers bought King Woolsey's Agua Frio Ranch at a tax sale and in 1869 built a flour mill there. That same year the partnership of Bowers & Bro. dissolved with Herbert remaining the post sutler and Nathan concentrating on the ranch and mill. Herbert Bowers remained Fort Whipple's sutler until his death in San Francisco on December 21, 1873. *Arizona Miner*, April 20, 1864; *Weekly Journal Miner*, June 20, 1867; November 11, 1869; December 18, 1869; December 26, 1873.

a chance.[4] The reading of these, if no better reason, kept me in my quarters most of the time. Occasionally, however, the desire to purchase something would take me there and I always found I was a very welcome guest. On these occasions I found the company frequently engaged in perpetrating jokes and "sells," Doctor Coues being the chief victim.

Coues was a very funny fellow, there is no denying. All the way out, on the march and in camp, we had been regaled with his puns and witticisms, many of them very excellent and some of them laughable only from their atrocity. But when he arrived at Fort Whipple and began to perpetrate his jokes at the sutler's, he waked up a few old jokers, who generally proved more than a match for him. In my rare visits to the back room, I learned that it was seldom safe to betray much interest in anything partaking of the mysterious which might be going on or to ask why, where, how or when, if a story was being told. Gravity and silence best became the casual visitor.

One man, George Cooler, who was on my payroll as spy and guide, was an inveterate joker.[5] He had scored dozens of sells against the doctor and had never once been made victim in return. He was a man of grave demeanor, whose face rarely relaxed into a smile and then but momentarily, while his most boisterous laughter never exceeded a single "Ha!" brought out with a jerk. He had been an old Dragoon sergeant many years before, then corral master at Santa Fé, leaving the last place to try the Arizona mines.

The doctor had laid many and deep pitfalls for Cooler, but had in every instance been caught in his own trap. On the last occasion,

4. Christian Bernhard Freiherr von Tauchnitz published the first volume in the Tauchnitz Edition of *British and American Authors* in 1841. His aim was to provide affordable editions of popular authors with a concentration on sales to European readers. By the end of 1864 his firm had published a total of 751 volumes. *Complete Catalogue*, 3, 144.

5. George Cooler, a native of Holland, enlisted in the U. S. Mounted Rifles on June 11, 1852, and was discharged as a sergeant after his second enlistment expired on May 27, 1862. When an attempt to win a commission as a captain in the 1st New Mexico failed, he spent two years as a wagon master shuttling freight for the army. Cooler spent most of 1864 as a miner in Arizona before signing on as a civilian employee for Lieutenant Curtis at Fort Whipple for five dollars per day. Cooler became an accomplished guide and scout, leading several successful expeditions against the Apaches. His postwar career included stints as scout, wagon master, saloon owner, and deputy sheriff. Although blackballed when he attempted to join the local Grand Army of the Republic post, Cooler was admitted to the Pacific Branch of the U. S. Soldiers Home on May 16, 1895, and died there on July 16, 1904. Hayden Arizona Pioneer Biographies, Arizona State University; U. S. Army, Register of Enlistments, 1798-1914; Union Provost Marshal's File of Paper Relating to Individual Civilians, George Cooler, November 20, 1862.

he had jumped from his chair and vowed in the presence of the sutler and a dozen *camaradas de rancho* (mess companions) that if anyone caught him again, he would pay the whiskey for the whole crowd for a month. Instantly the company crowded around him and insisted on taking him by the hand, as in some manner binding him to his word and at the same time particularizing each person present as a claimant to the whiskey, whose rights thereto could not afterwards be disputed.

The doctor left the store and for a while kept strictly in his quarters in the evenings. Reflection probably convinced him that therein only was safety. But after a time he relapsed into his old habit and, after going to the sutler's for a week and finding no attempts were made to victimize him, he was even betrayed into boasting to me "that he guessed they had given him up as a bad job." I cautioned him against being too confident and told him that the very quiet of the jokers should be taken as proof that they had not forgotten him. Besides that, he did not fully realize all that free whiskey for that array of parched palates meant; they were not going to let such a chance go by unimproved and that his only possible safety lay in keeping out of the sutler's store. But the doctor, in this, as in every case where advice was offered him, went directly against it.

One evening about four weeks after the doctor had made his rash promise, I went to the sutler's for a small purchase and after making it was invited into the back room. Entering this convivial apartment, I found something over a dozen men gathered around a large circular table playing Freeze Out. Among them was the doctor. My entrance was greeted warmly and a place was made at the table for me to take a hand. As soon as I had got fairly seated, Captain John Thompson, who sat on my right, whispered, "Don't ask any questions, Curtis, if you notice anything strange."[6]

6. John Thompson was commissioned a first lieutenant in the 4th New Mexico on October 3, 1861, and was promoted to captain on April 4, 1862. He was transferred to the 1st New Mexico Cavalry on May 10, 1862, and commissioned major by the governor on June 25, 1865. Thompson mustered out on October 7, 1866, to accept a position as captain in the New Mexico Battalion and served in that organization until August of 1867. Captain Thompson was described in the following manner: "The Captain was a red-headed, sandy-whiskered, much freckled, bronzed Irishman. He commanded with much pride a band including as accomplished and finished bravadoes and buccaneers of the border as ever raided an Indian Rancheria, captured a Mexican fandango or shot up a frontier town." Thompson and Company K, 1st New Mexico Cavalry arrived at Fort Whipple on November 30, 1864. John Thompson Military Service Records; Wells, *Argonaut Tales*, 270; *Arizona Miner*, December 14, 1864.

"What's up?" I asked.

"They are going for the doctor tonight."

"Where's Cooler?"

"He'll be in soon. Watch him, but don't say anything."

The game went on amid general conversation and an occasional burst of laughter at the jokes of the doctor, who seemed to be in rare good spirits this evening. He punned everything and everybody seemed to fall headlong into his traps. His head was nearly turned at his success and he at last went so far as to banter the crowd at their want of success in "selling" him and so getting the free drinks. To this the answer was that his experience was making him sharp, but that his time would come before long. He burst into a reiteration of his former promise and even offered to make the one month two, but Captain Thompson told him he had better stick to the one, for he might in an unguarded moment be made the victim of a joke. He would find the appetite of an Arizona crowd for "tarantula juice" was something fearful, especially where it cost nothing.

After we had been playing for some time, Cooler entered from the shop, his head bound up with a handkerchief and holding his jaw in the palm of his right hand. No one took notice of or said anything to him. He walked into a far corner, seated himself near a small table, placed his forearm along the top and rested his hand on it. Presently the doctor asked, "What's the matter, Cooler?"

"Toothache," was the reply.

"Ache bad?"

"Like hell!"

"Have it out. I'll pull it for you."

"No. It's too good a tooth. Guess 'twill stop fore long."

This ended the conversation for some little time and the game went on, with the jokes and laughter as before. A dismal groan from poor Cooler at last drew attention to him again and the doctor said, "Draw up a chair, George, and take a hand. It will help you forget the pain."

"Can't. Tooth jumps like a billy goat."

"Try some salt and alum in it," said Captain Thompson.

"Try thunder!" said the suffering Cooler. "I've tried half a dozen things already. They don't do any good."

"Salt and alum's good, I know," said the sutler. "What do you say, doctor?"

"He better have it pulled and be done with it. Still, salt and alum often stops toothache," answered Coues.

"There's a box of salt in the other room, George," said the sutler. "Help yourself to all you want, but I have no alum."

"I'll give you an order on the hospital steward for the alum, if you care to try the remedy," observed the doctor, as he pulled in a trick.

"Well, I think I'll try it. Make out your order," and Cooler rose from his seat and went into the storeroom, from which he emerged in a few moments with a neat paper cornucopia which he placed on the table, with the remark, ""There's the salt. Now I'll go for the alum."

The doctor handed him the order and Cooler went out of doors. No sooner had he gone than a miner named Calkins looked up and said, "Wouldn't it be a good joke on George to change that salt for sugar?"

"By Jove!" exclaimed the doctor, jumping to his feet with such eagerness as to throw over his chair, "So it would. Where do you keep the granulated sugar, Bowers?"

"In a barrel under the farther end of the north counter," replied the sutler.

The doctor seized the cornucopia and disappeared into the storeroom. He was excited at any possibility of perpetrating a sell at the expense of the invincible joker, Cooler. The mere hint of a chance to tally one against his old enemy had caused him to spring at once to the front and take the whole matter into his own hands.

While the doctor was gone, the game went on as usual and I was not aware that any trick was about to be played upon him. I had had a hint from Thompson not to ask questions, but simply to observe and I had not the remotest idea that what had taken place was a part of a well-planned farce, in which the principal actor was entirely unaware that he was playing a part. Presently the doctor returned, placed the cornucopia on the table and resumed his place at Freeze Out.

Cooler now returned and placed beside the cornucopia a small package of alum. He had hardly done so when the doctor looked up and asked, "You don't know that I am a necromancer do you, Cooler?"

"Well, no, doctor, I have never discovered it," was the answer.

"But I am. I can play lots of tricks."

"Show us one, after I take this mess," said Cooler, taking up the two packages, as if to go out with them.

"Hold on a moment," and the doctor advanced quickly and, placing his hand on Cooler's arm, said, "I'll bet you something that I can make you a whiskey toddy with that salt."

"A salt one, yes."

"No, a sweet one."

"What shall we bet?"

"Drinks for the crowd," was chorused by the thirsty miners.

"Well, let it be drinks for the crowd," assented the doctor. "I'll bet you the drinks for the crowd I can make a properly sweetened toddy out of the contents of that cornucopia."

"Agreed," said Cooler, handing over the cornucopia. "Go ahead."

The doctor then took two tumblers, one of which he filled nearly full of water and emptied the cornucopia into it. He then began pouring the water from one glass into the other, all the time running over with funny remarks, keeping the party, which had gathered around him to witness the proceeding, in constant merriment. After a little impatience at the slowness with which the sugar dissolved, he placed the tumbler containing the water on the table, filled the other with an equal amount of whiskey and poured one into the other until the contents were well mixed. He then divided the whole equally between the two tumblers and grated a little nutmeg into each. Raising the tumblers with a beaming and self-satisfied smile, he passed one to Cooler with a profound bow, accompanied with the remark, "There, old fellow, what do you think of me as a magician?"

Cooler moved aside the handkerchief which had enveloped his jaw, raised the tumbler to his lips, threw back his head, poised the glass and, amid perfect silence, took a mouthful and instantly spit it upon the floor, exclaiming, "Salt or I'm a Dutchman!"

The doctor looked puzzled. He glanced at the glass in his hand in a blank manner, raised it to his mouth and drank. He sputtered, strangled, dashed the tumbler into fragments on the floor and exclaimed, "Sold again, by Jove!"

The crowd was unmerciful in its boisterous laughter and vociferous reminders that the doctor could bring on his month's allowance of whiskey at once, etc., etc. He stood it for a moment and fled. After he had gone, the only mysterious part of the joke was explained to me. When Cooler went out after the salt, he prepared two cornucopias. When he returned with the alum, he exchanged the one which Coues had filled with sugar for the second one, containing salt.

The next day the doctor was notified that if he would furnish ten gallons of whiskey to be kept on tap at the sutler's, he would be let off without further expense. He sent the ten gallons. I need not say, perhaps, that this ended the doctor's attempts at playing jokes and in consequence Cooler and his fellows ceased playing them upon him. He often told me afterwards that his Arizona experience took a heap of nonsense out of him.

Chapter 38

Life in Prescott

The sawed timber used in the construction of Fort Whipple during the first three months after our arrival was sawed by hand in a saw-pit or on trestles, with whipsaws and was, of course, very expensive. About the last of September a steam sawmill made its appearance, was set up in the forest and very soon afterward sawed lumber was plenty and cheap.[1]

One of the first consequences of the cheapness of material was the building of half a dozen houses and stores after the pattern familiar to Eastern eyes and the discontinuation of the erection of log houses. One liquor seller built a billiard hall about fifty by forty feet on the ground and fourteen feet high. Before setting

1. Thomas Sanders explained the advent of Prescott's first sawmill: "Up to this time the magnificent stand of yellow pine timber that grew around Prescott had only been cut into to secure a few house logs and the possibilities for a sawmill finally attracted two men by the names of G. W. Curtis and A. O. Noyes who were experienced sawmill men." Sanders continued: "They shipped one out of San Francisco that came by way of the Gulf of California and up the Colorado River to Bill Williams Fork where it was loaded on wagons and drawn to Prescott by oxen in the summer of 1865. It was delivered to a point about two and one half miles out of Prescott. The mill was designed to cut from twelve to fifteen thousand feet of lumber per day. There was such a demand for lumber in the building up of Prescott and the surrounding country that the operators did not have to deliver the finished product. The patrons would come to the mill and haul it away green." Bates, *Arizona Adventures*, 42–43.

up his tables, he determined to give a ball.[2] Accordingly, for some weeks there was much fluttering among the few representatives of the fair sex in Prescott and on the adjacent ranches. No lines were drawn in society and every woman was sure of an invitation. Among the men only was there likely to be anyone left out and that simply because there were more of them than the hall could accommodate.

The billiard hall was built very much like a New England barn of the common sort, the boards on the outside standing perpendicular and the cracks battened with strips about three inches wide. The inside walls were covered with thin cotton stuff, upon which wallpaper was pasted, so that to the eye they looked like substantial plaster, but yielded to the slightest touch. Overhead the cotton was left bare, looking quite like plaster. Benches of unpainted pine ran around the room, tin sconces for candles were fastened along the walls and chandeliers of the same material hung from the ceiling.

The whole number of women collected from Prescott and vicinity, from Skull Valley and other faraway ranches, numbered but twenty-seven and these were of all ages between ten and the greatest age acknowledged to by the sex. The gentlemen outmustered the ladies four to one. I regret my power of description is so limited, for this ballroom would afford much material for the portrayal of character and personal peculiarities. The men were drawn from every grade in life and from pretty much every quarter of our country and many parts of Europe. The women were of the Missouri, Texas and Northwestern types, uneducated and uncultivated. But one woman was present who had a legitimate claim to the title of lady. She was the wife of a doctor, who had sought the southwest for relief from a lung difficulty. She had lived in Washington, Philadelphia and Baltimore for many years, belonging to the best society of those places and was a well-educated and highly accomplished lady. Her house in Prescott was a favorite resort with the civil and military officials and a

2. This dance was held in The Quartz Rock on November 8, 1864. This was the new saloon built by William Hardy and operated by John P. Bourke, Charles Ott running Hardy's adjoining store. The "soiree" was deemed "quite a success," despite the dearth of women. In addition to dancing, the billiard table and stock of liquor proved popular until after midnight when the assembly marched off to supper. *Arizona Miner*, November 23, 1864; December 14, 1864.

place where we could refresh our memories with a glimpse of Eastern culture and refinement.

All the Western girls had called upon Mary Leib for advice as to their toilets.[3] The Ehle girls, who were here in force, had all been benefited by a suggestion from madam. They were the belles of the ball and Miss Olive was positively bewildering in her beauty. It was almost impossible to believe that a young woman possessing such a beautiful face and figure, with such an intelligent face, could be so ignorant and uncultivated in speech as she was. She was naturally graceful and ladylike in her manners and, if one saw her at a distance from which he could not hear her speak, he would never suspect her want of cultivation. On this very evening Barr came up to where I sat watching the dancing and said, "What might not a fellow be tempted to do if that girl only had an education?"

"You mean Olive?"

"Of course. I'd propose before tomorrow morning, Curtis, if she was only half as accomplished as she looks."

During the evening the fair Olive made a remark which I have often seen in the funny columns of the newspapers, but which, so far as she was concerned, was at the time original with her. Bob Postle was sitting by the side of the frontier belle, making himself a little more familiar with her fan, handkerchief and other knickknacks than she thought proper, when she suddenly turned and, giving him an indignant flash of her blue eyes, said, "Go slow, old hoss, or you may get hit."[4]

For reasons already mentioned, I cannot dance. I took a seat under one of the tin sconces and watched the participants in the festivities. Of course, in a ballroom where there were so many

3. Mary Catherine Smith was raised by Moravian parents and received a seminary education prior to her marriage to Charles Leib in 1852. A lady of culture and refinement, Mary followed her husband across the country and literally walked from Santa Fe to Prescott with the original detachment of troops assigned to Fort Whipple. Two years after the death of her husband in 1865, she married Hezekiah Brooks, a probate judge who had boarded with them. Childless, Mary and her new husband adopted a Yavapai toddler in 1869. She died in Prescott on November 18, 1891. Smith, *Captive Arizona*, 79-84.

4. Postle seems to have had additional problems with women. In 1865 he fell in love with a woman who did not return his affection. He engaged Sheriff John P. Bourke to plead his case, but the lawman, described as "gay and fascinating and popular among the ladies," seemed to charm the lady himself, despite having a wife in California. Postle took offense and intimated about Prescott that Bourke was a cad. Bourke demanded a retraction. Postle refused to back down. Cooler heads soon prevailed and bloodshed was averted, but both men were ridiculed in the press. Postle finally found the woman he had always wanted in September of 1867 when he married a fifteen-year-old neighbor. *Daily Alta California*, November 12, 1865; *Prescott Daily Courier*, May 20, 2001.

men and so few women, there was a constant demand for the hands of the ladies in the dance, so that they had little if any rest. All were kept constantly on their feet through the night and only the men seemed to get any relaxation. After the ball had been under way for about two hours, a Jew trader named Moses Barth entered with a lady on his arm and crossing the hall took a seat near me. In common with nearly everyone in the room, I took an occasional glance at the strange lady to see if she was anyone I had ever met before. In a community like that of Prescott, everyone for thirty miles around was well known to everybody else. The new lady was a stranger. She was dressed well, well-mannered and did not appear to be over twenty years old. She went upon the floor and danced several sets with Barth and friends to whom he presented her.

After a time there was considerable confusion in a distant part of the hall, in the midst of which I saw Doctor Charles Leib, Moses Barth and the strange young lady in earnest and somewhat excited conversation, which ended by the two last-named disappearing from the room.[5] At the beginning of the fracas, the Ehle girls came running to the bench on which I was sitting, laughing in a very boisterous manner.

"What is the matter?" I asked of Amy.

"Didn't you see that gal yere?"

"The one with Moses Barth?"

"Yis, that critter."

"Who was it?"

"Little Sol, the Jew."

"Impossible!"

5. Doctor Charles Leib had been appointed to West Point in 1842, but was forced to leave because of physical disability. He graduated from medical school in Philadelphia, but spent more time immersed in Illinois politics and newspapers. Leib received an appointment as federal mail agent, but sought a military career and received a commission as a first lieutenant in the 11th Infantry on May 21, 1861. Leib had made political enemies and his commission was rejected by the Senate. Appointed an assistant quartermaster in western Virginia, he found himself in financial difficulties and this commission was also rejected by the Senate. Ever the opportunist, Leib wrote *Nine Months in the Quartermaster's Department, or How to Make a Million* before he moved to New Mexico in 1863. He ran the *Santa Fé New Mexican* and acted as a surgeon at Fort Union prior to moving to Prescott in 1864. A political opponent in New Mexico said of him: "An imposter of the most arrant kind, he moves from community to community, making pretensions of the most lofty character, plants himself upon the people as a public pauper and thus lives as long as the different communities will subsist him." He died there on January 21, 1865. *San Francisco Bulletin*, March 23, 1865; *Arizona Miner*, November 23, 1864.

Solomon Barth. Photograph from James A McClintock's *Arizona*.

"Yis, 'twas him, all dressed up in wimmin's close. Looked first rate, though, didn't he? 'Bout the best lookin' gal in the crowd, t' my eye."

It was as Amy said. Moses and Solomon Barth were brothers, who kept a clothing store on the *plaza*.[6] Solomon was a little fellow in size, not more than seventeen years old and beardless as a girl. He had dressed himself from their stock of ladies' goods and millinery and come to the ball. When discovered, all the gentlemen and ladies were disposed to treat the matter as a joke, after the free and easy manner of the frontier, but Doctor Leib looked upon it as an insult to his wife and requested the masquerader to withdraw.

For a few moments after this occurrence the ladies and gentlemen remained seated or grouped in the corners, talking. Rising to go to Mrs. Leib for a moment, I had taken but a step or two when everyone behind me broke into loud laughter, the Ehle girls fairly screaming. Turning round to see what was the matter, another group, still behind me, began to laugh. Mary Leib approached and said, "Lieutenant, the back of your coat is covered with tallow which dripped from the candle under which you have been sitting."

I withdrew to an anteroom and, taking off my coat, found a mass of tallow heaped in ridges from my collar to the middle of my back. I was in dismay at my mishap and stood contemplating the ruin of my only uniform coat so far from a military tailor. At this juncture Mary Ehle, the oldest of the girls, entered and told me that if I would take it round behind the hall, I would find Nettie Osborne ironing.[7] By scraping the tallow off with a case knife, close to the nap, then laying a few thicknesses of straw wrapping paper over the place and letting Nettie run her hot flatiron over the paper, every vestige of the tallow would be taken out.

6. Solomon Barth crossed the plains to San Bernardino in 1856 and began freighting and trading in Arizona five years later. In 1863 he formed a partnership with Aaron Barnett and they opened stores in Prescott and Weaver, dealing in general merchandise. The *Arizona Miner* reported on September 7, 1864: "The store of Barth & Barnett on Montezuma street, next to the post office, is also a creditable building. The proprietors have a well assorted supply of goods, and are soon to have more from California, where Mr. Barnett has lately been. Barth & Barnett are enterprising young men." Although Solomon did have a brother identified variously as Moses or Morris, his conspirator in this practical joke may have been his partner Aaron Barnett. After a long career that included being captured by Indians and serving time in the penitentiary, in addition to making a fortune in trading and holding several political offices, Solomon Barth died at St. Johns, Arizona, on November 30, 1928. At one time Barth held title to the south rim of the Grand Canyon after signing a treaty for the land with the Navajo. Solomon Barth and Aaron Barnett, Hayden Arizona Pioneer Biographies, Arizona State University.

7. Nettie Osborne cannot be positively identified.

This was the substance of Mary's directions, but by no means her language. I followed it to the letter. Behind the hall, under a canvas awning which stood in rear of the kitchen attached to the saloon, I found a woman ironing at that late hour in the night. She took my coat and put it in order and in a few moments I returned to the ballroom relieved in mind and of the tallow.

The Territorial Legislature met with the first winter months. It was composed of the principal men of the territory, its members being drawn from nearly every state in the Union and from many foreign countries. There were fire-eaters from the South and cool-headed men from the North, men with no education and men with the best education to be had in our schools and colleges. *Cœlum non animum mutant qui trans mare currunt* (Those who run across the sea, change the sky, not their soul) may be true of those who cross the sea, but I need not mention what scape graces are often made out of good Sunday school scholars and members of the Young Men's Christian Association when they cross the continent. The mining regions of the West bring out the man's secret character. Napoleon said scratch a Russian and you will find a Tartar. Is it not equally true if you scratch a Christian you will find a heathen?

The Legislature held its sessions in a long log building, which was divided into two sections of fifty feet by fifty feet and fifty feet by thirty feet, respectively. The former was used by the representatives and the latter by the council. The logs of which the capital was built were of pine, neatly squared, laid up horizontally and dovetailed at the corners. Inside a pine floor was laid and benches for the members were placed in rows, made like those of the New England district schoolhouses. At one end was a small stage for the speaker, or president, upon which sat a single chair and table. Before the stage was another table for clerks and secretaries. There were no galleries for spectators, but benches ran around the walls, with an extra one or two each side of the stage for such visitors as chose to attend. No paint adorned room or furniture.

On many of the evenings during the session of the Legislature, mock sessions and lectures filled up the time. In a community almost destitute of the refining influence of ladies' society, men were thrown entirely upon themselves for amusements and I need not say that these were usually rough in the extreme. The mock sessions were rich, to say the least; the lectures, however, were fine, and would have done credit to any lecture course in New England. Only one of these was in the spirit of burlesque, but with a Josh Billings and a Petroleum V. Nasby lecturing cast we can overlook one lecture of this character in Arizona.[8] A man by the name of Anderson delivered a lecture on the Aztecs and produced at different points of his discourse skulls of horses, donkeys, buffalos and wolves, with a heterogeneous collection of bones from the osseous structure of all these animals, calling them parts of the Aztec anatomy.[9] He kept his audience in a roar throughout the lecture, but not a twinkle of mirth could be discovered in his own face. The gravity with which he held a big skull of a mule in his left hand, while with his right forefinger he called attention to the craniological developments of the celebrated Aztecan statesman and chieftain, Hual-poptl-quacktl-beetl, who once governed the province now called Arizona, was inimitable. At the close of the lecture, the bones were taken in charge by the audience, who fenced with the ribs, had shillelagh fights with the thigh bones and enjoyed themselves somewhat after the style of Bret Harte's *Society Upon the Stanislaus*.[10]

8. Josh Billings was the name under which Henry W. Shaw became popular as a folksy American author in the post-Civil War period. Although his father had been a congressman from Massachusetts and counted presidents and senators among his friends, Billings assumed the persona of a barely literate country hick whose characters spoke and wrote in mangled English. He made a fortune writing and lecturing as a peer of Mark Twain and Petroleum V. Nasby. Billings died in Monterey, California, on October 14, 1885. David R. Locke was an Ohio newspaper editor who wrote letters and topical comments under the pen name of Petroleum Vesuvius Nasby. Locke's satire skewered slavery and the over-indulgence of alcohol while promoting woman's suffrage. His misspellings became as popular as those of Josh Billings. During the war he raised a company for active service, but the Ohio governor refused to offer a commission because Nasby's letters were worth more to the Union cause. Locke died in Toledo on February 15, 1888. Geary, *Geary's Guide*, 13–14; *San Francisco Bulletin*, October 14, 1885; Smith, *An Inkwell*, 130–31; *New York Tribune*, February 16, 1888.

9. James Anderson was the chief clerk of the Arizona House of Representatives in the First Territorial Legislature when he gave this humorous account of the Aztecs on November 10, 1864. The editor of the *Arizona Miner* took notice: "His audience was convulsed with laughter over his dry jokes and comical illustrations. His wit was ready, and his sarcasm without malignity. The relics which he had accumulated for the Historical Society will be a rare addition to the museum of that institution." A lawyer "of considerable ability," Anderson had come from Placer County, California, which he had represented in the state legislature. While on a visit to his former home, Anderson walked into the *Auburn Herald* office on October 5, 1866, began to read a newspaper and fell over dead. *Arizona Miner*, November 23, 1864; *Weekly Journal Miner*, November 30, 1866; *Sacramento Daily Union*, October 16, 1866.

10. Following the early death of his father, Francis Bret Harte's family moved to California in 1854 and he knocked about the mining settlements until appointed secretary of the U. S. Mint in San Francisco. He started out setting newspaper type, began his own paper which proved unsuccessful, and became editor of the popular *Overland Monthly*.

In the eastern end of the capital building, up under the roof, a Lodge of Free Masons had established themselves, under a dispensation from the State of California.[11] The brethren of the mystic tie had found much difficulty in rendering their hall a non-conductor of articulate masonry. The wooden building, so closely constructed of solid timber, carried sound to the listening non-elect assembled in the rooms below like a telephone. The double partitions and floors, with a plentiful supply of sawdust, soon corrected things so that the doings of the lodge edified no one but the members. For the same reason that men assembled almost nightly in the legislative halls, the Masonic brotherhood assembled as often in their hall. When bona fide candidates did not present themselves, the brethren acted in that capacity in turn, until they became expert capricornians. They could not only ride the ordinary old billy goat of civilization, but they could stick to the back of the veritable Rocky Mountain bighorn himself, mounting with him the tallest mountains and dropping with him to the lowest valleys, without losing the seat.

My duties as quartermaster kept me quite closely to the post. The other officers were frequently absent on one duty or another, doing gallant and brave service against the Apaches. Barr was particularly successful and never went out in search of a thieving party that he did not come up with it and inflict severe punishment.[12]

His humorous and insightful sketches of life, particularly in the mining camps, proved immensely successful. He came east and joined the staff of the *New York Evening Post*, but also contributed articles to the *Atlantic Monthly*. Harte became estranged from his family and accepted several consular posts in Europe until his retirement in 1885. He continued to write, although without his earlier brilliance, until his death on May 5, 1902, at Chamberley, near Aldershot, England. *[New York] Daily People*, May 7, 1902.

11. The Aztlan Lodge of Free Masons was formally organized on July 23, 1865. The Prescott Masons had been meeting since 1864, but Charles Curtis, the first secretary, "left unwritten many items which would to-day be of great value to us." As early as September 27, 1864, fraternity members gathered at the Prescott cemetery to bury a miner named Hopkins who had died at Fort Whipple of typhoid fever. Masons who attended the services included Captain Anderson and Lieutenants Barr and Curtis, Governor Goodwin, several judges and the speaker of the House of Representatives. At that time there were discussions about forming a lodge at Prescott. Although Curtis does not mention the fact, he was also a charter member of the Arizona Historical Society when it was established on November 7, 1864. *Arizona Weekly Journal-Miner*, July 1, 1891; *Arizona Miner*, October 5, 1864; December 14, 1864.

12. There are records of two successful scouts by Lieutenant Barr. He left Fort Whipple on December 26, 1864, with thirteen men from the 5th Infantry and seven men from the 1st New Mexico Cavalry and returned on January 5, 1865. On January 1 his party surprised an Apache camp at noon, killing four and recovering two head of cattle. Barr led another scout of eleven men from the 5th Infantry and seven men from the 1st New Mexico Cavalry from January 20 to January 26. On January 24 there was a large skirmish with a band of Apaches which resulted in the deaths of twenty Indians and the wounding of several of

All pursuits were made on foot, for, as I have already mentioned, the number of horses had become so reduced that but few of the cavalry could be mounted. When the Indians jumped a ranche, the news could rarely reach us until the day after, so that the marauders would have a full days' start before a pursuit could begin. This, however, never seemed to prevent Barr from overtaking them and at last, in all desperate cases, it got to be the custom to send him. Everybody got to believing in his luck.

To see a detachment of heavily-armed and heavily-laden foot soldiers start out after the Apaches, a day after the thieves had successfully raided a ranche twenty miles away, certainly did not promise success. But under Barr's command no march ever failed of its object.

With the approach of winter the Indians became more quiet. Only when hunger made some of them desperate did they commit any thefts and these were generally trivial, merely the taking of a single animal or a small quantity of supplies, showing clearly enough that but a few were engaged. One night they stole a blooded stallion belonging to King Woolsey, which was kept at a ranche eight miles from Prescott.[13] The animal was very valuable and much prized by the owner. Next morning the carcass, minus the hind quarters, was found by the roadside, a short distance from the corral. I think more indignation was expressed in the barrooms and saloons of Prescott over the perverted taste for horse flesh which led the Apache to eat the noble steed, rather than keep him for his own riding.

So the winter passed away, mild, like nearly all Rocky Mountain winters, only stormy in March. With books and magazines,

---

Barr's party. One of these men, John Sands of Barr's company, died on February 22, 1865, as the result of an arrow wound in his shoulder. Elliott Coues gave details of the case in a paper on the nature and treatment of arrow wounds that he treated while at Fort Whipple. Unaccountably, Sands's case is referred to as "G. S., Co. F, 5th U. S. Inf." Post Returns, Fort Whipple, January, 1865; John Sands Pension Records; Coues, "Some Notes," 323–24.

13. King Woolsey was one of the notable pioneers of Arizona. He reached Yuma in 1860 with a horse, a rifle, a pistol, and five dollars to his name. Woolsey started working as a mule driver, soon owned his own mule team and within mere months had signed contracts to deliver hay to Union posts. Unionists considered him a Southern sympathizer although he did not support the 1862 rebel invasion and made a small fortune selling supplies to Federal garrisons. Woolsey led several expeditions against the Apaches that boosted his popularity, although his actions might now be considered brutal and inhumane. The Indians retaliated at one point by driving off stock valued at $10,000. Woolsey was repeatedly elected to the state legislature, lost a significant portion of his wealth in a mining operation and died on his ranch outside of Phoenix on June 29, 1879. Farish, *History of Arizona* 2: 215–224.

King Woolsey. Courtesy of Sharlot Hall Museum Library & Archives / SHM Photographs / PO-0467P.

the amusements I have mentioned, occasional calls upon friends at Prescott and an evening now and then in the back room of the sutler's store, the season passed away pleasantly. With spring we selected a large piece of ground in the river bottom and started a post garden. We dug a trench across the creek from bank to bank, about four feet wide, and filled it to the top with tamped clay. This made the water, which often, when the summer was dry, flowed through the loose sand without appearing on the surface, pour freely over the crest of the dam. By a ditch we took the water to our garden, for irrigating purposes. The garden was a success and we were all summer independent of the market.

Chapter 39

Fight at Red Rocks

After we had been at Fort Whipple some months, Captain Anderson was appointed colonel of a California regiment of Volunteers and left for San Francisco in February of 1865.[1] His successor appeared in the person of Captain John Thompson, of the 1st New Mexican Cavalry. This officer had been a private and non-commissioned officer in the Regular cavalry for many years. At the formation of Kit Carson's regiment—the above mentioned cavalry—a number of old sergeants of Regulars, who knew the Spanish language well, were appointed to commissions and Thompson was among them. With these officers it was nearly always difficult for the Regular officers to get along. We were constantly obliged, in order not to awaken their resentment and ill-will, to treat them with the greatest deference and respect. The familiarity in which

1. The *Arizona Miner* reported that Captain Allen Anderson received orders from the War Department on January 25, 1865, to report at department headquarters to be mustered as colonel of the 8th California. After completing the necessary paperwork, Anderson left Fort Whipple on February 9 for his new assignment with an escort commanded by Lieutenant Barr. The editor said of the captain: "He has endeared himself to our citizens by his genial manners and gentlemanly deportment since his arrival, and his efforts to subdue their Indian enemies." To further show their respect for Captain Anderson, the citizens of Prescott sent the department commander a request that he and his new regiment be assigned to Fort Whipple. *Daily Alta California*, March 23, 1865; April 15, 1865.

we indulged among ourselves, regardless of rank, we dared not show toward these officers.[2]

Thompson was an uneducated man, who always fancied we were presuming on our superior acquired ability and made our lives as miserable as he possibly could. He took, for some reason of which I am still in ignorance, a decided antipathy to me and left no opportunity unimproved to annoy me. As quartermaster and commissary, my duties belonged strictly to the post and I was not by custom subject to detached service, except in a dearth of officers, occasioned by absence or sickness. With the New Mexican Cavalry, we numbered six officers, and it rarely happened that more than two were absent at any one time. This, however, did not prevent Captain Thompson from seizing every opportunity to send me out on difficult and dangerous service. One adventure consequent upon this disposition I will now relate.

My cattle herd was kept out grazing in the valley and on the hills to the north of the post, the sheep and goats to the south. The first were in charge of a Mexican named Antonio Jarrimillo, who had come with me from New Mexico.[3] He was a short, shock-headed fellow, whose Indian taint showed itself in his dusky skin, high cheekbones and grave and silent demeanor. Wrapped in a blanket, which was continued about his waist by a red woolen sash, his hands and arms never appeared to be visible, except when withdrawn to manufacture the *cigarritos* which he unceasingly smoked. Below the blanket a few inches of dirty buckskin breeches would be seen, confined at the knee by three horn buttons. His black, rough calves were naked and his feet covered by Indian moccasins. On his head he wore a broad-brimmed, low-crowned straw hat. My sheep were herded by a tall Pike County Missourian, of the most unsymmetrical pattern of that unsymmetrical race. His headgear was of

2. Captain Thompson's conduct was not exactly in accord with Regular Army regulations, as William Fourr remembered. Fourr explained how Thompson casually assembled men for an Indian scout: "While mining near Prescott I went on several scouting trips with the soldiers. Captain Thompson, the commanding officer who was a good friend of mine, would come into camp and say, 'You fellows want to go out with me? I've got lots of grub.'" On another occasion, Fourr told what happened to an Indian captive: "The next morning the captain set some of the soldiers to guard him, as they followed behind the rest of the troops. They were going to put him on some reservation or something. After awhile we heard a shot and the captain said, 'I am afraid my lambs got him.' Sure enough, when the soldiers came up they said that the Indian tried to get away and that they had shot him. Well, you know, he would have been an awful nuisance to guard all the way to the reservation." Fourr, "Reminiscences," 73.

3. Antonio Jarrimillo cannot be further identified.

straw, a steep-shaped hat, with a turned down brim, beneath which the most conspicuous object seemed to be a cob pipe, which he smoked with the same untiring persistence that the Mexican did his *cigarritos*. His nose was thin and slightly aquiline, his chin receding and covered with a spare yellow beard, his hair long and lanky, having the appearance of washed out and faded tow. His back made a regular outward curve from the back of his neck to his legs, while his breast made a corresponding inward curve. A pair of old butternut pantaloons, held up by one suspender, a dirty flannel shirt of uncertain color, over which was worn a long brown overcoat, open in front, made up the wardrobe of this man.

These two hopefuls had charge of my herd and flock, having strict orders never to go over a mile away and on no account to fall asleep on duty or leave their charges for an instant. These injunctions I have reason to believe were not strictly observed, as the rascals were afterward found to have occasionally sold an animal and pocketed the proceeds, reporting it strayed or stolen.

I was one afternoon sitting in my office writing, when Antonio burst in breathlessly exclaiming, "*Los Indios*! *Teniente, los Indios han arrebatado los ganados*!" ("The Indians! The Indians! Lieutenant, they have snatched the cattle!"). I went out immediately and, climbing to the top of the blockhouse, looked in the direction indicated by the Mexican. Far to the northeast, about four miles away, I saw the herd disappearing over a hill, driven by a small party of Indians on foot. Descending to the ground, I went to the commanding officer and reported, asking for a detail from the cavalry to go in pursuit of the marauders. In answer to this, the captain said he would send a party of infantry, with four days' rations. To my remonstrance that the delay necessary for the men to get their rations would enable the Indians to secure their booty and my request that cavalry might be sent without rations, in order to make a rapid pursuit, Captain Thompson exclaimed, "Take twelve men from the infantry, mount them on anything you have in the corral and make your own pursuit, sir!"

"Thank you, sir," I replied. "Tell the party with the rations to follow my trail."

"Perhaps I'll not send them," he said, as I disappeared into the sergeant's office to select my party. A long knowledge of F Company had made me well acquainted with every man in it, so I was not long in selecting twelve men who were good riders and brave soldiers.[4]

In fifteen minutes after the first alarm I was galloping out of the corral with twelve soldiers, armed with their rifles and carrying forty rounds of ammunition. The Mexican, Antonio, accompanied us to show the trail, a business with which he was well acquainted.

We rode down the valley and over the hill where I had seen the herd disappear, without delay. We passed several oxen which were too old to keep up under the sharp driving of the Indians, their bodies filled with rows of arrows on each side, still alive, looking frightened and in pain. We did not pause to shoot them, as in mercy we ought, for everything depended upon speed.

Over the hill, we found no difficulty in following the trail, the flying herd having turned up the soil so that even a greenhorn could not have gone astray. My Mexican seemed the only one who did not stick to the trail, seeming to use every effort to get us away from it, until one of the men suggested that he was afraid to come up with the Indians and was doing this to get us off the scent. I paid no further attention to him, but went off without him, and have never seen him from that day to this.

We were fast approaching the Red Rocks, to the west side of which the trail seemed to lead. On the right side of the road,

4. Although this story told by Curtis is generally true, the following account from the *Arizona Miner*, dated April 12, 1865, gives a slightly different version:

"On the morning of the 25th of March the herder in charge of the Government herd at Fort Whipple, came into the post and reported that Indians had attacked him and captured the heard [*sic*] within a mile of the fort. A detail of ten men and a citizen guide was made at once, with three days' rations, and sent in pursuit, under the command of Lieut. Abeytia. In the meantime, Lieut. Curtis, the Quartermaster, with three employés, pursued on horseback. He soon found the trail, and came up with an ox, left by the Indians, with eleven arrows in his body. The trail led directly to the eastern side of the red rocks, where it entered into a deep cañon. The Lieutenant lost the trail upon entering the rocks, and passed through them for two miles, without seeing an Indian. After returning to the post, one of his men, a Mexican, said that upon entering the rocks he saw thirty Indians, but did not dare to tell Lieut. Curtis, for fear he would attempt a fight.

"Two hours later Lieut. Abeytia entered the rocks at the same place, and found the Indians and stock. A desperate fight took place. The ten soldiers were opposed by over sixty warriors, who were soon reinforced by some thirty others, supposed to have been in pursuit of Lieut. Curtis. The Indians tried every way to outflank the soldiers, and get them into the bottom of the cañon, where they could have killed them off to a man. Lieut. Abeytia deserves great credit for his conduct during the fight, and the coolness with which he conducted the whole affair, and extricated the command from their perilous position. One soldier was killed, two others wounded, and twelve Indians were killed. More of the soldiers must certainly have been injured, but that during the whole fight the wind was blowing a gale, which must have broken the aim of the Indians with their light arrows." *Daily Alta California*, May 1, 1865.

five miles from Fort Whipple, on the route going north, is a granite formation called the Red Rocks, skirting the way for a distance of eight miles. It appears to be an irregular wall, breaking into occasional pinnacles from 200 to 300 feet high, and in no place being less than seventy-five feet high. This wall encloses a large area in which grow pine trees and cedars, with beautiful open glades and a clear crystal brook running through the whole. The enclosure is eight miles long, five miles wide, and there are only two points where it is possible to enter it, one on the north side where the brook debouches into the plain, and one at the southeast angle where a narrow entrance, which will not allow two horsemen to enter it abreast, are the only means of ingress.

It was toward this last entrance, five miles from the fort, that all the hoof tracks tended. I saw at once that the Indians must be inside the rocks with the cattle and that if I wanted to retake them I must enter too. I led the way into the narrow portal, the walls of which my feet grazed as I rode through, followed in single file by my twelve men. Arriving inside, I found myself standing on a ledge of several hundred feet in extent, upon which my inexperienced eye could see no track or trail. I paused while my men gathered around me and our panting horses recovered their breath. Presently a gentle breeze from the south wafted the odor of cattle to our nostrils. The smell was unmistakably bovine. I called the attention of the men to it and, after a general sniffing of the breeze, they all agreed with me. To the south of us was a thick chaparral of dwarf oaks and thorn bushes through which the eye could not penetrate. I dismounted from my horse and clambered to the top of an irregular pinnacle, from which I could see over the tops of the trees. I strained my eyes to try to look into the opening beyond the waving branches, but for a long time without seeing anything suspicious. Just as I was about to turn away I saw an ox cross the opening and disappear behind a jutting boulder.

I slid down from my perch and ordered the men to secure their horses in the trees, which done, we began picking our way cautiously through the bushes. As we proceeded, we found plenty of proof that our cattle had gone this way—the branches of the trees were broken and the stubs were covered with bunches of hide scraped from their skin. After a few moments we got where we could look into an open space about fifty feet wide and several hundred feet long. At the farther end were clustered our cattle. On one side of the ravine, the side toward the interior of the Red Rocks, the wall was formed of irregular masses of granite, of all sizes and shapes, which were well fitted to afford concealment to an enemy. On the other side rose a steep slope, up which one might pass with some difficulty to the outside country.

I did not much fear the Indians, for Antonio, when I had examined him as to how many Indians were in the party that captured the herd, had said there were not over twenty. Besides, when I looked from the top of the blockhouse, I saw that there could not be over that number driving the cattle. As I looked from the underbrush into the ravine, where the cattle were gathered and quietly grazing, I could see that the hill on the left held no enemy, as it afforded no means of concealment, but what might be in the ragged rocks of the right side I was unable to guess, although I felt quite sure there were not many Indians. There was a chance, too, that finding they were so closely pursued and that they did not have a great advantage in numbers, they might have abandoned the cattle and fled by way of the northern entrance to the rocks.

I ordered the men to push on with me from rock to rock, along the right side. We took advantage of every obstacle which would afford us concealment and protection from the fire of an enemy should there be one. Step by step we crept along until at last fifty feet intervened between us and the chaparral from which we emerged, when suddenly the air was filled with the demoniac notes of the Apache war whoop. We were corralled!

For a moment, which seemed an age, it seemed as if my heart would not get back on its right place and my eyes take in the situation. I am not of that temperament that I can preserve the coolness which the novel writer gives to his Indian fighters when the war whoop first bursts on my ear. My heart will not stay down and I always wish I was somewhere else. The surprise over, however, I recover my coolness and have no difficulty in doing the best I can. And so it was this time. I encouraged my men and made the most of our shelter. I got them well back toward the perpendicular rock and hastily threw up the loose stones between the boulders to afford a shelter. Arrows began coming in from both sides of us, showing that a party of Indians must have been concealed in the chaparral as we came through, in order to catch us in this trap.

We could see no enemy, but we had no difficulty in hearing them. It seemed as if at least 300 throats were swelling with the infernal yells that rent the air. We crouched low and peered out of the crevices of our fortification. For a long time we saw no Indians, but presently Tom Cleary's rifle spoke and I saw a redskin leap out of his hiding place and drop limp among the rocks. "First blood for us, Liftinent," said Tom, as he coolly began loading.

"And the second, be jabbers!" exclaimed Cleary's bunky, Hoey, as in answer to the crack of his rifle an Apache dropped from a high rock to which he had been crawling to get a downward shot into our rifle-pit. He had hardly uttered the words when an arrow flew into the crevice through which the rifle was thrust and went nearly through his arm, between wrist and elbow.

"The third for the divils, Tom," said Hoey coolly. "Will you pull it out for me?"

"Don't pull it out, George," answered Cleary. "If ye do th' barb'll stay in the flish and its pizened. Push it through."

"Is that the way it's done?" asked Hoey. "Then I'll cut it within an inch of me arm, for I don't care about pushing a full yard of Ingins weapin through the flish." Saying this, Hoey coolly cut off the arrow shaft within three inches of his arm and as coolly pushed the stone-headed missile through the flesh and placed it in his pocket, "as a keepsake."[5]

For some time after the killing of the two Indians nothing occurred. Even the war whoops ceased and a novice might have thought the enemy had gone. But I feared they were only changing their tactics, dreaded lest they might find some means of scaling the wall behind us and so compel us to run into the open space, where we should be entirely exposed to their murderous fire. I hoped that the captain had not adhered to what he had said

5. Doctor Coues explained that on Apache arrows "the heads were all of stone, quite small and sharp, and very brittle, so that they usually shivered when they struck a bone and the fragments were not easily removed. They were only held in place with gum in the shallow notch at the end of the small hardwood stick that was set in the large reed, and thus were always left in the wound when the stick was pulled out. It is within my certain knowledge that they were in some cases poisoned; the common opinion was that the septic substance was derived from a deer's liver into which a rattlesnake had been made to inject its venom, and which was then left to putrefy in the sun." Coues, *Zebulon Pike* 2: 747.

when I left the post, but had sent the infantry. I often raised my eyes to the top of the hill on the other side of the ravine, hoping that I might see the bluecoats coming to the rescue.

It was getting past the middle of the afternoon and already the shadows were deepening in the bottom of the ravine. Our anxiety was fast increasing, for we knew if help did not come before night, our chances for escape were small. Hunger and thirst, intensified by the situation, began to prey upon us. I was reviewing the chances of help and how long it would take the soldiers to secure their four days' rations and make the five mile march to the Red Rocks, when my further reflections were suddenly interrupted by the falling of a small stone from the ledge over our heads. Looking upwards we saw six of the savages had affected a lodgment on a shelf above us. Before we could raise our pieces to fire, a half dozen arrows came down upon us, instantly killing two men, and slightly wounding three more, including myself. There was nothing for it now but to break into the open space and try a run for the hill opposite. As I have already mentioned, I am lame in the left leg and hence not very good in a race. Accordingly, I said to my men, "Never mind me, men, save yourselves."

"We'll die with the Liftinent, if it comes to that," said Cleary. "But we'll not desert him."

"That's so," answered Hoey and the men restrained their pace to mine. The war whoops had begun again when we discovered the Apaches on the rocks and as we appeared in the open the arrows flew like rays of light. As we neared the middle of the space, I said, "Face about and go backwards. They will hardly dare show their heads if they think it will draw a bullet."

I had hardly spoken these words when an arrow struck me in the side. I stood still a moment, saw my men face about and my eyes sought the summit of the hill. Just then I saw Barr's head appear above the crest, heard him shout, "Hold on, Curtis, old boy, we are here!" heard the shouts of the men, the rattle of the musketry and I fell, to know no more until I waked up in my bed at the post.

My wound was not bad, but the *Arizona Miner*, which went to press that evening, printed a paragraph to the effect that I was "mortally wounded." This paragraph went east and was copied by the Eastern papers. Letters from relatives and friends began to pour in to the commandant, making inquiries about me, chiefly anxious to know if I died possessed of property. A few paid some fine tributes to my memory and one doubted whether I was wounded at all, venturing the surmise that I inserted the paragraph myself to create a sensation. So goes the world.[6]

All of my 300 cattle were retaken but five. Of the Indians, five were known to be killed. Our loss numbered three, one man of the twelve I took in pursuit dying of his wounds after reaching the hospital.

I never saw Antonio again after I lost sight of him near Red Rocks or the horse upon which he was mounted. After the fellow had gone, there were plenty of people to tell me that he was in the habit of sleeping when in charge of the herd. There is no doubt but he was asleep when the Indians crept up and run it off.

The reader is perhaps anxious to know how Thompson came to send the detachment of infantry after the remark he made as I was leaving his office. Barr told me that he did actually countermand the order and returned the men to their quarters. This stirred up the feelings of my fellow Regular and he went to the commanding officer and remonstrated with such success that he secured the remainder of F Company and came to the rescue. A lucky thing for us.

6. Curtis must have been injured in this encounter since news that he had been wounded did make its way to New England. On April 17, 1865, L. A. Beale of the *Boston Evening Transcript* wrote the following inquiry to Colonel Gardiner Tufts, Military Agent for the State of Massachusetts:

"Very meagre intelligence has been received (through the columns of the Arizona Miner—no date) by the friends of Lieut. Chas. A. Curtis of the Fifth U. S. Infantry, stationed at Fort Whipple—that he (Lt. Curtis) was relieved of the Quartermaster's Department, Jan. 30, and subsequently fell, mortally wounded, in some sort of a battle. No particulars given.

"His friends are anxiously seeking further information concerning his fate, and so I write you to request that you would be so kind as to ascertain if any official intelligence of like character has been received at headquarters. Lt. Curtis was largely interested in the mines, being reported worth half a million."

This fortune reportedly amassed by Curtis was mere rumor. When appointed as military instructor at Norwich University in 1870, the Federal census listed him as owning no real estate and only $700 in personal property. L. A. Beale to Gardiner Tufts, April 17, 1865, Letters Received by the Adjutant General; 1870 U. S. Census, Vermont, Washington County, Northfield.

Chapter 40

Politics and Punishment

My post life went along smoothly, until the Secretary of the Territory, Richard C. McCormick, found it necessary that he should go to New York on business. Before he left, he made an arrangement with me to edit his paper, the *Arizona Miner*. It was not to be known to anyone but the foreman of the office that I was the editor and the paper was to be kept strictly out of politics until the secretary should return.

The new duty had its fascinations for me and I took great pleasure for some time in playing editor, but the attempt to keep my connection with the *Miner* a secret failed. My style, or something, betrayed me, probably sentiments which I was heard to utter in private, appeared in the paper and aroused suspicion, but however it may have come about, Captain Thompson one day charged me with being the editor and I did not deny it.

Soon after this a candidate began to stir for the election as delegate to Congress. He was a scion of a rich Connecticut family named Joseph P. Allyn, who had traveled extensively in Europe, had obtained an associate judgeship in Arizona and settled there for his health. He was evidently a consumptive. Governor Goodwin had gone to San Francisco, so that the coast was clear for Allyn. He soon made friends with our captain, who, being a Volunteer, was interested in politics and secured his assistance in the campaign.

The captain called upon me one day and proposed that I should use the *Miner* to support Judge Allyn for Congress and order my eighty civilian employees to vote for him. When I answered that it would be a gross betrayal of Secretary McCormick's confidence, as well as a departure from the practice of Regular officers for me to be concerned in a political campaign, he replied that the judge would make it for my interest to assist him, that he would present my name and urge me for a staff appointment, a promotion it was known I wanted. I would not promise.

An attack was then made upon me in another way. A Union League Club had been formed in Prescott, at a time when the Secessionists in the country had threatened to capture the territory, and all Union men, including the officers and a few of the best non-commissioned officers of the garrison had joined it. All of my quartermaster's men were members. One evening I was summoned to a meeting of the club and when I got there I found an attempt was to be made to coerce me into using the newspaper in my charge for the support of Judge Allyn. I patiently heard all the arguments without replying and then moved that the club adjourn sine die. Captain Thompson made a somewhat sarcastic speech on my motion and advised me to withdraw it, as it was sure of defeat. I insisted upon it being put, it having been seconded by Sergeant Linstock, the same man who was lost with me in the hills of Los Valles Grandes. I had never seen the day when the enlisted men of my company were not friendly to me and I felt sure, by this act of the sergeant, where the other non-commissioned officers present would be when the vote should be tried. I was not as sure of the corral men or officers. The vote was put. Every quartermaster's man, all the soldiers and Barr voted with me.[1] The Union League adjourned by a two-thirds vote. This was a temporary triumph only, for the next day the commanding officer sent me on escort duty beyond Hell Cañon, as far as Bill Williams Mountain, a trip which took me away from my editorial duties for three

1. The post return for Fort Whipple showed that fourteen civilians worked for Lieutenant Curtis in 1865—nine in the quartermaster department and five in the subsistence department. Returns from Military Posts, 1806-1916.

weeks. It was no great loss to the readers of the *Miner*, however. I had discovered a Bowdoin College man among my quartermaster's men, a man whose style was unknown to our doughty captain. I threw the editorial mantle over his shoulders and left.[2]

My trip to the *cañon* was not of special interest, but as I have begun to tell all my adventures in Arizona, I suppose this must not be left out. I started about three o'clock in the afternoon, with fifteen soldiers, to escort a dozen men with their six wagons, who were going out to establish a camp near San Francisco Mountain. A turnpike company had been chartered by the Legislature the last winter to build a road from Prescott to the crossing of the Colorado Chiquito. These men were going to begin the work. The region around Bill Williams Mountain and beyond was not considered dangerous. It was a borderland between the Navajos on the north and the Apaches on the south. My first camp was at the north end of Red Rocks, the second at Bob Postle's, the third in Rattlesnake Cañon and the fourth at Bill Williams Mountain. As we crossed Rattlesnake Cañon, a fresh bear trail led up the northern ascent and several of my men asked to go and look for the bear. I did not think it prudent to reduce my force or run the risk of the men getting lost, should they stray from the road. Getting lost and never getting found is a frequent experience with soldiers in the Far West and I hesitated to allow my men to run any risks. We had not gone a half mile farther, however, before we saw a large grizzly bear scrambling up a steep ascent on the right of the road, apparently the same animal that had made the tracks we had observed below. I let the men go for him and they soon brought him down, thoroughly riddled with bullets. We took off his skin and fastened it over the wagon sheet, but did not take the carcass. It was too old and strong flavored.

We camped at night in an extensive meadow on the north of Bill Williams Mountain. This peak, though second in importance of the three principal mountains in this section of the territory, is far less lofty than its neighbor, Floyd, which is next in height to San Francisco Mountain. A fine stream flowed from the mountains

2. A politically motivated correspondent from Prescott wrote on July 20, 1865: "The editorship of the *Arizona Miner*, the only paper in our Territory, has been dropped by Lieutenant Curtis. It is now supposed to be edited by one Hamilton, late of the Los Angeles *Star*, said to be of strong secesh proclivities, and seriously threatened by an attack of Alcatraz confinement. The paper is the organization of our Territorial Administration, and the office is the center of Copperhead cogitations." *Sacramento Daily Union*, August 2, 1865.

and wound through the middle of the meadow, which was some 400 acres in extent and bears a good growth of grama grass. The surrounding hills and mountainsides were covered with fine pines and spruces. A few antelope were grazing on the far off side of the meadow as we turned into camp from the road, but they fled away into the forest like the wind when they saw us.

We were to stay at the mountains over one day before starting on our return. On the morning of this day, I permitted three of the men to go hunting for some black-tailed deer which had been seen on the edge of the meadow at daybreak. They were gone all day and at night two only returned. They brought a fine deer, but could tell nothing of their comrade. I ordered a fire built on an elevation which overlooked the country and had it kept burning all night, so that if the lost man should see it, he would come in. The night passed away and he did not return. I then directed several men to hunt for him and ordered them especially not to go out of sight of the fire. That they might see it in the daytime, pine and spruce branches were put on to make a dense smoke. The second day went by and all the men returned at night but the lost one. Next morning, just as we were hitching up the mules to leave, the missing soldier staggered into sight. I sent a saddle mule to bring him up to the fire. When he reached us, he appeared to be completely exhausted and in a starving condition. He could give no account of his wanderings or how he came to lose sight of his comrades. He had grown nearly insane with fear when his eyes caught sight of the smoke and he returned to camp.

I returned to Fort Whipple the morning after the *Miner* publication day, having been gone fifteen days in all. I had not hurried, but used the time in hunting and one day at Postle's in fishing. I had hardly got settled in my room when on April 26th I received an order from Captain Thompson relieving me from my duty as quartermaster and appointing the Mexican lieutenant, Antonio Abeytia, in my place.[3] I made no objections or remarks, but went

3. A native of Santa Fe, Antonio Y Abeytia was commissioned a first lieutenant in the 1st New Mexico Cavalry and was promoted to captain prior to his muster out on September 30, 1866. He was brevetted captain in the U. S. Volunteers "for gallantry in battle with Apaches in Arizona on the 24th of March, 1865." Abeytia moved to Socorro in 1871, ran a store that sold general merchandise and held several minor political offices. He was president of the Socorro County Bank when he died in that city on December 19, 1885. Despite his tense relations with Curtis, one editor remembered Abeytia as "well educated and a genial companion." Haines, *New Mexico*, 290-93; *Official Records*, ser. 1, 48, pt. 2, 1248; *Santa Fé Daily New Mexican*, November 19, 1873; *Galveston Daily News*, December 31, 1885.

Lieutenant Curtis in his office at Fort Whipple with Vic at his feet. Sketch from *Harper's Young People*

to work to take an inventory of the Government property in my hands in order to turn it over to my successor. In three days this was accomplished and I found myself once more attached to F Company for duty. I was not allowed to idle in the post, however, for on the second day after I finished the transfer, I was ordered to go to La Paz, a town on the Colorado River, 170 miles distant, "to inquire into the practicability of establishing a provost marshalship there." While I was reading the order and mentally reflecting that the captain was determined I should not run the

Miner, Barr entered and asked, "What do you suppose Abeytia has done?"

"Told all the corral men to vote for Allyn," I answered.

"Right. He just notified them if any man refused to vote for Allyn, he would discharge him."

"Did they agree to do so?"

"They have said nothing so far."

I began to get ready for my journey. A four-mule ambulance was furnished me, provided with three inside seats, the middle one so constructed that it could be let down to fill the space between the others and afford a comfortable bed. An escort of ten men and a corporal, detailed from the cavalry and infantry and mounted on the horses of the quartermaster's department, were ordered to report to me. Knowing from my order that I was to cross the Xuacaxella Desert, I called upon Captain Thompson to inquire about the water over that route and whether I should need to take along water kegs.[4]

The captain received me very affably, went on at some length to show me that he had done me a great service in relieving me from the quartermaster duty, assured me that I was of an adventurous turn, needed the excitement of field service and that he was showing special confidence and trust in me in sending me on this trip to La Paz. In regard to water on the desert, he said an expressman had just arrived from that route and reported water in three places on the plain, where it had gathered from the recent abundant rains. As for kegs, he did not see how he could possibly consent to any being taken by me, as he was contemplating an expedition in the direction of Green Valley and the Tonto Basin and should need every barrel and keg he could obtain.

I made no further effort to secure kegs, but took the captain's word that there was plenty of water on the desert and proceeded to complete my preparations for the journey. It was a green thing to do, to attempt to cross a desert without some means of carrying water to provide against accident. I have often since wondered at myself for being so inconsiderate, so unlike myself in other cases, so ready to fall into what now appears to me to have been a trap.

4. There seems to be no record of a region by this name, but Curtis may have relied upon a bad translation of what is now called the Coachella Desert.

Next day, about three o'clock in the afternoon, I started out of the fort by way of Prescott. A road had been constructed from that town, almost due north, running along the east side of Granite Range for some eight miles, when it passed through the range, a little west of north, to Mint Creek, from which point it turned a nearly acute angle and passed through Skull Valley. The ride from Fort Whipple to Mint Creek was fifteen miles long. Here we stopped for the night. The soldiers picketed their horses, my driver hobbled the mules and one man proceeded to get our supper of fried bacon, biscuit baked in a Dutch oven and coffee. On the seat in front of me I had a large roll containing a wool mattress, four blankets and a pillow. When night came, I let down the middle seat, unrolled the bedding, closed the curtains of the ambulance and had a very snug and private bedroom. The men slept in the grass by the roadside. They were well supplied with blankets, which were carried in the ambulance with the rations and cooking utensils.

In the morning we started for Skull Valley. The road for ten miles was a gradual ascent through a rough country, generally wooded, the hills rising on each side of the wheel tracks. As all this region was dangerous, I took the usual precautions against attack. Two men rode constantly in advance about 300 yards from the ambulance, two more rode the same distance behind and the remaining six, with the corporal, rode on each side of the carriage. When the country opened into a plain, this order was not strictly observed, for reason that cavalry is fretted in trying to maintain the pace of a trotting team. In this case, I directed the escort never to go more than half a mile beyond me or fall back more than that distance and never to lose sight of my carriage. This enabled the men to put their horses into a canter, dash ahead the proper distance, then drop into a walk until I overtook them and got half a mile beyond, when they would dash up again and so on as long as the country was open.

A ride of twenty miles took me to the Ehle ranche. As my wheels rattled up to the house, the whole family of girls poured out of the doorway and besieged me with questions until I was perfectly bewildered. I accepted their invitation to dinner and entered the house, where I found time to answer all the questions they could ask. I found Mr. Ehle had put considerable ground under cultivation and that vegetation promised good results. He reported that he had seen no Indians since last fall and thought they had finally disappeared from this section of the country.

Dinner at Skull Valley was furnished the enlisted men in the kitchen, while the officer was entertained in the family room. In the opinion of the Ehle family, there was no social or any other difference between officer and man and there is no doubt but the one received as many smiles as the other. Olive seemed to be the only one who showed a preference for a shoulder strap; she evidently had aspirations and seemed to realize her lack of accomplishments and education. The other members of the family knew each man of my escort and addressed him by his given name. Olive made the distinction of calling them by their surnames.

Dinner over, I took my seat in the ambulance, the men mounted their horses and we were ready for a start. The girls, with the exception of Miss Olive, crowded around the wheels, noisy in their farewells, good wishes and injunctions "to tak' car' yerself and don't let the Injins git yer skelp." Olive stood pensively in the doorway, fine-looking in her plain calico, for hers was a form and face that did not need setting off to make them attractive. At last she came forward and, going round to the side of the ambulance opposite to where her sisters stood, dropped a little note upon my seat. In another instant we were off. As soon as I was well clear of the house, I picked up the note so rudely scrawled, so badly spelled and read a wish that I would buy the writer some schoolbooks in La Paz and any others which I thought would benefit her to read. Poor Olive! Under favorable circumstances, among people who talked well and behaved well, with the advantages of school, everything was possible for her, but it seemed to me that the mere possession of books, without a competent instructor in the wilds of Arizona, would do her but little good. I pocketed the note, however, with the determination to get the books, even if I should be obliged to send to San Francisco for them.

We had journeyed but a short distance beyond the Ehle ranche when a horseman dashed into the wagon road, from the trail out of Prescott over which I rode in my search for Ferrin. He proved to be the mail carrier between Prescott to La Paz. He rode along the side of my carriage for some distance, talking about the dangers of the road and the escapes he had several times made. At last we came to where the road turns off sharply to the west, at right angles to the course it had followed since leaving Mint Creek. Here it entered Bell's Cañon, a deep ravine which separates the Kendrick Mountains on the north from the Weaver Mountains on the south. Just at the point of turning, stood the log house of a farmer. The mail carrier said he had a package for Richard Bell, who lived there, and suggested that if I wanted any eggs or chickens for supper this was a good place to buy them.[5] Accordingly, I rode up to the front door of the house and waited for someone to answer the mail carrier's knock. A woman came to the door, who proved to be Mrs. Bell. To the inquiry for Mr. Bell, she said that he and Cornelius Sage had started for La Paz three days before.[6] I asked her if she was alone and she said there was no one in the house but the wife of Mr. Sage. Mrs. Bell was a young woman, who had been but a few months married. She talked like a person of education and I afterwards learned that she was from Ohio and had received good school instruction.

I bought a couple of chickens, as many dozen eggs, bade goodbye to the ladies and started on. The road for the first mile or so after leaving Skull Valley climbs quite a steep grade. When I left the ranche, the mail carrier had wished me a pleasant journey and dashed off up the ascent at an easy canter. He had been gone but a short time when my advance guard shouted for me to look out. Moving forward in the driver's seat, I saw the mail carrier standing on a pinnacle by the wayside at the highest point of the road. Thinking he might have seen Indians, I dismounted my men, got the ammunition box into the rear of the ambulance, opened it and made a few other preparations for a fight.

5. William Fourr, an early miner in the Prescott area, remembered Richard Bell: "Bell lived in Bell's Canyon somewhere near Skull Valley and used to bring us beef. He was a jolly fellow and played the banjo. You know how miners are; some nights they would be all down in the mouth and swear that they were going to throw up everything and go back to California, then Bell would come along and play his banjo and sing some of his 'nigger' songs and in the morning they would have forgotten all about going. Bell was killed while going home from one of his trips to our camp." Fourr also remembered that Captain Thompson "asked us if we would go with him to bury a man by the name of Bell. As a matter of fact the mail carrier had buried him and we reburied him for the coyotes had dug him up." As late as 1896 the exact spot was still visible: "The spot is marked by a few stones only. It is in a lonely place in the canyon and is within a few feet of the wagon road. His remains are buried where he fell." Bell and Cornelius Sage were murdered on May 3, 1865. Fourr, "Reminiscences," 74; *Weekly Journal Miner*, February 19, 1896.

6. Cornelius Sage had been appointed sheriff of Yuma County on December 21, 1864, and officially took office on January 1, 1865. He was the first lawman from Yuma County to be killed while in office. Sage and Richard Bell were murdered on May 3, 1865. Ball, *Desert Lawmen*, 353–54.

Slowly we worked up the hill to the top, where we found the mail carrier standing beside his horse.

"What is it?" I asked, as we came to a halt.

"There is something in the road down there by Ferrin's grave that looks like two dead men," was the reply.

"Take my glass and look," I said, handing him my field glass.

After a long and silent gaze, the mail carrier handed back the glass, saying, "Two dead bodies in the road, sir. I fear they are Bell and Sage."

We began the descent into the *cañon*, and after half an hour's time reached the pile of stones which marked Ferrin's grave. In the road, but a few rods beyond, lay the naked and mutilated bodies of two men. Both had been scalped and the leg of one had been eaten off by the wolves. One body, which was pointed out by the mail carrier as that of Mr. Bell, showed a man of six feet in stature and finely proportioned; the other was that of a much smaller man, but one of a firm and compact build.

Our first thought was of the two women we had left but a mile and a half back, unconscious widows, but we could not turn back to tell them—that must be deferred until my return from La Paz. We dug a second grave, at the foot of Ferrin's, and dragged the two bodies to it in the manner once before described, tumbled them in, filled up the hole and built a second pyramid of stones.

Chapter 41

Into the Desert

The ride through the *cañon* was safely accomplished and night found us encamped at Willow Spring. This spring was surrounded with immense boulders of granite, so rotten that the pieces which had long been exposed to the weather would crush even in the hands. In fact, the bed of the spring and most the ground in the vicinity was composed of disintegrated granite. The spring would frequently fill up by the sliding in of the loose gravel, but it could easily be scooped out again. Water could be found almost anywhere within the space of a quarter of an acre by scooping away the gravel.

I met at this spring a Scotchman with his pack train, on his way to a mining claim near Prescott. I found him entertaining company through the long evening before bedtime. He had lived long in mining countries and possessed a fund of experience which seemed inexhaustible. The spring is also associated with a piece of wholesome discipline which I was obliged to administer and which I came near forgetting. One of the cavalrymen, by the name of Juan Trujillo, was a hard rider and did not take proper care of his horse.[1] In the first day's march, ending at Mint Creek, I saw that his

1. Juan Trujillo cannot be positively identified.

horse's back was swollen and ordered him to bathe and rub it, but he slighted the work. Next day, when we reached Ehle's ranche, one of the infantry soldiers received an injury by falling upon the pommel of his saddle. I therefore left the injured man at Ehle's with Trujillo's horse, which had grown worse during the second day, and put Trujillo on the other horse. Between Skull Valley and Willow Spring I kept my eye on the Mexican and soon saw that he abused his horse in many different ways. For one thing, he never dismounted at the steep ascents and descents, like the other men; he did not tighten the girth after leaving camp, until I ordered him to; riding his horse some time without the saddle blanket, which had worked out from under the saddle, and which he carried on his arm until I ordered him to replace it. When we arrived at the spring all the men bathed their horse's backs and rubbed them down, but this fellow threw himself on the ground and went to sleep. As soon as I put the guard on, I made Trujillo shoulder the saddle and walk post all night beside the sentinel, two hours on and one off. It cured him and the horse.

Our third day's journey was over a portion of the road so rough that we were unable to go faster than a walk, the slow walk of draught animals. The cavalry, which walked fast, was obliged to make frequent halts for the ambulance to come up. Small fragments of granite covered the whole face of the country, making a trotting gait impossible. When near a place now called Soldiers' Holes, because a few rifle pits were sunk there some time after I left Arizona, Corporal Duffy called my attention to some blood in the road.[2] I left the ambulance and examined the locality thoroughly. There had evidently been some kind of a skirmish here. There were the tracks of several horses and mules, easily distinguished by the shape of the shoe tracks, which had come along to this place from the west and gone no farther. There were signs showing that two men had fallen in the road and one of them had bled profusely. It was very evident that he must have bled to death. I could draw no conclusion. From appearances I judged that a party had been attacked, that one had been killed, the other two had escaped and another larger party had returned for the body.

The physical features of the locality were well adapted for a surprise. On the left of the road, going west, was a dense growth of

2. Corporal Duffy cannot be positively identified.

greasewood, a shrub which grows to the average height of four feet. This extended from the road to the mountains, a few miles distant. On the opposite side was an open plain bounded by mountains two or three miles away. In the greasewood were tracks of a large body of Indians, with a few also in the road, but there was no proof that an Indian had been killed. The tracks came from and returned to the mountains.

We drove on towards the west, ruminating on the tragical incident which had evidently occurred no longer ago than yesterday and wondering if we should ever know the particulars. Although this section of the march was not more than twenty-five miles, our rate of progress was so slow that the day was nearly passed before we reached our stopping place on Date Creek. For several miles before we came to the crest, we had seen the top of the line of cottonwoods show itself above the edge of the plain across which we slowly journeyed. Fatigue, thirst and hunger made the miles seem double.

At last we turned down in the valley, winding close along the side of a hill on our left, and presently came in sight of a large log house on the riverbank. Simultaneous with our appearance, a war whoop rent the air, coming from a dense grove of willows behind the house, at the same time the door of the house opened and eleven men rushed out, apparently overjoyed to see us. When I heard the war whoop, I had halted and dismounted my men instantly, expecting a fight, but no Indian appeared nor was the whoop repeated.

I found this ranche belonged to a man by the name of Colonel Marcus D. Dobbins.[3] I do not remember the names of but two others, who were there at the time of my arrival. One of them was a Scotchman, by the name of L. C. Gray, a wealthy trader who had a house at La Paz, and a branch store at Prescott and an assayer of Prescott, by the name of Charles Borger.[4] The rest of the men

3. Curtis mistakenly identified Colonel Marcus D. Dobbins as Mr. Hopkins. Dobbins had come to California during the Gold Rush in 1849. He was commissioned lieutenant colonel of the 5th California on September 12, 1861, and resigned on October 31, 1862. A prospector and rancher in Yavapai County, Dobbins moved to Yuma County where he served in the territorial legislature and as that county's district attorney. He died in Arizona City on August 28, 1871. *California Men*, 676; *Arizona Citizen and Weekly Tribune*, September 9, 1871; *Daily Alta California*, September 19, 1871.

4. L. C. Gray had mercantile establishments at La Paz and Prescott. On October 28, 1864, the territorial legislature granted Gray, Charles O. Cunningham, Joseph Tyson, and their associates the right to survey, improve and operate a toll road from La Paz to Prescott.

were miners and hired men in the employ of Dobbins. Gray was a sharp-featured man, with a slight stoop in his shoulders, about fifty years old, of a reticent temperament, with nothing to indicate more than ordinary pluck or generosity of character. Borger was fresh, rosy-faced, well made and somewhat effusive in conversation. Dobbins was a gigantic specimen of the Maine Yankee, generous and companionable.

I had hardly got out of my carriage when Borger cleared up the mystery of the tracks and blood near Soldiers' Holes. The story, stripped of embellishment, the frequent interruptions of Dobbins and an occasional one by Gray amounted to this. On the day before Gray, Borger and a California businessman named Charles O. Cunningham had left Date Creek, where they had stayed all night, for Prescott.[5] Gray was mounted on a young and high-spirited black horse, Borger on a mule and Cunningham on a California bronco. They rode along quietly until they reached the place already described. At this point Borger was a little in advance, with his carbine resting across his thighs, between his body and the pommel, whistling a melody, with no suspicion of danger. Gray and Cunningham were riding side by side a few paces behind, engaged in conversation. Suddenly a flight of arrows, with a few rifle bullets, burst out of the greasewood on the right, killing Cunningham instantly and causing the mule to throw Borger into the road. Free of their riders, the mule and bronco ran out upon the plain.

His account of the ambush on May 3, 1865, appeared in the *Daily Alta California* and differs in some minor details from Curtis's account. A second attempt by Gray to reach Prescott ended in yet another ambush. When within twenty miles of Prescott, Gray's party, consisting of a mail carrier and four soldiers, was attacked by roughly 100 well-armed Indians. Two soldiers were wounded, one mortally, but Gray and the rest finally reached Prescott. Curtis mistakenly referred to Charles Borger as "a Jew trader of Prescott, by the name of Rosenberg." Borger had left La Paz to set up an assaying office in Prescott in the summer of 1864 and his newspaper advertisement read: "Assays made of all kinds of ores, and guaranteed correct." Borger was also a partner in the Harcuvar Copper Vein with his two traveling companions, L. C. Gray and Charles O. Cunningham. Borger moved to California after the war. *First Legislative Assembly*, 21; *Daily Alta California*, May 28, 1865; June 21, 1865; *Arizona Miner*, August 10, 1864; Hassler, "Cunningham," 265.

5. At this point Curtis, with no journal or letters to which he can refer, understandably confuses the sequence of events some fifteen years after their occurrence. Bell and Sage, whose bodies Curtis claimed to have found earlier, were killed by Indians on the same day as Cunningham, whose story he will relate next. Curtis mistakenly referred to Charles O. Cunningham as "a lawyer named Hamilton." Cunningham had come to California during the Gold Rush and served for a time as a judge in Los Angeles County. During the war Cunningham moved his operations to La Paz where, after briefly engaging in the freighting business, he raised stock and speculated in gold, silver, and copper mines. His family lived in San Francisco while he sought his fortune in Arizona. Hassler, "Cunningham," 253, 255, 260–62, 265.

Now occurred one of those incidents which have made men heroes in all ages of the world. Out of a thousand men, but few, if any, could be found who would not have sought to save themselves in such a place as this. Gray saw one companion dead in the road, the other rolling in the dust, but alive. To the left was the open plain and safety, to the right was almost certain death. But this canny Scotch trader was made of the mettle that would not permit him to turn his back on a fellow creature in distress, even to save his own life, when there was a chance of rescuing him. He dashed his spurs into his horse, flew to Borger's side, stooped till he caught his coat collar in his vice-like grasp, shouted "Jump!" and with a herculean exertion flung him across his horse, behind the saddle, and fled out upon the plain amidst a whirlwind of arrows about his head and shoulders. Once out of shooting distance, he put Borger on his feet and went and caught the mule and bronco, which were grazing a little distance off. The two men then returned to Date Creek, where the rancheman and miners joined them to recover the body of Cunningham. They found the body stripped of its clothing, mutilated and the head scalped. He was brought in and buried near the house.

The party had hardly finished their rude funeral services when the band of Indians broke in upon them. Luckily, no one was hurt in the onset and all succeeded in getting into the house, where they had remained in a state of siege up to the time of my arrival.

From all that I could learn of the civilians there were some 200 Indians in the vicinity of the ranche. Doubtless this was an exaggeration, but I had no means of learning the true numbers. Accordingly, I began to make dispositions for a defence should we be attacked during the night. Dobbins signified his intention to leave the ranche and go to La Paz with me next day, where he would stay until the Indians were sufficiently subdued to make Date Creek a safe place of residence.

I was asked to take command of the entire party and do with them as I pleased during the night. I might pause here and demonstrate the impossibility of doing much with a body of citizens where everything depends upon vigilance and discipline, but I will spare the reader. I assembled the eleven men and told them I should put them on guard over one post and, in order that they might not lose much sleep, I should divide the time into eleven equal parts of less than an hour each and they could draw lots for the time of detail. I took some pains to impress it upon them that under no circumstances whatever were they to leave their post while they were on duty. With this injunction and a few other minor directions, I made my dispositions and got into my blankets, which I, for the night, placed on the ground.

I did not sleep much. I lacked confidence in my civilian guard. Three different men, during the night, left their posts. I saw the whole proceeding each time from my bed. First the man would pause and look earnestly around, particularly in my direction. Then he would tip-toe into the kitchen to light his pipe. That was always the temptation. No sooner would the culprit disappear than I would take his place on beat and be there, walking back and forward, when he appeared with his freshly lighted pipe. The soldiers plodded their two-hour tours faithfully.

The night passed away without disturbance and morning brought us evidence that the Indians had departed. Dobbins furnished a good breakfast for the whole party and after doing it ample justice we got ready for the road and started. Most of the men went down the creek by a route which passes Mount Ives, along Bill Williams Fork, to the valley of the Colorado. Gray, Borger and Dobbins alone accompanied me, the latter riding the horse of the late Cunningham. I drove about a mile west of the house to the crossing, where we forded the creek and struck into the Date Creek Mountains, following a new road which had recently been opened by Dobbins and which was not yet completed. The distance to the point where the road descended into the plain was twelve miles, through a very rough country. In many places we were obliged to fasten lariats to the top of the carriage, so that the men, by holding the ends and walking along the upper side, could prevent it from rolling down the declivity.

Date Creek is so named on account of the large number of the date plant which grows in that region. It is of the same family as the mescal, except that the spikes are not so fiercely barbed, nor so stiff. The stalk, which grows from the centre, attains an altitude of only three or four feet and bears a fruit about as long and as large as a banana, but more resembling the cucumber in shape. Three rows of black seeds, piled up like three piles of three cent pieces, run through the centre, from end to end. The fruit is softer and more jelly-like when ripe than the banana and very sweet. Sugar and syrup is often made from it. Who first named this fruit a date I am unable to say. It certainly resembles it in nothing.[6] At the time of my visit to Date Creek, the plant was green and not very tempting. In November of the same year, in another part of the territory, I ate a large number of them. The ripest were always covered with ants, which seemed to hold their sweets in high appreciation. The plant grows in plain and on mountainside, in the most barren and sandy regions, where it rains but seldom.

Once down upon the level of the Xuacaxella Desert, our team broke into a trot and we rolled swiftly along, with a fair prospect of soon crossing the ninety miles between the Date Mountains and the southern extremity of La Paz, provided we met with no drawbacks. After a few miles, Gray and Dobbins said good-bye and took a bridle road which led into the mining country near Wickenburg. Borger accompanied me, being the only person in my party who had ever been over the desert. I had obtained all the information possible from Captain Thompson before starting and from every person whom I met on the road who had ever taken this route.

We had not been long riding over the desert before the subject of water was broached and I found that Borger had grave doubts about there being any on the road except at Cisternas Negras and Tyson's Well. He had come from La Paz by another route, but made up his mind as to the scarcity of water from the fact that there had been no rains for a long time. I began to realize my situation and find that I was in a bad predicament, if there should be no water at the water holes beyond Cisternas Negras. To add to my perplexity, I found Borger had no canteen, having lost his in the Indian attack at Soldiers' Holes and taking no pains to secure another at Date Creek, because he supposed I would have a cask in the ambulance. We had eaten a breakfast of salt beef and bacon and the weather being exceedingly warm, the canteens did not long contain water.[7]

6. We extend a special thanks to Dr. Steve O'Kane, University of Northern Iowa, for his detective work in identifying this date plant as the banana yucca (*Yucca baccata*).

7. There were three popular stories about the Arizona heat. The first related how dogs could be seen hopping around because the ground burnt their paws. A second claimed that Arizona hens laid hard-boiled eggs. The third told of a soldier who died and went to hell, but came back for his blankets because the infernal region was so much colder than Arizona. Coues, *Spanish Pioneer* 1: 148.

A water hole in the Arizona desert. Courtesy of Ben Wittick, Palace of the Governors Photo Archive (NMHA/DCA), Negative #015527

The Xuacaxella Desert, or Cactus Plain, as Lieutenant Wheeler in his exploration had called it, extends north and south, parallel to the Colorado River. Between the river and the desert stretches a range of mountains and on the eastern side a range also borders the plain. The road which I traveled was near the western side, where long spurs of the mountains run out into the plain like points, capes and promontories into the sea. The first day's ride, after leaving

Date Creek, took us past three of these points. When we began to suffer from want of water, Borger had told us that in one of these points was situated the Black Tanks, so we rode along patiently expecting to quench our intolerable thirst when we should reach a point which when we first saw it, seemed to be almost on the horizon. Arriving there, however, we were informed that the next point was the place and that was in the dim distance ahead. When we reached the second, we found that the Black Tanks were in the third point.

I lost my patience, said some rude things to Borger and I could hear some impatient oaths drop from the men as disappointment succeeded disappointment. We had left Dobbins's ranche at four o'clock in the morning, with canteens filled. Our passage over the twelve miles through Date Mountains had averaged about two miles per hour, which made it near ten o'clock when we reached the road on the plains. The day was one of the most sultry I have ever known, with not a breath of air stirring. My canteen was empty when I got through the mountains and my mouth was as dry as an autumn leaf as soon as the last drop of water was gone. The men, cantering their horses beside the carriage, were gray with dust and generally miserable, the horses and mules streaming with foam and perspiration.

And so the day passed away, until, at five o'clock, we reached the third point, which Borger now recognized as positively the one in which we should find the Black Tanks. In fact, there was ample evidence that we had made no mistake this time. All about the roadside where we drew up was evidence that this was an old camping ground, for the ashes of many campfires were everywhere scattered around. On our right was the high promontory containing the Black Tanks; a short distance to our left was a small island rising abruptly from this terrific sea. We were not long in getting to the ground and asking for the place where we were to find water. To this question we received the comforting answer that the Black Tanks were two miles off the road and that all our animals would have to be driven that distance. Leaving a few men to guard the wagons, I started with the rest for the Tanks, driving the horses and mules, not forgetting to take a quart dipper along for my own use. I did not stop to examine the features of the landscape as I went, but I will here give the result of after observations.

From our camping place to the Black Tanks the distance was two miles, along a level interval, stretching between the mountain range on our right to a low range of hills on the left. All of this, to the full width and nearly a mile in depth, was filled with the *Cereus giganteus*, a cactus of the general average height of forty feet, cigar-shaped and rarely having a branch, although occasionally as many as three.[8] The cacti stood near together, about the usual distance of forest trees. The trunk of this species is dodecahedral when it leaves the ground and the ridges increase upwards by bifurcation and addition to the largest circumference of the tree, which is from fifteen to eighteen feet from the ground and where usually the few branches are given off. Here the ribs increase often to thirty in number and from this point decrease upward to the number of eighteen or twenty. The wood at the base of old specimens becomes a perfect hollow cylinder and from thence upward to the first branches, instead of being solid, it becomes a reticulated network of bundles of reeds surrounding a central pith. The ribs are armed from top to bottom with frightful-looking spikes, which grow uniformly regular and intersect each other so that the hand cannot touch the trunk without receiving injury.

Perhaps a more homely description of this cactus may be better understood. Suppose a small circle of ten inches in diameter to be described on the ground. Then take round poles of two inches in diameter and forty feet long, set them up around the ring and we have a fair resemblance to the *Cereus giganteus* as it appears after it has died and the wind has blown the dried bark and pith away. The ranchemen often use these poles for palings for fences. Cover the poles with a rind, or bark, of the color and smoothness of a green pumpkin, arm its ridges with thorns, each pole making a well-defined ridge from top to bottom, and you have the cactus. It should swell gradually from the bottom to the centre and diminish from the centre to the top, precisely like a cigar.

This cactus is found as far north as Latitude 34° and south to near Latitude 28°, in the vicinity of Guaymas, Sonora, Mexico. The fruit is called by the Mexicans, *pitajaya*, pronounced pit-a-hi-yah, and is eaten by the Indians and settlers of the regions where it grows. Conserves and syrup are made from it and preserved for use in the winter. It is pleasant to the taste in a fresh state.

8. The Saguaro Cactus.

The fruit grows near the top of the tree, at an altitude of twenty-five to fifty feet, and being very large and pulpy, if permitted to ripen and drop to the ground, would burst and be unfit for use. The Indians use a long slender pole, with a fork at the end, so contrived that the berry can be plucked and brought within reach. Birds and insects, particularly the ant, get all that man does not gather.

This cactus forest gave the landscape near the Cisternas Negras a very peculiar appearance. Their novelty and dissimilarity to any other was somewhat pleasing, but that gradually wore off and the monotonous columns, with their frightful spikes, engendered a feeling of repulsion.

Chapter 42

Water in Several Forms

Once before I found that I could not tell an adventure without introducing my constant companion, Victoriana. Vic had come with me, as usual, and had alternately run or rode as the whim struck her or as the danger from Indians permitted. She had shared a portion of the contents of my canteen and those of several men, but notwithstanding this indulgence, she was the greatest sufferer from thirst of any in the party. When I started for the Tanks, she trotted beside me. Our road took us through the cactus forest for some distance and then we came into an open valley, the soil of which was disintegrated granite, covered with fragments on every side. Here grew a cactus, one of the thousand varieties of that unpleasant plant that I had never before seen. It was like nothing else but handfuls of cambric needles, lying in bunches all over the ground. Examination showed no body to which they adhered. In the green state they looked like bunches of needle-like thorns irregularly piled up; dry they were in small, yellow, loose clusters, blowing about the surface of the ground.

Vic had not gone half a dozen steps after leaving the grove of giant cactus before she put her foot on a bunch of *Cholla*. The thorns ran far into her foot. She tried to remove the bunch with her teeth and instantly her tongue, lips and gums were thrust full of the needles. She was in great misery, but I was thirsty and could not stop to relieve her. In her distress, she rolled on the ground and filled her body with the spines until she howled with pain. Still I pressed on toward the water tanks. A walk of two miles along the south side of the mountain brought us at last to a ravine up which we turned to the north. As I raised my eyes to the mountain, I saw that it had been cleft from summit nearly to base as if with a wedge and I could see the blue sky through the cleft beyond. In this mountain rent we were to find water, water deposited in natural reservoirs in the rainy season, in millions of gallons, reservoirs which never became dry through the long arid summers.

We ascended a considerable height and well into the crevice before we came to the first deposit of water. As soon as I reached it I dipped up a quart and swallowed the whole, about as soon as I could pour it down, all the men doing the same. By this time the horses and mules were drinking and we went higher up where we found a larger reservoir, deep and clear, in a cleft whose perpendicular walls rose to the summit of the mountain and whose farther end was some hundreds of yards away. As I dipped up my second quart, I had time to observe that the water was full of animalcule, which wriggled and jerked through its limpid depths in a most stomach-provoking manner. But I was too thirsty to be squeamish and another quart followed the first. Some way the water did not seem to go to the right place and I concluded not to go on filling myself up, but simply moisten the mouth from time to time until the flow of saliva should begin again.

Here my attention was attracted to Vic. She had crept up to my feet, close to the edge of the water, no longer crying with pain, but the picture of much endurance and humility. She was lame in every foot, her tail and body were filled with *Cholla* needles and her mouth and tongue literally so pinned together with them that she could not lap the water. I sat down on a convenient stone, drew a jackknife from my pocket, which contained a general assortment of carpenter's tools, surgeon's instruments and culinary kit and selected a pair of tweezers. Taking Vic in my lap, I proceeded to draw the spines one at a time from her mouth. One of the peculiarities of the *Cholla* is that, while it goes in with the utmost ease and regularity, it comes out with pain and reluctantly. If left too long, the moist flesh swells them so that they split and cannot be extracted without great difficulty, often causing bad ulcerations. I found many of the thorns ran entirely through the tongue and lips. As I drew them out, the dog would whine, often crying out loudly with pain, the blood flowing freely with each extraction.

After a considerable time had passed, I got Vic into such a condition that she could drink and deferred further surgery until I should return to the ambulance. The men who had come to the spring had brought every cooking utensil, canteen and pail which would hold water and had carried them back to camp. When I was ready to return, I fastened my pocket handkerchief to the dog's collar and led her so that she would avoid the *Cholla*. In camp I finished drawing the thorns.

Supper over, I took an axe and went into the cactus grove for the purpose of examining thoroughly a specimen of the *Cereus giganteus*. Naturalists had long known that there was a bird which made a practice of tunneling into the top of this cactus and they had concluded that it was for the purpose of nest building.[1] I had a theory of my own and meant now to test it. I found, upon examination, that the cactus had hardly any roots. Indeed it seemed marvelous how it could stand up in a gale of wind. I selected one with a hole in the top and cut it down, but found no sign of a nest. Two others were examined with the same result. The holes appeared to be excavated into miniature caverns, but there was no evidence of nest building. I then cut off a section of the top, about four feet long, and stood it upright on the ground. With a long knife I cut a piece out of the top, which was as soft as a melon, so as to leave a saucer-shaped depression. This filled immediately with clear but slightly bitter water. I made up my mind that in this desert region the bird tunneled the cactus for water. Of course, I am not sure of this, but it opens a question for the naturalist to answer.

We passed the night in sound slumber, waking at four o'clock. The animals were driven to the Tanks by half a dozen men, who brought back a quantity of water for breakfast and to fill our canteens. At half-past five we resumed our journey, the road striking out toward the centre of the plain. The weather was a repetition of yesterday, but we had taken the precaution to eat lightly of

1. The Gilded Flicker.

bacon and to be more sparing in the use of water. That Vic might not require much, I fastened her in the ambulance, greatly to her disgust. The day passed along without much suffering from thirst. The road was generally smooth enough for rapid traveling, but there were occasional stretches where we did not make over three miles an hour. About three o'clock in the afternoon we came to the Hole in the Plain which Captain Thompson had told me I should find filled with water and where I had intended to stay all night. Not a drop of water—nothing but two or three acres of mud—and Tyson's Well a long day's journey ahead!

Had there been any grass at the place I should have stopped for at least an hour to graze the stock, but there was not a blade of anything in the vicinity which a horse or mule would eat. I concluded to push on. We drove for the rest of the day and just at nightfall a horseman overtook us, who proved to be Mr. Gray, the hero of Soldiers' Holes. He curbed his horse alongside of the ambulance and asked me several questions about my last camp and what provision I had for taking water. When I told him my situation, he looked troubled for a moment, but presently said, "Keep up your courage, lieutenant, it is not far to Tyson's now. You will get there early in the morning. Good-bye." And he galloped off into the gathering darkness.

I unrolled my bedding upon the ambulance seats and lay down to sleep. There was no use in my sitting up. I might as well be asleep as awake. The escort was the real sufferers and I found it was not easy sleeping knowing they were riding along, hungry, thirsty and tired. Long before daybreak the mules had ceased to respond by a trot to the stirrups of the driver or to the blows of his whip. Nothing but a walk could he get out of them. When it grew light enough to see anything, I found the country was barren and stony and the surface considerably undulating.

Reaching the top of a roll we strained our eyes in the hope of seeing some light which would indicate that we were approaching Tyson's. I took the glass and looked, but could see nothing save the long barren plain before us. I ordered one of the horsemen to take the whip and stir the mules into a trot. After much belaboring, he succeeded in quickening their speed for an instant, only to have them drop back into their old pace when he stayed his hand.

I began to see that there might be a necessity of abandoning the ambulance and walking. Visions of straggling and dying of thirst began to flit through my brain. There was a chance, of course, that out of the whole party one might get through and bring back water to the others, but there would be great suffering at the best, if not death.

We had descended into a basin and were wearily struggling on when the ambulance stopped. One of the mules had refused to go any farther. Two of the soldiers were already dismounted, leading their worn-out and broken-down steeds slowly along. It was eight o'clock in the morning and the sun was beginning to broil us after the old style. We had drank the last of our water on the previous afternoon and our tongues could hardly articulate plainly. I got out of the carriage, but, before giving an order to unharness and unsaddle, concluded to walk to an elevation a few rods in advance and take one more look for Tyson's Well. Borger accompanied me.

Walking along the road, we presently came to a ravine in which water had run in the rainy season. On the bank of this were a few yuccas, which concealed a part of the opposite bank from my sight. As we came up to them and were about to step down into the ravine, Borger exclaimed, "There are three barrels over there, lieutenant!"

Looking up, I saw three barrels standing by the roadside on the farther bank of the ravine. Borger ran to them and presently raised a letter, which had been held down upon the head of a barrel by a stone, saying, "Here's a letter, and it's for you! By Jove, it's in Gray's hand, too! It's water, yes, water!" and Borger sat down on the ground, overcome. "Excuse me," he said presently, "but I can't help it. That Gray is the *whitest* man in Arizona."

I had got my letter open and read:

> Lieutenant C. A. Curtis,
> Sir:
> Please accept three barrels of water with my compliments.
> L. C. Gray

Need I say that my eyes ran over at this unexpected good fortune? Or need I say that Gray—God bless him wherever he may be!—always fills a grateful niche in my memory. Water—three barrels—126 gallons! That meant a gallon to every man and ten to every animal! It meant rest, speed and safety!

I sent back Borger to tell the men of our good luck and tell them to get the ambulance up to where the barrels stood. By another piece of good fortune, there was abundance of dried grass and, in some very low places, green grass where we stopped. The animals were turned loose and, after a considerable struggle with the thirsty creatures, we succeeded in giving each one his share of water. Then we proceeded to get our breakfast, after which all the men but myself went to sleep. I had slept some during the night and could sleep as we should drive along, so I chose to do what guard duty was necessary while we remained in camp.

The men dozed along until noon, when one after another they aroused and began to busy themselves getting dinner. At two o'clock we caught up the animals, gave each a feed of grain from a bag or two in the ambulance and got ready for the road. At three o'clock we drove up the height from which I had started to take a look for Tyson's Well when the barrels were discovered. At the top the driver cracked his whip, the mules started promptly into a trot, the horses of the escort broke into a canter and amid the clatter of hoofs and rattle of wheels, we sped on our way as fresh as if we had just left Fort Whipple. So much had three barrels of water done for us.

In the language of Private Tom Cleary, who was one of my escort and whose language drew an audible "Amen!" from the soldiers about him as he took the first hearty drink from the water drawn from the barrels: "May that same man Gray never want for a soft hand to smooth his last pillow or plenty of masses for the repose of his soul!"

A ride of eighteen miles from where we had found the barrels, estimated from the number of hours we were on the road, brought us to Tyson's Well. Here the mystery of the water being left by the roadside was cleared up. Gray had reached the well the evening before and had hired a man to take three barrels of water in a wagon and go until he should meet me. He had then continued his journey to La Paz. The man had gone eighteen miles, left the water and returned, reporting that he went twenty-five miles and had seen nothing of us. He had shirked his duty somewhat, but we could be none the less grateful to Gray, for there was little doubt but the opportune finding of the water had saved us from great suffering, if not from death.

Tyson's Well was sunk on a dead level, by the side of a dry bed of what in the season of rain might be a brook and certainly had been a stream at some time. It was about thirty feet deep, the water being raised by a windlass having a crank at each end, which drew one bucket up and sent another down regularly every few minutes. During the time that I stopped at the well on my trip to La Paz and on my return, I noticed that the monotonous creak of the windlass never ceased. I heard it all through the evening and each time that I awoke in the night. Ten cents was charged for each animal that drank and the number of wagon trains, pack trains and herds of cattle going to and from the mines and ranches seemed innumerable. There was one house at the well which contained a barroom, storeroom, a sleeping apartment which would accommodate a large number of persons, a granary, a kitchen and a dining room.

I ordered a supper for myself and men and, while it was preparing, made a tour of the place to see what it was like. I saw two great stacks, one of straw and the other of grass. There was also a large corral, divided into several small yards, in which sheep and cattle were secured for the night. The house was surrounded by a fence made of the reeds of the *Giganteus* cactus. The posts were of cedar, brought from the mountains and set into the ground without being trimmed, except to the extent of removing the bark. Six horizontal and parallel rails constituted the fence.

When bedtime came I placed my bed on the ground outside of the house, with the pillow against the *adobe* wall, being one in a long row of guests; men who were in all sorts of business and from many places accidentally met here for a night. For some little time before we fell asleep, conversation was held from bed to bed, but at last the conversation lagged, until I fell off in the midst of a story which my right-hand neighbor was telling of a trip over the big bend of the Gila River and which his own increasing drowsiness made drag as wearily as did my mule team just before we reached the barrels. The moon shone so brightly that each time I awoke in the night, I could tell the hour by my watch. As I woke to a brief consciousness the creak of the windlass, the braying of mules and donkeys, the bleating and bellowing of sheep and oxen could be heard mingled with vociferations of men in English and Spanish as they drove the thirsty animals to the trough or drove away those who had been supplied.

Chapter 43

La Paz

In the morning we took our breakfast, gave a receipt to Colonel Charles Tyson for the water and forage furnished our animals and resumed our journey.[1] I am not sure of the distance from the well to La Paz or precisely the hour of day when I reached there. I only remember that the road was good, down a slightly descending grade, and that we rolled over it without delay or trouble of any kind. I found La Paz a town situated about a mile and a half from the flowing current of the Colorado River, but having several small lagoons, or bays, some up nearly to the buildings. There was but one street, running north and south, with an occasional court, along which was built the town. One hotel, two saloons and possibly a dozen stores made up the business portion of the place. There were few residences, as there were few ladies, the single men living in their places of business.[2]

1. In 1856 Charles Tyson built an adobe fort on the site of what is now Quartzsite, Arizona. Although never a regular military post, Fort Tyson did offer protection from the Mojave Indians. The well that offered the best water on the route from La Paz to Prescott was finished in March of 1864. As Tyson's Well grew in importance to travelers, it became an important stage stop on the overland road to California. *Grand Canyon State*, 361; *Arizona Miner*, March 9, 1864.

2. An earlier visitor to La Paz had noted the haphazard construction of the town: "No one street, if such it could be called, ran parallel with another. No two building lots were of precisely the same size. No two tenements were accurately on a range. Everything

La Paz, at the time I visited it, was the only place on the Colorado River above Fort Yuma which could claim to be a town. The steamboats plying on the river stopped and landed great quantities of freight for the mines. These stores had been shipped from San Francisco, by way of the Gulf of California, to the mouth of the river, where they were re-shipped for the various landings above by a line of sternwheelers belonging to the Colorado Navigation Company. It was by this line that the military supplies reached Fort Whipple, after it was transferred to the Department of California, our landing place, however, being at Fort Mojave, 150 miles above.[3]

As I rode into town, Gray invited me to be his guest while I should remain there. He also gave me the use of a large corral, where my animals could be kept and where my men could build a fire and cook their rations. Gray kept bachelor's hall. His house stood in rear of his store and was about sixty feet square. Through the centre from end to end ran a passage, from which opened four rooms on a side. In five of these rooms his four salesmen and himself were quartered, the other three were for his guests. The passage through the house was open at the extremities, so that it was the sitting room of the family, a light breeze always blowing through it and the weather rarely being cold enough for a fire or even an overcoat.[4] At the eastern end, which was the end farthest from the street, a floor about twelve feet deep and the whole width of the house—in fact, an outside extension of the floor in the passage—was laid and provided with settees and chairs. When the sun had

about the place was in shiftless confusion, and, if laid out properly on a map, the town would have resembled, as nearly as anything, a cobweb drawn and blotted by a young child on a rumpled piece of paper." The importance of La Paz lay in its location on the Colorado River, although that waterway later changed its course and the site is now a ghost town. *San Francisco Bulletin*, September 24, 1864.

3. Fort Mojave (also known as Fort Mohave) was established April 19, 1859, on the Colorado River at Beale's Crossing near the head of the Mojave Valley. The post was erected as the result of an 1858 Mojave Indian raid on an emigrant train bound for California. Fort Mojave was burned and abandoned on May 31, 1861, when the garrison was transferred to protect Union interests in Southern California, but re-occupied on May 19, 1863. Federal troops protected settlers and stage lines from Indian depredations and outlaws until the fort was finally abandoned by the army in 1890. *Soldier and Brave*, 73; Frazer, *Forts*, 11–12.

4. About the time that Curtis reached La Paz, a mining engineer complained about the weather there: "We have very hot weather here to judge from the thermometer which ranges from 90 deg. to 105 deg. Yesterday it stood 110 deg. in the shade. In my room it was 94 deg. So you see we can keep cool if we want to take care, for in a house judiciously constructed and properly kept and conducted, it should not have been over 85 deg. I hear nobody complain as yet, and everybody is astonished not to feel the heat more." *San Francisco Bulletin*, May 18, 1865.

sunk into the west along through the evening, this floor would be a general place of assembly for many of the citizens, who would smoke and talk on various topics until bedtime.

The next morning after my arrival I made the tour of the town and made the necessary inquiries about establishing a provost marshal's office. I found the town very quiet, most of the traders being Northern-born men, no one being disposed to make trouble for the military authorities. Gray, whose opinion was worth consideration, came as near laughing as I ever saw him when I asked him what he thought of the matter. I made a few memoranda and then devoted myself to seeing the sights. The town possessed no attractions in itself worth mentioning, but the presence on the streets and in the stores of a number of Mojave, pronounced Mo-har-vy, Indians was exceedingly interesting.[5]

These men were fine looking, generally tall and well-proportioned and showing a considerable degree of intelligence. For clothing they wore a string of buckskin around the body, with a piece of cotton cloth about six inches wide attached to the string in front, below the umbilicus. This cloth passed between the legs and was secured to the string behind, making what is popularly known as breechcloth. The scanty clothing showed their fine proportions to the greatest advantage. Their eyes were large, shaded by long lashes. In their noses and ears many of them wore ornaments of bone, ornaments that could be removed at pleasure, as I frequently observed. The hair was not allowed to grow long, rarely falling below the neck. Bright bands or handkerchiefs were worn on the head, but nothing else. There are no Esaus among the Indian tribes, their skin always smooth.

The women may be said to be generally handsome. The high cheekbones and flatness of the features are not according to our ideas of female loveliness, but there were many faces of a decidedly European oval to which one could make no objection. Their scanty

5. The Mojave people lived in the Mojave Valley in Arizona and California, but in 1859 they split into two communities, the largest settling on the Colorado River Reservation in 1865. The Mojave had little technology beyond what was necessary for subsistence farming. This attitude toward craftsmanship was in part attributable to the fact that all property of a deceased individual was destroyed at his death, thus leaving no personal possessions to pass on to the succeeding generations. Individuals did not own much but every family "had its designated plot of land, marked by boundary stakes which were painted or feathered. The early dwellings were open-sided, flat-roofed shades." The phonetic rendering of Mojave is Mō'hävē. Stewart, "Mohave," 55, 57, 59; Grey, *Tales from the Mohaves*, 4.

Mohave Woman. Courtesy of Library of Congress.

drapery, too, which was almost as slight as that of the men, showed there was no fashionable makeup or padding to their fine figures. It is doubtful whether a community of white people could show so many fine-looking women, healthy and finely-proportioned.[6] The women who had passed the age of twenty were usually stout, with fat, good-natured faces. Younger than this they are graceful and elegantly shaped. Their only article of dress consisted of a petticoat made of strips of cottonwood bark. I am not quite sure that I can describe this garment fully. My acquaintance with the Mojave belles was not sufficiently intimate for me to examine their dressmaking closely. They wear a cord about the hips, with strips of soft bark of uniform width, usually about an inch wide, hung over it. Supposing a cord sufficiently long to go around the body should be suspended like a clothesline from one point to another, then take ribbon one inch wide and cut it up into pieces of twenty-four inches long, hang these over the cord so that the ends shall all be even below and hang them one over the other until they are so close that no gust of wind will separate them so that you can see through them. Now tie this around the hips, bustle it behind so that it will stick out about eight inches, and you have a fair sample of the Mojave women's only garment.

I have twice said that Indian garments are fastened about the hips. This is true, for they never fasten anything at the waist. I well remember a little Indian girl whom we captured in one of our fights and gave to an officer's wife to rear and what difficulty that excellent lady had for a long time in preventing the dusky maid from sliding her skirts down upon her hips, after the manner of her tribe.

There is a raciness, volubility and mirthfulness about the Mojave that I have never seen in any other tribe. I was surprised also to find that they could sing sweetly. This was really a great and

6. Men generally wore breechclouts woven from strands from the inner bark of the willow tree and cottonwood tree while their women wore knee-length skirts of willow bark. Two other visitors to the Colorado River valley agreed with the assessment of Curtis regarding the beauty of the Mojave women. One remarked: "You may search the galleries of Italy for models, the Venus de Medici thrown in, and anywhere here I will match you an Indian girl, with prouder step, more delicately turned foot and ankle, exquisite hands and the bust of a Cleopatra, who walks in her native costume of striped bark, utterly unconscious, in her innocence, of the lavish display she is making of her charms." Another man noted that the Mojave women, "short-plump, smiling and good-looking, draped coquettishly from the loins down to the knees—leaned against the sunny side of the houses and amused themselves by ogling the strangers." Stewart, "Mohave," 59; Paterek, *American Indian Costume*, 175; *Sacramento Daily Union*, June 24, 1865; *San Francisco Bulletin*, September 24, 1864.

unlooked for surprise to me. I had known many tribes of Indians and had heard much of their monotonous chanting, but had never heard them imitate the singing of the white man until now. I was walking along the sidewalk when I came to a group of six Mojave girls sitting flat at a corner, playing a game of cards. They had jointly purchased a red flannel shirt and were playing to see which one of their number should own it. Their musical laughter, their graceful manners, their fine figures and apparent unconsciousness of the admiration they excited kept me for a long time watching them. It was at this time, while one of their number was dealing, that the girl in the shirt burst out singing "Gentle Annie" and was immediately joined by all the rest. Snatches of many popular airs followed this, with an attempt to give the English words, which was comical to the extreme. I watched the fluctuations of the game until the shirt was pulled off one pair of graceful shoulders to be placed on another for half a dozen times and the game was broken up with the original wearer in possession.

Later in the day I met the same group, painted and tinted from their toes to their foreheads in a most fashionable manner. Pigments of all colors had been used, there did not seem to be a square inch of their bodies which was not covered by some device and these devices were as artistic as the finest laces worn by white ladies. After displaying themselves before the stores and hotel for a while, the laughing and singing bevy went to the lagoon, plunged in and swam along for a few moments like so many mermaids, returning to the shore free of all paint, their brown bodies sparkling with crystal drops of water. Going back to their boudoirs they again bedecked themselves and, varying the patterns from those previously put on, appeared again on the street for a short time and again washed themselves in the river. This was repeated several times during the day and apparently gave the girls as much pleasure as a watering place belle takes in changing her dresses several times during the day, until she has shown her entire wardrobe to an admiring public.

The married women tattoo their chins with several vertical blue lines and wear a necklace with a single large seashell in front, curiously wrought.[7] Many of the shells have been handed down in

7. Margot Mifflin's *The Blue Tattoo: The Life of Olive Oatman* contains several illustrations of Mojave facial tattoos. Both men and women tattooed their chins as well as painted their faces. Stewart, "Mohave," 62–63.

families for several generations. The babies form an interesting feature in these groups. Those which are very young are carried in a wooden frame, shaped like an old style watch case, which can be carried in the hand as conveniently as a reticule, stood against a building or hung up in a tree, while the mother busies herself with her domestic or fashionable affairs. When a little older, the infant is taken out of the case and borne about on its mother's hip, naked as a cupid, sitting astride of the projecting petticoat, their legs and arms clinging closely to the mother's waist. They are wide awake babies and it is a curious sight to see them peering out from under their mother's arms, with an apparent desire to see all that is going on.

On the second day after my arrival at La Paz, I took a ride with Gray ten miles up the river to visit the Mojave village. All along the road we met men and women riding swiftly and easily on spirited horses. Many of the men were tinted with paints, the warriors invariably wearing a red line across the forehead. A few dandies painted their faces black and spotted it with white in curious designs, adding pendants in nose and ears. Several wore leather bracelets on the left arm, trimmed with bright buttons and beads, a kind of tunic made of fringed buckskin hung from the shoulders, beautiful plumes of eagles' feathers, sometimes white and sometimes colored red, tied to a lock of hair and floated from the top of the head. Strings of beads and seashells were worn as ornaments.

The soil all along our route seemed exceedingly fertile. Wheat, beans and corn were growing in many places. There were no evidences of water ditches or that the Mojaves irrigated the land. We passed several granaries, cylindrical in shape with conical roofs, in which corn, mesquite beans and *tornillas* (screwbean mesquite) were stored. The houses were well constructed and seemed warm and comfortable. They were built on dry soil, usually sandy, and were about thirty or forty feet square. The walls, about two feet thick, were of wickerwork filled with straw, the roofs were thatched, covered with two feet of earth and supported by stout cottonwood posts. Around the inner walls I saw large earthen pots, which upon examination proved to be full of corn, beans and meal for the use of the household. In front of the house was a large open shed or piazza, covering as much space as the house itself. Under this the Indians find shelter from rain and sun in the summer season. In the winter season fires are sometimes built in the centre of the house, the smoke rising to a small aperture in the centre of the roof. Around this they sleep, protected from the cold. The favorite resort, however, seems to be the housetop, where I saw numbers gathered on every house which I passed.

The mesquite bean, which forms a principal article of food, needs a description. Everyone has seen the locust tree which forms an ornament in so many dooryards and knows that it bears a small flat pod, in which are a few shrunken beans. The mesquite belongs to the same family, *Acacia*, and any person who has seen the first cannot help recognizing the last, from the similarity. Indeed, the only noticeable difference to the casual observer lies in the fact that the mesquite is a shrub and not a tree and that the pods are plump and the beans full. The meal made from these beans is rich and slightly saccharine. It is the principal article of food with the Indians of the Colorado and Gila, pronounced He-lar, Valleys. One of the most interesting articles of kitchen furniture was the mortar. This was made of a block of granite, the cavity in the top being worn with beautiful regularity into a conical shape, six inches across and about eighteen inches deep. The pestle was of polished green stone, a foot and a half long and four inches in central diameter. With this machine all the meal and flour for the family is made.

During my visit to the Mojave village I saw no one at work. Groups were upon the housetops watching us as we wandered about, laughing often so that the air rang with their merriment or singing songs which they had learned of the white men. On the ground, parties of men played at an exciting game with hoops and poles. The hoop is made of rawhide or wound buckskin and is six inches in diameter. The poles are straight and about fifteen feet long. One man sets the hoop rolling along a level course, two men chase it halfway and at the same instant attempt to throw the poles through the hoop from opposite sides. The one succeeding scores. Target firing and archery were going in several places.

Returning to La Paz after dinner, I strolled with Vic down to the banks of a lagoon. Here I discovered a novel raft of Mojave manufacture. It was a huge flat bundle of cane grass and rushes, bound together, in equal distances of a foot each, with withes. A pole lay on it, so I stepped aboard with my dog and poled myself some distance towards the river. The raft was very buoyant and easily handled. Landing where the lagoon emerged into the Colorado, I strolled down the shore and presently came to a steamboat tied up to the bank. It proved to be the *Cocopah* on her way down the river from Fort Mojave, drawn up here to take on some passengers and freight.[8] It was my first sight of a steamboat since I left the Missouri River some years before. I went on board and in the saloon on deck found Judge Allyn very much under the influence of corn juice. He explained to me, between his hiccoughs, that he was on an electioneering tour, had been up to La Paz while the boat had stopped, had made a speech and that "Everythins a'right—goin' t'whip hell out t'ole Goodwin, bet yer life! Overwhelmin' 'jority (hic)."He had arrived just after I went on my visit to the Mojave villages and had made a speech in the open air before the hotel. Drinking with his friends had brought him to the condition in which I found him. His remark about Goodwin was the first hint I had received that he was to be a candidate, a hint fully corroborated when I returned to Gray's, after seeing the *Cocopah* swing off and steam rapidly away on the swift current. I learned that Governor Goodwin and General John S. Mason, our new district commander, had arrived at Fort Yuma a few days ago and that the former had at once had announced himself a candidate for Congress.[9] He had gone along the southern road to

8. J. Ross Browne reported on the conditions encountered on the Colorado River by steamboats during this period: "In January, 1865, the Cocopah, under command of Captain [David] Robinson, one of the most experienced pilots on the river, was nearly two months making the trip from Fort Yuma to Fort Mojave, and the draught of this boat was not over 24 inches. She was compelled to transfer all her freight to barges after passing La Paz. On the return trip from Fort Mojave to Fort Yuma, without any freight whatever, she took nine days to make a distance of less than 300 miles down stream. The great difficulty arises from the constant shifting of the channels, caused by the caving of banks, deposits of sand in new places, and consequent changes in the direction of the current." Browne, *Mineral Resources*, 466.

9. John S. Mason graduated from West Point in 1847 and was commissioned second lieutenant in the 3rd Artillery on July 1. Promoted to first lieutenant on September 7, 1850, he served as regimental quartermaster for four years (1854-1858) before attaining the rank of captain in the 11th Infantry on May 14, 1861. Commissioned colonel of the 4th Ohio on October 3, 1861, Mason became a brigadier general on November 29, 1862, and received four brevets prior to leaving the Volunteer force on April 30, 1866. He commanded the District of Arizona from April 1, 1865, until April 30, 1866. Commissioned major in the Regular Army on October 14, 1864, and lieutenant colonel on December 11, 1873, he served in several infantry regiments until his final promotion to colonel of the 9th Infantry on April 2, 1883. Mason retired on August 21, 1888, and lived quietly in Washington, D. C. until his death on November 29, 1897. Heitman, *Historical Register* 1: 695; Cullum, *Biographical Register* 2: 186; *Evening Star*, November 30, 1897.

Tucson, and after visiting all the towns and mining districts, would return to Prescott and await the result of the election. This news pleased me. The governor was from my state, Maine, and had once represented a district in Congress. His loyalty and patriotism was above question and I had no doubt of his election. I congratulated myself that I had not fallen into the trap of turning over the *Miner* to Judge Allyn's support.

The third day of my stay in La Paz I made my preparations to start for Fort Whipple. I borrowed three ten-gallon kegs from Gray, which I was to turn over to his agent in Prescott. He was very glad to lend them to me for the sake of saving the cost of their transportation to a point where they would sell at a large advance over what they would bring at La Paz. The desert had no terrors for us, now that we were acquainted with it and had means for taking water. In the afternoon I drove to Tyson's Well and stayed there until six o'clock in the evening, when I watered all the animals, filled my kegs and started. We drove all night, arriving at the Hole in the Plain in the morning. Here we stayed all day, the animals grazing and not suffering much for water. The next night I drove to Black Tanks and all my troubles were over for this trip. I remained at the Tanks all day and till the next morning.

Just as we were ready to start, we were startled by hearing a discordant yelling from the eminence which I have described as an island in the desert. Looking up we saw two Indians looking down upon us. We made signs for them to approach and at last they mustered confidence enough to do so. They were squalid, wretched-looking creatures, with splay feet, large joints and diminutive figures, but had bright eyes and cunning faces. They proved to be Hualpais, pronounced Hwat-pys, and were great contrasts to the fine-looking and stalwart Mojaves whom we had recently seen.[10]

10. These people were originally referred to by the Americans as Hualapais, but they are now generally known to anthropologists as Walapai. They lived undisturbed in northwestern Arizona south of the Colorado River until the 1850s when four different government expeditions crossed their lands. The Walapai foraged while traveling over their extensive territory, living in brush shelters in summer and more substantial structures in the winter. The establishment of Fort Mojave in 1859 brought a temporary peace between white settlers and the Walapai, although the discovery of gold near Prescott in 1863 brought in a flood of prospectors and settlers that drove them from their homes. The so-called Hualapai War, actually a series of guerrilla skirmishes, was fought between these Indians and the U. S. Army from 1865 to 1870 with survivors sent off to reservations. McGuire, "Walapai," 25, 27, 32–33; McMillen, *Making Indian Law*, 6.

My journey back to Fort Whipple was without particular incident. I called to see Mrs. Bell, but found she had learned of her husband's death and had gone to Prescott. The Ehles were as demonstrative as ever and as hospitable. I gave Olive the few books which I had purchased for her and told her she would receive a few more from San Francisco in a few weeks.

Arrived at Fort Whipple, I made no report of my trip, either written or verbal, nor was I ever asked for one. I think I needed no better proof than this that I was sent to La Paz simply to get me out of the way.

Chapter 44

Major Thompson's Scout

Shortly after these incidents, Major Thompson announced his intention of going on a grand Indian hunt.[1] Great preparations were made and much consultation was had with Weaver, Cooler and other mighty hunters of the red man, as to routes, water places, Indian haunts, etc. The civilians had been loud in their complaints of our inaction and the old boast that a party of Western plainsmen and hunters were worth thrice their numbers in soldiers was iterated and reiterated in our hearing with a persistency only equaled by their want of modesty.

This is an old boast of the amateur frontiersman, and one which the Eastern editor, who knows as much about Indian warfare as he does of the military science of the antediluvians, frequently supports

1. John Thompson had received a commission as major from the New Mexican governor on June 25, 1865, but a notation in his military service record indicates that he never mustered or received pay at that grade. Although Thompson always claimed to have been mustered in at that rank by Lieutenant Curtis, official correspondence proves otherwise. Curtis reported "that he did not muster Captain Thompson into the service as Major 1st New Mexico Cavalry, but that he wrote to him at Maricopa Wells informing him that he must comply with certain requirements specified in the letter before he (Curtis) could muster him (Thompson) into service in that grade." The War Department ruled that Thompson was prohibited from mustering in as major since cavalry regiments reduced below the minimum strength were not entitled to three majors and the 1st New Mexico Cavalry already had two majors on its rolls. Thomas M. Vincent to B. L. E. Bonneville, June 12, 1866, John Thompson Military Service Records.

by sneering at the ability of the Regulars to fight Indians, recommending Government to employ a troop of men who do not exist in any great numbers outside the pages of the cheap novelette.[2]

We had been for some time unable to take the field for want of shoes. The Government had failed to keep us supplied with many things during the fall of our first year in Arizona, even keeping us so short of food supplies that we were for a month on half rations of everything but meat.[3] Shoes, the most necessary article of clothing in a march, for some reason or other were a long time withheld. The Arizona country was a severe one for sole leather. On all expeditions of over a week in length, the men were required to take an extra pair of shoes, to provide against accident. When we had become reduced to one pair to each man and those somewhat worn, we could not take the field in that cactus-studded land, the very soil of which was chiefly disintegrated granite.[4]

After abusing us to a considerable extent, the grumblers decided to try an expedition of their own. A mass meeting was held in Prescott and a company of over 200 volunteers was organized to go on a big hunt for redskins. The famous frontiersman was in

2. As if to illustrate this point made by Curtis, one resident of Prescott complained: "The military are doing nothing, and less than nothing against the Apaches. Their presence with a considerable stock has induced the Indians to come in near the town and camp." J. M. Swetnam went into more detail: "About the middle of September [1865], Lieut. Baty [Abeytia], with sixteen men, was detailed by the commander of Fort Whipple for the protection of the settlers of the Verde valley. But they were of little use, several of the men, from one cause and another, being unfit for duty, and the lieutenant commanding was a coward. On the way down, within seven miles of the settlement, the soldiers were attacked by the Apaches, the commissary wagon captured and burned, one or two troopers wounded, and two government mules killed. It was a notorious fact through the country that Indians would not hesitate to attack a party of troopers double the number of a party of settlers or miners that would be left unmolested; the reason being that the soldier had little heart in the fight and up to the days of General Crook [he arrived in 1871] were poorly commanded, while the settlers and miners were fighting for their homes, their honor and life itself." A third writer said merely that the military attempt to track down the Apaches was "a stupendous humbug and a useless waste of money." *Milwaukee Sentinel*, December 4, 1865; Farish, *Arizona* 4: 243–44; *San Francisco Bulletin*, November 27, 1865.

3. This problem continued long after the war ended. A letter written from Prescott in November of 1865 explained the situation facing General John Mason who had succeeded General Carleton: "He, like the rest of us, has been living on promises. It appears to me that the Commissary and Quartermaster's Departments are, just now, the slow coaches—as I understand there is very little provision in Fort Whipple, and it is useless to send out men on half rations, loaded down as they will be, with gun, blanket, ammunition and grub." *San Francisco Bulletin*, December 7, 1865.

4. Thomas Sanders explained how men would try to prolong the life of their precious shoes in Arizona: "We made everything last as long as we could and when the soles of our shoes began to wear out we would get a piece of rawhide and, with the hair side out, we would put it on our shoes to help along. Laced over our shoes with a buckskin thong, it would not take long to wear the hair off and bye and bye the hide too would be worn out over the rocks." Bates, *Arizona Adventures*, 28–29.

Pauline Weaver. Sketch from Edmund Wells' *Argonaut Tales*.

force in this organization—if long hair, broad-brimmed slouched hats, belts filled with revolvers and knives, buckskin suits fringed down the sleeve and leg, boastful language and huge oaths were any indication. It was worthy of notice, however, that those old comrades of Carson who were living in the vicinity of Prescott—Walker, Weaver and Grey—did not join the contemplated expedition, but frequented the post and often indulged in quiet laughter at the great preparation.[5]

A leader was selected, in the person of a Southern-born gentleman, immensely popular with the sympathizers with the Southern cause, Mr. King Woolsey. As soon as he was elected, he put the party into shape for marching and one afternoon the cavalcade, with much caracoling and display of horsemanship—pi-rooting and pe-rancing, Pauline Weaver called it—passed through our post, on their way to win undying laurels against the Apaches. They were, there is no denying it, a fine-looking set of men and they were well-mounted and well-armed, but they lacked the one thing which will always make the soldier superior to the mob, whether it be in Indian warfare or in the riots of our great cities—they lacked discipline. They ran their organization as they would run a caucus or a town meeting. They elected their own officers and they could remove them or disobey them at their own sweet will.

As this much-heralded organization passed the fort, they were loud in their boasts of what they intended to do and what lessons they would teach us. When they had fairly turned their backs, Pauline Weaver remarked with a smile, "Them youngsters shoot off their mouths too much. They won't get a scalp."

At the second camp, the volunteers went into a committee of the whole as to what route they should take and got into such a wrangle that half bolted the convention and returned quietly to Prescott. The rest, continuing under King Woolsey, went south into the valley of the Salinas, where they butchered thirty-two

5. Joseph R. Walker was one of those frontiersmen who seemed to be larger than life. One historian summarized the imposing Walker's career as a "Santa Fe trapper, Spanish captive, Indian fighter, Missouri sheriff, Southwest trader, captain under Bonneville into the mountains, breaker of the trail from Salt Lake west across the Great Basin to Monterey, desert guide for emigrant parties, California rancher and stock raiser, [and] first of the Arizona prospectors who opened the Prescott region." Broken down by his years on the frontier, Walker spent his last years living with a nephew in Ygnacio Valley, California. When he died there on October 27, 1876, Walker's only request was that his headstone should recognize him as the discoverer of Yosemite Valley. Sabin, *Kit Carson Days*, 119–20; *San Francisco Bulletin*, November 6, 1876.

Tonto Apaches, whom they treacherously attracted into their camp by showing a white flag. This dastardly act covered the great Woolsey expedition with infamy. Few members of it were afterwards known to willingly acknowledge their connection with it or vaunt the superiority of the frontiersman over the Regular.[6]

When it is remembered that from the time of his entering the army until old age incapacitated him for further service, the whole military life of most officers, except the few months leave allowed once in five years, is spent in the Indian country in constant intercourse with the red man, either in peace or war, it cannot be disputed that he has plenty of opportunity to know more of Indian warfare than any other class of men. Many officers have spent as much time upon the frontier as Carson and his fellows.

But to return to Major Thompson's expedition. Shoes had arrived in generous numbers and it was decided to follow the Indian into his secret haunts and punish him thoroughly for his numerous thefts and murders. There were no loud notes of preparations for everything was got in order for the march at the time appointed.

The major determined to take the greater part of the garrison on this expedition and expressed his intention to be gone ten days. The day before he was to start, he notified me that I would go also. There was no special need of my services on the trip. I had been regularly relieved from my company when I was made quartermaster and there was plenty of duty for me at the post at this particular time, but the major could not forego the opportunity of putting me to an inconvenience. Accordingly, he ordered me verbally to be ready to march with the command at daylight next morning. Except for some delay in the making out and forwarding of my monthly papers, I had no objection to going on the Indian hunt. In reality I liked it, but I objected to what I felt to be the real reason for the major's order. However, I said nothing, but secured the help of a private soldier to assist my clerk on the papers and got myself ready for the march.

Next morning, soon after reveille, the cavalry and infantry started on foot. The horses of the cavalry troops, from one cause

6. Another writer agreed with this assessment of Woolsey's Indian scout: "The expedition was not a successful one; no Indians were killed; trouble arose among the men; the party divided; some left and returned home before the main body, and all, when they got back, were dissatisfied and grumbling. Woolsey, I believe, did the best he could under the circumstances, but the trip lost him many friends." *Daily Alta California*, August 29, 1865.

and another, had become so reduced in numbers that less then half of the men could be mounted in case of an emergency. For this reason the troop was compelled to do duty as infantry. No wagons were taken, as the route was to be over a country too rough for wheels, but instead we took pack mules for the transportation of ammunition, provisions and cooking utensils. Lieutenant Abeytia was left to command the fort in our absence, with barely enough men to furnish a guard for two posts.

The first day's march was in the direction of Postle's ranche and was about ten miles in length, ending somewhere on the stream which rises in the Red Rocks. The next day we passed Postle's quite early in the morning, then turned down the valley of the Rio Verde, not following the banks of the river as on the fishing excursion, but taking the upper country, above the walls which enclose that stream. Neither did we generally march along heights or tablelands from which the river could be seen, but followed valleys which ran parallel to its course, barely rising into sight except when it became necessary to do so in passing from one valley into another.

All the officers and the two guides, Cooler and Weaver, were mounted. The doctor and myself usually rode together, sometimes in advance and sometimes behind, just as the notion took us. As I had no command and was purely ornamental, I had no fixed place, but could go where I chose, just so that I did not lose sight of the column. The doctor had received positive orders not to fire his shotgun at the birds until we should be on the return march. Accordingly, he confined himself strictly to the route and made no excursions to the right and left, as he otherwise would have done.

Soon after leaving Postle's, we crossed a small tributary of the Rio Verde, which Weaver told us was the last water we should see until we reached camp at night. A short halt was made to enable the men to take a drink and fill their canteens. After all had done so and the march was resumed, I dismounted to fill my canteen and while doing so the doctor rode up from Postle's, where he had halted to pay his respects to "P & B." Without dismounting, he gave his horse the rein, so that the beast could drink. Noticing that the doctor showed no intention of filling his canteen, I asked, "Did you get some water at Postle's?"

"Got a drink," was the reply.

"I mean, did you fill your canteen?"

"No, there's no need to, plenty of water on the route," and the doctor started his horse through the rivulet.

"You are mistaken, doctor," I said. "Weaver says we shall see no more water this side of the night camp."

"I don't care! I shan't need any water," saying which, Coues dashed into a gallop and was gone.

Our march all day was through a parched country, which bore nothing but the cactus and the yucca in their many varieties, with occasional clumps of *piñons* and junipers. We halted occasionally for the scouts to go to the tops of the ridges and look for Indians. By great care we did not once show ourselves, so that the enemy, had he been anywhere in the vicinity, could not have seen us. The weather was warm and I knew before we had been many hours of the march that the doctor, who was riding beside me, was wishing he had some water. He was an inveterate smoker and enjoyed his pipe as much as any person I ever knew. This alone would cause him to need water more than a person who did not use the weed in any form. I was a little tantalizing, perhaps, in the frequent shows I made of taking long swigs at the canteen and shaking the limpid fluid so that the breaking water should reach his ear. At last, after about four hours had passed, the doctor exclaimed, "For God's sake, Curtis, give me a drink of water."

"Certainly, doctor," I replied. "Why did you not ask for it before?"

"By Jove, I was ashamed to!"

Here he applied his mouth to the aperture and did not remove it until nearly half of the contents had gone down his parched throat.

"It seems very odd to me, doctor," I said, seizing the situation to deliver a lecture, "that you will never take any advice from me. Did I ever give you any wrong advice?"

"No, you never did, that is true."

"Recall all the scrapes and misfortunes you have met with since we first met on the Rio Grande and see if I ever advised you any way but what was right."

"No, you never did, old fellow, but then I always thought you were playing the superior to me, on account of your greater experience."

"Not a bit of it, doctor. When I first joined, I noticed that the older officers always let the newcomers severely alone, never advising or cautioning them about anything, but letting them blunder into all sorts of scrapes and acquire wisdom by experience. I determined that I would do differently and tell a new man what to avoid and what to do. You were my first chance and I believe up to today you have never taken my advice in anything."

"I guess that's true, but you can rest assured I shall keep my canteen filled after this and I'll try to take the advice too."

When camping began to be thought of, Major Thompson directed Cooler to mount the ridge and ride along until he could see a break in the river wall, and, when he did, come back to the column and report. Cooler at once disappeared and we continued our march for a full hour before he returned and reported an opening through which we could approach the bank of the Rio Verde. We at once turned at right angles with the course we had pursued during the day and, rising to the crest of the ridge, caught a glimpse of the bright green grass and willows of the river valley about five miles away, through what appeared to be a notch in the wall.

An hour's march increased the notch to a gap of half a mile in width and the country sloped gently through it to the river side. Once in that part of the valley, enclosed between the walls, we turned to the right and bivouacked on a broad green space against the perpendicular wall. The men had come well provided with lines and hooks. In a few moments after we had unloaded the mules and turned all the stock loose to graze, the banks of the stream were lined with men fishing for the "Gila trout" and not long after the fish were sizzling in the fry-basins of a dozen groups of men.[7]

I took a walk along the valley and found the same features existing here which I have mentioned as existing in that portion of the valley near Postle's ranche—the regular succession of beaver dams, one flowing into another. Returning to camp, I took care of my horse, as did all the officers except Doctor Coues, and then went to bed. The doctor, who had ridden all day, was not able to

7. A letter described the idyllic nature of this site: "The first camp on the river was in an open valley, filled with willows, walnut trees, grape vines and currant bushes. The water ran full and free over two large beaver dams, each damming water about six hundred yards in extent, abounding in myriads of fish, which the soldiers caught by hundreds, affording a luxury for supper not common in these parts." *Sacramento Daily Union*, August 16, 1865.

see that he ought not to put the care of his horse upon a man who had marched on foot since daybreak. I was so much vexed with his want of ordinary perception that I went to sleep without inflicting upon him a chapter of my advice.

We had not been under the blankets but a few moments when a drenching thundershower began to fall and soon penetrated to the skin. We slept well, however, and did not wake until called to breakfast. As I crawled out of my steaming blankets, I caught sight of George Cooler on his knees before the fire, holding a long-handled skillet with both hands and gazing with great intentness into the sizzling depth. Presently he gave a quick toss. A thin and supple disk flew into the air, turned over and fell neatly into the skillet, which was suspended for a moment more over the fire and then the contents were added to a pile of griddlecakes on a platter near by.

"What are you making, George?" shouted the doctor, as he raised himself into a bent position, resting on his hands and blinking sleepily towards the fire.

"Bromides!"

"What's a bromide?"

"Come and see for yourself."

Without stopping to get into his pantaloons, the doctor approached the fire, peered into the skillet, ran his hand through his frowzled hair and said, "Those are flapjacks."

"Yes, flapjacks, slapjacks, flannel-cakes, pancakes and *bromides*!"

"But where did you get such a name as bromide?"

"Don't know. That's what the miners call 'em."

At breakfast we had bacon, fish and bromides and did ample justice to the meal. At its close we rolled up our wet bedding to be packed on the mules and got our horses ready, all except the doctor who asked a soldier to wait upon him. As soon as everything was ready, we retraced our steps to nearly the same place from which we had turned off to the river the evening before and resumed the regular course of our march. No incidents occurred on this day to make it different from the preceding and with evening we again found ourselves in camp by the river side.

At this camp the doctor asked a soldier to unsaddle his horse, water and picket him out. The doctor lazily threw himself on the ground as soon as he was out of the saddle and, drawing a book from his pocket, began reading. Presently he called out to another man, "Sullivan, bring me a dipper of water!"[8]

"Never mind, Sullivan," said Major Thompson, "I'll get the water," and before the doctor could recover from his surprise, the major brought him a tin cup filled with water. Rising to his feet, the doctor took the cup and said, "Major, you do me much honor. I did not intend you should get it. I meant Sullivan should wait on me."

"Yes, I know what you meant, but I have been riding all day and Sullivan has been walking. He is very tired and I am not particularly so."

And so the doctor had learned another lesson, as usual knocked into him. From this time out on all our marches he waited upon himself whenever he rode and the men walked.

Next morning Barr punched me with a fishing pole while we were still in our blankets. Looking towards him, he pointed me to the fire and placed his finger on his lips. I raised my head so that I could see clearly and beheld the doctor at the fire with the skillet, in the same position in which I had seen Cooler the previous morning. He gave the skillet a toss, a bromide leaped into the air and fell into the fire. Taking a quick glance around, the doctor seized a small stick and punched the cake into the ashes out of sight. Then he poured another quantity of batter into the skillet and began as before. This time the bromide went up and came down half in the skillet and half out. Turning it in he finished cooking it and added it to the diminutive pile beside him.

"That's the fifth he has finished," whispered Barr, "and there are twenty-one in the ashes."

"It's lucky flour does not cost us as much as it does the miners," I said.

"And that our march is not a long one," added the lieutenant.

But the doctor kept improving and finally six fritters in succession came down squarely into the skillet. With the finishing of the last, the doctor gave a yell of delight, which aroused everybody, and shouted, "Oh, no! I can't make a bromide, can I?" at the same time flipping one into the air and in his excitement letting it fall flat into the fire.

"No, I should think not," replied Major Thompson, "if that is a specimen of your making."

8. Sullivan cannot be positively identified.

Everybody laughed and the doctor blushed. However, he did well next time and shortly made no mistakes. Barr was wicked enough in the midst of his triumph to dig out the twenty-one misflings from the ashes and present them to the doctor in the midst of his self-congratulation.

The two next days' marches brought us, without seeing any Indians, to our last camping place on the river. Here the break in the wall was over a mile in extent and a beautiful level valley, of a mile in width, stretched along the western side of the stream. The river took a sharp bend to the south from the eastern course which it had hitherto pursued, plunging into a *cañon* with upright walls which closed upon it close down to the water. In the face of a cliff, about a hundred feet high, which looked up the valley, was an opening about fifty feet high and forty feet wide, shaped like a gothic arch. This opening led into a cave a hundred feet deep. I manufactured a torch and explored it. It was the former home of cave dwellers. The whole interior was built up in rooms, story above story. On the top of the cliff, above the cave, was the trace of a ruined town, plainly indicated by the broken walls and scattered pottery. The valley had once been populated and I could not help thinking what a fine ranche might be taken up here when once the Apache should be put down.

Next day we started on our march to Fort Whipple, not retracing our steps, but through the Black Hills and across the plains. The day's march was through an exceedingly rough country, in many places all the officers and the guides dismounted to lead their horses. This was done not only because it was a kindness to the animals, but because it was safer for the rider. The doctor, however, had early declared his intention to stick to his horse. "To ride was what he bought him for and he meant to do what he pleased with him."

Along in the afternoon, we began the descent of a spur of the mountains, the road running along the side of a declivity and very steep, as well as stony. As usual, all dismounted but the doctor. He rode stolidly along, smoking his pipe, and indifferent to all advice. When within fifty yards of the bottom, the path crushed away beneath the horse's feet, causing him to fall over sideways. The doctor was unable to disengage himself from the saddle and went down with the horse, rolling completely over with him once.

A dozen of us leaped to the rescue, expecting to find the doctor crushed or his limbs broken. The horse had sprung to its feet and began cropping the grass before we reached the spot. The doctor lay in the red soil motionless and we feared dead. We got hold of him, raised him and he burst into a loud, hysterical laugh, the laugh of nervousness and shame. We looked him over thoroughly and found nothing had happened more serious than the destruction of his meerschaum and the splitting of the stock of his shotgun.

We were now going through a country believed to be a good mining region but which, on account of the Indian hostilities, had hitherto been prospected but little. The officers of the army were as much interested in the discovery of gold as anyone else and never went out on an expedition, which was likely to take them through the mountainous country, without being provided with the means of examining and testing the specimens collected. Some of the best mines in Arizona were discovered by army men. All through the Black Hills we neglected no opportunity to prospect for lodes.

On the second day after we left the river, we entered a valley in which the Mescalero Apaches had recently been cooking mescal, the plant from which they get their name.[9] The mescal is of the genus *Yucca* and family *Liliaceae*, having leaves about the length of a bayonet and a little wider, radiating outward and upward from the earth to the height of about two feet. The edges of the leaves are bordered with sharp and stiff points, which will penetrate shoe leather, if one thrusts his foot against it. From the centre grows a stalk about as big as a broom handle, to the height of eight or ten feet, which bears a lily-like flower. In selecting the mescal for food, the plants which have not flowered are chosen, the others are worthless.

To prevent wounding the hands, a very long knife is used to separate the plant from its roots. By thrusting the knife under the leaves close to the surface of the earth, it can be freed and the leaves or spikes can then be removed, one at a time, until the head or heart is disclosed, which is about the size of a rutabaga turnip.

9. Edmund Wells explained the popularity of mescal: "Scattered over the mountain slopes, fields or patches of mescal grew, the baked heart of the young growth yielding a nutritious fibrous bread of sweet flavor and in appearance resembling the old fashioned baker's section of ginger cake. It was a great winter food for the Apaches, and in fact, was relished by the hungry white hunters and trappers fortunate enough to procure it from the Indians." Wells, *Argonaut Tales*, 320.

This, when sliced, is turnip-like in appearance and in the raw state tastes like a chestnut.

I shall never forget my experience in tasting mescal. At this camp I had taken my carbine and gone out to look for some ruins, which I had heard were in the vicinity. On my arrival I "husked" a mescal, cut myself a generous slice and came into camp eating it. Major Thompson saw what I was doing and cautioned me not to eat more, as it would salivate me. The caution came too late. My mouth was exceedingly sore for a week after.

The Indian method of preparing the vegetable for food is quite simple. They build a pyramid of stones, over which they light a fire and continue it until the rocks are red hot. The fire and ashes are then swept away and the heads of mescal are piled over the stones, until a pyramid about eight feet high is raised. This is covered with straw and turf and left for forty-eight hours. At the end of that time, the mescal heads will mash like potatoes and are rolled out into mats, which a slight fibrous tissue keeps from breaking, to dry. When dry the mats are made up into rolls. A party of Mescaleros on a journey, or the warpath, is seldom without a mat of mescal, rolled up and slung across the back. The Mexicans make a whiskey from the same plant.

At this camp we had some difficulty in finding water. There was every evidence that the Mescaleros had been there a short time before we arrived. The fact, too, that this was a favorite locality for preparing mescal showed that there must be water somewhere in the vicinity. We made the most diligent search and it was not until three hours and much of our patience had been spent that we found it. The spring, which had no surface outlet, had been filled with stones which they had heaped up to resemble a mescal kiln.

Our last camp was on the edge of the plain. Here we found horrible evidence that the Indians must be aware of our march and of their intention to defy us. Not only was the spring defiled, but we found two dead white men, but recently killed, hung up by the heels near it. Two forked sticks were set up in the ground and a pole placed across the top, seven feet from the earth. The ankles of the bodies were fastened to the pole, so that their heads reached within two feet of the ground. A fire had been built beneath the men and they had died from this fiendish method of torture.

On a mound separated by a valley from the mountain and well advanced into the plain, are some ruins of the Aztecs or some other ancient people. We learned a long time after that a party of miners engaged in prospecting had camped at the spring the day before we reached it. After eating their dinner and before resuming their journey, two of their number started to see the ruins on the mound. When near the top, a party of Indians concealed in the ruins seized them as prisoners. The rest of the miners did not dare to attempt a rescue, but escaped and went on to the Bradshaw mining region, from which place the story reached us the next spring.

At this camp, Major Thompson determined to send me back to Fort Whipple to make up my papers, while he turned back into the mountains for two days more hunt. The next day at sunrise the command turned into the mountains a little to the south of where it came out and I started at a canter across the plain to Fort Whipple. Three days afterwards the major returned, well pleased with his campaign. By turning back at the ruins, he had met a large party of Indians and had given them a terrific whipping, with no loss on the part of the military.

Chapter 45

Last Days at Fort Whipple

Once more established in my quarters at Fort Whipple, for several weeks I did no duty outside of the garrison. I learned from many sources that there was much discontent among the employees in the corral at the actions of the commanding officer and his quartermaster, in ordering them to vote for Judge Allyn. I also learned that during my absence all my acts as quartermaster had been closely investigated, my clerk having received a pecuniary offer if he would furnish any information which could be the means of bringing me before a court martial. This proposition of my friend Thompson fell through, as my management of the Government funds and the property placed in my charge had been honest, if not at all times the best. To my face the major was affability itself, for he had no reason to believe that I was in possession of any information in regard to his investigation of my duties. He often came into my room with his pipe and made a great pretence of friendship. He never left, however, without informing me with great positiveness that "Allyn would be elected." To this I made no reply, for it was no business of mine who should go to Congress. I had a personal friendship for Governor Goodwin and no liking for Judge Allyn, but not being a voter and, what was a still stronger reason, being an officer of the army, I had no right to meddle in the interests of either candidate.

A month after my return from La Paz, Governor Goodwin and General Mason arrived in Prescott and took up their residence in the gubernatorial mansion, the general taking the southern side and the governor the northern. The second day after his arrival, all the officers of Fort Whipple waited upon the general in full dress, to pay our respects.

General John S. Mason. Courtesy of Massachusetts MOLLUS Civil War Photographs, United States Army Heritage and Education Center.

General John S. Mason was a graduate of West Point and at the time I met him held in the Regular service the rank of major and in the Volunteers the rank of brigadier general. He had been in active service in the East, doing his last active duty at Antietam and Fredericksburg. He is now lieutenant colonel of the 4th Infantry. We found him a pleasant gentleman, of reserved manners and handsome features. After staying a short time we returned to the fort.

The idea suggested itself to me to present my grievances to the general and ask his intervention between the major and myself, but I could not bring myself to do it. I felt I had been misused, but I could not complain.

One day, a week after our official visit to General Mason, I mounted my horse and rode to Prescott to make a call upon the governor. I stayed there perhaps an hour and was in the act of mounting to return, when the general came out of his quarters and said, "Mr. Curtis, wait a moment."

He went back to his office and presently appeared with an unsealed official envelope in his hand.

"There, sir, is an order which I think will please you."

"Thank you, sir," I replied. "I think I need something to please me."

"You are at liberty to read the order, only seal it afterwards and deliver it to Major Thompson. Come and dine with me tomorrow."

"Shall be happy to do so, sir," I replied and was off at a gallop. As I flew through the town my heart was bounding at the thought that the tide in my affairs had taken a turn. The courtesy of the general had meant something, there was no doubt. Evidently some friend had told him of my difficulties. When I got fairly out of town, I checked my horse into a walk, pulled the order from my jacket and read as follows:

Headquarters District of Arizona,
Special Orders, No. 23

I. 1st Lieut. Antonio Abeytia, 1st New Mex. Cav. is hereby relieved from duty as Quartermaster and Commissary at Fort Whipple, and will turn over immediately all property and funds pertaining to those departments now in his hands to 1st Lieut. C. A. Curtis, 5th U. S. Infantry.

II. 1st Lieut. C. A. Curtis, 5th U. S. Infantry, is hereby detailed for duty as Quartermaster and Commissary at Fort Whipple, and will receive from 1st Lieut. Antonio Abeytia, 1st New Mex.

Cav., all property and funds pertaining to those departments now in his hands.

III. Major John Thompson, 1st New Mex. Cav., is hereby relieved from duty as Post Commander at Fort Whipple and will proceed with Company M, 1st New Mex. Cav. to Maricopa Wells, where he will establish a camp, and await further orders. He will send in requisitions immediately for such transportation and supplies as he may need for the march.

By order of Brig. Gen. Mason.
(Signed)
John Green, Captain & Adjt. Genl.[1]

Of course, it is not necessary to assure the reader that the above order afforded me much pleasure. If I have failed to convey an idea of the many annoyances put upon me by Thompson, it is because I do not like to dwell upon them. This action of General Mason is in itself sufficient proof that something of an unpleasant nature, to say the least, had been going on, something which he thought it his duty to rectify.

I sealed the order and as I entered the fort, left it at the adjutant's office. I did not intend to let anyone know that the contents of the order were already in my possession, but await its regular promulgation. I will explain to the unmilitary reader that this order was written on three sheets of paper because there were three officers affected by it. One sheet, with the date, signature, etc., contained only that portion referring to Lieutenant Abeytia and was sent to him, another containing the part in which I was personally interested came to me and a similar one went to the major.

I had been sitting in my room but a few moments when Thompson burst in with his extract of the order in his hand, exclaiming somewhat noisily, "Well, Curtis, I have got what I have been wanting for a long time!"

"What is that, major?" I asked.

"I am going to Maricopa Wells!"

"Isn't that generally considered a disagreeable place?"

1. John Green was commissioned first lieutenant in the 4th Ohio on June 4, 1861, and was promoted to captain on June 11, 1862. At the request of his old colonel, now General John Mason, Green was assigned to his staff as captain and assistant adjutant general on March 11, 1863. Brevetted to major for his wartime service effective March 13, 1865, he was mustered out on August 15, 1866. Green moved west and was last heard from while residing at Council Bluffs, Iowa, in 1886. Heitman, *Historical Register* 1: 473; Kepler, *Fourth Regiment*, 244.

"Bless you, no!"

"I have always heard so and I think I once heard you say you had rather go to hell than go there."

"No, Curtis, it must have been some other place. Maricopa is just delightful. I wanted to go there." With the most unblushing effrontery the major began reading his order: "*By request* Major John Thompson is hereby, etc.," pretending that he had obtained the order by asking for it. I did not tell him I knew he was telling an untruth and he has never to this day known that I had the first reading of the order.

Three days from the receipt of the order, Major Thompson with all the New Mexicans left for Maricopa and on the morning of the same day I went to the corral and ordered the corral master to assemble all the quartermaster's employees, as I had a word to say to them. In a few moments all had gathered in front of the stables, when I made the following brief and eloquent speech:

"Men, I have called you together to say that there shall be no interference on my part with your voting for delegate to Congress. Choose your own candidate and I assure you no man shall be discharged for exercising his rights of citizenship."

"Then, by George, three cheers for Governor Goodwin!" exclaimed the corral master.

Three rousing cheers were given by all the men without an exception. Probably no speech during the campaign converted such a per cent of Allyn men to Goodwin as did mine. The election, which occurred soon after, brought the governor in with a good majority.

About the first of September a company of California infantry arrived and took the quarters recently vacated by the Mexicans. We also learned that there was a cavalry company *en route*, which would arrive before the month passed. The Regular company was very much reduced by expiration of term of enlistment and by death, several having died in hospital during the winter from mountain fever and a few in the fights with Indians. The company did not number in September more than twenty-five.

A few days after my return from an Indian hunt, a company of cavalry arrived from the direction of Fort Mojave. It had been raised in the vicinity of Oroville, in Butte County, California and was under the command of a young man of Southern birth, named Ebenezer C. Ledyard.[2] He was something of a gasconader, but anyone who took him for a coward on this account would make a serious mistake. He was thoroughly acquainted with his duty as an officer, being perfect in drill and holding proper ideas of discipline. Had he been appointed to the Regular service or to a company of Veteran Volunteers, schooled to discipline by long active service, he would have been considered an excellent commander. But he had the misfortune to know his proper place as an officer before his company had learned it and outgrown their disposition to refer all questions of discipline to the company caucus, or town meeting. In the first flush of their military enthusiasm, while in camp at Oroville under the daily instruction of the captain, they had taken up a contribution, purchased a gold-hilted sabre and presented it to their young officer, amid much parade and self-laudation. This was his first mistake, the acceptance of the present. By the acceptance, he gave every man a claim, in the man's mind, upon his favor. When the actual hardship of military life began, when the officer found himself, by his position and by the rigid requirements of the army regulations, isolated from the men; when they had learned that from him proceeded all the orders imposing what they looked upon as unnecessary hardships, then they began to dislike him; to kick against him; to aid an indiscreet lieutenant in opposition to him; and to do many things which longer service caused them to look back upon as foolish, to say the least.

Captain Ledyard was very proud of his gold-hilted sabre, never failing to call the attention of his visitors to it and keeping it displayed conspicuously upon the wall of his quarters. He seems never to have suspected that the men who gave him this present were regretting it and already planning to recover it, but he left his quarters hours at a time, open and unoccupied, with no fear that the sabre would be lost. One evening, however, while he was in Prescott, his quarters were entered, the sabre stolen and disposed of so that he never again saw it. It used to hang on a wall

2. Ebenezer C. Ledyard enlisted as a private in the 1st Louisiana on December 26, 1846. He served in Mexico and on December 24, 1847, was commissioned second lieutenant, mustering out on July 6, 1848. Commissioned captain in the 1st California Cavalry on March 2, 1865, Ledyard served in Arizona until ordered back to California for muster out on May 22, 1866. After leaving the service, Captain Ledyard moved to Mexico where he married and started a family. After contracting tuberculosis, he moved to Tucson and committed suicide there on July 11, 1878. *Mexican War Veterans*, 55; *California Men*, 89; *Arizona Enterprise*, July 27, 1878; *Arizona Star*, July 11, 1878.

of his cabin, the centre of a group of carbines and revolvers, neatly disposed in a warlike rosette. A common sabre was substituted for the stolen one, so that the theft was not known until the captain wished to show it to a visitor some time in the afternoon of the day after his visit to Prescott.

I have always felt sorry for Ledyard. He never was appreciated by his men at his true value. Had he been in the field where "lead was in the air," there is little doubt but what his bravery would have compelled the respect of his men, as has been the case with many other officers similarly situated, but he came into service the last year of the war and went out before his men had time to appreciate him. The Regulars at the post liked him and there was not a man among them who did not smile at the fancied wrongs of the cavalry troop.

My mention that Ledyard should not have received the present is not to be taken as an indication that I think it improper to take presents. I think it very proper and know that it is very acceptable for the officer to receive a present at the close of the campaign or the war, when there can be no mistake as to the motives of the givers and when the officer cannot fail to have his heart stirred by this delicate appreciation of his merits. There are many officers of the late war who have such presents, more dear to them than the complimentary orders of their superiors and more carefully cherished. But a present to the untried officer is a mistake. It trammels him from the outset and it leads the givers to look upon him as ungrateful whenever the rigid requirements of discipline demand that he should be harsh with them.

With the advent of Ledyard's company, my military career at Fort Whipple was drawing to a close. Before I left New Mexico, I had been granted leave of absence to go East "to get married." Circumstances over which I had no control and, which seem to have secured full control over the young lady whom I had hoped to enlist in the service of Hymen, caused me to neglect to take up my leave. When I was suffering under the continual harassing of Major Thompson, I bethought me of this leave of absence, which was waiting my acceptance. I applied for permission to take it up. The request, owing to the bad mail facilities and the many military channels through which it must pass from the time it left my hands until it returned, was a long time in going to Washington and coming back and, when it finally did so, it was saddled with the condition that I could leave whenever General Mason could spare me. Upon applying to him, I learned that I must remain at Fort Whipple until I had thoroughly straightened out the confusion in the quartermaster and commissary departments, made by the Mexican lieutenant whom Thompson had placed in charge.[3] I therefore went rapidly to work to get things into good condition, so that I could avail myself of the furlough.

With General Mason's arrival, several new regiments of California Volunteers were distributed through Arizona for the purpose of bringing under subjection the numerous bands of Apaches scattered through the almost inaccessible fastnesses of the territory. Besides the white troops, a company of Maricopa Indians was organized for scouting service and placed under the command of a German, Lieutenant Charles Reidt.[4] The Maricopas are a tribe living in the southern part of the territory and very nearly resembling the Pueblo Indians of the Rio Grande.[5] They cultivate the soil,

3. J. M. Swetnam recalled that when the first load of barley was taken to Fort Whipple in late summer of 1865 the farmers asked to be paid eighteen dollars per hundred pounds, the same price as if the grain had been freighted from California. Quartermaster Curtis, noting that the barley was subpar, remarked: "Don't think I want it at any price." Swetnam related how he and his neighbors in the Verde valley had risked their lives to raise the grain and complained about Curtis's refusal to purchase their crop. Curtis listened patiently, and then said: "Come back in an hour and I'll see what can be done." Upon his return, Swetnam learned that the lieutenant would buy all their barley at seventeen dollars per hundred pounds, an arrangement joyfully accepted by the sellers. Farish, *History of Arizona* 4: 239-40.

4. Charles Reidt was commissioned second lieutenant in the 1st Arizona and his company mustered in on September 2, 1865. With the exceptions of officers, his company, B, was composed entirely of Maricopa Indians. Reidt served as quartermaster and clerk at Fort McDowell after the war. After leaving the military, he purchased the land known as Mission Camp some thirty-five miles east of Arizona City (now Yuma). On Christmas Eve 1870, three Mexican desperados burst into the station and murdered Charles Reidt, the station cook Tom Oliver, and relief driver James Lytle. Mrs. Reidt was seriously wounded. The attackers ransacked the building and made off with half a dozen horses. The killings prompted a diplomatic confrontation between the Arizona governor and Mexican authorities. Some newspaper coverage referred to Reidt as "Reed" and others have confused Charles with his brother August, a lieutenant colonel in the 27th Pennsylvania. However, in 1872 August wrote to the adjutant general for information about Charles's death so that the family could settle some inheritance issues in Germany. McClintock, *Arizona* 1: 194; *Weekly Journal Miner*, January 7, 1871; *Arizona Citizen and Daily Tribune*, March 15, 1873; *San Diego Union*, December 25, 1873.

5. The Maricopa people are very similar and likely related to the Mojave and Quechan Indians. There seems to be some difficulty identifying the Maricopa in the historical literature and it is now used as a generic term unless specifically referring to the Opa people. The Maricopas lived in the Gila River valley, where they allied themselves with the Pima people, and numbered approximately 400 during the Civil War. The Gila River Reservation was set up for them in 1859. They practiced agriculture, supplemented by hunting and gathering. In the winter the Maricopa built permanent structures reinforced by soil so Apaches and other groups called them "sand-house people." Harwell and Kelly, "Maricopa," 71, 75, 79; Ezell, *Maricopas*, 26.

have large herds and flocks, but do not build houses. They wage no wars but defensive ones and are a peaceful and happy people. Nearly all the grain used by the military forces for foraging the stock was purchased of these Indians and their near relatives, the Pimas.[6] Our flour also was ground from wheat of their raising. It was not my fortune to visit that part of the territory where they lived, so I know little of them except from hearsay and reading.

The company of Maricopas numbered about one hundred, was organized as infantry, having Springfield rifles, and wore the uniform and accoutrements of the white soldier. As Lieutenant Reidt understood the Maricopa language, he made a translation of the schools of the soldier and company into that tongue but retained the English commands. After the red company had become proficient in drill, they were marched to Prescott to be reviewed by General Mason in the square before the governor's house. All the officers from Fort Whipple were invited to be present to witness the display. Accordingly, all of us except the one whose turn it was to be officer of the day went up to district headquarters some little time before the hour appointed.

While waiting for the review, the conversation turned upon the availability of the American Indian for military purposes. I found that there had for a long time been an opinion entertained by the army that the Indian might be used as a light cavalryman to good advantage and that this view had been laid before the President and Congress in several reports. The love of the Indian for display, for horseflesh, for dashing service and adventure would then be humored and, at the same time, he could be made to have a love and feeling of patriotism for the country. Some doubt as to the practicability of turning the Indian into an infantryman was expressed. His tastes were decidedly against plodding foot service. The Maricopas, however, being an agricultural people, possessing

6. Although generally known as the Pima people, they were actually the Upper Pima to differentiate them from a lesser-known group in Mexico. The Pima are further divided into Pima and Papago, although there is so little difference between the two that one village was actually classified as Pima in winter and Papago in summer. Living along the Gila River allowed the Pima to become proficient agriculturalists, leading them to become an important source of supply for the U. S. Army, especially after the establishment of a mill and trading posts in 1859. By 1857 they not only fed the army, but joined in active field operations, leading one writer to note that they had acted "with even more efficiency than a frontier military." In that same year the Pima united with the Maricopa to repel a Yuma invasion and that alliance "thoroughly vanquished the Yumas, leaving almost no survivors." Ezell, "History of the Pima," 149–50, 156–58; Dunnigan, "Lower Pima," 217; Shaw, *A Pima Past*, 6.

but few horses and not especially given to horsemanship, might be used as foot scouts, but it was thought doubtful whether any amount of service or discipline could make them stand up in line like a white man and fight an enemy face to face.[7]

The question has been often asked me whether the Indian will fight an open battle with the white man, where there is an even chance of success for both sides. History of Indian warfare in the states east of the Mississippi give many instances where the red man took his life in his hands and fought as desperately and gallantly for victory as the pale face. In the Florida War, in the sieges of Government forts, the Seminoles chopped away the gates with axes under the fire of the garrison, new men picking up the axes as fast as their comrades fell. In the Tippecanoe Campaign the Indians fought gallantly on the field. But in the Far West, the cases are rare where the red man fights unless all the advantages are on his side. The knowledge of this was the chief cause of the apparent reckless exposure of our lives in Arizona, the reason why small bodies would go through an Indian-infested country without fear. Everyone felt that so long as he avoided all chances of ambuscade, he was safe. To my knowledge, no Indian in New Mexico or Arizona ever attacked white men unless in the nature of a surprise or where they had a positive assurance of victory through their overwhelming numbers.

When the hour came for the review, the Maricopa Company of Arizona Volunteers arrived and was formed in front of the governor's house. When the general came out of his quarters, the "Present Arms!" was given with an accuracy and precision which won our admiration at the staff. The men of the company were fine-looking physically, looking strange only in their red complexion, high cheekbones, broad faces and their thick, bushy hair, which stood out full beneath their small soldier caps. The manual of arms was gone through with finely, eliciting much applause from the spectators.

7. Edmund Wells wrote of his personal experience with these Native American soldiers: "The recruits were robust, vigorous and athletic young men, quite humorous, and very jocose in magnifying their own valor and lack of courage in the enemy—white, red or Mexican. They were dramatically inclined and gave us pantomime exhibitions of ambushing the enemy and the attacks upon them. Just before going into battle they would go through the exercise of physical lubrication, consisting of rubbing their armpits, elbows, wrists, hip and knee joints with sand to make them supple and submissive to the dexterous use of the bow and arrow and the lance, and flexible in their dashing attack, and fleetness of escape in case of defeat." Wells, *Argonaut Tales*, 386.

The commands were in English, the captain rattling an occasional explanation in Maricopa like a native. At last the command "About face!" was given and the whole company faced in the opposite direction, revealing to our astonished eyes the fact that every Indian had cut a piece out of the seat of his uniform trousers about eight inches square. This revelation was greeted with peals of laughter, which, however, did not disturb the imperturbable Indian gravity or cause a man to turn his head.

"Well, the Indian peculiarities will show themselves in spite of everything," exclaimed Doctor Coues.

"Is that what you call them?" asked Barr. "I thought they were buttocks."

The drill went on and closed with a review in platoons, showing excellent proficiency in everything. The company was then dismissed and shortly afterwards marched to the south. In the war of the fall and winter, these Indians did good service scouting in small detachments, never regaining their company organization, but scattered to various posts throughout the country.

About this time there was an auction sale of lots in Prescott. Commissioners had taken up a section of the public lands for the town, had laid it out in streets, naming those running east and west after historical characters of the Spanish conquest, as Cortéz, Coronado, Montezuma, etc., and those running north and south after modern dignitaries who had had something to do with the Territorial organization, as Carleton, Goodwin, McCormick, etc. The lots along the streets were staked out and sold to the highest bidder, one-third of the price bid to be paid down and the rest whenever the Washington authorities should confirm the action of the commissioners. Several of the army officers who had laid up a little money purchased these lots. I bought three. When I left the territory, I placed them in charge of an ex-Volunteer officer who had set up as a lawyer after the expiration of his term of service. There proved to be some informality in the action of the town commissioners and Government ordered a relocation. My lawyer relocated in his own name and is now in possession of my three lots. This luck attended all the investments made by the Regulars.

I was possessed of 4,000 feet of gold mining claims, mines that assayed well and promised indefinite wealth, but absence and relocation extinguished my title to these also after I left the territory.

Governor Goodwin having been elected to Congress, it was necessary for him to go to Washington to occupy his seat. Doctor Coues, having completed his collection of 1,600 birds and 250 distinct species for the Smithsonian Institution, was ordered east, to make up his reports and superintend the stuffing and mounting.[8] I, having received my leave of absence, was anxious to get away as soon as possible. To save myself the expense of a trip to Los Angeles, I asked Coues to take me along in the ambulance assigned to him and he consented. The governor, the doctor and I met one evening at the rooms of the general and arranged for the party going east to leave on Monday, the 23rd of October, 1865. We were to have an ambulance with three seats, an army wagon and an escort of twelve cavalry and as many infantry.

My servant, Joseph Cain, who had waited upon me faithfully since I joined at Fort Craig, had been discharged from the service a few weeks before the date appointed for our departure and had expressed a desire to accompany me east. Feeling grateful to Cain for his long service, his honesty and for what he had done to put me in possession of the horse Two Bits, I decided to take him along. We needed a cook for our mess on the road and a general servant to take care of our luggage and Cain volunteered to serve us in both these capacities.

I purchased the supplies necessary for the ambulance party and had them made up in convenient packages for stowing in the wagon and also secured the necessary cooking utensils for our kitchen service. I called on all the friends I had made in Prescott and bade them good-bye. I rode to all the points of interest, to take one last look at them and lastly went into the company quarters to take each man by the hand who had served under my command since I had joined as a second lieutenant. There had been no familiar

8. On July 26, 1865, Coues lamented that he could have done more, explaining that "all through the season I was ordered off on Indian scouts and had no chance. Indeed, the Indians have all along cramped every movement; were it not for them, my collections would have been much larger and more varied." In addition to numerous Indian scouts, Coues then confessed that "being partially sick and partially lazy, I have done but little." Actually Coues was anything but lazy and he provided a treasure trove of information to scientists during his lifetime. A number of his specimens were described in *Key to North American Birds* which first appeared in 1872 and in many editions prior to his death. Dall, *Baird*, 381.

intercourse during these years, but officer and man had respected each other and had formed ties which could not be broken without some emotion. The good wishes of these men and the assurances of their regards were very pleasant to me. I shall not forget them soon. In fact, I believe I can recall the name of every private in F Company from John Bergen, the tallest man on its right, to George Hoey, the shortest on the left.

Chapter 46

Doctor Coues in Charge

The evening before we were to leave Fort Whipple, Governor Goodwin was in my room, having ridden down from Prescott to consult with me in relation to some matters connected with the outfit for the journey. We were seated at a table busy with figures and plans, when Doctor Coues burst into the room, flourishing a paper above his head and exclaiming, "Here's my order placing an ambulance, wagon and an escort of twenty-four men in my charge, to accompany me as far as San Bernardino! Now, Curtis, I'll show you how to march! None of your lying over half the time to graze, getting up before daylight and halting at noon, but we'll just go kiting!" Uttering this in a crescendo, accompanied by a boyish terpsicherous demonstration about the room, he departed full as suddenly as he had entered.

When he had gone, the governor said, "I thought you were to have command, Curtis?"

"No, I'm on leave after tomorrow."

"But that fellow will use up every animal before we have been on the road two days."

"It is his escort," I replied. "I have no authority when I am on leave. He can do just as he pleases."

"Can't you assume command?"

"Not under ordinary circumstances. If we are attacked by Indians, I shall consider it my duty to. But I am not entitled to transportation when on leave and am altogether a guest of the doctor's."

The governor soon after left for Prescott. Next day at ten o'clock, our ambulance drove up to the great gates of the post to take up the passengers. On the front seat rode the driver, John Martin, and José Duran.[1] The latter was a Mexican lad of fourteen, who had accompanied Doctor Coues from New Mexico as a servant. The doctor placed himself on the middle seat, while the governor and I located ourselves upon the rear seat. All the officers of the garrison surrounded the carriage to bid us good-bye. Most of them were the newly arrived Volunteer officers, with whom our acquaintance had been brief. Barr was the only one with whom I was really loath to part. I felt as if I should never see him again. He had always stood by me in all my difficulties like a brother and I trust I was no less loyal to him. I have never seen him since. Shortly after I left, he was ordered with the non-commissioned officers of F Company to New York and soon after resigned his commission.

During the early hours of the morning, Doctor Coues had been exceedingly busy in making preparations for the journey. He had been in the corral and condemned the selection of a wagon for our transportation, demanding the use of another not one whit different in any particular. He had inspected the mules, insisting on having rapid travelers and had kept the corral men in a high state of excitement and indignation the whole morning. He took his seat in the ambulance with an air of command which was somewhat amusing, running over with talk to the crowd surrounding us and boasting of the short time he should take to reach the Pacific coast. When the cavalry escort appeared—the infantry detachment had already started with the wagon—the doctor ordered the sergeant in command to place one-half of the men on the right side of the ambulance, the other on the left and ride himself in advance of the leading mules. This "spike escort," as Cooler at once dubbed it, caused some laughter at the doctor's expense. A team of horses or mules with a single leader is called a "spike team" in the West.

1. John Martin and Jose Duran cannot be positively identified.

At last all the parting words had been said and we were off. We passed down the bluff into the main road and were driving rapidly away, when a horseman overtook us, who proved to be a mounted orderly from district headquarters. Riding up to the side of the ambulance on which I sat, he passed me an official document. I opened and read the following order:

Headquarters, District of Arizona,
General Orders Prescott, Arizona Ter.
October 23, 1865.

I. 1st Lieutenant C. A. Curtis, 5th U. S. Infantry, is hereby directed to take command of the escort this day furnished to Assistant Surgeon Elliott Coues, U. S. Army. He will continue in command until his arrival at San Bernardino, Cal., where he will, after a proper rest, send the transportation back to Fort Whipple in charge of the sergeant of the escort.

II. The leave of absence granted 1st Lieutenant C. A. Curtis, by virtue of Special Order No. ---, dated at these Headquarters, October 19, 1865, is hereby amended to take effect upon the arrival of the Lieutenant at San Bernardino, Cal.

By Order of General Mason,
(Signed) John Green,
Captain and Asst. Adj't Gen.

So the doctor was not in command after all. I quietly put the order in my pocket and said nothing. I saw the governor's hand in this. He had feared the consequences of the doctor's rash plan for the march and had reported his youthful excitation to the general, who had in consequence issued this order. For me it was an excellent thing. For now my furlough, instead of beginning with my departure from Fort Whipple, would begin some sixteen days later, that being the time usually consumed in the journey, quite an item of extension when added to the time to be spent back East.

About five miles from the fort we came to a ranche, where the doctor halted the ambulance and escort to inquire for some eggs and milk for our dinner. Finding he could get them, he entered the house to trade. As soon as he was gone, I turned to the governor and said, "I suppose you know the nature of the order the general sent me."

"Yes, for I requested him to issue it."

"On many accounts I am sorry you did so."

"Why?"

"Well, for one thing, the doctor would have so enjoyed having the command. He has anticipated it for a long time and the escort is really his, anyway. I am here accidentally. If I were elsewhere he would certainly be in command unless the general had placed the sergeant in charge."

"But, Curtis," said the governor, "he is not fit to command. He would use up every animal in three days, if he marched as he says he intends to."

"I think he can be managed, governor. What he most dislikes is being advised or interfered with in any way. Now, if you do not object, I think I see a way in which this may be managed so as to leave him the honor and pleasure of the command, and still have everything go just as well as if I took charge myself."

"How?"

"This way. After he returns to the carriage and we have got well on the road, you ask me what are the military methods of traveling with an escort—why we rest so much of the time, why we should march early in the morning, rest during midday, drive again in the evening, etc., etc. I will give you an exhaustive lecture on the subject and the doctor will listen."

"But will the doctor follow the method?"

"Never you fear. He would not lose the opportunity to show his knowledge of the proper way, so long as it does not appear that he is advised. You will see that he will ask me no questions and that he will appear not to listen to me. But he will listen all the same."

"Can you shirk the command after receiving that order?"

"I'll take the risk. Of course I will take command in an emergency or, if I find the doctor doing anything foolish, I shall let him know I have the authority, but I really should like to have him command this escort and never know I had anything to do with it."

"Do as you please, Curtis," answered the governor. "I do not care who commands, so that we get through safe and sound."

The doctor returned with his eggs and milk and we started on. We had not gone far when the cavalry sergeant reported that two of his horses were unable to go on. We halted and examined them. They proved to be sick with dysentery and a closer examination showed that all the horses were sick with the exception of three. When asked the reason why such stock had been sent out on a long and fatiguing march, the sergeant said it was the result of a quarrel between Captain Ledyard and his first lieutenant. The captain had been unwell for a few days and the lieutenant was in charge. Doctor Coues and myself were friends of the captain and not admirers of the lieutenant, hence the sick horses. We consulted for a few moments as to whether we should return, but finally concluded to send the cavalry back to the fort and go on with the infantry.

Once more on the road, the governor asked the questions I had suggested and I gave a dissertation on marching through mountains and over plains and deserts at considerable length. The doctor whistled, hummed, petted his dog and showed every evidence of inattention, but he listened nevertheless and through the greater part of the journey observed every rule I set down.

It is not my intention to follow consecutively the incidents of my journey to the California coast. This portion of my Western experience is not so indelibly impressed upon my mind as other parts. When one drives a carriage through a country, he will remember all its features, the crossroads, the guideboards, the mountains and hills, the villages and even the farmhouses, but when one is a passenger many of these things will escape him. On the march from the Rio Grande to Fort Whipple, I was quartermaster in charge of the train, always on the lookout and near the wagons in every struggle through the difficulties of fords, ascents, descents and rough road generally—nothing escaped my observation. But on my journey from Fort Whipple to the Pacific, I was a passenger on a comfortable back seat, often sleeping through the early morning drives and rarely looking out closely, unless the country presented some special features to be admired.

Our first day's drive was over a comparatively level road, in a generally northwestern direction. At the end of twenty-five miles, we halted at a tollgate which stood at the mouth of a mountain pass, four and a half miles long. A turnpike company, chartered by the Arizona Legislature in 1864, had graded, bridged and walled a road from Prescott to Hardy's Landing, on the Colorado River. That is, they had improved all the bad places, making the road easy and practicable for the heaviest loaded wagons. The tollhouse stood on the side of the gate toward us, a log building of one story and about forty feet square. It was occupied by an elderly man, who lived there alone.

We descended from the ambulance just as the sun was setting and were hospitably received by our host. The mountain air added a keenness to the October cold and we were glad to gather by the large open fireplace, in which burned a pitch-pine fire, sending a dancing glow into every recess of the dark interior, showing a small counter with shelves behind it, containing bottles of liquors and cans of edibles, in one corner, and a fur-covered bed in another. A few deer's horns fastened to the ceiling sustained the armory and wardrobe of the establishment and a few rude chairs and blocks, sawed from the ends of logs, furnished the means of sitting.

Our wagon had followed us closely all day. The escort rode in it and the mules were trotted wherever the road was smooth. There was a corral behind the house, with a generous haystack, where the animals were secured for the night. The soldiers soon built a rousing fire, at which they proceeded to cook their supper and Cain built another to cook ours. He spread a section of a canvas shelter tent on the ground for a table and, when supper was called, we sat down upon the ground and ate. As we were to sleep under the sky for some time, we thought it best not to accept the toll-gatherer's invitation to sleep inside, but began at once by sleeping out of doors upon the ground. Our beds were therefore arranged in localities to suit each individual, a sentinel posted and everything made secure for the night.

Before bedtime we sat around the campfire listening to the tales of the toll-gatherer, an old mountaineer, whose life was brimming with adventure and whose opportunities for relating them were so rare that he could not neglect an occasion like this for monopolizing the campfire talk. The evening's amusement was continued, after the last story had been told, for a brief time longer by Cain, who, after the dishes had been washed and culinary department put in order, got out his fife, took a seat on a jutting crag of the mountain just above the ridgepole of the cabin and went through his whole repertoire of martial music. When the last note ceased we were all in bed and shortly asleep. Cain's fifing was the regular thing every evening, from this time until we reached San Bernardino, and I never think of this ride without giving a large place to Cain's musical solos.

Next day, at daybreak, we resumed our journey. The great gates swung open and we entered a narrow defile, from which the mountains rose steep on each side. This pass was four miles and a half long and debouched into Williamson Valley, along its southern side, near old Camp Rawlins, the ruins of which stood but a short distance to the left of the road. Over this part of the road we traveled at a trot for about sixteen miles, when we entered Aztec Pass, a defile lying between the Juniper Mountains on the north and the Santa Maria Mountains on the south. The pass was twelve miles long and brought us to the headwaters of a small stream called Trout Creek. We camped for dinner on this, in Muddy Cañon, forty miles west of the tollgate. After dinner the road was exceedingly rough, so that we accomplished but eight miles more before sundown. I will mention that our dinner was eaten at three o'clock. The camping place was at Fort Rock, so called on account of an eminence with a fort-like summit, standing to the left of the road. Here we had a slight scare from Indians, a party of about thirty showing themselves on a neighboring hillside about suppertime and yelling lustily. This caused us to move a little farther into the plain and take extra precaution in securing the mules for the night. We saw nothing more of them, however.

Next morning, while breakfast was being prepared, the doctor shot two ducks in a pool formed by the spring at which we camped and the governor shot half a dozen California quail on the plains. The latter are distinguished from Eastern quail by a black plume over an inch in length set in the back of their heads. Our drive for this day was barely twenty-five miles. We took dinner at The Cottonwoods and camped for the night at Dry Tanks. Why called dry I am unable to explain. We certainly found abundance of water there.

October 26th we dined at Hualpais Spring and at four o'clock P.M. reached Beale's Springs, high up in the pass through the Cerbat Mountain range. This spring was walled with stone, enclosing a space about ten feet square, and was running over with an abundance of pure water.

Next morning we crossed the divide and descended to a plain which stretched for over thirty miles to the Black Mountain range. This plain was covered with sand, in places loose and drifting, in others hard as a macadamized road. Huge yuccas, branched and towering to an average height of forty feet, were scattered over it, together with clumps of *Larrea*. It was here that I plucked dates similar to those described at Date Creek and which were now ripe. I found them delicious and palatable. We took dinner in the midst of the plain, under the shade of a yucca. These trees grow in small clusters or groves, with shining leaves, branching like a wide-spread fan. They are of all heights, from twenty to even fifty feet, the trunks being from a foot and a half to two feet in diameter. The leaves grow upon the outer extremity of the branches and each year as they die are folded back to give place to a new set. In this way the trunks attain great size. These dead leaves clustering closely to the trunk of a yucca are very combustible. I have often fired them in the night and sent the flames flashing up the tree to the outermost branches.

Evening found us at Union Spring, in the pass through the Black Mountains. This spring is said to have been discovered by a mule. One of the early Government exploration parties had halted on this barren plain, all their water gone, and were consulting whether they had better risk pushing on, trusting to find water in the black hills before them, or return to Beale's Springs. A pack mule which was grazing a little distance away from the party suddenly raised its head, brayed and then "lit out" at a gallop in the direction of the Black Mountain range. A herder pursued, but did not overtake the animal until he found him with his nose in Union Spring, far up in Union Pass. The herder rode back and informed the party of the discovery. That mule had smelt water fifteen miles.

My most vivid recollection of Union Spring is connected with an Arctic or mountain mosquito we found there. It was so cold during the night that water froze in buckets, but these mosquitoes sang and bit all night.

We crossed the mountains at daybreak and rode down a greatly undulating plain to the Colorado River at Hardy's Landing. Here we found a large trading station, wholesale and retail, belonging to a trader named William H. Hardy.[2] As this was one of the principal

2. In 1849 William H. Hardy joined a wagon train bound for California and was elected its leader, being bestowed with the title of captain by which he was known his entire life. Successful mining operations led him to open a store and his experience led him to settle at what was known as Hardyville, a mail station and ferry on the Colorado River some seven miles north of Fort Mojave. Hardyville was the northernmost point of navigation on the Colorado, so all supplies and passengers heading for Arizona by boat landed here. Hardy became a wealthy man and expanded his business to include freighting, operation of toll roads and a mercantile establishment in Prescott. He eventually lost his fortune, left Arizona in 1905 and died at Whittier, California on June 23, 1906. *Prescott Evening Courier*, June 28, 1906; *Prescott Daily Courier*, February 9, 2003.

William H. Hardy. Courtesy of Sharlot Hall Museum Library & Archives / SHM Photographs / PO-2138P.

river crossings for California and Arizona travel, as well as the steamboat landing point for military stores, the station was excellent for trade. The buildings were of *adobe*, one story, covering some acres of ground. We arrived here early in the day and were to remain until next morning. Accordingly, I borrowed a horse and rode to Fort Mojave, a few miles down the river.

I was hospitably received by the Volunteer officers at the fort and shown over the quarters and storehouses. The buildings were of *adobe* and *jacal*, situated on high ground which overlooked the Colorado, flowing half a mile below. I passed a pleasant day and returned to Hardy's Landing in the evening. When bedtime came, I spread my blanket on the floor in a room which, as I remember it, must have been a hundred feet long and fifty feet wide, the roof being upheld by a double colonnade of pillars. This whole space was piled with all sorts of goods in bulk. Somewhere in the centre I found a place to sleep and had no difficulty in losing consciousness as soon as my head touched the pillow.

Early in the morning I awoke to find Mr. Hardy standing beside my bed, holding one of my boots in his hand, which he was examining.

"Rather a poor boot, lieutenant," he said.

"It ought to be," I replied. "I bought it in Boston in 1862."

"Haven't worn it ever since?"

"No, I ripped the upper leather in Santa Fé a year after the purchase and have been obliged to wear army shoes or cavalry boots ever since. Have tried nearly every trader in New Mexico and Arizona, but can't find a man to fit me."

"I see," said Hardy, "your instep is high."

"Just so. I wear the boots in a carriage because they are easy and the hole does not bother me."

"Well, lieutenant, I believe I have something that will fit you. I have a pair of boots, the last in the case, which have been on my hands for four years. Can't find anybody that can wear them."

"Bring them here and I will try them on," I said, and Mr. Hardy disappeared down one of the passages between the surrounding boxes, barrels and bales. Presently he reappeared with a pair of sixes, which I put on and found fitted me like gloves.

We were ferried over the river at noon, on the 30th of October, in two trips of the flatboat. This boat was pulled over by a rope which stretched across from shore to shore, being arranged so that it could be slackened to the bottom whenever the steamboat passed, not oftener than once in a fortnight.

We rode twenty-five miles to Pai-Ute Springs, where we stayed all night. Next morning we started early and rode a long distance during the day, some sixty miles in all. As we considered ourselves well out of the hostile Indian country, we did not ride so closely to our wagon and escort as we had east of the Colorado. Just at nightfall, when several miles in advance of the wagon, we emerged from a dense wood, rode up a slight elevation and halted at a spring known as Government Hole, on the edge of a plain. This plain extended for a long distance before us towards the west. On the left it rose gradually to a high wooded ridge, on the right it sloped for two or three miles to a deep valley. As soon as we arrived, our driver turned the mules loose and accompanied by José went up the ridge to gather wood for our campfire. The governor took a double-barreled shotgun and went down the valley to the right to look for quail. The doctor sat down on the grass a few rods away and proceeded to skin and stuff a few birds, which he had shot on the drive. I had mixed a quantity of *pinole* (ground parched corn and sugar) in a quart cup and sat down by the carriage to read a novel.

After a considerable time had elapsed, so that the driver and José were well up the ridge, the governor far down the valley and the doctor and myself thoroughly absorbed in birds and books, I heard the doctor give a sudden exclamation and, raising my eyes, saw sixteen Indians approaching from the direction of the plain, not thirty paces away. I sprang to the carriage to secure my arms, the doctor caught his revolver from its case, but as we did so we saw the Indians were holding their weapons above their heads, advancing and chorusing, "How, how, how." At precisely this moment we heard the crack of the wagon driver's whip and the jar of the wagon wheels over the stones in the woods behind us.

Later reflection has convinced me that these Indians were camping at the spring, when the sound of our ambulance coming through the woods suggested that they should hide, until they could see the nature of the party approaching. They accordingly withdrew to a little ravine, scarce three feet deep, some thirty or forty paces west of the spring. There they lay concealed until our party arrived and scattered and, just as they might have been upon the point of attacking, they heard the noise of the coming wagon and escort. This, undoubtedly, decided them to play friends.

The Indians approached with extended arms and soon were shaking hands in the most friendly manner with the doctor and me. Some were armed with bows and arrows, a few with lances but none had firearms. They were clad in loose cotton shirts, with a belt around the waist and none possessed any other article of apparel except the chief, who wore two pairs of cotton trousers and several shirts, all ragged and fluttering. Evidently they had been out hunting and most of them bore trophies of their success, in the shape of hares and field rats. The heads of these animals were thrust up under the waist belts, the bodies dangling below. The chief approached me and, placing his finger upon my shoulder, said in broken Spanish, "*Es usted un capitán*?" ("Are you a captain?").

I replied in the affirmative, not thinking it worth while to explain the difference between a captain and a lieutenant.

"*Soy un capitán, tambien, un gran, montón capitán*" ("I'm a captain, too, a very great, heap captain").

Then he asked me where we were from and where we were going. After I had answered all his questions, I asked a few and learned that the party was Chemehuévis, one of the great Pai-Ute nation, speaking a language bearing no resemblance to their neighbors, the Mojaves.[3]

While I was talking with the chief, the doctor had been bargaining with the Indians for some of their hares. For a quantity of bread and sugar he succeeded in procuring half a dozen and soon had them in the hands of Cain, to be dressed for supper.

I returned to my novel, taking a seat in the ambulance for a more comfortable perusal. The Indians withdrew a short distance towards the ridge and began to get fuel together for a fire. In a few

3. The traditional territory of the Chemehuevi people was in southwestern Utah, although they gradually moved southwest into the Mojave Desert and on into the Chemehuevi Valley in California. Closely related to the Southern Paiute, their geographical location led them to adopt many of the elements of Mojave culture, such as elements of language, agriculture and technology. In fact, many of the Chemehuevi geographical names appear to have been borrowed from other languages, notably the Mojave. The Chemehuevi and Mojave warred against one another in 1865. When the former lost, they fled into the desert for several years before many of them settled on the Colorado River Reservation. Kelly and Fowler, "Southern Paiute," 368–70; Laird, *Chemehuevis*, 119.

moments there were three columns of smoke rising from as many fires—the escorts, the officers and the Indians, all were busily engaged cooking supper. The doctor busied himself for some time concocting the rabbit stew, choosing, as he termed it, "to engineer it" himself and the savory fumes were wafted into the ambulance, provoking my appetite and making me wish that supper would speedily come. The novel, however, was interesting, and the perils of heroine and hero soon made me unconscious of the affairs of the cuisine, when I was aroused by a shout from the doctor, "Oh, Curtis!"

"What is it?" I asked.

"Come here a moment."

He was at the Indian fire with the ambulance driver and José, all standing and watching the proceedings of the sixteen Chemehuévis, who were sitting closely about the fire. I left the ambulance and joined the group.

As I took my place behind the circle of red men, I saw that the fire had been raked clear of all brands and smoke-yielding material and was now a bed of glowing coals. Each Indian had selected a field rat from the collection in his belt and now proceeded to lay it on the coals without dressing or in any way disturbing its anatomy. He rolled the rat over once or twice, took it up again, brushed all the singed fur from its skin, pinched the forelegs off close to the body, the hind legs at the ham joint and replaced it on the coals. The rat was now turned over a few more times, then taken off and held daintily in the left hand, while with the right the Indian plucked off the flesh and placed it in his mouth, leaving in the hand only the head, with the ribs and their contents. I expected at this point the skeleton would be thrown aside. But no, it was replaced on the coals for a moment longer, taken off and deposited as before in the left hand, the right forefinger was thrust dexterously into the bowels, the intestines quickly wound about the finger in a huge reeking gob and thrust into the mouth. As I saw the evident intention of the first Indian who reached this part of the eating process, I had begun to feel uneasy at the stomach. The doctor, who well knew the delicate nature of my digestive operation, was so demonstrative in calling my attention to each step of the process that the Indians began to notice me. Accordingly, the one who popped the first gob into his mouth, looked up at me and thrust out his dirty tongue, exclaiming, "*Bueno*!"

This finished me. Hare stew or any other edible did not go down my throat that night. The doctor was immensely delighted. He felt as if the whole scene had been of his own contriving and that he had now got even with me for all old scores. At several meals after this, little José was instructed to say "*Bueno*!" just as we would get fairly at table. I was under the necessity of privately bribing him before he would cease. When our time for going to sleep arrived, we requested the Indians to withdraw to a greater distance and strengthened our guard. We also hobbled the mules. Next day when we arose, no Indians were in sight.

Chapter 47

A Change in Command

We got away before sunrise and with a good road soon passed over the seventeen miles between Government Hole and Soda Lake. As we turned round a big rock, we first beheld, down a long shelving shore, what appeared to be a frozen lake covered with snow. Had it been mid-winter and I had never before heard of this celebrated natural curiosity, I could have easily made up my mind that I was looking upon an ice-covered pond. Here were all the features—a dead level, with points of land reaching out into it, bold and shelving shore and what appeared to be an island at the farther extremity. In fact, there was nothing wanting to make it appear to be a lake. It is called a lake in all geographies and still it is simply a bed of sand. Probably an alkaline lake, of the nature of the Dead Sea or Salt Lake, once rippled here, but the winds of centuries had blown it full of dust, which, gathering gradually at the bottom, had raised it until it became the surface. Over the whole was a thick incrustation of soluble salts.

Soda Lake lies in the centre of what is known as the Great Basin, the general elevation being 3,000 feet above the ocean, while the surface of the lake is 1,116 feet. The Mojave River, rising in the San Bernardino Mountains, 160 miles west, flows to this lake and sinks. In reality it sinks many miles before it reaches the lake, never showing water on the surface of its lower course except in the wettest season, but the water flows on, nevertheless, deep down in the sand.

We rode down the shore and drove upon the lake, our wheels crisping through the alkaline crust with an audible sound. It being November, the evaporation was much less than at midsummer, consequently as we approached the western shore of the lake, where the Mojave River comes in, the water could be seen rising through the sand and encroaching upon the surface. To avoid swamping in the quicksand, we made a considerable detour to the right and rode along the shore to the soda spring where we were to halt for the night.

Our camp on the evening of Thursday, November 2nd, was on the western side of Soda Lake, under the side of a bluff about fifty feet high, upon which stood an earthwork thrown up many years before by a detachment of soldiers, as a defence against the Indians. Close under the edge of the bluff was a spring of crystal water, which poured a visible stream out of the bank in a column some four inches in diameter, making quite a large brook. The stream found its way to the edge of the lake, forming a marsh for several rods along the shore. In this marsh grew a dense mass of reeds, in which myriads of birds were rustling and fluttering in their search for seeds. It was also the breeding place for countless billions of ravenous mosquitoes, as we learned when night fell.[1]

Going to the spring for a drink of water, I was cautioned by both the ambulance driver and Governor Goodwin to drink sparingly of it, as it often acted as an emetic, and always as a cathartic. Being exceedingly thirsty, I could not deny myself less than a pint and a few minutes afterward threw it up, with the entire contents of my stomach. Within a half hour's time, this was the experience of nearly every man in our party.

My attention was early called to what appeared to be a bumblebee flying about the mules and keeping them constantly thrashing

1. Doctor Coues described their arrival at Soda Lake: "Before us lay a dead-white sea of salty efflorescence, where the lake had evaporated or sunk in the sand, leaving its saline matter. It was dry, except toward the middle, where dark green masses of Tulé reeds, contrasting with the snowy whiteness all around, showed that a little water was left. Our animals, like ourselves, were exhausted; one poor creature, cruelly over-tasked, had given birth to a foal, and lay groaning by the wayside, unable to rise. The water was too nauseous to drink, and hardly answered to cook with." Coues, *Northwest Birds*, 537.

and stamping. Closer observation showed that the insect was a fly. I succeeded in killing one with a blow of my hat and found it to be a veritable fly, quite as large as a bumblebee.

For two days before reaching this camp, the governor and ambulance driver had detailed to us all its peculiarities and particularly dwelt upon the difficulties of the drive for a distance of ten miles beyond the lake. This portion of the road was covered with loose drifting sand, sand which every brisk wind heaped in drifts and sent in clouds through the air, as Northern residents are accustomed to see snow drift and blow in mid-winter. No track remained visible a few moments after a team had passed. Our recent drives had been long and tiresome, so we had concluded to remain here overnight and not attempt the ten miles of sand until the next day. Big stories were told us of the difficulties of the road and how wagons in crossing it without loads left water barrels buried by the roadside, to use when they should return loaded and have the bad luck to get stalled in the sand. The location of these buried barrels was shown by rods with a piece of cloth or cotton fluttering from the top.

Until our arrival at this camp, Doctor Coues had given us no trouble. My plan of lecturing to the governor had worked well. The doctor had listened and carried out the routine just as I should have done had I commanded. He had demurred a little against the proposition of staying at Soda Lake after only a seventeen mile drive, when ten more would bring us to a fine spring, good grazing ground and no mosquitoes. But the advice of the driver and governor prevailed and he decided to stay.

During the long afternoon I amused myself by going out upon the bed of the lake and sinking holes in the crust, to see at what depth I could find water. I found water would flow perceptibly fast at two feet below the surface. As before mentioned, the only water which flows into this so-called lake comes from the Mojave River. This river was for a long time celebrated among the Western explorers because of the various opinions entertained in respect to its course and continuous flow to the Colorado. There is what appears to be a dry bed of a stream running from the Colorado in the direction of Soda Lake and this was for a long time looked upon as its outlet. Lieutenant Whipple, in his expedition of 1853, followed the dry bed for some distance from the great river, but owing to scarcity of water took another course into the Great Basin for the last third of the distance. At one camp on the Mojave he called the Mojave chiefs, Cairook and Iritaba, into consultation and drew a map on the sand an elevation of the Colorado River and adjacent country, completing the imaginary river from the Soda Lake to the Colorado.[2] The Indians seemed to understand his questions and replied that such a river had existed. Another expedition, under Lieutenant Robert S. Williamson, sometime later, demonstrated the fact that the Mojave is not a tributary to the Colorado, but a river without connection with the sea, sinking in the dry sands of Soda Lake.[3]

Evening arrived and the mosquitoes settled down upon us with ravenous appetites. The governor, the doctor and I took our blankets a dozen rods back of the campfire and lay down for sleep. No sooner were we prostrate and still than the winged pests settled upon every bit of flesh which showed outside our coverings. This caused us to draw our blankets over our heads. In this situation we would drop asleep, but the air would soon become stifling,

2. Cairook, chief of the Mojaves in the 1850s, stood six feet six inches in height and was regarded as "a truly magnificent specimen of the Mojave Nation." Cairook was friendly with the whites and acted as a guide for Lieutenant Amiel Whipple (1853) and Joseph Ives (1858), generously pointing out the location of water holes on their surveys. In 1858 a Mojave attack on a wagon train that killed eighteen immigrants brought retaliation from the federal government that included the establishment of Fort Mojave on the bank of the Colorado River in 1859. The fort commander insisted that Cairook and several other prominent leaders should give themselves up as hostages at Fort Yuma to insure the Mojaves would keep the peace. Later that year Cairook and several other hostages were killed while trying to escape. Iritaba was a sub-chief under the Mojave chief Cairook and also acted as a guide for surveys conducted by Lieutenants Whipple and Ives. He became a close friend of the white settlers, but after succeeding Cairook in 1859 persuaded many of his followers to leave the Mojave Valley. When the Mojaves were threatened by white incursions, Iritaba and a Pima chief named Antonio Azul traveled to California and thence by sea to Washington, D. C. to witness the white man's country. Having seen all the largest cities on the Atlantic seaboard and visited with President Lincoln, Iritaba came home dressed in "a Brigadier General's hat and outfit," bedazzled with ribbons and stars and looking exactly like "a full-fledged European Count or Duke." His followers thought his stories of the white world were all lies and Iritaba lost much of his influence. He died on May 3, 1874, near La Paz. Smith, *The Mojaves*, 76, 86; Spicer, *Cycles of Conquest*, 269-70; Ricky, *Indians of Arizona*, 100-101; Stewart, "Mohave," 55–70; Thrapp, *Frontier Biography* 2: 704–05; *Los Angeles Star*, May 21, 1864.

3. Robert S. Williamson graduated from West Point in 1848 and was assigned to the Topographical Engineers as a brevet second lieutenant. Promoted to second lieutenant on October 26, 1853, and first lieutenant on April 20, 1856, he spent much of his pre-war career on western surveys, including railroad routes to California along the 32nd and 35th Parallels. Promoted to captain on August 6, 1861, Williamson was transferred to the Corps of Engineers on March 3, 1863, and promoted to major on May 7, 1863. Elevated to lieutenant colonel on February 22, 1869, he retired on June 23, 1882, after having received two brevets for his Civil War service. Colonel Williamson died in San Francisco on November 10, 1882. Cullum, *Biographical Register* 2: 209–10; *1883 Army Register*, 357.

Iritaba (right) and friend. Courtesy of Library of Congress.

causing us to throw aside the blankets and then the mosquitoes would settle, when we would awake.[4]

Each time that I awoke I could hear the movements of my companions, the thrashings of the doctor often being accompanied by Sunday School phrases. At last, when we had stood the torture for nearly two hours, the doctor burst out of his blankets, exclaiming, "I'm not going to stand this, I'm going on!" and started for the campfire.

The governor and I hastened after him and begged of him not to disturb the men. The governor reiterated all that had been said of the ten miles of sand, adding much more and doing everything possible to prevent the doctor from doing anything rash. We reminded him we were equal sufferers with him and that we were willing to undergo the petty annoyance of the mosquitoes rather than dare the dangers of the sands in a dark night, when we could not tell where we were going. But nothing would stay the doctor. He approached the sleeping men, whose fatigue was so great that they did not mind the bites, and began kicking them to arouse them. The governor said in an undertone, "Curtis, you must show your order."

"I hate to do it, governor."

"But you cannot avoid it, unless you want to see the outfit wrecked."

I took the doctor to the expiring brands of the campfire, threw on a branch which leaped at once into a flame and showed him General Mason's order. He read it through silently, dashed it to the ground, returned swiftly to his blankets and disappeared in their folds. The few men who were aroused sank back to sleep and the governor and I went to the top of a hill nearby where we found but few mosquitoes and passed the night in talk.

The doctor's command had ended. All his fun was over. No one regretted this more than I. Had it not been for Soda Lake

4. Doctor Coues also remembered the mosquitoes at Soda Lake: "After a poor meal, we lay down with gloomy thoughts. But sleep was impossible, though wrapped never so closely, head and all, in our blankets. We contended with a blood-thirsty swarm of mosquitoes, wafted like a cloud from the stagnant pools. Every breath of air seemed to vibrate to the continuous hum of the insects; it was open onslaught, as well as stealthy attack, with them, as we huddled around the camp-fire, on the side to which the smoke was wafted, enveloped in blankets, and impatiently waiting the day. We were bitten on every exposed point; for days afterward our hands and faces were sore and swollen, inflamed by the tiny drops of poison instilled into each wound." Coues, *Northwest Birds*, 537.

mosquitoes, it is doubtful whether he would ever have known that I was really in command from Fort Whipple to San Bernardino. With morning the men arose, looking as if they had just come through a siege of smallpox. The very mules looked blistered, they had been so terribly bitten. After breakfast we started. Our experience corroborated all that had been said of the sand. The wheels sank to the hubs, the mules barely moved and nearly the whole day was consumed before we struck solid earth in the Mojave Valley. About the middle of the drive, when our carriage barely seemed to move in the deep sand, the doctor suddenly found speech—for his disappointment had kept him silent hitherto—"Well, gentlemen, I own up! If I had started last night, I should never have got across this." From this moment he cheered up, and was the old genial companion he could be when he chose. We took lunch as soon as we got to the spring, rested an hour and drove on to The Caves, arriving there a little after ten o'clock at night, some twenty miles from the lake.

The next day, Saturday, we arrived at Camp Cady, where we found a garrison of three Volunteer companies.[5] The officers had just received a wagonload of fresh vegetables from San Bernardino. Among these were potatoes, an esculent of which I had not tasted once a season for three years. We stayed over Sunday and ate potatoes. The officers were more than hospitable. The commandant, Captain B. R. West, had been landlord of the Washington House on Pennsylvania Avenue in Washington and knew how to entertain guests courteously.[6] He had those potatoes cooked in every fashion known to travelers—boiled, baked, fried, mashed, hashed,

5. Curtis and his traveling companions reached Camp Cady on November 4, 1865. Doctor Coues made the following diary entry for that day: "Half a day's pull through heavy sandy and gravelly washes brought us to this God-forsaken Botany Bay of a place, the meanest I ever saw yet for a military station, where four officers and a handful of men manage to exist in some unexplained way in mud and brush hovels. The officers were Capt. [Benjamin R.] West, Lieut. Forster [James G. Foster], Lieut. Davidson [James Davison], and Dr. Lauber [M. L. Lawber]—glad enough to see us—or anybody else." Coues, *Spanish Pioneer* 1: 242.

6. Captain Benjamin R. West was commissioned captain in the 4th California on September 19, 1861, and served in that capacity until mustered out on February 19, 1866. West had formerly served in Mexico as a second lieutenant in a company of volunteers raised in Maryland and the District of Columbia. When the Civil War began, he was engaged in mining at Horsetown in Shasta County, California. Captain West evidently made significant upgrades at Camp Cady since he was praised by the department commander in 1866 when an inspection revealed thirty-five adobe houses with assorted outbuildings. After the war he served as a deputy U. S. marshal before returning to his home state of Maryland. Heitman, *Historical, Register* 2: 72; *Baltimore Sun*, July 28, 1847; Hunt, *Army of the Pacific*, 31, 263; *Records of California Men*, 617, 1870 U. S. Census, Santa Clara County, California.

Boston-chipped and Saratoga-chipped and supplied us generously with everything.

Monday we bade our kind entertainers good-bye and rode to Grape Vines, a place so called on the principle of *lucus a non lucendo*, because there was not a grapevine within a hundred miles of there. Here a military expressman met us with the news that Secretary McCormick would be at Lane's Crossing of the Mojave, on Wednesday. On the following day we reached a point where the river flowed a brisk and living stream and each succeeding ten miles seemed to show an increase in its volume. Reversing the rule of Eastern rivers, where the body of water increases as it approaches the mouth, the Mojave increased in size as we neared its source.

Ranches began to appear with the running water. Every few miles we passed thrifty farms, with outbuildings, corrals, stacks and water ditches for irrigation. We were evidently nearing civilization.

Wednesday we reached Lane's ranche. The proprietor of this ranche had been a surgeon in the army, but had resigned rather than serve against his native South. He had married a wife of Spanish descent, who held a title to a vast tract of land on the upper waters of the Mojave. The house was of wood and well-constructed. As we rode up to the door, we met McCormick and wife, who greeted us warmly. We had been looked for about this time and, as soon as Doctor Aaron Lane's spyglass had discovered us ten miles down the valley, a turkey and concomitants was put to roasting and extra preparations made for our entertainment.[7] As soon as we could get down from the ambulance and wash off the dust of travel, we were invited to a dinner fit for a king. California wine, from the San Bernardino Valley, was among the viands, the first I had seen.

After dinner the governor and secretary spent the afternoon in arranging Territorial and mining business, as the former was to leave Arizona for some years and it was already decided by the powers that McCormick was to be his successor. While these

7. A New Hampshire veteran of the Mexican War, Aaron G. Lane came to California and in 1858 settled on a ranch on the main crossing between the Northern Arizona settlements and San Bernardino. He made a sizeable fortune in providing supplies and grain for freight wagons, both government and civilian, and mining at Silver Mountain. When a fire destroyed his settlement in 1867, Lane rebuilt and continued to harvest immense crops of hay, barley and corn until his death on his farm in September of 1883. *[Victorville] Daily Press*, April 26, 2010; Almendral, *Victorville*, 7.

two immersed in papers, the doctor went out shooting birds and I remained behind to talk with Margaret McCormick of Eastern matters.[8] From her I first learned of my promotion to the title of Brevet Captain and from her hand I received as a present my first captain's shoulder straps.

On the following day we bade adieu to our friends who were traveling east and resumed our journey to the west. We rode from eight o'clock in the morning to four in the afternoon, encamping at Martin's ranche.[9] On the next day we found ourselves, after a short drive, standing at the summit of the Cajon Pass of the San Bernardino Mountains, looking down upon a valley thousands of feet below, which extended from the base to the Pacific Ocean, visible to the naked eye sixty miles away. Our ascent up the valley of the Mojave had been so gradual that I was surprised to find myself standing on the crest of a mountain range. The grade for most of the distance, after leaving Soda Lake, had been about 80 feet per mile and during the last day it had increased to 180 to the mile. The difficulties attending railroad building over this route seemed to be right here at the Cajon Pass—the difficulty of getting down to the plain below.

We bridled all four of the wheels of the ambulance and started down the descent. To the foot of the gravelly ridge the natural inclination was very nearly forty-five degrees, but the road had been graded along a spur so that the fall was 820 feet to the mile. This distance brought us to an *arroyo* in a deep ravine from which point our rate of descent was 250 feet in two miles. Continuing downward, the road grew more winding and rougher and somewhat steeper, being 500 feet in three miles and a half. Then came four

8. Margaret Griffiths Hunt married Richard McCormick in Rahway, New Jersey, on September 27, 1865. A few days later the newlyweds sailed for California, then traveled overland to Prescott, Arizona, where Richard resumed his position as secretary (soon to be governor) of the Arizona Territory. Although the McCormicks lived in the governor's house from their arrival, Margaret did not officially become first lady of the territory until her husband's confirmation as governor on April 10, 1866. Following a trip to California, she died in childbirth on April 30, 1867. Margaret McCormick recorded in her diary on Wednesday, November 8, 1865: "This morning we started for the first crossing of the Mojave which we reached at about noon and to our delight found Gov. Goodwin and party." On the following day she wrote: "Spent the day quite pleasantly, having been well entertained by Capt. Curtis." This notation confirms the account by Curtis about his brevet promotion although the War Department would not make it official for many months. Tessman, "Personal Journal," 41–46.

9. Doctor Coues wrote of this last portion of the ascent to Cajon Pass: "The pass is a narrow, deep, and tortuous cañon, the roughest I have ever traversed on wheels; there was 10 miles of this from the tollgate to Martin's ranch." Coues, *Spanish Pioneer* 1: 245.

miles of about one hundred feet to the mile and we had reached the plain below.

From the mountain the road ran through a chaparral of *Acacia*, gradually descending towards the town of San Bernardino. Occasionally we started a herd of horses or cattle, which in a semi-wild state were grazing on these immense tracts, sending them scampering and excited into the brushwood. Chaparral cocks and hens now and then dashed across the road in advance of the ambulance, a pretty wild fowl of the pheasant family. The male of the species, crossed with Spanish cock-fighting stock, produces a hybrid not often beaten in the cock-pit by the best pure-blooded chickens. Several trains, the first we had met since leaving Fort Whipple, laden with goods for the Arizona traders, were beginning their long and slow journey eastward. They stopped us to enquire when the escort would return, so that they could avail themselves of its protection. An arrangement was made for them to consolidate at Hardy's Landing, where the escort would overtake them with little or no delay, as it could travel faster than they.

San Bernardino at the time I saw it, in 1865, was a thirsty town originally settled by a Mormon emigration, deserters from the polygamous customs. There were but few people living in the valley who were not of the Mormon faith, the only places for religious worship being maintained by that sect. I cannot now recall its population, but should suppose the number of inhabitants in the business portion must have been between 2,000 and 3,000.

We drove to a hotel and descended from the ambulance for the last time. The day was Saturday, November 11th, just nineteen days after we left Fort Whipple. The escort went round to a military station on the outskirts of the town, occupied by Volunteers, to take a rest of five days before returning.

After dinner I strolled about the town, sightseeing. Over the fences along the roadside I could see oranges, lemons, figs and peppers hanging ready for the pickers. In one place I came upon a huge wine press, from which spouted the juice of cartloads of ripe grapes, which were drawn into the yard by farmers. The wine pressing seemed to be done much as the cider pressing is done in New England. Each farmer brought in his grapes, paid for the pressing, either in money or in wine, and drove away with his barrels of new wine. Close by was a distillery in which the pomace was placed after the press had squeezed all the wine possible from it and from this was distilled brandy—brandy as crystal as the purest water. This was a surprise to me, simply because I never had considered it. All the brandy I had ever seen was colored and here it was colorless. The proprietor of the wine press and distillery, a corpulent Frenchman, explained to me that brandies originally got their colors from the woods of which the barrels were made at the place of shipment or storage. This had given them their commercial color, which imitations must bear in order to deceive the customer.

Before leaving Fort Whipple, I had been instructed by the district quartermaster to buy a couple of mules for him and send them to Prescott by the escort. Accordingly, on Sunday afternoon, the governor, the doctor and I rode out to the ranche of Pishon and Tuttle, four miles distant, to make a friendly visit and buy the mules. Pishon was an old acquaintance of mine. He had been colonel of the California cavalry serving in New Mexico and had been mustered out by me at Fort Whipple in the fall of 1864. I am tempted to tell his story.

One hundred and ten miles north of San Bernardino, at the summit of Tejon Pass, stands Fort Tejon.[10] Some years before the Civil War, this fort was occupied by a troop of the 2nd Dragoons. In this troop were two sergeants; one, Nathaniel J. Pishon, was born on the Kennebec in Maine; the other, Minor C. Tuttle, on the Mohawk in New York—both of them six feet high, straight as Indians, handsome men.[11] Tuttle was married to the daughter of

10. Established on August 10, 1854 near California's Tejon Pass, the garrison of Fort Tejon was charged with protecting friendly Indians at the nearby Tejon Indian Reservation and pursuing hostiles through the neighboring mountains. The fort was perhaps best known for Edward F. Beale's 1857 experiment of establishing camel caravans from Fort Tejon to Drum Barracks on the California coast. Fort Tejon was abandoned on June 15, 1861, and the camels were sold in California two years later. Fort Tejon was re-occupied on August 17, 1863, by California troops, but finally abandoned on September 11, 1864. The post was eventually purchased by Beale who converted the fort's buildings to houses and stables. *Soldier and Brave*, 94-95; Frazer, *Forts*, 32–33.

11. Nathaniel J. Pishon was appointed an ordnance sergeant in the U. S. Army on January 26, 1859, after over sixteen years of service in the 1st Dragoons. He was commissioned a captain in the 1st California Cavalry on February 24, 1862, and mustered out on November 23, 1864. For a time his company commander was James H. Carleton, who commanded the Department of New Mexico and became Pishon's brother-in-law. One of the pioneers of San Bernardino, he married the widow of his friend Minor C. Tuttle and held several political offices. After his first wife's death, Pishon moved to Oceanside, California, where he died on March 18, 1898. Minor C. Tuttle enlisted in the 1st Dragoons at Jefferson Barracks on February 17, 1846. He re-enlisted on July 19, 1851 and again on August 13, 1856. Following his discharge on August 13, 1861, Tuttle and his wife Caroline joined Nathaniel Pishon in running their ranch near San Bernardino. Minor Tuttle represented San Diego County in the California Senate for two terms, 1863–1864 and 1865–1866,

a fellow soldier, a German. In the cavalry scouts for Indians and on other duty, these sergeants had gone south to the valley of the San Bernardino River and had noticed its advantages as a farming country. They took up a ranche together and, that it might not be jumped, placed Caroline, the wife, upon it. There she remained developing the land and more than supporting herself until the sergeants' term of enlistment expired and they were once more citizens.

The fast friends and old comrades went to work at once in putting their farm in order. When I visited it, there was a fine house and substantial outbuildings, with every evidence of comfort and ease in the household. At a dinner which had three courses of meat, a turkey and fish, I was told that everything except the salt was raised upon the ranche and there was hardly a condiment or edible usually seen upon a good hotel table that was not before us.

When the war broke out, Pishon offered his services to his country and became colonel of Volunteers. While he was in Arizona, he one day showed me a letter from Tuttle, asking his advice whether he should be a candidate for senator in the California Legislature.

"What are you going to say to him?" I asked.

"I've advised him already," was the reply.

"What did you say?"

"Don't be a blamed fool."

"I don't think it is evidence of idiocy if he runs for senator."

"Perhaps not, but I cannot bear to think of Tuttle's being beaten."

He was not beaten, however. He received the biggest vote that had ever been cast for any candidate in San Bernardino and, what was better, received a re-election. When I visited him, he was just on the point of leaving for the Capitol.

I was constantly struck with the perfect accord with which these two men worked. They differed in nothing. They had a common money drawer, in which each put the results of his trades or investments or from which he drew whenever he had need, without question or comment. Each rejoiced in the other's

---

prior to his death at San Bernardino on March 10, 1867. Masich, *Civil War in Arizona*, 17; Letters Received by the Adjutant General, C. H. Ogle, January 10, 1858; *California Men*, 117; *Los Angeles Herald*, March 20, 1898; Registers of Enlistments; Davis, *Political Conventions*, 659.

success and grieved over his failures. There were no children in the family. Both men were devoted to Caroline, as they invariably called her. I shall not forget the delicacy with which I was consulted by the colonel at Fort Whipple about a suitable present to his comrade's wife when he left the service. I learn that one of the faithful friends died a few years after my visit to San Bernardino and that two years after, the survivor, Pishon, married the widowed Caroline.

There is another incident to relate of my acquaintance with Colonel Pishon. In 1871 I took the steamboat at Burlington for Fort Ticonderoga, on Lake Champlain. After a brief stop on the New York side, I crossed to a hotel at the Shoreham Landing and looked for a passage to Shoreham Village, where I could take the mail wagon for Brandon. The landlord reported that he had nothing in his stable but a four-year-old colt. All the other horses were away and he would trust no one to drive the colt but himself. To induce him to take me to Shoreham, I offered three times the usual rate, which resulted in his deciding to go. On the drive and when near the end of our journey, he asked me if I had ever been in California and mentioned that he had a brother-in-law in San Bernardino. I replied that I had been in California and in San Bernardino, also that one of the best men I ever knew and whose friendship I valued highly, Colonel Pishon, lived there.

"Colonel Pishon! That's the man—he's my wife's brother!" exclaimed my driver. Then followed a host of questions, which were barely answered when we arrived in Shoreham. When I offered to pay the landlord for my ride, he refused to take anything and said "he could not take a cent from a friend of the colonel's."

We stayed at Pishon's ranche overnight, bought the mules Monday and returned to town. The semi-weekly mail coach from San Bernardino to Los Angeles was to leave on Tuesday. Monday evening a ball was given at a hotel near the one at which we were guests and I looked in for a few minutes to see the style of the Mormon girls. They were generally coarse and ruddy, with no education or conversational powers.

Tuesday morning I left the town, mounted on a seat on the roof of the Concord coach, from which perch I could see the country as we rolled swiftly along. Our road led through a rich country, much of it under active cultivation. A talkative driver explained everything and told us of many tragedies enacted at the old Spanish ranches along the roadside. We passed through Cucamonga, Spadra and San Gabriel, arriving at Los Angeles in the evening.

Here we learned that there would be no steamer for San Francisco for a fortnight and that the stage route was so beset by highwaymen as to be very unsafe. There was nothing for it but to stay over, even if I curtailed my leave of absence in the States by two weeks. During the fortnight I spent my time between Drum Barracks, on the coast twenty miles distant, at the residence of a local nabob, Phineas Banning and in Los Angeles.[12] I rode to several ranches in the country and visited two wine cellars.

The visit to the wine cellars deserves a separate paragraph. One morning Governor Goodwin and Lieutenant Samuel Munson, of the 9th Infantry, called at my room and invited me to go with them to the wine cellar of Don Mateo Keller (Matthew Keller in Ireland, where he was born, but the Spanish Californians had turned the Matthew into the Spanish Mateo, with the prefix Don, by which name and title he doubtless is still known if living).[13] Keller was a

12. To counter Southern sympathizers in California, Phineas Banning and Benjamin Wilson, a former mayor of Los Angeles, donated land for a Federal garrison at what would soon be called the town of Wilmington. Camp Drum was officially named on January 13, 1862, for Major Richard C. Drum, adjutant general of the Department of the Pacific. Constructed at a cost of close to a million dollars, Camp Drum became the largest supply depot in Southern California. Renamed Drum Barracks, the post became unnecessary after the war and the land reverted to Banning and Wilson. Phineas Banning sailed for California in 1851 at the age of nineteen and landed at San Diego. In 1852 he commenced a freighting operation between Los Angeles and San Pedro. Recognizing the importance of the San Pedro harbor, Banning founded the town of Wilmington and built the Los Angeles and Wilmington Railroad to facilitate the growth of his town. Although wealthy from his army shipping contracts and a general in the state militia, Banning never pursued a political career. He died in San Francisco on March 8, 1885. Robinson, *Los Angeles*, 91–93; McGroarty, *Los Angeles*, 13–14.

13. Born in the East Indies, Samuel Munson enlisted as a sergeant in the 5th Maine on May 6, 1861, and was promoted to second lieutenant on May 27. He mustered out on September 4, 1861, but had meanwhile received a commission as second lieutenant in the 9th Infantry on August 5, 1861. Promoted to first lieutenant on December 31, 1862, Munson served as regimental quartermaster and simultaneously as assistant quartermaster of Volunteers with the rank of captain. Promoted to captain in the 9th Infantry on September 28, 1865, he mustered out of his volunteer rank on June 27, 1866. He remained in the army and died at the home of his mother in Farmington, Maine, on October 2, 1887. Don Mateo Keller, a native of Ireland, acted as a trader and accompanied the army during the Mexican War. Naturalized in New Orleans in 1849, Keller came to Los Angeles the following year and started in business packing and shipping grapes. He soon expanded his business to include the raising of grapes and by the Civil War had concentrated on the production of wine and brandy. His extensive land holdings and beverage production did not diminish the excellence of his products. One editor stated that "younger and more active men have surpassed him in the quantity of wines and brandy which they have made, but none have turned out a better quality." Keller died in Los Angeles on April 11, 1881. Heitman, *Historical Register* 1: 736; *New York Tribune*, October 4, 1887; *Los Angeles Herald*, April 12, 1881.

large manufacturer of wines, brandies and brandy and wine bitters, doing an extensive business with the principal cities of the nation. We walked to his place of business and entered the counting room, where we were obliged to wait for him about ten minutes. Presently a stout gentleman of ruddy countenance and Celtic features entered and was introduced as Don Mateo Keller. He had the least suggestion of a brogue in his speech and spoke Spanish and French with the same facility that he did English.

After chatting a few moments, he ordered a workman to light a lamp and show us to the cellar. We went down a dark, stone staircase some fourteen feet and found ourselves in what we were told was a cellar twelve feet wide and a hundred long. There were rows of barrels tiered high on each side of the cellar, leaving a passageway of some six feet in width from end to end. There were occasional alcoves to the right and left, also filled with barrels. Now I had never taken a pledge to "handle not nor taste not," so thought it no harm to taste of the vintages of each year for twenty years back and all the different wines made from different grapes of each year, as well as the brandies distilled from each grape.

Don Mateo preceded us with a wooden mallet and a long tin tube.[14] Each one of the visitors carried a tumbler. Pausing before a particular vintage the Don would give us a little lecture on the grape from which the wine was pressed, the date of barreling it and end by removing the bung with a few smart raps on the barrel. The tube, which was about two feet long and open at each end, was thrust into the wine. When filled, the upper aperture was closed by the thumb, the tube withdrawn and held over a tumbler. By removing the thumb from the tube, the wine would flow freely until it was closed again. Barely a teaspoonful was placed in each glass and no one thought of any harm in simply tasting. But before we reached the other end of the cellar, we had gone through all the stages of hilariousness, boisterousness and foolishness and we were helped unsteadily up a staircase to a carriage and driven to a hotel. We probably tasted of some hundred kinds of wines and brandies, being in the cellar for three hours. Of course, so many tastes made a number of glasses of the most powerful "stone-fence" before we got through.

14. This device is known as a wine thief.

Chapter 48

California and Home

I have not hitherto mentioned that my dog Vic was a passenger in the ambulance from Fort Whipple to San Bernardino. Neither have I said anything of the doctor's black and tan terrier Nellie, which had been with him from the Rio Grande to the Rio Colorado and to the Pacific Ocean, the two sleeping cozily in the bottom of the ambulance or gamboling by the side of the team as we trotted over the plain or crept slowly through mountain passes. I left Fort Whipple with the full intention of bringing my dog to the States. She had been my inseparable companion since I left Santa Fé for Los Valles Grandes. I changed my mind, however, before I had been long on the road. She was a constant care and I began to see that she would be a great encumbrance during a five months' leave, when I should be constantly upon the wing. The doctor was going directly to Washington, where he would be on duty, so he determined to keep his.

Vic was the favorite dog. The governor often held her for hours in his lap and the driver would pull up his team to extract a cactus thorn from her foot without a hint from me, while the doctor was obliged to ask for a similar favor. Long before I reached San Bernardino I determined to give Vic away, if I could find someone whom I could feel sure would treat her well. When I visited Colonel Pishon and the Tuttles, I found both the gentlemen and their lady took a liking to the animal and each asked me for her at different times. I concluded I could find no better home for my pet and reluctantly gave her away. It was an act I regretted a short time afterwards and have never ceased to regret since.

Vic was a beautiful dog and her education had been carried to as high a point as possible with canine nature. She seemed to understand conversation and the experiment has been tried many times of telling her to do things in an ordinary tone of voice and in common phrase. Many a time I have sat in my saddle, pulling on my gloves preparatory to a start, while she has been leaping, running and barking in anticipation of the pleasure of a trip with me and I have said in an ordinary tone, "No, my little girl, you must stay at home," or some similar phrase, for I used to say a great many things to her analogous to "baby talk." No sooner would I say this than Vic would crouch down disconsolately, never attempting to follow as I rode away, but if I added, without change of voice or looking back, "Well, you may go if you want to," she would resume her gambols and fly along the road before me, the happiest dog alive. She would close a door if I pretended to shiver, bring me my slippers when I pulled off my boots, sit up and *salute a la militaire* and do many things beside. She was always as neat as the most exactingly clean housewife could wish, never entering my quarters if wet or muddy unless invited and never getting upon the bed. She never barked nights, in fact, she was an exceedingly accomplished dog. I was very fond of her, more than I ever was of any other animal or ever expect to be.[1]

A little more than a fortnight after my arrival at San Bernardino, the steamer sailed for San Francisco. At three o'clock on Wednesday, November 29th, Governor Goodwin and I took seats on top of the Wells & Fargo express coach at the Bella Union Hotel, in Los Angeles. The many friends whom we had made during our short stay crowded up to bid us Godspeed and wish us a pleasant journey, friends of brief acquaintance, but, like all Far Western acquaintances, genial and generous without stint.

1. Vic died of old age in 1873, having been the mother of only one litter of puppies during her lifetime. *Virginia [Minnesota] Enterprise*, July 5, 1895.

The ride was twenty miles long, ending at Wilmington, on the coast. The road ran over an unfenced country, much of it low meadowland, upon which large flocks of wild geese—gray and white—were cropping the grass without paying the least attention to the coach which whirled rapidly past not thirty yards from them. At Wilmington we found a small, flat-bottomed steamboat ready to take us to the steamer, which was swinging at anchor under the lee of Dead Man's Island, a couple of miles away, there being no harbor at Wilmington.

In fact, our Pacific coast, in its long reach of 1,200 miles, possesses but four important harbors which are safe for shipping at all times: the mouth of the Columbia, San Francisco, San Diego and Humboldt Bay. All the other ports are upon the open, unprotected coast or in bays which afford shelter only against certain winds. At Wilmington the steamer changes her anchorage to different sides of Dead Man's Island, according to the direction of the wind. In November and March, when high winds are frequent, it often passes without stopping.

When the small boat paused under the lofty sides of the steamer, I saw Doctor Coues looking down upon us from the upper deck. He had stayed at Drum Barracks the whole fortnight and had not been with us during our visits in and about Los Angeles. A stepladder was lowered to the shore boat and we all ascended to the deck of the *Orizaba*. Cain still accompanied us, acting as body-servant to the governor and myself. He carried our small baggage to our stateroom and then retired to the steerage.

I saw the little Mexican boy, José, watching everything with round-eyed wonder. Born in New Mexico, the largest body of water he had ever seen was when he crossed the Colorado River. To see a body of water which presented no limit on its western side but the sky filled him with a boundless surprise, which found its expression in numberless questions. Everything had been fairyland to him since we came into the San Bernardino Valley. The well-furnished house of Pishon and Tuttle, the gilded and papered parlors and dining rooms of the hotels had been marvels of beauty and richness compared with the interiors of the mud houses he had known in his own town and the canvas tents and log quarters of the army. Now the steamer, with its richly-carpeted saloons, its upholstered furniture, its polished mahogany walls and ceilings, its brilliant chandeliers, etc., was to him as marvelous as the witcheries produced by the wonderful lamp of Aladdin are to an American boy. The ponderous engines and wheels, the glowing fires in the furnace room, the towering masts, gaily bedecked with flags, all filled him to the brim with curiosity and delight.

Evening had fairly descended upon us before the steamer started. José had barely a chance to go the rounds with me to see the engine start, the wheels revolve and the *Orizaba* gain headway before the increased motion of the ship, as she left the lee of Dead Man's Island, unsettled his stomach and he went to bed quite seasick. I put the little fellow comfortably into his bunk, did what I could to prevent his being very sick and left him. In the saloon I found supper ready and my friends seated at table. The governor was in excellent spirits, but I soon discovered that the doctor did not respond, but was fast paling about the gills. I am an exempt as regards seasickness, never having known the sensation, so I did not sympathize with my fellow traveler. As I looked at him, his face suggested my feelings at Government Hole, when the Chemehuévis cooked and ate rats. I looked across the table, and said "*Bueno*." The doctor sprang precipitately from the table, overturning his chair as he did and fled to his stateroom, belching audibly as he ran. His stomach was in too delicate a condition to think of what formerly had not affected him. He was so seasick that we did not see him again before we reached the Golden Gate. José recovered the second day out and came on deck when the line of the coast was but a dim streak on the horizon. His first remark after he had taken a sweeping view of the ocean was, "Where has the land gone?" Soon after he asked, "When shall we get off?" much bewildered at the extent of the ocean.

Off Santa Barbara, while we were at breakfast, a strong smell of petroleum pervaded the ship, suggesting the thought that one of the waiters had broken a lamp in the saloon, but when I got on deck the source of the odor was apparent. The ocean on every side was covered with oil which comes up from coal oil deposits at the bottom. We could see the oil rise to the surface, break and spread its iridescent hues over the waves. Many efforts have been made along this coast to sink oil wells, but with little or no success. At Los Angeles, hardly a gunshot from the *plaza*, the earth is covered with naptha, hardened by exposure until it resembles resin or the concrete of which sidewalks are made. In fact, it is used for sidewalks throughout the city and for roofs.

We touched at two points on our way up the coast, but as it was in the night I saw nothing of the places. A sharp gale was blowing from the north during the whole trip. When we reached the entrance to San Francisco Bay and it was necessary to turn at right angles with the wind, the captain of the ship set a sail or two to keep her from rolling. I had read in nautical tales of sails being blown out of the bolt ropes, now I witnessed a piece of new canvas burst with a report like a gun and fly away on the wind in ribbons and strings. This was the result of carelessness in loosening it, however, for a less strong sail held when it was properly hoisted. From rolling in a most violent manner before the sail was set, the steamer no sooner felt the strain of the canvas than she ceased rolling, became steady and was soon passing through the Golden Gate into smooth water.

We arrived in San Francisco on Friday, December 1st, in good time for the steamer which was to sail for Panama on the 10th. We took a hack for the Occidental Hotel and domiciled ourselves there for the short time we expected to stay in the city. In the afternoon I visited military headquarters and found that my arrival had been looked for with some anxiety for a number of days, as several of the Volunteers whom I had mustered out at Fort Whipple were in the city, having lost their papers and being unable to draw their retained pay and savings until a new set could be made up. I was accordingly at once ordered to duty, another bit of good fortune, for it would make my leave begin when I should sail, so that my delay at Los Angeles was really a gain.

Saturday morning I went to work and made up most of the papers before night. Sunday forenoon I attended service at Trinity Church and in the afternoon, like all good San Franciscans, went out to Woodward's Gardens. This, however, was an accident with me. After dinner I took José with me for a walk through the city. We passed along Montgomery Street to Market Street. As we entered the latter I saw a railroad station, with a locomotive and cars, just on the point of starting. I ran to the train and took a seat, with no idea where it was going. I only thought I should like to give José a new sensation, besides I knew that wherever the train might go it must return. José took his seat without question and waited, making no remarks.

When the train started he rose, looked eagerly about a moment and then resumed his seat, asking me, "where the horses were that were drawing us and if American horses went as fast as this." As this was a local train, belonging to a city company, the cars were constructed with seats on the top. In answer to José's question I took him to the platform and we ascended the stairs to the roof. From that point the locomotive, with its escaping steam and clanging bell, could be plainly seen. Of course, a boy who have never beheld the cars, or heard of them, was astonished. His astonishment, however, was not expressed so as to attract attention, but was simply whispered in my ear. José was a very intelligent boy and readily adapted himself to the circumstances in which he was placed. The doctor had dressed him at a clothing store on Saturday, so that he made a neat appearance. I have spoken of him as being the doctor's servant. This was hardly the fact. He was more of a companion and after the two reached Washington, José was sent to school and is now an accomplished young gentleman of good education.

After a ride of ten minutes the cars stopped and I noticed that everybody seemed to be leaving the train for a building which stood a few rods to the right, decked with flags of all nations, colors and designs. Acting upon impulse, as I had done in taking my seat in the cars, I hastened with the throng towards the house. The crowd was decidedly foreign in appearance, the German element predominating. Women of all ages, many of them holding a baby in their arms and tugging a toddler by the hand, were pushing to the doorway with great eagerness. Paying the fee demanded by a doorkeeper, José and I hurried through the building to a rear door where we found a spacious park, shaded by large trees, in the branches of which hung more flags and beneath the shade of which an immense crowd was gathered. Before we could take in all the surroundings, there was a murmur, a rush and a big balloon burst into sight over the treetops, showing an acrobat suspended below it by his legs. As he mounted swiftly skyward, he went through a dozen dizzy feats upon a horizontal bar which hung below the globe. José stood for a moment transfixed with amazement, his hat in his hand, that his vision might not be obstructed and then exclaimed, "*Los Americanos saben mucho—los Mejicanos nada*!" (The Americans know a lot, the Mexicans nothing!).

This seemed to be a culmination of the surprises which had overwhelmed the little Mexican boy since he left Fort Whipple. Everything in San Francisco was more attractive and more wonderful than what had formerly seemed so wonderful and attractive in Los Angeles. For a few days I took him constantly with me to see the city streets and the harbor.

I arrived in San Francisco just after the great earthquake of 1865, when the hotel walls and ceilings were still cobwebbed with the cracks opened by that severe wrenching and doors were jammed in the casings. People were nervous and looking for more shakings, those living in brick houses searching for wooden ones. In a visit to San Francisco in 1875, it was my fortune to be the guest of several wealthy gentlemen at different times. Each showed me the provisions he had made in the construction of his house against earthquakes. All the houses were of wood, few of the wealthy class building of anything else. A building of this material can be put together so that it will roll downhill without falling to pieces, while a brick or stone building will shatter and crumble. The chimneys, clamped and bound with iron, were attached firmly to the timbers.

On the 10th of December Doctor Coues and José left for New York. Governor Goodwin and I were to remain until the 20th. My father had gone to California in the early days of the discovery of gold and my mother, sister and three brothers had gone later. Father and two brothers were still living in the north part of the state, far up the valley drained by the Sacramento. I obtained leave of the commanding general, after completing my business, to go up the river. It was before railroads had been built to any great extent. The first stage of the journey from San Francisco had to be made by steamboat. These craft were splendid specimens of their kind. Californians, who are somewhat given to boasting, pronounced them superior to those of the Hudson River, but they were inferior in many respects, size especially.

I took the *Chrysopolis* at the foot of California Street at four o'clock in the afternoon and began my journey. It was over forty miles through San Francisco, San Pablo and Suison Bays to the mouth of the river. Probably no steamboat in American waters ever carried so many representatives of different nationalities and showed so many phases of social life among its passengers. Almond-eyed Chinamen and squalid Digger Indians jostled the blond-haired Englishman and the vivacious Frenchman; the Faro and Monte bank gamblers brushed the elbows of clergymen; bedizened, painted and overdressed members of the demi-monde sat on the same settee with the modest schoolgirl. Contrast reigned, affording the student of human nature a fine field for observation.

At Sacramento, next morning, I took the cars for Lincoln, then came a stagecoach ride to Marysville, where I expected to find a railroad to Oroville. But one of the big rains peculiar to this country had a few days before swept most of the railroad out of existence. Miles and miles of roadbed had been washed into the murky river and had gone downstream, to fill up the channels with their deposit. I was forced to stage it to Oroville, where I hired a team and went to my father's.

Down in the bottom of a *cañon*, beside the rushing and roaring current of Feather River, I found the new home of my family, where my father had lived for ten years, where my mother had died, where my sister had married and where one brother had mysteriously disappeared, never to be heard of again in this life. A younger brother, whom I had last seen a little fellow of ten years, now a fine young man of seventeen, was the only one of the family at home. Although not expecting the visit, he knew me at once. After a little conversation, we went to find another brother, two years younger than myself. A brisk climb up the mountainside into an oak grove brought to view a man in the top of a tree, boring an auger hole into the trunk. He was securing a hive of wild bees and was boring to ascertain the depth of the cavity in which they had built their comb.

This was the other brother. Without stopping his auger, he said, "You'll find some new wine in that watering pot, Charles, help yourself."

At the foot of the tree I saw a small garden watering pot, with the sprinkler removed. Raising it, I wished him a speedy descent with the hive and took a drink from the spout.

In time the hive was secured and lowered to the ground. The brother followed and gave me a warm grasp of the hand and welcome. We went to the house, took chairs by a glowing open fire and spent the rest of the day in talking and living over the scenes of our childhood. A little after dark, there came a shout from the other side of the river. It was father. I went down to the riverside, loosed the ferryboat and crossed for him alone. The meeting was an unexpected one to him, but, like the boys, he knew me at a glance.

I stayed four days and talked and listened all the time when I was not asleep, visiting all the localities of which I had read in the California letters. We grew boyish again and did many things simply for the fun. I never shall forget with what pains we dragged a skiff up the river, taking advantage of the eddies, and sometimes drawing over a point, in order to enjoy a ride down in mid-current, the two Californians impelling and guiding the boat with a pair of long-handled shovels.

At the end of the fourth day I started on my return, the youngest brother with me. He was to go to the States to school. The railroad had been repaired, so that I passed over it from Oroville to Marysville. At the latter place I took a sternwheeler to Sacramento. The river was high and running like a mill sluice, so we were not long in reaching Sacramento. There I took the *Chrysopolis* and returned to the coast.

On the 20th of December, 1865, I left San Francisco for Panama, occupying a stateroom jointly with the governor. There were a goodly number of passengers on board. Among them was a minister of Maximillian, Emperor of Mexico, on his way to Washington, and Sir Lambton Loraine, Flag Lieutenant of the British Pacific Squadron, on his way to England.[2] The last gentleman became quite well known afterwards as the English admiral who compelled the Spanish authorities to respect the American flag in the *Virginius* Affair. New York granted him the freedom of that city. He was a pleasant gentleman and used to seek me for the purpose of asking questions about our army organization, the war, government, etc.

The trip to Panama was exceedingly pleasant, for days there was scarcely any motion to the ship and consequently no seasickness.

2. Sir Lambton Loraine assumed his title in 1852 following the death of his father. That same year he joined the British Navy and served as a sub-lieutenant on Queen Victoria's yacht. Loraine was promoted to lieutenant in 1858 and commander in 1867. While in command of the *Niobe* on the West Indian Station, Commander Loraine famously saved the lives of American sailors imprisoned in Santiago, Cuba, during the *Virginius* affair. He was rewarded by an enthusiastic greeting in New York and promotion to captain in 1874. He received several government appointments later in life and died in England on May 13, 1917. *1917 Annual Register*, 171; *New York Herald*, February 7, 1874; *London Times*, May 15, 1917.

An empty wine bottle set up on its nose would stand a long time before the ship would tip enough to throw it down. Christmas Eve there was a ball and the dancers found no difficulty in keeping their feet, appetites were excellent and everybody felt well. Winter clothing, which we wore when we embarked, had to be gradually reduced as we went south, until when I entered Panama Bay I was clad in linen pantaloons and coat, a straw hat on my head and a big palm leaf fan in my hand. It was New Year's Day and the whole Isthmus seemed to be out in holiday attire.

We embarked at Aspinwall on the Caribbean coast on a new steamer, this being her first trip, sailing in the evening. As we put to sea, the French Consul was sending off fireworks in honor of the day. The sky thickened as we sailed on and morning found us in a tremendous gale. The engine, which ordinarily made sixteen strokes a minute, now made but four and a half. Every few minutes a wave would take us under the guard with a blow like a sledgehammer, bringing a crash of crockery to our ears from the pantry. Nearly all the passengers were sick, except me. I stayed on deck hours watching the storm. I saw the wave strike that tore the entire upper deck off, from the bow to the pilothouse, and another which stripped the larboard wheel of its covering, leaving it as exposed as a windmill. Occasionally a sea would break through the after gangway, up to the knees of the passengers, saturating the carpets of the saloon with salt water. In the midst of all this turmoil of the elements, a man died in the steerage, who proved to be a professor at Dickinson College in Pennsylvania. Fare in the steerage was $45 and in the cabin $310. He had consulted economy instead of style. The dead body was sewed in a canvas sack, with iron weights at the feet, and placed on a plank on the starboard side of the gangway. A Presbyterian minister, pale and miserably seasick, read the Episcopal burial service. The ponderous engine ceased its pulsations while the service was being read and, amidst the roaring, rushing and seething of the waves and the shrieking of the gale through the cordage, the dead man slid into the watery depths.

As we journeyed north, we increased our clothing, as we had before reduced it. All hilarity had disappeared, the few passengers who were able to be about generally spent their time in reading their Bibles, praying and resolving to lead new lives if suffered to reach the shore in safety. Some were so sick as to be entirely reckless of what became of them, lying on the carpet of the saloon and rolling about with the motion of the vessel. The officers were rarely seen below during the gale. I ate my meals at a long table, one of the three passengers who came down regularly to a table that had once seated thirty. The first sign of improving weather that I noticed was the entrance of the first officer to dinner, rubbing his hands, and looking as if the barometer had predicted a change. Before night the blue sky was in sight and as I sank off to sleep the steadiness of the ship was perceptibly increased and the throbs of the engine faster.

Next morning everything was serene. The penitent sinners of the day before were contemplating a renewal of their pleasures as soon as they should reach New York, without a thought of their promises. Seasick patients appeared at breakfast with ravenous appetites and visited the parts of the ship which showed the force of the water. On the Pacific side of the Isthmus a paper had been circulated and signed, thanking the captain for his efficient management of his steamer, the excellence of the food, the politeness of the waiters, etc. On the Atlantic side, the gallant fellows who stood at their post when the least neglect would have sent us to the bottom got no thanks. This has been the regular thing for years. The captains of the Pacific always got the praise, those of the Atlantic the censure. It was a purely gastronomic matter. On one side nobody was sick, so all had good appetites, hence praised everything. On the other side all were sick and had no appetites, hence nothing suited.

We arrived in New York Harbor on the 12th of January, 1866. It was frozen from Sandy Hook to the piers. A soft southerly breeze softened the ice and we crushed our way up to the wharves. At the Fifth Avenue Hotel, the governor, Cain and I separated.

Bibliography

Books and Articles

Acts, Resolutions and Memorials, Adopted by the First Legislative Assembly of the Territory of Arizona. Prescott: Arizona Miner, 1865.

Alexander, Francelle E. *Among the Cottonwoods: The Enduring Rio Abajo Villages of Peralta and Los Pinos, New Mexico before 1940*. Los Ranchos, NM: Rio Grande Books, 2012.

Almendral, Dylan M. *Victorville*. Charleston, SC: Arcade Publishing, 2013.

The Annual Register, 1917. London: Longmans, Green, and Co., 1918.

Arizona: A State Guide. New York: Hastings House, 1940.

"The Axolotl." *The Scientific Enquirer* 3 (April 1888): 64–66.

Bailey, Garrick A., and Gloria A. Young. "Kansa." *Handbook of North American Indians*, 13, pt. 1 (Washington, DC: Smithsonian, 2001): 462–75.

Ball, Larry D. *Desert Lawmen: The High Sheriffs of New Mexico and Arizona, 1846–1912*. Albuquerque: University of New Mexico Press, 1992.

Barnes, Will C. *Arizona Place Names*. Tucson: University of Arizona Press, 1988.

"BARNUM et al. v. BARNUM et al." *The Southwestern Reporter* 24 (St. Paul: West Publishing Company, 1894): 780.

Bates, Al, ed. *My Arizona Adventures*. Prescott, AZ: Prescott Corral of Westerners International, 2003.

Bierman, John. *Dark Safari*. New York: Alfred A Knopf, 1990.

A Biographical Congressional Dictionary. Washington, DC: Government Printing Office, 1903.

"Biographies of Members of the Legislature of 1868." *Transactions of the Kansas State Historical Society, 1907–1908* 10 (Topeka: State Printing Office, 1908): 265–279.

Blackmar, Frank W., ed. *Kansas, A Cyclopedia of State History*. Chicago: Standard Publishing Company, 1912. 2 vols.

Boatner, Mark M. *The Civil War Dictionary*. New York: David McKay Company, 1959.

Bodine, John J. "Taos Pueblo." *Handbook of North American Indians* 9 (Washington, DC: Smithsonian, 1979): 255–67.

Brandt, Elizabeth A. "Sandia Pueblo." *Handbook of North American Indians,* 9 (Washington, DC: Smithsonian, 1979): 343–50.

Breihan, Carl W. *Quantrill and His Civil War Guerrillas*. Denver: Sage Books, 1959.

Brown, J. Willard. *The Signal Corps, U. S. A. in the War of the Rebellion*. Boston: U. S. Veteran Signal Corps Association, 1896.

Brugge, David M. "Navajo Prehistory and History to 1850." *Handbook of North American Indians* 10 (Washington, DC: Smithsonian, 1983): 489–501.

Bryan, Howard. *Albuquerque Remembered*. Albuquerque: University of New Mexico Press, 2006.

"Bulls," *The Herd Register and Breeders' Journal of the American Guernsey Cattle Club* (October 1903), 13.

Callaway, Donald, Joel Janetski, and Omer C. Stewart. "Ute." *Handbook of North American Indians* 11 (Washington, DC: Smithsonian, 1986): 336–66.

Castel, Albert. *General Sterling Price and the Civil War in the West*. Baton Rouge: Louisiana State University Press, 1968.

Coffin, Selden J. *Record of the Men of Lafayette: Brief Biographical Sketches of the Alumni of Lafayette College*. Easton, PA: Skinner & Finch, 1879.

Complete Catalogue of the Tauchnitz Edition of British and American Authors. Leipzig: Bernhard Tauchnitz, 1905.

Condition of the Indian Tribes. Washington, DC: Government Printing Office, 1867.

Connelley, William E. *A Standard History of Kansas and Kansans*. 3 vols. Chicago: Lewis Publishing Company, 1918.

Coues, Elliott. *Birds of the Northwest: A Hand-Book of the Ornithology of the Region Drained by the Missouri River and Its Tributaries*. Washington, DC: Government Printing Office, 1874.

Coues, Elliott. "Extract From Journal of Elliott Coues' First Journey to the West." *Bird-Lore* 4, no. 1 (January-February 1902): 8.

———. "My Only Indian Massacre." *Forest and Stream* 50 (June 25, 1898): 505.

———. "Some Notes on Arrow-Wounds." *The Medical and Surgical Reporter* 14, no. 17 (April 28, 1866): 321–24.

———, ed. *On the Trail of a Spanish Pioneer*. 2 vols. New York: F. P. Harper, 1900.

———. *The Expeditions of Zebulon Montgomery Pike*. 3 vols. New York: F. P. Harper, 1895.

Cox, J. Randolph. *The Dime Novel Companion: A Source Book*. Westport, CT: Greenwood Press, 2000.

Crampton, C. Gregory. *The Zunis of Cibola*. Salt Lake City: University of Utah Press, 1977.

Cullum, George W. *Biographical Register of the Officers and Graduates of the U. S. Military Academy.* 2 vols. New York: D. Van Nostrand, 1868.

Curtis, Charles A. "A Cavalry Veteran." *War Papers Read Before the Commandery of the State of Wisconsin, Military Order of the Loyal Legion of the United States*. Milwaukee: Burdick & Allen, 1914. vol. 4: 31–50.

———. *Captured by the Navajos*. New York: Harper & Brothers, 1904.

Curtis, Edward S. *The North American Indian*. 20 vols. New York: Johnson Reprint Corp., 1970.

Cutright, Paul R. *Elliott Coues: Naturalist and Frontier Historian*. Urbana: University of Illinois Press, 1981.

Dall, William H. *Spencer Fullerton Baird: A Biography*. Philadelphia: J. B. Lippincott Company, 1915.

Davis, W. M. *Biographical Memoir of John Wesley Powell 1834–1902*. Washington, DC: National Academy of Sciences, 1915.

Davis, Winfield J. *History of Political Conventions in California, 1849–1892*. Sacramento: California State Library, 1893.

De Aragon, Ray John. *Padre Martinez and Bishop Lamy*. Las Vegas, NM: Pan-American Publishing, 1978.

DeMallie, Raymond J. "Sioux Until 1850." *Handbook of North American Indians* 13, pt. 2 (Washington, DC: Smithsonian, 2001): 718–60.

Dictionary of American Biography. 21 vols. New York: Charles Scribner's Sons, 1928–1937.

Dictionary of American History. 5 vols. New York: Charles Scribner's Sons, 1940.

Dunnigan, Timothy. "Lower Pima." *Handbook of North American Indians* 10 (Washington, DC: Smithsonian, 1983): 217–29.

Dutton, Bertha P., and Miriam M. Marmon. *The Laguna Calendar*. Albuquerque: University of New Mexico Press, 1936.

Edelman, Sandra A. "Pueblo San Ildefonso." *Handbook of North American Indians* 9 (Washington, DC: Smithsonian, 1979): 308–16.

Edelman, Sandra A., and Alfonso Ortiz. "Tesuque Pueblo," *Handbook of North American Indians* 9 (Washington, DC: Smithsonian, 1979): 330–35.

Eggan, Fred. "Pueblos: Introduction." *Handbook of North American Indians* 9 (Washington, DC: Smithsonian, 1979): 224–35.

Eicher, John H., and David J. Eicher. *Civil War High Commands*. Stanford, CA: Stanford University Press, 2001.

Ellis, Florence H. "Isleta Pueblo." *Handbook of North American Indians* 9 (Washington, DC: Smithsonian, 1979): 351–65.

———. "Laguna Pueblo." *Handbook of North American Indians* 9 (Washington, DC: Smithsonian, 1979): 438–49.

Ellis, William A. *Norwich University*. Concord, NH: Rumford Press, 1898.

———. *Norwich University, 1819–1911*. 3 vols. Montpelier, VT: Capital City Press, 1911.

Ezell, Paul H. "History of the Pima." *Handbook of North American Indians* 10 (Washington, DC: Smithsonian, 1983): 149–60.

———. *The Maricopas: An Identification from Documentary Sources*. Tucson: University of Arizona Press, 1963.

Farish, Thomas E. *History of Arizona*. 4 vols. Phoenix: Filmer Brothers, 1916.

Flint, Richard, and Shirley Cushing Flint. *Documents of the Corondao Expedetion, 1539–1542*. Albuquerque: University of New Mexico Press, 2012.

Fourr, William. "Reminiscences of William Fourr." *Arizona Historical Review* 6, no. 4 (October 1935): 68–84.

Fowler, Loretta. "Arapaho." *Handbook of North American Indians* 13, pt. 2 (Washington, DC: Smithsonian, 2001): 840–62.

———. *Araphoe Politics, 1851–1978*. Lincoln: University of Nebraska Press, 1982.

Frazer, Robert W. *Forts of the West*. Norman: University of Oklahoma Press, 1965.

Garcia-Mason, Velma. "Acoma Pueblo." *Handbook of North American Indians* 9 (Washington, DC: Smithsonian, 1979): 450–66.

Gardiner, C. Harvey. *William Hickling Prescott: A Biography*. Austin: University of Texas Press, 1969.

Geary, James. *Geary's Guide to the World's Greatest Aphorists*. New York: Bloomsbury USA, 2007.

General Orders and Circulars, Adjutant General's Office, 1891. Washington, DC: Government Printing Office, 1892.

Gibbon, Guy E. *The Sioux: The Dakota and Lakota Nations*. Malden, MA: Blackwell, 2003.

Goldfrank, Esther S. *The Artist of "Isleta Paintings" in Pueblo Society*. Washington, DC: Smithsonian, 1967.

Grey, Herman. *Tales From the Mohaves*. Norman: University of Oklahoma Press, 1970.

Hafel, LeRoy R., ed. *French Fur Traders and Voyageurs in the American West*. Lincoln, NE: Bison Books, 1997.

Haines, Helen. *History of New Mexico*. New York: New Mexico Historical Publishing Co., 1891.

Hale, Edward E. "Coronado's Discovery of the Seven Cities." *Proceedings of the American Antiquarian Society* new series, 1, no. 1 (April 1881): 236–45.

Hall, Sharlot M. *Cactus and Pine*. Boston: Sherman, French & Company, 1911.

"Harriette Louise Hughes Curtis." *The Granite Monthly* 56, no. 3 (March 1924): 171.

Harwell, Henry O., and Marsha C. S. Kelly. "Maricopa." *Handbook of North American Indians* 10 (Washington, DC: Smithsonian, 1983): 71–85.

Hassler, David W. "Charles O. Cunningham: California-Arizona Pioneer 1852–1865." *Arizona and the West* 27, no. 3 (Autumn 1985): 253–68.

Heitman, Francis B. *Historical Register and Dictionary of the United States Army*. 2 vols. Washington, DC: Government Printing Office, 1903.

Heyman, Max L., Jr. *Prudent Soldier: A Biography of Major General E. R. S. Canby 1817–1873*. Glendale, CA: Arthur H. Clark Company, 1959.

Hill, W. W. "Navajo Salt Gathering." *The University of New Mexico Bulletin*, No. 349, Anthropological Series, 3, no. 4. (February 1, 1940): 1–31.

The History of the Town of Montpelier. Montpelier, VT: A. M. Hemenway, 1882.

Hoig, Stan and Wilbur S. Nye. *The Kiowas & The Legend of Kicking Bird*. Boulder: University Press of Colorado, 2000.

Horgan, Paul. *Lamy of Santa Fe: His Life and Times*. New York: Farrar, Straus and Giroux, 2012.

The Houghton Mifflin Dictionary of Biography. Boston: Houghton, Mifflin Company, 2003.

Hughes, J. Patrick. *Fort Leavenworth: Gateway to the West*. Topeka: Kansas State Historical Society, 2000.

Hunt, Aurora. *The Army of the Pacific, 1860–1866*. Mechanicsburg, PA: Stackpole Books, 2004.

———. *Kirby Benedict: Frontier Federal Marshal*. Glendale, CA: A. H. Clark Company, 1961.

Hunt, Roger D., and Jack R. Brown. *Brevet Brigadier Generals in Blue*. Gaithersburg, MD: Olde Soldier Books, 1997.

Hutton, Paul A., and Durwood Ball, eds. *Soldiers West: Biographies from the Military Frontier*. Norman: University of Oklahoma Press, 2009.

Hyde, George E. *Life of George Bent Written from His Letters*. Norman: University of Oklahoma Press, 1968.

———. *The Pawnee Indians*. Norman: University of Oklahoma Press, 1974.

"In Memoriam." *Transactions of the Wisconsin State Horticultural Society* 19 (Madison: Democrat Printing Co., 1889): 222–24.

Ingstad, Helge. *The Apache Indians: In Search of the Missing Tribe*. Lincoln: University of Nebraska Press, 2004.

Iverson, Peter, and Monty Roessel. *Diné: A History of the Navajos*. Albuquerque: University of New Mexico Press, 2002.

Jordan, Ewing. *University of Pennsylvania Men Who Served in the Civil War 1861–1865, Department of Medicine, Classes 1816–1862*. Philadelphia: No Place, n.d.

Jowett, John, William Montgomery, Gary Taylor, and Stanley Wells. *The Oxford Shakespeare:* Oxford: Oxford University Press, 2005.

Julyan, Robert H. *The Place Names of New Mexico*. Albuquerque: University of New Mexico Press, 1996.

Kane, Adam. "James H. Carleton" in Paul A. Hutton and Durwood Ball. *Soldiers West: Biographies from the Military Frontier*. Norman: University of Oklahoma Press, 2009.

Kavanagh, Thomas W. "Comanche." *Handbook of North American Indians* 13, pt. 1 (Washington, DC: Smithsonian, 2001): 886–906.

———. *The Comanches: A History, 1706–1875*. Lincoln: University of Nebraska Press, 1996.

Keegan, Marcia. *The Taos Pueblo and Its Sacred Blue Lake*. Santa Fe: Clear Light Publishers, 1991.

Keen, Effie R. "Arizona Governors." *Arizona Historical Review* 3, no. 3 (October 1930): 7–20.

Keleher, William A. *Maxwell Land Grant*. Santa Fé: Rydal Press, 1942.

———. *Turmoil in New Mexico, 1846–1868*. Santa Fe: Sunstone Press, 2008.

Kelly, Isabel T., and Catherine S. Fowler. "Southern Paiute." *Handbook of North American Indians* 11 (Washington, DC: Smithsonian, 1986): 368–97.

Kepler, William. *History of the Three Months' and Three Years' Service of the Fourth Regiment Ohio Volunteer Infantry*. Cleveland: Leader Printing Co., 1886.

Kimberly, Robert L., and Ephraim S. Holloway. *The Forty-first Ohio Veteran Volunteer Infantry in the War of the Rebellion*. Cleveland: W. R. Smellie, 1897.

Klauber, Laurence M. *Rattlesnakes: Their Habits, Life Histories, and Influence on Mankind*. Berkeley: University of California Press, 1972.

Kluckhohn, Clyde. *The Navajo*. London: Oxford University Press, 1946.

Knack, Martha C. *Boundaries Between: The Southern Paiutes, 1775–1995*. Lincoln: University of Nebraska Press, 2001.

Lambert, Marjorie F. "Pueblo Pojoaque," *Handbook of North American Indians* 9 (Washington, DC: Smithsonian, 1979): 324–29.

Lamphere, Louise. *To Run After Them: Cultural and Social Bases of Cooperation in a Navajo Community*. Tucson: University of Arizona Press, 1977.

Lange, Charles H. "Santo Domingo Pueblo." *Handbook of North American Indians* 9 (Washington, DC: Smithsonian, 1979): 379–89.

Laird, Carobeth, and George Laird. *The Chemehuevis*. Banning, CA: Malki Museum Press, 1976.

Leland, Joy. "Population." *Handbook of North American Indians* 11 (Washington, DC: Smithsonian, 1986): 608–19.

"Letters, Extracts from Correspondence, Notices, &c." *The Ibis*, ser. 2, 1 (October 1868): 535–38.

Levine, Frances. *Our Prayers Are in This Place: Pecos Pueblo Identity Over the Centuries*. Albuquerque: University of New Mexico Press, 1999.

Levy, Buddy. *Conquistador: Hernan Cortes, King Montezuma, and the Last Stand of the Aztecs*. New York: Bantam Books, 2008.

Levy, Jerrold E. "Kiowa." *Handbook of North American Indians* 13, pt. 2 (Washington, DC :Smithsonian, 2001): 907–25.

Loew, Oscar. "The Moquis Indians of Arizona." *Popular Science Monthly* 5 (July 1874): 351–56.

McClintock, James H. *Arizona, Prehistoric—Aboriginal—Pioneer—Modern*. 3 vols. Chicago: S. J. Clarke Publishing Company, 1916.

McGroarty, John S. *Los Angeles From the Mountains to the Sea*. 3 vols. Los Angeles: American Historical Society, 1921.

McGuire, Thomas R. "Walapai." *Handbook of North American Indians* 10 (Washington, DC: Smithsonian, 1983): 25–37.

McManamon, Francis P., Linda S. Cordell, Kent G. Lightfoot, and George R. Milner. *Archaeology in America: An Encyclopedia*. Westport, CT: Greenwood Press, 2009.

McMaster, Richard K. *Musket, Saber, and Missile: A History of Fort Bliss*. El Paso: Complete Printing, 1974.

McMillen, Christian W. *Making Indian Law: The Hualapai Land Case and the Birth of Ethnohistory*. New Haven: Yale University Press, 2007.

McNitt, Frank. "Old Fort Wingate: The Inspection Reports." *El Palacio* 78, no. 2 (June 1972): 30–36.

Masich, Andrew E. *The Civil War in Arizona: The Story of the California Volunteers, 1861–1865*. Norman: University of Oklahoma Press, 2006.

Mexican War Veterans. Washington: Brentano's, 1887.

Mifflin, Margot. *The Blue Tattoo: The Life of Olive Oatman*. Lincoln: University of Nebraska Press, 2009.

Miller, Darlis A. *The California Column in New Mexico*. Albuquerque: University of New Mexico Press, 1982.

———. "Los Pinos, New Mexico: Civil War Post on the Rio Grande." *New Mexico Historical Review* 62, no.1 (Winter 1987): 1–31.

———. "The Perils of a Post Sutler: William H. Moore at Fort Union, New Mexico, 1859–1870." *Journal of the West* 32, no. 2 (April 1993): 7–18.

Mills, J. Harrison. *History of the Arkansas Valley, Colorado*. Chicago: O. L. Baskin & Company, 1881.

Miner, H. Craig, and William E. Unrau. *The End of Indian Kansas: A Study of Cultural Revolution, 1854–1871*. Lawrence: Regents Press of Kansas, 1978.

Minge, Ward A. *Acoma*. Albuquerque: University of New Mexico Press, 1976.

Minutes of the New Mexico Bar Association. Santa Fe: New Mexican Printing Co., 1894.

Moore, John H. *The Cheyenne*. Cambridge, MA: Blackwell, 1996.

———, Margot P. Liberty, and A. Terry Straus. "Cheyenne." *Handbook of North American Indians* 13, pt. 2 (Washington, DC: Smithsonian, 2001): 863–85.

Moorhead, Max L. *New Mexico's Royal Road: Trade and Travel on the Chihuahua Trail*. Norman: University of Oklahoma Press, 1958.

Morgan, Robert. *Boone: A Biography*. Chapel Hill: Algonquin Books, 2007.

Mumey, Nolie. *Old Forts and Trading Posts of the West*. Denver: Artcraft Press, 1956.

Murphy, Lawrence. "Cantonment Burgwin, New Mexico 1852–1860." *Arizona and the West* 15, no. 1 (Spring, 1973): 5–26.

Official Army Register for 1866. Washington: Government Printing Office, 1866.

Official Army Register for 1883. Washington: Government Printing Office, 1883.

Oliva, Leo E. *Fort Larned on the Santa Fe Trail*. Topeka: Kansas State Historical Society, 1982.

———. *Fort Union and the Frontier Army in the Southwest*. Santa Fe: National Park Service, 1993.

Opler, Morris E. "The Apachaean Culture Pattern and Its Origins." *Handbook of North American Indians* 10 (Washington, DC: Smithsonian, 1983): 368–92.

———. "Mescalero Apache." *Handbook of North American Indians* 10 (Washington, DC: Smithsonian, 1983): 419–39.

Ortiz, Alfonso. "San Juan Pueblo." *Handbook of North American Indians* 9 (Washington, DC: Smithsonian, 1979): 278–95.

Page, Charles D. *History of the Fourteenth Regiment, Connecticut Vol. Infantry*. Meriden, CT: Horton Printing Company, 1906.

Parks, Douglas R. "Cheyenne." *Handbook of North American Indians* 13, pt. 1 (Washington, DC: Smithsonian, 2001): 515–47.

Parmentier, Richard J. "The Mythological Triangle: Poseyemu, Montezuma, and Jesus in the Pueblos." *Handbook of North American Indians* 9 (Washington, DC: Smithsonian, 1979): 609–22.

Paterek, Josephine. *Encyclopedia of American Indian Costume*. New York: W. W. Norton & Co., 1994.

Pérez de Villagrá, Gaspar. *Historia de la Nueva México 1610: A Critical Annotated Spanish/English Edition*. Albuquerque: University of New Mexico Press, 1992.

Pettis, George H. *The California Column*. Santa Fe: New Mexican Printing Company, 1908.

Portrait and Biographical Album of Otoe and Cass Counties, Nebraska. Chicago: Chapman Brothers, 1889.

Pritzker, Barry M. *A Native American Encyclopedia*. New York: Oxford University Press, 2000.

"Radium—the Benchmark for Alpha Emitters." *Los Alamos Science* 23 (November 23, 1995): 225–233.

Report of the Annual Meeting of the State Bar Association of Wisconsin. Madison: Taylor and Gleason, 1901.

Records of California Men in the War of the Rebellion, 1861–1867. Sacramento: J. D. Young, 1890.

Remley, David. *Kit Carson: The Life of an American Border Man*. Norman: Universityof Oklahoma Press, 2011.

Report of J. Ross Browne on the Mineral Resources of the States and Territories West of the Rocky Mountains. Washington, DC: Government Printing Office, 1868.

Report of the Adjutant-General of the State of California, From November 30, 1865, to November 1, 1867. Sacramento: G. W. Gelwicks, 1867.

Report of the Secretary of the Interior. Washington, DC: Government Printing Office, 1865.

Reports of Cases Argued and Determined in the Supreme Court of the State of Kansas. Topeka: Kansas Publishing House, 1880.

Reports of Explorations and Surveys to Ascertain the Most Practicable and Economical Route for a Railroad from the Mississippi River to the Pacific Ocean. Washington: Beverley Tucker, 1856.

Ricky, Donald B. *Indians of Arizona: Past and Present*. Santa Barbara, CA: American Historical Publications, 1999.

Robinson, John W. *Los Angeles in Civil War Days, 1860–1865*. Norman: University of Oklahoma Press, 2013.

Rodee, Marian, and James Ostler. *Zuni Pottery*. West Chester, PA: Schiffer Publishing, 1986.

Roessel, Robert A., Jr. "Navajo History, 1850–1923." *Handbook of North American Indians* 10 (Washington, DC: Smithsonian, 1983): 506–23.

Rose, Carol. *Giants, Monsters and Dragons*. New York: W. W. Norton, 2000.

Sabin, Edwin L. *Kit Carson Days (1809–1868)*. Chicago: A. C. McClurg & Co., 1914.

Sando, Joe S. "Jemez Pueblo." *Handbook of North American Indians* 9 (Washington, DC: Smithsonian, 1979): 418–29.

———. *Nee Hemish, A History of Jemez Pueblo*. Albuquerque: University of New Mexico Press, 1982.

Schroeder, Albert H. "Pecos Pueblo." *Handbook of North American Indians* 9 (Washington, DC: Smithsonian): 430–37

———. "Pueblos Abandoned in Historic Times,." *Handbook of North American Indians* 9 (Washington, DC: Smithsonian, 1979): 236–254.

Shaw, Anna M. *A Pima Past*. Tucson: University of Arizona Press, 1974.

Simmons, Marc. *Following the Santa Fe Trail*. Santa Fe: Ancient City Press, 1984.

———. "History of Pueblo-Spanish Relations to 1821." *Handbook of North American Indians* 9 (Washington, DC: Smithsonian, 1979): 178–93.

Simmons, Virginia M. *The Ute Indians of Utah, Colorado, and New Mexico*. Boulder: University Press of Colorado, 2000.

Simpson, James H. *Journal of a Military Reconnaissance, From Santa Fé, New Mexico, to the Navajo Country*. Philadelphia: Lippincott, Grambo and Co., 1852.

Smith, Edmund B. *Governor's Island: Its Military History Under Three Flags, 1637–1913*. New York: By the Author, 1913.

Smith, Gerald A. *The Mojaves: Historic Indians of San Bernardino County*. San Bernardino: San Bernardino County Museum, 1977.

Smith, Stephen. *An Inkwell of Pen Names*. Philadelphia: XLibris Corporation, 2006.

Smith, Victoria. *Captive Arizona, 1851–1900*. Lincoln: University of Nebraska Press, 2009.

Soldier and Brave. Washington: Government Printing Office, 1971.

Speirs, Randall H. "Nambe Pueblo." *Handbook of North American Indians* 9 (Washington, DC: Smithsonian, 1979): 317–23.

Spicer, Edward H. *Cycles of Conquest: The Impact of Spain, Mexico, and the United States on the Indians of the Southwest, 1533–1960*. Tucson: University of Arizona Press, 2006.

Stanley, F. *The Fort Thorn, New Mexico Story*. Pep, TX: F. Stanley, 1965.

Stevens, T. Rorie. *The Death of a Governor*. Jacksonville, TX: Jayroe Graphic Arts, 1971.

Stevenson, Matilda. *The Zuni Indians: Their Mythology, Esoteric Fraternities, and Ceremonies*. U. S. Bureau of American Ethnology, Twenty-third Annual Report, 1901–1902. Washington, DC: Government Printing Office, 1904.

Stewart, Kenneth M. "Mohave." *Handbook of North American Indians* 10 (Washington, DC: Smithsonian, 1983): 55–70.

Strong, Pauline T. "Indian Pueblo of San Felipe." *Handbook of North American Indians* 9 (Washington, DC: Smithsonian, 1979): 390–97.

Tedlock, Dennis. "Zuni Religion and World View." *Handbook of North American Indians* 9 (Washington, DC: Smithsonian, 1979): 499–508.

Tessman, Norm. "The Personal Journal and Arizona Letters of Margaret Hunt McCormick." *Journal of Arizona History* 26, no. 1 (Spring 1985): 41–52.

Thirty-ninth Annual Reunion of the Association of the Graduates of the United States Military Academy. Saginaw, MI: Seemann & Peters, 1908.

Thompson, Jerry D. *Texas and New Mexico on the Eve of the Civil War*. Albuquerque: University of New Mexico Press, 2001.

Thompson, Jerry D. *A Civil War History of the New Mexico Volunteers and Militia*. Albuquerque: University of New Mexico Press, 2015.

———, ed. *New Mexico Territory During the Civil War*. Albuquerque: University of New Mexico Press, 2008.

Thrapp, Dan L. *Encyclopedia of Frontier Biography*. Norman: University of Oklahoma Press, 1988. 3 vols.

Tittmann, Edward D. "The Exploitation of Treason." *New Mexico Historical Review* 4 (1929): 128–48.

Toxological Profile for Radium. Washington, DC: Agency for Toxic Substance and Disease Registry, U. S. Public Health Service, 1990.

Trenholm, Virginia C. *The Arapahoes, Our People*. Norman: University of Oklahoma Press, 1970.

Twitchell, Ralph E. *The History of the Military Occupation of the Territory of New Mexico from 1846–1851*. Denver: Smith-Brooks Co., 1909.

———. *The Leading Facts of New Mexican History*. 2 vols. Cedar Rapids, IA: Torch Press, 1912.

Unrau, William E. *Indians of Kansas: The Euro-American Invasion and Conquest of Indian Kansas.* Topeka: Kansas State Historical Society, 1991.

———. *The Kansa Indians: A History of the Wind People, 1673–1873*. Norman: University of Oklahoma Press, 1987.

Wallace, Andrew, and Richard H. Hevly, eds. *From Texas to San Diego in 1851: The Overland Journal of Dr. S. W. Woodhouse, Surgeon-Naturalist of the Sitgreaves Expedition*. Lubbock: Texas Tech University Press, 2007.

War of the Rebellion: A Compilation of the Official Records of the Union and Confederate Armies. 128 vols. Washington, DC: Government Printing Office, 1893.

Warner, Ezra J. *Generals in Blue*. Baton Rouge: Louisiana State University Press, 1964.

———. *Generals in Gray*. Baton Rouge: Louisiana State University Press, 1959.

Weatherington, Ronald K. *Ceran St. Vrain: American Frontier Entrepreneur*. Santa Fe: Sunstone Press, 2012.

Wells, Edmund. *Argonaut Tales*. New York: Grafton Press, 1927.

Wharfield, H. B. *Fort Yuma on the Colorado River*. El Cajon, CA: n. p., 1968.

White, Leslie A. *The Pueblo Indians of Santo Domingo, New Mexico*. Millwood, NY: Krauss Reprint, 1974.

———. *The Pueblo of San Filipe*. Menasha, WI: American Anthropological Association, 1932.

Whitman, William, and Marjorie W. Whitman. *The Pueblo Indians of San Ildefonso: A Changing Culture*. New York: AMS Press, 1969.

Whittaker, John C. *Flintknapping: Making and Understanding Stone Tools*. Austin: University of Texas Press, 1994.

Williamson, G. R. *Frontier Gambling: The Games, the Gamblers and the Great Gambling Halls of the Old West*. Charleston, SC: Indian Head Publications, 2011.

Witherspoon, Gary. "Navajo Social Organization." *Handbook of North American Indians* 10 (Washington, DC: Smithsonian, 1983): 524–35.

Wolf, Charles B. *Sol Barth of St. Johns: The Story of an Arizona Pioneer*. No Place: 1st Books, 2002.

Woodbury, Richard B. "Indian Town of Zuni." *Handbook of North American Indians* 9 (Washington, DC: Smithsonian, 1979): 467–73.

Woolf, Charles M. "Albinism Among Indians in Arizona and New Mexico." *American Journal of Human Genetics* 17, no. 1 (January, 1965): 23–35.

Worster, Donald. *A River Running West*. New York: Oxford University Press, 2001.

"Writers of the Day." *The Writer* 12, no. 3 (March 1899): 42–45.

Young, M. Jane. *Signs from the Ancestors: Zuni Cultural Symbolism and Perceptions of Rock Art*. Albuquerque: University of New Mexico Press, 1988.

Newspapers

Albuquerque Daily Citizen
Arizona Citizen and Daily Tribune [Tucson]
Arizona Citizen and Weekly Tribune [Tucson]
Arizona Enterprise [Prescott]
Arizona Miner [Prescott]
Arizona Star [Tucson]
Baltimore Sun
Boston Journal
Breckenridge [Kentucky] News
Brooklyn Daily Eagle
California Farmer and Journal of Useful Sciences [San Francisco]
Chicago Inter-Ocean
Cincinnati Daily Gazette
Crisis [Columbus, Ohio]
Daily Alta California [San Francisco]
Daily National Intelligencer [Washington, D. C.]
Daily New Mexican [Santa Fe]

Daily People [New York]
Daily Union [Washington, D. C.]
Denver Post
Denver Rocky Mountain News
Evening Star [Washington, D. C.]
Galveston Daily News
Hartford [Connecticut] Daily Courant
Indianapolis Sentinel
Jamestown [New York] Journal
Kansas City [Missouri] Star
Kansas City [Missouri] Times
London Times
Los Angeles Herald
The National Tribune [Washington, D. C.]
Newport [Rhode Island] Mercury
New York Evening Post
New York Herald
New York Times
New York Tribune
Omaha World Herald
[Portland] Oregonian
Philadelphia Inquirer
[Cleveland] Plain Dealer
Plymouth [New Hampshire] Record
Portland [Maine] Daily Press
Prescott Daily Courier
Prescott Evening Courier
Prescott Journal Miner
Pueblo [Colorado] Indicator
Rio Grande Republican [Las Cruces, New Mexico]
Sacramento Daily Union
[Sacramento] Weekly Rescue
St Albans [Vermont] Daily Messenger
St Albans [Vermont] Messenger
San Diego Union
San Francisco Bulletin
San Francisco Call
[Santa Fé] New Mexican
[Santa Fé] Daily New Mexican
Springfield [Massachusetts] Republican
The Tech [Cambridge, Massachusetts]

[New Orleans] Times-Picayune
Tucson Daily Citizen
Virginia [Minnesota] Enterprise
Waterloo [Iowa] Evening Courier
[Atchison, Kansas] Weekly Champion and Press
[Prescott] Weekly Journal Miner
Wisconsin Cardinal [Madison, Wisconsin]

Index

H

I

J

K